WORKOUTS AND TURNAROUNDS
THE HANDBOOK OF RESTRUCTURING AND INVESTING IN DISTRESSED COMPANIES

WORKOUTS AND TURNAROUNDS
THE HANDBOOK OF RESTRUCTURING AND INVESTING IN DISTRESSED COMPANIES

Edited by
Dominic DiNapoli
Sanford C. Sigoloff
Robert F. Cushman

BUSINESS ONE IRWIN
Homewood, Illinois 60430

© RICHARD D. IRWIN, INC., 1991

All rights reserved. No part of this publication may be reproduced, stored in a retrieval system, or transmitted, in any form or by any means, electronic, mechanical, photocopying, recording, or otherwise, without the prior written permission of the copyright holder.

This publication is designed to provide accurate and authoritative information in regard to the subject matter covered. It is sold with the understanding that neither the author nor the publisher is engaged in rendering legal, accounting, or other professional service. If legal advice or other expert assistance is required, the services of a competent professional person should be sought.

From a Declaration of Principles jointly adopted by a Committee of the American Bar Association and a Committee of Publishers.

Project editor: Margaret Haywood
Production manager: Diane Palmer
Artist: Mike Benoit
Compositor: TCSystems, Inc.
Typeface: 11/13 Times Roman
Printer: Arcata Graphics/Martinsburg

Library of Congress Cataloging-in-Publication Data

Workouts and turnarounds : the handbook of restructuring and investing in distressed companies / [edited by] Dominic DiNapoli, Sanford C. Sigoloff, Robert F. Cushman.
    p.   cm.
    Includes index.
    ISBN 1-55623-335-3 — ISBN 1-55623-465-1 (Price Waterhouse version)—ISBN 1-55623-511-9 (GE Capital's Corporate Finance Group version)
    1. Corporate turnarounds—United States—Management. 2. Corporate reorganizations—United States. 3. Corporations—United States—Finance. 4. Securities—United States. I. DiNapoli, Dominic.
II. Sigoloff, Sanford C. III. Cushman, Robert Frank, 1931-
HD58.8.W68   1991
658.1'6—dc20   90–43802

Printed in the United States of America
       3 4 5 6 7 8 9 0   AGM   7 6 5 4 3 2 1

PREFACE

Corporate debt continues to grow. More and more companies face financial trouble. The distress of these highly leveraged businesses has become the meat upon which a new and emerging industry is feeding—the "Workout and Turnaround Industry." For those cognizant of the latest initiatives, initiatives that are extremely complex due to the many variables that have to be considered, investment opportunity and profit opportunity abound.

For those who have the ability to identify these opportunities, to structure their investments, and to orchestrate the stakeholdings, "Turnarounds" will undoubtedly become the "Investment of the 90s," just as LBOs are the "Investment of the 80s."

Workouts and Turnarounds is a guide to the current trends and latest developments in both restructuring and investing in distressed companies and the strategies and tactics to be employed when playing the restructuring game. It is coauthored by nationally recognized lawyers, accountants, workout and LBO turnaround specialists, and the bankruptcy experts who are, today, in the trenches, analyzing the viability of investing, and stabilizing, financing, restructuring, and enhancing corporate value, with the end game of realizing new and increased profits.

Dominic DiNapoli
Sanford C. Sigoloff
Robert F. Cushman

ABOUT THE EDITORS

Dominic DiNapoli is the partner responsible for Price Waterhouse's bankruptcy and restructuring services in the northeast region. He has significant experience in formal and informal reorganizations on behalf of debtors and creditors. As the lead partner in restructuring assignments, Mr. DiNapoli has provided services that include development and review of business plans, valuation, and expert testimony.

In addition to client engagement responsibilities in reorganizations and negotiated workouts, he has participated in the preparation and dissemination of data on financially distressed corporations and the development of practice guides for providing professional assistance to financially troubled companies. He has also given instructional presentations to corporate and financial institutions active on creditors' committees, and has provided technical assistance to practice offices serving parties in interest in bankruptcy proceedings.

Mr. DiNapoli has represented creditors in many of the largest Chapter 11 cases ever filed, including Drexel Burnham Lambert Group, Inc. and Lomas Financial Corporation. He is a member of the Association of Insolvency Accountants and is a certified public accountant licensed in New York and New Jersey.

Sanford C. Sigoloff is an internationally renowned expert in the field of corporate crisis management. With such successful reorganizations as Wickes, Republic, and Daylin to his credit, Mr. Sigoloff is at the leading edge in a field of management that is expanding dramatically as the corporate excesses of the 80s come home to roost in the 90s.

Mr. Sigoloff is chairman, president, and chief executive officer of Sigoloff & Associates, Inc., a crisis management and consulting firm based in Santa Monica, California.

Robert F. Cushman is a partner in the national law firm of Pepper, Hamilton & Scheetz and is a recognized specialist and lecturer on all phases of real estate and construction law. He serves as legal counsel to major construction, development, and bonding companies and has represented many of these entities in major construction default and workout situations.

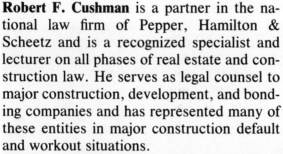

Mr. Cushman is the coeditor of *A Guide for the Foreign Investor; Business Opportunities in the Far East; Handbook for Raising Capital; The Handbook of Joint Venturing;* and *High Tech Real Estate*—all published by BUSINESS ONE IRWIN—as well as many other handbooks and guides in the insurance, real estate, and construction fields.

Mr. Cushman, who is a member of the Bar of the Commonwealth of Pennsylvania and who is admitted to practice before the Supreme Court of the United States and the United States Claims Court, has served as executive vice president and general counsel to the Construction Industry Foundation. He is a founding member of the American College of Construction Lawyers.

ABOUT THE AUTHORS

Edward I. Altman is the Max L. Heine Professor of Finance at the Stern School of Business, New York University. He has an international reputation as an expert on corporate bankruptcy and credit analysis.

He was named Laureate 1984 by the Hautes Etudes Commerciales Foundation in Paris for his accumulated works on corporate distress prediction models and procedures for firm financial rehabilitation and was awarded the Graham & Dodd Scroll for 1985 by the Financial Analysts Federation for his work on default rates on high yield corporate debt.

Dr. Altman's primary areas of research include bankruptcy analysis and prediction, distressed securities, credit and lending policies, risk management in banking, corporate finance, and capital markets.

Gregory E. Bardnell has directed many engagements resulting from the restructuring of the petroleum and financial services industries. The petroleum industry experience has included due diligence reviews relating to the acquisition of exploration, production, refining, and marketing assets and operations, as well as engagements directed toward restructuring organizations. The financial services engagements have primarily  been a result of the investigation and litigation involving insolvent thrifts in Texas.

Some of Mr. Bardnell's major projects include the acquisition reviews of refining and marketing assets of major refiners/marketers of petroleum products. One such project involved Venezuelan Petroleum Holdings, Inc.'s acquisition of certain assets/stock of Citgo Petroleum, Champlin Refining, and Unocal.

Mr. Bardnell is a certified public accountant and a member of several professional and business organizations. He graduated from the University of Texas at Austin with a B.B.A. in accounting.

Gregory A. Bray is a senior associate at Gendel, Raskoff, Shapiro & Quittner, specializing in bankruptcy reorganization and business workouts. Mr. Bray received his B.A. from the University of California at Los Angeles in 1980 and his J.D. from Loyola Marymount University in 1984.

Denis F. Cronin has been a partner at Wachtell, Lipton, Rosen & Katz since 1978. He holds an A.B. degree from Colgate University and a J.D. from Fordham University. He was a member of the board of editors at *Fordham Law Review* and is a frequent lecturer, panelist, and author.

Mr. Cronin is working or has worked on major cases, such as Texaco, Western Union Corporation, Resorts International, Wheeling-Pittsburgh Steel Corporation, Western Company of North America, Wickes Companies, Inc., Continental Airlines, and White Motor Corporation.

Carmen R. Eggleston is senior manager with Price Waterhouse in Houston, specializing in the tax issues associated with restructuring and bankruptcy. Ms. Eggleston was a member of the tax practice for 12 years before joining the reorganization and litigation services group. She has counseled both debtors and creditors as to the tax consequences arising from debt forgiveness income, the change of ownership rules for preservation of tax loss carry forwards, and the application of the original issue discount rules. She has also counseled on the tax consequences relating to the creation of a liquidating trust and the validity of certain IRS tax liens. Ms. Eggleston has worked on individual and corporate restructurings and testified in court. In addition to her tax specialization, Ms. Eggleston also works on the general accounting and economic issues relating to a restructuring. She has worked on restructurings such as MBank, Southmark, Texas Specialty Flat Roll Inc., Lomas Financial Corporation, Wilson Foods, Greyhound, Mr. Fred Erk, and Virginia Specialty Stores.

Ms. Eggleston is a CPA and member of national and state professional and business organizations. She graduated from Rice University with a B.A. in economics and managerial studies. She also received her Master of Accounting degree from Rice University.

James D. Epstein is an attorney with Pepper, Hamilton & Scheetz in its Philadelphia and New York City offices. He specializes in mergers and acquisitions, with a particular emphasis on leveraged buyouts, including restructuring leveraged buyouts.

Mr. Epstein earned A.B. and A.M. degrees from the University of Pennsylvania in 1980 and a J.D. degree from Emory University in 1983.

Carter S. Evans is a senior vice president in the financial restructuring group at Shearson Lehman Brothers, Inc. He has been involved with the restructurings of Chrysler Corporation, Navistar, White Motor, Texaco, A.H. Robins, Manville, Itel, Southmark Corporation, MCorp, and General Homes Corporation, among others. Recently he has been advising Federated Department Stores and Allied Stores.

Prior to joining Shearson in 1987, Mr. Evans was a vice president and group head in Chemical Bank's Credit Division. After college, he bagan his career with Price Waterhouse & Company in New York. He is currently chairman of Duckwall-ALCO Stores and a director of Timex Group, Ltd.

Mr. Evans holds a B.B.A. degree in accounting from Emory University.

Michael O. Gagnon is a partner in audit practice at Price Waterhouse. He is the managing partner for the litigation and reorganization consulting group for the New York metropolitan area.

As an auditor, Mr. Gagnon has participated in, supervised, managed, and directed audits and performed related services for entities in a wide range of industries and businesses. He has provided litigation consulting assistance, including testifying as an expert witness, in such areas

as damage assessment, accounting issues, audit fraud, and contract disputes.

Mr. Gagnon received a B.A. in economics and accounting from the College of the Holy Cross, where he was the winner of the National Association of Accountants top accounting graduate award. He is a certified public accountant and a member of the American Institute of Certified Public Accountants and of the New York State Society of Certified Public Accountants.

Richard J. Giacco served as associate general counsel of Safeguard Scientifics, Inc., from late 1984 until July 1990, when he became vice president of Axess Corporation. He had worked previously as an associate attorney with Morris, Nichols, Arsht & Tunnell in Wilmington, Delaware.

Mr. Giacco is a graduate of Widener University Law School (J.D., 1980) and the University of Virginia (B.A., 1976).

Peter J. Gibbons is a C.P.A. and the lead technical specialist partner for Price Waterhouse's reorganization and bankruptcy specialty practice. He is in its Philadelphia office and has devoted full time to the specialty practice for over 10 years.

Mr. Gibbons is president of the Association of Insolvency Accountants and is a member of the AICPA AcSEC Task Force on Accounting for Entities in Bankruptcy.

S. Fain Hackney is an associate in the business reorganization and finance section of Duane, Morris & Heckscher. Mr. Hackney specializes in bankruptcy law, business reorganization, and creditors' rights.

Mr. Hackney graduated from Middlebury College in 1983 and received his J.D. from the University of Pennsylvania Law School in 1987. He is a member of the Philadelphia Bar Association and the Pennsylvania Bar Association.

He has been involved in such bankruptcy cases as St. Joseph's Hospital and Swann Oil Company and in various out-of-court workouts.

Adam C. Harris is a fifth-year associate in the creditors' rights department at O'Melveny & Myers. Mr. Harris is the associate with primary responsibility in connection with O'Melveny's representation of the Official Committee of Unsecured Creditors in the Eastern Air Lines Chapter 11 case. Mr. Harris has also assisted in the representation of secured and unsecured creditors in other Chapter 11 cases, such as Allegheny International, Inc. and Western Company.

Mr. Harris graduated from Emory University in 1982 and received his J.D. from Georgetown University Law Center in 1986.

Stephen J. Hopkins's background includes nine years of experience with Nightingale & Associates, Inc.; a wide range of finance-related responsibilities with General Electric Company; and CFO of an AMEX company during its Chapter 11 reorganization.

As a principal of N&A, Inc., he has held interim management responsibilities as CEO of Worlds of Wonder, Inc., CFO of Evans Products Company, and acting CFO of several other companies.

He received his B.S. from Ohio State University in banking and finance and is a graduate of GE's general management courses.

John F. Horstmann III is a partner in the business reorganization and finance section of Duane, Morris & Heckscher. Mr Horstmann specializes in bankruptcy law, corporate reorganization, out-of-court workouts, and creditors' rights.

Mr. Horstmann graduated from St. Joseph's University in 1973 and received his J.D. from Villanova University School of Law in 1976. He is a member of the American Bar Association Section of Corporation, Banking, and Business Law; the Subcommittee on Corporate Reorganization and Bankruptcy; and the Pennsylvania Bar Association and the Philadelphia Bar Association.

Mr. Horstmann has been involved in such bankruptcy cases as Penrod Drilling Company and Placid Oil Company, Wickes Companies, Inc., Brooks Shoe Manufacturing Company, and Abbotts Dairies of Pennsylvania and has represented various companies and lenders in out-of-court workouts.

Donald R. Joseph is cochair of the international insolvency group of Baker & McKenzie, the world's largest law firm, having approximately 50 offices in the United States, Australia, Hong Kong, Europe, Canada, Mexico, South America, and throughout the Pacific Basin. Through its extensive network of offices, Baker & McKenzie participates worldwide in domestic and international insolvency and workout matters for creditors, debtors, trustees, receivers, and other affected parties.

Mr. Joseph has drawn upon the expertise of his colleagues in several of the firm's offices for assistance in preparation of the chapter entitled "The International Workout and Turnaround." Mr. Joseph practices out of the firm's San Francisco office.

Francis J. King is a partner in Price Waterhouse's valuation services group in New York. He has conducted numerous seminars for the Tax Executive Institute on valuation issues ranging from corporate liquidations to business valuations.

Mr. King has a B.S. in civil engineering and an M.B.A. in finance and marketing.

Raymond H. Kraftson has been vice president and general counsel of Safeguard Scientifics, Inc., and entrepreneurial technology company, since 1980. He was admitted to the Virginia Bar in 1967, the Pennsylvania Bar in 1970, and the Missouri Bar in 1971.

Mr. Kraftson graduated from the University of Pennsylvania (B.A., 1962) and the College of William and Mary (J.D., 1967), where he was managing editor of the law review and a W.A.R. Goodwin Scholar.

He is a director of several corporations and institutions. He was coauthor of the chapter "Corporate Joint Ventures" in *Handbook for Raising Capital* (Homewood, Ill.: Dow Jones-Irwin, 1986).

Francis J. Lawall, an attorney with the international firm of Pepper, Hamilton & Scheetz, has extensive experience in bankruptcy and creditor's rights related matters, including the reorganization of large financially distressed companies in the textile, clothing, and construction materials industries. In addition to the foregoing, he has extensive experience in the reorganization of companies plagued with mass toxic tort liabilities and has lectured and published works on various bankruptcy related issues.

Mr. Lawall is a graduate of Temple University (B.A. and M.A.) and Temple University School of Law.

Harvey R. Miller is a comanaging partner of Weil, Gotshal & Manges, a national law firm headquartered in New York City. Mr. Miller has had extensive experience and participation in bankruptcy reorganizations, workouts, and turnarounds.

He has served as attorney for Continental Airlines Corporation, Eastern Air Lines, Inc., Texaco, Inc., Global Marine Corporation, The Western Company of North America, and Revere Copper and Brass, Inc., among others, in pursuit of reorganization under United States bankruptcy law. He has also represented creditors' committees and trustees, as well as major secured creditors in cases such as W.T. Grant Company, Storage Technology Corporation, Federated Department Stores, Inc., and White Motor Credit Corporation. In addition, he has participated as attorney in many out-of-court workouts and turnarounds, including Armco, Inc., Chrysler Corporation, International Harvester Corporation, and Ideal Toy Corporation.

During the 1970s, he was special counsel to the New York Stock Exchange in connection with the turnaround and workout of member organizations in financial difficulties. In addition, he has lectured and written extensively on the subject of debtors' and creditors' rights.

J. Gregg Miller is a partner in the Philadelphia office of Pepper, Hamilton & Scheetz, where he has concentrated his practice primarily in the areas of bankruptcy and creditors' rights law since joining the firm in 1969.

He received his undergraduate degree from Yale College in 1966 and his LL.B. from the University of Pennsylvania Law School in 1969.

In January 1983, he addressed the American Bar Association's Section of Tort and Insurance Practice on the subject of "Bankruptcy—Crisis in the Construction Industry," and he wrote the bankruptcy chapter in *The McGraw-Hill Construction Business Handbook*, 2nd edition (New York: McGraw-Hill, 1985).

He has had extensive experience in construction bankruptcies and in mass toxic tort bankruptcies. In mass tort bankruptcies, he has represented four asbestos manufacturers and distributors as debtors-in-possession in Chapter 11 proceedings.

Mark A. Neporent is a partner in Schulte Roth & Zabel, where he works in the bankruptcy and business reorganization department.

Mr. Neporent graduated from Lehigh University (B.A., with honors, 1979) and from Syracuse University of Law (J.D., cum laude, 1982). He was lead articles editor of the Syracuse University Law Review. In 1982 he was admitted to the Connecticut Bar and, in 1983, to the New York Bar.

Mr. Neporent is a writer and lecturer; he is a coauthor of "Lender Liability in Connection with Leveraged Buyouts" (New York: Practicing Law Institute, 1987, 1988, and 1989).

William J. Nightingale is an operations-oriented general management executive combining successful corporate management and consulting experience.

Mr. Nightingale founded the general management consulting firm of Nightingale & Associates, Inc., headquartered in New Canaan, Connecticut, in 1975. The firm focuses on the turnaround of troubled companies, divestitures, interim management, corporate and financial restructurings, and asset recovery management. Clients range from medium-sized private companies to large public corporations. The firm operates throughout the United States and overseas.

Prior to founding N&A, Inc., Mr. Nightingale was president and CEO of the Bali Company, Inc., and, before that, vice president of finance of Hanes Corporation.

Mr. Nightingale received a B.A. in economics from Bowdoin College and an M.B.A. from Harvard Business School.

Theodore G. Phelps recently left his position as senior manager of corporate reorganization with Price Waterhouse to cofound the Wilson Phelps Group, a firm with offices in New York and Los Angeles, specializing in turnaround consulting. Over the past 15 years Mr. Phelps has assisted over 70 companies in their efforts to reorganize, either as an independent consultant or as a member of management.

M. Freddie Reiss is the partner responsible for Price Waterhouse's reorganization and bankruptcy services in the western region. He has provided extensive service as financial advisor to law firms in litigation and reorganization matters, including forensic accounting investigations, preference and fraudulent conveyance analyses, debt restructurings, solvency, and use of cash collateral. He was chairman of the Los Angeles Litigation Services Committee and is a member of the Association of Insolvency Accountants.

Mr. Reiss is a C.P.A. and received his B.B.A. degree from City College of New York.

Jeffrey S. Sabin is a graduate of Cornell University (B.S., magna cum laude, 1974) and Boston College (J.D., cum laude, 1977) where he was executive articles editor of the *Boston College International and Comparative Law Journal*.

Mr. Sabin is a partner in Schulte Roth & Zabel and head of its bankruptcy and creditors' rights department. He coauthored "Lender Liability in Connection with Leveraged Buyouts" (New York: Practicing Law Institute, 1987, 1988, and 1989). He was a faculty member of the Practicing Law Institute program, Lender Liability Litigation, in 1987, 1988, and 1989.

David A. Sands is a former manager in the Price Waterhouse corporate strategies group. He specializes in workout and turnaround consulting engagements for middle market companies. Prior to joining Price Waterhouse, he was employed by Seidemann and Associates, where he gained broad experience in financial consulting.

Mr. Sands is a graduate of Ohio State University and a certified public accountant.

Robert S. Seidemann serves as director of the Price Waterhouse corporate strategies group in the Cleveland area. He has assisted in the turnaround of numerous companies experiencing difficulties and has guided many from the brink of insolvency to profitability.

Prior to joining Price Waterhouse, Mr. Seidemann was president of Seidemann and Associates, a pioneering firm in the turnaround and workout discipline. The firm was nationally recognized as a leader in prebankruptcy and bankruptcy consulting.

He has been responsible at both Seidemann and Associates and Price Waterhouse for devising strategies for companies facing unique problems or growth opportunities and, with his entrepreneurial insight and negotiating skills, has played a vital role in solving many of his clients' problems.

Bernard Shapiro is a partner at Gendel, Raskoff, Shapiro & Quittner, Los Angeles, California. He is a member of the Advisory Committee on Bankruptcy Rules of the Judicial Conference of the United States and vice chairman, National Bankruptcy Conference. He is also a member of the Financial Lawyers Conference and Executive Committee, Section on Commercial Law & Bankruptcy, L.A. County Bar Association.

In 1980, Mr. Shapiro was adjunct professor at UCLA Law School and in 1978, visiting professor, Boalt Hall (UC Berkeley). He has authored various law review articles and lectures for the California Continuing Education of the Bar (CEB), Practicing Law Institute, American Law Institute, and the American Bar Association.

Michael S. Sitrick is chairman and chief executive officer of Sitrick and Company, a public relations firm specializing in corporate, financial, crisis, and transactional communications. One of the nation's most accomplished and experienced communications strategists, Mr. Sitrick has successfully developed and implemented programs for numerous troubled companies, operating both in and out of Chapter 11, as well as a variety of companies engaged in hostile and friendly takeovers.

Prior to founding Sitrick and Company, Mr. Sitrick served as senior vice president of communications at Wickes Companies, Inc., at one time the largest nonrailroad company to file Chapter 11. Before joining Wickes, Mr. Sitrick headed communications and government affairs for National Can Corporation; he was an officer and group supervisor of one of Chicago's largest public relations agencies; and an agency deputy department head and public information officer for the City of Chicago in the Richard J. Daley administration.

Mr. Sitrick holds a B.S. degree in business administration and journalism from the University of Maryland, College Park, Maryland.

William A. Slaughter is a partner with the Philadelphia-based law firm of Ballard, Spahr, Andrews & Ingersoll. A graduate of Yale University (1975, cum laude) and Yale Law School (1979), he has specialized in bankruptcy, workouts, and turnarounds for over 10 years.

Mr. Slaughter's practice is presently concentrated in financially troubled companies in real estate development and syndication, health care, and manufacturing, and in companies burdened with the defense of mass tort litigation.

Donald E. Thomas is the Price Waterhouse partner responsible for bankruptcy and restructuring services in the central region. He has a diverse business background, which includes consulting, investment banking, commercial banking, and industry experience as president and chief executive of a private company.

Mr. Thomas has had extensive consulting experience in complex financial restructurings, bankruptcies, mergers and acquisitions, and litigation testimony. Some of the recent bankruptcy and restructuring engagements that he has been involved with include: Southmark Corporation, Wilson Foods Corporation, Greyhound Lines, Inc., Circle K Corporation, First RepublicBank Corporation, The Western Company of North America, Kaiser Steel Corporation, MCorp., and Kroh Brothers Development Corporation.

Mr. Thomas, a certified public accountant, holds a B.A. degree in economics from Austin College and an M.B.A. degree in finance from the University of Texas at Austin.

Myron Trepper a graduate of Brooklyn Law School in 1968, is a partner in the firm of Willkie Farr & Gallagher in New York and heads the firm's bankruptcy and reorganization practice. He has practiced bankruptcy law exclusively since 1971, with a substantial concentration in the representation of debtors in reorganization proceedings under the Bankruptcy Code and its predecessor statute. He has been involved in many major

reorganization cases, including those of The Charter Company, Towle Manufacturing Company, and LTV Corporation, and he was part of a team of lawyers that represented Pennzoil Company in the Chapter 11 proceedings of Texaco, Inc.

Mr. Trepper has represented the Trump organization in its acquisition of the Eastern Airlines Shuttle and in connection with the Chapter 11 proceedings of Resorts International. He is presently lead counsel to Integrated Resources, Inc., in its pending Chapter 11 proceedings and is acting as an advisor to the Edward J. DeBartolo Corporation in connection with the Federated and Allied Chapter 11 cases. He has appeared on numerous panels and has lectured before trade and business organizations and associations.

Ronald G. Vollmar is a partner in the reorganization and litigation services group of Price Waterhouse. He has extensive experience with both in and out of court corporate reorganizations and related litigation and financial reporting issues.

Mr. Vollmar received both his bachelor of science in business administration and master of accountancy degrees from Bowling Green State University.

Barry S. Volpert is a vice president and head of workouts and restructurings at Goldman, Sachs & Co. He has extensive experience with corporate reorganizations, in and out of Chapter 11, representing companies, creditors, and others and investing as a principal. Recent transactions he has participated in include, among others, Eastern Air Lines, L. J. Hooker, First Executive, and Concurrent Computer. He has also worked on

numerous leveraged buyouts, recapitalizations, and mergers and acquisitions.

Mr. Volpert graduated summa cum laude from Amherst College, where he was a member of Phi Beta Kappa, and then worked as a newspaper reporter for the *Singapore Straits Times* while on a Luce fellowship. He earned a J.D., magna cum laude, from the Harvard Law School, where he was an editor of the *Harvard Law Review*, and an M.B.A. from Harvard Business School, where he was a Baker Scholar.

Jane Lee Vris is an attorney at Wachtell, Lipton, Rosen & Katz, practicing in the creditors' rights department. She specializes in workouts, Chapter 11 reorganizations, and corporate finance. She has participated in such workouts and reorganizations as Allis-Chalmers, A. H. Robins, LTV, The Western Company of North America, Allied Stores and Federated Department Stores, and Ames.

Ms. Vris is a member of the American Bar Association, the New York State Bar, The Association of the Bar of the City of New York, and the Bar of the District of Columbia.

She received her B.A., magna cum laude, from the University of Pennsylvania and her J.D. from New York University School of Law in 1983, where she was managing editor of the law review.

Carol A. Weiner is an associate at Schulte Roth & Zabel in its bankruptcy and creditors' rights department. She specializes in the area of Chapter 11 claims trading.

Ms. Weiner graduated from the University of Michigan (B.A., with high honors, 1983) and its law school (J.D., 1986). She was admitted to the New York State Bar in 1987.

David R. Williams is senior manager at Price Waterhouse in Denver. He has significant experience in consulting financially troubled companies, including engagements in numerous industries such as bank holding companies, real estate firms, savings and loan associations, insurance companies, and mortgage bankers. He also has extensive experience in debtor and creditor financial restructurings, acquisition due diligence, leveraged buyouts, and bankruptcies.

Mr. Williams received a B.S. in accounting from the University of Arizona. He is a member of the American Institute of CPAs.

Linda G. Worton is an attorney with the Philadelphia-based law firm of Ballard, Spahr, Andrews & Ingersoll. Her legal practice emphasizes workouts, turnarounds, and Chapter 11 reorganizations, representing both debtors and creditors.

Ms. Worton received her B.A., magna cum laude, from Duke University in 1984 and her J.D. from the University of Pennsylvania Law School in 1988.

She is admitted to practice in the Commonwealth of Pennsylvania, the State of Florida, and the United States District Court for the Eastern District of Pennsylvania. Ms. Worton is a member of the Pennsylvania Bar Association, Philadelphia Bar Association, the American Bar Association, and the Eastern District of Pennsylvania Bankruptcy Conference.

Joel B. Zweibel is a senior partner and co-head of the creditors' rights department at O'Melveny & Myers. During his career, Mr. Zweibel has represented official creditors' committees in many of the largest Chapter 11 cases ever filed, including, among others, Texaco, Eastern Air Lines, Lomas Financial, and Public Service Company of New Hampshire, and has also represented groups of secured and unsecured bank creditors in such cases as LTV, Braniff, and Baldwin-United.

Mr. Zweibel is a member of the National Bankruptcy Conference and chairman of its Committee on Avoiding Powers. Mr. Zweibel is also the former chair of the New York City Bar Association Committee on Bankruptcy and Corporate Reorganization, a coauthor of Herzog's Bankruptcy Forms and Practice, and a contributing author of the Collier Bankruptcy Practice Guide.

CONTENTS

INTRODUCTION
Sanford C. Sigoloff   1

1   IDENTIFYING A TROUBLED COMPANY
M. Freddie Reiss and Theodore G. Phelps   7

Early Warning Signals.   Stages of a Troubled Company.   Causes of the Problems.   Indicators of Financial Health.   Actions.   Conclusion.

2   DETERMINING THE LIKELIHOOD OF A TURNAROUND
Robert S. Seidemann and David A. Sands   44

Introduction.   Crisis Management.   The Crisis Management Team.   Steps toward Recovery.   Creditor Relations.   Conclusion.

3   WORKOUT OR BANKRUPTCY?
William A. Slaughter and Linda G. Worton   72

Introduction.   Warning Signs and the First Steps toward Reorganization.   Workout Out of Court.   Chapter 11 Bankruptcy Reorganization.   Moving from a Workout Mode to a Bankruptcy Filing.   Workout or Bankruptcy—The Decision Making.

4   FINANCING ALTERNATIVES FOR THE TROUBLED COMPANY—AN OVERVIEW OF AVAILABLE OPTIONS AND THEIR BENEFITS, PERILS, AND PITFALLS
Harvey R. Miller   97

Introduction. Asset Sales. Secured Financing. Employee Stock Ownership Plans. Exchange Offers. Equity Infusion. General Expense Reduction. Conclusion.

5 **RESCUE FROM THE DEAD: A TURNAROUND IN PROGRESS**
Raymond H. Kraftson and Richard J. Giacco   138

Background. Should We Get Involved in a Turnaround? Executing the Turnaround. Conclusion.

6 **TAX CONSIDERATIONS OF AN OUT-OF-COURT OR CHAPTER 11 REORGANIZATION**
Peter J. Gibbons and Carmen A. Eggleston   152

Introduction. Tax Consequences to the Debtor. Other Debtor Tax Considerations. Tax Consequences to the Creditor.

7 **LIQUIDATION OPTIONS FOR TROUBLED COMPANIES**
Francis J. King   200

Introduction. A Taxonomy of Assets. Fundamentals of Valuation. The Valuation of Intangible Assets. The Valuation of Tangible Assets. The Valuation of Going-Concern Value. Summary of Analytical Framework. Market Data on Asset Liquidations.

8 **REORGANIZATIONS AND THE SECURED CREDITOR**
Denis F. Cronin and Jane Lee Vris   244

Introduction. Overview. The Secured Claim. Avoiding Powers. Adequate Protection. Confirmation, Classification, Voting. Secured Creditor's Section "1111 (b) Election." Conclusion.

9 **OTHER CONSIDERATIONS IN DEALING WITH A TROUBLED COMPANY**
John F. Horstmann III and S. Fain Hackney   302

An Overview of Pension, Employee, and Retiree Benefits Considerations in the Context to Troubled Companies. An Overview of Environmental Considerations in the Context of Troubled Companies. An Overview of the Federal Plant Closing Act. Conclusion.

10 **STABILIZING THE WORK FORCE: CONTROLLING THE INFORMATION FLOW**
Michael S. Sitrick   329

The Need for Effective Communication in Crisis Situations. The Braniff Way versus the Wickes Way. Developing a Crisis Communications Program. How to Hire Public Relations Counsel.

11	**HOW TO TURN AROUND A CORPORATION PLAGUED WITH MASS TOXIC TORTS**
	J. Gregg Miller and Francis J. Lawall 341

Introduction. Parties. Planning for Bankruptcy. Future Claims. Claims Bar Date. The Plan of Reorganization. Confirmation of the Plan. Voting on the Plan. Cramdown. The Trust Fund. I.R.C. Section 468B Tax Issues.

12	**THE ROLE OF THE UNSECURED CREDITORS' COMMITTEE IN WORKOUTS AND REORGANIZATIONS**
	Joel B. Zweibel and Adam C. Harris 363

Formation ot the Unsecured Creditors' Committee. Powers and Duties of Creditors' Committees. The Creditors' Committee as Ally or Adversary. Conclusion.

13	**THE LAWYER'S ROLE IN REPRESENTING THE DISTRESSED COMPANY**
	Myron Trepper 400

Understand the Business. Understand the Legal Entity and Debt Structure. Develop an Understanding of Cash and Financing Resources. Involving the Constituencies. Advising the Board of Directors. Counseling Management. In or Out of Court. Prepackaged Chapter 11. Chapter 11—The End or the Beginning? Conclusion.

14	**THE ACCOUNTANT'S ROLE IN THE WORKOUT ENVIRONMENT—REPRESENTING THE DEBTOR**
	Donald E. Thomas 434

The 1990s—Future Opportunities for Accountants. The Changing Role of the Accountant. The New Role of the Accountant. Present Value/Recovery Matrix of Restructuring Alternatives. Conclusion.

15	**THE ACCOUNTANT'S ROLE IN THE WORKOUT ENVIRONMENT—REPRESENTING THE CREDITOR**
	Dominic DiNapoli 456

Introduction. Creditors Need Their Own Accountants. Accountant's Role—Representing the Creditor in an Out-of-Court Workout. Accountant's Role—Representing the Creditor in a Bankruptcy Proceeding. Determining if a Workout or Chapter 11 Is the Proper Course of Action. Conclusion.

16 THE INVESTMENT BANKER'S ROLE IN THE WORKOUT PROCESS
Carter S. Evans 473

Evaluating the Situation and Getting Management to Come to Grips with the Problem at Hand. Preparing the Business Plan. Determining Debt Capacity. Credit Agreements. Exchange Offers. Term Loan Agreements. Valuation of the Business. Conclusion.

17 CONSIDERATIONS FOR INVESTING IN TROUBLED LEVERAGED BUYOUTS
Robert F. Cushman and James D. Epstein 490

Introduction. Capital Structure—Reasons for Financial Difficulties. Participants in an LBO Restructuring. Federal Tax Issues in a Restructuring of an LBO Company. Fraudulent Conveyance Issues.

18 OPPORTUNITIES FOR INVESTING IN TROUBLED COMPANIES
Barry S. Volpert 514

Introduction. Increased Investment Opportunities in Troubled Companies. Identifying Opportunities. Methods for Investing in Troubled Companies. Investment Risks. Analyzing Opportunities: Case Study. Conclusion.

19 ANALYZING FINANCIAL STATEMENTS FILED WITH THE SEC
Michael O. Gagnon 543

Introduction. Reporting Requirements of SEC Registrants. Analysis of Reports Filed by SEC Registrants. Examples of Distressed Companies.

20 UTILIZING CASH FLOW STATEMENTS AS AN ANALYTICAL TOOL
Gregory E. Bardnell and David R. Williams 562

Introduction. Cash. Solvency. Generally Accepted Accounting Principles (GAAP). The "Old" Statement of Changes in Financial Position. Statement of Cash Flows. Ratio Analysis. Quality of Cash Flows. Nonreporting/Nonrecurring Items. Sample Review. Prospective Information. AICPA Guidelines. Cash Management Orders. Conclusion.

21 ANALYZING CHAPTER 11 FIGURES
Ronald G. Vollmar 597

Introduction. Schedule of 20 Largest Unsecured Creditors. Operating Reports. Plan of Reorganization. Disclosure Statement. Utilization of Cash Flows. Conclusion.

22	**EVALUATING MANAGEMENT**	
	William Nightingale and Stephen J. Hopkins	612

Introduction. General Functions of Management. Management Requirements in a Crisis Situation. Initial Evaluation of Management Effectiveness. In-Depth Evaluation of Management Competence. Effective Management and the Use of Outside Consultants. Conclusion.

23	**PURCHASING FINANCIALLY DISTRESSED COMPANIES BEFORE BANKRUPTCY—PITFALLS**	
	Bernard Shapiro and Gregory A. Bray	631

Introduction. General Rules of Successor Liability in Stock Transactions and Asset Purchases. Successor Liability for Failure to Give Advance Notice of the Transaction to the Seller's Creditors: The Bulk Transfer Laws. Attacking the Transaction for Inadequate Consideration: The Fraudulent Conveyance Laws. The Hot Goods Rule: The Seller's Violation of Federal Labor Laws Can Preclude the Purchaser from Selling or Using Goods. Representations and Warranties by the Distressed Seller: Structuring the Transaction to Maximize the Purchaser's Potential Recovery Should They Be Breached. Conclusion.

24	**INVESTING IN DISTRESSED SECURITIES**	
	Edward I. Altman	663

Supply of Distressed Securities. Distressed Security Investor Profile. Returns on Distressed Securities Investment Strategies. A Defaulted Debt Index. Market Value Weighting and Return Bias. Diversification Benefits: Correlation With Other Securities. Market Importance and Outlook. Glossary of Terms.

25	**LEGAL CONSIDERATIONS OF PURCHASING SECURITIES**	
	Jeffrey S. Sabin, Mark A. Neporent, and Carol A. Weiner	686

Introduction. What Constitutes a Security in a Bankruptcy Case. Rights of Equity Security Holders under the Bankruptcy Code. Trading of Claims in Bankruptcy. Section 1145 of the Bankruptcy Code.

26	**INTERNATIONAL WORKOUTS AND BANKRUPTCIES: ADDITIONAL CONSIDERATIONS**	
	Donald R. Joseph	719

Introduction. The U.S. Debtor Having Assets Abroad. The Foreign Debtor Having Assets in the United States. The Model International Insolvency Cooperation Act. Conclusion.

INDEX   **757**

INTRODUCTION

Sanford C. Sigoloff
Sigoloff & Associates, Inc.

The 80s was the decade when the entire nation got hooked on business. Young and old alike, we came to realize that a good business saga has as much to do with human dynamics as it did with a healthy balance sheet. We read the business pages for drama—the same reason we usually read the sports pages.

When we use "the 80s" casually as a term of derision, we tend to forget there was another part of the decade. As horrifying as the excesses of the late 80s were, it is important to remember they began either as refreshing insights or as much needed reforms. It was only as the decade evolved that they were perverted by greed and venality.

We've had decades like the 80s before—the Roaring Twenties were giddy on money and the thrill of spending it; and other decades worshipped businessmen and mistook speculation for investment. We had the conglomeration madness of the 60s and its resultant damage to American initiative. Nothing really was new—not being overweight with debt, not the arrival of the junk bond, not even the obsession with paper profits. We needed a new business vocabulary that reflected the decade's greed and moral laxity; terms that emerged from the financial heights and pits, including raider, entrenched management, management buyout, leveraged buyouts, risk arbitrage, junk bonds, vultures, white knights, squires, strips, PIKS, fradulent conveyance, default rate, and turnaround. Our genius for creating acronyms like DINK (double income no kids), NIMBY (not in my back yard), and MEGO (my eyes glazed over) added to the babblespeak of the times.

Junk bonds proved to be the ideal weapon for exploiting a weakness in corporate America that raiders had detected quickly. They saw an inefficient stock market that valued many large companies at prices well below what became known as their *breakup value*. By using war chests of junk bonds, takeover artists could pay a premium to shareholders and still stand to profit from dismantling their target.

Thanks in large part to Drexel Burnham Lambert, the 1980s became the decade of the deal. In 1986 alone, approximately 4,000 takeovers, mergers, and buyouts were completed in the United States, at a record total cost of some $236 billion. While some takeovers shook up overly complacent managers and led to useful restructuring, much of the raiding served only to distract corporate America from its real work of developing and improving products and services. In the view of Wall Street's critics, hundreds of deals were driven by the fees and stock payoffs they would generate. This was not the way Wall Street traditionally operated, but, in that hotly competitive environment, many firms followed Drexel's lead. Last year, interest payments of nonfinancial corporations amounted to almost 25 percent of pretax income, up from approximately 14 percent in 1979.

"In a period of slow growth like we have now, unwinding the excesses of the 1980s is going to result in some major problems," says noted economist Henry Kaufman. He sees companies reducing capital expenditures to save money, thereby penalizing future productivity gains and limiting their ability to compete. He also predicts that a new era of more rigorous government oversight of the financial system and markets is at hand.

Drexel's demise becomes the symbol that officially ends the go-go era of financial deregulation, of debt-heavy takeovers and leveraged buyouts that together produced the improvidence of the 1980s on Wall Street and in corporate boardrooms. Their departure, coming on the heels of the massive taxpayer bailout of the nation's thrift industry and the recent eruption of real estate loan problems at many of the nation's banks, has reignited worries that the entire U.S. financial system is a debt-laden house of cards. Few experts forecast a collapse—unless the United States suffers a jolting recession that would make it hard for companies to service their soaring debts. Yet the unprecedented debt buildup has left behind major headaches. The debt binge of the 1980s is over, and a new conservatism has taken hold. Growing demand, shrinking profits, and intense competition are turning once manageable debt loads into crushing financial burdens. Those who said the borrowing couldn't go on forever were right.

Shedding the excesses of the 1980s will be painful for both borrowers and lenders. But the process may be inevitable. A healthy financial system, in which the frugal savings of individuals are matched to the dreams of borrowers, is critical in a modern capitalist economy. If savings can't be tapped, investment withers. If borrowers fritter away other people's money, wealth is destroyed. It is said that the relationship between debtors and creditors forms the ultimate foundation of capitalism. Today, debtors, creditors, and regulators have begun the task of firming up that foundation.

As the credit contraction begins, the economy is likely to undergo some profound changes. Spending will slow, and economic output will be dampened. Savings hopefully will increase and ultimately fuel a rise in business investment. The transition from extravagance to prudence will not be easy, however, and, while it will bring positive results, these may not be apparent for some years.

The pullback in lending and borrowing is bound to have a marked impact on the economy, if only because debt had so dramatic an effect on economic growth in the 1980s. Easy credit built office towers, shopping malls, and housing developments. It also financed the leveraging of corporate America, including some $500 billion transformed from equity into debt. That conversion is one important factor behind the 1980s' consumer spending spree.

With global competition so fierce, companies find it difficult to raise prices. What's more, their debt burdens are pinching profits hard, since interest payments are now absorbing a record 30 percent of cash flow. In addition, some highly leveraged companies are discovering they can no longer sell assets at heady prices to reduce their onerous debt obligations.

All that will change. First, spending by consumers, already slowing, is likely to fall well below the 3.5 percent annual rate of increase it averaged in the second half of the 1980s. Indeed, consumer spending, adjusted for inflation, fell by about 0.1 percent in the fourth quarter of 1989. Consumers are not about to go on another borrowing binge. Some economists predict that people might retrench as residential real estate values slump in many parts of the country. Mortgage loans at least 30 days overdue rose to 5.0 percent during the third quarter of last year, up from 4.5 percent in the previous quarter. Installment loan delinquencies climbed to more than 2.8 percent at the same time—just short of the record attained during the 1974–75 recession. Business, too, is cutting back on its borrowing and spending plans. Business investment grew at a 4.4 percent rate from the fourth quarter of 1988 to the fourth quarter of 1989. But in the final quarter of last year, capital spending dipped to a 3.0 percent annual rate. Investment should be flat to slightly lower this year, several Wall Street economists predict. The reason: the current squeeze on corporate profits and corporate cash flow.

The result of this is an economic growth rate over the next few years that is likely to run below the 2.6 percent pace of the past decade. As corporations work down their debts, for instance, their newfound conservatism most likely will tend to ensure that growth remains slow.

But even as companies shun investments in the face of high capital cost, their shareholders will continue to push managers to pursue such strategies as restructurings, leveraged buyouts, and takeovers to achieve higher returns. This forces management to pull back on long-term investment and to increase investor payouts. Foreign companies, by contrast, spend far more on long-term investments, because their cost of capital is much lower and their focus less short term.

Over time, and in good market conditions, reducing the cost of capital and shrinking corporate leverage will remove a huge impediment to investment in factories, as well as in research and development. Deleveraging many companies should let them recapture cash flow now diverted to interest payments, and, ultimately, higher investment rates should help improve U.S. companies' productivity and international competitiveness.

While the new conservatism will be a plus in the long run, it will claim many victims besides bankrupt Federated/Allied Stores and

Drexel Burnham Lambert. Rating agency Standard & Poor's Corp. estimates that about $15 billion of bonds could go into default this year, up from $6 billion in 1989. Small and medium-sized companies, even sound ones, are often getting cool responses from lenders.

Many of these collapsing businesses will go through the process of repair, redirection, and resuscitation euphemistically called *turnaround*.

The turnaround process (sometimes referred to as *corporate renewal*) has become a field in itself, employing specialized managers and consultants, as well as professionals from the fields of law, accounting, and finance. Turnarounds are often described as dramatic and unpredictable at best. In an economy fueled by LBOs and debt, the use and importance of turnarounds will grow even further as Chapter 11 actions become increasingly important in American business practice.

While awareness of turnarounds has become widespread, the industry and its participants have lacked historical perspective and formal definition of something that is a complicated process, not merely a single event. The terms *turnaround* and *workout* are used interchangeably, and have become synonymous with an industry that is growing, not only in size, but in the sophistication and specialization of its participants.

Concurrent with specialization comes a vocabulary of terms usually signalling a subtle shift in emphasis. Crisis management is active in everyday corporate life as management directs financial and nonfinancial resources to cope with competition, factory schedules, product line pricing, labor relations, and the like. To a turnaround practitioner, crisis management usually means *acute distress* that prevents, inhibits, or threatens the well-being of the enterprise. If the crisis is severe and viability is at risk, corrective actions range from going into bankruptcy to the restructuring of management, ownership, operations, and the balance sheet. Broadly speaking, the term *restructuring* today connotes debt-equity conversion, bank agreement covenant modification, interest rate adjustments or deferrals, and creation of new or modification of old debt instruments concurrent with these management and operational redirections.

The events of the 80s wrought numerous disturbing new trends in the areas of corporate distress. For example, the increase in LBO activity from $18 billion in 1984 to $73 billion in 1989 is shadowed closely by an increase in business failures from 11,000 cases and $4.6 billion in 1980 to 50,000 cases and $36 billion in 1989.

The effect of burdensome institutional debt in contributing to failures has increased from 2.1 percent of cases in 1984 to 9.0 percent in 1988, reflective of the excessive leveraging taking place at the time.

In addition, the size of bankruptcies has changed dramatically as well. In 1987, Kaiser Steel for $706 million and Cook United for $70 million were the first and tenth largest bankruptcy cases, respectively. This compares to Lomas Financial for $6.7 billion and Maxicare for $710 million in 1989 as the first and tenth largest cases, respectively. The *tenth* largest case in 1989 would have been bigger than the *largest* case in 1987, emphasizing dramatically the changing face of these kinds of cases.

In the future, the bankruptcy courts increasingly will become a forum for what have not been traditional bankruptcy court issues. The Texaco-Pennzoil litigation, the A. H. Robbins/Dalkon shield litigation, and the Manville/asbestos resolutions might be seen as harbingers of cases to come, where legal issues are the primary driver of a given case. We are also not far from seeing the first cases driven by environmental or international trade issues as further examples of the rapidly evolving role of the bankruptcy court in resolving some of the havoc wrought by the socioeconomic changes of the 80s. Increasingly, the turnaround/workout process will become a mirror reflective of the mistakes and excesses of our time.

In the preparation of this handbook, we have attempted to match topics and authors that bring both the academician's and practitioner's views to the readers. If the 80s were the "deal years," then the 90s will be the "repair and regrowth years."

CHAPTER 1

IDENTIFYING A TROUBLED COMPANY

M. Freddie Reiss, CPA
Price Waterhouse
Theodore G. Phelps, CPA
Wilson Phelps Group, Inc.

EARLY WARNING SIGNALS

Business organizations do not generally become financially troubled overnight. Usually the problems that result in financial distress are cumulative and have built up over a long period, sometimes years. Although it often seems that a single event, such as the bankruptcy of a large customer or a technical innovation by a competitor, is the triggering of a company's troubles, more often this is the straw that broke the camel's back.

The ability to predict financial problems early enough to implement meaningful remedial action is, therefore, of great importance. Unfortunately, many of the indicators of future problems are looked at as merely day-to-day problems of running a business, and are, therefore, ignored as early warning signs of impending or future disaster. It may be true that isolated incidents are generally no more significant than that. But when these incidents seem repetitive and begin falling into familiar patterns, more serious attention must be devoted to the enterprise to determine the causes of the problems and the solutions needed to solve these problems early enough to avert financial disaster.

A number of quantitative models have been developed to predict the possibility of bankruptcy in later years, most notably the Altman analysis, or "Z" score. While such models are of great value and are relied upon heavily by many banks and other lenders, there are qualitative events or trends that also serve to predict upcoming trouble or problems.

At times it is difficult to distinguish early warning signs of financial difficulty from the actual causes of such problems, since they do cross over to a great degree. An early warning sign that is allowed to continue unabated might itself become one of the causes of the problems the organization is facing.

STAGES OF A TROUBLED COMPANY

The stages of a troubled company may arbitrarily be defined as early, immediate, and late. It must be emphasized that the progress through these three stages is a continuum, and no one event or circumstance can be pointed to as a transition point from one stage to another. There is, therefore, a great deal of crossover, and the definitions are by necessity somewhat arbitrary and will differ by industry. For example, a 30-day payable might be quite acceptable to a steel vendor but prompt a lawsuit by a supplier of perishable products.

Early

In a company entering the early stages of financial distress, isolated inefficiencies in the production and distribution functions begin to occur more frequently and form patterns. Shipments slow down somewhat and quality slips a bit.

In like manner, inventories build or remain constant as sales stagnate or begin to decline. There is some erosion in margins, but management is generally not concerned, feeling that the situation will correct itself "next month" or "next quarter." Payables might be extended about 15 days beyond normal terms, but, beyond getting a few phone calls from concerned vendors, no problems are perceived by management.

Cash balances are falling, but with a little stretching all immediate obligations are met. The bank, if concerned at all, might ask a few questions but generally is reassured by management responses.

Intermediate

In the intermediate stage of a troubled company, production problems become more acute. Actual material shortages are now occurring as management attempts to conserve cash by reducing inventories. Quality problems are generally more frequent, and gross margins are slipping noticeably.

Collections are still slowing, and working capital lines are close to or at their limits. Vendors are passing 60 days past due and are demanding payment prior to extending new credit. Some vendors are demanding cash on delivery or cash in advance. New trade credit is difficult to obtain as the industry becomes aware of the company's paying habits.

Cash balances are dangerously low, and meeting payroll becomes a weekly challenge. The company's bank is becoming very concerned at this point and generally asks for a meeting at which the bank expects the management of the company to produce a plan for recovery. The company's credit facilities are in technical default with respect to covenants, and servicing the debt becomes more and more difficult by the day.

Employee morale is falling as they observe the problems that the company is experiencing. Rumors are circulating concerning the company's problem. Some of the better people are looking for other jobs or have already left.

Late

A company in late decline is generally in chaos. Production schedules are routinely not met as orders are rescheduled in an effort to ship those orders that have become high priority, because of customer paying habits or, more often, threats by valued customers to purchase elsewhere if schedules are not kept. Quality problems have become the norm, and returns and rework factors are rising. There is a general inability to maintain an efficient production schedule, because of chronic material shortages or outages.

Collections continue to slow as quality problems and requests for credits by customers cause the value of the accounts receivable to deteriorate. The company's working capital lines may be overdrawn at this point, because receivables previously used as collateral have become ineligible because of their age. The company is now on C.O.D. with nearly all of its vendors, and many of them are demanding C.O.D. plus a portion of the past due balance prior to shipment. Those vendors who have received N.S.F. checks are now demanding certified checks or cash prior to accepting new orders. Several vendors have filed lawsuits to which the company can offer no defense.

Cash balances are now negative as the company plays the float. Daily overdrafts are reported by the bank to the company, and covering those overdrafts becomes the full-time occupation of the company's controller. Because of this, financial reporting has become nonexistent or haphazard at the best. The bank may have turned the credit over to its problem-loan people, who are demanding more and more frequent meetings.

Employees are now leaving in increasing numbers. Layoffs are arbitrary and frequent. People are now trying to do more than one job with little success and less direction from management. Collapse of the business is imminent.

The above is a somewhat abbreviated odyssey through the stages of a declining company. Obviously much more is going on during this process, and no company will have the same experience.

Certain threads, however, are consistently present in all stages of a company in decline. Management becomes increasingly ineffective, unable to deal with the slightest deviations from the norm. Employee morale continues to worsen as it loses confidence in the ability of management to turn things around.

The customers of the company become increasingly impatient as they are offered excuse after excuse for poor quality, late shipments, incorrect or missed orders. The loyalty upon which the company could once depend is now replaced by customers impatiently waiting until they can jump to another source.

The creditors of the company are also increasingly frustrated as promise after promise is broken, telephone calls are not returned, and checks are routinely returned for lack of funds. Creditors left with no other resort will finally sue the company, knowing full well that their chances for recovery of the monies due them are next to nothing.

Secured lenders of the company have progressively lost all confidence in management and are wondering whatever possessed them to make the loan in the first place. Their entire emphasis has now shifted to recovering their principal. If there exists a possibility that a commercial finance house will pay the bank off, the bank will take every opportunity to encourage the company to take this financing, even though it may involve significantly higher carrying charges and further impair the profitability and cash flow of the company. Absent the ability to get paid off from another source, the bank will attempt to work things out with the company but may demand additional collateral, the employment of a crisis consultant, collateralized personal guarantees, and higher interest rates to cover the increased risk of dealing with an ailing company. Communications with the lender have become much more formal, and the bank's attorney is now involved, whether or not he or she is present at meetings.

CAUSES OF THE PROBLEMS

The underlying causes of financial decline can be loosely separated into internal causes and external causes. Internal causes are those generally controllable by the management of the company, while external causes are typically not controllable, or at least controllable only in a limited sense by management.

Internal Causes

Ineffective Management
By far the most frequently cited reason for company failures is incompetent or ineffective management. The management of a company, along with its directors and ultimately its shareholders, is responsible for everything that goes on within the company. Every function and, by implication, every failure of a function is ultimately under the control of and, thereby, the responsibility of management. It is the responsibility of management to ensure the existence of proper manufacturing controls so that goods and services are

purchased at the lowest possible price, that quality is maintained, that products and services are delivered on time, and that customer complaints are adequately and promptly handled. It is the responsibility of management to see that adequate information systems are so designed and implemented that it has the essential information available to it in a reliable and timely fashion to enable it to carry out its function. It is the responsibility of management to see that accounts receivable are collected within the terms extended by the company, and that the bills are paid on time. If financing is needed, it is the purview of management to seek out such financing on the most favorable terms available and to see that it is repaid according to the terms agreed upon. It is also the responsibility of management to identify its own errors and to take corrective action. The buck stops with management, or the bucks stop altogether. It is a big job, and it is a job that all too often is not taken seriously enough by those to whom it is entrusted.

Financial difficulties can result from unrealistic expectations of management or of ownership. For example, an overappraisal of the manner in which a product will be accepted in the marketplace might lead to an overexpansion of facilities. Then if the anticipated sales are not realized, the company is saddled with idle facilities and often with the debt associated with them.

Frequently, especially in entrepreneurial enterprises wherein the owner is also the chief executive officer, unrealistic expectations can lead to extravagances that are not supportable by the profits the organization can reasonably be expected to achieve. The availability of debt financing sometimes aggravates this problem. More than one entrepreneur has built himself a Taj Mahal for an office only to realize too late that the Taj Mahal is a tomb.

Extravagances do not have to be of a personal nature. It is not uncommon to visit the factories of troubled companies and find some of the most sophisticated and technologically superior equipment in the industry standing idle, because of lack of sales due to some other problem that cannot be addressed by superior technology, such as products with waning life cycles or with quality problems caused by the use of substandard materials in manufacturing.

Businesses often outgrow the ability of their founders to effectively manage them in the face of increasing sales. It is not uncommon for such persons to overestimate their abilities to continue to manage the business as it continues to grow. Even when they recognize the need to bring new talent on board, they often lack the skills to determine who they should hire and to manage them once they are hired. When problems begin to manifest themselves, they often are unable to recognize that they have problems and lack the depth of experience with this to deal with them.

Finally, when financial problems have manifested themselves, and cash flow becomes unmanageable, it is a natural tendency for management to blame nearly everyone other than itself. To do otherwise is to admit failure, and that is a bitter pill to swallow. Suddenly the bank that extended the loan last year is now cold and unsympathetic, suppliers are difficult to deal with, and the employees are not performing as well as they should. The fact of the matter is that the bank wants to be repaid, the vendors want to be paid for the goods and services they have provided, and the employees are probably not doing anything different than has been demanded of them all along.

Undercapitalization—A Major Cause
Probably the major reason for business failures after poor management is undercapitalization. While it can be argued that undercapitalization is a reflection of management's inability or unwillingness to recognize the limitations imposed upon the business by inadequate capital, it makes sense to treat undercapitalization as a separate subject.

It is theoretically possible in physics to sustain perpetual motion, except for the existence of friction. By like analysis, one might suppose that it would be possible to sustain business operations without capital. Friction does exist, however, and the theory is not supported in fact. The existence of capital in a business enterprise, among other things, provides an equity cushion for losses, differences in the timing of expenditures, and the receipt of cash for sales made previously. The judicious use of debt reduces the need for as much capital as would be necessary in the event that debt were not used. This is the reason for accounts receivable and inventory financing. A general rule is the more capital the better, within a relevant range. Fortunately, in the companies under consideration here, that range is always relevant.

Capital is also a measure of the ability of a business to withstand adversity, such as losses from bad debts, obsolete or ruined inventory, theft, and the like. Finally, capital is a means by which losses can be absorbed without the necessity of going out of business. Businesses have found another way to finance losses, which is the creation of more debt, much to the chagrin of those extending the credit.

A healthy business can become undercapitalized if it is experiencing rapid or uncontrolled growth or both. Such growth can, besides making the business unwieldy from a management standpoint, cause the capital of the business to be insufficient to sustain the business at the new levels. Rapid growth often sees critical short-term assets converted into less liquid or illiquid long-term assets (e.g., machinery and equipment used to sustain higher shipping levels). At the same time, higher levels of receivables and inventory strain cash further, forcing the company either to borrow against its current assets or to otherwise increase debt (e.g., by stretching its payables).

A business that is undercapitalized is always teetering on the brink of disaster, and usually not much is needed to move it over the line. Recognizing this is not going to improve the situation. Our history is full of stories of businesses started on a shoestring and turning out to be immensely successful enterprises. The stories neglect to state, however, that most of these businesses replace the shoestrings with capital infusion either from outside or from the retention of profits.

Excessive Leverage

A very pertinent corollary to undercapitalization as a major cause of business failures is that of excessive leverage. Capital can be small, because it is small, or because the debt is disproportionately large. Over the past decade and a half, leveraged buyouts have moved us from the sublime to the ridiculous with respect to debt-financed enterprises. Improperly used, a leveraged buyout can destroy a well-managed profitable enterprise by burdening it with incredible debt service. It will have a sensitivity to interest rates so onerous as to cause a company to reassess its prospects of survival with as low as a one point change in interest rates. The underlying business operations of the company might remain just as profitable, or more so, than they were prior to the leveraged transactions, at least in terms of earnings before interest and taxes; but when the debt service is figured in, the company might very well be insolvent in terms of meeting its debts as they mature. In such cases, the turnaround effort is simply one of restructuring the financing, provided that payment of the debt service up to the time of the restructuring has not created other problems, such as defaulting on subordinated debt or the overextending of trade creditors or the like.

A more likely scenario involving leveraged buyouts is one wherein the company falls somewhat short of its business plan, management does not perform entirely as expected, and the business is not as profitable as it was projected to be, or, in some cases, maybe it has taken a loss. Leveraged buyouts will continue to be a topic of conversation and debate in the insolvency world as more and more of them continue to fail. Also, excessive leverage will continue to be a major cause of business failures for the foreseeable future.

Failure to Penetrate Key Markets

The failure of a business to penetrate key or targeted markets brings into question the very reason for the enterprise's existence. Many companies have but one or two product lines that are targeted at a single market. In the event this market is not reached, the business likely will begin to fail. In a similar manner, the failure of a newly introduced product by a mature business can lead to severe problems, particularly if the company has a large up-front investment in the new product or innovation.

It is important for a company to have a "disaster plan" for dealing with the failure of a product to reach its market. Such a plan should address alternative markets, abandonment of the product line, and the resultant downsizing of the company. During this planning process, management will often see opportunities to minimize the risk. For example, when planning the disposition of an expensive piece of machinery, and the resultant losses accompanying such a disposition, management may see the advantage of outsourcing that particular stage of production until the product proves itself in the marketplace.

Lack of Product Innovation

Depending upon the industry, every product has a lifetime. This might be exceedingly short, as in the electronics or computer industries, or quite long, as in agricultural implements. The failure to take into account product life cycles has led many companies to become complacent and to take their markets for granted. Then, when someone else comes along with the proverbial better mousetrap, they are forced to scramble just to keep up in a market where they may have been dominant. It is imperative that producers remain up to date with present technology to provide for their customers' demand for the best and most innovative products available.

Large Concentration of Customers

Keeping one's eggs in one basket is a proscription not limited to egg ranchers. It often happens that a company develops a very small group of customers that provide the bulk of the company's sales. Although there are advantages to this, these are far outweighed by the possibility that one or more of those customers might encounter its own problems and not be in a position to pay its bills on time or to continue to order at previous levels. This sets up a daisy chain, which has the effect of the customer's problems becoming the supplier's problems. Clearly, spreading this risk among a larger customer base is a good strategy to follow. Product diversification is also a good defensive strategy. Also, reliance on a very large customer may leave the company unable to negotiate proper margins. While such relationships help propel young companies to fast growth, they can ultimately be their undoing as well.

Limited Sources for Strategic or Scarce Materials

A corollary to avoiding overdependence upon a single customer or group of customers is to assure to the greatest extent possible that alternative sources of supply exist for scarce or strategic materials or products. This is particularly pertinent to the company already experiencing some difficulty, in that sole source vendors are able to exert an inordinate amount of leverage in such situations by refusing to ship unless they are paid, even when the majority of other suppliers may have agreed to more lenient terms. In the less extreme situation, sole source vendors are in a position to demand prices that are not competitive. It always pays to shop around for the best price, terms, and quality, and, whenever possible, a company should have several sources of supply for its raw materials.

Poorly Planned Incentives for Retaining People
Today, especially as businesses become more dependent upon technology and on people who are skilled at making use of technology, the procuring and retention of quality personnel has become an increasingly important factor. Not adequately planning for the type of incentives that will lead to the retention of highly qualified employees is one of the more leading causes of quality problems, particularly in enterprises where quality is a major component. High turnover is expensive in any company, and, the more specialized the training, the more expensive it is to lose trained people. This is not only applicable to middle management people but to all levels.

Lack of Planning by Budgeting
Ignoring the budgetary process in business planning can and does lead to disastrous consequences. Today, it is imperative that a company know where it is going as well as the price of the journey. Generally speaking, troubled companies are those wherein this process has either been ignored or poorly implemented.

The budgetary process in a well-managed company is a dynamic one, in which nearly every level of management participates. Several budgets are normally prepared, including capital budgets, budgets of selling and G&A expenses, and manufacturing cost budgets. A great deal of thought must go into the sales forecast, because it drives many of the other budgets. At its best, the budgeting process brings together all of the best talent in the company to produce a product that will serve both as an operating plan for the ensuing period and as a measuring device to measure progress toward achieving the company's stated goals and objectives. However, when the process is improperly carried out, not carried out, or, worse, carried out and then ignored, the enterprise is working in the dark—with no scale by which to measure its effectiveness.

Lack of Management Information Systems
Lack of timely and correct data and the systems to provide it is a leading cause of business failure. Companies that do not have an accurate picture of product costs cannot make wise pricing decisions.

The systems for gathering such data, compiling it, and reporting it in a form usable by management are often inadequate to the task, either because of poor design or improper implementation. Often the systems are designed without due attention having been given to proper controls to ensure the integrity of the data. The systems themselves might contain flaws in the manner in which the information is processed once it has been gathered.

A company's management information system is an essential element in its success, not to say its survival, and the efficacy of these systems should be reviewed not only at the time of the original implementation of the system but at any time the system is modified, and then periodically thereafter. As processes that the system are designed to measure change, so must the information systems change as well.

It is generally a good idea to involve the company's auditors in the ongoing review of its management information systems, because their perspective, particularly as it relates to internal controls, is of great value. It is easy to understand how often entrepreneurial-based companies are driven by sales marketing and ignore information systems. However, a balance of priorities must exist.

Lack of Timely Internal Reporting
Timely reports to management concerning the profitability of a business, as well as its financial position, are of paramount importance. The delay of these reports reduces the usefulness of the information, in that it cannot be used to make the daily decisions necessary to keep a business operating. To the extent that decisions are made without this information, or with stale information, the chances are multiplied that mistakes—costly mistakes—will be made. Although the lack of timely internal reporting was previously described as a symptom of a troubled company, again there is a crossover between cause and effect. Poor decisions are usually made pursuant to a lack of pertinent information, rather that to sheer incompetence. Most managers will make the correct decision

when in possession of timely and correct data. It must be added that the unavailability of timely and accurate internally generated financial statements is a leading cause of lenders becoming disenchanted with a borrower. They assume, and rightfully so, that a company without such reports is headed for trouble, and they will then act accordingly.

External Causes

Again, the purist will assert that "excellent" management will be prepared for all eventualities no matter how calamitous. It is true that management has become more cognizant of external factors than it was in the past (e.g., preparing disaster recovery plans), and, with the aid of sophisticated computer analyses, preparing "what if" types of scenarios is more feasible that it was in the past. More realistically, however, it is reasonable to assume that at least some of the following factors are likely to take the majority of companies by surprise and cause havoc on their finances.

Legislation or Politics
More than ever before, legislative and political influences are affecting business. Where in many cases new opportunities are created by such actions, in others entire industries can be adversely affected. To illustrate, in the case of asbestos, an entire new industry, that of removing and disposing of asbestos, has been created, while one of the nations largest producers of asbestos was forced into Chapter 11 reorganization simply to deal with the rash of lawsuits brought about by the discovery of a link between that material and certain types of lung cancer. The disposal of toxic wastes, while it has created an entire industry whose charter is to dispose of these materials safely, also has imposed conditions on some industries so stringent as to put them out of business. Even if some of these circumstances could have been foreseen, it is doubtful that many of the adversely affected companies could have raised the money to correct their particular situations.

In today's environment, more than in any time in our history, legislative fiat is likely to impose burdens on industry that cannot be accommodated either by the normal operating cash flow of a company or by borrowing. Although it is difficult to determine what might come next, it is not at all difficult to foresee that legislative and political factors will become a larger, not a smaller, part of our economic surroundings.

Industry Conditions
General conditions within an industry can have a ripple effect on those who supply that industry. Therefore, a supplier to one of the large automakers can be adversely affected by the economic fortunes of its large customer. Moreover, a shopkeeper in a community that is made up largely of auto workers will be affected by a slowdown in the automobile industry. This is a simplified account of the manner in which industry conditions not controllable by management can, nevertheless, affect the operations of a business.

General Economic Conditions
General economic conditions (e.g., the rate of inflation, interest rates, the balance of trade) and the general economic health of the nation as a whole can have a profound effect on individual companies and their financial well-being. Consumer psychology about inflation and recessions can sometimes be self-fulfilling prophecies. If the dollar is "high" in international trade, exporters may suffer while importers flourish. While management can make contingency plans for some aspects of general economic conditions, often the consequences are so pervasive that it is impossible to escape the adverse effects resulting from such changes.

Labor Problems
Labor problems are another factor that is primarily external to the company but can affect its very existence. It is altogether possible for a business that is nonunion to be so damaged by, say, a trucking strike as to have to shut its doors for lack of ability to obtain needed materials and supplies. This is clearly beyond the ability of management to control. While it is possible to develop alternative means of having product delivered, it is doubtful that such can be done without severe effects on the profitability of the enterprise.

Labor problems need not only involve organized labor. In areas of the country there is a real shortage of certain types of skilled and unskilled labor. It is entirely possible that a large plant might open in a community, thereby drawing away much of the labor that had previously serviced the businesses there. When a labor shortage becomes acute, the company is faced with having to pay more to retain its employees, with finding a way to bring people into the work force who might live farther away than what is considered to be a normal commute, or with having ultimately to move.

Regulatory Issues
Closely related to political and legislative concerns are regulatory issues. The proliferation of regulatory involvement in business reached a new high in the last 20 years and shows no real signs of abatement. Occupational health and safety issues have led to new regulations, which cost hard dollars to implement. Factories have been forced to retrofit existing machines with enhanced safety features, while at the same time paying more for new machines that already have these features. While the motive is laudable in most cases, such regulatory edicts generally do not provide financing to those affected. In this instance, a cash-poor company may be forced to borrow at high rates or to defer payments to other creditors merely to remain in compliance with the law.

Foreign Competition
While doing business in the United States becomes more expensive because of various legislative and regulatory concerns, increased competition from countries where these concerns do not weigh as heavily, where labor costs are considerably cheaper, and where national tax policy might be more friendly to business than our own is, are competing head on with American industry. The results in many cases are that entire markets have been lost to foreign competition. In some cases it might be impossible, in spite of excellent management, to continue in some lines of business. In such instances, management might be doing its best to recognize the problem and cut its losses by leaving the marketplace or by shifting production overseas.

Innovative Technology Leading to Obsolescence
A company that does not invest in research and development is likely to find itself disadvantaged by more innovative competitors, be they foreign or domestic. In some instances, entire industries will change or become obsolete, and, in those cases, it is quite

probable that a company might not survive. It then becomes the job of management or those professionals it employs to apprise the shareholders of this circumstance so other alternatives might be pursued. These alternatives might include sale of the company, purchase of another product line, or liquidation. Diversification of products has become quite evident in some of our larger industries. Many tobacco, oil and gas, and automotive companies, to name a few, have actively diversified their products and services.

Natural Disaster
No one can determine when a natural disaster might occur, although companies can and many do develop disaster recovery plans for salvaging what can be saved following such an occurrence and by resuming business as quickly as possible. No doubt, some loss will be suffered, and it may be necessary to take unusual measures to ensure the survival of the business following a natural disaster. Clearly, adequate insurance and well-planned contingency alternatives can alleviate the strain.

Shifting Consumer Preferences
Consumers are fickle, and a shift in consumer preferences can and does destroy markets. Anyone who doubts this should check on the most current prices of pet rocks. More specifically, look at athletic shoes in the 1980s; Reebok grew while Nike struggled with its product and, at the end of the decade, L.A. Gear was pushing both for market share.

Limited Sources of Supplies of Strategic Materials
Scarce or strategic materials, if used in a product made or sold by a company, can become a serious factor in the company's ability to continue to produce or sell the product at an economical price. The scarcity and resultant high cost of gasoline in the early 1970s had a severe impact on the recreational vehicle industry, as an example.

Decreasing Market for Products or Services
Markets can be affected by demographic factors. As our population ages, the market for products geared toward a younger population, while it won't disappear entirely, is liable to shrink significantly; so, while market share as a percentage of the total market is now

decreasing, the total market might be getting smaller. Conversely, many companies have catered to the longevity of our senior citizens by developing products or services that meet their needs. As an example, certain real estate developers have built retirement communities, having in mind active senior citizens retiring at earlier ages.

INDICATORS OF FINANCIAL HEALTH

Quantitative Indicators

Any number of quantitative tools exist that are helpful in assessing the financial health of an institution. While many are merely indicative, some models are actually predictive of financial problems. The more traditional are financial analysis tools, mainly ratios, which only serve to illustrate events as they stand at a particular moment in the history of the company. Far more important from a predictive standpoint is the trend of such calculations over a period. Thus, if working capital continues to decrease, or the debt to worth ratio shows an increasing trend over several periods, the ability of a company to continue—absent stringent measures—becomes questionable.

Debt to Worth
This ratio has gained significant attention of late as a result of the concern for junk bond financing during the 1980s. The debt to worth ratio is computed by dividing total debt by the total net worth of the company, and it is expressed as a ratio, such as 3.5 to 1 (3.5:1). A high debt to worth ratio indicates the extent to which the company is leveraged. A steady trend of increase in this ratio generally indicates a pattern of losses and is cause for concern. Clearly, many acquisitions were structured with extremely high debt-equity ratios and require significant growth in cash flow and aggressive asset dispositions to occur. Many of the troubled companies of the current decade will need to restructure acquisition debt as the aggressive growth projections, or changes in interest rates, quickly result in defaults.

Working Capital

Defined as the difference between current assets and current liabilities, this measurement determines the extent to which a company is able to meet its current obligations. Low or negative working capital indicates an inability to meet current obligations as they mature, which in itself is one definition of insolvency. Often, working capital is expressed as a ratio between current assets and current liabilities. Certain current assets are difficult, if not impossible, to readily convert to cash. An example of such an asset is prepaid insurance. Another ratio seeking to give recognition to the fact that certain current assets are not liquid is the quick, or acid test, ratio. This computation excludes from current assets those not readily convertible to cash. A trend of declining working capital, or a trend of deteriorating working capital ratios, is a certain predictor of financial distress.

Increased Aging of Receivables and Payables

Increased aging of receivables or payables is generally expressed as number of days sales or purchases outstanding, or as turnover ratios. An increase in the number of days (or months) that accounts receivable are outstanding indicates a deterioration in the manner in which the firm is managing its receivables, generally its second most liquid asset. Or, it might indicate a decline in the financial health of the company's customer base—an equally disturbing circumstance. Increases in the aging of payables indicates that the company does not have the cash available to liquidate its payables according to terms—and also has serious implications about the company's ability to obtain further trade credit.

Financing Long-Term Assets with Short-Term Money

Financing long-term assets with short-term money does not make financial sense. Therefore, when this practice is observed, it usually indicates a problem, whether simply ignorance or incompetence on the part of management, or the inability to obtain more appropriate financing. In the extreme case, bank loans that have matured either because of time or because of acceleration will appear as all current on a company's balance sheet, possibly wiping out working capital. In this particular instance, the company is using short-term money to finance losses that, in reality, can only be recovered by subsequent profitable operations. To illustrate, acquisitions with balloon payments within a few years may come due before the company has enough financial success to allow either refinancing the debt or equity placements.

Inordinately High Financing Costs
It is a simple fact of financial life that, the more you need money, the more you are going to pay for it. In the case of companies in need of financing, the price they pay for such financing is in great part a reflection of the lender's perception of the risk involved in extending the credit. Inordinately high financing costs are an indicator that someone (although possibly not the management of the company) feels that the company is either in trouble or heading in that direction. The cost of financing must be compared to profit margins, since slow collection of low margin products will ultimately erode profitability.

Slowing Turnover of Inventories
Slow turnover of inventories as measured against industry averages at its best indicates a purchasing function that is not being adequately managed or controlled. In the worst case, building inventories can reflect obsolescence, declining sales, or incorrect bookkeeping practices. A pattern of increasing days sales in inventory is a predictor of future cash problems. Awareness of inventory buildup and critical decisions, such as plant closedowns or slowdowns, is vital. The financing cost of bloated inventories will accelerate a company's deterioration.

Profitability Measures
A number of measures of the operating efficiency of a company exist, loosely referred to here as *measures of profitability*.

   Declining Margins. Gross profit is the difference between the total sales and the cost associated with those sales for a company in a given period. The costs in question may be the cost to manufacture a product, or simply the cost of buying a product or service for resale. In either case, this profit margin, when decreasing as a percentage of sales, indicates that costs are either not being effectively controlled or that pricing is not keeping up with necessary or unavoidable increases in costs. Gross profit margins are important indicators of management efficiency, in that many of the factors entering into costs are controllable by management. Controllable costs include scrap factors, overtime, material usage, to name just a few. In other cases, increases in costs are not avoidable. Inflation heads this list, along with increases in the general wage level per collective bargaining agreements, increases in materials prices, and so on. These types of increases must be answered by corresponding increases in the prices of the company's goods and services if margins are to be maintained. It is altogether possible that in some cases such costs cannot be passed on to the customer, and the result is that margins will be depressed until such time as the customer is willing to pay more, or unless some extraordinary cost-cutting measures can be implemented. Pressure on margins, especially from wage increases, must be offset by productivity enhancements.

Declining Profits. Declining profits are certainly a result of declining margins; but it is possible to have a situation wherein margins remain stable, while profits are declining. In such a case, it is selling or general and administrative expenses or interest expenses that are causing declining profitability. Corporate overhead must be carefully monitored and such issues as centralized or decentralized management must be determined in light of industry and competitive pressures. It is interesting to note that no trend seems to be evolving about the location of top management. Some companies are staying close to or at key factory locations, while others are moving executive offices closer to financial sources or markets.

Declining Sales. Declining sales can result from any number of reasons, including decreased demand, quality problems, and problems in delivering the merchandise in a timely fashion. Whatever the reason, declining sales indicates a problem or problems that are a definite precursor of future financial difficulty, if not addressed in a timely manner. Sales analysis on a timely basis, including comparisons with prior periods, must be carefully scrutinized so management can react quickly to unfavorable indicators.

Declining Per-Unit Sales Values. Sales may remain constant in absolute values, while per unit values are declining. Put more simply, the company is selling more for less. This results in declining margins, which was addressed earlier. An interesting subset of this problem is constant unit sales with increasing prices and, therefore, increasing margins. While increasing margins are generally a good thing, increasing margins when unit sales are remaining constant or declining may be a harbinger of future problems, because it might indicate shifting customer preferences among a significant proportion of the company's sales base, which will eventually, if continued, result in lower overall sales. It is certainly a phenomenon that bears further investigation. Too often, especially for fast-growing retailers, the sales per store is overlooked when overall sales is growing. A slowdown in mature markets may indicate early troubles and should not be ignored.

Z Score. The Z score, developed by Professor Edward I. Altman in the late 1960s, measures corporate health and, thereby, propensity for business failure, by combining five financial ratios together after assigning appropriate weighing to each. The Z score is calculated as follows:

$X1$ = Working capital/Total assets
$X2$ = Retained earnings/Total assets
$X3$ = E.B.I.T./Total assets
$X4$ = Market value of equity/Total liability
$X5$ = Sales/Total assets
Z = Overall index

$Z = 1.2(X1) + 1.4(X2) + 3.3(X3) + 6(X4) + 1(X5)$

According to the model, if the score is above 2.99, the company is considered to be healthy. If, however, the score is below 1.81, the company is unhealthy and the probability of failure is high. Scores falling between 1.81 and 2.99 are in a gray area and bear further study.

Qualitative Indicators

Qualitative factors, while observable, do not lend themselves easily to numerical analysis. These factors affect the efficiency with which the company pursues its objectives, strategies, the relationships it has with its customers and suppliers, and the manner in which it deals with its employees. No one of these factors is a predictor of financial distress; but, when observed in connection with several others over a significant time, financial problems in the future are predictable.

Production Problems
It is almost a given that a manufacturing company that becomes a turnaround candidate had experienced various production problems or stoppages.

Late Shipments
Companies that routinely fail to shop products or to deliver services on time are experiencing problems relating to scheduling, inventory control, purchasing deficiencies, and the like. Late shipments will eventually lead to loss of revenues as customers find more reliable suppliers. Shipping late increases the amount of time that the company's resources are invested in work in process inventories, thereby increasing the financing costs of the business and leading to slower cash flow and depressed profits. Backlog and other important sales data become inaccurate and unreliable with late shipments. It is important to segregate and identify each of the causes of late shipments, including purchasing delays, supplier problems, manufacturing errors, and similar causes.

Incorrect Shipments
Shipping the customer the wrong merchandise, or the right merchandise in incorrect quantities, likewise leads to customer dissatisfaction, to the added expense of restocking, to increased shipping costs, and so on. A company that routinely ships the wrong product to its customers runs the risk of customer frustration building to such a level that they will eventually seek more efficient sources of supply. This may also be an early warning of either management abuse and attempts to prebook sales. Incentive programs ill conceived may cause bogus shipments.

Returns
A high rate of returned product is indicative of poor quality or a mishandling of the shipping function. A customer who repeatedly has to return product for whatever reason will soon seek other

sources. A high rate of returns increases expenses, since the customer is only going to pay for shipping costs once. Therefore, the company must absorb the additional shipping costs associated with the return and reshipment of the order. Follow-up on high returns may be indicative of more serious problems, which should be reviewed. If customer returns become excessive, the company might have to readdress its "right of return" policies.

Unusual Allowances
The granting of excessive or unusual allowances indicates any number of problems. It might mean that the company is attempting to "buy" the market with special allowances. If so, these allowances are more properly classified as a sales or marketing expense, rather than as an adjustment to the sales price. Heavy use of sales allowances may be a method the company has devised to compensate customers for previous shipments of poor-quality merchandise or of late shipments. Large allowances should be approved at an appropriate management employee level to limit possible defalcations.

Rework
Rework, whether done prior to shipment, because quality control measures have detected the defects, or because the defects have been caught by the customer, is an overhead item that increases the product cost and, thereby, depresses margins. It results from either inattention during the manufacturing process, poor inbound inspection, inadequately maintained machinery or tooling, or quite possibly from ill-designed manufacturing processes. Although it is not possible to eliminate rework entirely from any manufacturing process, it is a margin-eroding factor; and the presence of rework in the excess is indicative of problems that will manifest themselves in declining margins, slow shipments, and customer dissatisfaction. Employee morale problems may manifest themselves in poor production work habits, which may be evident by the need for excessive rework. Factory supervision and attention to production report information can alert management staff to this type of early warning sign.

Scrap Factors Increasing
Some scrap is inevitable in any manufacturing process, and, in the initial costing of any new product, scrap must be factored into the equation. In designing the manufacturing process, and the tools and

fixtures to be used, scrap factors must be minimized to obtain maximum usage of materials. Whenever scrap standards are being exceeded, the causes might include poor maintenance of tools or dies used in the manufacturing process, incompetence of fabrication or assembly personnel, poor product or manufacturing process design, or inaccurate determination of the scrap standards themselves. High factory turnover rates and inadequate training may also result in a high scrap factor. Regardless of the cause, depending upon the industry, scrap factors can have a tremendous effect on gross margins. Again, it should be closely watched as an early warning sign to management.

Customer Dissatisfaction with Products or Services
The primary reason for an enterprise's existence is to sell products or services to its customers at a profit. When the company's poor performance on any number of fronts has caused customer dissatisfaction to become the hallmark of its relationship with that customer, or with a number of customers, it has endangered its very existence. Customer dissatisfaction shows in many ways, including slow payment of amounts owed to the company, a fall-off of orders, aggressive price negotiations, or, in the extreme, a refusal to deal with the company at all. If customer dissatisfaction becomes widespread, the failure of the enterprise is almost a foregone conclusion. As an early indicator of future problems, customer dissatisfaction may not manifest itself to an outsider; but it certainly is known to those within the company who deal directly with those customers. Management attention to customers and maintenance of open communications is essential. As companies grow larger, there is a tendency for top management to spend less time with key accounts or to understand their future product needs. Many a turnaround has succeeded where management recognized the need to revisit the policies that made the company successful in its entrepreneurial stage. This usually included aggressive client service, marketing, and timely product deliveries.

Deferred Maintenance
Deferred maintenance in capital intensive firms is a time bomb. Companies that use this method of increasing cash flow are simply

deferring losses or inadequate profits to future periods. Moreover, this practice can and does lead to severe problems as machinery or equipment becomes unreliable or unsafe. In the extreme, deferred maintenance can lead to manufacturing downtime, poor product quality, and accidents, including loss of life. A standard for maintenance in capital intensive industries can generally be determined by examining industry averages. If this standard is routinely higher than the actual experience in the company in question—especially when accompanied by rising expenses for unscheduled repairs, manufacturing downtime, product quality considerations, or safety problems—it is a fair assumption that this company is headed for problems in the not too distant future.

Low Morale
Low morale among employees, while difficult to quantify, is easily observed. Absenteeism and tardiness are usually higher when things are not right in a company. Poor attention to detail both in the factory as well as in the office indicate that the employees are not motivated to do a good job. Cynicism directed toward management, customers, suppliers, or other employee groups within the company becomes common and is easily observed. Employees who routinely turn out late or inadequate work product, particularly if this was not characteristic of the individuals in the past, have lost motivation and, more importantly, have lost confidence in the management of the company to deal with its problems. Low employee morale from the top down is a definite indicator of future problems.

High Employee Turnover Rate
An increasing rate of employee turnover is a manifestation of low morale among employees. People routinely seek job satisfaction and will leave when it is not present. Normally the best and brightest will leave first, leaving those who previously might have functioned well to handle jobs for which they may not be qualified. Under such conditions, it is difficult to recruit and retain good people, and a high turnover rate might even lead to an increased general wage scale while productivity and profitability are falling.

It might be said here that low or nonexistent turnover could be an indication that general wage rates are too high, particularly when the profitability of the enterprise is lower than normal. If the management of a company has made a conscious decision to "share the wealth" by paying higher than normal wages to retain good people, this cannot really be criticized, because it is simply a manifestation of a policy adopted by management. Employee turnover is a factor that can be and is managed in a profitable enterprise. However, if accompanied by other indicators of financial problems, particularly by falling profits, then it can safely be assumed that the situation is not under the control of management, despite protestations to the contrary. While salary or other compensation incentives are usually identified as leading factors to morale, many studies have demonstrated that nonmonetary factors are more likely to cause employee dissatisfaction, especially in the service sector.

Accidents

Accidents in the workplace are commonplace among companies that are headed for trouble. Management inattention, poor maintenance of machinery and equipment, harried production schedules—all contribute to an environment where safety considerations are not a high priority. In addition to the cost in human misery, lost time, increased insurance rates, lawsuits, and the like, the toll exacted on employee morale is extreme. People do not want to work in an environment where their safety or even their lives are in jeopardy. A reputation for maintaining an unsafe workplace will lead to increased scrutiny by regulatory agencies and, ultimately, to an erosion of the customer base.

Other Indicators

Numerous other factors illustrate impending problems in companies. Many of them, while readily apparent to outsiders, are not so apparent to those within the company. This occurs because the problems evolve slowly and are not readily brought to the attention of management by quantifiable means. Many of these problems rest with management itself, which, because of its focus on handling the problems that are the result of these factors, fails to examine the actual causes, instead handling these manifestations as they arise, rather than controlling events in a way to prevent the problems in the first place.

General Inability of Management to Control Events
In troubled companies, management becomes controlled by events instead of controlling those events. This is simply another way of saying that management is not in control at all; and indeed, in extreme situations, chaos seems to be the order of the day. This condition is soon perceived by employees, suppliers, and customers, and it leads to an erosion of confidence. It is difficult, sometimes impossible, for management to regain control when the situation has deteriorated to this extent, and many times the only workable solution is a replacement of some or all of the management in question. Putting out "fires" constantly can ultimately become the norm. Eventually, the pressure and resultant stress will undermine management objectives.

Management Becomes Reactive instead of Proactive
Good managers, be they executives or middle managers, are in control of their time. They anticipate events, plan their responses to those events, implement those responses, and monitor the results, thereby learning from the process so they can more effectively deal with those events in the future; this is *proactive management.* In a troubled company environment, managers from the top down are no longer proactive. Instead, they become *reactive:* they wait for things to happen to them and then react in whatever manner seems to be the most expedient at the time. They many times develop a siege mentality, wondering either privately or aloud, What's next? Such a management style, or lack of same, leads to a chaotic situation wherein the perception of employees, customers, and suppliers is that nobody is in control. People and organizations do not like to deal with this type of company, and will not, unless it is absolutely necessary—and, even in that case, will take the first available opportunity to make a change. Such a situation contributes to the inability of salespeople to garner top prices for the company's products, for purchasing agents to negotiate favorable pricing on the materials they buy, and for managers to attempt to maintain high standards of morale and quality of work among their employees.

Lack of Timely and Accurate Information

Management cannot perform its role in a vacuum. Effective management requires timely and accurate information. This is true not only of financial information, which is generated by an accounting department, but of production figures, information concerning the market for the company's products or services, information concerning the company's competitors—the list is endless. The lack of this kind of information leads to the inability of management to determine where the company has been, where it is, and where it is going. It is quite common in troubled companies that information systems become deficient or, in the extreme, nonexistent. Reasons for this vary. Many times, the pressures created by the inability to pay bills on time, get materials when needed, or increased returns, rework, or quality problems will result in the personnel who are responsible for producing management reports delaying the completion of such reports to answer the more pressing needs of the moment. While expedient, this process has disastrous consequences to management's ability to plan events.

An unfortunate sidelight to the lack of timely and accurate information is intentionally misstated information. It is common that the management of companies in trouble indulge to some extent in misleading themselves as well as outsiders who depend upon such information. In the extreme case, this constitutes outright fraud. As has recently come to light in the Minscribe bankruptcy filing, extreme senior management pressure for performance resulted in many fictitious sales practices.

The means by which information is misstated are myriad. Unexplained adjustments to inventories, sales accruals not supported by shipping documents, and unbooked credits are a few of the more common ones. When an outside lender is involved, such as a bank or finance company that has a security interest in the assets, which are being reported at inflated levels to present higher than actual profits, that lender is being misled about the value of his collateral. Worse than that, such misstatements lead to the lender making unsecured or undersecured advances to the company. The presence of these types of misstatements in a company's books and records is a sure indicator that something is amiss, and, again it is quite possible that the underlying motive in such cases is of a fraudulent nature.

Short-Range Planning Is Difficult
Short-range planning is important in any organization, but in a company experiencing financial problems it is essential. Without the ability to forecast short-range cash needs, for example, the firm may not make its next payroll. Without timely and accurate information concerning short-term cash needs, collapse is imminent. In general, the more limited the company's cash resources the more essential is the ability to plan in the short term. In extreme situations, cash needs must be planned on a daily basis. Information concerning purchase commitments, shipping schedules, and required payments, such as rent utilities and debt service, must be instantly available—and it must be correct. Unfortunately, management attention on continuous long-term profit growth as an obsession often causes inattention to short-term capital needs to finance aggressive expansion.

Long-Range Planning Is Impossible
Long-range planning of new product development and introduction, capital acquisitions, penetration of new markets, or dropping a product line also requires timely and accurate information. Many companies have experienced disastrous failures because such information was not available or was incorrect. Most wrong decisions are made because of faulty or unavailable information. While long-term planning is not essential to the short-term survival of an enterprise, the long-term health of the organization cannot be managed without it.

Inability of Company to Pay Its Debts as They Mature
Such an inability is the ultimate manifestation of a company in trouble. This is not an early warning sign; but it is frequently the only warning sign that is noticed by management, which until this is evident has been complacent and nonresponsive to earlier symptoms. By the time this has happened, virtually every other warning has either been ignored or dealt with ineffectively. Illiquidity is the result either of poor management of a company's assets or undercapitalization. In the former, earlier indicators have been ignored, for whatever reason, and the company is now on a downward spiral, which can only be halted by extraordinary measures that are not ordinarily in the set of management skills ordinarily

possessed by most managers. The ability to raise capital or negotiate credit facilities is difficult at best if attempted after vendors have initiated collection activities and the credit rating has already been tarnished.

Trade Creditors Demanding Cash on Delivery

Trade creditors provide short-term and generally interest-free financing to their customers. This is the cheapest and most readily obtained financing that a company can find, and it is also the easiest to abuse. Trade creditors, depending upon the industry, and the overall effectiveness of their own credit and collection function, are generally slow to respond to their customers by extending terms to them beyond normal or stated payments. However, the increasing insolvencies, especially among LBOs, has increased the scrutiny by credit managers on terms and size of debt lines for customers.

Payroll Taxes Paid Late or Not at All

Not paying payroll taxes when they are due is the ultimate refinement of the art of corporate suicide. This type of financing is not only dangerous to the company itself but will result in liability being attributed to corporate officers, directors, and even employees if they are part of the process. This type of financing should be avoided at all costs, even to the shutdown of the business. The government treats those who employ this type as little more than criminals and exacts severe penalties when it becomes aware of this. It is one of the most common reasons for a company filing for Chapter 11 protection. Such taxes are ordinarily not dischargeable in a bankruptcy. One of the more insidious aspects of this problem is that, often, the taxing authority does not become aware of the problem for several months, leading to management complacency. When the hammer falls, and it will, the company may be unable to pay the taxes, along with the substantial penalties accompanying them. This initiates a process that many times is the precursor to bankruptcy and the possible demise of the company. It cannot be emphasized enough that withheld payroll taxes should never, not even in the most desperate of circumstances, be viewed as an alternative method of financing the company.

Deteriorating Relationship with Banks or Lenders
Banks and other secured lenders have become increasingly sophisticated, through the use of computers and financial models of predicting problems, and more often than not the lender is the one that informs the company that it is having problems. A deteriorating relationship with a lender is a serious problem itself and, if not resolved, can and often does lead to the bankruptcy or demise of the company. The violation of financial covenants, often referred to as *technical defaults* (as opposed to actual defaults in the payment of scheduled debt service payments) is a serious matter.

Financial convenants are written into loan agreements for a purpose: of assuring the lender that the company will manage its affairs in such a manner to give maximum assurance that the debt will be repaid as scheduled. Too often, violation of these covenants is treated by the company and even the lender in a casual manner, and the only action taken is that the lender grants a waiver so the financial statements of the company can be issued without reclassifying the debt as current.

Lenders also like to be informed of events concerning the health of their credits. The inability or the unwillingness of the company to communicate negative information to its lenders can only result in a relationship not conducive to the effective working out of the company's problems. Unfortunately, as often happens, lenders are surprised when problems arise that cannot be hidden, such as writs of attachment, tax levies, N.S.F. checks, or overdrafts. This is probably as much the lenders' fault as that of the borrower, but this is of little consequence. Lenders have a great deal of power in such a situation and will use it to protect their interests. It behooves the company to keep its lenders informed of all significant events affecting the company and to prevent in every way the lenders' being surprised. It is damaging to the credibility of a borrower to be informed about the result of bank audits or collateral review of problems that the borrower should have known beforehand. Once destroyed, trust and credibility are difficult if not impossible to regain. Being asked to find a new banking relationship as a result of credibility is often going to further exacerbate the problem. As the results of lenders' liability suits seem to be moderating, one can expect quicker and more pressing bank reaction to credit abuses. To repeat, it is to the advantage of the borrower to be informed about the progress of the company, and to keep its lenders informed as well.

External Reporting Indicators

A company's independent auditors will generally issue a report on the company's financial statements soon after the close of its fiscal year. Late reports by auditors are often an indication of various types of problems that might be facing a company. A late report might result from serious problems in the company's books and records, resulting in the necessity for additional audit procedures.

The refusal of a bank or other lender to waive violations of certain lending covenants might lead to the reclassifying of long-term debt as a current obligation. This is a serious situation, which might lead to a qualified opinion in the auditor's report. Aside from the implications that the bank may be considering calling its loan, the presence of a qualified opinion is reason for concern. A "going-concern" opinion is the auditor's expression of his or her concern that the company may be unable to continue in business in the ensuing period. Other types of qualified opinions might reflect disagreements with management concerning the treatment of certain accounting issues—for example, the method of estimating bad debts or inventory adjustments.

It is common for auditors to produce for management a report on internal control. The presence, year after year, of the same comments in such reports is an indication that the company does not take such issues seriously, or that it has been unable to confront and satisfactorily resolve these issues. A management report that year after year contains comments relating to internal control issues is definitely a warning sign worth close attention. While audited financial statements are historical and, therefore, may be late indicators of business problems, senior management should carefully scrutinize the results of the audit and require meetings with the auditors to understand any problems arising in the audit process. The time it takes management to close its books, the frequency of audit adjustments, and the materiality of the differences in the audited results to management reports should be carefully evaluated.

Probably the most significant thing to realize about the Z score is that virtually every financial analysis program presently being used by banks to analyze financial statements calculates the Z score; therefore, it is being looked at in most credit-making decisions. Accordingly, despite the controversy about whether this or other scoring devices are too mechanical, management may wish to consider its use to see how others are evaulating the company.

ACTIONS

Immediate Steps

Once the determination has been made that a company is in financial trouble, quick and decisive action must be taken to isolate the problems and keep them from becoming more severe. The very survival of the company might very well depend on how management reacts once it recognizes that a problem exists. This is not a time for weak, indecisive management. Instead, management must respond in a positive manner to address the crisis.

Generally speaking, management must become more autocratic during a turnaround, making, many times, unpopular decisions and implementing them without a great deal of input from the ranks. In terms of management philosophy, Theory X management becomes the rule of the day.

The immediate strategy in a turnaround situation calls for maximizing the company's cash flow in whatever ways are possible. In the severest of situations, this may call for selling off or liquidating profitable segments of a business to bring in needed cash and keep the business going.

Take Control of Cash

Cash, not profit, is the lifeblood of a company in financial distress. Management must resist the temptation to hold something back for the future. First the managers must ensure that a future will exist. This calls for tough decisions and implementation. Receivables must be collected at a faster rate than before, and inventories must be turned into receivables as quickly as possible. It may be necessary to offer deep discounts to customers to induce them to buy up excess inventories and pay cash for them. Unneeded assets, such as machinery or equipment, should be sold as quickly as possible to raise cash.

Cash must not only be generated but be conserved. When a company has been losing money for any period, particularly when it has moved into a negative equity position, those losses have been financed by increased debt, either secured, trade, or in most cases both. The only manner in which that debt can be repaid is out of future profits if the company is to survive. The cash raised by the liquidation of assets should be put into financing the current operations of the company. This means that debts must be rescheduled. The creditors likely will not be eager to participate in such restructuring; but generally, when faced with the unpleasant alternatives of bankruptcy and liquidation, they can be persuaded to enter into negotiations with the company's management. Secured lenders would likewise prefer to work out the company's problems over a liquidation scenario and will generally participate in a turnaround plan.

Concurrent with efforts to generate cash, steps must immediately be taken to reduce expenditures. All personnel not immediately necessary to run the company over the next 60 to 90 days should be released. Purchase commitments should be examined and, if not absolutely necessary for immediate production, be deferred or cancelled. All unnecessary expense items should be cancelled. Steps should be taken to review the insurance needs of the company, with an eye toward reducing coverage where possible, and otherwise reducing overall insurance expense.

Subleasing of unneeded office or warehouse space might reduce occupancy cost. In short, cut deep.

Management has a tendency to approach cost cutting the way one might approach peeling an onion, a layer at a time. This will not work. Cuts, particularly in the area of personnel, should be accomplished as quickly and as deeply as possible. New budgets should be established and adhered to religiously. No area should be sacred.

If concessions are required of the hourly work force, the salaried work force must follow suit. And management should trim back its own salaries and perks as well.

After the layoffs and other cost cuts have been made, the remaining employees should be assured that management has taken positive steps to maximize the likelihood of success. They should be encouraged to consider themselves part of the team and to contribute what they can in suggesting and implementing further steps to conserve cash and generate profits. They must be convinced that management has regained control of the situation, and that they are needed and valued. They should not be guaranteed that their jobs are safe. This would be less than honest—and they would not believe it, anyway. They can, however, be assured that, if the company performs according to its short-term business plan, further layoffs should be unnecessary.

In the extreme case, it may be necessary to seek protection under Chapter 11 of the Bankruptcy Act to facilitate the turnaround process. This is particularly indicated in cases where creditor cooperation is not forthcoming, where lawsuits have been filed and the litigants show no intention of forebearing, or where there exist substantial payroll tax delinquencies. It must be emphasized that Chapter 11 is a radical step not to be taken lightly. It is and it should be the last resort of a company in trouble. The statistics of small companies emerging from Chapter 11 intact and reorganized is not high.

Engage Competent Professionals
As early as possible in the turnaround effort, the company should avail itself of the best professional help available. A competent attorney or law firm specializing in bankruptcy and insolvency issues is a must. His or her advice and counsel will be invaluable during the process, as will his or her ability to effectively negotiate with the various creditor groups. One can be assured that the secured lenders, as well as other creditors, will be competently represented in this area.

In addition, it is generally good practice to engage a professional who is experienced in consulting with financially distressed companies. These individuals are variously known as *turnaround consultants, workout consultants,* or *crisis managers*. They may be freelance or part of a larger consulting or accounting firm. Their reputations are generally known to local attorneys and secured lenders. If management does not have knowledge of these people, either its banks or attorneys can generally provide a list of several reputable firms or individuals.

Professionals specializing in providing services to financially distressed companies are by no means inexpensive, and they generally demand a substantial up-front payment or success bonuses. While the expense may seem prohibitive, the chances of a successful workout are vastly enhanced by their participation. It has happened on more than one occasion that banks have made funds available for the engagement of such professionals, even though the loans are in jeopardy, indicating the value they place on such involvement.

Short-Term Business Plan
A short-term business or operating plan should be prepared immediately after the workout begins. This plan should cover a relatively short period of time, generally 13 weeks, but in no case more than a year. The plan should endeavor to properly time all anticipated receipts and expenditures. It will be used in negotiations with various groups of creditors and others in interest, and, noticeably, the company's progress will be rigorously compared to the projections contained in that plan. As emphasized earlier, cash flow projections are the heart of this plan, because the major thrust for the immediate future is to maximize cash.

Liquidation Analysis
A liquidation analysis should be prepared in conjunction with the short-term business plan. This analysis should show as accurately as possible the projected results of liquidating the company's assets and using the proceeds to pay off debts in the order of their respective priorities. Good-faith estimates of auction costs and administrative expenses should be made and included in this analysis, which will be used in negotiations with the company's secured and unsecured creditors and will provide a basis for future financing. It is important that this be completed as accurately as time allows. It may be necessary to use the services of appraisers and valuation experts in more complex cases.

Intermediate Steps

Turnarounds are similar to administering first aid. The first step is to stop the bleeding and then move to less-critical steps. Once cash flow has been stabilized, the more fundamental causes of the company's problems can be addressed as time and budgetary considerations allow. Inadequate information systems should be addressed. Inefficiencies in manufacturing areas can be dealt with, along with production control and scheduling functions. While inventories must remain under control, now is the time to round out unbalanced inventories and attempt to return the production line to a more normal operation. If feasible, the company should implement "just in time" purchasing techniques to maximize inventory turnover, thereby reducing the carrying cost of inventories.

As the company returns to profitability, management must guard against complacency and continue to take whatever steps necessary to run the operation as lean as possible. New product development should be undertaken only if a fairly high rate of certainty exists that the product will immediately contribute to the bottom line. Longer-range planning becomes more important as the company gets back on its feet.

CONCLUSION

To briefly summarize this chapter, the early warning signals of a company in decline are not very loud at first, and they may be confused with the day-to-day problems of "just running a business." If ignored, these problems form patterns that become discernible as sales and margins fall, cash becomes tighter, and the customers, creditors, and employees of the company continue to lose confidence in the ability of company management to control its affairs.

Most of the problems of declining companies are caused by the inability or the unwillingness of management to face up to its problems and take corrective action in time to avert disaster. Lack of accurate and timely information exacerbates the situation, and this cannot be generally corrected in a hurry if it has been allowed to deteriorate for any length of time. In distressed companies it is not uncommon for top management to not even be able to come up with an accurate bank balance at any given time.

While some of the causes of decline might be external to the company and, therefore, to a greater or lesser extent not controllable by management, the majority of companies that fail do so either because of poor management or undercapitalization, with the emphasis on the former, rather than the latter.

CHAPTER 2

DETERMINING THE LIKELIHOOD OF A TURNAROUND

Robert S. Seidemann
David A. Sands
Price Waterhouse

INTRODUCTION

The focus of this chapter is the turnaround process. Although every company and every crisis scenario is unique, the actions necessary to implement a successful turnaround are remarkably similar. A turnaround is best described as an analytical process supplemented by creative strategies.

    We will begin with an explanation of crisis management techniques that form the basis for any successful turnaround. Next will be a description of the crisis management team, how it is selected, and who are the "players." The third section of this chapter will be an analysis of the turnaround process, or the steps towards recovery. We will complete the chapter with some practical considerations for developing good relationships and negotiating with the various classifications of creditors that must be addressed during the turnaround process.

CRISIS MANAGEMENT

Crisis management involves developing and implementing a specific plan of interrelated action steps designed to turn negative cash flow into positive cash flow. The plan must be implemented in an orderly, expeditious manner and be based on calculated probabilities of success with alternative fallback strategies available as needed. To be effective, the process must have a beginning, a middle, and an end. There must also be specific goals and objectives for each phase of the process.

Several differences distinguish crisis management from the day-to-day management process. The main difference is that crisis management is tightly focused on the problems at hand. Crisis management must also consider outside constraints, such as lack of financing or deficient management skills.

Recognition that problems exist and acceptance that the solution lies outside the ordinary course of business is a prerequisite for implementing true crisis management. Unfortunately, the company managers are often the last to recognize that serious problems or possibly even a crisis exists. Therefore, they often fail to undertake prompt action.

Failure to recognize the existence of serious operating problems is the result of psychological denial and unrealistic expectations. Managers tend to ignore obvious signs of trouble by dismissing them as temporary setbacks that are beyond their control. Often, they believe that improvement will magically occur. This is most frequently manifested in overly optimistic projections that include unexplained sales growth, margin improvements, or inventory turns.

Another typical management failure is to understate the scope and severity of the problems or the crisis. Traditionally, management is only willing to implement cosmetic changes, and it understates the corrective actions necessary. This failure results in either the existing problems creating a crisis or the severity of the crisis increasing. The key to crisis management is that management must accept the company's plight and develop a plan to deal with it, rather than being defensive.

Ideally, crisis management techniques should be employed *before* there is a crisis. Crisis management techniques are best used to avert the crisis; therefore, they should begin at the first sign when "business as usual" is no longer working for a company. If started early enough, crisis management can be used to avoid drastic survival actions that are necessary for the short term but potentially harmful in the long run. For example, capital investment that is necessary to improve long-term productivity may need to be postponed if crisis management is not implemented quickly enough.

As mentioned earlier, management usually looks unrealistically for outside factors to rectify a crisis situation. As a result, the managers spend all of their time "fighting fires," such as creditors demanding payment, that are common in a crisis situation. By doing this, management believes it is practicing crisis management, but this is not the case. True crisis management goes beyond addressing the symptoms of the crisis. It involves the development of a plan to rectify the underlying business problems so the company can return to successful operations.

Each crisis situation is different. Companies in need of crisis management are in various stages of deterioration, and the crisis symptoms are different, as are the actions necessary to solve the underlying problems. There is no formula for a turnaround, but the progression of the process is generally common to most companies.

THE CRISIS MANAGEMENT TEAM

The key determinant of the success or failure of any turnaround attempt is the quality of the management team. For this reason, assembling the crisis management team is the most important aspect of the process. While it is impossible to outline a "one size fits all" roster for the turnaround team, special characteristics are common to a quality crisis management team. In this section we will analyze these characteristics and discuss the team selection process.

The first critical factor in the selection of the crisis management team is the structure of the organization. If the company has an independent board of directors, a special committee of outside directors should be formed. Its purpose is to monitor progress and report to the full board. The first duty of the committee is to select the crisis management team and assist them in establishing overall goals. The committee should not be involved in the daily operations of the crisis management team, but the members should receive regular progress reports and continue to shape strategy. For the sake of expediency, the reporting and communications between the team and the committee should be less formal than normal. If, as in the case of many privately held middle market companies, there is no outside board of directors, the crisis management team will have to be chosen by the company's shareholders or chief executive officer.

The need to establish an independent committee is obvious. At this crucial time when a company's existence is in doubt, it is critical to have independent and objective leadership. It is also important that the committee is not tied down by preconceived opinions of daily operating management. When building the team, the committee should review the following questions:

1. Can present management make a successful transition to crisis managers?
2. What types of skills and experience are needed to supplement present management?
3. Should outsiders be brought in to round out the crisis management team?

When reviewing the qualifications of present management to lead a turnaround, there are three important factors. First, do the managers really possess the skills and experience necessary to lead the company through this difficult process? Second, can they be objective in their analysis and decision making? Third, have they accepted the need for a change in course and demonstrated the willingness to implement what may be drastic changes?

After determining the qualifications of the present management, the committee must evaluate the resources from the outside that are needed for the crisis management team. Some of the necessary personnel additions will become full-time permanent managers. The search for these individuals should begin immediately, since the process is difficult and time consuming. The final members of the crisis management team will be outside professionals, who will serve in an advisory capacity. The need for outside professionals is determined by the nature and severity of the problem and the level of expertise of management. Several groups of outside professionals generally are considered for inclusion on the crisis management team. The most common groups include accountants, attorneys, management consultants, investment bankers, and professional crisis managers. The roles of several of these professionals are detailed in subsequent chapters, so we will focus here on the outside crisis manager.

There are two broad categories of crisis managers. The first are managers in the truest sense. These individuals typically become employees of the company and assume key management posts for the duration of the turnaround process. They are compensated as full-time employees and could receive an additional "success fee" based on the results achieved. The second type of crisis manager is typically known as a workout or turnaround consultant. The consultant does not become an employee of the company. Instead, he or she provides an objective viewpoint and critical direction to the crisis management process. Turnaround consultants are generally compensated on an hourly rate. They may also negotiate additional success fees in some circumstances.

The decision to hire a full-time crisis manager or a turnaround consultant is never easy, but it is of critical importance. Basically, if the present CEO or another manager is not suited to lead the crisis management team, a full-time crisis manager is needed. If, on the other hand, a crisis leader surfaces out of present management, retaining a turnaround consultant might be desirable. The key advantage to retaining either a full-time crisis manager or a turnaround consultant involves the objectivity that an outsider can contribute, as well as previous crisis management experience.

Whether the leader of the crisis management team emerges from within the existing management group or is brought in from the outside, leadership and implementation skills are of primary importance. The committee may be able to help set direction for the team, but it will be the responsibility of the chief executive officer to implement the strategy and ensure the success of the turnaround process.

The CEO should be involved in the selection of the remaining team members, to the extent practical. When selecting the team members, it is important that they have the ability to work with the

CEO. Prior differences of opinion with the CEO do not disqualify anyone from becoming a member of the turnaround team; in fact, they may even be a positive trait. The problem is that, as companies begin to encounter trouble, executives sometimes develop a distrust for each other that prevents them from working together effectively. There is no room for this on the crisis management team.

No two crisis management teams are alike, and the selection process may be limited by a lack of talent. It is important that the team encompasses each of the critical functional areas of the company. Team members must also possess strong management skills to leverage their individual efforts.

Typically, the crisis management team will include members with the following responsibilities:

Sales and marketing: Most turnarounds involve significant changes in the company's product line and sales mix. This manager must help the crisis management team reexamine the product line, and he or she will be responsible for integrating the resulting changes throughout the sales force. It is also important for this manager to help the company define the market for new and existing products. Finally, the sales and marketing manager will be responsible for upgrading the sales force by replacing or eliminating poor performers and providing greater accountability.

Operations: The operations manager must be an integral part of the product analysis process. The operations manager must implement improvements in the manufacturing process and in other cost reductions.

Finance: A strong chief financial officer is an indispensable member of the crisis management team. The CFO must take a leading role in preparing accurate cash flow forecasts and in identifying and implementing short-term cash flow improvements. The CFO also has the responsibility of dealing with the various categories of creditors. The CFO must provide other members of the team with accurate and meaningful management reports and translate the turnaround plan into realistic projections.

Human relations: The human relations manager must perform several critical functions. This HR manager will be responsible for implementing any necessary staff reductions and maintaining the lines of communication with remaining employees. He or she will also support the other managers in the effort to retain key employees.

The role of the chief executive officer is to oversee the efforts of the crisis management team, as well as the daily management of the company.

Once in place, the crisis management team must work within the hierarchy of the organization to achieve results. The team must, however, avoid being caught up in the politics of the organization. The committee and the full board should encourage the crisis management team to communicate freely with them.

Privately held companies where stockholders also function as senior management represent a unique challenge in the attempt to develop an effective crisis management team. As we discussed in the previous section, management is often the last group to recognize the existence of serious problems that have resulted in a crisis. Management is generally a large part of the problem, due to the managers' unwillingness to accept the changes necessary. Often subordinates recognize the problem and are powerless to make the changes necessary, because their bosses own the company.

When this is the case, it is important for an outsider to exert indirect influence over the management group. The most likely party to perform this function is the company's bank. As a secured creditor, the bank is sometimes the only party available to push hard for changes. This is usually done by first requesting a business plan from the company. If the bank is still not satisfied, or if a business plan previously submitted by the company lacks credibility, the bank may recommend outside workout consultants. Usually, banks will provide the company with at least three qualified firms and allow the company to choose which, if any, they will retain. Referring several firms allows the bank to avoid charges of exerting undue control over the company and allows the company to hire the firm with whom it feels most comfortable.

We have been retained in this way on numerous occasions and, in these cases, there are two goals that are at least as hard to attain as the development and implementation of the turnaround plan. First, management must be convinced to accept the consultant as a member of the team, not the bank's. Second, management must be convinced of the severity of the problems and accept that substantive operating changes will be necessary to correct the situation. An outsider specializing in and experienced at workout and turnaround engagements can be invaluable in accomplishing this second goal.

Selection of the crisis management team is the most important facet of the turnaround process. Almost all crisis situations result from a breakdown in management control, and, in every circumstance, the road to recovery lies in strong and effective management.

STEPS TOWARD RECOVERY

The steps toward recovery vary for every company, but every turnaround must begin with a plan. Although developing the plan is important, the real trick is to effectively implement the plan. As we previously discussed, the process cannot begin until management has accepted the fact that serious problems exist. Timing is critical, so the process must begin immediately before the deterioration becomes irreversible. Once the problem is recognized and a crisis management team is formed, either formally or informally, there should be an orderly and fast-paced process put in place.

This section is a discussion of the key elements of developing and implementing a turnaround plan. The steps outlined here often occur simultaneously and there is a great deal of overlap.

Problem Identification

As a first and extremely important step, the problems must be clearly identified; many turnarounds are doomed to fail for not doing so. The mistake most managers make is to look outside the organization for the source of the problems. The "likely suspects" are usually the first to be rounded up by a management grasping at straws. These often include poor economic conditions, increased competition, higher costs for labor and materials, loss of a key customer, or a hundred other outside factors. These external factors may be present, but the real problem is the company's failure to operate successfully in today's world. For example, a common lament is that increased competition has resulted in lower sales and margins. The real problem may be the company's cost structure, lack of advanced manufacturing techniques, an obsolete core product, or failure to develop new products for emerging markets. The other problem with identifying outside factors as a source of the crisis is that it allows management to hinge a turnaround on outside factors beyond the managers' control. Management often plans for an unreasonable increase or an increased margin despite evidence to the contrary.

Two major categories of problems are encountered in the turnaround process. Each problem can generally be described as either "at the root" of the crisis or as a "result" of a problem that is at the root of the crisis. This distinction is critical—to make sure one is addressing not the symptoms but the disease itself. Problems that are a result can be solved without a turnaround taking place. This is because these are symptoms, and the problem at the heart of the crisis remains unsolved and will cause the "result" problems to reoccur.

Two of the most common examples of result type problems are overleverage and high employee turnover. With the exception of some leveraged buyouts, most companies become overleveraged because of poor financial planning or poor financial results. Recapitalizing the company may be necessary, but that does not mean a turnaround has taken place. The root problem, usually operations, must also be addressed. Another common problem found in most crisis situations is high employee turnover. Again, this is usually not the core problem but the result of deeper management and organizational issues.

To truly identify the problems at the root of a crisis, management must accept the current economic conditions and identify the weaknesses within the organization and the changes that must be made. The analysis process should begin from the ground up, and no aspect of the company's operation can be spared or overlooked. The problem-identification stage is ongoing throughout the turnaround process. As one problem is solved, others are identified.

Several other mistakes are commonly made during the problem-identification process. The first, which we previously discussed, is to underestimate the scope of the problems. This leads to "half-way" solutions, which may slow the decline but will not result in a turnaround. The second major mistake management often makes when reviewing the operations is to accept certain assumptions as facts. This is usually the result of the managers' own biases. When looking for the problems at the source of the crisis, everything about the company must be objectively reviewed, and nothing can be considered sacred from being damaged or eliminated.

Stopping the Bleeding

Concurrent with the identification process, the company must take whatever steps are necessary to turn its negative cash flow into positive cash flow or at least a breakeven. As long as cash flow is negative, the timeframe for implementing a turnaround plan and the options available to the company will continue to shrink. Management's credibility with outside parties also erodes with negative cash flow. To reverse the negative cash flow, the crisis management team should focus its efforts in three areas:

1. Getting a handle on cash.
2. Creating time and money.
3. Eliminating expenses.

The focus of each of these areas is different, but the overall goal is twofold. First, the crisis management team needs to understand the company's current cash flow and be able to anticipate future problems. Second, the crisis management team must identify and implement creative short-term strategies that provide the breathing room necessary to implement a longer-term turnaround plan.

Getting a Handle on Cash

Strong cash management during the crisis management and turnaround process cannot be overemphasized. Many fundamentally sound turnaround plans have been undermined because the company ran into a cash shortage, which resulted in irreversible damage to the company's operations. Liquidity problems can be managed if they are properly forecasted. Cash management responsibilities should be delegated to one member of the crisis management team. Getting a handle on cash begins with an assessment of the current cash availability and the known emergency payments coming due. To determine the cash availability, the crisis manager needs to understand the company's commercial banking relationships. The variations in banking relationships are almost endless, and they determine the company's availability to cash. Some examples of the questions that need to be answered:

- Does the company have a controlled disbursement account? Controlled disbursement accounts are bank accounts set up in another city with an affiliate of the primary bank. These accounts provide an extra day of float on payments, because checks presented to the affiliate bank are not cleared through the main bank until after the close of business.
- How quickly can the company access customer payments? Should it utilize lock box services provided by most banks? What is the cutoff time for processing deposits?
- If the company uses asset-based financing, how often is the formula recalculated? What is the deadline for loan requests?

The next step in the cash management process is to establish a simple system to track the cash balance. Many companies fail to monitor their cash position, only to be surprised when they receive a call from their bank that their accounts are overdrawn. This system can usually be as simple as a rolling balance calculation, similar to the way individuals record checks and deposits in their checkbooks.

The final step involved in getting a handle on the cash is to prepare a short-term cash flow projection and then use the cash flow to plan disbursements and monitor results. The cash flow projection can be started with a projection period as short as 14 to 30 days and should ultimately cover a rolling 60-day period, which should be updated weekly. The real advantages to using a cash flow projection are that future cash shortages can be identified and payments can be prioritized.

Creating Time and Money

Time and money are the two prerequisites for implementing the turnaround plan. Time and money create a platform that effective management can leverage into the turnaround plan. An understanding of the techniques used to create time and money is also an area where experienced crisis managers can add substantial value to a company. There are two sources of time and money for any company: the balance sheet and the income statement. The following is a discussion of several strategies for each statement.

Balance Sheet Strategies

The overall balance sheet strategy is to *liquidify* the company. This is done by "pulling the assets up" and "pushing the liabilities down." The following discussion presents strategies that should be considered for the categories commonly found on the balance sheet. Pulling the assets up refers to the process of generating cash from the asset side of the balance sheet.

Cash. In some cases, consolidating cash accounts may be appropriate. Keeping an imprest balance in special accounts, such as payroll or freight accounts, may seem like a small item, but these can represent nonproductive uses of a very scarce resource. A positive bank balance and a negative book balance kept tightly in control and properly supervised is good cash management.

Accounts Receivable. One of the most amazing things about a troubled company is that its accounts receivable aging often mirrors its payables aging. Solid management and follow-up of customer balances is often one of the first things to be neglected when the crisis strikes. Many companies are also willing to accept undue credit risks in an effort to bolster falling sales. Even if accounts receivable are part of the formula for an asset-based loan, the bank is advancing less than 100 percent and probably disqualifies receivables over 90 days and all foreign accounts. Develop a program to collect from overdue accounts; send reminder notices and place collection calls. If the account won't pay, demand cash in advance or C.O.D. terms. In any scenario, especially a crisis, the company is better off with a lost sale than a bad debt.

Other Receivables. Take notes receivable to your bank or a factor and try to discount them for cash. Eliminate employee advances and collect shareholder loans. Creditors will almost certainly pursue collection of a shareholder loan if the company fails, so arrange for payment when the company needs cash.

Prepaid Expenses. Such items as insurance and certain local taxes are usually payable in advance for periods up to one year. The amount paid that relates to future periods is referred to as a *prepaid expense*. Work to turn these into accrued liabilities. Investigate financing terms.

Inventory. Inventory should be reviewed very carefully. Many companies calculate their overall inventory turns and are quite satisfied when they meet or exceed industry norms. A closer inspection usually reveals a serious problem.

Typically, a large portion of a troubled company's inventory is slow-moving or obsolete. The overall calculation masks the slow-moving portion, because the good portion is turning rapidly due to lack of goods. An analysis of the inventory should be directed at identifying slow-moving items. All slow-moving inventory should be liquidated for cash immediately.

Property, Plant, and Equipment. There are several strategies that should be considered to generate working capital from plant, property, and equipment. The most obvious is to attempt to sell excess equipment. Other possibilities include sale/leaseback arrangements for major assets, performing subcontractor work on underutilized machines, moving to a smaller facility, or subleasing facilities to others. Do not be concerned about possible "book losses"; cash is primary in a crisis. Profit and loss in the accounting sense is secondary in importance to cash flow at a time of crisis.

Other Assets. The possibilities include borrowing against the cash surrender value of life insurance policies and recapturing deposits from vendors no longer being utilized. Any nonmaterial investments or securities in other companies should be put up for sale.

Pushing the liabilities down refers to the process of delaying payments for existing obligations or liabilities. The goal initially is to avoid paying or settling existing liabilities faster than new ones are created. If a company is paying off more liabilities than it is creating, it is effectively in a self-liquidation mode. This may be appropriate as part of an overall "downsizing" program, the goal of which is to pare down to a profitable level; but if the company does not carefully control the process, a full liquidation may eventually be the only alternative left. Many of the strategies for pushing the liabilities down are also discussed in the following section, which addresses creditor relations.

Accounts Payable. An extensive discussion of dealing with trade creditors is included in the following section. However, several key concepts must be considered. The most important principal is what we refer to as the *one-for-one* theory. The concept of the one-for-one theory is that, for every cash payment made to a creditor, an equivalent amount of value in product is received in return. When creditors begin to realize a company has financial difficulties, they naturally try to reduce their exposure. This occurs most commonly in the form of limiting access to credit. Typical examples include such demands as payment of all past-due invoices prior to shipment of new product. These types of demands usually mean that the company is effectively paying a "premium" for the value received. One simple example will demonstrate the cash flow impact of this premium. Let us assume the company purchases $40 worth of raw materials that are processed and sold for $100. The overdue balance with the vendor is $60. The following illustrates the difference between applying the one-for-one theory versus paying such a premium.

	One for One	Past-Due Invoices
Sales	$100	$100
Payment to vendor	40	60
Manufacturing cost	20	20
SG&A expense	30	30
Cash flow	10	(10)

As the above example illustrates, the company loses cash on the sale if the one-for-one theory is not followed. This result would not be reflected on the profit and loss statement. Eventually, the company will exhaust its resources if this procedure is repeated and will be forced into a bankruptcy or a liquidation. Past-due trade creditors must be convinced that past-due balances cannot be repaid out of cost of sales but only out of profits generated by a successful workout. The one-for-one theory must be in place until adequate positive cash flow permits a reasonable repayment plan to be instituted for all the past-due creditors.

The second important concept to keep in mind when dealing with trade creditors is that a small number of vendors make up the majority of the dollar value. It is extremely important to identify these critical vendors and deal with them effectively. Communicate with them frankly about the extent of the problem and help make them part of the solution.

Income Statement Strategies

Creating time and money through income statement strategies is closely tied to operations analysis, which is discussed later. However, several key points need to be made. During this phase of the turnaround process, it is important to develop strategies and take actions that improve cash flow, even if they are detrimental to book earnings, as mentioned earlier. Many of the strategies are closely related to the balance sheet strategies discussed above. One example is to sell excess inventory at less than cost. While this generates a book loss, the cash can be put to productive use in a profitable segment of the company. Another example might be to choose the outright sale of an idle plant over a lease arrangement, even if the lease payments have a higher discounted cash flow value. Other strategies to improve cash flow involve postponement or deferral of expenses, as well as identifying cost reduction opportunities. Any discretionary expenses should be deferred or eliminated.

Eliminating Expenses

The differences between this process and the strategies introduced above in the section Creating Time and Money are somewhat more subtle. But, we make the distinction for a very important reason. While the purpose of this process is usually to help stop the bleeding, here we begin to make permanent structural changes in the way a company operates, as opposed to the previous strategies, which are more temporary means of alleviating cash flow problems. The structural changes resulting from this process are really the beginning of the transition from crisis management to implementing the turnaround.

We have previously stressed how important it is to set aside preconceived notions and inbred prejudices about how the company should operate, and this area of eliminating expenses is where it is absolutely critical to do so. To be effective, the process should begin from the ground up, with what is commonly referred to as a *zero-based budget*. In fact, "elimination of expenses" is the wrong way to approach this process. If management starts with the company's current cost structure and looks for cuts, the managers will usually fall woefully short of what can be accomplished. This is because the expenses will all appear rational in the framework of the organization. To be done effectively, the expense elimination process must begin with the assumption that the company is starting over.

The first step is to identify the company's mission or purpose for existence. Identify the key products or services being provided to customers. Once this is done, expenses should be added back selectively on the basis of what is reasonable and necessary to accomplish the mission. The result will be the ideal expense structure for the company.

The second step is to then compare the ideal structure to the existing one.

The final step is to implement the changes that will transform the company into its ideal structure.

Usually, one of the keys to expense elimination is a reduction in the work force. If this is done correctly, management can avoid many of the negatives of layoffs and dismissals and, possibly, even realize unexpected benefits, such as increased efficiency. If the reductions are not handled well, there can be serious adverse consequences. It is important to identify and make all the cuts at once, if possible, to treat the employees who are let go with respect, to review and streamline the work for the employees who are left, and to reward them when possible.

Developing and Implementing the Turnaround Plan

Developing and implementing a turnaround plan requires many of the skills normally utilized in strategic planning for a healthy company. The differences are that the turnaround plan must be focused primarily on correcting current weaknesses and on considering existing constraints, and the turnaround plan must be developed and implemented in a very short timeframe. It is absolutely essential that the managers responsible for the plan have the ability to communicate the objectives throughout the organization and follow through on the implementation of the plan. The process of devising the turnaround plan should begin as soon as the state of crisis is identified, since the crisis management techniques discussed above are the first step towards implementing the turnaround plan. Once management begins to adequately address the crisis issues, the managers can begin analyzing longer term strategies. The following is a discussion of this process based on our extensive experience with numerous turnarounds.

Assessing the Prospects

The causes and seriousness of the crisis and related problems have a dramatic affect on the strategies that can be employed. Before proceeding with any strategy, management must assess the prospects for survival and ultimate turnaround. There are two primary considerations to analyze:

- What level of deterioration has been reached as a result of the crisis?
- How effectively can the company compete in today's marketplace?

After analyzing the above, a clear picture of the company's current status and future outlook comes into focus. This picture helps dictate the alternatives available to the company and their attractiveness. Several alternatives might need to be considered:

Liquidation sale: Some companies reach the point of no return. This occurs when the business has deteriorated to the point where the revenue stream is insufficient to support the replenishment of inventory and minimum operating expenses, and there are no assets left to sell. Liquidations can be accomplished in various ways, including formal bankruptcy proceedings, secured party sales, or out of court.

Merger: This is generally appropriate when the company has a viable core business, but it requires additional capital to survive or grow.

Bankruptcy or composition: This alternative, if successful, allows the company to compromise certain of its liabilities and remain in business. An analysis of these options is presented in Chapter 3.

Operational Analysis

As we previously discussed, a successful turnaround involves major operational changes. This is the phase of the turnaround where the necessary changes are identified. During the operational analysis, management must begin with a reexamination of the core business. Every division, product line, and individual item must be analyzed. This analysis usually identifies unprofitable or peripheral areas of the business. Downsizing the business by eliminating these unprofitable and noncore aspects of the business, through a sale or disposal, has several advantages. The primary advantage is that the business should be more profitable; but another advantage, often equally important, is the liquidity improvement that results. Downsizing the company provides liquidity in two ways. First, the company has excess assets after the downsizing, which can be sold, and second, the downsized operation requires less working capital. On a precautionary note, management must always be careful not to use the benefit of cash flow from downsizing to avoid needed changes, because the excess cash flow will eventually end once the appropriate level is reached. Instead, management should take advantage of the opportunity to put into place the changes needed for a successful turnaround during the downsizing period.

The Turnaround Business Plan

After the groundwork has been laid, the crisis management team must distill its efforts into a turnaround business plan and then work to implement the plan. Although the plan need not be a formal publishable document, all plans must have certain characteristics. The objectives should be realistic and concrete and be accompanied by specific completion dates. The steps necessary to accomplish the objectives should be well thought out, and there should be a methodology for measuring success or failure. The plan must include financial performance targets and fallback strategies for unexpected developments. The plan must also be split into short-, medium-, and long-term segments.

The short-term plan will generally include the weekly cash flow projections, previously discussed, and strategies for dealing with the major crisis issues. The short-term plan period is when management learns to work within the crisis management environment and reestablishes lost credibility with outsiders by addressing the important issues. This is a time to regain control of the business.

The medium- and long-term plan should include the analysis of the core business and the strategy for the business going forward. It is used as a tool to guide management and as a budget. The long-term plan can also be used to obtain new financing or to seek a merger partner. Usually longer-term financial projections are prepared in this process. At least two sets should be developed, using different economic assumptions.

CREDITOR RELATIONS

As previously mentioned, developing and maintaining good relationships with the various classes of creditors are critical to the turnaround process. As also discussed earlier, the concept of time and money is part of the platform on which a turnaround is built, and creditors can provide both. Let's begin with some general guidelines for creditor relations and then follow up with specifics for each class of creditors.

The goal of all creditor relations activity is to develop "partnerships" with the key creditors. If key creditors buy into the process, they are a tremendous asset; if relationships become adversarial, creditors can squeeze liquidity and divert management attention away from rebuilding the business. The keys to good creditor relations are to maintain open communications, to avoid surprises, and to not make promises that cannot be kept. The extent that credibility has eroded, because of a previous lack of candid communication, must be dealt with. Outsiders can provide assistance to management in rebuilding credibility.

All successful creditor relations begin with open communication. Without an ongoing dialogue, creditors will naturally assume the worst and act accordingly. Unfortunately, many managers avoid open communication at the time when it is most critical. This avoidance arises from the irrational belief that a problem ignored will somehow go away. It is also very difficult for management to openly discuss the company's problems, especially if the managers have not recognized or admitted to themselves the existence or magnitude of the problems.

Avoiding surprises is an extension of open communication. All successful relationships are built on trust, and nothing can undermine trust as quickly as a nasty surprise. An early warning of bad news allows a company to minimize the damage by framing the setback in the most positive light possible. Advance warning can also build confidence in management, because creditors are more assured that management can recognize problems early.

The final element of successful creditor relations is to avoid making promises that cannot be kept. When dealing with a creditor, the first instinct is to "tell them what they want to hear." This is the easy way out; the creditor believes it will receive a promised payment and the debtor believes the creditor will go away, at least for a while. Unfortunately, this comes back to haunt the company and damages long-term relationships.

The nature of the relationship with the individual creditors, and the strategies for dealing with them, varies according to their status. The discussion below presents the general classifications of creditors encountered in a turnaround situation and the key considerations for developing a good working relationship and for conducting negotiations.

Banks and Other Financial Institutions

Three key elements determine the nature of the relationship and the negotiating strategy. The first element is whether the loans are fully and properly secured by the assets of the company or by outside guarantees. The second is the bank personnel assigned to the loan. The third element is the past history between the bank and the company.

As "senior" lenders, banks usually seek to collateralize their loans by obtaining a security interest or mortgage on the assets of the company at the time the loan is made. It is important to immediately determine if the "security" at the time of the crisis is sufficient to pay off the loan balance, in the event of a liquidation, and the excess collateral value above the loan balance. When a bank is fully secured, it is generally more inclined to support the company's turnaround efforts. The reasons are fairly straightforward. The bank's loss exposure is minimal, and it has a strong desire to avoid a forced liquidation. Forced liquidations are costly and time consuming. The bank's actions may be questioned by other creditors and they can create large amounts of negative publicity. There is also the possibility of a lender liability lawsuit (to be discussed in a later chapter), if the bank has or is perceived to have acted in bad faith. If the bank is not fully secured, it will generally be less supportive of the turnaround process, since every dollar lost reduces recovery if the company must be liquidated.

In addition to security from the company's assets, banks have often sought to protect their loans to privately held and middle market companies by having principals or officers of the company personally guarantee repayment. These personal guarantees have been almost standard operating procedure for most middle market lenders, without regard to the financial condition of the borrower or the guarantor. In addition to providing additional security for the loan, the banks believe that the guarantors would be more diligent in seeing that the loan will be repaid if their personal assets were at risk. For example, the banks have a greater assurance of keeping the guarantor involved in the responsibility of collecting the loan balance, in case of liquidation or dissolution of the debtor.

Two recent court cases, *In re V. N. Deprizio* and *In re Coastal Petroleum Corporation,* have adversely impacted the appeal of personal guarantees if the borrower ends up in bankruptcy. In both cases, the court ruled that lenders can be saddled with insider status if the loans were personally guaranteed by an insider. The term *insider* refers to officers, directors, and others who can control the actions of the company. Inclusion as an insider extends the preference period from 90 days to one year. A *preference,* loosely defined, is a payment made to one creditor to the detriment of the other creditors. There are two significant factors that limit the potential preference recovery. First, the loan must be less than fully secured by the assets of the company, and second, the bank must have received more than it would have received from a Chapter 7 liquidation.

The following example illustrates the danger of these rulings. Assume a bank loans money to a company and the loan is guaranteed by the president of the company. Within a year of filing bankruptcy, the company makes several unscheduled loan payments. The bankruptcy trustee could seek to recover all payments received by the bank within a year of the filing. Without the personal guarantee, the recovery period would only extend to 90 days prior to the filing.

The second factor that has an effect on the relationship with the bank is the department assigned responsibility for the loan. The flexibility in negotiating with the bank could be limited once responsibility for a loan is transferred to the bank's workout department. The workout department within different banks may carry various names, such as Special Assets or Loan Administrator, but every major bank has a workout department that is set up to collect problem loans. In the past, workout departments usually concentrated on liquidating borrowers to collect whatever possible on a loan. Recently, banks have assigned more experienced personnel to their workout departments who are more flexible in dealing with borrowers; but the primary goal of the workout department is still collection. Once a loan has been transferred to a workout office, the relationship between the borrower and the lender can change substantially.

The third factor that influences the present banking relationship and negotiating position is the previous history of the professional relationship. If the company has a long-term association with the bank and with a loan officer who understands their business, there will probably be more flexibility than if the bank has had bad experiences with a management that has consistently failed to meet projections or the bank's expectations. Banks also develop what we refer to as *lender fatigue* as a result of dealing with a consistent problem loan. This is generally reflected in the form of an attitude change by the banker. The onset of this problem will usually result in a crucial blow to the banking relationship.

The company's relationship with its bank is substantially different than with other creditors. Often, the bank is owed the largest amount of any creditor, it has a security interest in the company's assets, and it has a high level of access to management and to the company's financial records. Cultivating the bank as a "partner" is critical to the turnaround process. It is more important than ever that the loan officer understands the company's business. The loan officer should also receive regular updates on the status of the turnaround. By working closely with the loan officer, and also the manager of his department, the company has an advocate at the bank. The better the loan officer understands the company and its problems and proposed solutions, the more likely the bank's management will be willing to work with the company through the workout into the turnaround.

In certain circumstances, the bank may be willing to make additional loans to support the turnaround process. However, this usually occurs only when there is equity left in the assets pledged to the bank, when the company and the bank have a longstanding relationship, when the bank perceives the problems as temporary, when management has proposed a workable turnaround plan, and when there is utmost confidence in management.

Usually, the bank is unwilling to advance additional loans, but it will continue lending to the company on the basis of existing terms. However, the bank may insist on changing some of the terms of the loan. Typical modifications may include the following:

- Establishment of a cash collateral lock box account, where customers remit accounts receivable payments directly to an account that the bank uses toward loan repayment. This forces the company to make daily draws on available credit lines.
- Daily reporting of accounts receivable and inventory balances, and the requirement of support documentation for new sales.
- Eliminate certain services, such as controlled disbursement accounts or access uncollected funds.
- Increase the interest rate, facility, fee or other charges.
- Lower advance rates for accounts receivable or inventory, or both.

Trade Accounts Payable

Developing good relationships and negotiating with trade creditors is critical to the turnaround process. Trade creditors usually have the most to lose if the turnaround is unsuccessful, since their claims are unsecured. They also have the most to gain if the company turns around. They receive payment for their outstanding invoices, and the company continues to be a customer for their goods and services. Dealing with trade creditors presents a unique problem, because there are so many of them and responding to numerous inquiries can be extremely time consuming and can divert management attention from important turnaround tasks. These factors must be balanced against the need for ongoing goods and services from vendors. If several key vendors refuse to work with a troubled company, the turnaround effort is almost certainly doomed.

Any successful program for dealing with trade creditors begins with the identification of key vendors. The definition is simple: a *key vendor* provides goods or services needed to operate the business that are not readily accessible from another source. Dealing with creditors is difficult, so narrowing the field to a select few helps make the process easier.

Once the key creditors have been identified, the remaining group should be broken down into ongoing and discontinued vendors. The knowledge of the trade creditor group gained through this exercise is an important lever in the negotiations.

After the creditors have been segregated into groups, the company must develop a plan of attack. *Attack* is the key word here, since the company cannot afford to be passive, because of the need for goods and services from its vendors. The plan should begin with open communications. No one likes to deal with upset vendors demanding payment. It is a natural reaction to ignore phone calls and correspondence; but this only pushes them into drastic actions, such as lawsuits or even filing involuntary bankruptcy proceedings. It is important that *every* phone call receive a prompt reply. At the early stage of the crisis, this will help buy the time necessary to bring about the turnaround. This is also the only method of having a positive influence on the actions the vendors may decide to take.

Unfortunately, answering these calls takes an inordinant amount of time. Several strategies can help alleviate this problem. First, by having the accounts payable clerks take all calls, many vendors will be satisfied temporarily just to have made contact with an employee of the company. Second, the team member responsible for cash management should set aside a specific period of the day for dealing with vendors that are not satisfied with reaching the accounts payable clerk. Doing this ensures that the remainder of the day can be devoted to problem solving.

Once a member of the crisis management team begins discussions with creditors, some general guidelines should be adhered to. First, you should be conciliatory and reasonable. Make sure the creditors know that you understand that they are upset. Acknowledge their claim, if it is not in dispute, and emphasize that your company appreciates the good past relationship and wishes for this to continue. Give them credible explanations for the problem and emphasize the hard work being put into a solution. Make them realize that they are not alone, and that they will be treated fairly. In some instances, it may even be appropriate to remind them of past sales volume that you have paid for, and that *they* made a conscious decision to sell to you on credit. Be careful at this point, since it can be inflammatory.

There are also several key "do nots" to this process. Do not lie to them about when to expect payment or make a promise that cannot be kept. Never make a payment because the creditor screams louder than anyone else. Finally, you should emphasize to the creditor that the company intends to meet its obligations and has no plans to seek bankruptcy court protection. Most sophisticated creditors realize their chance of recovery is severely damaged and delayed by bankruptcy proceedings, and they will work with the company to avoid this unless they suspect management fraud. If it is apparent that the full obligation cannot be repaid, the company must consider either an out-of-court workout or a bankruptcy filing. These considerations are discussed in the next chapter.

Payments to ongoing creditors should only be made in accordance with the established cash flow projections and priorities in return for new goods or services. There is both a legal and a practical consideration for this. The legal consideration is to avoid creating preferences. Preferences are the result of paying certain creditors to the detriment of others. The more important practical reason is that every dollar is needed to purchase goods and services during the turnaround.

Specific negotiation tactics for creditors depend on their classification and their willingness to work with the company. Critical vendors require the most care, because they have been identified as necessary for the business to continue. If these vendors are willing to continue selling on open terms, the company should attempt to try to preserve this. Usually, by the time the crisis is recognized, these vendors have been extended past their limit. The key is to try to develop a "partnership" type of relationship with these creditors. Remind them of many successful years of dealings. Unfortunately, these creditors have a great deal of leverage at their disposal. The best strategy is to try to employ the one-for-one theory. If they accept this arrangement, they have an opportunity to earn a profit on their sales to the company without assuming additional exposure. Even if the turnaround fails they may make enough profit to cover part or all of the subsequent accounts receivable write-off.

Several other methods can be explored to keep product flowing from a key supplier. One possibility is to have the debtor's customers with good credit pay for materials drop-shipped to the debtor, and deduct the cost from the purchase price.

Creditors that will continue to provide goods or services, as one of several sources, provide slightly different problems and opportunities. As with critical suppliers, it is important to utilize available cash for new purchases. One possibility is to pay cash or C.O.D. for purchases. Identify the suppliers that are willing to support the company and use them to the fullest extent possible.

The final group is the creditors that are not needed to move forward. This can occur because the vendors' products or services were substandard or they were suppliers for a segment that is being discontinued. The key to negotiating with these creditors is to allocate as little cash as possible for either settlement or pacification through the workout process.

Other Unsecured Creditors

This group includes mezzanine lenders and bondholders. The holders of these debts can include private investors, insurance companies, investment banks, and commercial banks. Often, these creditors hold equity in the company through warrants or options.

The strategy to be used for these creditors will be determined by the company's cash flow. During the first stages of the turnaround, payment will often need to be deferred. This is only possible if the creditors believe management is capable of turning around the business.

One option for these creditors is to convert their obligations to equity. Usually, this equity can be in the form of preferred stock. Preferred stock offers numerous advantages to the debtor. The biggest advantage of converting debt to preferred stock to equity is the effect on the company's balance sheet. After the conversion, the revised balance sheet may improve the company's ability to obtain trade credit. If cash flow or restrictions from the company's bank prevent the payment of dividends, they can be accumulated as cumulative dividends. Preferred stock can also carry a stated redemption date or retirement schedule similar to a note.

CONCLUSION

Running a business in the midst of a crisis can be a stressful and emotionally trying experience for even the most seasoned and talented manager. Successfully implementing a turnaround is one of the most satisfying accomplishments a manager can achieve. In this chapter, we have endeavored to provide practical guidance and advice that can be used to enhance the likelihood of successfully coping with an existing crisis—or to avert in the future a more pervasive crisis.

The primary element of successful crisis management is early recognition of the problems. Crisis managment techniques must be implemented before the deterioration of the company becomes irreversible. True crisis management begins once management recognizes that critical problems exist and the solutions lie outside the current operating methodology. The sooner management realizes this, the less dramatic the needed changes will be. Until management recognizes the need for change, the managers are simply fighting fires, not practicing crisis management. During the crisis period, management must create time and money through the techniques we described, such as the one-for-one theory. The goal of crisis management is to stabilize the business and to achieve an initial breakeven and subsequent positive cash flow.

The groundwork for the turnaround process is laid during the crisis management stage. Management must leverage the time and money that has been created into a long-term turnaround. The managers must accept the need to implement changes and the responsibility for identifying and implementing these changes. Most turnarounds are built around a refocusing on the company's core business. Management must take the steps necessary to strengthen or rebuild the core business and restructure the organization properly to support this core business.

CHAPTER 3

WORKOUT OR BANKRUPTCY?

William A. Slaughter, Esq.
Linda G. Worton, Esq.
Ballard, Spah, Andrews & Ingersoll

INTRODUCTION

For many corporate executives, the prospect of having a business with serious financial difficulties has always been akin to being caught in a plane crash. It was something they read about but that only happened to other people. Words like *workout* and *bankruptcy* were not in the minds of CEOs of large corporations . . . that is, until today.

Today we hear leading businessmen predicting that during the next 10 years we will see the deleveraging of corporate America and an overwhelming amount of workout business.[1] We read that bankruptcy is now a business strategy—a way to solve a problem.[2] Large businesses are finding themselves in the position of deciding whether to reorganize through an out-of-court workout or by filing for bankruptcy.[3] Increasingly, they are opting for bankruptcy.

This chapter will address some advantages and disadvantages

of bankruptcy, compared to an out-of-court workout, and will discuss some of the major issues to be considered by a troubled company and its creditors in making a choice between a workout and bankruptcy.

WARNING SIGNS AND THE FIRST STEPS TOWARD REORGANIZATION

Warning signs of an impending workout or bankruptcy may come in many forms. The first clue may come in the form of increasing day-to-day business problems; an uneasy board of directors; fundamental and adverse changes in a company's competition, customers, and markets; worsening relations with lenders and other creditors; persistently unfavorable press and analyst reports; or an increasingly nearsighted focus to the business planning process.[4] The final clue that a reorganization may be necessary is generally the discovery that the business can no longer meet its current debt obligations as they become due.

The inability to meet debt requirements, however, is often a symptom of more fundamental problems in the business. Thus, the cause of the problems must be defined and clarified to determine the steps necessary to permanently remedy the problems. The inability to meet debts and associated financial difficulties may be related to such problems as lack of proper management, inadequate working capital, overleverage, unsuccessful investments, an unpredicted economic downturn, a change in the segment of the economy in which the company does business, or a combination of such factors. Unless the situation calls for *immediate* relief, management should perform a careful analysis of the problems before taking steps toward a fundamental reorganization. Once the underlying causes of the problems have been identified and management has begun to focus on possible solutions, it may be that the remedy required is simply an infusion of new management or additional cash. If the business is still operating at a breakeven point or better, but profits are decreasing, management may choose to hire a business consultant before calling bankruptcy counsel. A reorganization, whether in or out of bankruptcy court, is only one alternative available to help remedy the underlying financial problems; it is not a remedy itself.

WORKOUT OUT OF COURT

Workout is a term that has come to connote negotiations outside of bankruptcy or other court proceedings, between a debtor and its creditors, seeking to achieve an extension of debt or a composition of debt, or both. Normally, the purpose of the workout is to persuade creditors to give a debtor some breathing room by extending the time within which payment is required or by reducing the amount to be paid in satisfaction of an obligation. The key to a successful workout is the willingness of all or substantially all of a debtor's major creditors to participate in and assent to the proposed workout.

To successfully negotiate a workout, the debtor must develop a business plan to show creditors that, with a little more leeway in terms of time, lowered interest rate, and/or increased financing, the debtor will be in a position to pay creditors more than the creditors would receive if they pursued rights and remedies to which they are otherwise entitled. The contents of a workout plan will depend upon the nature of the business, the source of the problem, and the proposed solution to the problem. However, a creditor will generally require financial projections before it considers a plan that proposes a substantial modification of the terms of the debtor's obligations.

The key to a successful business plan is to ensure that it demonstrates three things: *(a)* its own feasibility, *(b)* its fairness, and *(c)* that it is better than the alternative — usually bankruptcy reorganization or liquidation. If creditors are persuaded that a debtor's business plan is feasible, fair, and provides a greater return than any other alternative, their economic self-interest will dictate support of the plan. It is often necessary for a debtor to overcome often irrational resistance to an out-of-court workout by creditors who, by virtue of their past experience, harbor feelings of distrust and resentment toward the debtor and who feel that the debtor has not lived up to its commitments in the past. Without the three fundamental elements — feasibility, fairness, and advantage over other alternatives — an out-of-court workout will be doomed from the start.

Out-of-Court Workouts — The Benefits

If an out-of-court workout can be implemented successfully and quickly, it is almost always preferable to the alternative of bankruptcy, from the standpoint of both the debtor and its creditors. The preference for an out-of-court workout exists principally for two reasons: first, noncourt workouts are almost always less expensive to administer than a bankruptcy; and second, neither the debtor nor its creditors are burdened by the rules, restrictions, and public scrutiny that a bankruptcy creates.

An out-of-court workout can often provide the debtor with the opportunity and the means to correct cash flow problems and operate at a profit. It is a way that the management can sit down and develop a strategy to remedy the problems that are affecting business operations. The debtor can then work with its creditors to so negotiate its plan that the plan is satisfactory to those parties involved. The debtor has the option of dealing with each creditor separately or with all of its creditors together. Both the debtor and its creditors enjoy a great deal of flexibility in developing the structure of the workout.

In an out-of-court workout, the debtor avoids court scrutiny in developing the terms of the plan and in operating its business. A lender may require certain operations and accounting reports as a condition to a loan, but the debtor is obligated to do only what it agrees to do. The debtor does not open its accounting records for public scrutiny the way it would in a bankruptcy proceeding.[5]

It is generally advantageous for a debtor to keep its financial troubles private. Where a debtor can meet its payroll and pay its trade creditors on a current basis, it is better to negotiate for credit with its secured creditors without alarming the trade creditors. If a trade creditor suspects that a business is in financial trouble, it may demand adequate assurance of future performance and may suspend further credit, requiring cash on delivery or other similar arrangement. Similarly, employees may panic, spreading rumors regarding the company's financial position or seeking jobs in what they perceive to be a more stable business. And, of course, bankruptcy can be a public relations nightmare affecting all aspects of the troubled company's business: employees, customers, suppliers, creditors, and shareholders. By contrast, an out-of-court workout offers a debtor the opportunity to deal solely with the creditors that are affected by the problem, without subjecting either the debtor or its creditors to the scrutiny of the bankruptcy court or to public scrutiny generally.

Finally, because the workout is generally faster to accomplish and involves fewer parties (and, therefore, fewer lawyers) than a bankruptcy, it is often less costly to administer; consequently, it is usually significantly less expensive than a bankruptcy reorganization.

Out-of-Court Workouts — The Risks

The debtor takes certain risks in attempting a workout when the business is in serious financial trouble. First, and usually most important, is the "holdout problem." The holdout problem occurs where a debtor spends a great deal of time and expends large sums of money in legal fees to negotiate a business plan only to find in the end that the entire plan is jeopardized by a few stubborn creditors' refusal to accept it. A creditor may try to use its role as a holdout to create leverage for itself and obtain preferred treatment, or it may choose to pursue its legal rights, possibly in ways that substantially impair a debtor's ability to operate.

There is no *sure* solution to the holdout problem. One *possible* solution is the development of a plan that includes some, but not all, of the debtor's creditors. However, the debtor then runs the risk that participating creditors will attempt to improve their ultimate economic recoveries at the expense of the nonparticipating creditors. In such a case, the nonparticipant may try to pull the rug from under the debtor (and the participating creditors) by seizing property or accelerating debt, or both, and may try to undo what it perceives to be the damage of the workout by filing an involuntary petition in bankruptcy and taking advantage of a bankruptcy trustee's avoiding powers (discussed later). In addition, the debtor runs the risk that creditors otherwise willing to participate in the debtor's proposed workout will back away if they perceive that holdouts are receiving better treatment.

The structure of an out-of-court workout is almost always shaky. Workout participants are more than conscious of the possibility of a bankruptcy filing and must incorporate into the deal the possible consequences of the filing. Each party takes the chance that, in the event of a bankruptcy, the terms of the workout may be void or may actually harm its position. For example, if a creditor receives a transfer from the debtor within the 90-day period before the bankruptcy filing, the transfer may be deemed a "preference" and avoided, so the creditor loses the benefit of the transfer. Moreover, if the creditor becomes overly involved with the debtor's operations, the creditor may be deemed an "insider"[6] of the business. As an insider, the preference period increases from 90 days to one year,[7] and the creditor's claim may be subordinated to other claims.[8]

In addition to the risk of a bankruptcy filing, workout participants are conscious of many other risks involved with committing to a workout. While the debtor is working out its troubles with one group of creditors, its problems continue to mount with other groups. For example, a debtor with cash flow problems may turn to its principal lenders first. But, while the debtor is negotiating an extension of credit with its lenders, the employees may be preparing to strike, litigation of claims against the company may be continuing, interest on unpaid obligations may continue to accrue, and trade vendors may be increasingly unwilling to continue to supply the debtor on credit terms beneficial to the debtor.

The debtor may be overwhelmed by the number of issues it must address and may be unable to assess all of its liabilities. The workout offers some relief but may not be enough. The debtor may need some breathing space to develop a feasible plan of reorganization and negotiate the plan successfully. An out-of-court workout may offer that breathing space, to the extent the participants agree to it, but it does not offer the extensive protection that a bankruptcy filing provides.

CHAPTER 11 BANKRUPTCY REORGANIZATION

When a company can no longer meet its debt obligations and is unable to restructure its indebtedness, management may turn to the United States Bankruptcy Code for relief.[9] The Bankruptcy Code offers two avenues of relief for a business — Chapter 7 liquidation and Chapter 11 reorganization.

Under both Chapter 7 and Chapter 11, the debtor begins a voluntary bankruptcy by filing with the clerk of the bankruptcy court a simple petition stating that it desires to initiate bankruptcy proceedings.[10] With certain exceptions, any (1) individual, partnership, or corporation that (2) resides or has a domicile, place of business, or property in the United States may file for relief under Chapter 7 or Chapter 11.[11] Once the case has commenced, the debtor is required to file with the clerk of the bankruptcy court a list of creditors, schedules of assets and liabilities, a schedule of current income and expenditures, and a statement of the debtor's financial affairs.[12] As such, the administration of the estate begins. In a Chapter 7 case, the objective is to liquidate the estate under the aegis of a trustee and to distribute the proceeds of the liquidation to the debtor's creditors in accordance with the Bankruptcy Code. In a Chapter 11 case, the objective is to reorganize the debtor in such a way that its business will continue to operate and creditors will receive more than they would in a Chapter 7 liquidation.

After the debtor files the necessary information with the court, the debtor begins administering the case and creditors begin negotiating their claims. The bankruptcy court appoints an unsecured creditors' committee, consisting of the seven largest unsecured creditors that are willing to serve on the committee.[13] On request of any party in interest, the court may also order the appointment of any other committees necessary to assure adequate representation of other creditors and parties in interest.[14] Once appointed, the committee works to protect the common interests of those it represents. A committee appointed under the Bankruptcy Code has the authority to, among other things, (1) consider whether the business should continue to be operated, (2) determine whether the court should be asked to appoint a trustee or examiner, (3) conduct an investigation of the financial affairs of the debtor, and (4) consult generally with the debtor or trustee in the administration of the case.[15] Subject to bankruptcy court approval, a committee may employ its own lawyers, accountants, and other agents to perform services for the committee, and those professionals are paid from the assets of the debtor's estate.[16]

Most managers will make an effort to continue to operate the business and to reorganize the business affairs in Chapter 11, rather than giving up control to a trustee and having a trustee liquidate the company. Similarly, equity security holders and creditors will prefer Chapter 11 to Chapter 7, because they realize that a company's assets are generally worth more in an organized and ongoing business than in a liquidation sale. The party filing the bankruptcy petition has the option to file under either chapter, but any party in interest may request that the court convert the case from a Chapter 7 to a Chapter 11 or vice versa.[17]

Chapter 11 — The Benefits

A Chapter 11 reorganization offers many advantages to a debtor that an out-of-court workout cannot provide. Generally, Chapter 11 offers two crucial commodities that often cannot be otherwise obtained: *(a)* time and *(b)* the ability to impose a reorganization plan binding on all creditors (even nonconsenting creditors) so long as the requirements of the Bankruptcy Code are met. Specifically, Chapter 11 gives a debtor:

- The ability to restrain creditors from seizing the debtor's property or canceling beneficial contracts and to stay judicial actions against the debtor.
- The ability to continue to operate the business effectively without interference from the creditors.
- The ability to borrow money by granting liens on the debtor's assets equal to or superior to the liens of existing creditors.
- The ability to avoid certain transfers that occurred prior to the filing of the bankruptcy petition.
- The cessation of interest accrual on debts that were unsecured as of the filing date.
- The ability to propose and negotiate a single plan with all of the debtor's creditors.
- The power to bind dissenting creditors to a reorganization plan that meets the Bankruptcy Code standard.
- The receipt of a discharge by the bankruptcy court of all prepetition claims treated under the reorganization plan.

The Automatic Stay
One of the main advantages of Chapter 11 over out-of-court workouts is the protection of the automatic stay. The automatic stay, as its name suggests, occurs automatically upon the filing of a bank-

ruptcy petition, without the need for affirmative action by the bankruptcy court or anyone else. The stay is a debtor's best friend, protecting the debtor from a broad range of actions, allowing the debtor to maintain possession of its property, and giving the debtor breathing space to reorganize itself.[18]

The automatic stay prohibits all entities from the commencement or continuation of any judicial, administrative, or other action or proceeding against the debtor that was or could have been commenced before the commencement of the case; the enforcement against the debtor or its property of any judgment obtained before the commencement of the case; any act to obtain possession or control of the debtor's property; any act to create, perfect, or enforce any lien against the debtor's property; any act to collect, assess, or recover a claim against the debtor that arose before the commencement of the case; and the setoff of any debt owing to the debtor that arose before the commencement of the case.[19] The stay is automatic upon the filing of the petition and remains in effect until vacated by the court or until the earliest of the time the case is closed, the case is dismissed, or the debtor's discharge is granted or denied.[20]

Any party in interest may obtain relief from the automatic stay but only for "cause" and only after notice and a hearing.[21] Although the Bankruptcy Code requires the bankruptcy court to rule on an interested party's request for relief from the automatic stay within 30 days of the filing of such a request, bankruptcy courts hesitate to grant such relief in the early stages of a case, particularly where the granting of relief will effectively prevent the debtor from developing a plan of reorganization.

Thus, the automatic stay provides the first key element—time—that often is not available to a debtor attempting to resolve its financial difficulties out of court and without the protection of the Bankruptcy Code.

Operating the Business as a Debtor-in-Possession
Subject to certain limitations discussed below, in a Chapter 11 case, the debtor continues to operate its business in the normal course. While the Bankruptcy Code provides that a distinct legal entity called *debtor-in-possession* is created upon the commencement of a Chapter 11 proceeding, as a practical matter the debtor's existing

management and board of directors remain in control of the company's day-to-day operations and maintain control over the direction of the company's reorganization.

Transactions out of the ordinary course of business (e.g., major asset sales), however, require bankruptcy court approval upon notice to creditors. The creditors' committee has general oversight responsibility, and the committee, through its counsel, necessarily becomes a "player" in the proceedings. Moreover, any interested party may request that the court appoint a trustee to take possession of the debtor's property and to operate the business if it can demonstrate that it is "in the interests of creditors, equity security holders, and other interests of the estate."[22] However, absent gross mismanagement, fraud, or other palpable wrongdoing, appointment of a trustee in a Chapter 11 case is an extreme measure that is infrequently exercised.

Once the debtor becomes a debtor-in-possession, it must be able to effectively operate the business, which normally requires access to cash. The Uniform Commercial Code concept of a "floating lien" has made it commonplace for loans to be secured by *all* of the debtor's property, including real estate, fixtures, equipment, inventory, accounts receivable, and the proceeds thereof, regardless of when acquired. If the debtor is in default on a secured loan, nonbankruptcy law entitles the secured creditor to take possession of the collateral securing the loan to satisfy its claim.[23] The automatic stay prevents a secured creditor from seizing property; but it does not automatically grant the debtor the authority to use, sell, or lease the encumbered property or the cash proceeds of the encumbered property. Such "cash collateral" may not be used unless and until the secured party consents to its use or until the court, after notice and hearing, authorizes its use.[24] If a secured party objects to the use of the cash collateral, the court may still authorize its use upon finding that the secured party's position is "adequately protected."

Thus, at the outset of most bankruptcy cases, the debtor and its secured creditors negotiate, within the framework of the Bankruptcy Code's concept of "adequate protection," the terms under which the debtor continues to use the cash generated in its business. This provision governing use of cash collateral is one of the many examples of the way the Bankruptcy Code seeks to create a balance in the bargaining position between a debtor and its creditors by adding some weight to the debtor's side of the scale. In bankruptcy, the debtor has the power (with bankruptcy court approval) to use property that outside of bankruptcy could only be used with a creditor's permission. Where, in an out-of-court workout, a lender may bring a debtor's business to a screeching halt by turning off the flow of cash, in a bankruptcy that threat is lessened by the debtor's ability to have the court authorize use of the creditor's collateral.

In essence, the debtor is able to operate its business and is able to use property of the estate even when that property is subject to a lien. The Bankruptcy Code prevents secured creditors from seizing property and allows the debtor to use the property in the ordinary course of business and thereby to carry on business as usual while it attempts to reorganize its debt. The elimination of the threat of seizure and the use of the encumbered property enables the debtor to continue to generate cash, gives the debtor time to negotiate with creditors, and removes the undue leverage a secured creditor often has by virtue of its right to seize collateral.

Obtaining Postpetition Credit

For a debtor in bankruptcy, the ability to obtain additional credit to assure continued business operations may be as critical as its ability to use its own property. A debtor may obtain unsecured credit in the ordinary course of business, either through the purchase of goods or services or through the borrowing of money, without court approval.[25] To encourage third parties to provide such unsecured credit to a debtor, the Bankruptcy Code provides that any creditor providing unsecured credit in the ordinary course of business during the bankruptcy is automatically deemed to have a first priority administrative claim, which assures the creditor payment ahead of prepetition claims.[26] Where a debtor is unable to obtain unsecured credit, the Bankruptcy Code permits the debtor, with court approval, to obtain credit on a secured or special priority basis by granting the creditor priority over all other administrative expenses.[27] And, if the debtor is still unable to obtain credit by offering the creditor priority over administrative expenses, then the debtor may offer the creditor a lien on unencumbered property of the estate[28] or a lien senior to an existing lien, provided that the interest of the displaced lienor is adequately protected.[29]

Where a highly leveraged company is facing financial difficulties, it is often difficult to obtain additional financing outside of bankruptcy, because all of its assets are encumbered and existing lenders are unwilling to agree to a new lien on a par with, or superior to, their interests. Thus, the super-priority available in bankruptcy may be a useful tool for the debtor to obtain new financing. Such interim financing may be the key to a reorganization, by providing enough cash to allow the debtor to operate during the reorganization process.

Avoiding Powers
The creation of a debtor-in-possession grants the debtor certain "avoiding powers" under the Bankruptcy Code. The avoiding powers give the debtor the opportunity to recover funds or interests that were transferred by the debtor, either voluntarily or involuntarily, before the commencement of the case. The property recovered then goes back into the debtor's estate for the benefit of all creditors. In this respect, as in many others, the debtor acts as a trustee for its own creditors. The debtor may invoke three types of avoiding powers: (1) the preference provisions of the Bankruptcy Code, (2) the fraudulent conveyance provisions of the Bankruptcy Code and relevant state law, and (3) the equity power of the bankruptcy court.

Preference Provisions. Section 547 of the Bankruptcy Code enables the debtor to avoid *(a)* any transfer of property of the debtor to or for the benefit of a creditor; *(b)* on account of an antecedent debt; *(c)* made while the debtor was insolvent; *(d)* within 90 days before the date of the filing of the bankruptcy petition (or between 90 days and one year before the filing, if the creditor was an insider); *(e)* if the transfer would enable the creditor to receive more than the creditor would receive in a liquidation under Chapter 7 had the transfer not been made.[30] The term *transfer* is defined loosely to include "every mode . . . of dispensing of or parting with property or with an interest in property, including retention of title as a security interest and foreclosure of the debtor's equity of redemption."[31]

The preference provisions thus allow a debtor to bring back into the estate funds transferred in payment of old debt during the three-month period before the bankruptcy. Such funds may provide an additional source of working capital and may be used in a reorganization plan to fund payments to all creditors.

Fraudulent Conveyance Statutes. Another potentially powerful tool for the recovery of property transferred prior to a bankruptcy filing are the state and federal fraudulent conveyance laws.[32] Three general statutory schemes may be applicable to a fraudulent conveyance action:[33] (1) Section 548 of the Bankruptcy Code,[34] (2) the Uniform Fraudulent Conveyance Act (UFCA),[35] and (3) the Uniform Fraudulent Transfer Act (UFTA).[36]

In essence, each of the three statutory frameworks provides that a conveyance may be avoided where: *(a)* a prepetition transfer was made, *(b)* without the exchange of property for the reasonably equivalent value, and *(c)* the debtor was insolvent or was rendered insolvent (or left with unreasonably small capital to conduct its business) as a result of the transfer.[37] A transfer may be avoided either as an intentional fraudulent conveyance, where property was transferred with actual intent to hinder, delay, or defraud creditors, or as a constructive fraudulent conveyance regardless of intent.

Increasingly, fraudulent conveyance attacks are now being used to challenge recently concluded leveraged buyouts, where the debtor has incurred an obligation or suffered liens attached to its assets to facilitate a transfer of ownership, without any direct benefit realized by the debtor itself or its general creditors.[38] Like the preference provisions, the fraudulent conveyance statutes allow the debtor to escape from transfers made or obligations incurred prior to the filing of a bankruptcy petition, to undo a prepetition restructuring, and to create a potential source of funding for the debtor's current attempt to reorganize.

Equitable Subordination. A third way in which a debtor may recover property is through the equitable subordination of claims.[39] The subordination of a claim alters the priority of claims and the order of distribution of proceeds of the debtor's estate as prescribed in the Bankruptcy Code. Equitable subordination is an equitable remedy left primarily to the discretion of the bankruptcy judge, and it is generally applied where: (1) the claimant engaged in some kind of inequitable conduct, (2) the conduct resulted in injury to other creditors or conferred an unfair advantage on the claimant, and (3) the subordination of the claim would not be inconsistent with the general provisions of the Bankruptcy Code.[40]

Preference actions, fraudulent conveyance attacks, and equitable subordination claims each offer the debtor the unique opportunity to recover funds, undo transactions, and alter the priority of claims. In some cases, the mere threat of the use of such avoidance powers may be just what is needed to encourage reluctant creditors to negotiate toward a reorganization that is fair to all.

Prepetition Claims and Interest Accrual

Where a debtor suffers from severe cash flow problems, the greatest benefit of bankruptcy may be the provision of the Bankruptcy Code that relieves the debtor of any immediate obligation to pay prepetition claims. The Bankruptcy Code actually prohibits the debtor from paying prepetition claims and suspends any interest accrual on those claims.[41] Only a fully secured creditor is entitled to interest on its prepetition claim; but even the secured creditor is entitled to such interest only to the extent that the amount of its claim does not exceed the value of the collateral securing its claim.[42]

This cessation of interest accrual may save the debtor a great deal of money, and it creates a strong incentive for an undersecured or unsecured creditor to negotiate more easily so a plan of reorganization can be consummated quickly.

The Plan of Reorganization

The principal objective of Chapter 11 is the development, negotiation, and confirmation of a plan of reorganization. For 120 days after the filing of the bankruptcy petition, the debtor has the exclusive right to propose a plan of reorganization.[43] If the debtor fails to file a plan within the 120-day exclusive period,[44] the debtor may still file a plan and seek its acceptance and confirmation; but at that point any creditor or party in interest may file a competing plan and independently seek its confirmation.

The Bankruptcy Code imposes relatively few rules governing the contents of a debtor's plan of reorganization. The plan must divide the debtor's creditors into classes depending upon the nature of their claims, must propose a prescribed treatment of each class of claims, and must provide a means for execution of the plan. Beyond that, a debtor and its creditors are free to pursue any type of reorganization that is feasible.

The reorganization may involve a sale of assets, infusion of new capital, restructuring of debt, issuance of new securities, or the merger of the debtor with or into another company.[45] The Bankruptcy Code strives to facilitate the types of transactions that are often included within plans of reorganization by making the transactions easier and less costly than they would be outside of bankruptcy. For example, the Bankruptcy Code permits the sale of assets free of transfer and similar taxes;[46] and it permits the issuance of securities without compliance with certain requirements of the federal securities laws, provided that the transactions are accomplished in connection with a bankruptcy plan.[47]

Once a plan is proposed and filed, the proponent of the plan sends the plan and a disclosure statement relating to the plan (akin to a proxy statement) to all creditors and interest holders for their vote. To be confirmed (i.e., approved) by the court, a plan must normally be accepted by each of the classes of creditors and interest holders whose claims are impaired under the plan.[48] Acceptance by an impaired class of creditors requires the affirmative vote of at least two thirds in amount and one half in number of the creditors within such class who actually vote on the plan.[49] Once confirmed, a plan is binding upon all creditors (regardless of how an individual creditor may have voted), and a debtor is discharged from any obligation it had in respect of such creditors' claims, other than the obligation to perform in accordance with the plan. Thus, bankruptcy solves the "holdout problem" by providing a mechanism by which the debtor may bind classes of creditors by majority vote and avoid the need for unanimous or near-unanimous agreement of creditors.

In addition, in certain instances, a plan may even be "crammed down" the throats of a class of creditors that votes against the plan. To be crammed down upon a rejecting class of claims, the court must find that the plan is fair and equitable and that it does not discriminate unfairly against the dissenting class. For secured creditors, the fair and equitable and nondiscrimination requirements demand that the creditor retain its lien on the debtor's property (or on the proceeds of the sale of the property) and receive on account of its claim deferred cash payments having a present value at least equal to the value of the secured creditor's collateral.[50] To be crammed down upon a class of unsecured claims or junior interests, the fair and equitable and nondiscrimination provisions require, at a minimum, observance of the *absolute priority* rule—that is, no class junior to the nonaccepting class may receive or retain any interest or property under the plan.[51]

The cramdown provisions of the Bankruptcy Code are one of a debtor's most potent sources of leverage over creditors. Obviously, it is a source of leverage available only in a bankruptcy proceeding.

Chapter 11—The Risks

Time and Expense

Perhaps the greatest disadvantage of pursuing a bankruptcy case, rather than an out-of-court workout, is the time and expense involved in a Chapter 11 reorganization. The Bankruptcy Code does not provide any time limit for the duration of a Chapter 11 case. The length depends on such factors as the size of the debtor, the number of creditors, the reasonableness of the parties, and the starting point on the petition date. A debtor with a confirmable plan and cooperative creditors may have the plan confirmed within a few months, while a debtor with many competing creditors, a low cash flow, and large operations may take years before it is able to develop a plan and obtain court approval. Thus, it is difficult to estimate the average amount of time a bankruptcy case takes, but it is safe to say that it generally consumes more time than an out-of-court workout.

More time means greater expense—particularly where such professionals as lawyers, accountants, appraisers, business consultants, investment bankers, and others may be necessary to the successful completion of the bankruptcy reorganization. Moreover, the Bankruptcy Code explicitly contemplates that, in a bankruptcy case, the debtor will be responsible not only for the cost of its own lawyers and other professionals but also for the cost of professionals retained by the creditors' committee and by any other committees that may be appointed in the case.[52] In large bankruptcy cases, professional fees may be enormous. In the Johns-Manville case, for example, professional fees cost the company nearly $200 million. In cases involving small to medium-sized companies, the administrative expenses associated with the bankruptcy are generally not as large in raw number but may well be even larger in proportion to the company's size and its available cash. It is not unusual for bankruptcy administration costs to be so overwhelming as to be a major obstacle in a reorganization. While out-of-court workouts also involve hefty professional fees, it is fair to say that the transactional costs are significantly lower than the related costs in bankruptcy.

Loss of Control

The management, board, and shareholders of a distressed company inevitably suffer some loss of control when a debtor files for bankruptcy. The concept of a "debtor-in-possession" is unique, in that the debtor-in-possession owes a fiduciary duty to the creditors and the debtor's "estate,"[53] notwithstanding those managing the estate may have an interest that is adverse to that of the creditors or the estate, or both. Consequently, management may find itself in some uncomfortable situations.

For example, management is charged with the duty of pursuing any lawsuits the debtor may have.[54] These lawsuits may include suits against lenders, equity security holders, or management itself. If management fails to bring the suits, the creditors' committee may do so with the bankruptcy court's approval.[55] Consequently, management may face the unpleasant task of suing the shareholders of the company or even management.

Management may also find that its financial interest in the debtor has been significantly decreased or eliminated. The Bankruptcy Code subordinates equity claims to other claims, which effectively forces equity security holders to sacrifice their right to distributions until all other creditors are paid in full. Insiders' claims are not automatically subordinated, but bankruptcy courts generally subject such claims to very close scrutiny.[56] Where creditors challenge an insider's claim, courts will consider such factors as whether any misconduct has occurred and whether the insider's misconduct gave rise to the claim.[57] The insider has the burden of proving the fairness and good faith of the claim once the claim is challenged.[58] Thus, the managers may find themselves defending their own interests and managing a company in which they have little or no interest.

In addition, management may find that it has lost a great deal of its authority in rendering decisions. Although the debtor has the authority to continue to operate its business without further order by the court, the Bankruptcy Code imposes certain restrictions on the operation. First, a debtor may use, sell, or lease property without court approval *only* in the "ordinary course of business."[59] If a lender has a mortgage on or a security interest in the property, the property cannot be used, sold, or leased unless the creditor consents or the court determines that the creditor's interest is adequately protected against loss.[60] The debtor-in-possession must obtain court approval, inter alia, to use, sell, or lease property or cash subject to a lien;[61] to obtain credit financing;[62] to set salaries of officers and other employees of the debtor;[63] and to employ professionals, such as accountants, lawyers, and business consultants.[64]

Management may also find that business opportunities are stalled or missed because of bankruptcy procedure. For example, a debtor may not sell substantially all of its assets while in a Chapter 11 proceeding if it is outside of a plan of reorganization, unless the debtor demonstrates to the court that it has substantial business justification or some type of emergency.[65] Thus, management may be forced to justify its decision and to wait for court approval before it can close a deal. The process of obtaining court approval generally takes at least 30 days from the time the request is filed, and, in a fast-moving business environment, even 30 days may be a very long time to wait. But the debtor-in-possession must accept the fact that every move outside the ordinary course of business will take longer to accomplish and may be scrutinized by the court.

In addition, the debtor is required to file periodic reports concerning the debtor's financial affairs and condition, receipts and disbursements, profits and losses, and other data pertaining to the debtor's ongoing operations.[66] This reporting requirement contributes to the debtor's loss of control, as well as to the expense of the reorganization.

The debtor may suffer an even greater loss of control where the court removes the debtor's control over operations and assets or removes the management itself. On request of any party in interest, and after notice and a hearing, the court may order the appointment of a trustee for cause, including fraud, dishonesty, incompetence, or gross mismanagement of the affairs of the debtor by current management, either before or after the commencement of the case or if such appointment is in the interests of creditors, any equity security holders, and other interests of the estate.[67]

Stigma

Although less a factor in the 1990s than in the past, a stigma is attached to a bankrupt business. While the out-of-court workout of a business is rarely headline news, the filing of a bankruptcy petition can make the front page if the company is large enough. The mere filing of a bankruptcy, even in today's environment, will invariably have a detrimental effect upon a debtor's relations with customers, suppliers, employees, creditors, and shareholders. Suppliers are reluctant to sell to, and customers are reluctant to buy from, a company in bankruptcy, particularly where they can deal with that company's competitors on essentially the same terms. By the same token, the publicity and uncertainty attendant to the initiation of a bankruptcy case make it more difficult for a debtor to maintain a capable work force, particularly where employees can move elsewhere; and it is always the most well-qualified employees that have the greatest mobility and are, therefore, most likely to jump ship at the crucial moment.

Even after a successful bankruptcy reorganization (as opposed to a successful workout), the bankruptcy stigma can remain with the company, depressing the company's securities and making it more difficult for the company to obtain credit. On the other hand, perceptions are changing and will continue to change. Toys "R" Us, Inc., emerged from the Interstate Department Stores bankruptcy with its stock trading for as little as 12.5 a share, but 10 years later it sold for 300 times that amount.[68] More recently, Storage Technology's 11.625 percent bonds sold for $500 per $1,000 of face value after the company filed for bankruptcy in 1984. Thirty-two months later, the bonds were worth $1,300.[69]

More and more we hear bankruptcy referred to as a *strategy*, rather than a *last resort*. However, many businesses still avoid bankruptcy based upon the stigma alone.

MOVING FROM A WORKOUT MODE TO A BANKRUPTCY FILING

The key to a successful workout or reorganization, whether in court or outside of court, is early detection. Managers must try to detect signs of deterioration before the business reaches a point of emergency. Managers must dare to ask the question "What if . . .?" And when managers foresee the possibility of bankruptcy, they must begin to take precautions just in case the company will ultimately seek bankruptcy relief.

Management should be particularly careful to monitor the business and to document any changes in performance. Managers should be conscious of the fact that, if a workout or bankruptcy happens, in all likelihood every decision, disclosure, and course of action will be examined under the "litigation microscope" at some point in the future.[70] The importance of accurate recordkeeping cannot be overemphasized.

At this preliminary stage, managers should also be conscious of special problems relating to subsidiaries, parents, or other affiliates with major debt. If the financially troubled affiliate is in default or is a significant guarantor of the distressed debtor, the managers must consider the potential for parallel bankruptcies. The domino effect can create complex problems for a debtor who is not prepared.

Once a bankruptcy is imminent and it becomes a question of "when," rather than "if," managers must begin to think about possible bankruptcy counsel, financial advisors, and special counsel to the directors. The Bankruptcy Code has strict guidelines concerning conflicts of interest, and managers may find that they need separate counsel for shareholders, directors, the debtor, and affiliates or subsidiaries of the debtor. One attorney can no longer represent all of the related parties, regardless of the friendly relationship between these parties. Significant amounts of cash will have to be available to employ the attorneys, because each will require a substantial retainer.[71]

In addition, the debtor will need to build up cash reserves to sustain operations postpetition. If cash is subject to a lien, the debtor must be prepared for a fight over the use of that cash. And, even where the debtor is ultimately successful in the fight, the fight itself may prevent use of the cash until the court resolves the dispute.

WORKOUT OR BANKRUPTCY—THE DECISION MAKING

Generally, most experts agree that a debtor should consider other options before filing for relief in bankruptcy and should not turn to bankruptcy until the 11th hour.[72] However, every case must turn on its own set of circumstances. If a creditor has a foreclosure date set to enforce a lien on all of the debtor's property, the debtor may have no choice but to seek bankruptcy relief. On the other hand, if a real estate investor debtor has three properties and the creditor intends to foreclose on the one property pulling the others down, the debtor may choose to let it go, rather than drag the others into Chapter 11. Directors of corporations and general partners of limited partnerships may also face a dilemma where the Bankruptcy Code offers needed protection against creditors, but may precipitate claims against management by shareholders or limited partners.

A distressed debtor must consider all of the variables and evaluate the benefits and risks of a workout and a bankruptcy reorganization. But above all, the debtor must evaluate the source of the problems and determine what it hopes to accomplish through reorganization. Absent such a considered approach and coherent strategy neither a bankruptcy nor out-of-court workout is likely to succeed.

ENDNOTES

1. **See,** for example, "The 'Vulture Capitalists' Are Circling," *Business Week,* Sept. 5, 1988, p. 84.
2. *Id*.
3. Such companies as Eastern Airlines, Texaco, Johns-Manville, Federated Department Stores, REVCO, Guehauf, Dart Drugs, and Mushroom King have had their financial troubles covered extensively by the press.

4. R. Moir, "Counseling the Corporation in Financial Crisis," *The Colorado Lawyer*, April 1988, p. 631.
5. A debtor in bankruptcy is required to file with the bankruptcy court lists of all of its assets, liabilities, cash flow statements, names of equity security holders, executory contracts, leases, and any other information local rules may require. The information becomes a matter of public record.
6. If the debtor is a corporation, an "insider" includes: directors, officers, or persons in control of the debtor; partnership in which the debtor is a general partner; general partner of the debtor; and a relative of the general partner, director, officer, or person in control of the debtor. 11 U.S.C. § 101(28)(B). If the debtor is a partnership, an "insider" includes: a general partner in the debtor; a relative of a general partner in, general partner of, or person in control of the debtor; a partnership in which the debtor is a general partner; and a general partner of the debtor, or person in control of the debtor. 11 U.S.C. § 101(28)(C).
7. 11 U.S.C. § 547(b)(4)(B).
8. 11 U.S.C. § 510(c). For a discussion of the avoidance powers, **see** the text accompanying endnotes 30–40.
9. A debtor may file for bankruptcy relief under state insolvency/bankruptcy laws or under federal bankruptcy law. This chapter shall address only *federal* bankruptcy law under the United States Bankruptcy Code, 11 U.S.C. § 101 *et seq*. (1989), hereinafter referred to as the "Bankruptcy Code."
10. 11 U.S.C. § 301. A bankruptcy may be either voluntary or involuntary. 11 U.S.C. §§ 301, 303. When a debtor initiates the proceedings (i.e., files the petition), the case is a voluntary bankruptcy. 11 U.S.C. § 301.
11. 11 U.S.C. § 109. The Bankruptcy Code lists certain types of entities that may not file for relief under Chapter 7 (e.g., banks, insurance companies, railroads) and certain types of entities that may not file for relief under Chapter 11 (e.g., banks, insurance companies, stockbroker, commodity). 11 U.S.C. § 109(b).
12. 11 U.S.C. § 521.
13. 11 U.S.C. §§ 1102(a)(1), 1102 (b)(1).
14. 11 U.S.C. § 1102(a)(2). For a general discussion of committees in a Chapter 11 proceeding, **see** Trost, "Business Reorganizations under Chapter 11 of the New Bankruptcy Code," *The Business Lawyer* XXXIV (April 1979), 1309, 1314–15.
15. 11 U.S.C. § 1103(c).
16. 11 U.S.C. § 1103(a).
17. 11 U.S.C. §§ 706, 1112.

18. 11 U.S.C. § 362.
19. 11 U.S.C. § 362(a). **See** 11 U.S.C. § 362(b) for a list of actions not stayed by the bankruptcy filing.
20. 11 U.S.C. § 362.
21. 11 U.S.C. § 362(d).
22. 11 U.S.C. § 1104(a). The Bankruptcy Code defines "cause" to include fraud, dishonesty, incompetence, or gross mismanagement of the debtor's affairs by current management before or after the commencement of the case.
23. Uniform Commercial Code § 9-503.
24. 11 U.S.C. § 363(c)(2).
25. 11 U.S.C. § 364(a).
26. *Id.* This rule has some exceptions. For example, where a Chapter 11 case is converted to a Chapter 7 liquidation, the expenses incurred in the Chapter 7 case will take priority over the Chapter 11 case expenses. **See** 11 U.S.C. § 726(b).
27. 11 U.S.C. § 364(c)(1).
28. 11 U.S.C. § 364(c)(2).
29. 11 U.S.C. §§ 364(c)(2), 364(d).
30. 11 U.S.C. § 547.
31. 11 U.S.C. § 101(48).
32. Fraudulent conveyance laws are generally regarded as a creditor's remedy but may be employed by a debtor where, in a bankruptcy, the debtor is afforded all of the avoiding powers of a trustee for creditors.
33. The Bankruptcy Code permits a debtor to avoid any transfer that is avoidable under relevant state law. 11 U.S.C. § 544(b). Thus, the debtor may apply the state fraudulent conveyance statutes if they are more advantageous than those provided in the Bankruptcy Code.
34. 11 U.S.C. § 548.
35. UFCA §§ 1 *et seq.*, 7A U.L.A. 430 (1985). The UFCA was approved by the National Conference of Commissioners on Uniform State Laws and the American Bar Association in 1918. As of March 1, 1989, the UFCA was effective in Arizona, Delaware, Maryland, Massachusetts, Michigan, Montana, Nebraska, New Mexico, New York, Ohio, Pennsylvania, Tennessee, the Virgin Islands, and Wyoming. **See** 7A U.L.A. 100 (Supp. 1989).
36. UFTA §§ 1 *et seq.*, 7A U.L.A. 643 (1985). The UFTA was approved by the National Conference of Commissioners on Uniform State Laws in 1984, and has replaced the UFCA in a significant number of states. As of March 1, 1989, the UFTA was effective in Arkansas, California, Florida, Hawaii, Idaho, Maine, Minnesota, Nevada, New Hampshire, New Jersey, North Dakota, Oklahoma, Oregon, Rhode Island, South

Dakota, Texas, Utah, Washington, West Virginia, and Wisconsin. **See** 7A U.L.A. 120 (Supp. 1989).
37. UFCA *supra* n. 35 § 7; UFTA *supra* n. 36 § 4(a)(1); 11 U.S.C. § 548(a)(1). The UFCA uses the term *fair consideration* rather than *reasonably equivalent value*. UFCA *supra* n. 35, §§ 4, 5, 6. **See** UFCA *supra* n. 35, § 3 for the definition of fair consideration.
38. **See** R. Cieri, "An Introduction to Legal and Practical Considerations in the Restructuring of Troubled Leveraged Buyouts," *The Business Lawyer* XXXXV, 333, 352–68, for a discussion of fraudulent conveyance laws applied to LBOs.
39. **See** 11 U.S.C. § 510(c).
40. **See** *Pepper* v. *Litton*, 308 U.S. 295 (1939); *Benjamin* v. *Diamond*, 563 F.2d 692 (5th Cir. 1977).
41. 11 U.S.C. § 506(b).
42. *Id.*; *United States Savings Association of Texas* v. *Timbers of Inwood Forest Associates, Ltd.*, 484 U.S. 365, 108 S. Ct. 626 (1988).
43. 11 U.S.C. § 1121.
44. The exclusivity period may be increased or reduced for "cause." 11 U.S.C. § 1121(d).
45. **See** 11 U.S.C. § 1123.
46. 11 U.S.C. § 1146(c).
47. 11 U.S.C. § 1145(a).
48. 11 U.S.C. § 1129(a). Generally, a class of claims is impaired unless the plan leaves unaltered the legal, equitable, and contractual rights of the claimants in the class. 11 U.S.C. § 1124.
49. 11 U.S.C. § 1126.
50. 11 U.S.C. § 1129(b)(2)(A).
51. 11 U.S.C. § 1129(b)(2)(B). The one significant exception to the absolute priority rule is that a junior class may retain an interest in the debtor notwithstanding the objection of an impaired senior class if the junior class makes a substantial and tangible new contribution to the debtor to assist in the funding of the plan. **See** *Norwest Bank Worthington* v. *Ahlers*, 108 S. Ct. 963 (1988). This exception allows equity security holders to retain their interest in the debtor where classes senior in priority are impaired, provided that the equity security holders make a contribution to the plan.
52. 11 U.S.C. § 1103.
53. 11 U.S.C. §§ 1107(a), 1108.
54. 11 U.S.C. §§ 1107(a), 1106, 704.
55. 11 U.S.C. §§ 1103(c)(5), 1109(b).
56. **See** *Pepper* v. *Litton*, *supra* n. 40 (held dealings of insiders are subject to rigorous scrutiny and, where any of their contracts or engagements

with the debtor are challenged, the burden is on the insider to prove good faith and inherent fairness).
57. For a discussion of equitable subordination of claims, **see** A. Herzog & J. Zweibel, "The Equitable Subordination of Claims in Bankruptcy," 15 Vand. L. Rev. 83, 101-2 (1961).
58. **See** *supra* n. 56.
59. 11 U.S.C. § 363(c)(1).
60. 11 U.S.C. §§ 363(c), 363(e).
61. 11 U.S.C. § 363.
62. 11 U.S.C. § 364.
63. 11 U.S.C. §§ 105, 1107(a). **See** *In re Hooper, Goode Realty*, 60 Bankr. 328, 331 (Bankr. S.D. Cal. 1986) (held court has power to review salaries paid to debtor's officers under Sections 105 and 1107(a) of the Bankruptcy Code).
64. 11 U.S.C. §§ 327, 328.
65. **See** *In re Lionel Corp.*, 722 F.2d 1063, 1070 (2d Cir. 1983) (good business reason must exist before a sale of a substantial part of the estate is permitted outside plan); *In re White Moter Credit Corp.*, 14 Bankr. 584 (Bankr. N.D. Ohio 1981) (same).
66. 11 U.S.C. §§ 1106(a)(1), 704(8). Typically, courts require proof of insurance, proof of new bank account, biweekly or monthly operating reports with cash flow statements, tax statements, profits and loss statements, and account receivable levels.
67. **See** *supra* n. 22.
68. **See** *supra* n. 1.
69. *Id.*
70. Moir, *supra* n. 4, 631-2.
71. *Id.* at 632.
72. **See**, for example, *Id.*

CHAPTER 4

FINANCING ALTERNATIVES FOR THE TROUBLED COMPANY—AN OVERVIEW OF AVAILABLE OPTIONS AND THEIR BENEFITS, PERILS, AND PITFALLS

*Harvey R. Miller**
Partner
Weil, Gotshal & Manges

INTRODUCTION

The 1980s was a decade accented by increased sources and availability of financing, which led to increased activity in mergers, acquisitions, leveraged and management buyouts, and friendly and hostile takeovers. Billions of dollars of debt was issued to finance these transactions, and, as an incident to many of such transactions, billions of dollars of equities were retired. The wisdom of many of

---

* The author gratefully acknowledges the assistance and huge contribution of his associates, Stephen D. Lerner, Jay A. Dorsch, and Johnson C. Ng.

such transactions will now have to withstand the scrutiny of the 1990s about whether the transactions were too highly leveraged, overpriced, or ill-conceived. Indeed, the 1990s may be known as the "Age of Deleveraging."

Those transactions of the 1980s that fail the test of time will require financial and operational restructuring to avoid the occurrence of default and, possibly, the commencement of reorganization or liquidation cases under the Bankruptcy Code[1] or other applicable laws.

Financial and operational restructurings are euphemisms used to connote the process of a "workout" or "turnaround." In legal parlance, it usually involves the recapitalization and rehabilitation of a troubled business outside the context of a formal court-supervised reorganization or liquidation. While no specific rules exist, most workouts and turnarounds invariably involve exhaustive and fragile negotiations among the representatives of the troubled business and its lenders and creditors (secured and unsecured), and, sometimes, other "interested" parties. The success of the negotiations requires (1) mutual recognition and acknowledgment of the priorities among competing creditors, lienholders, and holders of claims and interests in the business entity and (2) efficient and calculated use, and often redeployment and disposition, of the assets of the troubled business entity—all against the backdrop of what might occur or be achieved if formal proceedings were commenced under the Bankruptcy Code or other applicable laws.

This chapter reviews various financing alternatives for the troubled business entity. It is by no means an exhaustive analysis of the means or alternatives available. The types of transactions discussed in this chapter represent some of the techniques most frequently considered and used by troubled business entities in the effort to restructure and rehabilitate themselves.

Six different alternatives dealing with financial distress are discussed: (1) asset sales, (2) secured financing, (3) employee stock option plans (ESOPs), (4) exchange offers in conjunction with the use of high-yield bonds, (5) capital infusion by new or existing equity interest holders, and (6) contraction of ordinary expenses and capital expenditures.

ASSET SALES

General Considerations

The sale of assets of the troubled business may appear to be the easiest and most productive means of raising necessary cash. However, the business must be careful to avoid the disposition of critical assets with attendant violence to its ability to continue to operate the business. The selective divestiture of assets should serve the dual purpose of raising necessary funds and stemming unnecessary losses and expenses relating to the business operations. Targeted assets may include, among others, subsidiaries and affiliates acquired through mergers or leveraged buyouts that are redundant and not in line with the entity's core business, or such assets that may have more value to a prospective purchaser than to the troubled business entity.

To maximize the return from the sale of assets, business alternatives must be evaluated and implemented. These alternatives may include: (1) sale of the whole or part of a division on a going-concern basis; (2) liquidation of some or all parts of a division or subsidiary; (3) sale of certain assets of the business as the foundation for a future merger or joint venture; and (4) reorganization and redeployment of the existing assets in the perspective of the establishment of a feasible business operation, after taking into account current market values and market liquidity.

Formal appraisals of assets to be sold should be obtained before conducting a sale. Generally, three types of valuation are necessary: (1) going-concern value, (2) orderly liquidation value, and (3) forced sale value. The valuations are used as predicates for the development of the strategy to be pursued.

Inherent in the process are the preparation of offering memoranda; locating, contacting, and screening potential purchasers; determining how the sale or sales should be packaged to maximize recoveries (e.g., sale in bulk or by lots), depending upon the nature of the assets. As a part of the process, the entity must give consideration to the advisability of engaging investment bankers, financial advisors, and other specialists. Critical to such consideration is a determination of what value is added by the use of such professionals, as well as the legal standards applicable to the proposed asset disposition program.

Treatment of Existing Encumbrances

In most, if not all, financially troubled businesses, existing assets are subject to layers of liens and encumbrances in favor of creditors and, often, subject to contractual restrictions and requirements. As a sale of assets may trigger a default and, possibly, acceleration of debt, it is imperative that such encumbrances and convenants be properly dealt with prior to any action that might jeopardize the ability of the business to continue operations. In that context, however, a business may be able to achieve its objective of raising cash through asset sales without having to use the proceeds to satisfy outstanding debt.

The troubled business's leverage may lie within the rights and protections afforded to debtors under the Bankruptcy Code. Generally, the informal restructuring and workout phase is undertaken in the perspective of what might occur and what would be available if formal bankruptcy proceedings were commenced. Thus, the provisions of the Bankruptcy Code form the backdrop to the negotiations for an informal rehabilitation and restructuring. The respective constituencies engage in an analysis of their relative strengths and weaknesses in a hypothetical case under the Bankruptcy Code and, in particular, under Chapter 11 of that code. As a consequence, creditors must take into account the protective provisions incorporated into the Bankruptcy Code for the benefit of the debtor and its estate, including, without limitation, the automatic stay against creditors' actions as set forth in Section 362 of the Bankruptcy Code and the ability of a Chapter 11 debtor in possession to use cash collateral with permission of the bankruptcy court.[2]

The troubled business must also take into account the creditor protective provisions contained in the Bankruptcy Code and the restrictions that would be put upon its operations by reason of those provisions.[3] Thus, for example, the troubled business must consider that sales outside the ordinary course of business require approval of the bankruptcy court. In this context, the financially troubled business must consider the advantages and disadvantages of commencing a formal bankruptcy case. If it is important for the business to have the opportunity to sell property free and clear of liens and encumbrances, then a formal bankruptcy case becomes more attractive because of the provisions of Section 363 of the Bankruptcy Code.

Given the "threat" posed by the potential bankruptcy scenario, the leverage and protection afforded the troubled business as a debtor and the corresponding possible delay and detriment to secured creditors, there may be sufficient inducement for secured creditors to consensually agree with the troubled business to permit assets to be sold in a way that will enable the rehabilitation and turnaround of the business. Conversely, if the secured creditors are insistent upon attaching and receiving the proceeds of sales of collateral security, the troubled business may be compelled to seek relief under the Bankruptcy Code to achieve its objectives.

Fraudulent Transfers and Conveyances

Invariably, creditors—both secured and unsecured—will seek additional (or initial) collateral security protection from a troubled entity engaged in a workout. However, if the workout fails or a formal bankruptcy case is commenced, the assets transferred[4] to such creditors, whether for cash or for debt forgiveness, may be subject to a fraudulent transfer or conveyance attack.

Fraudulent transfers and conveyances may be voidable under both state debtor and creditor laws and the Bankruptcy Code. Generally, three statutory scheme are applicable:

1. The Uniform Fraudulent Conveyance Act (UFCA).[5]
2. The Uniform Fraudulent Transfer Act (UFTA).[6]
3. The Bankruptcy Code.[7]

Although there are minor differences in the language used in the several statutes, generally, two types of transactions may be challenged: (1) transfers made with the *actual intent* to hinder, delay, or defraud creditors of the transferor;[8] and (2) *constructively fraudulent* transfers, in which the transferor did not receive "fair consideration"[9] or "reasonably equivalent value,"[10] *and* the transferor was either insolvent or became insolvent as a result of the transfer,[11] *or* the transferor retained "unreasonably small capital to continue to operate its business,"[12] *or* the transferor intended to incur or believed it would incur debts beyond its ability to pay as such debts mature.[13]

Fraudulent conveyances challenged under the actual intent standard are measured against the "badges of fraud" derived from the English Statute of Elizabeth cases[14] as indicia of actual intent.[15] In transfers in which constructive fraud is alleged, two tests must be satisfied: (1) adequacy of consideration and (2a) insolvency, or (2b) small capital, or (2c) inability to pay debts as they mature.[16] Courts applying this standard usually look to the consideration received by the transferor, rather than the value imparted by the transferee or the selling stockholders of the debtor.[17] This analysis is sound, because fraudulent conveyance laws are intended to protect creditors of the debtor. Moreover, courts construing the "small capital" factor usually use a cash flow analysis and allow expert testimony to establish the capitalization requirements of businesses similiar to that of the debtor.[18] Occasionally, some jurisdictions have combined the insolvency and "unreasonably small capital" factors into a single analysis.[19]

In the perspective of the foregoing, to minimize the exposure to fraudulent conveyance attacks both before and as a result of a workout, participants must be aware of the laws relating to fraudulent conveyances and transfers and must maintain all necessary documentation relating to the transfer, including compilation of due diligence reports, credible appraisals of the property transferred, and appropriate analyses of the transferors existing and future projected financial conditions.

Fiduciary Considerations

In managing the business of a corporation, directors owe fiduciary duties of care and loyalty to the corporation and its stockholders.[20] If the corporation is solvent, directors may be liable for breaching the duty of loyalty—entire fairness or absence of self-dealing—to the stockholders by taking into consideration the interests of other parties.[21] Conversely, if the corporation is or becomes *insolvent,* the fiduciary duties of directors are expanded to extend to the protection of the entire community of interests in the corporation—stockholders and creditors alike.[22] However, the enlargement of the class of beneficiaries to whom directors' fiduciary duties are owed when a company is insolvent does not change the standard of care to be exercised by the directors—informed business judgment.[23]

When the directors propose to sell all or substantially all of the debtor's assets, they must act with the prudence of informed businessmen.[24] Although there is no precise definition of what "substantially all" means, the general consideration is whether the sale effectively puts the entity out of business, or what portion of the operating assets (a qualitative test), rather than gross assets (a quantitative test), will be sold.[25] In many states, a sale of substantially all corporate assets may trigger the requirement of a stockholder vote and sometimes stockholders' appraisal rights. In addition, the sale may be attacked by creditors under the relevant fraudulent transfer or conveyance statutes and other laws applicable to such sales.[26]

Therefore, it is advisable, if not imperative, that the board and management must evaluate the proposed transactions from the perspective of the facts and applicable principles of law, including appraisals of the assets to be sold. Only after due deliberation and the exercise of business judgment in good faith will management and the board protect themselves and the transaction from the successful attacks of creditors and stockholders.

Negative Impact of Asset Sales

A thorough analysis should be taken to determine the costs and benefits of the sale of assets before embarking on such a divestiture. The advantages of cutting expenses related to the operation of the particular asset, in the form of reduced mortgage interest expenses, maintenance costs, and rental payments, may be outweighed by the disadvantage of slowing down overall production, reducing sales, and triggering severance pay provisions embodied in labor contracts or pursuant to applicable laws. Above all, it may affect the financially troubled entity's ability to effectively reorganize if a Chapter 11 case becomes necessary. Care must be taken that the sales program does not result in the disposition of the most productive assets, with the consequence that further reorganization efforts are stymied.

SECURED FINANCING

General Considerations

The financial distress of a business may be the result of many factors, including general economic conditions, political events, national disasters, and the like. In some situations, the financial stress may be identified as temporary and curable, if additional funds can be obtained to finance current operations. Absent an equity/capital infusion, usually the only source of such funds is to collaterally secure repayment of new and existing borrowings by granting liens against and security interests in the assets of the business—asset-based and secured financings. Asset-based lenders place heavy emphasis on the nature and value of the collateral security as the source of repayment. The analysis of the value and liquidity of the collateral security transcends the review of the borrower's general financial condition. Of paramount importance is the ability of the lender to realize on the collateral security if the borrower defaults and, thus, requires consideration of what legal and practical obstacles may delay or prevent resort to the collateral security.

Before deciding whether assets should be encumbered to secure financing, a debtor must evaluate the costs and consequences of granting liens and security interests, including, among others, the cost of such acts, the covenants (affirmative, negative, and restrictive) to be imposed, and the potential reactions of other parties. A natural consequence of the hypothecation of business assets, even for short-term cash relief, is increased surveillance by the lenders of the entity's financial condition and administration. Typically, in situations of closely held corporations, lenders may require principal stockholders to personally guarantee outstanding borrowings.[27] If the assets of the debtor are subject to encumbrances but the current value of such assets exceeds the underlying debts, the debtor may be able to obtain additional financing. In those circumstances, the debtor may have to negotiate with the prior lienholder and the new lender the terms of an intercreditor agreement that will provide for the rights and priorities of the respective parties.

If a debtor has pledged all of its assets in a workout and the workout should thereafter fail, the lack of free assets will severely hamper the ability of the business to fashion a feasible economic plan sufficient to support a plan of reorganization under Chapter 11 of the Bankruptcy Code. Notably, since transactions entered into between the debtor and its lenders may be subject to challenge under the fraudulent conveyance/transfer laws and the preference provisions of the Bankruptcy Code, [28] all parties to a workout must be vigilant in protecting their rights in order to participate effectively.

Types of Collateral Pledged in Secured Financings

1. *Tangible Personal Property:* Equipment (if held or used primarily in the debtor's business); inventory (if held for sale or lease or to be furnished under contracts of service).
2. *Intangible Personal Property:* Accounts (representing rights to payment for goods sold or leased or for services rendered); chattel paper (writing evidencing a monetary obligation and a security interest in or lease of specific goods); documents of title (warehouse receipts, bills of lading, and the like); instruments (drafts, notes, commercial paper, and so on).
3. *Real Property, Fixtures, and Improvements:* Fixtures are items that become so related and attached to real property that an interest in them arises under the real property law.[29]
4. *Proceeds and After-Acquired Property:* Proceeds may include whatever is received upon the sale, exchange, or other disposition of the collateral security. Both proceeds and after-acquired property are typically pledged as additional collateral security for a receivables or inventory-based financing. The Uniform Commercial Code generally recognizes the validity of after-acquired property clauses in security agreements, but the Bankruptcy Code severely limits their application.

Any of the items described above may be used as collateral security for an asset-based financing.

Accounts Receivable Financing Methods

Although cash is "king" and the most liquid asset, accounts receivable also are highly liquid assets and may be readily pledged or assigned as collateral security for a financing. There are at least three methods by which receivables can be used as a source to procure financing: (1) conventional accounts receivable financing, (2) bank financing, and (3) "off balance sheet" financing.

1. *Conventional Accounts Receivable Financing:* Conventional receivables financing involves three parties: borrower, lender, and account debtor (i.e., the borrower's customer). The structure of such financing typically involves a revolving loan, in which the lender advances funds to the borrower based upon a formulated percentage of "eligible receivables" outstanding at any one particular time (usually in the range of 85 percent of such receivables, depending upon the industry).[30] Receivables are eligible for hypothecation to the lender only if they meet certain standards, including the nature of the account debtor and the collectibility of the receivables within a prescribed time period. The lender, thus, must pay particular attention to the creditworthiness of the account debtors to determine the financial eligibility of the borrower and the appropriate amount or level of advances. Depending upon the borrower's business, numerous other factors will influence the eligibility of a receivable.[31] Typically, the borrower will be required to advise its account debtors to remit payments in respect of accounts receivable directly into a "lockbox" account maintained by the lender. The borrower will provide the lender with daily reports of its accounts receivable and collections in connection with such receivables. Accordingly, the lender can look to both the borrower and the account debtor for recovery. Lenders also should reserve the right to modify the borrowing base formula to account for changes in the borrower's business and to cease making further advances upon the occurrence of specific events of default.

2. *Bank Financing:* In connection with bank financing, the bank lender obtains a floating lien in the borrower's receivables and proceeds but does not receive daily reports and turnovers of collections. Instead, the lender receives periodically (usually monthly) reports from the borrower, which list the amount of outstanding receivables. The eligibility of receivables and adherence to formula advances are often somewhat more casual here than in the conventional method of accounts receivable financing. This "loose" arrangement, however, can be modified if provided for in the loan and security agreement, and if the lender believes it needs tighter controls.

3. *"Off Balance Sheet" Financing:* This type of financing involves the "sale" of receivables, rather than the use of such receivables as a base for a secured loan. The sale can be without recourse to the borrower. The borrower's customers need not be notified, and the borrower usually collects and services the accounts. Accounting is ordinarily done on a monthly basis, in which the moneys due from the buyer/lender are netted against the outstanding collections due from the seller/borrower (sometimes referred to as *batch processing*). The buyer pays either the full or discounted prices for the receivables, depending on their creditworthiness.

The characterization of the transaction is derived from the fact that the seller has no fixed obligations to the buyer as a borrower would to a lender.

A Business Entity with an Existing Receivables Facility and a Need for Additional Working Capital

If a pro forma liquidation analysis of a financially troubled debtor demonstrates that a receivables-based lender will recover less than it would on a "going-concern" basis, the troubled debtor may possess the leverage to seek additional working capital from the lender. Moreover, the possibility that the debtor may seek protection under Chapter 11 of the Bankruptcy Code and obtain authority to use cash collateral[32] to meet its urgent financial needs is often a sufficiently meaningful pressure point to persuade the accounts receivable lender to extend further credit in the effort to avoid resort to protection under the Bankruptcy Code.

In some cases, the accounts receivable lender may be persuaded to modify the "borrowing base" advance formula by allowing an "overadvance" (i.e., lending money in excess of the eligible receivables base). However, the debtor may have to preserve the lender's right to "pull the plug" if changes in financial condition adversely impact the lender's position. Of course, if the lender feels uncomfortable in making additional cash advances, it may demand that the entity pledge other assets, in addition to receivables, to secure the overadvance, assuming such assets are available. If such assets exist and are encumbered, it may be necessary, because of contractual restrictions against subordinate liens or security interests, to enter into an intercreditor agreement allowing for such subordinate liens and security interests.

Quite often, the lender may require that such additional collateral security also cross-collateralize both the existing indebtedness and the new advances. Cross-collateralization may present problems for existing lienholders. The impasse may be resolved, however, if, for example, the accounts receivable lender agrees to release its lien or security interest in respect of the new collateral security once the entity gets "back into formula."

Voidable Preferences and Lender Liability Considerations

Every lender that obtains additional collateral security for preexisting indebtedness in a workout situation must be aware that the transfer of such property may be subject to a preference attack in a subsequent bankruptcy case pursuant to Section 547 of the Bankruptcy Code. Section 547(b) sets forth five elements that a bankruptcy trustee (or a debtor in possession) must establish to avoid any transfer of property of the debtor: (1) the transfer was to or for the benefit of a creditor; (2) the transfer was made for or on account of an antecedent debt; (3) the debtor was insolvent[33] at the time of the transfer; (4) the transfer was made within 90 days immediately before the commencement of the bankruptcy case, or within one year if the transfer was made to an insider;[34] and (5) the transfer has the effect of increasing the amount the creditor would have received under a Chapter 7 liquidation case. In respect to certain prepetition transfers, however, Section 547(c) sets forth various exceptions to voidability: contemporaneous exchanges for new value, transfers made in the ordinary course of the debtor's business, perfected purchase money security interests, and subsequent advances in running accounts.[35]

An accounts receivable lender is protected from a preference attack under Section 547(c)(5), unless it improves its position during the 90 days prior to the commencement of the bankruptcy case. Improvement can be measured by comparing its position (collateral to loan value) 90 days before the date of the commencement of the bankruptcy case and on the date of the commencement of such case. The extent of such an improvement is subject to the trustee's powers of avoidance.

A secured lender who advances money to a troubled entity in exchange for new collateral security obtained during a workout should maintain full and accurate documentation evidencing that the debtor received reasonably equivalent new value[36] for the exchange. Failure to do so may open the doors to a litany of fraudulent conveyance and voidable preference attacks by the trustee or, indeed, by creditors. Conversely, a troubled entity's threat of impending bankruptcy and concomitant preference problems for lenders who insist on obtaining additional collateral security may permit the entity the opportunity to resolve its difficulties.[37]

Finally, secured lenders must consider the extent to which new demands upon the entity may place them in a position of "controlling" the entity. Control may occur if the lender acquires voting stock in the entity or if additional affirmative and negative covenants are required from the entity in a workout that effectively placed control in the lenders, and that control is exercised. A "control" person is not only subject to a potential preference liability for an extended one-year insider period but, in more serious situations, the exercise of actual control and domination over the debtor with damage to other parties may lead to the equitable subordination of the lender's claim to claims of other creditors or, indeed, disallowance.

EMPLOYEE STOCK OWNERSHIP PLANS

An employee stock ownership plan (ESOP) is a tax-qualified employee benefit retirement plan whose assets are required to be primarily invested in stock or securities, or both, of the sponsoring employer. In recent years, ESOPs have become more popular as a vehicle of corporate finance and may enhance the financing of the financially troubled company in conjunction with a restructuring of the compensation and benefit package of its employees.

Leveraged ESOPs have been established primarily as a vehicle to permit the buyout of major stockholders of closely held corporations, to prefund 401(k) plans of public corporations, and to facilitate management buyouts that incorporate a leveraged ESOP as part of a total financing package. As discussed below, the decision to establish a leveraged ESOP and implement it requires careful scrutiny to determine whether the benefits of an ESOP outweigh its cost as an employee benefit plan and its compliance with the technical requirements for ESOPs.[38]

Structure of Leveraged ESOPs

General Description

An ESOP is a type of defined contribution retirement plan that is qualified under Section 401(a) of the Internal Revenue Code of 1986, as amended (the Code), and is specially designed to invest in employer securities.[39] ESOPs can be nonleveraged, in which case an employer contributes employer securities (or cash and the plan purchases employer securities) to be held under the plan. Alternatively, an ESOP may permit borrowing for the purpose of allowing the ESOP to buy employer securities. The latter type of ESOP is known generally as a *leveraged ESOP*.[40] The use of a leveraged ESOP enables an employer to initially repay a loan with tax deductible dollars, thereby reducing the overall cost of the borrower's financing.

In a typical leveraged ESOP structure, the ESOP either borrows funds directly from a lending institution or from the employer itself, which has borrowed the funds from a lending institution and then extended the loan to the ESOP on substantially similar repayment terms to its own loan (hereinafter referred to as a *back-to-back loan*). The ESOP then utilizes the borrowed funds to purchase common or convertible preferred stock from the employer or from existing stockholders. The employer guarantees the loan by the lender to the ESOP or obligates itself on the back-to-back loan and, if necessary, grants a security interest in collateral to the lender.[41] The lender may also be granted a security interest in the stock held by the ESOP. In addition, the employer generally obligates itself to make fixed contributions over a period of time to the ESOP in sufficient amounts so the ESOP is in a position to amortize its loan.

An ESOP loan must be without recourse against the ESOP, and the only assets of the ESOP that may serve as collateral for the loan are qualifying employer securities acquired with the proceeds of the loan (or that were used as collateral on a prior ESOP loan repaid with funds from the current loan). The lender also has limited rights against the ESOP assets to satisfy the loan obligation, and it can only levy against the loan collateral those contributions designated for loan payments and earnings on the collateral. If the ESOP defaults on the loan, the value of the plan assets used to satisfy the loan cannot exceed the amount of the default. Thus, a lender will not be allowed to retain any amounts transferred in satisfaction of the loan that exceed the amount due under the loan; any excess must be returned to the ESOP. In addition, if the ESOP loan is from a disqualified person[42] (such as in a back-to-back loan), the ESOP loan can only be declared in default if there is a failure to meet the payment schedule (which eliminates cross-default provisions).

An ESOP must pass through to participants the voting rights on publicly held securities allocated to the accounts of participants. Participants in plans of employers whose voting stock is not publicly held must have the right to direct the stock allocated to their account on certain major corporate matters, such as a merger, recapitalization, or liquidation.[43]

Limitations on Acquisition of Stock by ESOP— Contributions to ESOP and Allocation of Stock

The amount of stock that can be purchased by an ESOP (which determines the amount the employer can borrow) is limited by restrictions on annual contributions and allocations to participants. The maximum amount that can be purchased is a function of the maximum annual contributions permitted and the term of the ESOP loan.

At the time of the initial purchase of stock by an ESOP with borrowed funds, all of the stock held by the ESOP is unallocated, and, as described above, generally is used to collateralize the ESOP loan, which must be nonrecourse with respect to any other assets of the ESOP. Stock held by the ESOP is allocated to the accounts of participants under the ESOP as the loan is amortized. This allocation normally is based on the compensation of participants in the plan. Generally, under Section 415 of the Code, annual allocations for ESOPs are limited to the lesser of 25 percent of each participant's compensation or $30,000.[44] For years commencing on or after January 1, 1990, not more than $209,200[45] of compensation of each participant can be considered in making allocations. The limitation on allocations to participants, which is based on the covered payroll of the ESOP, in effect limits the rate of amortization of an ESOP loan. Thus, the more labor intensive an employer is, the more its ESOP can borrow. The amount of allocation is based upon the original cost of the stock purchased by the ESOP and not upon market value at the time of allocation. If stock is used as collateral for an ESOP loan, the loan must provide for the release each year of stock so that stock may be allocated to participants. Generally, stock is allocated to participant accounts over the term of the loan as it is repaid.

Because of the limitation on allocations under Section 415 of the Internal Revenue Code, annual contributions to an ESOP to satisfy loan amortization for a year are limited to 25 percent of covered payroll of the ESOP plus interest payments.

Distribution Requirements

A participant's account balance under an ESOP must be distributed within one year after a participant's retirement, disability, or death, or, in the event a participant terminates employment at an earlier point in time, five years after the participant's termination of employment. However, if a portion of a participant's account is attributable to stock purchased with an ESOP loan that has not yet been repaid, such amounts can be deferred until the total loan has been repaid. In addition, with respect to stock acquired after December 31, 1986, participants over age 55 with 10 years of participation in an ESOP will be permitted to direct the trustee, during the six-plan-year period which begins with the date the age and service requirement is satisfied, to invest up to 25 percent of their account balance in three investment alternatives that must be provided by the plan sponsor. The diversification right is increased to 50 percent of a participant's account balance in the final year of the election period.

Participants entitled to their benefits under an ESOP must be allowed to demand that their benefits be distributed in the form of employer stock.[46] If the stock is not publicly held, the participants must have the right to require that the employer repurchase the stock under a fair valuation formula (the "put option").[47] The payment terms, which must provide for interest payments on the unpaid portion, must be reasonable, and they usually would feature periodic payments starting 30 days after the put is exercised for a term not extending over five years.

The put obligation can place a severe cash drain on the financially troubled employer who must fund the obligation. In analyzing an ESOP transaction for a financially troubled company, an emerging liability study must be prepared relating to the employer obligation on puts from ESOP participants and from the diversification requirements to determine if the company has sufficient cash flow to satisfy its obligations under the loan. The older the employees are, the more important the study is, because cash to fund the put option and the diversification rights will be required much sooner than if the work force was comprised of younger employees. The put obligation of the employer and the diversification requirement could be funded in whole or in part from supplemental deductible cash contributions to the ESOP designed to build a cash reserve to satisfy the put obligation. Building such a cash reserve necessarily would reduce the contributions to the ESOP that are utilized to amortize the ESOP loan.

The put obligation should be considered as any other obligation of a company in determining the feasibility of an ESOP transaction. The value of a leveraged ESOP is in part determined by measuring the present value of the put obligation against the present value of the tax deductions to the employer from contributions to the ESOP to amortize the ESOP loan.[48] While a leveraged ESOP creates a tax deferral to enable an employer loan to be repaid with tax deductible dollars, the value of that deferral is limited by the put obligation, the extent to which the financially troubled employer can utilize the tax deductions, and the dilution of the equity interests of current shareholders.[49]

Tax Incentives for Leveraged ESOPS

Tax Deductible Repayment of Principal
Subject to certain limitations, annual contributions to an ESOP are tax deductible. In the case of a leveraged ESOP, these tax deductible contributions are used to amortize the principal on the ESOP's loan, which results in the loan being repaid with tax deductible dollars, thereby reducing the overall cost of the loan.

Exclusion of 50 Percent of Interest Income
If certain organizations lend money to an ESOP, either directly or through a back-to-back loan to enable the ESOP to buy employer

stock, 50 percent of the interest paid on the loan is excluded from the income of the lending organization, provided the ESOP owns more than 50 percent of (1) each class of outstanding stock of the corporation issuing the securities or (2) the value of all of the corporation stock ("50 percent requirement"). The 50 percent requirement was recently enacted and, for the most part, will probably limit this tax benefit to ESOP loans for closely held companies where employees are purchasing the entire company.

A lender will receive the interest exclusion with respect to a loan to an employer if, within 30 days after such loan, the employer contributes to an ESOP employer securities equal in value to the loan proceeds and the loan term is not more than seven years. This provision permits a nonleveraged ESOP to be used, with the lender receiving the interest exclusion.

The lender must be a bank, insurance company, corporation actively engaged in the lending business, or a mutual fund. Loans cannot be made between members of the same controlled group or between a plan and the sponsoring employer or a member of the employer's controlled group. The provision is intended to encourage the lender receiving the tax break on the interest income to pass through its tax savings to the ESOP in the form of a lower interest rate on the loan.

Loans to ESOPs to refinance earlier loans that qualified for the interest exclusion will qualify for the interest exclusion, provided the loan term is limited to seven years.

Deferral of Gain on Sale to ESOP

The gain on the sale to an ESOP or worker-owned cooperative of certain qualifying stock of closely held businesses will be deferred if (1) the proceeds are reinvested in certain securities of U.S. corporations actively engaged in business and (2) the ESOP must own at least 30 percent of each class of the stock outstanding or 30 percent of the total value of stock outstanding immediately after the sale.[50] The deferral is an elective provision for individuals, partnerships, and S corporations and, if utilized by the seller, would essentially allow him or her to roll over the gain on the securities sold to the ESOP and defer it until he or she ultimately sells the securities in which he or she reinvests. The taxpayer's basis in the new securities is reduced by the amount of gain deferred on the stock sale to the ESOP.

If the ESOP sells the stock within three years of its acquisition and either the number of shares held by the ESOP decreases to less than the number held by the ESOP at the time of the deferral sale, or the value of shares held by the ESOP has declined to less than 30 percent of the value of all similar stock outstanding, the employer is generally subject to a 10 percent penalty tax on the amount realized by the ESOP on the disposition.[51]

Deduction of Dividends

A corporation (which could be the sponsoring employer or a corporation within its controlled group) paying dividends on employer stock held by an ESOP can take a deduction for dividends paid on such stock. Normally, a corporation receives no tax deduction for dividends paid on its own stock. To obtain the deduction, dividends must be paid in cash to plan participants, or paid to the plan and paid out to participants within 90 days after the end of the plan year, or utilized to amortize an ESOP loan.[52] Such dividends are not considered an "annual addition" for the Section 415 limits on allocations and, thus, can be used to increase the amount that the ESOP can borrow.

Because of the deductibility of dividends, the use of convertible preferred stock is frequently considered in structuring an ESOP. Convertible preferred stock becomes particularly attractive when used as part of a 401(k) plan combined with an ESOP. In such case, the convertible preferred stock purchased by the ESOP is used to match (when released from the suspense account) employee tax deferred contributions.

Net Operating Loss

Prior to July 13, 1989, the limitations on the use of a company's net operating loss carryforwards and certain tax credits following a change of more than 50 percent of its ownership did not apply where the change in ownership resulted in an ESOP owning 50 percent or more of a company.[53] The Omnibus Budget Reconciliation Act of 1989, however, has repealed this special ESOP benefit for acquisitions of employer securities after July 12, 1989, unless the acquisition was made pursuant to a written binding contract in effect on July 12, 1989.

Fiduciary Considerations

Fiduciary Responsibility Rules
The rules governing the conduct of plan fiduciaries are generally set forth in Section 404 of ERISA, which requires a fiduciary to discharge its duties with respect to a plan "solely in the interest" of, and for the "exclusive purpose" of, providing benefits to plan participants and their beneficiaries. Section 404 of ERISA also requires that a fiduciary discharge its duties with respect to a plan with the care, skill, prudence, and diligence under the circumstances then prevailing that a prudent man acting in a like capacity and familiar with such matters would use in the conduct of an enterprise of a like character and with like aims (the "prudent-expert" rule).

Application of Fiduciary Rules to the Purchase of Stock by ESOP
ERISA defines the term *fiduciary* to include any administrator, officer, or trustee of an employee benefit plan. The *named fiduciary* of a plan is the fiduciary designated in the plan that can direct the trustee to make investments for the plan or appoint investment managers to make such decisions, in the absence of such decisions being made by the trustee, if provided by the trust agreement. The ESOP should have an independent trustee, independent financial advisers, and independent counsel.[54]

The trustee (as named fiduciary), based in part upon an independent fairness opinion, must determine whether the proposed transaction is prudent and in the best interests of the participants of the ESOP and whether the purchase price represents more than "adequate consideration."[55] Particular attention must be given by the ESOP fiduciaries to "cheap" stock set aside for management and others in a leveraged buyout to determine whether the allocation is fair from the perspective of the ESOP. In making such determination, the trustee would be required to act "solely in the interest" of the plan participants and beneficiaries and in accordance with ERISA's prudent expert rule.[56] The bank trustee may ask to be indemnified by the employer for any liability it may incur as a result of the proposed transaction.[57]

In summary, the fiduciaries of an ESOP must act "prudently" and "solely in the interest" of the ESOP participants and beneficiaries when deciding whether to invest the assets of the ESOP in employer stock. If the acquisition or the continued holding of stock by an ESOP is *not* prudent and solely in the interest of the ESOP participants and beneficiaries, the ESOP fiduciaries could be held personally liable for any loss resulting from breach of their fiduciary responsibilities, notwithstanding that the acquisition of the stock was exempt from the prohibited transaction restrictions of Section 406 of ERISA by virtue of the statutory exemption described above.[58] In this context, if management has failed to take all actions necessary to insure an unbiased decision-making process, the DOL may require a restructuring of the transaction in favor of the ESOP.[59] In addition, a nonfiduciary (which could be a lender) that participates in a transaction with knowledge that the transaction constitutes a fiduciary breach could be required to return any unjust enrichment or make the plan whole.[60]

Restructuring Employee Benefits

Freezing current employee wages and benefits in exchange for implementation of an ESOP may be used by management of a financially troubled company to obtain short-term labor concessions. The mechanics of structuring an ESOP in this situation are similar to a leveraged ESOP, with the addition of reductions in current cash outlays for benefits and compensation that are replaced with employer stock. The transaction can be structured so that the savings from the wage and benefit reduction can be used to pay down the principal and interest on the loan.

As an alternative to a leveraged ESOP, companies have negotiated reductions in cash wages and benefits in exchange for stock contributions to an ESOP. Because it is unlikely that the timing between wage reduction and stock allocation will coincide, the restructuring should be carefully planned to meet the particular needs of the employer and its employees.

EXCHANGE OFFERS

Nature of the Transaction

In an exchange offer, existing security holders are requested by the issuer to exchange their outstanding securities for new securities of the debtor. In debt-for-debt exchanges, the proposed new security may be a bond with a lower interest rate, a longer maturity, or modified convenant provisions. In equity-for-debt exchanges, the new security will be either a preferred or common stock. An exchange offer may, of course, involve the swapping of a combination of debt and equity securities for existing outstanding debt securities.

Many exchange offers undertaken or attempted recently relate primarily to the restructuring of acquisition debt (i.e., debt obligations incurred to finance an acquisition or leveraged buyout). In any of such situations, the acquirors of the new business contributed relatively little equity to the corporate capital, and their investment is often minuscule in comparison with the debt obligations created in connection with the acquisitions. Hence, the restructuring of this indebtedness essentially is the conversion of debt into equity, making bondholders into equity interest holders of the restructured entity. When the debt securities are publicly held, participants in an exchange offer that is conducted as part of a turnaround workout must consider the applicability on the Trust Indenture Act of 1939 against the backdrop of the Bankruptcy Code.

The Trust Indenture Act of 1939

The Trust Indenture Act[61] prescribes a relationship among the issuer, its bondholders, and the indenture trustee. The trustee usually has little discretion under the indenture. While the indenture agreement may empower the trustee upon the issuer's default to accelerate the maturity of the bonds, foreclose upon the collateral, if any, or resort to whatever remedies are provided for under the indenture, the trustee is not authorized to make compromises with the debtor without the bondholders' consent, as provided in the applicable indenture. Further, Section 316(b) of the Trust Indenture Act specifically prohibits majority bondholders from making binding modifications of core terms (principal amount, interest rate, and maturity) of the bond issue without the consent of all other bondholders. However, certain restrictive convenants may be modified by specified majorities, as set forth in the indenture.

If the bonds are in the hands of a few institutional investors, restructuring of the outstanding debt is tantamount to renegotiating a private loan—the 100 percent consent requirement for indenture modification may not pose an insurmountable obstacle. Conversely, if the bonds are widely held, it is almost impossible for the debtor to obtain the necessary consent of every bondholder to waive those provisions of the indenture requiring such consent.

Dissenting bondholders that choose not to participate in a workout/turnaround exchange offer are not bound by the terms of the proposed restructuring, and their rights are preserved under the original indenture agreement. These bondholders will benefit from their nontender if the entity succeeds in exchanging the old debt with new equity securities, because they will continue to hold their claims against the debtor and, at that time, such entity may have greater financial viability, creating a better prospect for full recovery on the existing claims. However, if enough current holders reject the exchange offer and hold out, it is possible that the consent level percentage requirement needed to carry out the proposed exchange offer will be defeated. Typically, an exchange offer requires 85 percent to 90 percent of the holders to accept the exchange and tender their securities to consummate the exchange offer.

To overcome the problem of holdouts, the debtor may appeal to all bondholders by conferring some immediate cash benefit upon the tendering bondholders, thus imposing a burden on the nontendering bondholders. Although this strategy is primitive and may become costly, it has some coercive effect on the borderline holdouts.

Another persuasive technique for influencing holdouts to accept the exchange offer may involve the offering of a new security that is senior to or matures earlier than the target issue. The fear of losing a priority position, should the debtor later commence or be subject to bankruptcy, may induce holdouts into tendering their bonds. To obtain a senior security, holders may be requested to forego current interest payments or other features of the existing debt securities. This method may be used, even though the underlying indenture prohibits the issuance of senior debt. Because the Trust Indenture Act does not prohibit majority consent to modify noncore provisions of the indenture agreement, the issuer can obtain the "exit consents" of exchanging bondholders to vote to change a restrictive convenant that prohibits the issuance of senior securities. This will bind the minority holdouts to the modification. If the exchange is successful, which would usually leave less than 15 percent of the target bonds outstanding, the thin residual will further reduce the "tradeability" of the holdout bonds. This result may have the effect of forcing the minority holders into accepting the proposed exchange.

While the above techniques may diminish the holdout effect, they may raise issues of fairness and subject the participants to drawn out litigation. In this context, the Bankruptcy Code may provide a legitimate means of persuading the holdouts to accept the exchange offer without running afoul of the legal rules and regulations. This may be accomplished through the use of the "prepackaged Chapter 11."

Prepackaged Chapter 11 Reorganizations

The Bankruptcy Code provides a unique, and as yet relatively unused, method for accomplishing an exchange offer as part of a Chapter 11 reorganization case. Section 1126(b) of the Bankruptcy Code permits the debtor to conduct a prepetition solicitation of the acceptance of a proposed plan of reorganization.[62] Thus, in an appropriate case (typically a simple capital structure and few "impaired"[63] classes of claims and equity interests), the company seeking to accomplish an exchange offer can propose as an alternative a plan of reorganization that has the same result as the proposed exchange offer (e.g., a debt-for-debt or equity-for-debt swap).

Under this technique, the exchange offer is proposed and the solicitation materials apprise all holders that, if the requisite level of acceptances is not attained, the debtor entity may resort to protection under the Bankruptcy Code. As part of this tactic, a proposed plan of reorganization under Chapter 11 will be part of the solicitation materials, and holders of the debt securities will be apprised that acceptance of the exchange offer will also constitute an acceptance of the proposed plan of reorganization under Chapter 11 if it becomes necessary to commence a Chapter 11 case.

The advantage of the alternative of a prepackaged Chapter 11 is that while a relatively high percentage of holders is required to tender in a typical exchange offer, for that offer to become effective only two thirds in amount and a majority in number of the holders voting or accepting the exchange offer is necessary to bind *all* holders under a Chapter 11 plan of reorganization.[64] The commencement of a Chapter 11 case in which less than the specified percentages of holders can bind the entire class may be daunting enough to result in the attainment of the requisite percentage of acceptances. However, even if this percentage is not reached, the issuer is not left without an attractive course of action. If, for example, a 90 percent acceptance level is required to complete the exchange offer and only 75 percent of the holders tendered, the issuer cannot complete the exchange offer but will likely have the votes necessary to accomplish a successful plan of reorganization under Chapter 11. At that juncture, the issuer can consider the possibility of commencing a Chapter 11 case and moving with expedition to confirm the plan of reorganization included as part of its solicitation materials. A prepackaged Chapter 11 case may be expeditiously completed and, if properly administered and programmed, should be completed within three to six months.

Securities Laws' Concerns

In an exchange offer, the debtor proposes to replace the existing outstanding securities with new securities; the issuance of the new securities may be subject to the application of federal and state securities laws that require disclosure and compliance with other provisions of such laws.

Rule 145 of the Securities Act of 1933[65] (the 1933 Act) establishes registration procedures for certain kinds of corporate reorganization transactions and provides, in part, that an "offer for sale" shall be deemed to occur when "there is submitted to the security holders a plan or agreement pursuant to which such holders are required to elect, on the basis of what is in substance a new investment decision, whether to accept a new or different security in exchange for their existing securities." If a transaction constitutes such an offer for sale, registration of the new securities under the 1933 Act may be required. However, Rule 145 also provides exemptions from the registration requirement if the transaction falls within other statutory exemptions of the 1933 Act. For example, Section 3(a) (9) of the 1933 Act provides that "[e]xcept with respect to a security exchanged in a case under title 11 [of the United States Code] any security exchanged by the issuer with its existing security holders exclusively where no commission or other remuneration is paid or given directly or indirectly for soliciting such exchange" is an exempt security and is not subject to registration requirements. A close analysis of the foregoing reveals that the Section 3(a)(9) is rather narrow if the exchange is done in a non-bankruptcy workout/turnaround. First, it prohibits the payment of a commission or remuneration in connection with the solicitation and, thus, reduces the probability of the success of this exchange offer. If the debtor's securities are publicly held, the retention of professionals to assist in the solicitation of acceptances will not be possible. Second, the exemption is available only if the exchange is exclusively with existing holders. If the debtor also wishes to sell the securities to new investors to raise financing, the exemption will not be available. Third, the exemption is only for the transaction and not the subsequent disposition of the securities issued. Thus, even if the exchange is exempt from registration, holders of securities received under this section must qualify for another exemption if they later decide to sell without registration. Rule 144 and Section 4(l)[66] of the 1933 Act are the provisions that apply to whether there exists a "safe harbor" for resale of the newly issued security.

In contrast, if the debtor wants to propose the exchange offer within a bankruptcy case, Section 1145(a)(1) of the Bankruptcy Code exempts from registration the issuance of securities pursuant to a plan of reorganization in exchange for claims against or interests in the debtor entity. The exemption is also applicable to the registration requirements under the Trust Indenture Act of 1939 if the debtor proposes to issue short-term commercial notes that mature not later than one year after the effective date of the plan.[67]

Of course, while outside the scope of this chapter, the "antifraud" and "full disclosure" provisions under both the 1933 Act and the Securities Exchange Act of 1934[68] apply with full force to any exchange offer, even though it may satisfy the statutory exemption from registration.

Use of High Yield ("Junk") Bonds in Exchange Offers

High yield bonds, sometimes characterized as "junk bonds," are noninvestment grade corporate securities. They have been used extensively in the early and mid-80s to provide "mezzanine" financing for many corporate takeovers and leveraged buyouts.

High yield bonds may provide for a variety of financial techniques to deal with payment of debt and are often described by the financial technique used: deferred-interest bonds, zero-coupon bonds, payment in kind (PIK) notes, delayed convertible subordinated notes or bonds, and resettable interest rate bonds. Each of the debt instruments has one feature in common: the issuer promises to pay interest sometime in the future on currently forgone interest, and the purchaser bought with the expectation that he or she would be paid in full according to the stipulated terms. In recent years, this expectation has been met with a high level of frustration.

The high yield bond market, currently, is in a state of gridlock, its liquidity being compared to that of glaciers.[69] This is especially true with respect to the "lower tier" debentures that were issued by lesser-known companies without proven financial track records. Among the many factors that precipitated the collapse of this once active market were the "insider trading" scandals of the late 1980s, as well as the tightened governmental regulations dealing with financial institutions, and, in particular, savings and loan associations that require the divestiture of high yield bonds currently in the portfolios of such institutions.[70] As a consequence, the ability to use high yield bonds as part of a proposed exchange offer has been severely diminished. Many regulated financial institutions holding existing high yield bonds may not exchange such bonds for the proposed new high yield bonds because of federal regulations.

The use of exchange offers and high yield bonds in such exchange offers has been further diminished by a recent decision by the United States Bankruptcy Court for the Southern District of New York. In *In re Chateaugay Corp.*, 109 Bankr. 51 (Bankr. S.D.N.Y. 1990) ("LTV"), the bankruptcy court held that the original issue discount (OID) on a debenture which had not "accreted" prior to the commencement of the case constituted unmatured interest and, thus, was not an allowable claim under Section 502(b)(2) of the Bankruptcy Code. OID is the difference between the proceeds received by the debenture issuer (before issuance expenses) and the face amount of the debenture repayable at maturity. As such, OID represents additional unmatured interest on the bond. The bankruptcy court decision is based primarily on the language of Section 1273 of the Internal Revenue Code[71] and the legislative history of Section 502(b)(2) of the Bankruptcy Code, which provides, in part, that "any portion of prepaid interest that represents an original discounting of the claim" will be disallowed if that portion of the claim "would not have been earned on the date of bankruptcy."[72]

In the perspective of the LTV decision, holders of high yield bonds—which are often issued at a rather steep discount to reflect the risk of nonpayment and, thus, may be OID securities within the meaning of the LTV decision—that participate in a workout/turnaround exchange offer may potentially wind up with a smaller claim if the issuer thereafter is subjected to a case under the Bankruptcy Code. Thus, pending the outcome of appeals from the *LTV* decision, the use of debt-for-debt exchange offers involving high yield bonds has been substantially diminished.

Tax Considerations: Income from Cancellation of Debt

An entity generally "receives" income for tax purposes when its debts are reduced or canceled (COD income).[73] An entity is not, however, taxed on COD income to the extent that such entity is insolvent immediately before the cancellation of debt occurs. Insolvency exists if its liabilities exceed the market value of its assets. If the entity is a partnership, it is the insolvency of the partners, not the partnership, that counts. COD income is included in income for tax purposes to the extent the entity is made solvent by the cancellation of debt, but is entirely excluded (even if the debtor is made solvent) if the cancellation occurs in a bankruptcy case, rather than an informal workout/turnaround. Accordingly, it may be preferable, from a tax perspective, for an exchange offer to occur in a bankruptcy case and as part of a plan of reorganization.

However, there is a price exacted for the exclusion of COD income, whether in or out of bankruptcy. The debtor must reduce certain favorable tax attributes (various tax credits, net operating loss and capital loss carryovers, and the tax basis of its assets) by the amount of COD income excluded. This reduction of tax attributes can be avoided, however, if the debtor's exchange, in whole or in part, for stock and certain tests are satisfied relating to the amount of stock distributed and the allocation of the stock among different classes of creditors. This rule, like the general rule for excluding COD income, applies only if the debtor is in bankruptcy, or to the extent the debtor is insolvent.

If tax attribute production is avoided by issuing stock to creditors in an exchange offer, the debtor must take care that a change of control does not occur that would result in a limitation on the debtor's use of its tax attributes. For this purpose, a change of control occurs if, within any three-year period, stockholders increase their ownership of the debtor's stock by more than 50 percentage points. In such circumstances, however, special rules are available that may make a bankruptcy case a more favorable form from a tax perspective.[74]

EQUITY INFUSION

Potential Sources

When a company faces financial distress, one way to seek relief is to find new investors that are willing to infuse new capital into the debtor entity. An alternative is to search for assistance from existing lenders and creditors. In addition to requesting a moratorium on principal and interest payments, the debtor entity may propose to undertake an equity-for-debt swap (as described earlier in the Exchange Offer section), transferring current debtholders into future equity interest holders.

Further, the troubled debtor may look to vendors and trade creditors (for whom their continuity in business is dependent on the debtor's viability), customers (for whom the debtor is an important source of supply) and its employees (for whom their current and future income are conditional upon the continued viability of the entity); perhaps these entities, driven by the principles of symbiotic survival and economic reality, may be willing to take an equity position in the debtor. Finally, under appropriate circumstances, the financially troubled entity may request governmental assistance—this is especially applicable if the collapse of the debtor may affect the gainful employment of thousands of workers and potentially have a domino effect, causing other entities financial distress. The bailout of the Chrysler Corporation in the early 1980s by the government is representative of the foregoing situation. Such situations are rare.

Typical Considerations

If the new equity interest holder is a regulated financial institution, upon the infusion of the new equity the capital structure of the new debtor will have to be modified so that the equity ownership by such financial institution will not exceed regulatory limitations.[75] This may cause the establishment of several classes of equity securities so the equity participation will conform to the relevant federal and state regulatory guidelines. Options and warrants may be considered as an alternative to circumvent the problem and as a means of inducing the new investor/lender to participate through a combination of debt and equity investments.

If the new investors come in as joint venture participants or potential merger partners, they may seek to immediately influence management of the debtor. Depending on the amount of investment and their share of equity in the debtor, they may gain effective control over current management. Moreover, they may demand a position senior to the existing equity holders, or, if feasible, even over unsecured creditors. In a nonbankruptcy context, however, it is almost impossible to obtain senior or equal status with secured creditors. Quite often, investors experienced in seeking out and investing in financially troubled entities are able to identify the entity's problems and fashion proper remedial courses of action, which may rescue it from the onset of a formal bankruptcy case. While such investors may be willing to endure the current illiquidity of their investment, they will likely seek indemnification from the debtor and its stockholders to protect their position, and, in the more extreme cases, they may even attempt to bind the debtor to contracts that are beneficial to their own businesses (e.g., the purchasing of raw materials and other products from such investors), hence insuring a market and outlet for their own products. While the existing management and equity holders of the debtor may resist such "overbearing intrusions" of the new investors, they may not have any real choice and conclude that survival requires a sacrifice of reduced control.

Creditors of the debtor, secured and unsecured, should also consider the effect of such additional financing as may be furnished by the new investors. The additional financing or investment may require subordination by existing creditors, with a loss of asset preferences. The creditors also may be requested to waive default provisions in loan agreements, or restrictive and other covenants that might adversely affect their legal rights against the debtor but will enable the infusion of new moneys from the financing or investment. Creditors will have to consider the advantages and disadvantages of the give-ups requested. If they conclude that the new investors will provide the wherewithal that will enable the curing of the financial distress of the debtor, then they will stand to benefit from the concessions requested.

GENERAL EXPENSE REDUCTION

Many factors may cause a debtor to incur economic turmoil. While it is important for management to raise the necessary financing to meet operational costs, it is equally crucial that an effective general expense reduction program be implemented to stop monetary hemorrhaging. However, before any drastic actions are taken to curtail expenses, management should try to identify the causes that have triggered the financial crisis. The following are typical causal factors:

- General market turndown or industrywide problems not primarily attributable to the entity. For example, recessions, inflation, stock market crash, floods, or other natural disasters.
- Overexpansion or diversification to new areas that are not related to the entity's main line of business; management lacks qualified personnel to supervise the daily operations of the new business area.
- Excessive debt due to overleveraging; cash flow is inadequate to meet debt obligations.

- Inadequate control over financial reporting and ineffective management communication programs.
- Depressed sales due to fierce competition, inferior products, market share shrinkage, or change in customers' tastes and needs.
- Poor labor relations, excessive wages, featherbedding, and other employee-related matters.
- Antiquated equipment and machinery resulting in noncompetitive production and costly maintenance.
- Disadvantageous contractual commitments with suppliers, vendors, and customers.
- Environmental and other tort liabilities.

The foregoing is not exhaustive or fully comprehensive. Management of a debtor must be constantly vigilant about the costs of its operations and should conduct a thorough analysis based on the particular facts of the business of the debtor and then determine what, if any, cost-cutting programs should be effected. Among such programs are:

- Identify and sell off divisions of the debtor that are no longer profitable. This may include the sale of the "crown jewel" if it is ascertained that current corporate resources are insufficient to support its growth and maintenance.
- Close and consolidate plant and warehouse locations that are underutilized.
- Abandon costly research and development programs possessing only speculative and marginal success projections.
- Freeze hiring, lay off excess personnel.
- Relocate corporate headquarters and branch offices to less-expensive commercial spaces.
- Refinance high interest debts if current rates are favorable and such refinancing is feasible.
- Exchange obsolete and nonproductive machinery with modern equipment to stay competitive.
- Analyze and, where appropriate, effect salary and wage reductions. Review collective bargaining agreements and seek appropriate concessions.

Management must be alert to evaluate countervailing effects that may result from imprudent cost-slashing programs. Excessive cuts in labor and financial budgets may have both psychological and economic impact upon the debtor. Notably, employees who are uncertain of their prospects of continued employment may no longer be willing to contribute extra efforts and, thus, severely diminish their output. Their reduced-incentive work affects production, which in turn depresses the amount of articles or services available for sale. Declining receipts from sales necessitate further labor and budget cuts and may cause an irreversible downward spiral that may precipitate the necessity to resort to protection under the Bankruptcy Code.

In addition, termination of employees may trigger severance pay clauses or other pension-related benefit provisions in employment or collective bargaining agreements or pursuant to applicable laws. Further, sales, closures, or other disposition of corporate assets may involve the payment of substantial professional fees (e.g., investment bankers, brokers, auctioneers, attorneys, accountants, appraisers, and so on) and penalties relating to premature termination of leases and contracts. Continuity of normal business operations may be impaired. Care must be exercised to assure that the cost-cutting programs do not have the effect of destroying the core business of the debtor and, thus, precluding the possibility of successful reorganization under Chapter 11 of the Bankruptcy Code. Consequently, a careful balancing of all of the benefits and disadvantages relating to the proposed expense reduction program must be undertaken before the program is effectuated and implemented.

CONCLUSION

Participants in the deleveraging, restructuring process should, in addition to the more technical matters discussed above relative to the various financing alternatives, bear in mind the following "pointers" to partake in the workout effectively and constructively.

First, be realistic. Participants should realize that erroneous or overly optimistic projections about the debtor made in the past cannot be changed now. Accordingly, the restructuring of the troubled debtor will have to be based upon a new set of valuations, which may not be as favorable.

Second, be assertive, yet also be willing to make compromises when and if necessary. Rationality must prevail. Concessions and compromises are essential in the workout/turnaround. The objective is that all parties in interest be treated equitably, and that the actions taken yield the greatest benefits for all concerned.

Third, be active, rather than reactive. Passivity will not enhance the effectiveness and economic returns of those involved.

Finally, be flexible. The workout rules are ad hoc. They change as the process progresses. The debtor, as well as the creditors and other parties in interest, must not view a proposed restructuring plan as static. Creativity and imagination are key factors in a successful workout/turnaround. Rigidity is incompatible with the changing circumstances that occur in almost every workout/turnaround.

ENDNOTES

1. 11 U.S.C. § 101 *et seq.* (the Bankruptcy Code).
2. 11 U.S.C. § 363(c).
3. **See** generally, 11 U.S.C. §§ 361, 362(b), 363(c), 363(e), 1102, 1104, 1111(b), and 1112.
4. A transfer of assets is construed broadly to include every mode, direct or indirect, voluntary or involuntary, of disposing of or parting with property of the debtor's estate. 11 U.S.C. § 101(50).
5. UFCA was approved by the National Conference of Commissioners on Uniform State Laws (Conference) and the American Bar Association in 1918. As of March 1, 1989, the UFCA remained in effect in Arizona, Delaware, Maryland, Massachusetts, Michigan, Montana, Nebraska, New Mexico, New York, Ohio, Pennsylvania, Tennessee, the Virgin Islands, and Wyoming.
6. In 1984, the Conference replaced the UFCA with the UFTA. As of March 1, 1989, the UFTA was adopted by the following states: Arkansas, California, Florida, Hawaii, Idaho, Maine, Minnesota, Nevada, New Hampshire, New Jersey, North Dakota, Oklahoma, Oregon, Rhode Island, South Dakota, Texas, Utah, Washington, West Virginia, and Wisconsin. Because few cases have been decided under the UFTA, the discussion in this chapter focuses primarily on UFCA and the principles developed under the Bankruptcy Code.
7. 11 U.S.C. § 548 sets forth what has commonly been characterized as the federal fraudulent conveyance law. 11 U.S.C. § 544(b) empowers a

trustee (including a debtor in possession) to void any transfer of an interest of the debtor in property that is voidable under applicable state law by a creditor holding an allowed unsecured claim. Thus, a trustee may take advantage of the longer statute of limitations provided for by UFCA and UFTA.
8. UFCA § 7; 11 U.S.C. § 548(a)(1).
9. UFCA § 3. Under the UFCA, fair consideration inquires into the adequacy of consideration and that the consideration not be disproportionately small, compared to the property exchanged by the transferror. Furthermore, good faith is required of the transferee.
10. 11 U.S.C. § 548(a)(2)(A). The Bankruptcy Code considers only the reasonableness of equivalent value and does not require good faith. However, the legislative history does seem to intend substantive changes from the UFCA and, in fact, appears to be a modern articulation of the UFCA's "fair consideration" test. **See** 1978 U.S. Code Cong. & Admin. News 5787.
11. UFCA § 4; 11 U.S.C. § 548(a)(2)(B)(i).
12. UFCA § 5; 11 U.S.C. § 548(a)(2)(B)(ii).
13. UFCA § 6; 11 U.S.C. § 548(a)(2)(B)(iii).
14. 13 Eliz., c.5 (1571). For a case describing the various elements constituting "badges of fraud," **see** generally, *In re Steele*, 79 Bankr. 503 (Bankr. M.D. Fla. 1987). The following elements, *inter alia*, are considered to be "badges of fraud": (1) the transfer involves substantially all of the debtor's assets, (2) the conveyance is made while legal actions are pending against the debtor, (3) the transaction is secretive and (4) the transferee acts as a trustee for the debtor with respect to the transferred property.
15. *United States* v. *Tabor Court Realty Corp.*, 803 F.2d 1288, 1305 (3rd Cir. 1986), *cert. denied*; *McClellan Realty Co.* v. *United States*, 483 U.S. 1005 (1987).
16. **See** endnotes 9–12, *supra*, and accompanying text.
17. *In re Ohio Corrugating Co.*, 70 Bankr. 920 (Bankr. N.D. Ohio 1987).
18. *Credit Managers Ass'n. of Southern California* v. *Federal Co.*, 629 F. Supp. 175 (C.D. Cal. 1985).
19. *United States* v. *Gleneagles Investment Co.*, 565 F. Supp. 556 (N.D. Pa. 1983), *aff'd*; *United States* v. *Tabor Court Realty Corp.*, 803 F.2d 1288 (3d Cir. 1988).
20. *Unocal Corp.* v. *Mesa Petroleum Co.*, 493 A.2d 946 (Del. 1985).
21. *Revlon, Inc.* v. *McAndrews & Forbes Holdings*, 506 A.2d 173 (Del. 1985).
22. *Pepper* v. *Litton*, 308 U.S. 295 (1939). **See also** *Commodity Futures Trading Commission* v. *Weintraub*, 471 U.S. 343 (1985).

23. *In re Xonics, Inc.*, 99 Bankr. 870 (Bankr. N.D. Ill. 1989).
24. *Smith* v. *Van Gorkim*, 488 A.2d 858 (Del. 1985). Of course, sales of less than substantially all assets also require care and prudence, but the standard arguably is not as high as would be required of sales involving all assets of a business.
25. See, for example, *Katz* v. *Bregman*, 431 A.2d 1274, *appeal refused sub. nom., Plant Indus. Inc.* v. *Katz*, 435 A.2d 1044 (Del. 1981); *Gimbel* v. *Signal Companies, Inc.*, 316 A.2d 599 (Del. Ch. 1974), *aff'd*, 316 A.2d 619 (Del. 1974).
26. For shareholders' appraisal remedies, **see**, for example, Del. Gen. Corp. Law § 262; Cal. Corp. Code § 1300; New York Bus. Corp. Law § 623(h)(4); Rev. Model Bus. Corp. Act §§ 13.01-1303, 1320-1328, 1330-1331. For fraudulent conveyance statutes, **see** endnotes 5–7, *supra* and accompanying text.
27. A lender that obtains payments from the principal stockholder-guarantor of a debtor company may be subject to a one-year preference period of limitations for insiders under the Bankruptcy Code. **See** *Levitt* v. *Ingersoll Rand Financial Corporation*, 874 F.2d 1186 (7th Cir. 1989).
28. Fraudulent conveyance concerns are discussed on pages 101–2. Preference considerations will be discussed *infra*.
29. The Uniform Commercial Code essentially incorporates state statutes and case law to establish a definition of "fixture." UCC § 9-313(1)(a). A few states have adopted a so-called institutional doctrine for classifying fixtures. Under this doctrine, the test is to determine "whether the item in question is somewhat integral to the operation of something built on the real estate irrespective of its ease of removal." Speidel, White, and Summers, *Commercial Law* 126, 4th ed., 1987 (West Publishing). Due to the lack of a uniform definition of "fixture" among the states, White and Summers have jokingly proposed that "anything that cannot be moved by one man in one hour armed with a crescent wrench is a fixture." Ibid.
30. Notably, revolving credit loans often involve a pledge of inventory and equipment in addition to receivables. Thus, the amount of an advance will depend not only on the amount of eligible receivables but, usually, a broader "borrowing base" comprised of eligible inventory, equipment, cash, and other pledged assets.
31. For example, (1) if there are no outstanding disputes between the account debtor and the borrower, with respect to the goods supplied or the services rendered; (2) the particular receivable should not be more than a specified number of days old, as measured from the date of invoice ("aging of receivables"); (3) the collection of the receivables should be legally enforceable and not subject to offsets or counter-

claims; (4) the sales should be to unaffiliated companies of the borrower (this is to avoid the extinguishment of intercompany debts in the event of consolidated bankruptcy cases filed by the borrower and its affiliated customers).
32. 11 U.S.C. §§ 363(a)(1) and (c)(2).
33. Insolvency is presumed for the 90-day period immediately prior to the commencement of a bankruptcy case. 11 U.S.C. § 547(f).
34. "Insiders," as defined in 11 U.S.C. § 101, include, among other entities, relatives of an individual debtor and directors and officers of a corporate debtor.
35. 11 U.S.C. §§ 547 (c)(1), (c)(2), (c)(3) and (c)(4), respectively.
36. "New value" means "money or money's worth in goods, services, or new credit, or released by a transferee of property previously transferred to such transferee in a transaction which is neither void nor voidable by the debtor or the trustee under any applicable law, including proceeds of such property, but does not include an obligation substituted for an existing obligation." 11 U.S.C. § 547(a)(2).
37. See *Coral Petroleum, Inc.* v. *Banque Paribas-London*, 797 F.2d 1351 (5th Cir. 1986) (The protection thus afforded the debtor in [§ 547] often enables him to work his way out of a difficult financial situation through cooperation with all of his creditors).
38. To take advantage of the tax benefits of an ESOP, the ESOP must satisfy the detailed statutory provisions of the Internal Revenue Code of 1986, as amended, that apply to all tax-qualified retirement plans as well as code provisions that are specific to ESOPs. These provisions cover employee participation, vesting of benefits, contributions, terminations, distributions, and the conduct of parties who interact with the ESOP. A discussion of most of these rules is beyond the scope of this chapter.
39. Code § 4975(e)(7).
40. This discussion does not describe the requirements for nonleveraged ESOPs, which are more lenient than the requirements for leveraged ESOPs.
41. Under Statement of Position on Accounting Practice for Certain Stock Ownership Plans, 76-3, December 20, 1976, the ESOP loan should be reflected as a liability on the balance sheet of the corporation with an offsetting debit in stockholders' equity equal to the amount of the loan. This could have the effect of violating financial ratio covenants of existing debt.
42. A "disqualified person" is defined under Code § 4975(e)(2) to include a fiduciary of the ESOP, an entity providing services to the ESOP, the sponsoring employer, and certain related or affiliated parties.
43. Code § 409(e).

44. Code § 415(c)(1).
45. The amount of compensation may be adjusted by the Secretary of the Treasury. Code § 401(a)(17).
46. Code § 409(h)(1)(A). The plan can provide that benefits may be distributed in cash or stock and not risk disqualification, provided that a participant must have the right to receive stock if she so requests.
47. Code § 409(h)(1)(B). Consideration should be given to including a "floor" for the put option equal to the original purchase price by the ESOP of the stock, as adjusted by the operating income or loss of the employer without regard to the ESOP. **See**, for example, the Parsons Corporation and Blue Bell leveraged buyouts. Without a floor, it is possible the ESOP shares could be valued at an amount substantially less than the original purchase price, putting older employees in a disadvantageous position.
48. If the ESOP repurchases stock (from a cash reserve), rather than the employer, the after-tax cost of such purchases will be reduced. Of course, the contributions of cash to the ESOP (to build up a cash reserve) will, in turn, increase the value of the accounts of participants and the ultimate benefits distributed.
49. An employer with publicly held stock, as described above, would not have a put obligation. The cost of an ESOP to such an employer would be measured in terms of a dilution of other common stockholders.
50. Code § 1042. In addition to providing deferral of gain, Section 1042 should provide a means to obviate any potential ordinary income tax treatment if stock were redeemed by the employer corporation. The Internal Revenue Service has consistently held that such a transaction is a sale, rather than a redemption, governed by Code §§ 302 or 304, provided that certain conditions as set forth in Rev. Proc. 78-18, 1978-2, C.B. 49, are met.
51. Because the 10 percent penalty tax is imposed on the employer where there is a disqualifying disposition by the ESOP, under certain circumstances it may be advisable to negotiate stock transfer restrictions on the stock purchased by the ESOP.
52. Code § 404(k).
53. Code § 382(l)(3)(c).
54. Section 401(a)(28) of the code requires that an independent appraiser must be used by an ESOP for any transaction in securities that are not traded on an established securities market.
55. Tender offers by ESOPs for stock publicly traded above the market price should be restricted to purchases from unrelated parties to avoid violating the adequate consideration requirement in purchasing stock from related parties.

56. The Department of Labor (DOL) has taken the position in several ESOP transactions that, notwithstanding no more than adequate consideration would be paid for stock by an ESOP, the ESOP fiduciaries must participate in the negotiation of a transaction to be sure the ESOP is being treated fairly in relationship to other parties involved in the transaction. For example, in the Blue Bell and Raymond Engineering ESOP transactions, the DOL was concerned that management employees participating in the leveraged buyouts were receiving very attractive investments at the expense of the ESOPs involved. In the ill-fated Scott-Fetzer transaction, the DOL initially refused to acquiesce in the terms of the transaction, because it believed the terms were unfair to the ESOP.

57. Although an employer may generally indemnify or purchase insurance on behalf of plan fiduciaries, the DOL has taken the position an employer may not indemnify the fiduciaries of ESOPs. This is because a plan may not indemnify a fiduciary, and the indemnification by an employer, where the plan owns a controlling interest therein, may be viewed as an indirect indemnification by the plan itself.

58. See, also, legislative history to ERISA, in which Congress emphasized the need for special scrutiny in reviewing loans to assure that the interests of participants and beneficiaries will be served. H.R. No. 93-1280, 93d Cong., 2d Sess. (1974) at p. 313.

59. See endnote 56, *supra*.

60. See *Thornton* v. *Evans*, 692 F.2d 1064 (7th Cir. 1982); *Freund* v. *Marshall and Isley Bank*, 485 F. Supp. 629 (W.D. Wisc. 1979); *Donovan* v. *Dougherty*, 550 F. Supp. 390 (S.D. Ala. 1982).

61. 15 U.S.C. § 77aaa *et seq.*

62. 11 U.S.C. § 1126(b) provides that "a holder of a claim or interest that has accepted or rejected the plan before the commencement of the case under this title is deemed to have accepted or rejected such plan . . . if (1) the solicitation of such acceptance or rejection was in compliance with any applicable bankruptcy law, rule, or regulation governing the adequacy of disclosure in connection with such disclosure; or (2) if there is not any such law . . . such acceptance or rejection were solicited after disclosure to such holder of adequate information. . . . ''

Section 1125(a)(1) of the Bankruptcy Code defines adequate information as "information of a kind . . . that would enable a hypothetical reasonable investor typical of claims or interests . . . to make an informed judgment about the plan. . . . '' To insure that the out-of-court solicitation meets statutory requirements, the safest method is to insure that the disclosure documents are as complete as possible.

See *In re Metrocraft Pub. Services, Inc.*, 39 Bankr. 567 (Bankr. N.D. Ga. 1984);   **see also,** Merrick, *The Chapter 11 Disclosure Statement in a Strategic Environment*, 44 Business Lawyer 103 (1988).
63. A class of claims or interests is impaired unless (1) the legal, equitable, and contractual rights of the holders of such claims are left unaltered; or (2) the plan reinstates the debt and cures the default; or (3) the plan, on its effective date, provides cash payment to *(a)* a creditor, with an amount equal to the amount of the creditor's allowed claim, or *(b)* a stockholder with an amount equal to the greater of the redemption price or the liquidation preference of the equity interests. 11 U.S.C. § 1124.
64. 11 U.S.C. § 1126(c).
65. 15 U.S.C. § 77a *et seq.*
66. Section 4(l) states, in substance, that the provision of Section 5 [registration requirements] "shall not apply to a transaction for any person other than the issuer, underwriter or dealer." **See also** 11 U.S.C. § 1145(b) for a definition of a "non-underwriter."
67. 11 U.S.C. § 1145(d)(1). When the notes are for a term longer than one year and, thus, would come within the Trust Indenture Act of 1939, the debtor must file a qualified trust indenture. Ibid., for an extensive discussion of § 1145 and the securities laws and considerations in the bankruptcy context, **see** 5 Collier on Bankruptcy ¶¶ 1145.01-04 (15th ed., 1988).
68. 15 U.S.C. § 78a *et seq.*
69. *The Wall Street Journal*, October 16, 1989, at C1, C2, and C21.
70. **See** Financial Institution Reform, Recovery and Enforcement Act of 1989, Pub. L. 101-73, 103 Stat. 183 (August 9, 1989).
71. In substance, Code Section 1273(b) states that, if the debt instrument is exchanged for property which is regularly traded on an established market, the issue price of the debt instrument is the fair market value of that property. In addition, Section 1272 provides for the constant interest method of proportionately allocating the OID over the life of the debt instrument. There exists some question about whether the bankruptcy court properly analyzed the code in connection with the issue of exchange offers.
72. H.R. Rep. No. 95-595, 95th Cong., 1st Sess. 352-354 (1977);   S. Rep. No. 95-989, 95th Cong., 2nd Sess. 62-65 (1978).   **See also** *In re Allegheny Intern., Inc.*, 100 Bankr. 247 (Bankr. W.D. Pa. 1989) for a comparable analysis.
73. For a more comprehensive discussion of the tax treatment of COD income in exchange offers, **see** 26 U.S.C. § 108.

74. **See** 26 U.S.C. § 382(1)(5), (6).
75. **See** for example, 12 U.S.C. § 1843(c)(6). No bank holding company shall acquire shares of any company that includes more than 5 percent of the outstanding voting shares of such company.

CHAPTER 5

RESCUE FROM THE DEAD: A TURNAROUND IN PROGRESS

Raymond H. Kraftson, Esq.
Richard J. Giacco, Esq.
Safeguard Scientifics, Inc.

The editors' request to develop a chapter dealing with turnarounds came at an opportune time. While Safeguard Scientifics, Inc. (Safeguard) has been involved with turnarounds before, we are presently working on the most challenging in recent history. Within the context of this "work in progress," we hope to be able to communicate our approach on how to decide if a turnaround should be attempted and on how to execute the turnaround plan.

BACKGROUND

Safeguard has a number of entrepreneurial partners (both subsidiaries and investments) that develop and sell various communications and applications software products and services. One of our early investments (1981) was a small, passive one in a promising company that, through the vision of its founder, was developing a state-of-the-art system for the automation of the back-office functions of the banking industry. (We will refer to that company as "the Company" to protect the innocent). The mission was to build an organization that could design, develop, and install multimillion-dollar minicomputer-based systems that would leapfrog the competition and anticipate the needs of its banking clients in the 1990s. Competitive systems were generally completed in the 1970s and early 1980s.

The Company grew through equity investments, such as ours, and by up-front license funding from bank customers who realized that the Company's system would provide them a strategic edge in their recently deregulated and increasingly competitive business. The initial system developed by the Company, which addressed one back-office function, was reasonably successful and provided the financial and technological basis for the next step: a vastly more complicated full-function system. Like most entrepreneurial companies, it had the confidence that it could promise and deliver that system on the basis of breakthroughs that were much tougher to achieve than anticipated. The Company found itself in serious trouble when, in 1986, a high-profile project for an extremely high-profile customer fell apart. While there were a number of reasons for the failure, and the Company and other interested parties have different views of where to allocate the blame, the bad publicity eliminated the Company from consideration in the minds of the people whose decisions drive the Company's market.

Each decision to buy the type of system the Company offered takes at least a year to make, involves relatively large amounts of money, and represents a choice on which the career of a banking officer could be made or broken. In general, banking officers are risk averse and will frequently decide to buy the safest system, rather than the best or most advanced. Buyers also prefer a seller with strong financial statements because of a justifiable concern that the seller will be around to install, support, and maintain the system. The result of the 1986 failure, while tragic for the Company, was not surprising.

A downward spiral developed. Competitors trumpeted the failure. The Company had built up its overhead of people and space on its projections of success, and it had to make painful and expensive reductions as sales evaporated. The underlying rights to the first system the Company had developed had to be sold to raise cash. In addition, the expectations of other customers were not being addressed as desired. Faced with mounting losses, management felt itself forced to respond that it would deliver what customers needed only if the customers came up with additional funds. That approach produced angry and alienated customers instead of additional cash. The Company's hardware supplier and landlord were stretched and angry. But the news was not all bad. Dedicated employees worked hard to finish and stabilize the system for a number of loyal customers and succeeded in that effort in 1988. The Company also completed development of a new component to the system, which anticipated the globalization of the financial marketplace and which was virtually unique in the market. However, by that time, the Company was so financially shaky that even customers who liked and believed in the system would not consider it.

SHOULD WE GET INVOLVED IN A TURNAROUND?

Since Safeguard's initial investment in the Company was a passive one, its response to all the bad news prior to 1988 was simply to provide counsel, support, and advice to the extent it was requested, but it took no active role.

However, some of the Company's managers started to impress us in late 1988 that, despite all the negative publicity, the angry customers, and the past failures, they had developed a reliable and unique system that did indeed address customer needs for the 1990s. In fact, we began to get interested when an existing customer confirmed that the system turned out to be as advertised. There were also prospective customers very interested in the system but very nervous about the financial capability and overall condition of the Company.

We also took a hard look at competing products and became convinced that the Company was far ahead of the field. In fact, projections of costs required to bring any competitive products to the level of the Company's system indicated that the product, on an even playing field, could reasonably be considered a franchise for the near future. Impressed with the product, Safeguard began to consider seriously a turnaround campaign. While we, along with other investors, had been providing interim funding to keep the Company alive, our projection of the investment of time, money, and reputation involved in a turnaround was significant for a company of our size and other commitments. And, as valuable as the system might be, the system was only one aspect of the Company, and other assets, liabilities, and prospects had to be examined and weighed.

Our initial step was to conduct intensive due diligence. The first inquiry was directed at the market. Customers who had worked with the Company through the negative publicity confirmed that the system had been stabilized and possessed features that were not only crucial but otherwise not available from the competition. We also talked with dissatisfied customers and determined that their complaints could be addressed fairly if the Company was given sufficient time and support.

We sat down with the employees, a constituency as important as any other. Since crucial assets in any information business walk in and out of the door each work day, we wanted their input and some comfort that they would remain assuming fair treatment down the road. Finding and retaining quality people is a challenge for virtually every business, and we did not want to face material employee departures along with the multitude of other problems the Company would face. Their degree of loyalty to the objectives and success of the Company, given all its problems and layoffs, surprised us and indicated that material defections and bad blood would not be a problem during the turnaround effort.

We brought in a seasoned advisor to assess management. His background was in the field, and he had built up a number of successful management teams in the past. His task was to study the organization while analyzing the strength and weaknesses of the individual managers for their suitability for the tough road ahead. His input helped us to focus on where help was needed. He also helped us to focus on the fact that the Company has historically been run as a development house, rather than the systems management company it would have to become. A fundamental problem was that the Company had fallen into a pattern of promising and trying to deliver all things to all people, and that practice had to change.

We considered seriously making a formal bankruptcy proceeding a requirement of our proposal. Past experience indicated that as soon as a deep pocket appeared as a sponsor for the Company, dissatisfied customers and suppliers would line up for payment of real or imagined claims. However, while that process might have cleaned up some of the Company's liabilities on favorable terms, we felt that the perception of the Company to its conservative market, already tarnished, might be irreparably damaged by the filing no matter what emerged. Our alternative was to take a firm position with everyone from the past: that any money Safeguard invested in the Company would be directed to making the Company successful in the future and would not serve to satisfy past claims. We believed that such an approach, applied consistently, would elicit reasonable compromises of problems without a formal proceeding. To date, that approach has been successful.

We approached the Company's hardware supplier, which was troubled by very substantial nonpayments, to gauge whether it might consider some alternatives to satisfy its trade debt. Since the Company's system operated exclusively on that hardware system, the supplier would be a crucial player in the turnaround effort. We were able to convince the supplier to convert a substantial portion of its receivables into equity equivalents, in return for a structured payment of the rest and a seat on the board. Our participation in those negotiations helped to insure credibility.

The fact that the system operated only on the "platform" of that supplier (which was not one of the big three minicomputer suppliers) was another concern, because it significantly narrowed the market. We also believed that minicomputer technology itself might be on a course of being squeezed out of existence by advances in microcomputers and "distributed processing" between mainframes and microcomputers. In fact, a number of our other entrepreneurial partners are driving technologies that have contributed to this trend.

We also initiated our other standard legal and financial due diligence procedures and discovered two significant clouds. The first was litigation with former customers, both actual and threatened. While protracted litigation from former customers produces bad publicity, management distraction, and lost opportunities, it also generates significant cash requirements for legal fees and settlements (if appropriate), and it did not appear that there was insurance coverage. We did not intend to see our investment in the Company, necessary for working capital purposes, exit the Company to pay legal fees and settlements.

Financial due diligence revealed that the capital structure of the

Company had grown so complicated and generally unfavorable for a going concern that a recapitalization would be required. During the dark days when survival was questionable, the Company had swapped most of its equity for debt as a condition for further investment, and the balance sheet was excessively leveraged.

In late 1988, with its cash resources stretched paper thin and with no other capital sources available, the Company had approached its prior investors for additional cash. The investors eventually agreed to purchase a series of 8 percent senior subordinated convertible debentures with a 10-year maturity (Senior Debentures). There was one significant condition tied to the new money, however: the Company was required to offer to exchange a second series of subordinated debentures for the preferred and common stock the investors had acquired in past investments. The effect was to replace most of the equity on the Company's balance sheet with debt at the same time additional debt was being added and to telegraph a lack of confidence in the future of the Company as a going concern. The exchange transaction led to a number of headaches above and beyond the negative impact on the Company's balance sheet.

First, while stated interest on the second series of debentures (the Secondary Debentures) was a seemingly small 2.5 percent per year over a 20-year period, if the Company had been sold or had completed a significant public offering during that period, all future interest would accelerate. Had either trigger event occurred within the first few years, the return on the investment would have been extremely generous to the holders of the debentures and less than generous to any equity holder. For any prospective equity investor, the acceleration feature would have been particularly difficult to live with.

Second, the validity of the procedure used to make the exchange for the Secondary Debentures was uncertain under applicable state corporate law. At the time, a corporation without a sufficient earned or capital surplus could not repurchase shares from its holders, through debt instruments or otherwise. The Company decided to set up a sufficiently capitalized subsidiary, which then issued the debentures in exchange for the preferred stock. Following that transaction, the subsidiary merged into the Company, which resulted in the return of the preferred stock to the Company and the transfer of the obligations under the Secondary Debentures to the Company. The problem that surfaced after the transaction was that despite the apparent technical correctness of the subsidiary transaction, outside counsel for the Company would not issue an opinion that the transaction complied with applicable corporate law. The Company's auditors also questioned the transaction and, given the lack of confidence demonstrated by the Company's lawyers, advised the Company that any audit report it would issue would disclose the issue of the uncertain legal basis for the Secondary Debentures. The Company was then faced with additional problems involved with proceeding as a going concern without audited financial statements in an environment of concerned suppliers, customers, and potential investors where they were crucial. The six months of effort to rectify this situation are outlined later.

As a result of our due diligence work, we felt we knew most of the challenges and risks that a turnaround would entail. The system was a valuable asset, if it could be distanced from the prior bad publicity. It appeared that customers would buy the system, if the Company could find a sponsor with a good reputation and a financial commitment. The people were valuable, if wary, assets who had remained loyal in tough times and would likely flourish given success in a turnaround. Certain managers were tremendous assets who would also flourish; the rest were perceived as less valuable but possibly capable of the requirements of the turnaround if given a chance. We knew that the hardware platform issue might present a serious problem eventually and felt that a migration to other platforms could be accomplished given time and reasonable success. The litigation and balance sheet issues were problematic; but we felt, based on past experience, that they could be favorably dealt with, if sufficient effort and imagination could be applied.

EXECUTING THE TURNAROUND

By February 1989, we had decided to make the attempt to negotiate a turnaround package with the board of the Company. The timing was crucial, not only because the Company was out of cash but, more important, because a customer was ready to commit to the system, if a sponsor such as Safeguard stepped in. Past investors composed a majority of the board, and initially they felt that the valuation of the Company included in our proposal was insufficient. In fact, it was only 10 percent of the most recent valuation of the Company, only a year earlier, and a smaller fraction of prior valuations. It reflected our view that the investment was extremely high risk. Given that response, we invited any and all of the investors to take any or all of the proposed investment. Initially, one investor committed to make at least 80 percent of the overall investment, and two precious weeks were lost when that commitment fell through. At that point, the board agreed to our turnaround proposal.

The proposal consisted of a cash commitment and, more important, our commitment to become the Company's "corporate partner" and to put our reputation in the software industry on the line for the Company. The proposal required a firm commitment from management: it had to develop and communicate to us a plan to implement the turnaround and had to include us in the day-to-day implementation of the turnaround plan.

Top management possibly intended to live up to that requirement, but it was apparent to us in a few weeks that these managers were not doing so. Within that period, we also attended two key trade shows, which virtually all industry sales prospects attended and experienced, first hand, the negative image of the Company. While that was not news to us, we discovered that the same negativism had tainted most of the Company's sales force. Management and senior salespeople actually retreated from the floor of the shows to the Company's hospitality suite to commiserate about the Company's bad image and their bad fortune.

The combination of those experiences and the lack of commitment to our participation forced us to look at replacing a fair portion of the top management of the Company in March 1989, no less than a month after our turnaround proposal had been accepted. We simply believed that the leadership necessary for the turnaround would have to be found elsewhere.

One of our advisors had extensive industry contacts and was able to persuade a top manager at one of our competitors to talk with us about assuming leadership of the Company. It was a whirlwind courtship. While he initially did not consider seriously the prospect of working for the Company, he was looking for a challenge. We described our history of obtaining faith in the Company and its system, and Safeguard was also willing to stand behind the Company's commitments to him if it did not succeed. The essentials of his package were negotiated over a weekend in mid-February 1989 with the help of our key outside consultants, and we proposed and secured his election as CEO at a board meeting at the end of that month.

The election process required some finesse. We did not control a majority of the board, and we perceived that some of the directors might delay the decision. Since the Company needed a new leader immediately, we did not believe it was in the Company's best interests to deal with the uncertainty and further diversions that would have been caused by delay. We spent a great deal of time with the Company's founder and chairman (who was also the prior CEO) and key directors before the meeting and knew we had the founder's support and enough director votes before we went in. The CEO was given the opportunity to respond, which he declined, and was provided a fair severance package and immediate outplacement support.

With the change made at the top, things began to fall into place. The new CEO brought in, sometimes with our help, new managers where needed. He recommended promotions and recognition for loyal middle managers. The founder and chairman was placed in a position of higher visibility. We commenced a cooperative process of addressing the Company's liabilities and leveraging its assets.

One change that was dramatic in impact and relatively easy to implement was removing the physical clutter that had built up in the offices over the years and was highly visible after the contraction. It not only gave a less than professional appearance to the Company's customers and vendors but also served as a depressing reminder to the employees of the layoffs and other negative baggage of the past. Another change along the same lines was to remove most of the physical barriers between management and the rest of the Company, which, coupled with an open door policy, started producing better communications.

The Company went on the offensive against the bad publicity by setting up a number of "road shows" to promote the system and spread the word about our commitment and new management. The reviews were favorable and a sales pipeline began to develop. The customer that had been waiting for a viable sponsor to emerge ordered the system and the installation was successful. Another installation, which had been waiting in the wings, proceeded with a great deal of care and was successfully completed.

The process of attacking the liabilities continued. As noted earlier, the Company's hardware supplier converted most of the trade debt into equity equivalents, and the senior officer who served as a director worked with the Company toward making it a success. A subtenant for the empty space in the Company's building was located and placed in the building in conjunction with a plan to pay discounted back rent. The negotiations were difficult, sometimes frustrating, but the Company kept pushing and closed on them.

Dealing with litigation was more challenging. At the time we commenced our involvement, there was one lawsuit by a former customer in progress. As sometimes happens, there was bad blood on both sides and the litigation had taken on a life of its own. The Company's professional liability insurance carrier was equivocating about coverage and was not paying defense costs. Since the Company believed a recovery against it might not be covered by insurance and it had no money to contribute to a settlement, it felt it had no alternative but to fight. We took a hard look at the insurance coverage issue with a partner in one of our outside law firms who specialized in coverage issues, determined that the Company was under the wrong impression, and began a successful negotiation with the carrier on paying defense costs and contributing to a settlement. At the same time, we were presented with a combative plaintiff having no inclination to settle on a reasonable basis. An end run was required to change that. The plaintiff had been a "failed bank" and was under the operation of one of the federal regulatory agencies. We began to communicate with the agency and brought home the theme that we were trying to be reasonable, but that plaintiff's counsel seemed more interested in keeping the litigation alive than obtaining a reasonable resolution. Eventually that positioning had the desired effect, and with the participation of the Company's carrier and commitments from Safeguard, the Company was able to put this dispute behind it.

One of the changes we advocated for the Company was discarding the former "all things to all people on their schedule" approach and adopting a practice of setting reasonable priorities.

That new approach has helped the Company in general and specifically in dealing with threats of litigation. The disciplined approach has been to make all reasonable attempts to address the issues generating the threats and to demonstrate that, despite any perception of broken promises in the past, the system not only works but should be viewed as a crucial strategic tool. This approach has been productive with customers interested in solving their system problems, but it has not met with unqualified success.

Almost as soon as it became known publicly that the Company had a sponsor with deep pockets, two disgruntled former customers, which had not previously commenced litigation, made multimillion-dollar claims against the Company. Safeguard officers met with those banks and explained we had adopted a policy that our investment of new funds would be used only to assure the success of the Company, not to buy off claims from the past. Their response was "pay or we sue." Without Safeguard the Company might have collapsed under the threats, but we have the resources to deal intelligently with litigation. We let them know that unless their posture changed, we would see them in court. The suits are being dealt with by a litigation team put together by the Company and Safeguard. The customers' basic claims are that the system was not finished and did not work when they contracted to buy it five years ago, and they have conveniently overlooked that they knew that the system was not fully operational and had never been installed in institutions of their size. The Company believes they were sophisticated customers that must bear responsibility for their actions in the relationship, and that the claims will be resolved on a basis very favorable to it in the three to five years it will take to get to trial. The litigation has not, as threatened by the claimants, hurt the Company's sales efforts. Instead the Company has successfully negotiated the sale of its new product to an industry-leading institution in exactly the same contractual posture as the claimants. That product is being installed as this chapter is being written.

As noted earlier, six months of intense effort went into converting the substantial amount of debt on the Company's balance sheet into equity. The challenge was to persuade a number of investors (who are largely concerned with getting their invested money out of the Company with a reasonable rate of return and in short order) to convert debt into long-term preferred equity when the future of the Company is uncertain.

Fortunately, the advances the Company had made since we became involved alleviated at least some of the investors' concern over the future of the Company. It helped also that our continued funding of the Company had been made through a third series of subordinated convertible debentures, which were on equal footing with the Primary Debentures and senior to the Secondary Debentures, so a collective commitment by Safeguard and the investors to convert to equity would be an advantage for the investors.

After a lot of thought, analysis, imagination, and discussions with the investors, Safeguard was able to design and propose to the Company two new series of preferred stock, which we believed could address everyone's legitimate concerns. The first series (Series A stock) was designed to provide the holders the right to participate, through dividends, in a significant percentage of the Company's annual net earnings once the Company surpassed a significant cumulative earnings threshold. The threshold served to insure that the Company would be in a position to accumulate sufficient working capital before cash began to exit through the dividend payments. The dividends were also subject to a progressive cap, which increased each year the Series A stock remained outstanding. After eight years (equivalent to the maturity date of the Senior Debentures), if the stock had not been redeemed previously, a special dividend would be paid equal to the lesser of (1) a percentage of the Company's earnings for the five prior years or (2) the maximum dividend that would otherwise have been payable that year under the progressive cap, net of any prior dividends. The Series A stock was not convertible; but its mandatory redemption features were designed to cash the holders out if the Company, measured by different criteria, could do so and continue to retain viability. Importantly, the Series A was given a liquidation preference over the second series of preferred stock (Series B stock) proposed. The series B stock was expressly subordinated to the Series A stock also in respect to dividends. However, it offered favorable conversion rights to common stock and voting rights far superior to the Series A stock.

The two series were offered to the investors in an exchange offer that gave them and Safeguard the opportunity to swap any of the debentures for either Series A stock or a package of Series B stock and common stock. To help effectuate the exchange, the Company requested and received the agreement of its hardware supplier (which owned debentures but did not wish to participate in the offer) that, in the event the assets of the Company were sold within the year following the exchange offer, its liquidation preference would be treated as equivalent to the liquidation preference of the Series A stock.

Another important selling feature was Safeguard's willingness to exchange its debentures for the Series B stock and, thereby, provide the investors interested in the Series A stock a liquidation advantage that would not exist if the exchange offer was not successful. Since we are confident of the success of the turnaround, we were comfortable with our belief that, despite the loss of the preference, the greater long-term value will be found in the Series B stock. We felt also that it was crucial to making the recapitalization work.

The investor group, when presented with a fair plan that will give the Company some breathing room and reward the investors for their patience, has reacted favorably. All of the other investors elected to exchange for the Series A stock and Safeguard, as promised, elected to take the Series B stock.

The hardware platform issue has emerged as the most significant problem the Company now faces. While the Company has been successful in making four sales in the past year (after none in the prior 18 months), the perception in the market that the hardware on which the system operates may have no long-term future has been accelerated and reinforced by the highly publicized problems at several minicomputer makers, including the Company's supplier, during the summer of 1989. That development has chilled revenues, since buyers do not want to invest in a hardware system with a limited future unless they are comfortable that the system software will operate in the future on a major vendor's hardware platform. The Company knows it must respond to the market by implementing a translation of the system to the hardware the market feels comfortable with. The challenge is that the translation will take at least a year and will be a multimillion-dollar project, which the Company is not in a position to fund.

Fortunately, at the same time that the Company approached two minicomputer manufacturers to fund a translation of the system, the vendors started to realize that the Company's system was the best on the market and could help generate significant hardware sales. Safeguard was able to add credibility to the Company, because of our successes and contacts in the software business. One manufacturer is particularly interested in gaining market share in the banking business and has provisionally committed to fund a major portion of the translation project. One of the world's most reputable systems integrators has been sufficiently impressed by the Company and its products to offer to participate as project manager in the translation project. The arrangement is market-driven, in that a customer must decide to purchase the system on that hardware before funding commences, and the Company is confident that the decision will be made shortly.

CONCLUSION

In retrospect, we believe that the responses of the Company and Safeguard to the issues that existed at the time we decided to proceed with the turnaround have not only brought it back from the dead but have transformed it into a highly professional systems management business. We also believe that the turnaround efforts to date have positioned the Company to be able to deal with, and avoid becoming submerged by, the difficult issues any business on the edge of automation technology will face. The potential of the Company has now begun to be fully realized.

CHAPTER 6

TAX CONSIDERATIONS OF AN OUT-OF-COURT OR CHAPTER 11 REORGANIZATION

Peter J. Gibbons
Carmen R. Eggleston
Price Waterhouse

INTRODUCTION

The tax consequences from an out-of-court settlement or Chapter 11 filing can be significant and may impair a debtor's restructure plan if not carefully considered. In general, the tax considerations for an out-of-court settlement and a Chapter 11 filing are similar; however, more beneficial provisions are available for the company that has filed for bankruptcy. The restructuring or discharge of debt obligations and the voluntary (or involuntary) transfer of property in payment of debt have tax consequences for the debtor. Since the debtor is already experiencing financial difficulty, an unexpected tax liability or loss of tax attributes can wreak havoc on its financial condition. The filing of a bankruptcy petition also impacts the priority of the payment of taxes and interest or penalties associated with those taxes.

This chapter will discuss in general terms the tax consequences to the debtor resulting from debt restructuring or asset transfers. There is also discussion of Internal Revenue Code Section 382 about how a change of ownership can result in the loss or severe limitation of the debtor's tax attributes such as net operating loss carryforwards.[1] There is discussion of some of the complexities faced by a consolidated group of corporations when one or more of the members or ex-members file bankruptcy. In addition, there is a discussion on the resulting tax consequences to the creditor of the company from these actions. Taxation of debt forgiveness income is analyzed for solvent, insolvent, and bankrupt debtors. This chapter does not discuss the complexities that may face an individual who files bankruptcy. The term *bankruptcy* is used throughout for a Chapter 11 filing, since the Internal Revenue Code does not distinguish between the types of filings available under Title 11. The chapter is current as of October 8, 1990.

TAX CONSEQUENCES TO THE DEBTOR

Transfers of Assets in Satisfaction of a Debt Obligation

Nonrecourse Debt
The tax consequences of transferring an asset in satisfaction of a debt obligation depend in part on whether the debt is recourse or nonrecourse. In general, when property is acquired using nonrecourse debt financing, the property is the sole security for repayment of the loan. In contrast, when recourse debt is used, the creditor can hold the borrower personally liable for the debt in addition to holding a security interest in the property.

When property subject to nonrecourse debt is transferred in satisfaction of the debt obligation, the transaction will be treated as a sale or exchange for tax purposes. Tax gain or loss will be recognized by the debtor equal to the difference between the deemed sales price and the debtor's adjusted tax basis in the asset. The debtor will be deemed to have sold the property to the lender for the face amount of the debt.[2] The fair market value of the property at the time of disposition is not relevant in determining the amount realized.[3] Even if the fair market value of the property is less than the debt it secures, the full face value of the debt is treated as proceeds from the disposition.

If the fair market value of the property is less than the debt it secures, a portion of the debt has not been repaid and the debtor is generally no longer liable. This does not, however, generate forgiveness of debt income to the debtor, because the full face value of the debt is used to determine the sales price of the property. All of the debtor's potential gain on the transaction is recognized through the deemed sale of the property to the lender.

The debtor's adjusted tax basis in the asset includes the amount paid for the property, including the nonrecourse financing, plus costs of capital improvements to the property and capitalized interest and taxes, less any depreciation claimed on the property.[4] If the property is depreciable property, the debtor will typically realize a gain because of the past depreciation deductions.

Example 1

Debtor acquired an office building in 19x5 for $4.4 million. He paid $.4 million cash and obtained a $4 million nonrecourse note. The building was deeded back to the lender in 19x6 when its fair market value was $3 million. No principal payments had been made on the note. The adjusted tax basis of the building was $2.8 million due to $1.6 million of depreciation. The debtor will realize a gain of $1.2 million ($4 million − $2.8 million). Note that the fair market value of the property was ignored in the gain calculation.

The character of the gain or loss recognized by the debtor depends upon the nature of the asset in the debtor's hands. If the property is held as inventory for sale to customers in the ordinary course of business, the gain or loss will be ordinary. If the asset is used in the debtor's trade or business, the gain or loss will be treated as a Section 1231 gain or loss. Any other gain or loss will be treated as capital.[5]

Depreciation recapture provisions may apply to Section 1231 gain.[6] Prior depreciation deductions are recaptured as ordinary income to the extent of the gain. Any remaining gain in excess of the recapture is Section 1231 gain. All Section 1231 transactions for the year are netted. In general, if there is a net gain, it is treated as capital gain; if there is a net Section 1231 loss, it is treated as ordinary.[7]

Accrued but unpaid interest may be treated as a component of the face value of debt, depending on the creditor's rights to collect the interest. If the property securing the debt is the only security the lender can look to for payment of the interest, it will be considered part of the debt principal and will be included in the amount realized on the deemed sale of the property.[8] However, if the lender can also look to the debtor's other assets for payment of the interest, the interest will not be considered a component of the face value of the debt.

Recourse Debt

When property subject to recourse debt is transferred to a lender to pay off debt, the tax consequences depend upon the value of the property at the time of conveyance. The deemed sales price realized by the debtor will be the fair market value of the property.[9] The property is considered sold at its fair market value, rather than the face amount of the loan, because the debtor has personal liability for any remaining balance considered unpaid. This result is not changed if the debtor is relieved of his personal liability upon the transfer of the property. The realized gain or loss on the property will be the difference between the fair market value of the property and the debtor's adjusted tax basis. The adjusted tax basis includes the amount paid for the property, including the recourse financing, plus costs of capital improvements to the property and capitalized interest and taxes, less any depreciation claimed on the property as discussed above.

If the value or sales price of the property equals or exceeds the remaining loan balance, the debt will be paid off in full, with any excess returned to the debtor. If the sales proceeds are less than the remaining loan balance, the debtor may realize debt forgiveness income.[10] Debt forgiveness income will be recognized if the creditor does not enforce its right to repayment or the debtor is otherwise discharged from liability. The timing of the recognition of the debt forgiveness income is discussed on page 159.

Example 2

A debtor and lender structure an agreement whereby the lender receives in a deed in lieu of foreclosure an office building in full satisfaction of a recourse loan. The outstanding loan balance was $4 million and the fair market value was $3 million. The adjusted tax basis of the building at foreclosure was $2.8 million. On the transfer of the property, the debtor will realize a gain of $.2 million ($3 million − $2.8 million). The debtor will also have debt forgiveness income of $1 million ($4 million − $3 million).

When there is an asset transfer in satisfaction of recourse debt, it may be possible to realize both income and loss from one transaction. If in the above example, the debtor's basis in the property was $3.5 million, he would have a loss from the sale of the asset of $.5 million and discharge of indebtedness income of $1 million. Thus, the debtor would have generated $1 million of taxable income as a result of the asset transfer. The $.5 million capital loss generated would provide a tax benefit only to the extent of capital gains generated by other transactions. This result is likely to happen when the property is not depreciable, such as land held for future development that has declined in value lower than the outstanding debt.

The character of the gain or loss on the asset sale will be governed by the same rules as described for property subject to nonrecourse debt. Debt forgiveness income is ordinary income but may be eligible for special exclusions from taxable income based on a troubled debtor's financial condition, discussed below.

The total of the gain or loss on a transfer in satisfaction of a debt obligation does not change depending upon whether the debt is nonrecourse or recourse debt. The timing of the recognition of the income and the nature of the income (gain on sale of the property versus debt forgiveness income) will vary. These variances can significantly alter the tax consequences to the debtor since debt forgiveness income is subject to special rules and may be deferred or eliminated.

Debt Forgiveness Income

In General
The receipt of a loan does not generate taxable income for the borrower. When the borrower does not repay 100 percent of the loan proceeds, however, debt forgiveness income is generated. As a general rule, cancellation of debt generates taxable income for the debtor equal to the excess of the face amount of the indebtedness over the amount paid for its discharge.[11] If a debt is discharged with no payment, the entire amount of the debt is income. If debt is

satisfied by the transfer of an asset, the transaction is treated as if the asset were sold and the proceeds used to pay off the debt as discussed earlier. Section 108 provides three exceptions to this general rule. Income is not currently recognized when debt is discharged in a Title 11 case, when the taxpayer is insolvent, or when the debt is qualified farm indebtedness.

Qualified Farm Indebtedness
The Technical and Miscellaneous Revenue Act of 1988 amended Section 108(a)(1) by adding subsection (c) to exclude discharge of qualified farm indebtedness from gross income. Section 108(g) provides that a solvent farmer may exclude debt forgiveness income incurred directly in connection with the operation of the trade or business of farming or debt on property used or held in the trade or business of farming. The amount excluded cannot exceed the sum of the taxpayer's adjusted tax attributes and the aggregate adjusted bases of qualified farm property held by the taxpayer as of the beginning of the taxable year following the taxable year in which the debt is discharged.[12]

Insolvency
For income tax purposes, a debtor is insolvent when his liabilities exceed the fair market value of his assets. All of the taxpayer's debts are included in this calculation, except for contingent debt.[13] Even if a taxpayer owes amounts on a nonrecourse debt that is secured by property with a value less than the debt, the full value of the nonrecourse debt is included. All of the debtor's assets subject to the creditor's claims are valued for this calculation. Assets such as goodwill, management contracts, customer lists, and other intangibles must be considered, even if they are not reflected on the debtor's financial statements.[14] The debtor's insolvency is determined on the basis of the taxpayer's assets and liabilities immediately before discharge.[15] The debt forgiveness exclusion is limited to the amount of insolvency. Any debt forgiveness in excess of insolvency is currently recognized as income.

Example 3

Corporation X has $8 million of assets and $10 million of liabilities immediately before $1.5 million of the liabilities are forgiven. X will recognize no income from the discharge of indebtedness because the amount discharged is less than its insolvency. Corporation Y has the same assets and liabilities immediately before $2.5 million of its liabilities are forgiven. Y will recognize debt forgiveness income of $.5 million because the forgiveness exceeded the insolvency ($2.5 million debt forgiveness minus $2 million insolvency).

Interest

If interest was relieved in addition to principal, the debtor will recognize debt forgiveness income if he had previously deducted the interest expense and received a tax benefit from the deduction. For example, an accrual basis taxpayer deducts the interest expense as it accrues, rather than when the interest is actually paid. Since the debtor has received benefit of a tax deduction for an expense he will never pay, he must recognize debt forgiveness income upon relief from the liability to pay the interest. If the debtor did not deduct the interest expense or did not receive a tax benefit from the deduction, the relief of the liability will not generate debt forgiveness income. As discussed on page 156, accrued interest that is treated as a component of the face value of nonrecourse debt does not generate debt forgiveness income if it is relieved. Instead, it is treated as additional proceeds received with respect to the underlying property transferred.

Tax Benefit Rules

No income is recognized from the discharge of indebtedness to the extent that payment of the liability would generate a future tax deduction.[16] This provision is important because, in many reorganizations, one of the liabilities renegotiated is future rent or lease payments. To the extent these liabilities are reduced, no debt forgiveness income is generated. Also, under this rule, a cash basis taxpayer will not realize debt forgiveness income from the discharge of debt attributable to expense items such as interest, compensation, and utilities. Section 111 provides that recovery of an item that did not reduce tax liability in a prior year will not be included in taxable income. Therefore, if the debtor had expired net operating losses or paid alternative minimum tax, the forgiveness of a previously deducted amount may generate little to no debt income forgiveness. A deduction that arose in a taxable year in which there is an unexpired carryover will be deemed to have reduced tax liability, and thus the discharge income will be included in taxable income.[17] This result is not adverse, since the taxable income generated should be offset by the carryover amount.

Timing of Recognition
The timing of the recognition of income resulting from the cancellation of debt depends on the facts and circumstances of each individual situation. In general, the recognition of income may result from some identifiable event,[18] such as an agreement between the debtor and lender satisfying the debt,[19] the date of the judicial approval of a settlement,[20] or the running of the statute of limitations barring collection.[21] If the lender does not pursue the debtor or the debtor has no intention of paying, then income should be recognized in the year of nonpayment. If the debtor intended to pay but was later unable to pay, the income should be recognized in the year of the inability to pay.

Reduction of Tax Attributes
To the extent debt forgiveness income is excluded from the debtor's taxable income, there generally will be a corresponding reduction of the debtor's tax attributes.[22] Therefore, the effect is not a permanent exclusion of the income but a postponement of the debtor's gain. The benefit to the debtor is that he does not recognize currently the discharge of indebtedness income but recognizes the income later through a larger gain or smaller loss when the debtor's property is subsequently depreciated or sold. Most debtors will prefer this postponement, because of the obvious economic benefit of a deferral of tax obligations.

The debtor's tax attributes are reduced in the following order:

    a. Net operating losses incurred in the year of the discharge.
    b. Net operating loss carryovers to the year of the discharge.
    c. General business credit carryovers ($0.33 reduction per dollar of exclusion).
    d. Capital losses and capital loss carryovers.
    e. Basis of taxpayer's assets.
    f. Foreign tax credit carryovers ($0.33 reduction per dollar of exclusion).

The $0.33 reduction in the carryovers listed at *c* and *f* above is to compensate for the fact they offset tax due versus the other attributes that offset taxable income. The ordering of the reduction of tax basis of assets is prescribed by the regulations under Section 1017. The reduction is applied first to assets purchased with the proceeds; second, to property subject to a lien securing the indebtedness; third, to other long-term assets of the creditor; last, to accounts receivable and inventory. Even if inventory or accounts receivable were purchased with debt or are subject to a lien, they are always in the last category.

Example 4

A debtor and lender structure a loan workout whereby the lender receives a deed in lieu of foreclosure on an office building. The outstanding recourse loan balance is $4 million and the fair market value of the building is $3 million. The adjusted tax basis of the building is $2.8 million. The debtor is insolvent to the extent of $.8 million and the lender relieves the debtor of any further liability. The gain on the sale of the building is $.2 million ($3 million − $2.8 million). The gain from debt forgiveness is $1 million ($4 million − $3 million). The determination of the amount of debt forgiveness income that must be recognized currently is:

Gain from debt forgiveness	$1,000,000
Less: Amount insolvent	(800,000)
Recognized debt forgiveness income	$ 200,000
Required tax attribute reduction	$ 800,000

Before reducing the attributes listed above, the debtor's tax liability for the year of discharge must first be calculated. This allows a debtor to fully utilize her tax attributes in the taxable year of debt forgiveness. Therefore, if a debtor has gain assets that will be disposed of shortly, she should consider disposing of the assets in the taxable year of debt discharge so as to have her tax attributes fully available. Reductions in the bases of a taxpayer's assets will take effect as of the first day of the taxable year after the discharge of indebtedness takes place. The bases of the aggregate assets cannot be reduced below the debtor's remaining liabilities.[23] If the taxpayer does not have sufficient tax attributes to be reduced, or the reduction is limited by the outstanding liabilities, the excess is eliminated. There is no requirement to reduce future tax attributes or the tax basis of future assets acquired.[24]

Example 5

Z has assets with a fair market value of $19 million and liabilities of $26 million. Debtor corporation Z restructures its bank debt and realizes debt forgiveness income of $6 million. Z has a net operating loss of $4 million and its tax basis in its assets is $21 million. Since Z is insolvent immediately after the discharge, the full $6 million debt forgiveness is excluded from income. Since the debt forgiveness will not be recognized as income, Z will reduce its tax net operating loss to zero and allocate $1 million of basis reduction among its assets ($21 million tax basis in assets less $20 million liabilities). The remaining $1 million of debt forgiveness income disappears.

As an alternative to the order of the reduction in tax attributes described above, a taxpayer may elect to reduce the basis of depreciable property by all or a portion of the amount excluded.[25] The amount of the basis reduction is not limited by the remaining liabilities but may not exceed the tax basis of the depreciable assets. The basis reductions will be applied as of the beginning of the next taxable year. Basis reduction under these provisions is not a disposition; however, when the reduced basis property is disposed of, any gain related to the basis reduction will be subject to the depreciation recapture rules and will likely be ordinary income.[26] Once made, the election can only be revoked with the consent of the Secretary of the Treasury.

Example 6

Debtor corporation X has the following assets and liabilities:

	Tax Basis	FMV
Cash	$ 2,000,000	$ 2,000,000
Accounts receivable	18,000,000	12,000,000
Inventory	40,000,000	10,000,000
Depreciable property	15,000,000	5,000,000
Land	2,000,000	1,000,000
	77,000,000	30,000,000
Liabilities	$50,000,000	$50,000,000

The depreciable assets are real property with a life of 31.5 years. X has a net operating loss carryforward of $20 million. X restructures its debt and is relieved of $20 million. Since X is insolvent, the debt forgiveness income is not recognized. X makes the election to reduce the basis of the depreciable property first. X can choose to reduce the basis of the depreciable property in any amount up to $15 million, which is the actual tax basis of the property. X makes the maximum election. As a result, the depreciable basis is reduced from $15 million to zero and the remaining $5 million of debt forgiveness reduces the net operating loss carryforward.

By reducing the basis of the depreciable property, X has preserved a loss carryforward to shelter income earned after the reorganization and will instead recognize the $15 million debt forgiveness over the 31.5-year life of the depreciable assets.

The election is only available with respect to the taxpayer's depreciable property. Depreciable property includes property used in a trade or business or property held for the production of income. The allocation is limited to property for which a basis reduction would reduce the amount of depreciation or amortization for the next taxable year. Depreciable property also includes a partnership interest to the extent of such partner's proportionate interest in the depreciable property held by the partnership.[27] A parent company that files a consolidated tax return with its subsidiary may treat its interest in the subsidiary stock as depreciable property to the extent the subsidiary consents to reduce the depreciable basis of its assets.[28] In addition, a debtor may make an election to treat real property that is considered inventory in the hands of the debtor as depreciable property.[29] Once this election has been made, it may only be revoked with the consent of the Secretary of the Treasury.[30]

Restructure or Modification of Existing Debt

In General
Restructuring a troubled loan frequently involves modification of the underlying debt. Restructuring may include agreements between the debtor and lender to change the interest rate on the debt, defer or forgive interest payments, defer or forgive principal payments, extend the maturity date, change debt covenants, modify conversion features, change security provisions, or any combination of these changes.

Debt restructuring involves a variety of technical tax considerations. One issue is whether the modification is treated as an exchange of the old debt for a new debt instrument. If the restructuring is treated as an exchange, the debt modification may be a taxable transaction for the debtor and the creditor. Depending on the type of change made, the tax consequences for the debtor can include debt forgiveness income and the creation of new original issue discount (OID). The creation of OID will provide the debtor with future noncash interest deductions at the expense of having to recognize current debt forgiveness income.

In each situation, it will be necessary to determine whether the modification constitutes an actual or deemed exchange of the existing debt for new debt or is simply a continuation of the old debt under modified terms. The IRS's position is that the substance of the transaction, rather than the form, controls.[31] Therefore, it does not matter whether the modification of the debt was accomplished by altering the existing debt instrument or issuing a new debt instrument.

Original Issue Discount (OID)

An exchange of debt instruments is governed by Section 1274. Under Proposed Regulation 1.1274-1(c), a modified debt instrument is treated as a new debt instrument if the modified debt differs "materially in either kind or extent" within the meaning of Regulation 1.1001-1(a) from the terms of the old debt. The proposed regulations under Section 1274 state: "A payment to or from the lender (or a successor) not provided for in the debt instrument shall be treated as a modification of the debt instrument."[32] This seems to suggest that any alteration, however small, from the original terms of the debt can result in treatment as a new debt instrument.

An outright reduction of the debt by forgiveness of unpaid principal or interest was previously not considered an exchange of debt. The IRS, though, in a recent Revenue Ruling has stated that a reduction in interest rate or the stated principal of a debt obligation results in a taxable transaction.[33] The IRS has also ruled that a reduction in the interest rate equal to one half of 1 percent is a material modification resulting in a taxable exchange.[34] It is likely that any modification of the debt instrument will be challenged by the IRS as a taxable exchange. The only modifications that may escape challenge are those that provide for a deferral of interest or principal payments, or both, where interest still accrues on the unpaid portion. The courts, however, have not upheld the IRS's position and have found certain modifications to not constitute a change.[35] Since it is the IRS's position that seemingly minor modifications do constitute a change, a debtor will need to review the costs of litigation as a factor in taking the position that the modification was not a taxable transaction.

When the old debt is deemed to have been exchanged for new debt in a taxable exchange, the debtor will realize debt forgiveness income if the present value of the sum of payments to be made under the new debt instrument is less than the present value of the sum of payments to be made under the old debt instrument.[36] This happens despite the fact the stated principal of the two obligations may be the same. Effectively, the provisions reduce the stated principal amount of the new obligation and recharacterize it as interest. Therefore, a deferral of payments or a reduction in the future interest rate to be paid may generate forgiveness of debt income. The present value is calculated using the rate paid on comparable term (short-term, mid-term, or long-term) marketable obligations of the United States. To the extent the debt forgiveness income is attributable to a reduction in the interest rate or a deferral of the payments, there should be new OID generated on the new obligation. This new OID will be a future noncash deduction for the debtor.

The OID rules do not address the consequences resulting from a reduction of a market rate of interest when the debt was originated to a new market rate at time of renegotiation. Presumably, if the difference in the value of the two debt instruments results solely from a decrease in the interest rate to a rate that is still a market rate, then debt forgiveness income may be avoided. This should result because of the exception to the recognition of debt forgiveness income for an amount that would have given rise to a tax deduction. Future interest payments would be deductible; thus, debt forgiveness income should not arise when these payments have been forgiven.

Example 7

Debtor corporation T borrows $2 million at a 15 percent rate which is a market rate of interest at the date of borrowing. Three years later, interest rates have fallen so T renegotiates the interest rate on the debt to 12 percent. The decrease in the interest rate of 3 percent should not give rise to debt forgiveness income since the payment of that interest would have given rise to a tax deduction.

The determination of OID on the new instrument is also dependent upon whether the exchange is taxable or is considered a tax-free recapitalization. If both the old debt and the new debt are considered securities, the exchange should constitute a tax-free recapitalization. In general, if the original maturity of the debt exceeds 10 years, it should be considered a security. If the original maturity is less than 5 years, it should not be considered a security. The status of instruments with maturities between 5 and 10 years is unclear. The maturity test is just a rule of thumb and not the sole criteria.[37] Each debt instrument must be evaluated for the overall nature of the debt to determine its classification as a security. Debt instruments that are long term and depend in some part on the future profitability of the debtor are more likely to be found to be securities. If the new instrument is considered a security, there is a limit to the amount of new OID generated in a reorganization.[38] The new OID will be equal to the lesser of the OID computed on the new debt without regard to a limitation or the OID remaining on the prior debt. If either the old debt or new debt instrument does not qualify as a security, the exchange will not be a tax-free recapitalization.

Example 8

Assume old debt has a face value of $1,000 and original OID of $100. At the date of exchange, $8 of this OID has been amortized. Therefore, the adjusted principal amount is $908. The new debt has a face value of $1,000 and a fair market value of $850, determined using the present value method. If either the old or new debt is not considered a security, new OID is generated in a taxable exchange. The adjusted principal value of the new debt would be $850 and the OID would be $150. The debtor would recognize debt forgiveness income of $58 ($908 minus $850) for the reduction of principal. However, if the exchange is considered a tax-free reorganization, the adjusted basis of the new debt will be $908, and the new debt will have the same $92 of OID that the old debt had. The debtor will not recognize any forgiveness of debt income, because the adjusted principal of the new debt equals that of the old debt.

The creation of OID from the debtor's perspective is not always negative. If the debtor has expiring net operating losses or losses that are restricted under IRC Section 382, creation of OID may be helpful. There will be debt forgiveness income generated equal to the amount of the new OID. If the debtor's net operating losses carry over but are limited under the change in ownership rules, the debt forgiveness income should reduce the loss carryover at little or no cost to the debtor. This will allow the debtor to take future interest deductions over the life of the new debt.

No Deemed Exchange
If the modification did not constitute an exchange of debt instruments, the debtor continues to account for the debt instrument as before. If the modification was to defer interest payments, the debtor would continue to deduct the interest under his method of accounting. A cash basis debtor would only deduct the interest when actually paid, and an accrual basis debtor would deduct it as it accrues. The accrual basis debtor should be allowed to continue to deduct the interest, even if the payment of the interest was questionable.[39] The only exception would be if the debt was nonrecourse and the fair market value of the property was less than the principal amount of the debt.[40]

Applicable High Yield Discount Obligations
The Revenue Reconciliation Act of 1989 enacted Sections 163(e)(5) and (i) in response to concern over the tax favored treatment of high yield debt obligations in a leveraged buyout. The new rules apply to specified debt instruments whether issued in conjunction with a leveraged buyout or not. These rules apply to certain debt instruments issued with substantial OID that do not pay interest currently or that permit payment of interest in the form of additional debt instruments or in stock. In general, an *applicable high yield discount obligation* (AHYDO) is treated similarly to preferred stock and is subject to three special rules. First, the issuer may not deduct the OID until it is actually paid, while the holder must accrue the interest income under the normal OID rules. Second, a portion of the issuer's OID deduction will be permanently disallowed but will still accrue as income to the holder. Third, a corporate holder of the debt may be allowed a dividends-received deduction for the portion

of the OID income recognized that equals the OID deduction permanently disallowed to the issuer.

In general, to be classified as an AHYDO, a debt instrument must have four qualifying characteristics; (1) the debt instrument must be issued by a corporation; (2) the instrument must have a maturity date more than five years from the date of issue; (3) the yield to maturity equals or exceeds the sum of the applicable federal interest rate plus five percentage points; and (4) the debt instrument has significant OID.[41] The determination of significant OID is complicated and not clear-cut. Generally, if the payment of interest is substantially deferred, significant OID will result. Measurement of the significant OID is made at the time of issue and is based on the terms of the instrument assuming any payment required to be made is made on the last day permitted under the instrument.[42] Therefore, the determination of whether or not a debt instrument has significant OID is based on the original terms of the instrument regardless of whether or when the interest is actually paid.

The issuing corporation's deduction is disallowed permanently for the disqualified portion of the OID that is the yield in excess of the applicable federal rate yield plus 6 percent. The deduction for the remainder of the OID is deferred until the interest is paid. Payment with new or baby debentures or payment in stock is not considered payment for these purposes. Therefore, one of the benefits for the debtor for issuing instruments with OID has been eliminated. The debtor can no longer receive the beneficial cash flow from currently deducting the accrued OID.

Example 9

On January 1, 19x1, X corporation issues an AHYDO at an issue price of $100 and a yield to maturity of 20 percent when the applicable federal rate is 9 percent. The total return on the debt for the first year is $20 ($100 issue price times the 20 percent yield to maturity). The applicable federal rate plus 6 percentage points is 15 percent. Therefore, the disqualified yield is 5 percent (20 percent yield to maturity minus 15 percent). The ratio of the disallowed portion of the yield to the yield is 25 percent (5 percent disqualified yield divided by 20 percent yield to maturity). Therefore, the disqualified portion for the first year is $5 ($20 return for the year times 25 percent). The remaining $15 deduction is deferred until it is actually paid.[43]

This provision is generally effective for debt instruments issued after July 10, 1989. It does not apply to refinancings of debentures originally issued before July 11, 1989, provided that the refinancing does not extend the maturity date of the original instrument or result in an issue price that exceeds the adjusted issue price of the instrument. In addition, the refinancing cannot increase the stated redemption price at maturity or decrease the interest payments required to be made before maturity. If a bankruptcy reorganization plan had been filed before July 11, 1989, the provision also does not apply to an instrument issued after July 10, 1989, pursuant to a bankruptcy plan of reorganization provided the terms of the instrument do not exceed the required terms as specified in the reorganization plan filed before July 11, 1989.

Conversion of Debt to Equity

Prior to the Bankruptcy Tax Act of 1980, case law provided an exception to the general rule of debt forgiveness income. In the case of a corporate debtor issuing stock in satisfaction of its indebtedness, no cancellation of debt income was recognized. The exchange of stock for debt was considered to represent a continuation of the existing liability in a different form. The Bankruptcy Act of 1980 codified this rule with certain limitations. Congress's intent was that the provision of favorable tax treatment would encourage reorganization, rather than liquidation, of financially distressed corporations that had the potential for survival.

However, Congress did stipulate that this exception to the general debt forgiveness rule would not apply if only a de minimis amount of stock were issued. The de minimis exception was created so that the recognition of debt forgiveness income could not be circumvented.[44] The definition of what constitutes a "nominal or token" number of shares is somewhat vague. However, in IRS Technical Advice Memorandum (TAM) 8837001, the IRS looked to the legislative intent behind the provision and ruled that the determination should be based on the economic substance of the exchange and the creation of a real equity interest. If the debt for equity exchange is a sham that does not create a meaningful substitution of liability such that the creditor does not receive a real equity interest in the corporation, the equity for debt rule would not apply.

The stock involved in the TAM was not considered nominal or token because the interests on each side of the exchange were adverse, the value of the stock was significant in relation to the discharged debt, and the total consideration received by the creditors was almost twice the estimated liquidation value of the debtor.

With the enactment of the Deficit Reduction Act of 1984, Congress limited the equity for debt exception to a debtor in bankruptcy or to the extent the debtor is insolvent.[45] Now, a solvent corporate debtor must recognize debt forgiveness income when it issues stock for outstanding debt to the extent the outstanding debt exceeds the fair market value of the stock. The effect of this provision is to treat the solvent debtor as if he had satisfied the debt with an amount of money equal to the fair market value of the stock.

The IRS issued Revenue Ruling 90-87 which limits the stock for debt exchange where preferred stock with a set redemption and liquidation price is issued.[46] The stock for debt exception was ruled to apply only to the extent of the set redemption and liquidation price.

To the extent debt forgiveness income is not created under this exception, there is no required tax attribute reduction. This results because literal reading of the statute provides that the debt is deemed satisfied in full. This exception then is very beneficial for the debtor, since it avoids the recognition of debt forgiveness income both currently and in the future. By limiting this exception to debtors who have filed under Title 11 or to the extent the debtor is insolvent, Congress has created a strong tax incentive for a corporation to file for bankruptcy.

Example 10

Debtor corporation R has $8 million of assets, liabilities of $15 million and a net operating loss of $7 million. R negotiates a settlement to pay the creditors 65 cents on the dollar. If the payment is made in cash or cash and notes, R will realize $5.25 million of debt forgiveness income. Because R is insolvent, the debt forgiveness will not be recognized currently but will instead reduce R's net operating loss. If R had structured the settlement to be 30 cents in cash and 35 cents worth of common stock, no debt forgiveness income would be recognized nor would there be a reduction to the net operating loss.

Purchase Money Debt Reduction

Another exception to the debt forgiveness income rule provides that a purchase-money debt satisfied at a discount will be treated as a purchase price adjustment for a solvent taxpayer, rather than debt forgiveness income.[47] When a seller reduces the indebtedness incurred by a debtor in purchasing specific property, the purchaser does not recognize income but reduces his basis in the specific property to the extent of the debt reduction. This reduction in basis will also decrease any allowable depreciation and will increase any gain or decrease any loss to be recognized on the ultimate disposition of the property. If the debt or the property has been transferred to a third party, legislative history suggests that this purchase-money debt reduction exception does not apply. Presumably too, if the property has been depreciated below the amount of the forgiven debt, this exception to debt forgiveness income would be limited to the depreciable basis.

Example 11

X purchased property from Y for $.7 million, $.1 million was paid in cash and a note for $.6 million was given. X subsequently had cash flow problems and renegotiated the debt to $.5 million. X does not recognize taxable income from the debt forgiveness of $.1 million, but the basis of the property is reduced by $.1 million.

While the statute provides this exception only for solvent taxpayers, insolvent or bankrupt taxpayers may get the same result to the extent the unrecognized debt forgiveness income is applied to reduce the debtor's basis in his property.[48] This exception provides some benefit if the purchase property is long-lived property or is nondepreciable, such as land. The exception does not apply if the purchased property is inventory or accounts receivable.[49]

Acquisition of Debt by a Related Party

When a related party acquires the debtor's outstanding indebtedness, the debt will likely be treated as acquired by the debtor, rather than by the related party.[50] The law states that, to the extent provided by regulations, an acquisition of a debtor's debt by a related party will be treated as if acquired by the debtor. To date, no regulations have been issued. There has been one news release issued in 1982 and one court case applying the law in an individual setting.[51] The Congressional Committee reports for the legislation enacting this provision contain several examples of legislative intent. It is expected that, when the regulations are issued, they will require the related party acquisition to be treated as an acquisition by the debtor in almost all circumstances, and the regulations will be retroactive. The following example illustrates the legislative intent.

Example 12

Assume a parent corporation purchases for $900 on the open market a $1,000 bond issued at par by its wholly owned subsidiary. The subsidiary must account for a debt discharge amount of $100 for its taxable year during which the debt was so acquired. In the following year when the debt matures, the subsidiary pays its parent the full principal amount of $1,000. The subsidiary is treated as paying off $900 in debt and having paid a dividend of $100 to its parent corporation.[52]

Based on the news release issued in 1982, any exception to this general rule is expected to require three things. First, the debt was acquired in the ordinary course of the related party's trade or business. Second, the related party disposes of the debt in its ordinary course of business. And third, the related party does not transfer the debt to the debtor or any other related person.

The following persons are treated as a related party for purposes of this provision: (1) a member of a controlled group of corporations of which the debtor is a member as defined under Section 414(b); (2) a trade or business under common control with respect to the debtor as defined under Section 414(b) and (c); (3) either a partner in a partnership treated as controlled by the debtor, or a controlled partnership with respect to the debtor as defined under Section 707(b)(1); or (4) a member of the debtor's family within the meaning of Section 267(b). The definition of family for this purpose includes a spouse, children, grandchildren, parents, and spouse of a debtor's child or grandchild. It does not include brother-sister family attribution.

Acquisition of Debt by a Shareholder

If a shareholder acquires a corporation's debt and contributes it to the corporation, the corporation will be treated as if it satisfied the debt with an amount of money equal to the shareholder's adjusted tax basis in the debt.[53] Therefore, if the shareholder acquired the debt at a discount, and contributes it, the corporation will recognize debt forgiveness income equal to the discount.

This provision is not dependent on the timing between the acquisition of the debt and its contribution to the debtor. Therefore, when a shareholder who has held debt for a substantial number of years contributes it to a corporation, it will result in the debtor being treated as satisfying the debt in an amount equal to the shareholder's adjusted tax basis in the debt. This happens even if the fair market value of the debt is substantially lower than the shareholder's adjusted tax basis. Thus, for a shareholder who has a tax basis at or near face value of the debt, a contribution of the debt will avoid debt forgiveness income.

Change of Ownership—Section 382

In General
Congress has long been troubled by the acquisitions of loss companies whose sole or principal value results from their tax net operating loss carryforwards. Therefore, the Tax Reform Act of 1986 made significant changes to the rules regarding the availability of net operating losses and other tax attribute carryforwards for the companies in which a substantial change in ownership has occurred. These rules are extremely complex and a full discussion of them is beyond the scope of this chapter.[54] This discussion will highlight the rules and the provisions that are relevant to a troubled company.

In general, if there has been a 50 percentage point change in the loss company's stock ownership over a three-year period (testing period), the carryforward of certain losses and credits is limited. The annual limitation is equal to the long-term tax-exempt bond rate times the value of the loss company's stock immediately before the ownership change. The limitation determines the amount of tax attributes that can be applied against the company's annual income.

Because the value of a troubled company is usually not significant, this limitation can be severe. In addition, the annual limitation will be zero if the loss company does not continue its business enterprise at all times during the two-year period after the change date.[55] The test of the continuation of business enterprise will be met if the new owner continues the historic business of the loss corporation or if a substantial portion of the loss corporation's assets are used in the trade or business of the ongoing corporation.

Determination of Ownership Change

The stock of the company is divided into groups: each individual shareholder who directly or indirectly owns 5 percent or more of the company during the testing period and one or more "public groups." A public group consists of all the individual shareholders who directly or indirectly own less than 5 percent of the company. In general, there is an ownership change if the percentage of stock owned by a 5 percent owner (including a public group) increases in the aggregate by more than 50 percentage points over the lowest percentage of stock owned during the prior three years. There are special rules for determining 5 percent shareholders and for the aggregation and segregation of the shareholders in the public groups that are beyond the scope of this chapter. These rules are written harshly to find an ownership change whenever possible. Generally, with some modification, the constructive ownership rules of IRC Section 318 apply in determining stock ownership.[56] Stock owned by corporations, partnerships, or other entities is treated as owned proportionately by the individual owners.[57] Stock held by an individual is aggregated with stock owned by all family members and treated as owned by one person.[58] An option to acquire stock is considered stock if such treatment would result in an ownership change.[59]

The option attribution rule is applied selectively in a manner generally very unfavorable to the taxpayer. The rule only applies if it would create an ownership change. It is applied separately to each 5 percent owner and separately to each class of options. It is possible that the exercise of all outstanding options would not produce an ownership change, but the selective application of this rule would produce a change. In such case, only the selective options are deemed exercised.

Example 13

A and B own all the outstanding stock of X corporation. A owns 90 shares and B owns 10 shares. X issues options entitling each shareholder to purchase 15 additional shares of stock for each share owned. An ownership change has occurred. If B exercised his options and A did not, B would own 160 of the outstanding 250 shares of stock. B would increase his ownership percentage by more than 50 percentage points, causing an ownership change.

A similar rule applies to any contingent purchase, warrant, convertible debt, put, stock subject to risk of forfeiture, contract to acquire stock, or similar interests. Even if such option is contingent or not currently exercisable, an ownership change may occur because the contingency is ignored and the stock is deemed exercised at the date of grant.[60] Thus, if a loss corporation gives a creditor convertible debt, with a conversation ratio that is under water, the debt will be deemed to be converted at date of grant if the conversion would result in an ownership change.

If an option or similar instrument that generated a change in ownership lapses unexercised, or the owner irrevocably forfeits his right to acquire stock from the instrument, the option will be treated as if it had never been issued.[61] If this makes Section 382 limitation inapplicable, an amended return may be filed subject to the statute of limitations.

Consequences of an Ownership Change

The prechange tax attributes that are limited by Section 382 include but are not limited to net operating losses, built-in losses, and capital losses. Built-in losses are losses that have occurred economically but have not yet been realized for tax. For example, a tract of land purchased for $10 million that is now worth $6 million has a built-in loss of $4 million.

Any carryforward losses that are limited in any postchange year will be carried forward to the next postchange year until the loss is utilized or the carryforward expires. Thus, while not explicitly providing for the denial of loss carryforwards, the statute effectively treats some losses as disallowed, since they can never be utilized before expiration.

Example 14

Company S has a net operating loss of $2.5 million, which will expire in 10 years. S experiences a Section 382 change of ownership and the resulting annual Section 382 limitation is $.1 million. The loss may be utilized at $.1 million each year until it expires, for a total of $1 million. The Section 382 limitation results not only in the deferral of the utilization of the loss carryforward but in the expiration of $1.5 million of unused loss.

The limitation is based on the fair market value of the stock of the loss company immediately before the change.[62] If a redemption or other corporate contraction occurs in connection with an ownership change, the value of the corporation shall be determined after taking into account the redemption or contraction.[63] Any capital contributions made for the principal purpose of avoiding or increasing the Section 382 limitation will not be considered. Except as provided in regulations, any capital contributions made during the two-year period ending on the change date will be considered as made for the purpose of increasing the corporation's value and, thus, will be subtracted from the corporation's value.[64] This "anti-stuffing" rule is intended to prevent a loss corporation from circumventing Section 382 by increasing the value of the corporation with capital contributions immediately before a change occurs. As of publication date, no regulations have been issued, so all capital contributions within the prior two years may have to be excluded. It is expected when the regulations are issued they will provide an exception for capital contributions made for working capital or other business needs. Hopefully, these regulations will be retroactive.

If the new loss corporation has substantial nonbusiness assets, the value of the old loss corporation will be reduced by the excess of the value of the nonbusiness assets over the indebtedness attributable to those assets.[65] Nonbusiness assets are assets held for investment and not as an integral part of conducting the trade or business. A loss corporation has substantial nonbusiness assets if at least one third of its total assets are nonbusiness assets.

Elective Bankruptcy Rule
The Section 382 limitation may be escaped by a corporation in a Title 11 bankruptcy proceeding or a receivership, foreclosure, or

similar proceeding in a federal or state court. If the shareholders and creditors of the old loss corporation before the change own at least 50 percent of the voting power and value of the stock immediately after the change, then the general limitation rules of Section 382 do not apply even though there is an ownership change.[66] For purposes of this exception, only certain creditors are considered. The creditor must have held the debt for at least 18 months before the Title 11 or similar case or the debt must have arisen in the ordinary course of the old loss company's trade or business, and it must be continually held by the original creditor.[67] This limitation results in little benefit for a company with publicly traded debt, since, typically, as the company starts experiencing financial difficulties, there is extensive trading of its debt instruments. To determine whether 50% or more of the stock is held by shareholders and qualified creditors, the option attribution rules discussed on page 174 are applied. Specifically, options and similar interests will be deemed to be exercised if they cause the 50 percent test to be failed.[68]

Several special rules apply to the corporation implementing this bankruptcy exception to the Section 382 limitation. These rules apply a toll charge for the use of this exception. The prechange loss carryforwards must be recomputed as if no deduction were allowed for interest paid or accrued by the old loss corporation on indebtedness that will be converted into equity in the Title 11 proceeding. The interest is disallowed for each of the three taxable years preceding the taxable year in which the ownership change occurs and the prechange portion of the taxable year in which the ownership change occurs.[69] In addition, a corporation must reduce its tax attributes by 50 percent of any debt forgiveness income not recognized due to the exchange of debt for equity.[70] This provision partially revokes the exclusion of debt forgiveness income for bankrupt corporations, discussed earlier. Indebtedness for interest accrued but not paid by the old loss corporation that is converted to equity is not considered in reducing the tax attributes.

Since the general rule that the business enterprise must continue for two years after the ownership change is not applicable when the bankruptcy exception is utilized, the IRS issued Proposed Regulation Section 1.269-3(d). This regulation provides that unless the corporation continues to carry on more than an insignificant amount of an active trade or business during or subsequent to the bankruptcy filing, any acquisition of control of the company will be presumed to be for the principal purpose of the evasion or avoidance of income taxes. Strong evidence to the contrary will be needed to overcome the presumption. If the presumption cannot be overcome, the tax attributes will be eliminated.

Under this special bankruptcy rule, if the new loss corporation has another change of ownership within two years after the first change in ownership, the new Section 382 limitation will be zero.[71] In addition, based upon a literal interpretation of the statute, the bankruptcy exception rule will not apply to the first ownership change. This would result in a retroactive repeal of the beneficial bankruptcy provision. There is no definitive guidance about the congressional intent in drafting this provision. Until regulations are issued, there is exposure that a second ownership change will result in a retroactive repeal of the beneficial provisions for the first. Presumably, amended returns would have to be filed for the prior year returns.

If the bankruptcy exception rule does not apply to a company in Title 11 or similar case, the value of the company's stock is increased by any debt forgiveness for purposes of calculating the Section 382 limitation.[72] A loss corporation may elect out of the bankruptcy exception rule and have the regular Section 382 limitations apply.[73] A company may elect out of the exception if the increase in the limitation due to the increased value of stock from the debt forgiveness would be more beneficial than the 50 percent exception for debt forgiveness income. A company may also elect out of the bankruptcy exception if the creditors and shareholders were not willing to retain control of the company for two years. In this case, the limited loss carryforwards would be preferable to the complete disallowance upon the subsequent ownership change and possible retroactive repeal of the allowance for the first change.

ESOP Exception
The 1989 Tax Act repealed the exception to the ownership change rules for an employee stock ownership plan (ESOP). Previously, if an ESOP acquired 50 percent or more of the loss company, the increase in the stock ownership attributable to the ESOP was not counted in determining if an ownership change occurred.[74]

Forgiveness of Debt in Consolidated Groups

Frequently, troubled companies may not be independent but may be part of a consolidated group. One or more members of the consolidated group may be financially troubled. Usually, the related companies will have intercompany outstanding debt as well as different outside creditors. The existence of the consolidated group and related party debt complicates the tax implications of restructuring debt or realizing debt forgiveness income.

If a subsidiary has previously filed consolidated returns with its parent and subsequently files bankruptcy, it must continue to file as apart of the consolidated group.[75] However, if the affiliated companies have never previously filed a consolidated return, the bankrupt company will be prevented from filing a consolidated return.[76] The bankrupt member will continue to be a part of the consolidated group unless and until an actual change in stock ownership occurs that removes it from the group. The general rule for inclusion is ownership of 80 percent or more of the total vote and the value of the debtor corporation.[77]

Prior to the issuance of Treasury Decision 8924, the consolidated return provisions allowed for a loss when intercompany debt and stock became worthless. Now Treasury Decision 8924 provides that no loss can be claimed by the consolidated group on the worthless stock of a consolidated subsidiary. These rules are harsh because they do not allow for economic losses. They were soundly criticized during public hearings and may be modified to allow for true economic losses.

A recent bankruptcy court decision has also denied a parent company the ability to write off its subsidiary's stock.[78] Section 382 provides that, if a parent company writes off the stock of its subsidiary, it will be treated as a sale of the stock of the subsidiary on the last day of the taxable year and a reacquisition of it on the first day of the next taxable year.[79] The effect of this provision is to disallow the net operating losses in full, because the parent has just valued the company at zero. The bankruptcy court stated the net operating losses were assets of the subsidiary's bankruptcy estate and that the parent could not take any action to diminish the value of the asset. If the provisions of T.D. 8924 are repealed or loosened so that a parent is able to realize a loss on the write-off of its subsidiary stock, then there can be a conflict between tax law and this bankruptcy decision. For tax purposes, the loss on the stock must be claimed in the year it becomes worthless. If the stock becomes worthless while the subsidiary is still in bankruptcy, then the parent may be precluded from writing it off.

When filing a consolidated return, the members of the consolidated group are severally liable for the consolidated tax liability.[80] Thus, if one member of the group does not pay its allocated liability, other members of the group will be held accountable for payment of income tax liability allocated to the nonpaying member. Reg. Section 1.1502-6 provides for some limitations when a member leaves the consolidated group, but then states the limitations will be ignored if the full collection of the tax is in jeopardy. The parent of the consolidated group is the party responsible for paying the tax to the IRS and is also the responsible party in meeting and negotiating tax liability with the IRS. Thus, when a member has left a consolidated group and subsequently files bankruptcy, the former parent still continues in its role as negotiator with the IRS.

The debt forgiveness rules of IRC Section 108 are applied separately to each member of a consolidated group. The IRS, though, may be considering using regulations that would apply the provisions on a consolidated basis. Application on a separate company basis may be beneficial if one member has debt forgiveness that exceeds its tax attributes. For example, Z corporation has debt forgiveness of $1 million. Its tax attributes total $.75 million. The tax attributes are reduced to zero, and the excess debt forgiveness of $.25 million is eliminated. It does not reduce the tax attributes of another member in the consolidated group. However, separate application may be negative for the stock for debt exception. It would likely not apply if stock of the parent is given in exchange for debt of the subsidiary. The group may be forced to give stock of the parent, since the parent must own 80 percent or more of the subsidiary to continue filing consolidated tax returns.

The Section 382 limitations are also applied separately to each member of a consolidated group. However, the IRS is considering adopting regulations that would apply Section 382 on a consolidated basis. Until then, there is no clear-cut guidance on the application of the annual limitation. Is it done on a company-by-company basis or on a group basis? Regulations are expected to be issued by the end of 1990. In addition, the bankruptcy exception applies only if the company is in bankruptcy. Thus, if a subsidiary has filed, but its parent has not, the exchange of its parent's stock for debt won't meet this provision. If the parent has filed, then it will meet the provision, but, as just discussed, the stock for debt exception for debt forgiveness income may not apply. In addition, the statute is not clear about whether, in this circumstance, the subsidiary's creditors are combined with the parent's for purposes of determining the parent's 50 percent ownership test.

Bankruptcy Filing

General Tax Consequences
When a corporation or partnership files bankruptcy, a separate estate is created for bankruptcy purposes. However, this estate has no tax significance because it is not considered a separate taxable entity.[81] The corporation or partnership continues as the taxable entity even if a bankruptcy trustee is appointed. The corporation's tax attributes and taxable year remain unchanged by the bankruptcy proceeding. An individual filing bankruptcy is treated differently. The individual's bankruptcy estate is considered a separate taxpayer from the individual.[82] There are numerous tax considerations that arise when an individual files bankruptcy, which are beyond the scope of this chapter.

Typically, upon emerging from bankruptcy, the reorganized corporation will have either undergone a recapitalization or "E" reorganization and preserved its original corporate charter or transferred its assets to a new corporation in a transfer subject to the "G" reorganization provisions.

Debt Forgiveness Income
The special provisions regarding the nonrecognition of debt forgiveness income for a bankrupt debtor apply if the debt discharge is pursuant to a plan approved by the bankruptcy court.[83] Therefore, it is not sufficient that the discharge or forgiveness occurs during the period of the filing; the discharge must be pursuant to an approved plan or be granted by the court.

Example 15

Troubled Corporation filed for Chapter 11 protection on October 1, year 1. On February 4 of year 2, Troubled was able to negotiate a settlement with a secured creditor, whereby the secured creditor foreclosed on the property securing their debt and did not seek to file a proof of claim for the portion of their debt that exceeded the value of the property securing the indebtedness. When the debtors submitted their plan of reorganization to the court on December 12 of year 2, their plan did not include this transaction, since the transaction was completed. As a result, the debt discharge may not be discharged by the court, or pursuant to a plan approved by the court. Therefore, exposure exists that the debt forgiveness income would not be excluded pursuant to the bankruptcy exception.

In contrast to the insolvency exception, the amount excluded under this provision does not depend on the debtor's financial status. A solvent taxpayer who has filed Chapter 11 is entitled to exclude 100 percent of the debt forgiveness income from taxable income. This exception requires a tax attribute reduction described on page 159. See also page 158 for discussion of the tax benefit rule.

Federal Tax Claims
When a bankruptcy petition is filed, notice is automatically given to the IRS by the bankruptcy court. Generally, secured debts are satisfied first in bankruptcy. Then unsecured claims are satisfied in order of priority, as specified in Section 507 of the Bankruptcy Code. Administrative expenses are given highest priority among the unsecured debts. Most taxes incurred while the bankruptcy proceedings are in progress are considered administrative expenses and given highest priority. These priority taxes include income taxes, employee's withholding taxes, employer's share of employment taxes, tax penalties, interest on unpaid taxes, property taxes, excise taxes, and any claim attributable to an excess allowance of a quickie refund (such as a tentative net operating loss carryback) that was made after the filing of bankruptcy.

Claims incurred in the ordinary course of the debtor's business after an involuntary bankruptcy petition but prior to the appointment of a trustee or the entering of the formal order of relief are given second priority. Any taxes arising during this "involuntary gap" are second priority claims.

Third priority claims are unpaid wages earned within 90 days prior to filing of the bankruptcy petition to the extent of $2,000 per individual. Employment taxes related to these wages are also given third priority. Wages and related taxes earned prior to the 90-day period and in excess of the $2,000 limit would not receive any priority and would be classified with other unsecured claims.

Most other taxes owed to the federal government or a state or local taxing authority are given seventh priority in the bankruptcy proceedings. Seventh priority unsecured tax claims include income taxes incurred prior to bankruptcy filing for tax years with returns due within three years before the bankruptcy filing, income taxes assessed within 240 days prior to the bankruptcy filing, assessable income taxes that have not yet been assessed, and such compensatory penalties as the penalty for failure to withhold employment taxes. Any other tax claims not given a priority status would be classified with other general unsecured claims. Prebankruptcy interest has the same status as the associated tax. Postbankruptcy interest on both priority and nonpriority tax claims is given last priority.[84]

The Bankruptcy Code states that all unsecured taxes with priority must generally be paid in cash on the effective date of the Chapter 11 plan, with two exceptions. Seventh priority plans may be satisfied with deferred payments over a period not exceeding six years from the date the tax liability was assessed. Since the time period allowed to defer payments begins with the assessment of the tax, the deferral may be for much less than six years after the effective plan date for an early assessment date. The deferred payment must provide for a payment of interest to cover the cost of not receiving payment at the effective date. Alternatively, the bankrupt corporation may request an extension of time for payment under the provisions of IRC Section 6161(c) for 18 months, or up to 30 months in exceptional cases. The commencement of a bankruptcy proceeding gives the debtor a stay against issuances of assessments. The IRS can only issue an assessment if it gets the approval of the bankruptcy court. Priority tax claims against an individual are not dischargeable in a bankruptcy proceeding.[85] A corporation under

Chapter 11 can receive a discharge of a priority tax claim, but only if it is provided under the confirmed plan.[86]

The running of the statute of limitations on assessment and collection of tax from the debtor is suspended during the period of the bankruptcy.[87] The suspension of the statute is also operative for refund claims filed.

"G" Reorganization Provisions

A "G" reorganization is a transfer by a corporation of all or part of its assets to another corporation in a Title 11 or similar case, but only if, in pursuance of the plan, stock or securities of the new corporation to which the assets are transferred are given to the debtor's shareholders or qualifying creditors.[88] Assets must be transferred pursuant to a plan that has received approval of the court.[89] The business enterprise of the debtor corporation must be continued or a significant portion of the business assets must be used in its business after the transfer.[90]

If a reorganization qualifies as a "G" reorganization, the debtor corporation will generally not recognize gain or loss on the receipt of stock or securities of the other party to the reorganization.[91] A distribution of property to creditors is considered a distribution in pursuance of the plan of reorganization.[92] If substantially all the assets are transferred in a "G" reorganization, the acquiring corporation will succeed to and take into account the tax attributes of the transferor corporation, including the net operating loss carryforwards.[93] In addition, the basis of property acquired in a "G" reorganization will carry over to the transferee and may be increased to the extent any gain is recognized by the transferee on the transfer.[94] No loss will be recognized.

The important thing to note here is the requirement of a "G" reorganization that the creditor(s) transfers stock or securities of the debtor and receives, in exchange, stock or securities of the new corporation. If the creditor's debt is long term, it may qualify as a security, and, thus, the exchange will be tax free. If a creditor's debt is short term, it will likely not qualify, and the creditor's exchange will be taxable (see discussion on page 191). Thus, some creditors may receive tax-free treatment while others may have taxable transfers. The important test for the debtor is if the majority of the equity and security holders of the new corporation were security or long-term debt holders of the debtor (continuity of interest test)[95] then the transfer should qualify as a "G."

The creditors in a "G" reorganization holding debt that qualifies as a security generally will not recognize gain or loss on the exchange of their debt instrument. The two exceptions to this general rule are: (1) the creditor receives stock in exchange for accrued interest or (2) the principal value of the new instrument exceeds the principal value of the old instrument.[96]

Recapitalization or "E" Reorganization

When a corporation exchanges stock for its outstanding debt, the exchange may be treated as an "E" reorganization which is tax free. There are no specific provisions that must be met for the exchange to qualify as an "E" reorganization. The only limitation is that the debt should qualify as a security. As discussed before, this typically means it should have a life in excess of 5 years and preferably 10 years. The regulations give three examples of "E" reorganizations. These examples are not the only exchanges that qualify as an "E" reorganization, but rather they illustrate the types of exchanges that qualify. The first example is an exchange of debt securities for preferred stock. The second is an exchange of preferred stock for common, and the third is an exchange of common for preferred stock.[97]

"E" versus "G" Reorganization

Prior to the Tax Reform Act of 1986, a corporation would try to meet the requirements of a "G" reorganization upon emerging from a Chapter 11 proceeding. The reason for this was that tax rules provided for a more liberal allowance of the loss carryforwards than if the corporation had merely restructured itself using the "E" reorganization provisions. Now the Tax Reform Act of 1986 has eliminated the advantage of "G" reorganizations, and a recapitalization may be more beneficial. Theoretically, it should not matter whether creditors take control of a debtor corporation by capitalizing their debt or by creating and acquiring a new organization. However, this is a situation where form controls over substance.

A "G" reorganization can be difficult to achieve if few of the creditors hold an interest that qualifies as a security for the distribution requirements, if the reorganization lacks continuity of interest, or if the business enterprise is not continued. If these provisions are not met, then tax attributes, such as net operating loss carryover, would not survive the transfer. In a recapitalization, no continuity of interest or continuation of the business enterprise is required. It does not matter what creditor gets securities or equity interests to preserve the tax-free status of the debtor. The Section 382 limitation applies to both reorganizations equally. In addition, where the acquiring company files a consolidated return with one or more subsidiaries, the consolidated return separate-return-limitation-year (SRLY) rules that limit the utilization of losses of one member against another member's income will apply to a "G" reorganization, thereby further limiting the usefulness of the losses. The SRLY limitations do not apply in a recapitalization. For these reasons, a recapitalization may be more beneficial than a "G" reorganization.

Liquidating Trusts

Liquidating trusts may serve as a means to hold assets of the failing company for the benefit of its creditors. The troubled debtor may wish to sell its assets to pay its creditors, but the assets may not be easily sold except at unfavorable prices. The trustee is given the power to dispose of the assets in a reasonable time frame, with the proceeds going to the beneficiaries and to preserve the assets in the interim. In general, liquidating trusts are used where illiquid assets can only be converted into cash over a period of time.

For example, a company has agreed to a plan of bankruptcy reorganization with its creditors and shareholders. Pursuant to the plan, specified assets are to be set aside for the benefit of the unsecured creditors. These assets are not in high demand and would be difficult to sell rapidly except at distressed prices. Therefore, the assets are distributed to a liquidating trust, which will take the time to sell them at reasonable prices and distribute the proceeds to the creditors who are now the trust beneficiaries.

The major tax question involved in liquidating trusts is whether the trust will be considered a trust or a corporation for taxation purposes. A distinction is made between true liquidating trusts and business trusts. Business trusts are created to operate a profitable business and are taxed as corporations. In a business trust, the trustee has managerial power over the trust assets. If the trustee administers the assets in a trade or business, the trust will be considered a corporation. Even if the trustee does not use this managerial power, its mere existence will cause the trust to be taxed as a corporation.

A liquidating trust is organized for the primary purpose of liquidating and distributing the assets transferred to it, and its activities are all reasonably necessary to, and consistent with, the accomplishment of that purpose. It is treated as a trust for tax purposes because it is not designed to carry on a profit-making business, which would normally be conducted through corporations or partnerships.[98] The management powers of the trustee must be very limited for the trust to qualify as a liquidating trust.

Liquidating trusts are generally treated as grantor trusts. The trust is a pass-through entity, and all taxable events pass through to the grantor. If the debtor retains a reversionary interest in the trust, the trust income should be taxable to the debtor.[99] If the debtor does not retain a reversionary interest, the grantors should be the creditors who will benefit from the trust. It should be noted, however, the transfer of the assets to a liquidating trust in which the debtor has no reversionary interest may be considered to be a taxable event. This would trigger gain or loss to the debtor equal to the difference between the fair market value of the property and the debtor's tax basis in the property. The liquidating trust then would have a fair market value basis in the acquired assets.

OTHER DEBTOR TAX CONSIDERATIONS

Partnership Considerations

A partnership that files bankruptcy does not create a separate taxable entity, which was discussed before. Instead, the partnership continues to pass through to its partners all items of income and deductions. The special provisions for the treatment of debt forgiveness income depend on the taxpayer's status as insolvent or under bankruptcy proceedings. Since a partnership passes out all of its taxable income to its partners, the special provisions for debt forgiveness depend upon the financial status of the partner and not the partnership. Therefore, the filing of a bankruptcy proceeding by a partnership will not allow the individual partners to exclude the debt forgiveness income from taxable income and instead reduce their tax attributes. They may exclude the debt forgiveness only if they themselves are insolvent or in bankruptcy proceedings.

One significant consideration in restructuring the debt of a partnership is the impact to the individual partners. Many of the partnerships that were organized in the late 1970s and the early 1980s were funded with a substantial amount of debt. This debt allowed the partners to take deductions for losses for which they had not paid. A partner is entitled to deduct losses equal to his investment in the partnership plus his allocated share of partnership liabilities.[100] The result is that these partners typically have a negative investment in the partnership. The restructure or outright settlement of the partnership liabilities can create taxable income for the partners from two different sources. First is the creation of the debt forgiveness income, which will likely be recognized in full by the partners. Second, and probably the bigger consideration, is the recapture of the partner's negative investment in the partnership. Once the debt is restructured or settled, the partner's allocated liabilities are reduced by his proportionate share of the debt discharge or settled. If the sum of his recomputed liabilities plus investment is negative, the partner must recapture, as income, an amount sufficient to bring the sum to zero.[101] For many of these partnerships, restructuring the debt will generate substantial income for the partners.

Another significant consideration about a partnership is the allocation of income and deductions among the partners. Many partnerships allocate income and deductions in different percentages. In addition, many partnership agreements do not specifically provide for the allocation of debt forgiveness income. If the partnership agreement does not specify the allocation of debt forgiveness income and provides different ratios for the allocation of income and deductions, the partners who reported the deductions attributable to the debt may not be the partners who report the debt forgiveness income. Also, if there has been a loss on the transfer of an asset in satisfaction of a debt obligation, the partners who report the loss may not be the same as the partners who report the debt forgiveness income.

Example 16

Partnership AB has two partners, A and B. Income is shared 50/50 and losses are shared 90/10. AB purchased raw land for investment. The purchase price was $4 million and financed with $3.5 million of debt. The value of the land declined significantly, resulting in the partnership negotiating a settlement with the lender whereby the lender would receive the land valued at $1.5 million and continue to hold debt of $1 million. The partnership has a loss on the transfer of the land of $2.5 million ($4 million purchase price less $1.5 million value) and has $1 million debt forgiveness income ($3.5 million original debt less $1.5 million payment less $1 million debt left). The income and loss recognized by each partner would be as follows:

	A	B
Debt forgiveness income	$ 500,000	$500,000
Loss on transfer of land	−2,250,000	−250,000
Total	−$1,750,000	$250,000

(The loss on the transfer of the land will likely be capital and the debt forgiveness income will be ordinary, so the loss may not be able to offset the income.) This disparity in allocation results under the partnership agreement, even though the same transaction resulted in the recognition of the debt forgiveness income and the loss on the transfer of the land.

The filing of a bankruptcy proceeding by either the partnership or by one of its partners will not result in the termination of the taxable year of the partnership.[102]

S Corporation Considerations

An S corporation is a tax-advantaged corporation. It receives favorable tax treatment because it does not pay tax on its income. Instead, it passes through the taxable income or loss to its shareholders, who report the items in their individual returns.[103] To qualify for S corporation status, the corporation must be owned by individuals.[104] The filing of a bankruptcy proceeding by an individual transfers the ownership of the stock of the S corporation to a bankruptcy estate. A bankruptcy estate of an individual is deemed to be a qualifying shareholder; therefore, the bankruptcy filing by a shareholder of an S corporation will not result in the loss of the S status of the corporation.[105]

The bankruptcy filing or insolvency of an S corporation is similar to that of a regular corporation. So while an S corporation is similar to a partnership in that it passes out all items of income and deduction, the special treatment afforded debt forgiveness income depends on its financial status rather than the individual shareholder's.[106] Since an S corporation shareholder does not generally get to deduct losses from the S corporation based upon debt, there is not the same problem as with a partnership regarding the recapture of a negative investment in the entity.

If a restructuring S corporation wants to maintain its S status, it will be important to not give any equity interest to creditors that are not qualifying shareholders. In addition, it is also necessary to review the terms of any debt instruments given to creditors to ensure that the instruments would not constitute a second class of stock and, thus, disqualify the corporation from S status.

Alternative Minimum Tax and the ACE Adjustment

The discussion of the tax consequences and tax-attribute carryforwards has focused on the regular federal income tax and net operating loss carryforwards. A corporation may be able to avoid incurring a regular federal income tax but yet be subject to an alternative minimum tax. Alternative minimum tax is assessed at a 20 percent rate on a corporation's alternative minimum taxable income. This income is based on federal taxable income with certain adjustments and disallowance of expenses. Only 90 percent of alternative minimum taxable income can be offset by net operating loss carryforwards. For a corporate taxpayer, this will result in a tax rate of 2 percent for any year in which taxable income is generated (10 percent taxable income times 20 percent tax rate). Also, the alternative minimum tax net operating loss carryforward is typically less than the regular net operating loss carryforward because of disallowance of expenses and other adjustments to income. Thus with less losses to shelter income, alternative minimum tax will likely become payable before regular federal tax.

For tax years beginning after 1989, the alternative minimum tax adjustment is based upon "adjusted current earnings," or the ACE adjustment.[107] The Revenue Reconciliation Act of 1989 provides that debt forgiveness income not included in regular taxable income is also not included in ACE income.[108] Therefore, there should not be any adverse alternative minimum tax consequences from debt forgiveness income that was not recognized for regular tax purposes. The attribute reduction that occurs, because this income is not recognized, will also apply to reduce the alternative minimum tax attributes.

Acquisition of Profitable Company to Utilize Losses

Once a troubled company has been restructured and has maintained its tax attribute carryforwards, there may be thoughts to acquire a company that generates taxable income and cash flow. The company can fund its operations with the cash flow while avoiding paying tax on the income. No specific provisions disallow the utilization of the loss carryforwards, except for the general rule that if the principal purpose for the acquisition of a company is the evasion or avoidance of income taxes, then the losses will be disallowed.

However, if the thought is to acquire a company that has assets having a substantial unrecognized tax liability or built-in gain, there may be a limitation. The purpose for this type of acquisition from the restructured company's perspective is to purchase assets at a discount from fair market value because of the substantial tax liability, and then to use its tax-attribute carryforwards to shelter the liability. In 1987 Congress sought to limit the tax benefits of this type of acquisition with the enactment of Section 384. This section provides that if a loss company acquires a company with built-in gain, then that gain can only be offset by losses generated by the acquired company or future losses generated by the acquiring company. The threshold for the built-in gain limitation is the lower of 15 percent of the value of the gain corporation or $10 million.[109] Any net gain below this threshold is not subject to this limitation.

TAX CONSEQUENCES TO THE CREDITOR

Debt Modification

In General
A creditor will also realize tax consequences from a debt restructuring. The creditor can realize gain or loss on the deemed or actual

exchange of debt instruments, realize more interest income than provided under the agreement, and realize a bad debt deduction from forgiven principal. As discussed previously, debt modifications, such as changing the interest rate or the timing of the interest payment, providing for an equity kicker, or deferring principal payments, can result in the debt modification being treated as a taxable exchange of debt instruments. It does not matter if the exchange was made solely by means of modifying the existing debt instrument or entering into new agreements.[110]

The critical test is whether the creditor has received in substance an instrument that differs materially in kind or in extent to what he had before.[111] The mere fact that the new or modified instrument differs in value from the prior instrument is not conclusive in determining whether there has been an exchange. This is because the market value of the debt prior to the change is not determined solely by reference to the original terms of the debt instrument but also by the creditor's current financial condition. The determination that the exchange is taxable is not necessarily an adverse result. If the creditor will realize a loss on the exchange, it is better for the exchange to be taxable so the creditor can recognize the loss currently.

Original Issue Discount (OID)

The governing rules were issued in proposed format in April of 1986. Even though they are only proposed, they are indicative of the IRS's perspective on the treatment of debt modification. These rules alter significantly the ability to allocate payments between interest and principal. They require payments to be treated as interest to the extent of the accrued but unpaid interest on the debt. Next, payments are treated as prepaid interest to the extent designated by the parties. Finally, they are treated as payments of principal.[112]

The first test for the creditor is whether the exchange qualifies as a tax-free exchange. To qualify for tax-free treatment, the debt must be treated as a security instrument for tax purposes. A rule of thumb is that debt with a life of less than 5 years is not a security and, thus, will not qualify for the tax-fee treatment. Debt with a life over 10 years is usually a security for tax purposes and, thus, will likely qualify for tax-free treatment. The treatment for debt with a life between 5 and 10 years is unclear and depends on the characteristics of the instrument. The characteristics of the debt that are reviewed are those that delineate the amount and extent of the creditor's continuing interest in the affairs of the debtor and the risk associated with ownership of the instrument. If the interest is long term and dependent upon the future profitability of the debtor, it will be more akin to an equity interest and will likely qualify for tax-free treatment.

If a portion of the new debt is attributable to unpaid interest that has accrued during the creditor's holding period, then this portion of the new debt will not qualify for tax-free treatment.[113] This provision applies to original issue discount (OID) under the old debt instrument as well as interest called for under its term. The provision applies whether the creditor is on the accrual or cash basis method of accounting. As discussed earlier, payments first are allocated to accrued but unpaid interest. Therefore, the effect of these two provisions is to treat the portion of the debt attributable to interest as equal to 100 percent of the accrued but unpaid interest amount and to deny tax-free treatment on this part of the exchange. This forces the creditor to realize immediate income, regardless of the creditor's method of accounting and despite the fact that economically, the accrued but unpaid interest may have been forgiven in the terms of the exchange.

Example 17

Debtor had a note outstanding for $2,000 with a term of 20 years. The note has accrued but unpaid interest of $300. The note is renegotiated, with the creditor receiving a note with a new principal balance of $1,700. The $300 of interest will be deemed to be paid. If the exchange qualifies for tax-free treatment for the remaining portion of the debt, the creditor's basis in the instrument will be $2,300 ($2,000 original plus $300 interest). If the exchange does not qualify, then the creditor should realize a loss equal to $600 ($300 decrease in the principal of the debt and $300 of accrued interest, which will not be paid).

Both the new and the old debt need to qualify as securities for the exchange to receive tax-free treatment. In a tax-free exchange, gain realized on the exchange will be recognized by the creditor, only to the extent she receives property other than stock or debt that qualifies as a security. No loss will be recognized. Consequently, if other property is received and there is gain on the transaction, then the property is taxable to the extent of the lower of its fair market value or the gain on the exchange.[114] If the face value of the new debt is greater than the face value of the old debt, the excess in face value is treated as other property and, thus, may generate taxable gain despite the tax-free treatment.[115]

The face value of the debt is not determined by reference to the face value stated on the instrument. Instead, it is computed under the OID rules discussed previously (page 163). In a typical restructuring, the deemed face value of the new instrument is likely to be less than the deemed face value of the old instrument. Therefore, in the typical restructure, if the debt qualifies for tax-free treatment, the creditor would not be able to recognize a loss for tax purposes on the exchange.

If the exchange qualifies for tax-free treatment, no new OID will be created with respect to the new instrument. If the old instrument had OID, then it would continue to be amortized and included in income of the creditor as before. The creditor's basis and holding period for tax purposes in the debt will carry over. The basis will be increased for any gain recognized as a result of other property being transferred and decreased for any money or other property received.

If the exchange is taxable, the creditor will realize gain or loss on the exchange equal to the difference in value of the new instrument over his or her adjusted tax basis in the old instrument. The value of the new instrument is the present value of all payments due, including interest payments. Any loss will be recognized currently. In general, gain will be recognized on the installment basis as payments of principal (or deemed principal) are made. Gain will be recognized currently if the creditor elects out of the installment sale treatment or if the transaction does not qualify for installment sale treatment (e.g., if the debt is publicly traded).

Applicable High Yield Discount Obligation (AHYDO)
As discussed on page 166, the Revenue Reconciliation Act of 1989 was enacted to limit the use of high yield debt obligations in leveraged buyouts. The rules, however, were not limited to a leveraged buyout and apply to any high yield debt instrument. The main

impact to the creditor receiving this type of instrument is that a portion of the income may be eligible for the dividends received deduction. Thus, if the creditor is a corporation, it may be entitled to exclude 70 percent of the OID income recognized because of the dividends received deduction. The downside is that the creditor must still recognize the remaining OID income currently while the debtor has to defer his deduction until the interest is actually paid.

Property for Debt Exchange

When a creditor forecloses on property or receives property in a voluntary transfer, the exchange of the debt for the property is treated as a taxable exchange. It does not matter to the creditor if the debt is recourse or nonrecourse. The property received will have a tax basis equal to the fair market value of the property. Any excess of the amount of the debt over the value of the property will be a bad debt deduction for the creditor, unless the creditor is able to recover additional amounts from the debtor. The timing of the bad debt deduction depends on the creditor's rights with respect to recovering the deficiency on the debt, the debtor's ability to satisfy the deficiency, and the creditor's method of deducting bad debts for tax purposes.

A creditor that sold real property to the debtor, received a purchase money mortgage from the debtor, and reacquired the property in full or partial satisfaction of the debt is subject to special provisions. Generally, the creditor will not recognize gain or loss on the repossessing of the property and cannot claim a bad debt deduction. Instead, the creditor will recognize gain equal to the lesser of (1) the cash and fair market value of other property received before the repossession, to the extent this exceeds the gain reported prior to the repossession, or (2) the gain realized on the original sale reduced by the amounts previously recognized prior to repossession, plus amounts paid by the creditor in connection with the repossession. The basis of the reacquired property is the adjusted basis of the debt increased by the amount of any gain recognized plus amounts paid by the creditor in connection with the repossession.[116]

Example 18

The creditor sells property for $1 million in which his tax basis is $.8 million. The creditor receives $.1 million cash plus a note for $.9 million. The debtor makes several payments on the debt totalling $.1 million before the creditor repossesses the property. Prior to repossession, the creditor has recognized $40,000 ($.2 million cash times 20 percent) in gain and received cash of $.2 million. The creditor will recognize a gain of $.16 million ($.2 million less $40,000) on the repossession, and his basis in the reacquired property will be $.76 million [$.9 million original note less $.1 million payments less $40,000 ($.2 million original gain less $.16 million gain recognized)].

Stock for Debt Exchange

A stock for debt exchange may create tax consequences for the creditor. The question is whether the exchange qualifies for tax-free treatment. The test will be whether the debt qualifies as a security. As stated previously, debt with a life less than 5 years will likely not qualify. Debt with a life over 10 years will likely qualify for tax-free treatment. If the exchange qualifies for tax-free treatment, then the creditor's tax basis in the debt will carry over and become the basis in the stock acquired. If the transaction is taxable, the creditor will realize gain or loss on the transaction equal to the difference in the value of the stock compared to the creditor's tax basis in the debt. The gain or loss will be ordinary if the debt was entered into as a part of the creditor's trade or business. Otherwise, it should receive capital treatment.

Timing of the Bad Debt Deduction

The timing and character of the deduction for the nonpayment of debt depends on whether the debt qualifies as a security and is a nonbusiness debt or business debt. Nonbusiness debts must be completely worthless before a loss is allowed. Business debts can be deducted when they are partially worthless to the extent they are charged off during the year. Securites, if exchanged for an instrument qualifying as a new security, can result in deferral of gain or loss on the exchange.

When existing debt is exchanged for new debt or stock, the creditor realizes gain or loss on the transaction (except a tax-free exchange). There is no bad debt deduction. A bad debt deduction arises when existing debt is partially paid off with no current or future recovery or when the debt becomes completely worthless. The Internal Revenue Code does not define worthless. It generally has been interpreted to mean lacking current and future monetary value. If there is no current value but a prospect of future value, then the debt is not worthless. The filing for bankruptcy by a corporation may be indicative of its troubled status, but that may not be sufficient to allow for a bad debt deduction. If there will be partial payment to the unsecured creditors, then the deduction may be postponed until the confirmation of the reorganization plan. Only if a creditor will receive no payment does the filing of the bankruptcy plan prove the debt has become worthless.

If the creditor received stock in exchange for the debt and took a bad debt deduction with respect to the original debt, the stock is subject to recapture rules. Specifically, if the creditor realized gain on the disposition of stock, the creditor will have ordinary income equal to the lesser of the gain on the stock sale or the bad debt deduction. Any remaining gain would be eligible for capital gain treatment. This rule applies to any bad debt deduction taken whether before or during the reorganization proceeding. Likewise, the rule also applies to a partnership interest received in exchange for debt, where the debtor is a partnership, and to any income not recognized by the creditor because of its method of accounting.[117]

ENDNOTES

1. All section references in the chapter and IRC references below are to the Internal Revenue Code of 1986, and BC references are the Bankruptcy Code.
2. IRC Reg. Sec. 1.1001-2(a).
3. IRC Reg. Sec. 1.1001-1(b).
4. IRC Sec. 1011.
5. IRC Sec. 1221.
6. IRC Secs. 1245 and 1250.
7. IRC Sec. 1231.
8. *Allan v. Comm.*, 88-2 USTC, para. 9510 (CA-8, 1988).

9. IRC Reg. Sec. 1.1001-2(a).
10. IRC Reg. Sec. 1.1001-2(a)(1) and (2).
11. IRC Sec. 61(a)(12).
12. IRC Sec. 108(g)(3).
13. Connestoga Transportation [sic] Co., 17 TC 506 (1951).
14. Ibid.
15. IRC Sec. 108(d)(3).
16. IRC Sec. 108(e)(2).
17. IRC Sec. 111(c).
18. *Vanguard Recording Society v. Comm.*, 418 F.2d 829 (2d Cir. 1969), *K & S Electric Co., Inc. v. Comr.*, TC Memo 1969-291 (1969).
19. *U.S. v. Ingalls*, 399 F.2d 143 (5th Cir 1968), rev'g 272 F. Supp. 10 (N.D. Ala. 1967), and *Seay v. Comr.*, 33TCM 1406 (1974).
20. *Exchange Security Bank v. U.S.*, 492 F.2d 1096 (5th Cir. 1974), rev'g 345 F. Supp. 486 (N.D. Ala. 1972).
21. *North American Coal Corp. v. U.S.*, 97 F.2d 325 (6th Cir. 1938), aff'g 32 BTA 535 (1935), *Schweppe v. Comr.*, 168 F.2d 284 (9th Cir. 1948), aff'g 8 T.C. 1224 (1947).
22. IRC Sec. 108(b).
23. IRC Sec.1017(b)(2).
24. S. Rep. No. 1035, 96th Cong., 2nd Sess. (1980).
25. IRC Sec. 1017.
26. IRC Sec. 1017(d).
27. IRC Sec. 1017(b)(3)(C).
28. IRC Sec. 1017(b)(3)(D).
29. IRC Sec. 1017(b)(3)(E)(i).
30. IRC Sec. 1017(b)(3)(E)(ii).
31. Rev. Rul. 81-169, 1981-1 CB 429.
32. IRC Prop. Reg. Sec. 1.1274-1(c).
33. Rev. Rul. 89-122.
34. Rev. Rul. 81-169.
35. *Truman H. Newberry v. Comm.*, 4 TCM 576 (1945), Dec.14, 602, *Mutual Loan and Savings Co. v. Comm.*, CA-5, 50-2 USTC, para. 9420, 184 Fed. 161 (1950). Rev. Rule 53.
36. Rev. Rule 77-437, 1977-2, CB 28.
37. **See** Buttker and Eustice, *Federal Income Taxation of Corporations and Shareholders*, para. 14.31.
38. IRC Sec. 1275(a)(4).
39. Rev. Rul. 70-367, Technical Advice Memorandum 8642005, June 30, 1986.
40. S. Rep. No. 169, Vol. 1, 98th Cong., 2nd Sess. 225 (1984); GCM 39668 (Sept. 24, 1987).

41. IRC Sec. 163(e)(5) and (i)(3).
42. IRC Sec. 163(i)(3)(A).
43. H. Rep. No. 101-386, 101st Cong., 1st Sess. (1989).
44. IRC Sec. 108(e)(A).
45. IRC Sec. 108(e)(10).
46. IRB 1990-43.
47. IRC Sec. 108(e)(5).
48. Reg. Sec. 1.1017-1(a)(1).
49. IRC Sec. 1017(b)(3).
50. IRC Sec. 108(e)(4).
51. Announcement 82-138, IRB 1982-45.
52. S. Rep. No. 1035, 96th Cong., 2d Sess. 19,n.23 (1980).
53. IRC Sec. 108(e)(6).
54. Goldring and Feiner, "Section 382 Ownership Change," 66 *Taxes* 427 and 619; Silverman and Keyes, "An Analysis of the New Ownership Regs. Under Section 382," 68 *Journal of Taxation* 142 and 300, 69 *Journal of Taxation* H2.
55. IRC Sec. 382(c).
56. IRC Sec. 382 (l)(3)(A).
57. IRC Sec. 382(l)(3)(A)(ii)(II).
58. IRC Temp. Reg. Sec. 1.382-2T(h)(6).
59. IRC Sec. 382(l)(3)(A)(iv) and IRC Temp. Reg. Sec. 1.382-2T(h)(4).
60. IRC Temp. Reg. 1.382-2T(h)(4)(iii).
61. IRC Temp. Reg. 1.382-2T(h)(4)(viii).
62. IRC Sec. 382(e)(1).
63. IRC Sec. 382(e)(2).
64. IRC Sec. 382(l)(1).
65. IRC Sec. 382(l)(4).
66. IRC Sec. 382(l)(5)(A).
67. IRC Sec. 382(l)(5)(E).
68. Proposed Reg. Sec. 1.382-3(c)(1)
69. IRC Sec. 382(l)(5)(B).
70. IRC Sec. 382(l)(5)(C).
71. IRC Sec. 382(l)(5)(D).
72. IRC Sec. 382(l)(6).
73. IRC Sec. 382(l)(5)(H).
74. IRC Sec. 382(l)(3)(C)-R.
75. IRC Reg. Sec. 1.1502-75(a)(2).
76. IRC Reg. Sec. 1.1502-75(c),(d).
77. IRC Sec. 1504(a)(2).
78. *The Official Committee of Unsecured Creditors and Cold Spring Shipping, L.P.* v. *PSS Steamship Company, Inc.*, Bankr. S.D. NY, 107 Bankr. 832; 1989 Bankr.; 19 Bankr. Ct. Dec. (CRR) 1929.

79. IRC Sec. 382(g)(4)(D).
80. IRC Reg. Sec. 1.1502-6.
81. IRC Sec. 1399.
82. IRC Sec. 1398.
83. IRC Sec. 108(a)(1)(A).
84. BC Sec. 726(a)(5).
85. BC Sec. 523(a)(1).
86. BC Sec. 1129(a)(9)(c).
87. IRC Sec. 6503(b).
88. IRC Sec. 368(a)(1)(G).
89. IRC Sec. 368(a)(3).
90. IRC Reg. Sec. 1.368-1(d).
91. IRC Sec. 361(a).
92. IRC Sec. 361(b)(3).
93. IRC Sec. 381(a).
94. IRC Sec. 362(b).
95. IRC Reg. Sec. 1.368-1(b).
96. IRC Secs. 354(a)(2), 355(a)(3), 356(d)(2)(B), 351(d)(3).
97. IRC Reg. Sec. 1.368-2(e).
98. IRC Reg. Sec. 301.7701-4(d).
99. IRC Secs. 671-677, *In re Sonner* v. *U.S.*, USTC 85-2, para. 9810; *In re Holywell* v. *U.S.*, USTC 88-1, para. 9351.
100. IRC Sec. 704(d).
101. IRC Sec. 752(b), 731(a).
102. IRC Sec. 1399.
103. IRC Sec. 1366.
104. IRC Sec. 1361(b)(1)(B).
105. IRC Sec. 1361(c)(3).
106. IRC Sec. 108(d)(7).
107. IRC Sec. 56(c)(1)(B), 56(g).
108. IRC Sec. 56(g).
109. IRC Sec. 382(h)(3)(B)(i).
110. Rev. Rul. 81-169, 1981 CB 429.
111. IRC Reg. Sec. 1.1274-1(c).
112. IRC Sec. 1.446-2(d).
113. IRC Sec. 354(a)(2)(B).
114. IRC Sec. 356(a)(1).
115. IRC Reg. Sec. 1.356-3(a).
116. IRC Sec. 1038(c).
117. IRC Sec. 108(e)(7).

CHAPTER 7

LIQUIDATION OPTIONS FOR TROUBLED COMPANIES

*Francis J. King**
Partner
Price Waterhouse

INTRODUCTION

The relationship between a company and investors exists because of the ability of each party to satisfy the needs of the other party. The investor provides the company with the capital it needs to invest in plant, equipment, and operating assets. The company provides the investor with a means to apply his or her funds to the production of income and, therefore, with a return on his or her investment. The nature of the relationship between the investor and the company may take many forms. A traditional view of corporate finance would classify most investments as either debt or equity. In recent years, with the growth of highly leveraged financing and various forms of preferred stock, the traditional classifications have been somewhat obscured. Despite the recent trends in the capital markets, one major governing principle still holds: investors are motivated to provide their resources to a company by the prospect of receiving an acceptable return on their investment. What investors consider to be acceptable is determined by their perception of the riskiness of the investment.

---

* The author wishes to thank Steve Labrum, Yuli Tartakovsky, Jim MacCrate, and Bob Jones for their considerable assistance with the research and preparation of this chapter.

Risk may be described in several ways. At the most basic level, risk is simply the possibility that the investor will lose the money invested. A slightly more complex view of risk addresses the topic of volatility. A significant amount of financial and economic theory is based on the premise that an individual prefers to know that he or she will receive $100 a year from now, rather than having equal chances of receiving either $90 or $110. In terms of the expected return on an investment that an investor requires, additional compensation must be included to make the investor willing to bear uncertainty, all other things being equal.

The market relationship between risk and expected return leads to the need, from the perspective of an investor, to develop a means of assessing the risk associated with a prospective investment. One measure used is the *beta* of a common stock. The beta is a measure of the relative change in the value of a specific stock when the overall stock market moves higher or lower by a given increment. From an analytical perspective, it is useful to look beyond the beta and assess what characteristics of a company make it more or less risky than another.

The cash flow generated by a company is the most important measure of performance. Investors seek assurance that a company has sufficient cash not only to make payments of principal, interest, and dividends to investors but also to support the continued operations of the company. Investors are also interested in whether the company will have sufficient cash under various operating conditions. A company may prosper in times when its specific industry, or the economy as a whole, experiences expansion. However, prospective investors and lenders must evaluate whether the company will continue to have sufficient cash flow when conditions become adverse, such as when sales decline significantly or when the cost of raw materials increases sharply.

Seeing that the likelihood of a company's being able to generate sufficient cash flow is low, an investor or lender will perceive a greater degree of risk associated with the investment or loan. In response, the investor may either choose to seek an alternative investment or to negotiate for a high expected rate of return. As the perceived risk increases, the fundamental relationship between a company and the capital markets begins to break down. A point is reached at which money is either not available at all or is available only at interest rates that are very high and that will exacerbate the cash flow difficulties of the company.

When such a situation occurs, a company is often forced to abandon the capital markets and to look for other ways to generate the needed funds. The purpose of this chapter is to provide an analytic framework to identify and evaluate the options available to the management of a troubled company. This framework will address ways to use the assets of the company, through liquidation or refinancing, as a source of capital. When approaching the decision process, a manager will be faced with three central questions:

- Which assets may be used to generate capital?
- How much capital will they generate?
- What effect will a proposed transaction have on the company?

The following pages of this chapter address these three questions, with particular emphasis on the market valuation process.

A TAXONOMY OF ASSETS

The first step in the decision process is to identify the assets that potentially could be liquidated. An obvious starting point is the balance sheet of the company. The balance sheet will identify the asset categories that have significant book balances. Sole reliance on the balance sheet will lead to the omission of many potentially valuable assets that are either shown at insignificant values or are not shown at all. The purpose of this section is to discuss the various assets of a company that have potential market value.

A simple hypothetical company will be a helpful example in this exploration. Let us consider the situation of a fictitious company named Typical Industrial Manufacturer, Inc. (hereafter, TIM). For example purposes, let us suppose that TIM, which was highly successful 20 years ago, has fallen upon difficult times. TIM has two operating divisions, TIM Products and TIM Realty. TIM Products produces one very well-known consumer product in a single building, which serves as office, factory, and warehouse, located in a mid-size northeastern city. TIM Products relies on two raw materials, which are each purchased from sole suppliers with whom TIM Products has long-standing and strong working relationships. TIM Products has been highly stable but has not experienced major growth in recent years, as changing demographic trends have led to a slight reduction in the size of the target market.

TIM Realty was conceived eight years ago as a means to profitably invest the excess cash that was being generated by TIM Products and which was not needed for capital reinvestment. In its first three years, TIM Realty, which invests in residential and commercial real estate development projects, produced very strong earnings. As a result, management decided to expand the operations of TIM Realty and took on several types of debt to increase the capital available for investment.

Two years ago, two development projects failed and caused major losses at TIM. The repayment of the outstanding debt started to pose difficulties. Initially, TIM had no difficulty rescheduling some of the debt, based on the stable record and earnings performance of TIM Products. In the past year, TIM Products has experienced difficulty as a result of sales growth being flat and the need to replace a major piece of equipment. Now the banks and lenders are very concerned about the ability of TIM to repay its debt and are not willing to extend any new commitments. Management has concluded that, to avoid default, TIM must generate cash within three to six months. Furthermore, management acknowledges it can no longer turn to the equity markets or to unsecured lenders.

The balance sheet, as of the most recent year-end, was:

TIM, INC.
Balance Sheet
($000s)

Current assets	$ 10,000	Current liabilities	$ 25,000
Net P, P & E*	70,000	Long-term debt	65,000
Real estate investment	15,000	Other liabilities	5,000
Other assets	5,000	Shareholders' equity	5,000
Total	$100,000	Total	$100,000

*Property, plant, and equipment.

The management of TIM initially reviewed the balance sheet and concluded that the only potential lay in the liquidation of the real estate investment assets, which are not considered to be desirable, or in some transaction involving TIM Products' operating facility, including real estate and some excess equipment (the "Net P, P & E"). Over the past year, management had received a number of proposals for various transactions and had kept a file of these proposals. Interested in finding alternatives, management reviewed the file. The file showed that TIM owned many business assets that were attractive to other companies but which do not appear on TIM's balance sheet. Three proposals are summarized below.

Company A, which sold consumer products through similar distribution channels to similar customers, discovered that very few people in its target market had any recognition of its trade name. Company A found that the same people thought highly of the "Super Tim" trade name and would be positively disposed to other products bearing that name. Company A offered to purchase the rights to the name for $2 million on the understanding that TIM would retain the right to use the name for its own products.

Company B, which manufactured unrelated products, relied heavily on one of the two raw materials used by TIM Products. Recently, there was a reduction in the amount of the material that was available. Company B was unable to buy any of the material, because the supplier reserved all available stock for TIM Products, in accordance with a 10-year supply contract between TIM and the supplier. Learning that the contract was divisible and transferable, Company B offered $500,000 for a 50 percent participation in the contract.

Company C, which manufactured and distributed related products in the western region of the country, observed that TIM had only minimal distribution in this part of the country. C offered to buy the western operations, on a going-concern basis, including some of the specialized equipment that could be moved from TIM's production facility to C's own facility.

The example of TIM, Inc., demonstrates that a company may have many assets that are either undervalued or not valued at all on the balance sheet. Undervalued assets include assets that have been depreciated partially and that still have significant economic value, and assets that are shown on the financial statements at purchase price but that have appreciated since acquisition. Assets that are not shown on the balance sheet include fully depreciated assets and "intangible" assets, such as the trade name and supply contract (described above in the examples of the transactions proposed by Companies A and B). Companies may also have "going-concern value," which is part of what TIM would sell under the transaction proposed by Company C.

To fully answer the first question cited in the introductory section, it would be useful to summarize and distinguish the asset types that might be marketable. In this section we will identify assets in the three categories mentioned above: tangible, intangible, and going-concern. In the next section we will discuss what characteristics of these assets determine their value and then proceed to discuss how to answer the second question stated above, "How much capital will they generate?"

Tangible Assets

In broad terms, tangible assets, consistent with their title, are mostly physical assets, such as buildings, real estate, machinery, finished goods inventory, and raw materials. Tangible assets also include financial assets, such as cash, investment securities, and accounts receivable.

Intangible Assets

Intangible assets are more difficult to define. The Internal Revenue Service, which, for one specific tax purpose, needed to define intangible assets, found it more expedient to define them by example than by descriptive statement. In Internal Revenue Code Section 936(h)(3)(B), the IRS defines intangible property as "any:

   (i) patent, invention, formula, process, design, pattern, or knowhow;
  (ii) copyright, literary, musical, or artistic composition;
 (iii) trademark, trade name, or brand name;
 (iv) franchise, license, or contract;
  (v) method, program, system, procedure, campaign, survey, study, forecast, estimate, customer list, or technical data; or
 (vi) any similar item,

which has substantial value independent of the services of any individual."

This list excludes intangible assets that are linked to individuals, such as agreements not to compete and employment agreements, but which are widely accepted as valuable intangible assets. This list may be characterized as assets that are developed deliberately by businesses and that often involve a considerable development investment. Examples of *any similar item* include "financing" intangible assets, such as favorable leases and below-market interest rates on borrowing, and such items as order backlogs and an assembled work force. If one were to take any of these assets away from a company (through litigation, for example) then the company would experience lost revenues and increased expenses.

Going-Concern Value

Going-concern value represents the value of a company as an operating entity over and above the value of the identifiable tangible and intangible assets. In a typical corporate acquisition, the price paid exceeds the value of the assets acquired. This premium is attributed to goodwill on the balance sheet of the acquiring company. Going-concern value arises because the market value of an ongoing business takes into account the expectation that earnings will be sustained in the future, that new customers will be acquired, and that old customers will continue to buy the company's goods and services.

FUNDAMENTALS OF VALUATION

In our example of TIM, Inc., the company received offers to purchase three separate assets, including intangible assets and a portion of the company's going-concern value. If the management of TIM wishes to ascertain what is the most favorable offer, or even whether it should consider soliciting a completely different transaction, it requires a framework for such an analysis.

The first step in such a framework is to define the standard of value that is to be applied. The choice of the standard must suit the intended use of the results. For example, a highly troubled company that is desperately in need of funds might find the "forced liquidation" definition (see below) to be the most appropriate. Without clear definitions, a stated result may be interpreted very differently by different people in various circumstances. Several of the most widely used standards of value are "investment value," "fair market value in use," and "liquidation value," which includes both "orderly liquidation" and "forced liquidation."

Investment value is defined as the value of an asset to a specified purchaser who expects to realize synergistic benefits from the combination of the acquired business with the existing business.

Fair market value in use is defined as the price at which property would change hands between a willing buyer and a willing seller, when the former is not under any compulsion to buy and the latter is not under any compulsion to sell, both parties having reasonable knowledge of relevant facts. *Orderly liquidation* is the amount for which an asset could be sold, given a reasonable amount of time to find a purchaser. *Forced liquidation,* in comparison, is the price that could be realized at public auction with limited time to find prospective buyers.

While other standards are discussed below, including a standard that takes into account the circumstances of a troubled company that must undergo a forced liquidation, the following discussion of valuation procedures will be structured primarily in terms of the fair market value definition stated above.

Once the objective of the analysis is determined, the next step is to select appropriate analysis tools. Within the valuation field, three basic approaches to asset valuation are frequently cited: the income approach, the market comparison approach, and the cost approach. A sound analysis will usually involve the consideration of each approach and the selection of one or more approaches that are best suited to the asset in question. Each approach is described briefly below.

The income approach is used to determine the value of an asset based on the future cash flows that it is expected to generate. The cash flows that are attributable to the asset are projected, usually on a marginal (i.e., a before and after) basis, and are then discounted to their present value using a discount rate that appropriately reflects the prevailing interest rates in the market and the relative risk of an investment in the subject asset. The total present value of the future cash flows, after any final adjustments (described below), is taken to be an indication of the fair market value of the asset.

The market comparison approach is based on observed market prices in actual or proposed transactions involving similar assets. Consideration is given to factors that could lead to different values, such as the date of the transaction, the location of the assets under analysis, and differences in the condition of the assets. If several transactions involving highly similar assets can be found, this method is likely to result in the most reliable indicator of fair market value.

The cost approach is based on the assumption that a rational individual or organization would not purchase a given asset for an amount that is greater than the cost of replacing the asset. For example, if one is trying to value a particular type of structure for which no reasonable comparable transaction prices can be found, a useful indication of value would be what it would cost to build a similar structure, and then adjust the cost for the economic depreciation of the subject asset.

Having defined an appropriate standard of value and discussed several approaches to valuation, let us proceed to examine specific approaches to the valuation of certain assets. For purposes of organization, we will discuss the application of these valuation approaches to intangible assets, tangible assets, and going-concern value.

THE VALUATION OF INTANGIBLE ASSETS

The selection of the appropriate valuation approach for an intangible asset depends on the circumstances and nature of the asset. Within the list of intangible assets shown above, there are assets that are appropriately valued using each of the approaches mentioned above. A program or system that a company may have developed is likely to be unique. Clearly, no comparison with market transactions will be possible. A cash flow analysis may be difficult and inherently arbitrary if there is no associated clear and distinguishable revenue or expense stream. In such a case, the cost approach may be the only reasonable approach. In other cases, such as the two described below, cash flows can be projected reasonably, making the income approach valuable. A franchise is an example of an asset that is often sold in arm's-length secondary transactions. In such a case, the market comparison approach is appropriate.

Example 1: Approaches to Valuation

Let us return to our example of a troubled company, TIM, Inc., which must raise funds through the sale of assets. TIM had previously received offers, among others, to purchase its Super Tim trade name and a 50 percent interest in its raw material supply contract. While highly simplified, we present below an example approach to the valuation of these assets based on hypothetical data.

The management of TIM is interested in knowing what would constitute a fair market price for the sale of the trade name. Under the terms of the hypothetical proposed transaction with Company A, TIM's operations and costs will not be affected, since the proposed use of the trade name will be in geographic regions where TIM has no material market presence, and since TIM's use of the trade name will not be restricted. TIM's management is primarily interested in performing an analysis to indicate what price Company A would be willing to pay under fair market conditions. In this case, useful results can be achieved using the income approach, with secondary consideration of the cost approach.

As a first step in the analysis, TIM management used a three-year income and cash flow history for Company A as a basis for developing projections for A's income and cash flow for the next five years (see Table 1). This projection was performed on an "as is" (i.e., pretransaction) basis. The projections in Table 1 are adjusted to show "Cash flow to invested capital," which removes the effects of A's capital structure.

To simplify this example, we are assuming that the managements of both A and TIM share some apocalyptic vision under which the trade name would became worthless at the end of the five-year period.

The next step in the analysis is to develop a fair market required rate of return to apply to the investment in the trade name. A reasonable approach to the development of the required rate of return would be to calculate a weighted average cost of capital for Company A. Under fair market value assumptions, this should be based on the cost of capital for "typical" companies similar to A. Let us assume that we identified five companies that are comparable to A. Our objective is to use data from these companies to calculate

TABLE 1
Company A—Operating History and Projections

	Historical				Projected			
	1987	1988	1989	1990	1991	1992	1993	1994
Net revenues	$1,000	$1,010	$1,025	$1,040	$1,123	$1,213	$1,310	$1,415
Cost of goods sold	600	606	615	624	674	728	786	849
Operating income	400	404	410	416	449	485	524	566
Selling, general, and admin.	160	162	164	166	180	194	210	226
Interest expense	80	80	80	80	80	80	80	80
Earnings before taxes	160	162	166	170	189	211	234	260
Taxes	64	65	66	68	76	84	94	104
Net income	96	97	100	102	113	127	140	156
Add back:								
Depreciation	60	61	62	62	67	73	79	85
Interest expense	80	80	80	80	80	80	80	80
Less taxes on interest	32	32	32	32	32	32	32	32
Cash flow to invested capital	$ 204	$ 206	$ 210	$ 212	$ 228	$ 248	$ 267	$ 289

a required rate of return. This may be achieved by applying two well-known formulas from the field of finance: the capital asset pricing model (CAPM) and the weighted average cost of capital (WACC) formula.

The capital asset pricing model calculates a required rate of return to equity based on interest rates and the relative risk of the stock. In this example, let us assume that we ascertained that the five companies have an average stock beta (defined in the introductory section of this chapter) of 1.33. The CAPM is as follows:

$$Re = Rf + Beta \times (Rm - Rf)$$

where:

Re is the required rate of return on equity.

Rf is the current market risk-free interest rate (such as the yield on a U.S. Treasury bond).

Rm is the average rate of return on the stock market.

If current market observations show that Rf is 8 percent and Rm − Rf is 6 percent, then the required return on equity is calculated to be 8 percent + 1.33 × 6 percent or 16 percent.

This result is used as an input into the WACC formula, which may be stated as:

$$WACC = Re \times E + (1 - t) \times Rd \times D$$

where:

Re is as defined above.
E is the proportion of equity in the capital structure.
t is the total tax rate.
Rd is the cost of debt.
D is the proportion of debt in the capital structure.

Let us assume that an analysis of the financial statements of the five comparable companies showed that they have an average capital structure of 50 percent debt and 50 percent equity. We also ascertain that the total tax rate is 40 percent and the cost of debt borrowing is currently 10 percent. These values are substituted as follows:

$$WACC = 16\% \times 50\% + (1 - 40\%) \times 10\% \times 50\%$$

This calculation yields a WACC of 11 percent.

The third step in the analysis is to project the impact of the proposed acquisition on Company A's projected cash flow. Let us project that the trade name will lead to a 10 percent increase in revenues and cost of goods sold but will not affect S, G, and A or interest expense. The revised projections are shown in Table 2. The value of the trade name to Company A is the present value of the incremental revenues it will generate. Table 3 shows the difference between the cash flows determined in Table 1 and Table 2. Table 3 also shows present value factors, based on the 11 percent required rate of return (assuming that the cash flows are received at the midpoint of each year). The total present value of $141,000 represents the value to Company A of the trade name.

Another way to interpret the analysis is to say that if Company A were to evaluate the proposed purchase from a capital budgeting perspective, it would find that a project consisting of purchasing the trade name for $141,000 and receiving the proposed incremental cash flows would have an internal rate of return of 11 percent. If, as determined above, A faces a cost of capital of 11 percent (implying that its "hurdle" rate for investments should be 11 percent), then this proposed investment would just meet the acceptance threshold.

Before finally concluding that the price determined is the fair market value of the asset, we should consider another approach to valuation—the cost approach. Company A may believe that it has an alternative strategy: to invest in marketing expenses and create a trade name that would be as effective as the Super Tim trade name. If Company A approaches a marketing consulting firm and learns that it would cost $500,000 to achieve the same results, then the alternative may be ruled out. On the other hand, if the objective could be achieved for $100,000, then the fair market value of the trade name should be determined according to the cost approach, since Company A would not pay more for the asset than it would have to pay for a similar asset that is available.

Example 2: The 50 Percent Interest in the Supply Contract

The valuation analysis for the supply contract is somewhat similar to the analysis for the trade name. The basic approach will be to use a cash flow analysis, comparing "before" and "after" scenarios.

TABLE 2
Company A—Operating History and Projections (revised)

	Historical			Projected				
	1987	1988	1989	1990	1991	1992	1993	1994
Net revenues	$1,000	$1,010	$1,025	$1,144	$1,236	$1,335	$1,442	$1,557
Cost of goods sold	600	606	615	686	742	801	865	934
Operating income	400	404	410	458	494	534	577	623
Selling, general, and admin.	160	162	164	166	180	194	210	226
Interest expense	80	80	80	80	80	80	80	80
Earnings before taxes	160	162	166	212	234	260	287	317
Taxes	64	65	66	85	94	104	115	127
Net income	96	97	100	127	140	156	172	190
Add back:								
Depreciation	60	61	62	69	74	80	87	93
Interest expense	80	80	80	80	80	80	80	80
Less taxes on interest	32	32	32	32	32	32	32	32
Cash flow to invested capital	$ 204	$ 206	$ 210	$ 244	$ 262	$ 284	$ 307	$ 331

TABLE 3
Company A—Valuation of Trade Name

	Projected					
	1990	1991	1992	1993	1994
Cash flow to invested capital:					
From Table 2	$244	$262	$284	$307	$331
From Table 1	212	228	248	267	289
Cash flow from trade name	32	34	36	40	42
Present value factor (11%)	0.9492	0.8551	0.7704	0.6940	0.6252
Present value	30.4	29.1	27.7	27.8	26.3
Total present value	$141				

To avoid redundancy, we will not review the steps that are similar to those taken in the example described above. Two issues are important to discuss: the process of estimating the effect on cash flows and the impact of intangible asset amortization on taxes.

The projection of the cash flows that will result from the purchase of the supply contract involves uncertainty. If, for example, the raw material will be in abundant supply at low prices throughout the term of the contract, then the contract would not provide a benefit. On the other hand, if prolonged shortages occur that lead to supply interruptions and increased prices, then the contract provides a significant benefit. The objective is to develop an expectation of the likelihood of each possibility.

As an example, suppose that there is a 75 percent likelihood of Scenario A, under which there will be abundant low-cost supplies and a 25 percent likelihood of Scenario B, under which there will be major shortages. Management of TIM projects that Company B would experience annual operating results under each scenario as follows:

	Scenario A	Scenario B
Revenues	$100	$90
Expenses	80	90
Income before taxes	$ 20	$ 0

If the contract ensures that Company B is able to operate under the conditions of Scenario A, no matter what actually happens, one can estimate the benefit on an expected value basis. In other words, the contract has a 75 percent likelihood of providing no benefit and a 25 percent likelihood of providing a $20 pretax benefit ($12 after tax, assuming the same 40 percent marginal tax rate). On average, the contract provides a $3 after-tax benefit.

A second major consideration is that the price Company B is willing to pay will be affected by the fact that Company B will be able to take a deduction from taxable income for the amortization of the supply contract. To demonstrate the impact this amortization would have on fair market value, let us consider the cash flow data shown in Table 3 for the Company A example. Table 4 shows a revised version of Table 3, which is adjusted so that in each year the company takes a tax deduction for 20 percent (based on a useful life of five years) of the total present value of the cash flows. A comparison of Table 3 with Table 4 shows that the tax benefit will add

TABLE 4
Company A Example—Revised to Show Amortization Tax Benefit

	Projected				
	1990	1991	1992	1993	1994
Cash flow to invested capital:					
From Table 2	$244	$262	$284	$307	$331
From Table 1	212	228	248	267	289
Cash flow from trade name	32	34	36	40	42
Intangible asset valuation	41	41	41	41	41
Amortization tax shield*	16	16	16	16	16
Total cash flow	48	50	52	56	58
Present value factor (11%)	0.9492	0.8551	0.7704	0.6940	0.6252
Present value	45.9	43.1	40.4	39.1	36.5
Total present value	$205				

*Defined as the reduction in taxes due to the amortization.

significantly to the price a purchaser can pay for an asset and still meet his or her desired internal rate of return.

The preceding discussion provides a framework that the management of TIM, or any healthy or troubled company, might use to evaluate a contemplated liquidation of intangible assets. While intangible assets are very real economic assets, their value is highly contingent upon the conditions of the company to which they provide service. It is for this reason that the cash flow approach to valuation is often the most appropriate means of determining fair market value.

THE VALUATION OF TANGIBLE ASSETS

A troubled company that is forced to generate funds through the liquidation of assets will frequently look for opportunities in its tangible assets. Companies that own large office buildings, for example, have entered into various forms of transactions to receive the equity in the property. We will discuss real estate options at length below; but first, let us consider a few other liquidation options and discuss valuation methods that would be of service to the management of liquidating companies.

Returning to our hypothetical company, TIM, Inc., we see that it has three tangible assets that might be sold: accounts receivable, excess machinery and equipment, and its one building. In the general case of a troubled company, there may be other appropriate tangible assets; however, a discussion of these three will introduce many of the valuation issues and approaches that would be of interest to a management faced with other liquidation options.

Accounts Receivable

Accounts receivable, which in most cases are standard trade invoices that have not yet been paid, are relatively liquid assets. Many commercial banks have "factoring" operations that purchase receivables at a discount. The discount reflects two issues that detract from the value of the receivable. The first is the interest rate charged (implicitly through the accretion of the discount) from the time the factored proceeds are advanced to the company to the time the receivables are received by the factoring bank. The second component of the discount is an allowance for accounts that may prove to be uncollectible.

The factoring of receivables may be an attractive option for a troubled company, because the rate of return required by the factoring bank may be considerably lower than the cost of capital faced by a troubled company. On the negative side, the liquidation of receivables is not likely to have a material impact on the financial condition of the troubled company, since the net result is to provide access to funds which, without liquidation, would probably be received within about 30 days.

Excess Machinery and Equipment

Unlike liquid assets, financial assets (such as accounts receivable), machinery, and equipment are not always easy to sell, since they may be tailored to specialized circumstances or processes that are not well suited to the needs of likely purchasers. A major consideration in the assessment of the probable selling price is the amount of time available to find a buyer. In the field of valuation, a distinction is frequently drawn between asset valuations performed under conditions of orderly liquidation, when sufficient time is available to find a buyer who is willing to pay a fair price, and those performed under conditions of forced liquidation, when it is imperative that money be received as soon as possible and when a relatively low offer may be the best available.

To determine a value under orderly liquidation, one can refer to reference sources, such as used equipment manuals, or consult with equipment dealers. Such sources will quote a "value in exchange," a secondary market price which will be less than "value in use" and which considers the added value of installation and other related factors. It is not easy to measure the appropriate difference in value that should be expected under forced liquidation. Generally, an asset appraiser will estimate a discount based on information he or she has gathered during an appraisal career.

Real Estate

Real estate assets present several liquidation options:

- The property may be sold outright.
- The property may be refinanced.
- The owner may enter into a sale leaseback.
- The owner may find a partner and develop the property to its most advantageous use.

The sale of the property may be the best option, when the real estate market in the region of the subject property is active and values are increasing. In a weak commercial real estate market, the seller is often forced to accept a "purchase money mortgage," under which the buyer provides 20 to 40 percent of the purchase price and pledges to pay the remaining balance in the form of mortgage payments made directly to the seller. A troubled company that needs capital will not necessarily be best served if it is forced to accept a purchase money mortgage.

The second alternative mentioned above is to refinance the property. A bank, or other lender, is usually willing to provide financing for up to 70 or 80 percent of the value of the property. This option is preferable to the outright sale of the property, if the company desires or needs to retain occupancy. If there is an unpaid balance on an existing primary mortgage bearing a below-market interest rate, then the company may use a "wraparound" mortgage. A wraparound mortgage is a new mortgage but, unlike refinancings, leaves the original mortgage intact.

A sale leaseback transaction is attractive to a company that wishes to retain the use of the property but desires to receive a higher level of proceeds than would be available under a refinancing. This option may be the most attractive to a viable but troubled company, given the fact that it may be able to access 100 percent of the value of the property, compared with 80 percent under a refinancing transaction.

The final option is to redevelop the property for a completely different purpose. This option is attractive when the property occupies very valuable land. Recently, in New York City, the owners of a landmark structure went to court to sue the city's landmark commission for the right to destroy their property. This option is not often attractive but, in certain circumstances, it bears consideration.

The valuation of real estate also follows the three approaches outlined above (the income approach, the market comparison approach, and the cost approach).

The valuation of a sale leaseback is usually based on the income approach, since the value is determined both by the expected value of the property at the end of the lease and by the size of the lease payments that the seller agrees to. In this case, the cash flow forecast will consider lease payments, depreciation and taxes, and the required rate of return for the counterparty. If management performs a cash flow analysis and develops an estimate of the future market value of the leased property, then it can ascertain how much capital it should receive in a fair transaction.

The market comparison approach is very useful in real estate appraisal. Under this method, the subject property is compared with similar properties for which transaction prices are available. These prices are adjusted for differences in date of sale, location, size of the land lot and of the building, and the general condition of the property.

The cost approach, as described above, considers the costs of replacing the property, starting with a vacant lot and building a comparable property. The cost is then adjusted for the condition of the subject property. The cost approach is more complex to implement, certainly, compared to the market approach, and would generally be used when there are difficulties applying the other approaches.

The management of a troubled company should bear in mind that the distinction between orderly liquidation and forced liquidation, described above in the context of excess machinery and equipment, is equally applicable to real estate.

THE VALUATION OF GOING-CONCERN VALUE

An important option faced by the management of a troubled company is the sale of an entire operating unit of the business. The sale of a division, for example, may command a higher price than the sale of tangible or intangible assets because of the going-concern value of the business. A valuation of part of a business is a similar process to the valuation of the stock of a privately held company, for which there are relatively well-established valuation procedures.

The two most commonly used approaches are the market comparison approach and the income approach. To demonstrate the process of applying each approach, let us return to the example of TIM, Inc., and apply these approaches to determine a fair market value for the Western Division.

The Market Comparison Approach

The fair market value of the Western Division of Tim Products, known as WESTIM, may be estimated by comparing various operating and financial characteristics of publicly traded comparable companies with those of WESTIM. The process essentially involves the calculation of ratios of the market value of the comparable companies to the financial indicators. Although exact comparability is not attainable, the effects of dissimilarities in such characteristics as size, capital structure, and marketability can be taken into account through the valuation process.

To select comparable companies, one can refer to one or more of many publicly available data sources. Many of these sources classify companies according to Standard Industrial Classifications (SIC) Codes, which is a numerical system that identifies the nature of the business of a company according to definitions published by the Office of Management and Budget, a branch of the U.S. federal government. If we determine that the definition for SIC Code 3999, "Manufacturing Industries, Not Elsewhere Classified," best suits the business of WESTIM, we can use a database or other reference source to identify other companies also assigned SIC Code 3999.

The next step in the process is to review business descriptions for each comparable company identified by the database and exclude companies with significant operations in different lines of business. Since the objective is to perform a financial analysis of the comparable companies, we should also exclude companies that have not published financial reports for at least the last three and preferably the last five years, or which have experienced highly unusual or distorted (i.e., by a significant merger) results.

Let us assume that this process results in the identification of five good comparable companies. The historical income statements for these companies are adjusted to eliminate the effects of one-time items that are not indicative of future performance, such as gains or losses on the sale of assets, amortization of deferred items, or intangible assets. The income statements are adjusted to remove the interest paid on long-term debt and the associated tax deductions. This is done to eliminate the effects on income of the capital structure chosen by management.

Next, we determine the market value of the invested capital (debt plus equity) of each comparable company. Publicly quoted stock prices should be obtained and multiplied by the number of shares outstanding to obtain the market value of the equity. Debt should also be priced at its market value, or, if the interest rates are close to current market rates, the debt value may be estimated at book value. The resulting market value of the invested capital is then used to determine the market ratios. Typically, useful indications of value can be drawn from ratios of market value to book value, cash flow from operations, and net income. Furthermore, when using cash flow and net income, it is useful to calculate ratios based not only on current cash flow and net income but also on averages for the most recent three to five years. Example market value ratios for the comparable companies are shown in Table 5.

To apply the ratios determined in Table 5 to WESTIM, it is necessary to obtain the same financial data for WESTIM as was used for the comparable companies in the determination of the market ratios. Let us assume that WESTIM financial reports were examined and adjusted to remove nonrecurring items, resulting in the values shown below under "WESTIM Values." These values are then multiplied by the market ratios from Table 5 as shown below:

Indicator	Market Ratio	WESTIM Values ($000s)	Indicated Value ($000s)
Book invested capital	1.14	$23,000	$26,220
Net income	10.20	2,700	27,540
5-yr. avg. net income	11.70	2,400	28,080
Cash flow	7.80	3,100	24,180
5-yr. avg. cash flow	9.10	2,900	26,390
Average indication			$26,482

TABLE 5
Comparable Companies—Market Value Ratios

Company	Market Value ($000s)	Book Value ($000s)	Market Value Ratio	Recent Net Income ($000s)	Market Value Ratio	5-Yr. Avg. Net Income ($000s)	Market Value Ratio	Recent Cash Flow ($000s)	Market Value Ratio	5-Yr. Avg. Cash Flow ($000s)	Market Value Ratio
Comparable 1	$11,400	$12,000	0.95	$1,140	10.0	$1,000	12.0	$1,600	7.5	$1,333	9.0
Comparable 2	15,400	14,000	1.10	1,812	8.5	1,273	11.0	2,154	6.5	2,000	7.0
Comparable 3	12,350	9,500	1.30	1,372	9.0	905	10.5	1,357	7.0	1,118	8.5
Comparable 4	12,900	10,750	1.20	1,032	12.5	768	14.0	1,075	10.0	896	12.0
Comparable 5	14,950	13,000	1.15	1,359	11.0	1,182	11.0	1,625	8.0	1,444	9.0
Average ratio			1.14		10.2		11.7		7.8		9.1

The indications of value shown on page 221 represent estimates of the value of the total invested capital of WESTIM. The average indicated value of $26,482,000 should not be interpreted as the fair market value of the invested capital of WESTIM. Adjustments should be made for differences between the investment appeal, from the perspective of the investor, of WESTIM, and of the comparable companies used in the analysis.

The first major difference is that the value of a stock not readily marketable is less than a stock that is. The comparable companies are assumed to be publicly traded companies. An investor in these companies is able to buy and sell stock with relative ease through the stock exchanges on which the companies are listed. When investors consider buying WESTIM, they must face the fact that it will not be a simple matter of calling a broker if they want to sell their ownership interest. Various studies have been undertaken to verify this assumption. These studies (one of the most frequently cited is the SEC's *Institutional Investor Study* of letter stock transactions) have produced differing results, but generally support the claim that a "marketability discount" of between 20 percent and 30 percent is appropriate.

The second major difference is that the proposed acquisition of WESTIM would give the buyer a controlling interest in WESTIM. A controlling interest gives the buyer control over business decisions and the ability to access the cash flow generated by the business. In contrast, the stockholders of the publicly traded comparable companies only receive a dividend stream determined by the management of the companies. Market studies have been performed (e.g., see *Mergerstat Review,* published annually by W. T. Grimm and Company) that measure the difference between the price paid to take control of a company and the market value of the company immediately prior to acquisition. These studies generally support the conclusion that a "control premium" of 30 percent to 40 percent is appropriate when determining the fair market value of a controlling interest in a business.

These adjustments are applied to the indication of value determined from the market ratios to calculate an estimate of fair market value as follows:

Estimated Fair Market Value of WESTIM Using the Market Comparison Approach

	Value ($000s)
Preliminary indicated value	$26,482
Less marketability discount (25%)	6,621
	19,861
Plus control premium (35%)	6,952
Fair market value	$26,813

The Income Approach

The income approach is another important and widely used approach to going-concern valuation. The approach is based on the premise that the real value of a business to a purchaser is the "free cash flow" provided by the operations of the business. Free cash flow is the total cash flow generated by the business less the cash flow that must be reinvested to sustain the business, such as additions to working capital and capital investment in plant and equipment.

Cash flow projections are based on the historical records of WESTIM and on management projections. Table 6 shows an example five-year forecast of free cash flow, including projected additions to working capital and capital investments needed to sustain the projected business growth. Table 6 also includes a column labeled "Residual." The discounted cash flow approach to the valuation of a business assumes that the business will continue to operate indefinitely. The process of residual "capitalization" applies a basic mathematical formula to simplify the process of calculating the present value of the cash flows earned in all years after the specific five-year forecast period. The formula (a proof of which may be found in most basic finance textbooks) is:

$$\text{PV of cash flow stream} = \frac{\text{First-year cash flow}}{K - g}$$

where:

K is the discount rate.
g is the annual rate of growth of cash flows.

TABLE 6
WESTIM—Free Cash Flow Projections ($000s)

	1990	1991	1992	1993	1994	Residual
Net revenues	$10,000	$10,800	$11,664	$12,597	$13,605	$14,285
Cost of goods sold	5,000	5,400	5,832	6,299	6,802	7,143
Operating income	5,000	5,400	5,832	6,298	6,803	7,142
Selling, general, and admin.	1,000	1,080	1,166	1,260	1,360	1,429
Earnings before taxes	4,000	4,320	4,666	5,038	5,442	5,714
Taxes	1,600	1,728	1,866	2,015	2,177	2,285
Net income	2,400	2,592	2,800	3,023	3,265	3,429
Add back:						
Depreciation	625	675	729	787	850	893
Cash flow from operations	3,025	3,267	3,529	3,810	4,115	4,322
Less:						
Additions to working capital	250	270	292	315	340	357
Capital investment	500	540	583	630	680	714
Free cash flow	$ 2,275	$ 2,457	$ 2,654	$ 2,866	$ 3,095	$ 3,250

TABLE 7
WESTIM—Discounted Cash Flow Valuation ($000s)

	1990	1991	1992	1993	1994	Residual
Free cash flow	$ 2,275	$2,457	$2,765	$2,866	$3,095	$ 3,250
Capitalized residual						40,625
Present value factor (13%)	0.9407	0.8325	0.7367	0.6520	0.5770	0.5770
Present value	2,140	2,045	2,037	1,869	1,786	23,441
Total present value	$33,318					
Less marketability discount (25%)	8,329					
Fair market value	$24,988					

In this instance, the first year of cash flow used for capitalization purposes is 1995. We assumed that an ongoing growth rate of 5 percent would be achieved. Hence, the residual cash projection represents a 5 percent growth from the 1994 projection.

In Table 7, the present value of the cash flow projections is calculated using a 13 percent discount rate (chosen for example purposes). The capitalized residual is calculated according to the formula stated above—that is, the annual cash flow of $3,250,000 is divided by 0.13 − 0.05, or 0.08. The next step is to calculate the present value of all future cash flows, including the residual value. This results in a total present value of $33,318,000. The final step is to subtract a marketability discount of 25 percent, for reasons described above. The results of the discounted cash flow approach to the valuation of WESTIM indicate a fair market value of $24,988,000.

Reconciliation of Approaches

In the example of WESTIM, discussed above, we used two separate approaches to valuation on a going-concern basis. One approach resulted in a value of $26.8 million, while the other approach resulted in a value of $25.0 million. Clearly, the approaches are not expected to produce identical results. However, when the values are reasonably close, they provide strong support for a conclusion that a reasonable price at which to sell WESTIM should fall within a range of $25 million to $27 million (possibly plus or minus some additional estimation margin).

SUMMARY OF ANALYTICAL FRAMEWORK

In this chapter we have identified and discussed many of the assets that might be liquidated by a troubled company to raise capital. Using a hypothetical example to illustrate the process, we have described methods that may be used by management to assess a fair selling price for its assets under various scenarios. The decision process cannot be completed without a comparison and evaluation of alternatives. In the example of TIM, Inc., we considered a company with several options. If the management of TIM were to apply the methods and approaches described above, it would have a good basis for estimating and negotiating fair selling prices for the various assets. What TIM is still lacking is a basis for deciding which option is best suited to the needs of the company.

In the introductory section of this chapter we suggested three questions that might be asked by the management of a troubled company faced with liquidation options. The third question was, "What effect will a proposed transaction have on the company?" This question provides the framework for evaluating the options. The methods of valuation described above help to answer this question, in terms of the expected proceeds from the transaction. These methods may also be used to assess the total effect on the company.

Many companies adopt, as a corporate objective, a stated purpose along the lines of "maximizing shareholder wealth." Consistent with this purpose, management could compare its liquidation options by performing a valuation analysis (using the income approach described above in the section on going-concern value) of its own company under various scenarios consistent with each option. This approach will take into account both the proceeds from the transaction and the effects on the remaining company.

For example, if one compares the proposed transaction with Company A with the transaction with Company C, one notices that the Company A deal provides a net cash inflow of $2 million (the purchase price) while Company C provides an inflow of perhaps $25 million but takes away future cash flows, which, if TIM survives as an operating concern, would have a present value of $33 million (from Table 7). If TIM is in such great need that it must accept the offer from Company C, then there is no decision for management to make. On the other hand, if $2 million would be sufficient to solve a liquidity crisis and put TIM back on a profitable path then, based on a total net present value basis, Company C's offer could be the more attractive.

It is almost certainly the case that no template decision tool could be devised for problems of this nature. The framework developed above is intended only to identify analytical tools that could be used in the decision process. The management of a troubled company may also find it helpful to know, on a post-facto basis, how investors have interpreted previous decisions made by the management of various companies that liquidated assets. The final section of this chapter provides some market data on this topic.

MARKET DATA ON ASSET LIQUIDATIONS

A review of corporate successes and failures during the 1980s yields a myriad of strategies, approaches, and results. There is clearly no simple interpretation of this history that would support any formula or guideline for strategy in any given circumstance. The rapid growth of leveraged buyouts during the decade was fueled, in part, by the perceived benefits of realizing the "break-up value" of a company. Such transactions were founded on the premise that the process of asset liquidation, enhanced by cost reductions, would yield profits.

During the 1980s there was a dramatic increase in the level of corporate divestitures, as evidenced by the following data reported in *Mergerstat Review:*

Year	Divestitures ($ billions)
1981	$16.7
1982	16.1
1983	24.2
1984	29.4
1985	45.8
1986	59.9
1987	58.3
1988	69.6

There were many reasons for the growth in devestitures, including the liquidation of businesses acquired through leveraged buyouts and the 1980s trend by diversified companies to return to their core businesses.

The 1980s also saw many sales of assets by companies that either preferred not to have significant capital invested in certain asset categories or that chose to apply the capital to other areas of their business. For example, in August 1984, Security Pacific Corporation sold its 55-floor Los Angeles headquarters building for $310 million. Management of Security Pacific was quoted as saying that it did not have a specific need for the cash. Investors supported this move, because the stock price moved from a range of 20⅜ to 21 in July 1984 to a range of 20¾ to 24⁵⁄₁₆ in August.

The 1980s also provides many examples of companies that were experiencing difficult times and resorted to asset liquidations to try to solve their problems. We selected four companies whose actions, and the response of investors to those actions, provide useful insight concerning the potential for success of such strategies. The case studies selected here are Interco, Cooper Companies, Tyler Corporation, and USG Corporation. Stock charts of the companies are at the end of the chapter.

Interco

Interco—a retail conglomerate including several well-known brands, such as Ethan Allen furniture, Converse and Florsheim shoes, and London Fog apparel—was not a troubled company during the first half of 1988. Faced with the prospect of a hostile acquisition, the company adopted a poison-pill strategy that had the effect of making Interco a troubled company. Rather than accept a $70 per share offer from City Capital Associates, management implemented a leveraged recapitalization designed to provide $76 in value to shareholders. Shareholders received dividends of $38.60 in cash and $32.15 in preferred stock and junk bonds.

The task faced by Interco was to generate capital through the sale of assets. Unfortunately, management discovered that asset sales consistently generated less than expected. The junk bonds lost 40 percent of their value within a year, and the "stub" stock has lost most of its value. *Value Line* (December 1, 1989) placed the decline of the stock price in appropriate perspective by noting that "it is hard to make a case for buying stock in a company with no dividend, no earnings visibility, and a negative net worth of nearly $40 a share."

The September 11, 1989, edition of *Business Week* quoted Interco's new chief executive as saying "there are all kinds of options available to us." In light of the focus of this chapter, one may question whether the options that were available since the recapitalization were viable. If the transaction was based on assumed liquidation values that greatly exceeded what could actually be realized, then either the value of these assets changed as the company became troubled or they were overestimated at the outset.

As of the end of 1989, Interco had liquidated several businesses and was left with only a few businesses and some real estate. Analysts projected that the asset liquidation program would produce insufficient funds to repay the bank debt. In February 1990, the company received extensions from banks and had to renegotiate its bonds, giving equity to the bondholders.

USG Corporation
In a situation very similar to that of Interco, USG was subject to a hostile tender offer of $42 per share and implemented a restructuring financing. The restructuring transaction provided shareholders with $37 in cash, $5 in junk bonds, and a stub equity stock. To finance the shareholder dividend, significant bank loans and junk bond issuance were necessary.

USG's main subsidiary is U.S. Gypsum, which supplies about a third of the domestic demand for wallboards to the construction industry. Asset liquidations include the sales of Masonite Corporation, Kinkead, the Marlite Division, and Wiss, Jenney, Elstner Associates. USG is not considered to be beyond hope of survival, but it does have a difficult path ahead, given the slow pace of the construction industry.

What is interesting about this case is that the asset liquidation program may have been successful in creating shareholder wealth. The offer from Desert Partners would have given each shareholder $42. The recapitalization plan provided $37 in cash, $5 dollars in debt, and a share of stock, which was recently selling at $4.50.

Cooper Companies
Cooper Companies is a collection of companies involved in the manufacture and distribution of lenses. During the early 1980s, it

acquired several companies with operations in related fields. The company experienced troubles in 1988 and 1989 and implemented an asset liquidation program. In July 1989, the company sold Cooper Technicon, its largest business, for $477 million.

In this instance, the sale of core operations seems to have been very successful in terms of turning around a troubled situation. The stock chart shows that a gradual upward trend began in July 1989, coinciding with the sale of the largest division. As of year-end 1989, Cooper had significant cash accumulated and was actively looking for acquisitions to which it could profitably apply net operating loss carryforwards.

Tyler Corporation
Tyler, a diversified provider of industrial goods and services, sold Hall-Mark Electronics in 1988 and Reliance Universal in 1989. After the 1988 divestiture, it paid a special $10 per share dividend. Unlike the examples described above, Tyler did not undertake to liquidate assets because it was a troubled company. The sale and special dividend were consistent with a strategic objective of management.

Market data, as evidenced by the stock chart, shows strong approval of the liquidation policy. The stock price fell by only a little over four points at the end of August 1988, compared with the end of July 1988. Since the distribution, the stock price has moved modestly higher. The case of Tyler Corporation is an example of a successful strategic self-liquidation.

The four examples provide different perspectives on the effectiveness of asset liquidation as a management strategy. In the case of Interco, the defensive pressures may have led management to adopt overoptimistic expectations regarding the liquidation value of the business assets. One consideration described in a previous section of this chapter was the difference in value that may be realized under orderly liquidation, compared with forced liquidation. Clearly, the case of Interco was forced, hence lower values should have been anticipated.

USG, while in a situation similar to that of Interco, was able to stabilize itself without sacrificing its core business. This recapitalization transaction succeeded in creating shareholder wealth when compared with the competing tender offer. Cooper Companies became troubled through leverage and adverse business conditions. In this example, the company managed to stabilize itself through asset sales and appears to be headed in a positive direction. Tyler Corporation undertook a strategic divestiture and partial self-liquidation, which was very beneficial to its stockholders.

In these cases, the market data indicate that liquidation, under positive circumstances, can be beneficial. The lesson of Interco, namely that forced liquidation may produce disappointing results, indicates the potential for problems. One should not infer from a single example that the approach will never be successful; however, there are clearly some lessons that should be considered by the management of troubled companies considering liquidation options.

Analysis of the Domestic Airline Industry

The 1980s was a turbulent decade for the domestic airline industry as the effects of deregulation, which took place in 1978, and mergers have caused many significant and rapid changes in the nature of the business. Recent years have seen considerable growth, as evidenced by the 12 percent average growth rate of revenue passenger miles from 1985 to 1989. Despite the strong growth experienced by the industry as a whole, the experience of individual airlines has been highly varied. For comparative purposes we selected six airline companies with different characteristics and performance histories:

United Airlines.
Trans World Airlines.
Pan American.
Southwest Airlines.
Texas Air.
US Air.

The stock charts of these airlines are at the end of the chapter.

United, generally grouped with American and Delta, is one of the large, stable, and generally profitable airlines. In the early 1980s United, through its holding company Allegis, attempted to establish an integrated travel services company. It acquired Hilton International (purchased from Transworld Corporation in 1986) and Westin

Hotels (in 1970) and Hertz (in 1985) only to change course in 1987 and dispose of them.

Trans World Airlines has been a troubled airline throughout the 1980s. Between 1980 and 1987 it had only one year, 1984, in which it had a positive net income. In 1985, the airline was the subject of hostile acquisition by Carl Icahn, who took the company private in 1988.

Pan American, according to some analysts, has not made a good strategic decision in the last decade. During the 1980s the airline lost approximately $3 billion and frequently liquidated assets to provide necessary funds. Now, the airline is nearly out of assets and has a minimal chance of survival.

Southwest is something of a niche airline, with a preference for the smaller airports (such as Love Field in Dallas and Midway in Chicago) in the markets it serves. Originally, it served three Texas cities and expanded throughout the central region of the country. The airline was stable and profitable over the last decade, with a slight downturn caused by the termination of operations at TranStar Airlines, which Southwest purchased in 1985.

Texas Air Corporation, parent of Eastern and Continental Airlines, was a troubled company throughout the decade. Continental Airlines, acquired in 1982, went into bankruptcy proceedings in 1983 and emerged in 1986. Eastern also experienced difficult times. Purchased in 1986 for $640 million, it filed for bankruptcy in 1989 after selling the Eastern Shuttle.

US Air began the decade as a reasonably small northeastern carrier based in Pittsburgh. Through its acquisitions of PSA and Piedmont, it developed a national flight network. The airline has shown steady growth and profitability.

Asset Dispositions by Airlines

The airline industry is of particular interest in an examination of asset dispositions because of the many types of asset liquidations that occur. Airline assets that are regularly sold include:

Operating units—on a going-concern basis, such as the sale of the Eastern Shuttle to Trump.

Aircraft—outright and in sale leaseback, which is very common throughout the industry.

Air routes—such as the sale of the Pacific routes of Pan Am to United.

Landing slots—which are valuable at busy airports with limited traffic flow.

Gates—which are extremely valuable at congested airports with limited expansion capabilities.

Affiliated companies—such as the divestiture of the Allegis companies.

Other ground facilities—such as the sale of the Pan Am building.

Recent History of Asset Dispositions by Troubled Airlines

We reviewed recent histories of Pan Am, TWA, and Texas Air to ascertain which assets were selected for liquidation and how successful the liquidations were in terms of contributing to shareholder wealth. The stock charts of these three airlines are at the end of the chapter.

Pan Am

Major asset sales by Pan Am include the Pan Am Building, which was sold for $400 million in December 1980; International Hotels Corporation, sold for $500 million in September 1981; the Pacific routes, sold to UAL for $750 million in February 1986; and the sale of aircraft purchase rights in December 1988 for $115 million. In 1982, 1984, and 1986 it sold various aircraft for approximately $100 million.

Statements by analysts suggest that the prices received by Pan Am may not have been generous. The January 15, 1990, edition of *Business Week* suggests that UAL's revenues from the Pacific routes have grown by 22 percent annually and accounted for about $2 billion in 1989 revenues. The December 25, 1989, edition of *Forbes* estimates that the Pan Am Building is now worth about $1 billion, suggesting that it was a good investment for the purchaser.

A review of the six stock price histories below suggests that many airlines were experiencing upward trends throughout the decade. From 1986 to 1988, Pan Am suffered a continued stock price decline. While this was no doubt caused by the constant flow of poor operating results during this period, it also reflects investor expectations for the future. Clearly, these expectations reflect the loss of the Pacific business. The stock price evidence following the sale of the Pan Am Building is less dramatic, given similar patterns during this time period for other airline companies.

It is not supportable, given the large number of interrelated factors, to conclude that the market evidence indicates that the route sale was a poor liquidation choice for a troubled company. On the other hand, the evidence is at least consistent with this conclusion. According to the analytical framework provided in earlier sections of this chapter, one might explain this conclusion in terms of the third question: What effect will a proposed transaction have on the company? What Pan Am gave up was a component of the business that had the most potential to contribute future growth.

Trans World Airlines

TWA, which historically has shown operational similarities to Pan Am, and which has also experienced ongoing losses, adopted a very different approach to asset liquidation. Unlike Pan Am, TWA did not undertake divestitures that would have reduced the scale of operations, except for the sale in December 1986 of a 50 percent interest in PARS, its reservation system, and the sale of its Chicago to London route. Most liquidations were financing liquidations, including the sale of receivables and the sale leaseback of equipment. In February 1986, TWA sold $313 million of equipment trust certificates, essentially along the guidelines of a refinancing transaction as described earlier, in The Valuation of Tangible Assets. Market evidence on the 1986 transaction was not conclusive.

In January 1990, TWA sold 11 Lockheed L1011s and Boeing 747s for $210 million. This transaction followed the December 1989 sale to American Airlines of the Chicago to London route for $195 million. Unfortunately, the stock was privately held by this time so no market observation was possible.

Texas Air Corporation

Texas Air, while a troubled company for many years, liquidated very few assets until the need was critical. The only notable asset liquidations are the sale of landing slots at LaGuardia and Washington National airports for $63 million in 1986, the sale of the Shuttle in October 1988 for $365 million, the sale of Britt landing slots in

1989 for $35 million, and the December 1989 agreement to sell Eastern's profitable Latin American routes to American Airlines for $471 million.

The stock price chart for Texas Air shows a marked decline in 1987 to 1989 from the 1986 and early 1987 levels. Given the volatile market conditions in 1987, attribution to the purchase or sale of assets is doubtful. The decline in January 1990 seems to reverse a positive trend in 1989, perhaps (with similarity to the Pan Am case) reflecting the sale of the potential for profit and growth on the Latin American routes.

Recent History of Asset Dispositions by Other Airlines

Southwest Airlines and US Air

Southwest has shown stable performance in recent years, even though it is now facing somewhat reduced earnings prospects as a result of increased fuel costs and personnel expenses. In 1989, Southwest transacted a sale leaseback of aircraft. This move was not the result of necessity, since Southwest is considered to be a financially strong airline. US Air, like Southwest, has undertaken few asset liquidations. The purpose of including these two airlines in this analysis is to provide "control" examples for market comparison purposes. Any assessment of the asset liquidations by the troubled companies must be made with reference to overall market trends. Southwest, US Air, and United, as well as the Standard & Poor's 500 stock composite index (see chart at end of chapter), indicate trends in airline industry market values and in the overall movement of the market.

United Airlines

The divestiture of the Allegis companies was accomplished in 1987, when Hilton International was sold for $1.1 billion and Hertz was sold for $1.3 billion, and, in 1988, when Westin Hotels was sold for $1.3 billion. The stock price chart suggests that the sale of these assets was received positively by investors, implying both that the price was acceptable and that the remaining business had good growth and profit potential.

Summary of Data on Asset Liquidations for the Airlines

The purpose of the review of events in the airline industry was to demonstrate the variety of liquidation options that may be chosen by management, and which actually have been chosen in certain circumstances. This history is viewed relative to the market performance of the airline companies. Given that the industry has shown constant growth over the last decade and is projected to maintain strong growth, one would anticipate that companies would be reticent to liquidate business operations. The evidence provided above supports the conclusion that only the most troubled airlines have sold business operations (e.g., the Eastern Shuttle and the Pan Am Pacific routes). Less-troubled companies have opted for financing liquidations, such as TWA's equipment trust certificates.

In summary, the only recourse of a troubled company in need of capital may be to liquidate assets. This chapter has provided an analytical framework that could be used by management to evaluate and compare its options. A brief review of market data was included to address the question of whether investors have shown support or preference for certain choices. The conclusion is clearly that the appropriate choice depends entirely on the specific circumstances of the troubled company, with the possible caveat that the liquidation of core profitable businesses does not seem to be supported by market data.

238 Chapter 7

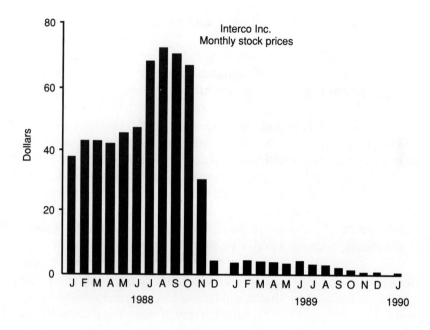

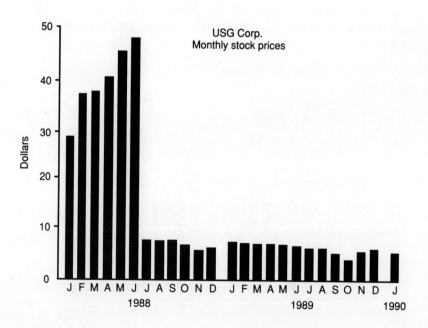

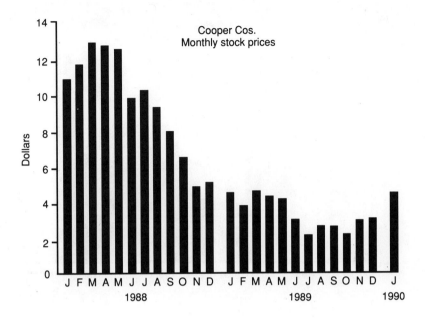

Cooper Cos.
Monthly stock prices

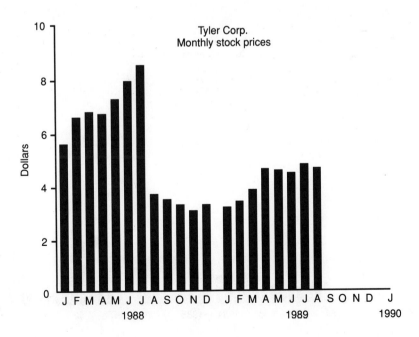

Tyler Corp.
Monthly stock prices

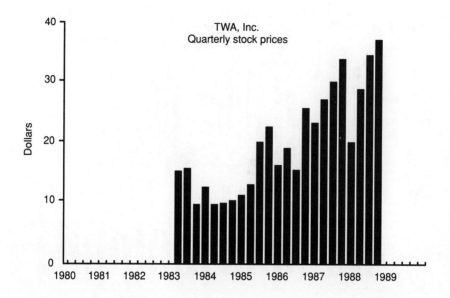

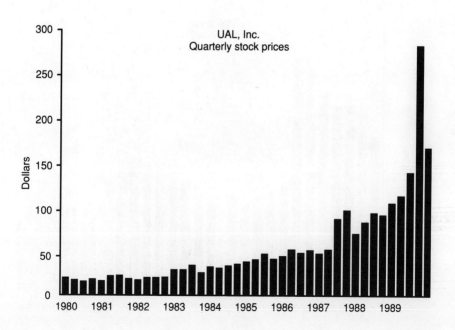

Liquidation Options for Troubled Companies   241

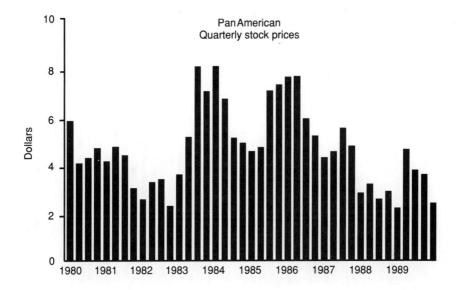

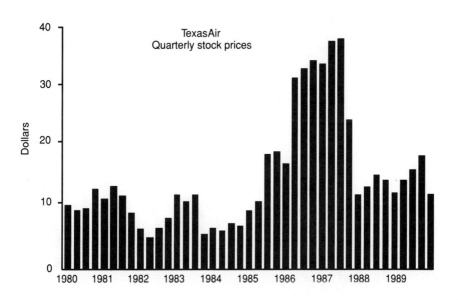

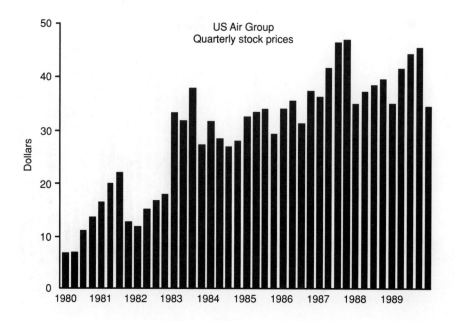
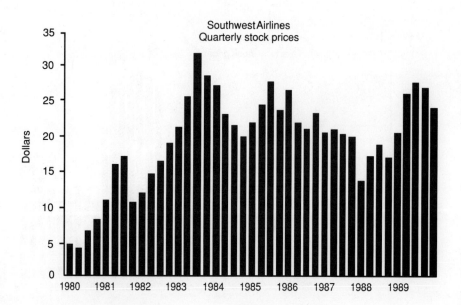

Liquidation Options for Troubled Companies **243**

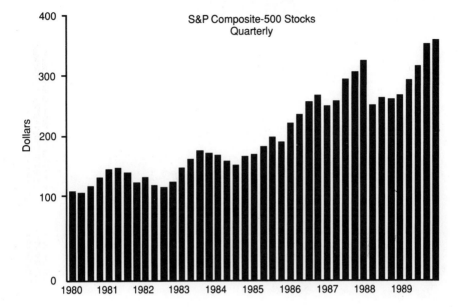

CHAPTER 8

REORGANIZATIONS AND THE SECURED CREDITOR

Denis F. Cronin, Esq.[*]
Jane Lee Vris, Esq.
Wachtell, Lipton, Rosen & Katz

INTRODUCTION

When a "troubled" company begins its long march toward restructuring its debt, in the usual case the secured creditor initially has an interested but somewhat passive role, observing from the sidelines the negotiations of the company with its unsecured creditors and shareholders. The reasons are simple: (1) the secured creditor is in a more formidable position because of its collateral than unsecured creditors or shareholders; and (2) if the secured creditor is to be asked to "share the pain" of a restructuring, whether out of court or pursuant to a Chapter 11 reorganization, serious consideration of any significant "contribution" of the secured creditor to the restructuring will only occur after substantial concessions have been made by the inferior unsecured creditor and shareholder interests.

As part of any proposal made by the troubled company to the secured creditor, after the concessions of these other inferior interests are shown, the secured creditor will be shown how, with its

---

[*] The authors gratefully acknowledge the assistance of Gregory A. Azzara, Esq., of Wachtell, Lipton, Rosen & Katz in the preparation of this chapter.

"contribution" to the restructuring effort, the company can successfully reorganize and regain its financial health without the need for a Chapter 11 reorganization. In the usual case, the company will also at the same time suggest to the secured creditor that a Chapter 11 proceeding would likely cause a thorough investigation of the perfection of its lien, the validity of its lien, and the value of the collateral, and that the Chapter 11 filing might not only have an adverse effect on prospects of the company's business but the prospects of the secured creditor's claim as well. If the secured creditor has not already done so, this discussion will then cause the secured creditor to focus on what exactly will happen to it and its collateral in a Chapter 11 case.

Whether in workout or in Chapter 11, the secured creditor's assessment of any restructuring proposal the company makes to it begins with a comparison of that proposal with the secured creditor's analysis of what might happen to its claim and its collateral in a Chapter 11 proceeding. Thus, the Chapter 11 comparison is the keystone to the secured creditor's judgment of whether to agree to restructure its secured claim, and, if so, on what terms. If the treatment proposed by the company in the restructuring for the secured claim is less favorable than the treatment to be accorded the secured claim in Chapter 11, the secured creditor will seek to improve its proposed treatment or reject the restructuring proposal, possibly precipitating a Chapter 11 filing.

While there are many uncertainties inherent in the Chapter 11 process, a number of fundamental issues are applicable only to secured claims that must be considered in any Chapter 11 case. This chapter will discuss the most important of these issues with a view toward highlighting the protections, risks, and uncertainties that await the holder of a secured claim in its actual or comparative journey through a Chapter 11 case.

OVERVIEW

The "purpose" of Chapter 11 of the Bankruptcy Reform Act of 1978, as amended,[1] in the words of Congress, "is to restructure a business's finances so that it may continue to operate, provide its employees with jobs, pay its creditors, and produce a return for its shareholders."[2] It would be inconsistent with that purpose to allow a debtor's secured creditors to foreclose on their liens, taking assets away from the debtor that are necessary to its operations. Nevertheless, the goal of fostering reorganization must be balanced against the secured creditor's lien on the collateral, a protected property right: "The secured creditor is entitled to realize his claim, and not have his collateral eroded by delay or by use of the estate."[3] Many of the Code provisions applicable specifically to secured claims are designed to balance these two interests, on the one hand, by staying actions against the debtor's property, and, on the other, by providing the secured creditor with "adequate protection" against erosion in the value of its collateral and "cramdown" provisions, which insure that it will realize on its claim an amount at least equal to the value of its collateral. Before examining these provisions, however, the secured creditor must first determine whether and to what extent its claim will be treated as a "secured claim" in the Chapter 11 reorganization process.

THE SECURED CLAIM

A claim against a borrower secured by a lien on the borrower's assets is not necessarily a claim entitled to special protection as a secured claim. A "secured" claim under the Code is one that is an "allowed" claim secured by a lien on property in which the estate has an interest. It is secured only to the extent of the value of the secured creditor's interest in the property.[4]

Allowed Claim

A claim is deemed "allowed" once the creditor has filed a proof of claim, unless a party in interest objects to the claim.[5] If a party objects to the allowance of the claim, the bankruptcy court determines the amount of the allowed claim.[6] In a Chapter 11 case, if a claim appears on the various schedules of liabilities the Code requires the debtor to file, and if it has not been scheduled as disputed, contingent or unliquidated, then a proof of claim for that claim is deemed to have been filed.[7] However, since a debtor may later amend its schedules, it is a better practice to file a proof of claim and not to rely, possibly to one's detriment, on the debtor's schedules.

Generally, claims for postpetition interest are not allowed.[8] There are exceptions. Some courts have allowed postpetition interest to accrue on unsecured claims when the debtor was solvent, reasoning that it would be more equitable to allow claims for postpetition interest than to permit the debtor (and thus, indirectly, the shareholders) to receive, in effect, a windfall to the extent of the value of that postpetition interest.[9]

In addition, the Code specifically provides that a secured claim may include postpetition interest to the extent of any value in the collateral in excess of the principal amount of the claim.[10] Most courts have held that postpetition interest accrues at the contract rate.[11] Postpetition interest stops accruing once it equals the excess value in the collateral.[12] Excess value is determined after deducting the value of any prior liens and without regard to any junior liens there may be on the collateral, and after deduction of certain costs and expenses of the estate that are charged against the collateral (discussed below).[13] The Supreme Court has recently determined that the statutory provision permitting postpetition interest on secured claims should be read to permit postpetition interest on both consensual liens (e.g., mortgage liens) and nonconsensual liens (e.g., tax liens), thus reversing Code cases (and diverging from act cases) that had not allowed postpetition interest to accrue on tax liens.[14]

Oversecured creditors are also entitled to include in the amount of their allowed claim, to the extent of the excess value in their collateral, "any reasonable fees, costs, or charges provided for under the agreement under which such claim arose,"[15] including attorney fees. The court determines whether any such amounts are "reasonable."[16] Secured creditors may be able to assert an unsecured claim for amounts that the court determines are not reasonable if the documents under which such claims arose provide for reimbursement of such amounts and if the contractual reimbursement provisions are enforceable under state law.[17]

Interestingly, a few courts have appointed official committees of secured creditors in Chapter 11 cases.[18] A consequence of these decisions is that costs and expenses of secured creditors' advisers acting as professionals retained by the secured creditors' committee will be compensated along with other committee professionals from the debtor's estate without regard to the value of the secured creditors' collateral.[19] A secured creditors' committee may be particularly appropriate when there exist numerous mortgage bondholders or similar types of secured creditors sharing an interest in the same collateral pool.[20] Additionally, an undersecured creditor may be able to participate in an unsecured creditors' committee, with the costs and expenses of the committee's advisers paid by the estate to the extent approved by the court.[21]

The costs and expenses that the trustee or debtor-in-possession may recover from the collateral, and which may be netted against the value of the collateral in determining how much postpetition interest and costs and expenses may be included in the allowed claim, if any, are "the reasonable, necessary costs and expenses of preserving, or disposing of [the collateral] to the extent of any benefit to the holder of such claim."[22] Expenses incurred in selling collateral (e.g., advertising and auctioneers' expenses) courts agree may clearly be deducted from proceeds of collateral. Beyond those readily identifiable expenses, courts have not applied a uniform rule specifying the costs and expenses which may be deducted from a secured creditor's collateral.

A few courts have been relatively generous in charging collateral, interpreting the Code as permitting expenses that enabled the debtor to continue as a going concern. Employing this standard, some courts have permitted the administrative expenses of a proceeding, including committee expenses and committee counsel's fees, to be charged against the collateral.[23]

Other courts have been more protective of secured creditors' interests, and, following the language of the Code more closely, have required that the expenses be incurred primarily for the benefit of the secured creditor, and that the creditor be directly benefited. Courts applying this standard are likely to test the benefit to the secured creditor quantitatively: an expenditure should be included only if the secured creditor would have received less from its collateral had the expenditure not been made.[24]

If a secured creditor consents to the expenditure of costs and expenses by the debtor, some courts consider the secured creditor to have also consented to deduction of those costs and expenses from its collateral. Not surprisingly, courts differ in their willingness to infer the secured creditor's consent to expenditures from its actions. A few courts have deducted costs and expenses when the secured creditor consented to the continued operation of the debtor's business, while others have found that a secured creditor only consents to those expenses that it caused the debtor to incur.[25]

The total amount of the costs and expenses of preserving or disposing of collateral is deducted from the value of the collateral in determining the extent to which a creditor is oversecured and, therefore, entitled to postpetition interest and the expenses provided for in its underlying loan documentation.

Lien on the Property of the Debtor's Estate

To be "secured," the allowed claim must be secured by a lien on (or security interest in) property in which the estate has an interest. Generally, only those interests that existed at the time the petition was filed become property of the estate.[26] With one exception, discussed below, prepetition liens do not extend to property acquired by the debtor after the filing. For example, notwithstanding any "after acquired" clause in the collateral documentation, a creditor's prepetition lien in all accounts receivable will not extend to accounts receivable generated after the petition.[27]

The one exception permitted by the Bankruptcy Code is a lien on "proceeds, product, offspring, rents, or profits" of collateral to the extent the prepetition security agreement so provided and to the extent the agreement is enforceable under applicable nonbankruptcy law (i.e., usually state law).[28] Thus, a lien will attach to cash the debtor received postpetition on account of a prepetition account receivable,[29] and a lien will attach to postpetition payments on a contract assigned prepetition to the creditor.[30] Whether particular property constitutes "proceeds, product, offspring, rents, or profits" of collateral is determined by state law.

The court can limit or deny altogether the exception permitting a lien on postpetition proceeds if the equities of the case compel that result.[31] A court could decide that it would be more equitable to let the debtor retain property free and clear if the debtor had improved the property through its time, effort, or money that would have otherwise been expended for the benefit of general unsecured creditors.[32] The equities may also favor the debtor if the secured creditor has sufficient collateral without resort to the postpetition collateral.[33] In weighing the equities, courts consider the policy imbedded in Chapter 11 of promoting the rehabilitation of the debtor.³⁴ The determination of whether the equities of the case argue for cutting off a postpetition lien lies in the discretion of the court and will vary from case to case.³⁵

Value of Collateral

An allowed claim secured by property is not necessarily wholly a "secured" claim. The claim is secured only to the extent of the value of the secured creditor's interest in the collateral. The remainder of the claim, if any, is an unsecured claim.³⁶ For example, a claim based on a $100 loan secured by collateral worth $60 is a secured claim in the amount of $60 and an unsecured claim for $40. The protection and treatment provided for secured claims under the Code will apply only to $60 of the $100 claim. The value of the secured claim will be reduced by the amount of any prior liens.

The method of valuing collateral, obviously an important predicate to a reorganization under Chapter 11, is nowhere prescribed by the Code. Instead, the Code provides generally that "value shall be determined in light of the purpose of the valuation and of the proposed disposition or use of such property."³⁷ Valuation is required in a number of circumstances, and a secured creditor may find that the amount of its secured claim will fluctuate throughout the case. A determination of value in one context is not binding precedent in another.³⁸

The more significant events in a Chapter 11 case that can require valuation of collateral are circumstances in which adequate protection must be provided to a secured creditor, preference actions, and confirmation of a plan either with the consent of a secured creditor or without such consent under the cramdown provisions of the Code. (Full coverage of these topics follows.)

The congressional committee reports evince Congress's intent that no one method of valuation be required for all purposes. Value is to be determined on a case-by-case basis.³⁹ The range of methodologies used by courts in valuing collateral runs the gamut from liquidation value to going-concern value. For example, when determining whether adequate protection exists in the context of a motion to sell collateral, a court will most likely use the proposed sale price of the collateral for its value.⁴⁰ In the context of a cramdown hearing, a court will more likely use a going-concern value.⁴¹ In other situations, a court may weigh whether the debtor is more likely to liquidate or reorganize successfully before choosing the appropriate standard.[42]

There is a relative paucity of decisions involving valuation of businesses and significant pieces of a debtor's property. This is not by accident: creditors and debtors generally prefer to negotiate an agreement on value than to leave such a significant determination to the court's discretion.

AVOIDING POWERS

The Code gives the trustee the power to avoid certain liens.[43] By virtue of these avoiding powers, a secured creditor may find that its lien is avoided and its claim is treated as wholly unsecured. The avoiding powers of the trustee are found primarily in (1) the so-called strong-arm provisions of the Code, (2) the provisions for avoiding preferential transfers, and (3) the provisions for avoiding fraudulent transfers (each discussed below).

Strong-Arm Provisions of the Code

Upon commencement of a case, the trustee may avoid any lien that a hypothetical lien creditor, judgment creditor, or bona fide purchaser of real property could have avoided on the date the case was commenced.[44] More simply, a trustee may avoid any lien that was not perfected, and was, therefore, not enforceable against other creditors of the debtor, prior to the filing of the petition.

A trustee will scrutinize the documentation relating to the secured creditor's collateral to determine whether all legal formalities for perfecting the lien in the collateral were observed. Generally, state law determines whether the lien was properly perfected.[45] For example, in a state that requires Form UCC-1s to be filed in two places, locally and centrally, a lien will not be perfected if the secured creditor filed its Form UCC-1 in only one place. A mortgage lien, too, will be unperfected if it has not been filed in the form and in the place required by state law. So, for example, if the signature of the debtor has not been acknowledged as required under state law, the mortgage lien will be unperfected even if the mortgage was filed in the correct place.⁴⁶ There may be an exception under applicable state law making the lien enforceable against creditors with actual knowledge, even though it was unperfected. Notwithstanding the existence of such an exception, the trustee will be able to avoid the lien under those circumstances for the benefit of all unsecured creditors, regardless of any actual knowledge it or any other creditor may have had.⁴⁷

The Code also gives the trustee whatever avoiding powers unsecured creditors are given by applicable state law.⁴⁸ State law, for example, permits unsecured creditors to avoid a lien that constitutes a fraudulent conveyance. In some states, the relevant statute of limitations is as long as six years. Although the Code provides for avoidance of fraudulently conveyed liens, the statute of limitations is only one year. With its expanded avoiding powers, a trustee could potentially avoid a lien utilizing the applicable state law fraudulent conveyance provisions if the one-year statute of limitations for actions brought under the bankruptcy fraudulent conveyance provisions had expired.

Preferential Transfers

The trustee may avoid the lien of a secured creditor (or payments made on account of such a creditor's claim) if the creditor's lien was granted (or payment was made) within a statutorily defined period before the petition was filed, and such grant (or payment) constituted a voidable preference as such term is defined in the Code. As will be more fully considered below, a fully secured creditor holding a valid lien, in contrast to an unsecured or undersecured creditor, generally cannot be found to have received a preference by a payment made to it within the applicable preference period.

Under the Code, the basic elements of a preference are a transfer: (1) of an interest of the debtor in property; (2) to or for the benefit of a creditor; (3) for or on account of an antecedent debt owed by the debtor before such transfer was made; (4) made while the debtor was insolvent; (5) made (*a*) on or within 90 days before the date of the filing of the bankruptcy petition or (*b*) between 90 days and one year before the date of the filing of the petition; and (6) that enables the creditor to receive more than it would receive if the case were a Chapter 7 liquidation case.⁴⁹

A payment to a secured creditor that was fully secured at the time of the petition cannot be recovered as a preference. No transfer on account of a fully secured claim could give the secured creditor more than it would receive in liquidation, since, in liquidation, the fully secured creditor would have received the entire amount of its claim.[50]

Even if all the elements of a preference are present, the transfer will not be avoidable if it was an ordinary course payment made on debt incurred in the ordinary course of business.[51] Courts have not been consistent in their determination of whether interest payments made on long-term debt within the applicable preference period can be recovered as preferences. Some courts have held that such interest payments fit within the exception; other courts have permitted the trustee to avoid such payments, reasoning that long-term debt is not incurred in the ordinary course of business.[52]

In the course of a workout, a creditor may agree to restructure its debt: it may agree to alter the interest rate, the principal amount, the payment terms, or to forego the protection of certain covenants. As part of this workout package, the creditor may receive some consideration in exchange: it may get collateral it did not previously have, it may get an increased interest rate, and it may even get a special one-time paydown of its debt.

Following the workout, there is a risk that any new collateral or payments of interest or principal that a creditor who participated in the workout receives under the restructured terms of its debt could be recovered as a preference. Payments in respect of long-term debt which was incurred by the debtor in the ordinary course of business or represents the consolidation of debt that was originally incurred in the ordinary course of business might be protected from attack as preferential transfers; nevertheless, a court may determine that the restructured debt was not incurred in the ordinary course of business, and that all payments on the restructured debt made within the applicable preference period are avoidable.[53]

Additionally, there is a risk that any consideration received by the creditor in the workout may be recovered if the Chapter 11 petition followed the consummation of the workout within the applicable preference period. Although the Code excludes from the preference avoiding powers transfers made in exchange for "new value," new value is narrowly defined.[54] *New value* means "money or money's worth in goods, services, or new credit, or release . . . of property"; but the definition specifically excludes the substitution of one obligation for another obligation.[55] Some courts have held that restructuring an existing obligation does not by itself constitute new value.[56] Creditors who received their collateral as part of a workout, therefore, may find their liens avoided in a preference action. It is worth noting that, if the recipient of an alleged preference can demonstrate the debtor was solvent at the time the transfer occurred, one of the basic elements of a preference (i.e., the debtor was insolvent at the time the transfer was made) would not be present and the transfer would not constitute a preference. The trustee, however, is assisted by the rebuttable presumption created by the Code that the debtor was insolvent during the 90-day period immediately preceding the filing of the petition.[57]

Secured creditors should also be aware of the possibility that they may be classified as insiders for purposes of the application of the preference provisions of the Code and, thereby, subjected to the one-year preference period applicable to insiders instead of the 90-day period applicable to noninsiders. In the case of a debtor corporation, the Code defines an insider as including any officers of the corporation, persons "in control" of the corporation, partnerships in which the corporation is a general partner, general partners of the corporation, and relatives of a general partner, director, officer, or person in control of the corporation.[58] Affiliates of the debtor and insiders of affiliates also are deemed to be insiders.[59]

Although most traditional creditors fall outside of the definition of insider, a creditor might be classified as an insider if it could be deemed to be in control of the debtor. It could also be subjected to the extended preference period applicable to insiders if it holds a guarantee from an individual or an entity that is itself an insider of the debtor. Several recent cases, reasoning that payments made directly to the creditor in respect of an obligation guaranteed by an insider benefit that insider by reducing the insider's obligations under the guarantee, have explicitly found that such payments are, therefore, subject to the one-year preference period.[60] An avoidance of a preferential transfer by the trustee results in the recovery by the estate of such a grant or transfer from its transferee for the benefit of the estate and, thus, for the benefit of all general unsecured creditors.

Fraudulent Conveyances

The trustee may also avoid, in whole or in part, the lien of a secured creditor (or recover payments made on account of such a creditor's claim) for the benefit of the estate if such lien was granted (or payment was made) in a transaction that constituted a fraudulent conveyance.[61] Both the Code and state law protect creditors from transfers of property that are fraudulent to the extent those transfers are intended to impair creditors' ability to enforce their rights to payment[62] or have the effect of depleting a debtor's assets at a time when its financial condition is precarious.[63] Fraudulent conveyance laws have been part of the legal landscape for over 400 years, and are embodied in state law in one of two forms: either the Uniform Fraudulent Conveyance Act (UFCA) or the Uniform Fraudulent Transfer Act (UFTA). They have recently become of greater concern to secured creditors, because they have been used successfully to attack the validity of security interests granted to secured lenders in leveraged buyouts.

The Code's provisions relating to fraudulent conveyances empower the trustee in bankruptcy to avoid any transfer of an interest of the debtor in property, or any obligation incurred within one year prior to the date of the filing of the bankruptcy petition in the case of intentional fraud and three instances of constructive fraud similar to those found in the UFCA, discussed below.[64] Under the Code, as in the UFCA, the existence of constructive fraud depends on lack of adequate consideration for a transfer combined with insolvency, unreasonably small capital, or intent by the debtor to incur debts beyond its ability to pay.[65] The main difference between the Code and the UFTA, discussed below, and the UFCA is in the phrasing of the consideration element in the definition of constructive fraud: the UFCA requires fair consideration, while the Code and the UFTA require a "reasonably equivalent value" in exchange.[66] In certain limited circumstances, a transferee who takes for value and in good faith may be granted a lien or may be permitted to retain any interest transferred or may be permitted to enforce any obligation incurred to the extent of value given to the debtor.[67]

As has been discussed earlier, the Code empowers the trustee to avoid a transfer made (or obligation incurred) by the debtor that is avoidable under state law by an unsecured creditor holding an allowed claim.[68] Consequently, with certain limitations, the trustee can avail himself of the fraudulent conveyance provisions of both the Code and state law.

The primary state statutes governing fraudulent conveyances are based on the newer UFTA and the older UFCA.[69] In simplified terms, the UFCA defines four types of transactions that are fraudulent and, therefore, avoidable by creditors. The first three are rules of "constructive" fraud, which define circumstances where transfers are deemed fraudulent whether or not the transferor actually intends to defraud creditors. Transfers are deemed fraudulent if they are made without fair consideration, and, at the time of the transaction, (1) the transferor either is insolvent or rendered insolvent, (2) is in business and is left with unreasonably small capital, or (3) anticipates incurring debts beyond its ability to pay.[70] The fourth and final rule embodies the concept of intentional fraud and enables creditors to recover property conveyed with an actual intent to hinder, delay, or defraud creditors.[71]

The UFCA contains two exculpatory provisions that protect innocent transferees and recipients of transfers from such transferees. Under the first of those exculpatory provisions, creditors cannot recover from a purchaser who purchased for fair consideration and without knowledge of the fraud.[72] Under the second, a transferee who paid less than fair consideration, but who did so without actual fraudulent intent, may retain the property or obligation as security for repayment of the consideration paid.[73]

As has already been mentioned, the application of fraudulent conveyance laws to leveraged buyout transactions has recently become a matter of great concern to secured creditors. The current majority view among the courts is that fraudulent conveyance laws are applicable to leveraged buyouts.[74]

In a standard leveraged buyout transaction, the acquisition vehicle borrows funds to purchase the stock of the target company. The target company then guarantees the loan and pledges its assets as security for the guarantee, or it may merge into the acquisition vehicle thereby assuming the primary obligation to repay the acquisition debt, again securing the obligations with its assets. Either way both the undertaking to repay the acquisition debt and the security granted for that undertaking constitute "transfers" of property of the target company. The target's granting of a security interest in its assets also constitutes a "transfer" of its property.

Because they constitute transfers of property, both structures of leveraged buyout transactions are susceptible to attack as fraudulent conveyances.

As already discussed, a fraudulent conveyance action can be premised on either actual or constructive fraud. Although lenders in leveraged buyout transactions are usually attacked on the ground of constructive fraud, it is possible for them to be sued on the basis of actual fraud, because, in determining the existence of actual fraud, at least one recent case has found that a state fraudulent conveyance statute looks to the *debtor's* intent.[75] However, even if a court were to conclude that a leveraged buyout constituted an actual fraud on the debtor's other creditors, a transferee who took without knowledge of the fraud and gave reasonably equivalent or fair value to the debtor probably would be protected from having the transfer attacked as a fraudulent conveyance.[76]

In determining whether a transfer is avoidable under the constructive fraud provisions of the Code and the UFTA, the first question is whether the debtor received "reasonably equivalent value" for the property transferred or the obligation incurred. This is a factual determination to be made on a case-by-case basis. At least one court found that the debtor, the target of a leveraged buyout, and its affiliates received no consideration in the transaction, because the loan proceeds were used to pay the target's stockholders for their shares, resulting in no direct benefit to either the target or its affiliates.[77] Another recent case has held that an upstream guarantee and pledge of assets by a subsidiary in connection with a restructuring of its parent corporation's obligations under an existing credit agreement were made without consideration.[78]

Similarly, under the UFCA, the debtor must have received fair consideration in return for the property transferred or the obligation incurred. Fair consideration requires that the transferee pay "fair equivalent" value in "good faith."[79] As a general matter, the tender of stock by selling shareholders in connection with a leveraged buyout does not in and of itself constitute fair equivalent value.[80] Good faith sometimes can be established by demonstrating that the transfer in question was arm's length.[81] It is worth noting, however, that several courts have held a transferee cannot be acting in good faith if it has knowledge of or participates in the fraud.[82]

The other elements involved in determining whether a leveraged transaction constituted a fraudulent conveyance (i.e., whether the transaction rendered the debtor insolvent, left the debtor with unreasonably small capital, or caused the debtor to incur debts beyond its ability to pay) are factual inquiries that will vary from case to case. Nevertheless, a lender who (1) obtained solvency letters, valuation opinions, and asset appraisals showing the debtor was solvent at the time the leveraged transaction occurred, and (2) can demonstrate that the revenue and cash flow projections it used in evaluating the loan were reasonable at the time the loan was extended, should be in a stronger position to rebut the financial elements of the fraudulent conveyance analysis than lenders who did not take such steps. Nevertheless, it must be emphasized that, if a court is considering these issues, the solvency letters, valuation opinions, cash flow projections, and the like were probably based on assumptions that turned out to be too optimistic. Having the benefit of "hindsight," the court may be skeptical of the reasonableness of some of these devices and the assumptions on which they were based.

Subordination

A secured creditor with a validly perfected lien, not avoidable under any of the trustee's avoiding powers, may nevertheless find its secured claim subordinated to the claims of general unsecured creditors. The Bankruptcy Code enables a court, after notice and a hearing, to subordinate part or all of an allowed claim, including a secured claim, to part or all of another allowed claim under principles of equitable subordination.[83]

Broadly stated, a claim may be equitably subordinated on one of two grounds. A claim can be subordinated if it could be recharacterized as an equity contribution (i.e., if it was made by an insider at a time when the debtor was undercapitalized). A claim, whether held by an insider or another party, can also be subordinated if the creditor engaged in inequitable conduct that either harmed other creditors or advantaged it.

Whether conduct was inequitable depends on the facts and circumstances and is, therefore, within the court's discretion to decide. Courts hold creditors who are insiders to a higher standard of conduct than others, because they are viewed by the courts as fiduciaries of the debtor, if not also the creditors. Creditors that are not insiders may nevertheless find their conduct judged by this higher standard if they exercised sufficient control of the debtor to be, in effect, deemed an insider. Conduct of a creditor that is not an insider or otherwise a party deemed in control must be egregious to be "inequitable." Once inequitable conduct is found, the claim is subordinated only to the extent necessary to offset the harm caused by the conduct.[84]

A discussion of all the circumstances in which claims have been equitably subordinated is beyond the scope of this chapter. The secured creditor (or purchaser of a secured claim) when assessing the value of its claim in Chapter 11 should review prepetition conduct and, for claims held by insiders, the capitalization of the debtor when the claim arose to determine whether there is any basis for subordinating its claim to the claims of the general unsecured creditors.

The Code also recognizes contractual subordination. If a secured creditor agreed to subordinate part or all of its claim or lien to another creditor, the agreement will be enforceable to the same extent as under nonapplicable bankruptcy law.[85]

ADEQUATE PROTECTION

"Adequate protection" is designed to protect the secured creditor from diminution in the value of its collateral during the pendency of the case, whether from erosion of the collateral's value or from the debtor's use of the collateral. This protection is grounded, to a limited extent, in the constitutional protection of property in the "due process" clause of the Fifth Amendment of the United States Constitution.[86]

Situations in which adequate protection must be provided, to the extent necessary to protect the value of collateral, include (1) when a court denies the motion of a secured creditor seeking to lift the automatic stay in order to foreclose on its collateral;[87] (2) when a trustee is permitted to use, sell, or lease a secured creditor's collateral;[88] and (3) when a trustee is permitted to incur indebtedness secured by a lien that is senior to, or has the same priority as, the lien of another creditor in the same property.[89]

The Code specifies that adequate protection may be in the form of (1) periodic cash payments or a single cash payment, (2) a lien on additional or replacement collateral, or (3) relief providing the secured creditor with the "indubitable equivalent" of its lien.[90] The forms of adequate protection specified are not exclusive. The debtor may fashion other forms of adequate protection subject to agreement of the secured creditor or, if it objects, to approval of the court. The Code explicitly rejects the grant of an administrative claim (one that has priority over all unsecured claims) as a form of adequate protection.[91] If, however, a secured creditor receives an acceptable form of adequate protection, which, in hindsight, did not adequately protect the secured creditor's interest in its collateral, the secured creditor is entitled to an administrative claim with priority over all other administrative claims.[92]

Valuation of the collateral (as well as valuation of any proposed additional or replacement collateral) is crucial in determining whether adequate protection is necessary and, if so, to what extent. As discussed above, no one method of valuation is prescribed by the Code, nor is valuation of collateral at any one point in a case necessarily determinative of value at any other point in the case.[93]

The Supreme Court has made it clear that value (and, therefore, the adequate protection to which a secured creditor may be entitled) does not include the value of immediate possession of the collateral.[94] While a secured creditor is entitled to protection from diminution in the value of its collateral during the case, the time value of the money a creditor may have received, had it not been stayed from foreclosing and realizing on the collateral, is not protected.[95] Note, though, that the time value of an oversecured claim is protected (perhaps more, perhaps less, depending on the applicable interest rates) by the statutory provision, discussed above, which specifically permits an oversecured claim to accrue interest postpetition to the extent of the excess value in the collateral.

A secured creditor may be tempted, in the context of an adequate protection hearing, to minimize the value of its collateral, thus reducing the "equity cushion," if any, and increasing the provision for adequate protection. The temptation should be resisted in most cases, however, since a creditor's testimony may come back to haunt it in a cramdown hearing (discussed later in this chapter), when it may seek to establish a higher collateral value.

Automatic Stay

The automatic stay is one of the chief procedural protections afforded a debtor by the Code. It is very broad and is designed to give the debtor "breathing space" in which to reorganize by staying all actions by creditors to recover on their prepetition claims.[96] Thus, the automatic stay prohibits a secured creditor from foreclosing on collateral included in the debtor's estate, whether it or the debtor is in possession of the collateral. The stay is effective immediately upon filing of the petition, whether filed voluntarily or involuntarily.

Effect of the Stay

The automatic stay protects all property of the estate. Property of the estate is broadly defined to include all interests, legal or beneficial, of the debtor in property as of the commencement of the case.[97] The jurisdictional statute grants courts worldwide jurisdiction over the estate's property.[98] Thus, even for the secured creditor with collateral in a foreign country, the automatic stay prohibits it from taking any action against that collateral. As a practical matter, when property is located in another country, a United States bankruptcy court may only be able to enforce the stay against such property if it has personal jurisdiction over the secured creditor or any of its property by threatening the creditor with a contempt citation. A foreign court with jurisdiction over the collateral may choose to recognize the automatic stay and also enforce it, effectively on behalf of the bankruptcy court, through principles of comity. It is also possible that the foreign court will choose not to enforce the automatic stay and permit the secured creditor to proceed against the collateral.

Conversely, a secured creditor with collateral in the United States and a debtor which is the subject of a reorganization proceeding under the laws of a foreign country may also find its actions against the collateral stayed by the automatic stay provisions of the Code. The Code permits a foreign trustee to commence an ancillary case in a United States bankruptcy court, and it permits the bankruptcy court to stay actions against property of the estate.[99]

There are exceptions to the types of actions blocked by the stay. Most do not have general applicability. To illustrate, one exception allows governmental actions to enforce police powers (e.g., a criminal prosecution) to continue.[100] Other examples are the ability of the Secretary of Commerce to foreclose a mortgage in a vessel,[101] and of the creditor with a purchase money security interest in the aircraft of an air carrier to foreclose.[102] However, one narrow exception is of general interest to secured creditors: the right to perfect certain liens postpetition.

The Code permits a creditor to perfect its lien postpetition if, under state law, the perfection would be deemed effective at an earlier time and would have given the secured creditor rights in the collateral superior to the hypothetical lien creditor.[103] To illustrate, in some states a mechanic's lien for services can be perfected after the services were rendered (within some statutorily prescribed time), and the perfection will relate back to such time. Perfection of purchase money security interests also can relate back to a time prior to the filing of the financing statement under the Uniform Commercial Code. In both cases, filing the requisite notice or financing statement under state law after the petition will not violate the stay so long as perfection relates back to a prepetition time.[104]

Courts have considered whether actions against third parties or property owned by third parties can be stayed. The circumstances in which courts have been willing to stay such actions generally are ones in which the interests of the debtor are perceived to be so intertwined with those of the third party that allowing the actions to proceed would impede the debtor's ability to reorganize or diminish the estate.[105] Technically, courts that have been willing to stay actions against third parties or their property have primarily relied on their broad equitable powers, rather than the automatic stay provisions, but the effect is the same. Thus, secured creditors have been stayed from going against guarantors and their collateral or officers or directors of the debtor in actions for which the debtor has indemnified them, whether directly through a contractual indemnification or through the maintenance of director and officer insurance.[106] Courts have generally let creditors whose claims were secured by letters of credit draw on them, reasoning that letters of credit are not property of the estate.[107]

Lifting the Stay

In the absence of a motion by a creditor to lift the automatic stay, it continues until the Chapter 11 case has been dismissed or closed or the debtor's liabilities discharged, whichever is the first to occur.[108]

Once property leaves the estate, it is no longer protected by the stay. If the trustee abandons (or sells) property subject to the liens of secured creditors, those secured creditors are no longer stayed from foreclosing on their liens.[109]

A creditor may move to have the stay lifted on one of two grounds: (1) for cause, including lack of adequate protection, or (2) if the debtor lacks equity in the collateral and the collateral is not necessary for an effective reorganization.[110] Valuation is obviously a crucial component of either basis for seeking relief from the stay.

As discussed above, adequate protection is a concept designed to protect a secured creditor from diminution in the value of its collateral. In these situations, the debtor must offer the secured creditor some form of adequate protection to compensate it for the loss in collateral value. Excess value in the collateral, or the "equity cushion," may provide sufficient adequate protection.[111] The obvious corollary is that adequate protection does not protect against any diminution in the equity cushion that the secured creditor may have enjoyed (or even bargained for) before the filing, since postpetition interest begins to erode the equity cushion once the petition is filed. Courts have required some form of adequate protection beyond the equity cushion, once postpetition interest has eroded it substantially.[112]

In some cases, the potential for deterioration in collateral and, therefore, in its value is obvious. Retail merchandise is a classic example of collateral that diminishes in value rapidly. Sometimes it is more difficult to determine whether there is any loss in collateral value that adequate protection should replace. A secured creditor with a lien in an operating manufacturing plant may persuasively argue that the going-concern value of the plant is diminishing, even though the liquidation value of the components of the plant—its building, its fixtures, the equipment inside—remains constant. Congress left it to the courts to decide whether the value to be protected is the going-concern value or the liquidation value of the collateral. Whether a secured creditor would be entitled to adequate protection in that situation is within the court's discretion and may, therefore, vary from case to case.[113]

Even if the value of the collateral is not diminishing, the secured creditor is still entitled to relief from the stay if the debtor has no equity in the property—that is, the value of the collateral is less than the claims secured by it, and the collateral is not necessary for an effective reorganization.[114] To determine whether property is necessary for an effective reorganization, the Supreme Court has made it clear that the reorganization should be more than a theoretical possibility; it must be a reorganization *"that is in prospect"* (i.e., "there must be 'a reasonable possibility of a successful reorganization within a reasonable time' ").[115] Courts have taken this language to heart and are continually exploring ways to improve management of a case generally to prevent excessive delays.

Procedure

The Code uncharacteristically prescribes specific procedures and time constraints for hearing and adjudicating a motion to lift the stay. Once a secured creditor has filed a motion seeking to have the stay lifted, the stay will automatically be lifted 30 days later unless the court has, within that time, either made a final determination denying the creditor's request or has made a preliminary determination that "there is reasonable likelihood that the party opposing relief from [the] stay will prevail."[116] If the court has made only a preliminary finding, the final hearing must begin within 30 days of the preliminary determination.

The Code provides for an expedited procedure if necessary to prevent "irreparable damage." The stay in such an emergency may be lifted *ex parte*—that is, without notice to any other party.[117] The Bankruptcy Rules, however, require that notice be given orally to the trustee and establish a procedure for reinstating the stay.[118] This is an extraordinary procedure to be employed only in extraordinary circumstances. An example is collateral such as a truckload of perishable food exposed to the elements standing unattended by the debtor or anyone else on an abandoned pier on a Friday night.

The Code also specifies who bears the burden of proof: the creditor seeking relief from the stay must prove that the debtor has no equity in the property; the trustee has the burden on all other issues.[119] The congressional record indicates that such a hearing is not the appropriate forum for determining counterclaims that the debtor may have against the secured creditor.[120] Assertions of, for example, lender liability will not be permitted to extend interminably the automatic stay hearing. As a consequence, however, the secured creditor should be aware that it could regain its collateral only to find later that it must defend against counterclaims such as allegations of lender liability.[121]

Disputes over the automatic stay inevitably require balancing the debtor's interest in reorganizing against the secured creditor's protected interest in the value of its collateral. Given the importance of the stay to a reorganization and the discretion courts have to select the applicable valuation methodology, it is difficult to predict whether a secured creditor will be able to foreclose on its collateral once a petition has been filed; certainly it should not assume so. However, as discussed throughout this chapter, the Bankruptcy Code has been fashioned to compensate the secured creditor for the loss of its right to foreclose by providing the secured creditor with adequate protection to protect it from diminution in the value of its property during the Chapter 11 case.[122]

Use, Sale, or Lease of Property

A trustee can generally use, sell, or lease a secured creditor's collateral without the creditor's consent. A trustee may dispose of collateral *in the ordinary course of business* without notice and a hearing (i.e., without the secured creditor's consent or court approval).[123] It may dispose of property *out of the ordinary course of business* after a notice and a hearing. The secured creditor has an opportunity to oppose the disposition of its collateral; but the court may approve the proposed use, sale, or lease over the secured creditor's objections.[124] "[N]otice and hearing" is a defined phrase meaning "after such notice as is appropriate in the particular circumstances, and such opportunity for a hearing as is appropriate in the particular circumstances." A hearing can be conditioned upon a party in interest requesting it; the secured creditor, therefore, may find that it must respond quickly to a trustee's motion to dispose of its collateral to have its objections heard.[125]

Property may be sold free and clear of all liens, with the lien attaching to proceeds of sale or the secured creditor otherwise receiving adequate protection for its collateral.[126]

"Cash collateral" is afforded special protection: it may not be used (or sold or leased), even in the ordinary course of business, unless the secured creditor consents or the court authorizes the disposition after notice and a hearing.[127] Thus, upon the filing of the petition, the trustee may not use cash collateral absent consent or court approval. Cash collateral is defined to include cash equivalents (e.g., securities and negotiable instruments). It includes the cash proceeds of collateral generated postpetition to which the prepetition lien is permitted to attach pursuant to the Code.[128] The trustee must segregate and account for all cash collateral.[129]

When collateral is sold over the objection of the secured creditor, the secured creditor nevertheless enjoys some protection. Unless the secured creditor consents, the collateral cannot be sold free and clear of liens for less than the value of liens against it.[130] The extent of the protection this consent requirement provides depends on what the "value" of the liens is, and courts have not been consistent in calculating that value. Courts have used the aggregate amount of the debt secured by the liens as the "value" of those liens. Calculated in this manner, the proceeds from the sale will always be sufficient to repay the debts secured by the liens.[131] Other courts have calculated the "value" of liens in the same manner as the secured claim is defined: the value of the liens is equal to the value of the property. With this method of calculating value, the proceeds will not necessarily be sufficient to repay all the debt secured by liens.[132] The required consent may be implied if a secured creditor fails to object timely to the sale, after it was given adequate notice.[133]

Adequate protection is another of the secured creditor's defenses: upon the secured creditor's request, the court must condition the sale, use, or lease of its collateral on the provision of adequate protection.[134] A common form of adequate protection for a secured creditor's interest in property that the trustee intends to sell is the grant of a substitute lien in the sale proceeds. Since valuation to determine adequate protection in the context of a motion to sell property will often be derived by reference to the sale price, a lien in the sale proceeds will frequently constitute adequate protection.[135]

It does not follow, however, that adequate protection will always be in the form of a lien on cash. First, the consideration paid for the collateral does not have to be cash, and a lien on proceeds will not, therefore, necessarily mean a lien on cash. Second, the form of adequate protection offered by the trustee does not have to be a lien on the sale proceeds. If, for example, the property is sold for cash needed in the debtor's operations, the trustee may offer another form of substitute collateral as adequate protection.[136]

As further protection, secured creditors are permitted to bid in the full amount of their claims at a sale of their collateral, not just the secured portion of their claim.[137] If, for example, a trustee seeks to sell manufacturing equipment for $75,000 and the equipment secures a claim for $100,000, which was valued earlier in the case as a $50,000 secured claim and a $50,000 unsecured claim, the secured creditor may bid in $80,000 of its claim to purchase the equipment, leaving it with a $20,000 unsecured claim.

Obtaining Credit

Under certain circumstances, a trustee may obtain financing postpetition, known as *DIP financing* (for debtor-in-possession), and may grant the postpetition lender a lien in property senior or equal to other liens in the property. However, a lien that is senior or equal to prepetition liens on collateral may be granted only after notice and a hearing, at which the trustee must establish that DIP financing cannot be obtained on any other basis. Such a lien may be granted only if the prepetition secured creditors can be given adequate protection for the amount by which the value of their collateral will be reduced by the postpetition lien.[138] Adequate protection in this situation is likely to be a substitute lien. DIP financing is treated in detail in Chapter 4.

CONFIRMATION, CLASSIFICATION, VOTING

An understanding of the process by which a plan of reorganization is confirmed provides important insights into the treatment accorded secured claims following the commencement of a Chapter 11 case. The code creates two confirmation procedures: one is consensual, the other authorizes the court to confirm a plan over the objection of creditors under its so-called cramdown powers. This section considers both of these confirmation procedures. This section also considers in some depth the issue of the classification of claims, a concept that can play an important role in formulating strategies to promote or hinder the confirmation of a plan. Classification is a significant issue for the creditors of a debtor, because, as will be discussed in connection with confirmation, voting on a proposed plan of reorganization is conducted on a class-by-class basis.

Before a plan of reorganization may be implemented, it must be voted on by creditors and confirmed by the court. Before a plan may be confirmed, the court must conduct a hearing to consider confirmation of the plan.[139] The purpose of this hearing is to insure that the plan complies with the statutory requirements of the Code governing confirmation. Those requirements are designed, in part, to protect the secured creditor's interest in its collateral.

Treatment of Claims and the Secured Creditor's Response

Secured claims can be handled in several ways by a proposed plan, and secured creditors, in turn, can react to such proposed treatment in several ways. A plan can propose to leave a secured claim "unimpaired." A plan can also propose to impair a secured claim. If the plan impairs a secured claim, that claim ultimately may be dealt with either through the consensual confirmation process or the involuntary cramdown procedures. In addition to the responses to a proposed plan available to secured creditors discussed in this section, secured creditors should also be aware of the election provided to them under Section 1111(b) of the Code, which is discussed later.

Leaving a Claim Unimpaired

As has been mentioned, a plan may propose to leave a secured claim unimpaired. If the court finds that the proposed plan, in fact, leaves such a class of claims unimpaired, it is presumed to have accepted the plan.[140]

The Code defines impairment broadly by stating that a class of claims or interests is impaired under plan unless one of the three exceptions set forth by the section of the Code governing impairment is satisfied.[141]

The first exception allows a class of claims to be considered unimpaired if the proposed plan "leaves unaltered the legal, equitable, and contractual rights to which such claim or interest entitles the holder of such claim or interest."[142]

The second exception allows the debtor to consider unimpaired those obligations on which it has defaulted by allowing the debtor to decelerate any claims that have been accelerated due to the debtor's default of a contractual term or applicable law.[143] Under this second exception, the debtor may decelerate claims only if the plan provides for the following: (1) the curing of any default, other than default that occurred as a result of an ipso facto bankruptcy clause (providing for a default solely because of the filing of the Chapter 11 petition); (2) reinstatement of the maturity of the claim or interest; (3) compensation to the holder of the claim or interest for any damages incurred by such holder in reasonable reliance on its right to accelerate; and (4) leaving the legal, equitable, and contractual rights of the holder of the claim or interest otherwise unaltered.[144]

The third exception provides that a claim is unimpaired if the claim's holder receives cash equal to the allowed amount of its claim on the effective date of the plan.[145]

The question of the appropriate amount of damages to be awarded under the second exception has engendered some litigation. Although the standard is not settled, there seems to be general agreement in the case law that damages include, at a minimum, any contract interest and late charges due on the date of the filing of the petition and attorney's fees and expenses incurred by the creditor in pursuit of a foreclosure judgment.[146] Other issues arising under the second exception have included whether a debtor needs to compensate the creditor for its opportunity costs or pay the postdefault interest rate on the accelerated debt provided for by the contract. The general trend in the case law seems to be that, to affect a cure and reinstatement under the second exception, the debtor need not compensate the creditor for its lost opportunity costs nor pay interest at the default rate.[147]

The potentially detrimental impact on secured creditors associated with the exceptions to the presumption created by the Code that a claim is impaired by the plan may not be immediately obvious, but at least two such possibilities exist. First, creditors who are deemed unimpaired under the cure and reinstatement provisions of the second exception will receive the original, possibly below-market, rate on their loan. Second, the cash-out provision contained in the third exception may hurt oversecured creditors holding claims with above-market rates, because it allows the debtor to leave unimpaired claims carrying higher than market rates by cashing them out at their face amount plus accrued interest, even though the actual market value of those claims, absent the potential for such a cash-out, may well exceed such amount.

Despite these potential pitfalls, however, creditors can generally expect that if the plan proposes to modify or eliminate any of the covenants contained in their loan documents, they will be considered impaired under the plan and, thereby, be eligible to vote on the plan. Case law interpreting impairment has found that, in assessing whether a plan impairs a claim, the concept of impairment should be interpreted broadly, and that the exceptions to impairment provided by the Code should be narrowly construed.[148] Case law has also found that any impairment or alteration of a creditor's legal, contractual, or equitable rights constitutes impairment.[149]

Treatment of Claims Impaired by the Plan

The more likely treatment to be experienced by a secured creditor in a proposed plan is for the secured claim to be impaired; the methods through which a plan may propose to impair a claim can be as varied as the creditors in a large case. In response to such proposed impaired treatment, the holder of a secured claim (like the holder of any impaired claim or interest) may consent to any method of treatment under the plan.[150] The holder of an impaired secured claim may also object to its treatment under the plan by voting against the proposed plan. As will be explained in connection with the discussion of voting and classification (see below), if such claimant is part of a *class* that rejects the plan, the plan can only be confirmed over the objection of that class if the court finds the plan meets the confirmation standards set forth in the cramdown provisions. If such claimant is part of an accepting class, the plan may still be confirmed over the claimant's objection, unless such claimant can show that it is receiving less for its claim under the plan than it would under a liquidation under Chapter 7.[151] A class of secured claims that is to receive nothing under the plan would be deemed to have rejected the plan, and the proponent of the plan would have to demonstrate compliance with the cramdown provisions before the court could confirm the plan.[152]

Voting and Classification

Voting

As already mentioned, voting in respect of a proposed plan is conducted on a class-by-class basis, and a plan can only be confirmed as a consensual plan if all the classes voting for that plan vote in the affirmative; if one or more classes reject a proposed plan, the plan can only be confirmed in accordance with the Code's cramdown procedures.

Acceptance of a plan by a class of claims requires the affirmative vote of not less than two thirds in amount and a majority in number of the allowed claims of creditors in that class *that actually vote*.[153] For a class of interests, acceptance is required by two thirds in amount only of voting interests.[154] Claims held by creditors whose acceptance or rejection of a plan was not in good faith, or whose votes were not solicited or procured in good faith or in accordance with the provisions of the Code, are not counted.[155]

Classification

Given the mechanics of the voting process, it should be clear why classification is an important issue for secured creditors: if a secured creditor who objects to a plan is placed in a class which, along with all the other classes voting on the plan, accepts the plan, the court can confirm the plan as a consensual plan despite that creditor's objections, unless that secured creditor is able to demonstrate it would receive less under the proposed plan than it would in a liquidation, the so-called best-interests test.

Secured creditors are rarely put in this position, however, because, as will be discussed below, secured creditors having the same collateral are generally each classified in a separate class by the plan, because of differences in priority and nature of their collateral from other secured creditors. Nevertheless, it is an important issue for secured creditors to be aware of, because some secured creditors, such as mortgage bondholders and secured creditors with security interests in the same collateral pool, may be classified together and, thereby, potentially affected by this result.

This result is also important to formulating an overall strategy for the confirmation of a plan, because it provides a mechanism outside of the cramdown process for dealing with junior claimants that oppose a plan supported by the secured creditors. If the plan proponent can successfully classify an objecting claimant in a class that would accept the plan, despite that objector's opposition, and all the other classes voting on the plan vote to accept the plan, the plan can be approved over that objector's opposition under the consensual confirmation provisions of the Code.

In general terms the provisions of the Code governing the classification of claims provide: (1) subject to certain exceptions, a plan may classify a claim or interest in a particular class only if such claim or interest is *substantially similar* to the other claims or interests in such class;[156] and (2) a plan must provide the same treatment for each claim or interest in a particular class, unless the holder of a particular claim or interest within a class agrees to less-favorable treatment than the other claims or interests in that class.[157] The phrase substantially similar has been construed to mean similar in legal character.[158] Claims and interests are not substantially similar; therefore, a claim cannot be placed in the same class as an interest. In general terms, claims are defined by the Code as rights to payments and rights to equitable remedies for the breach of performance, if such breach gives rise to a right to payment.[159] The term *interest* is not explicitly defined in the Code, but its use in the section of the Code governing cramdown and the legislative history[160] indicates that it should be interpreted to mean "equity security." As defined by the Code, equity securities include shares in a corporation, limited partnership interests, and certain types of rights and warrants.[161]

Secured claims cannot be classified together with unsecured claims, because the secured claims' right to recover from specific collateral renders them significantly distinct from unsecured claims.[162] Ordinarily, each holder of an allowed claim secured by a security interest in different properties of the debtor must be placed in a separate class.[163] If claims are secured by the same property, they may only be classified together if they are of equal priority.[164] It is not clear based on the language of the Code how the unsecured portion of an undersecured creditor's claim should be classified, but case law indicates that such claims should be classified with other unsecured claims.[165]

More generally, there is no requirement in the Code that all substantially similar claims be included within a particular class.[166] This point is very significant, because it provides a mechanism for dealing with the requirement that claims or interests in the same class must be treated equally. By classifying similar claims separately, a plan may treat similar claims differently, even though the Code would have required equal treatment for such claims if they had been classified together.

The question of the extent to which similar claims can be separately classified has been the subject of some dispute. As a general matter, the classification of the claims is within the discretion of the proponent of the plan.[167] Nevertheless, the plan proponent's discretion in classifying similar claims in separate classes is not without limits; it is unlikely that a bankruptcy court would permit the classification process to be used to cause a circumvention of the class voting process[168] or of the policies underlying the Code,[169] including the principle that similarly situated creditors should be accorded equal treatment.[170] It is also worth noting that classification cannot be used solely to insure satisfaction of the provision of a cramdown section requiring that at least one class votes to accept a plan.[171]

Confirmation of Plan

The section of the Bankruptcy Code governing confirmation specifies 13 requirements that must be met before a plan may be confirmed.[172] The proponent of a plan carries the burden of proving each element.[173]

Consensual
As has been discussed in connection with voting, a proposed plan may only be confirmed as a consensual plan if each of the classes voting on such plan accepts the plan or is left unimpaired by the plan.[174] One of the most important protections provided to creditors by the Code, in addition to the voting process, is provided by the so-called best-interests test. The best interests test essentially provides that each member of an impaired class of claims or interests must receive or retain under the plan property with a value, as of the effective date of the plan, at least equal to what the member would receive or retain if the debtor were liquidated under Chapter 7, unless (1) each member of the class accepts the plan or (2) the class is secured and the holder makes the election described in Secured Creditor's Section "1111(b) Election."[175]

The liquidation value of collateral is the amount such asset would bring at a sale less the costs of disposition; it assumes no future or a limited future for an asset's relationship to a going concern. (Liquidation values are generally lower than going-concern values, but exceptions to this general rule can arise when the debtor is not the optimal user of the asset.[176]) Thus, even though it may not provide complete protection for the secured creditor, where the liquidation value of a creditor's collateral is less than the amount of its claim, the best interests test provides protection to secured creditors by creating an absolute floor with respect to the distribution such creditor will receive in respect of its claims, even if such creditor is a dissenting member of an accepting class in a consensual plan.

Cramdown

If a plan meets all the standards for the confirmation of a consensual plan, other than acceptance by every impaired class,[177] the court still may confirm the plan under its cramdown power if: (1) the proponent of the plan requests confirmation, (2) the plan does not discriminate unfairly, and (3) the plan is "fair and equitable" with respect to the dissenting class.[178] Even if the cramdown process is employed, at least one class of impaired claims must accept the plan.[179]

Unfair Discrimination. The requirement that the plan not "discriminate" unfairly with respect to a dissenting class was initially intended to protect the rights of a dissenting class in a manner consistent with the treatment of other classes whose rights were interrelated with those of the dissenting class.[180] Although some courts have suggested that the unfair discrimination analysis is limited to the treatment of subordinated claims or interests,[181] the recent trend in the case law has been to broaden the concept of unfair discrimination, inquiring into whether the plan segregates two similar claims or groups of claims into separate classes and proposes disparate treatment for those classes.[182]

Fair and Equitable. Under the Code, a plan will be considered to be fair and equitable with respect to a rejecting class of secured claims if one of three alternative tests is satisfied:

(a) The secured creditor claimholder (A) retains the lien securing its claim to the extent of the allowed amount of its secured claim, whether the property subject to such lien is retained by the debtor or transferred to another entity, and (B) receives deferred cash payments totalling at least the allowed amount of the claim, having a value, as of the effective date of the plan, at least equal to the value of the secured creditor's interest in the debtor's estate, that is, the amount of its secured claim;[183]

(b) If the collateral is to be sold, all liens will attach to the proceeds of such sale, and they will be treated either under the method described in the preceding paragraph or under the method described in the following paragraph; or[184]

(c) The secured creditor receives the indubitable equivalent of its claim.[185]

Determining the indubitable equivalent of a claim can be a difficult and unpredictable process. The term *indubitable equivalent* is derived from a decision by Judge Learned Hand in which he analyzed the issue of adequate protection of creditors during the pendency of a debtor's reorganization.[186] The legislative history of the cramdown provisions indicates that abandonment of the collateral to the secured creditor or issuing replacement liens on similar collateral would satisfy the indubitable equivalent standard.[187] The legislative history also includes examples that would not satisfy the standard, such as the granting of unsecured notes or equity securities.[188] Beyond those situations, the determination of whether a plan will, in fact, give a creditor the indubitable equivalent of its claim is left to the court's discretion on a case-by-case basis.[189]

Valuation. Valuation is obviously fundamental to the cramdown process: the secured creditor's collateral must be valued, any substitute lien must be valued, and any proposed deferred cash payments must be valued. The legislative history of the cramdown provisions states a valuation will almost always be required in connection with a confirmation that is to occur pursuant to the cramdown power, because of the fair and equitable requirement.[190] As a general matter, at least one case has held that, in conducting such a valuation, the court should use a conservative standard of valuation to protect the interests of senior creditors.[191]

If the proponent of a plan proposes to cram down a class of secured claims by making deferred cash payments, the court is required to value the future cash stream so as to establish the present value of the deferred cash payments provided for by the plan, as of the effective date of the plan.[192] As a general matter, the case law has found that, in determining the present value of a secured claim, the appropriate discount rate is the current market rate of interest, and that this rate is to be determined by the court on a case-by-case basis.[193] The appropriate market rate to be used should be the prevailing market rate for a loan of equal term to that proposed in the debtor's plan, the quality of the collateral securing the indebtedness, the credit standing of the borrower, and the risk of subsequent default.[194] To determine the amount of the secured creditor's claim, a going-concern valuation of the reorganized entity based on a capitalization of the debtor's prospective earnings is the generally accepted method of valuation.[195] With respect to the question of what is the appropriate time to determine the value of a secured claim, the majority of cases have found that secured claims should be valued as of the effective date of the plan.[196]

Despite the existence of these general guidelines, however, it should again be emphasized that both creditors and debtors generally prefer to negotiate an agreement on value rather than leave such a significant determination to the court's discretion. The reasons for this preference include: (1) in valuing a stream of deferred cash payments, the court may select a discount rate different from that favored by either the debtor or the interested creditor; (2) in valuing a specific asset securing a creditor's claim, it may be uncertain whether the value ascribed to such an asset should be based on an appraisal, recent sales of comparable assets, or the present value of the earnings or cash flow that the asset is expected to generate in the future; and (3) when valuing a whole business, there can be a wide range of valuations (due to differences in forecasts, discount rates, and the like), any one of which a court could reasonably, though not necessarily predictably, select as its standard.

SECURED CREDITOR'S SECTION "1111(b) ELECTION"

The secured creditor's safeguard against erosion in the value of its collateral during the Chapter 11 case, adequate protection, has already been discussed. Protection in the plan confirmation process has also been discussed: the secured creditor is protected against treatment under a plan that does not provide for the repayment of the full value of the secured portion of its claim. If the payments are to be made over time, the present value of the payments must equal at least the value of the secured creditor's collateral when the plan becomes effective. One additional protection the Code creates is a mechanism for the undersecured creditor to enjoy the benefit of an increase in the value of its collateral after confirmation of a plan.

As we have seen, the Code bifurcates undersecured claims into two claims: a secured claim to the extent of the value of the collateral and an unsecured claim to the extent the debt exceeds the value of the collateral. However, the Code also permits an undersecured creditor to elect to have the entire amount of its allowed claim treated as secured in a Chapter 11 case.[197] Absent this election, the debtor could unfairly take advantage of a depressed market for the secured creditor's collateral. It could use the cramdown provisions of Chapter 11 to reduce the amount of the secured creditor's postconfirmation lien to the depressed market value of the collateral at the time of confirmation. The secured creditor's lien, once so reduced, would not extend to any increase in the value of the collateral postconfirmation. Instead, it would benefit the debtor by increasing its equity in the collateral by an equal amount. The secured creditor, however, would be entitled to an unsecured claim for the deficiency.

Prior to the enactment of the Code, nonrecourse creditors (i.e., creditors with a lien on property of the debtor's estate but with no right beyond its collateral for repayment) were subject to extraordinarily inequitable treatment: not only would their lien be reduced to the depressed market value of their collateral, their entire claim would be reduced. The nonrecourse creditor, unlike the secured recourse creditor, would have no claim against the debtor personally for the deficiency. To prevent this outcome, the Code converts a nonrecourse claim automatically to a recourse claim, thus entitling the creditor to an unsecured claim for any deficiency, unless the nonrecourse creditor makes the election to have its entire allowed claim treated as a secured claim.[198]

To expand upon an example given in the legislative history of the cramdown provisions, suppose the secured creditor loaned the debtor $15 million secured by real estate worth $18 million at the time of the loan. The real estate market subsequently became depressed and the collateral was now worth only $12 million. Absent election, the secured creditor would have a secured claim for $12 million and an unsecured claim for $3 million. The plan could be confirmed so long as the cramdown provisions for the $12 million secured claim and provision for the $3 million unsecured claim were made in the plan. As discussed above, the cramdown provisions for the secured $12 million claim would be satisfied if *(a)* it was secured by a lien and *(b)* the secured creditor received cash payments over time totaling at least $12 million and having a present value of at least $12 million. The remaining $3 million claim would be treated as an unsecured claim under the plan. If the real estate market recovered after confirmation and the value of the collateral increased to $15 million, the secured creditor's lien would still be capped at $12 million and the debtor would then have $3 million of equity in the collateral.[199]

If the secured creditor had made the election to have its entire allowed claim treated as secured in the foregoing example, the cramdown provisions for the secured claim could only be satisfied if *(a)* all $15 million was secured by a lien postconfirmation and *(b)* the secured creditor received cash payments over time totaling at least $15 million (not $12 million) and having a present value of $12 million. However, the obvious should be noted: having made the election, the secured creditor would have lost its right to an unsecured claim for $3 million and, with it, the right to vote and participate in any distribution made to the unsecured creditors.

Because, in either scenario, the present value of the cash payments to the secured creditor is capped at $12 million, the benefit to the secured creditor of making the election is not immediately evident, particularly since it will have given up its unsecured claim for the deficiency. However, if the secured creditor believes the reorganized debtor will default on its post-confirmation payment obligations to the secured creditor, the secured creditor may be better protected by making the election: the secured creditor who has made the election will have a secured claim of $15 million (less any post-confirmation payments) in any subsequent bankruptcy case or foreclosure proceedings, whereas the secured creditor who has not made the election will have a secured claim of only $12 million (less any post-confirmation payments), or $3 million less than the electing secured creditor.

The election must be made on a class basis. The minimum necessary approvals are the same for approval of the plan: two thirds of the amount of the claims in the class and one half of the number of allowed claims in the class must choose to make the election.[200] Once the election is made, it is binding on all members of the class.[201] (As noted above, the secured creditor will frequently be alone in its class.) Generally, the election may be made any time before the end of the hearing on the disclosure statement.[202] Once made, it is probably irrevocable, at least absent changes in the treatment of creditors under the proposed plan.[203]

There are limitations on the secured creditor's ability to make this election. The election may not be made if either *(a)* the collateral is to be sold during the case or under the plan or *(b)* the value of the secured creditor's lien in the collateral is of "inconsequential" value.[204] If the collateral is to be sold, the secured creditor (both recourse and nonrecourse) will be permitted to bid in the entire amount of its debt. Thus, its protected expectation of either receiving payment in full or its collateral is satisfied.

In determining whether to make an election, assuming it is available, the secured creditor must compare the treatment of secured claims to that of unsecured claims under the plan. It is possible, particularly if the value of the collateral is a small part of the secured creditor's claim, that the present value of the distributions made to the unsecured creditors under the plan will be greater, as a percentage of the secured creditor's entire claim, than the present value of the payments made on account of the creditor's secured claim after election.

In addition, the secured creditor should consider the potential strategic impact of an election. It may be easier for a plan to be confirmed without the consent of a class of secured claims than without the consent of the class of unsecured claims particularly if the value of the collateral is a small portion of the claim. To cram down a secured claim, it must receive cash payments equal to the secured claim with a present value equal to the value of the lien in the collateral. As suggested above, if the value of the lien is small, payments could be stretched over a long time. In contrast, for unsecured claims to be crammed down, either they must receive distributions (which need not be in cash) with a present value equal to the entire allowed unsecured claims or all junior classes of claims and all equity may not receive or retain anything under the plan. Depending on the amount of the secured creditor's deficiencies (i.e., the amount by which the secured creditor's claim exceeds the value of the collateral), the secured creditor may be able to block consensual confirmation of a plan if it retains its unsecured claims. Thus, even if the debtor could cram down the secured portion of this claim and the unsecured creditors were willing to approve the plan, the secured creditor could vote its unsecured claim, which may be controlling, against approval, forcing a cramdown of the unsecured creditors, too.

The undersecured creditor's election to have its claim treated as wholly secured is one more form of protection for its interest in receiving either its collateral or the value of its collateral. The election recognizes, in effect, that permanently fixing the value of the secured creditor's collateral at less than the amount of its claim, while giving the debtor the benefit of any increase in value, is an inadequate substitute for the secured creditor's right to foreclose on its collateral. It deprives the secured creditor of its ability to bid in its entire claim in a foreclosure and to wait for market conditions to improve before selling the collateral.

CONCLUSION

As discussed throughout this chapter, many determinations are made by a court in a Chapter 11 case that substantially affect the treatment of secured claims. Some of these determinations lie within the court's discretion. This discretion, combined with the inherent uncertainties in a Chapter 11 case generally, make precise analysis of the potential treatment of a secured claim in a Chapter 11 case extremely difficult. There are certain protections that the Code affords the secured creditor, as identified in this chapter, that will at the very least define for the secured creditor the minimum provision it can expect for its secured claim in a Chapter 11 case. The secured creditor should analyze this "worst case" scenario as a benchmark before accepting—or rejecting—an out-of-court restructuring proposal from a troubled company.

ENDNOTES

1. Hereinafter the Code. All statutory references are to the Bankruptcy Code unless otherwise specified.
2. House Report Rep. No. 95-595, 95th Cong., 1st Sess. 220 (1977) (hereinafter "House Report").
3. *Id.* at 181.
4. Section 506(a). A claim against the debtor that could be offset against an obligation owed by the creditor to the debtor is also a secured claim to the extent of such offset (i.e., to the extent it could reduce the creditor's obligation to the debtor).
5. Section 502(a).
6. Section 502(b).
7. Section 1111(a).
8. Section 502(b)(2).
9. **See,** for example, *In re Shaffer Furniture Co.,* 68 B.R. 827 (Bankr. E.D. Pa. 1987). Section 726 (a)(5) of Chapter 7 of the Code, concerning liquidation cases, expressly provides that postpetition interest be paid to unsecured creditors at the legal rate before any surplus is returned to the debtor. Although the provision is not expressly incorporated in Chapter 11 cases when creditors' claims are to be left unimpaired, courts have permitted postpetition interest on unsecured claims under general equitable principles.
10. Section 506(b).
11. It is unclear whether some of these rulings survive the recent Supreme Court ruling in *United States* v. *Ron Pair Enters., Inc.,* 489 U.S. 235 (1989), permitting postpetition interest to accrue on nonconsensual liens. **See,** for example, *Bank of Honolulu* v. *Anderson (In re Anderson),* 833 F.2d 834 (9th Cir. 1987) (interpreting section 506(b) to permit interest provided for in contract to accrue postpetition); *P.J. Taggars Co.* v. *Glenn (In re Glenn),* 796 F.2d 1144 (9th Cir. 1986) (same). However, other courts which specifically rejected interpreting Section 506(b) to permit postpetition interest only to the extent provided contractually nevertheless opted for the contract rate. **See** *In re Loveridge Mach. & Tool Co., Inc.,* 36 B.R. 159 (Bankr. D. Utah 1983).

12. See *Marine Midland Bank, N.A.* v. *Ladycliff College (In re Ladycliff College)*, 56 B.R. 765 (S.D.N.Y. 1985); *In re Bradley*, 94 B.R. 563 (Bankr. N.D. Iowa 1988).
13. *Id.;* **see,** for example, *Maimone* v. *Columbia Sav. Bank (In re Maimone)*, 41 B.R. 974, 983 (Bankr. D. N.J. 1984). However, note that, as observed by the court in *Maimone, supra,* if a senior secured creditor inequitably delays the proceedings to the detriment of junior secured creditors, there is a risk that the senior secured creditor's claims for postpetition interest will be disallowed.
14. *United States* v. *Ron Pair Enters., Inc., supra* endnote 11.
15. Section 506(b). Here, too, claims secured by junior liens on the collateral are disregarded when calculating excess value. **See,** for example, *Anderson* v. *First National Bank of Cobb County (In re Anderson)*, 28 B.R. 231 (Bankr. N.D. Ga. 1983).
16. **See,** for example, *In re B & W Management, Inc.*, 63 B.R. 395 (Bankr. D. D.C. 1986); *Crownover* v. *Manufacturers Hanover Comm. Corp. (In re Central Foundry Co.)*, 45 B.R. 395 (Bankr. N.D. Ala. 1984).
17. **See** *Liberty Nat'l Bank & Trust Co.* v. *George*, 70 B.R. 312 (W.D. Ky. 1987). However, the oversecured creditor is probably entitled to attorney's fees even if, under state law, such agreements are unenforceable. **See** *Unsecured Creditors' Comm.* v. *Walter E. Heller & Co. Southeast, Inc.*, 768 F.2d 580 (4th Cir. 1985).
18. **See** *In re Diversified Capital Corp.*, 89 B.R. 826 (Bankr. C.D. Cal. 1988); *In re Fidelity Am. Mortgage Co.*, 7 BCD 1186 (Bankr. E.D. Pa. 1981). But **see** *In re Wekiva Dev. Corp.*, 22 B.R. 301 (Bankr. M.D. Fla. 1982) (implying that secured creditors may not be entitled to a committee, at least to extent interests *inter se* not identical).
19. **See** *In re Diversified Capital Corp., supra* endnote 18 (court approved retention by a secured creditors' committee of secured creditors' attorneys).
20. **See** *In re Beker Indus. Corp.*, 55 B.R. 945, 949 (Bankr. S.D.N.Y. 1985).
21. There is conflicting law on this point. **Compare** *In re Walat Farms, Inc.*, 64 B.R. 65 (Bankr. E.D. Mich. 1986) (undersecured creditors may serve on unsecured creditors' committee) **with** *In re Glendale Woods Apts., Ltd.*, 25 B.R. 414, 415 (Bankr. D. Md. 1982) (undersecured creditors may not serve on unsecured creditors' committee).
22. Section 506(c).
23. **See,** for example, *United States* v. *Annett Ford, Inc. (In re Annett Ford, Inc.)*, 64 B.R. 946 (D. Neb. 1986).
24. **See,** for example, *General Electric Credit Corp.* v. *Peltz (In re Flag-*

staff Foodservice Corp. II), 762 F.2d 10 (2d Cir. 1985); *General Elec. Credit Corp.* v. *Levin & Weintraub (In re Flagstaff Foodservice Corp. I)*, 739 F.2d 73 (2d Cir. 1984); *Brookfield Prod. Credit Ass'n* v. *Borron*, 738 F.2d 951 (8th Cir. 1984).

25. **Compare,** for example, *In re Annett Ford, Inc., supra* note 23 (consent to continue business is consent to have expenses deducted from collateral); *Chee* v. *Dynamic Indus. (In re Waikiki Hobron Assoc.)*, 51 B.R. 410 (Bankr. D. Haw. 1985) (same) **with,** for example, *Cent. Bank of Montana* v. *Cascade Hydraulics & Utility Serv., Inc. (In re Cascade Hydraulics & Utility Serv., Inc.)*, 815 F.2d 546 (9th Cir. 1987) (consent to some expenses and cooperation is not consent to have other expenses deducted from collateral). **See,** generally, *In re Chicago Lutheran Hospital Ass'n.*, 89 B.R. 719, 730-31 (Bankr. N.D. Ill. 1988) (secured creditor should not have to obstruct reorganization process to protect against Section 506(c) costs).
26. Section 541(a)(1).
27. Section 552(a); **see,** for example, *First Nat'l. Bank* v. *Texas Tri-Collar, Inc. (In re Texas Tri-Collar, Inc.)*, 29 B.R. 724 (Bankr. W.D. La. 1983).
28. Section 552(b). The issue of what constitutes "proceeds, product, offspring, rents or profits" is complicated and beyond the scope of this chapter. It is worth noting at this juncture that even if a security agreement does not explicitly include a lien on proceeds, such a lien may exist as a matter of state law because Section 9-203(3) of the U.C.C. provides that unless a security agreement provides otherwise, it automatically gives the secured party the rights to proceeds provided by Section 9-306 of the U.C.C.
29. *Mercantile Nat'l Bank* v. *Aerosmith Denton Corp. (In re Aerosmith Denton Corp.)*, 36 B.R. 116 (Bankr. N.D. Tex. 1983).
30. See *Carlson* v. *W.J. Menefee Constr. Co. (In re Grassridge Indus., Inc.)*, 78 B.R. 978 (Bankr. W.D. Mo. 1987).
31. Section 552(b).
32. **See** *House Report, supra,* endnote 2, at 376-77.
33. *In re Vanas,* 50 B.R. 988 (Bankr. E.D. Mich. 1985).
34. **See** *United Virginia Bank* v. *Slab Fork Coal Co. (In re Slab Fork Coal Co.)*, 784 F.2d 1188 (4th Cir.), *cert. denied,* 477 U.S. 905 (1986); *id.*
35. *In re Slab Fork Coal Co., supra* endnote 34.
36. Section 506(a). A partially secured creditor may elect to have its entire claim treated as a secured claim, except in certain circumstances. For a discussion of this "election," **see** *infra* in this chapter, Secured Creditor's "1111(b) Election."
37. *Id.*

38. See Senate Report No. 95-989, 95th Cong., 2d Sess. 68 (1978) (hereinafter "Senate Report").
39. See *Senate Report, supra* endnote 38, at 53–54.
40. See, for example, *In re Fiberglass Indus., Inc.,* 74 B.R. 738 (Bankr. N.D.N.Y. 1987) (dictum); *In re The Kids Stop of America, Inc.,* 64 B.R. 397 (Bankr. M.D. Fla. 1986) (inventory should be valued at going concern value if debtor selling in ordinary course and liquidation value if debtor liquidating inventory); *In re Walkup,* 28 B.R. 225 (Bankr. N.D. Ind. 1983) (sale price best indication of value).
41. See discussion of fair and equitable standards contained in the section on confirmation *infra*.
42. See *In re Phoenix Steel Corp.,* 39 B.R. 218 (D. Del. 1984).
43. References throughout this chapter to the trustee should be considered also as references to the debtor in possession, as appropriate. If a trustee has not been appointed by the court (for "cause" or the interests of the creditors, the equity holders, or the estate) under Section 1104, then the debtor in possession has, generally, the rights, powers, and duties of a trustee. Section 1107(a).
44. Section 544(a) (1)-(3).
45. See, for example, *Stern* v. *Continental Assurance Co. (In re Ryan),* 851 F.2d 502 (1st Cir. 1988).
46. *Id.*
47. Section 544(a). However, if there are facts that would put all creditors on "constructive" notice of a lien under applicable state law, even if improperly perfected, the lien may be enforceable against the trustee. See *Probasco* v. *Eads (In re Probasco),* 839 F.2d 1352, (9th Cir. 1988).
48. Section 544(b).
49. Section 547(b). For a general discussion of the law of preferences, see Countryman, *The Concept of a Voidable Preference in Bankruptcy,* 38 Vand. L. Rev. 713 (1985); Hall, *Preferences and Setoffs: Sections 547 and 553,* 2 Bankr. Dev. J. 49 (1985); Note, *Preferences: Section 547,* 3 Bankr. Dev. J. 365 (1986); Nutovic, *The Bankruptcy Preference Laws: Interpreting Code Sections 547(c)(2), 550(a)(1) and 546(a)(1), 41 Bus. Law.* 175 (1985); 4 *Collier on Bankruptcy,* ¶ 547.01, *et seq.* (15th ed. 1990).
50. See, for example, *Braunstein* v. *Eastern Air Lines Employees Fed. Credit Union (In re Fitzgerald),* 49 B.R. 62, 65 (Bankr. D. Mass. 1985).
51. Section 547(c).
52. **Compare** *CHG Int'l Inc.* v. *Barclays Bank,* 897 F.2d 1479 (9th Cir. 1990) (interest payments on long-term debt were not intended to be

covered under the ordinary course of business exception); *Aguillard v. Bank of Lafayette (In re Bourgeois)*, 58 Bankr. 657 (Bankr. W.D. La. 1986) (principal and interest payments in respect of long-term debt are not within the ordinary course of business exception); *In re Acme-Dunham, Inc.*, 50 B.R. 734 (D. Me. 1985) (payments in respect of long-term debt do not qualify for the ordinary course of business exception); *In re Jackson*, 90 B.R. 793 (Bankr. D. S.C. 1988); *In re Control Elec., Inc.*, 91 B.R. 1010, 1017 (Bankr. N.D. Ga. 1988) **with** *In re Finn*, 909 F.2d 903 (6th Cir. 1990) (finding that payments in respect of long-term consumer debt which is incurred as part of a "normal financial relation" and which is not an "unusual action" taken during the "slide into bankruptcy" can qualify for the ordinary course of business exception); *Rinn v. MTA Employees Credit Union, Inc. (In re Butler)*, 85 B.R. 34, 36 (Bankr. D. Md. 1988) (long-term loans are "unquestionably" within a consumer debtor's ordinary financial affairs; preferential transfers made in respect of those long-term loans found to be qualified for ordinary course of business exception); Broome, *Payments on Long-Term Debt as Voidable Preferences: The Impact of the 1984 Bankruptcy Amendments*, 78 Duke L.J. 78 (1987).

53. See *In re Gull Air, Inc.*, 82 B.R. 1 (Bankr. D. Mass. 1988) (payments received under a restructuring agreement within 90 days of the debtor's filing of its petition were made in exchange for consideration and were not so unusual as to render them outside the ordinary course of business but were found to be outside of the ordinary course of business, because the restructuring agreement was part of the settlement of litigation initiated by the creditor upon the debtor's initial default); *In re Magic Circle Energy Corp.*, 64 B.R. 269, 273 (Bankr. W.D. Okla. 1986) (payments made within 90 days of the debtor's filing of its petition pursuant to a restructuring agreement executed by the debtor and the creditor who received the payments were in the ordinary course of business, because "[t]he mere restructuring of payment terms does not alter the fact that the underlying debt was incurred under normal circumstances"); *In re Gilbertson*, 90 B.R. 1006 (Bankr. D. N.D. 1988) (debtor's prepetition payment to creditor, made within 90 days of petition filing, pursuant to a deferral agreement entered into in connection with a restructuring negotiated between debtor and creditor was a transfer in the ordinary course of business).
54. Section 547(c)(1).
55. Section 547(a)(2).
56. **Compare** *In re Dempster*, 59 B.R. 453, 459 (Bankr. M.D. Ga. 1984)

(no new value given by creditor by renewing notes where those notes were secured by the same collateral that secured the notes they replaced, and no new funds were advanced) **with** *In re Spada,* 91 B.R. 668 (Bankr. M.D. Pa. 1988), *aff'd,* 115 B.R. 796 (M.D. Pa. 1989), *aff'd in part and rev'd in part,* 903 F.2d 971 (3rd Cir. 1990) (granting of mortgage to formerly unsecured creditor in connection with restructuring between creditor and debtor found not to be a preferential transfer, because the creditor gave "new value" by granting an approximately six-point reduction in interest rate and permitting the debtor to repay interest only for the first year of the loan and requiring the creditor to subordinate its mortgage if a lender were secured financing the construction of a project on the mortgaged property). On appeal in *In re Spada,* 903 F.2d 971, 977 (3rd Cir. 1990), the circuit court reduced the scope of the holding of the bankruptcy court by finding that the new value was granted to the debtor only to the extent of the value of the reduction in interest rate and the interest-only payment provision and, accordingly, that any value given by the debtor to the creditor which exceeded the amount of that new value would not qualify for the new value exception. **See,** generally, *In re Jet Florida Sys., Inc.,* 861 F.2d 1555, 1558-59 (11th Cir. 1988) ("[s]ection 547(c)(1) protects transfers only 'to the extent' the transfer was a contemporaneous exchange for new value"; a creditor seeking the protection of Section 547(c)(1) must prove with specificity the new value given to the debtor); *In re Robinson Bros. Drilling, Inc.,* 877 F.2d 32, 34 (10th Cir. 1989) (adopting the interpretation of the 11th Circuit in *In re Jet Florida Sys., supra); Drabkin* v. *A. I. Credit Corp.,* 800 F.2d 1153, 1155 (1986) (finding that a creditor's forbearance with respect to foreclosing on collateral does not constitute new value, and that a creditor's release of a lien, even if it is for the benefit of a third party, may constitute new value); *In re Finelli Jewelry Co.,* 79 B.R. 521, 522 (Bankr. D. R.I. 1987) (faced with a facially disproportionate exchange of value, the court found value in a contemporaneous exchange under Section 547(c)(1) must approximate the worth of the asset transferred to qualify as an exception to preference provisions); *In re Louisiana Indus. Coatings, Inc.,* 31 B.R. 688, 695 (Bankr. E.D. La. 1983) (new value requirement "implies at a minimum, some reasonable equivalence of value in the considerations flowing from the debtor to the creditor and vice versa"); *In re Duffy,* 3 B.R. 263, 266 (Bankr. S.D.N.Y. 1980) (forbearance from commencing repossession of collateral does not constitute "new value").

57. Section 547(f).
58. Section 101(30).
59. Section 101(30). The term *affiliate* is defined in Section 101(2).
60. See *Levit* v. *Ingersoll Rand Fin. Corp.*, 874 F.2d 1186 (7th Cir. 1989) *(In re De Prizio Constr. Corp.); In re Robinson Bros. Drilling, Inc.*, 892 F.2d 850 (10th Cir. 1989); *Ray* v. *City Bank and Trust Company (In re C-L Cartage Co., Inc.)* 899 F.2d 1490 (6th Cir. 1990); *In re Installation Serv., Inc.*, 101 B.R. 282, 284 (Bankr. N.D. Ala. 1989). See, generally, Note, *Trustee Recovery of Indirect Benefits under Section 547(b) of the Bankruptcy Code*, 6 Bankr. Dev. J. 403 (1989).
61. See Sections 548(a), 550(a); Uniform Fraudulent Conveyance Act (UFCA) § 9(1), 7A U.L.A. 427, 577-78 (1985). For discussions of the application of the law of fraudulent conveyances to leveraged transactions, see Sherwin, *Creditors' Rights Against Participants in a Leveraged Buyout*, 72 Minn. L. Rev. 449 (1988); Note, *Fraudulent Conveyance Law and Leveraged Buyouts*, 87 Colum. L. Rev. 1491 (1987).
62. See Section 548(a)(1); UFCA § 7, 7A U.L.A. 427, 509 (1985).
63. See Section 548(a)(2); UFCA §§ 4-6, 7A U.L.A. 427, 474, 504, 507 (1985).
64. Section 548(a).
65. The standard to determine whether a transaction left the debtor with unreasonably small capital is not settled, but one recent case has found that "[u]nreasonably small capitalization is not the equivalent of insolvency in either the bankruptcy or equity sense. . . . [the concept] encompasses difficulties which are short of insolvency in any sense but are likely to lead to insolvency at some time in the future." *In re Vadnais Lumber Supply, Inc.*, 100 B.R. 127, 137 (Bankr. D. Mass. 1989).
66. Section 548(a)(2); UFTA § 8(a), 7A U.L.A. 643, 662 (1985). Because very few cases have been decided under the UFTA, it is currently unclear whether the difference in phrasing of the consideration elements contained in the UFCA and the UFTA will be interpreted by the courts as being substantively different. One recent case, however, has found that " 'fair consideration' equals 'reasonably equivalent value.' " *Webster* v. *Barbara (In re Otis & Edwards, P.C.)*, 115 B.R. 900, 908 (Bankr. E.D. Mich. 1990).
67. Section 548(c). See also Section 550(b) for broader exculpatory provisions for secondary transferees.
68. Section 544(b).

69. The National Conference of Commissioners on Uniform State Laws revised the UFCA in 1985 and the new title is the UFTA. UFTA, 7A U.L.A. 643 (1985). As of the end of 1989, 24 states had enacted the UFTA while the UFCA was still in effect in the Virgin Islands, and in the following states: Arizona, Delaware, Maryland, Massachusetts, Michigan, Montana, New York, Ohio, Pennsylvania, Tennessee, and Wyoming. One major difference between the UFCA and the UFTA is that the UFTA contains a four-year statute of limitations, whereas the UFCA did not contain any statute of limitations. It should be noted, however, that some states, such as New York, included a statute of limitations in their enactments of the UFCA.
70. UFCA § 4-6, 7A U.L.A. 427, 474, 504, 507 (1985).
71. UFCA § 7, 7A U.L.A. 427, 509 (1985).
72. UFCA § 9(1), 7A U.L.A. 427, 577 (1985). The UFTA adopts the "reasonably equivalent value" standard used by the Code. UFTA §8(a), 7A U.L.A. 643, 662 (1985).
73. UFCA § 9(2), 7A U.L.A. 427, 578 (1985).
74. See *United States* v. *Gleneagles Inv. Co.*, 565 F. Supp. 556, 581 (M.D. Pa. 1983), *aff'd sub nom.*, *United States* v. *Tabor Court Realty Corp.*, 803 F.2d 1288 (3rd Cir. 1986), *cert. denied, McClellan Realty Co.* v. *United States*, 483 U.S. 1005 (1987) (hereinafter, *"Gleneagles"); Kupetz* v. *Wolf*, 845 F.2d 842 (9th Cir. 1988); *Wieboldt Stores, Inc.* v. *Schottenstein*, 94 B.R. 488 (N.D. Ill. 1988); *In re Ohio Corrugating Co.*, 70 B.R. 920 (Bankr. N.D. Ohio 1987). **See,** generally, Sherwin, *Creditors Rights against Participants in a Leveraged Buyout, supra* note 61; Kirby, McGuinness & Kandel, *Fraudulent Conveyance Concerns in Leveraged Buyout Lending,* 43 Bus. Law. 27 (1987). It is worth noting that, in *Kupetz,* even though the court found that the leveraged buyout in question was not a fraudulent conveyance, it did find on a more generalized level, under the California version of the UFCA, that: (1) when the parties to a leveraged buyout fully intend to hinder the general creditors and benefit the selling shareholders, the conveyance is fraudulent under the UFCA; (2) a transfer made by an insolvent debtor who does not receive fair consideration in exchange for that transfer is a fraudulent conveyance; and (3) if a transaction leaves a firm with unreasonably small capital, the transaction may be attacked on fraudulent conveyance grounds.
75. See *In re Pinto Trucking Serv., Inc.*, 93 B.R. 379, 386 (Bankr. E.D. Pa. 1988). (finding under Pennsylvania law that the conduct of the transferor (i.e., the debtor) must be established to be fraudulent, not the conduct of the transferee).

76. See *Stratton* v. *Equitable Bank, N.A.,* 104 B.R. 713, 726 (D. Md. 1989) ("a conveyance will not be set aside under § 548(a)(1) if the transferee . . . was without knowledge of the fraud and paid a fair consideration for the conveyance"); *Gleneagles, supra* endnote 74 (a conveyance will not be set aside under the Pennsylvania version of the UFCA, if the transferee was without knowledge of the fraud and paid a fair consideration for the conveyance).
77. See *Kupetz* v. *Continental Ill. Nat'l Bank & Trust Co.,* 77 B.R. 754, 761 (D. Cal. 1987), *aff'd,* 845 F.2d 842 (9th Cir. 1988).
78. *In re Osage Crude Oil Purchasing, Inc.,* 103 B.R. 256, 261-63 (Bankr. N.D. Okla. 1989). It is likely, however, that a downstream guarantee by a parent company of the obligations of a subsidiary will result in a sufficient indirect benefit to the parent company to constitute adequate consideration for the guarantee for the purpose of defeating a claim that the incurrence of the guarantee obligation constituted a fraudulent conveyance. **See,** generally, Note, *Guarantees and Section 548(a)(2),* 52 U. Chi. L. Rev. 194, 215 (1985). For a consideration of indirect benefits, **see** *Rubin* v. *Mfrs. Hanover Trust Co.,* 661 F.2d 979, 994 (2d Cir. 1981); *In re Xonics Photochem., Inc.,* 841 F.2d 198 (7th Cir. 1988). **See also** *In re Metro Communications, Inc.,* 95 B.R. 921, 933 (Bankr. W.D. Pa. 1989) ("indirect benefits *may* furnish fair consideration, *provided, however,* that the value received by Debtor is *reasonably equal* to the value of the obligation given"). **See also** UFCA § 3(a); *Cohen* v. *Sutherland,* 257 F.2d 737, 742 (2nd Cir. 1958).
79. UFCA § 3, 7A U.L.A. 427, 448-49 (1985).
80. See *Wieboldt Stores, Inc.* v. *Schottenstein, supra* endnote 74; *In re Roco Corp.,* 701 F.2d 978, 982 (1st Cir. 1983); *Hyde Properties* v. *McCoy,* 507 F.2d 301, 307 (6th Cir. 1974). But **see** *In re Anderson Indus., Inc.,* 55 B.R. 922, 927 (Bankr. W.D. Mich. 1985).
81. See *Bullard* v. *Aluminum Co. of America,* 468 F.2d 11, 13 (7th Cir. 1972).
82. See *Gleneagles, supra* endnote 74; *Wiebolt Stores, Inc.* v. *Schottenstein, supra* endnote 74.
83. Section 510(c)(1).
84. For general discussions of the principles of equitable subordination, see *Pepper* v. *Litton,* 308 U.S. 295 (1939); *In re Multiponics, Inc.,* 622 F.2d 709 (5th Cir. 1980); *In re Future Energy Corp.,* 83 B.R. 470 (Bankr. S.D. Ohio 1988).
85. Section 510(a).
86. Congress may, under its bankruptcy powers, abrogate contractual obligations. Obligations owed to unsecured creditors, therefore, may

be impaired. But the rights of secured creditors in specific property are property rights that Congress may not impair. *Louisville Joint Stock Land Bank* v. *Radford,* 295 U.S. 555, 589-90 (1935).
87. Section 362(d)(1); **see** subsection, Automatic Stay, *infra.*
88. Section 363(e); **see** subsection, Obtaining Credit, *infra.*
89. Section 364(d)(1)(B); **see** subsection, Obtaining Credit, *infra.*
90. Section 361.
91. *Id.*
92. Section 507(b).
93. **See** subsection, Value of Collateral, *supra,* and cases cited therein.
94. *United Sav. Ass'n* v. *Timbers of Inwood Forest Assoc., Ltd.,* 484 U.S. 365 (1988).
95. *Id.* at 371.
96. *House Report, supra* endnote 2, at 340.
97. Section 541(a)(1). Insurance policies, for example, can be property of the estate. **See** *Minoco Group of Cos.* v. *First State Underwriters Agency of New England Reinsurance Corp. (In re Minoco Group of Cos.),* 799 F.2d 517 (9th Cir. 1986).
98. 28 U.S.C. §1334(d).
99. Section 304(a) and (b).
100. Section 362(b)(4).
101. Sections 362(b)(3) and 546(b); **see** House Report, *supra* endnote 2, at 371.
102. Section 1110.
103. **Compare,** *Yobe Elec., Inc.* v. *Graybar Elec. Co. (In re Yobe Elec., Inc.),* 728 F.2d 207 (3d Cir. 1984) (no violation of stay; perfection relates back) **with** *In re Nicholson,* 57 B.R. 672 (Bankr. D. Nev. 1986) (postpetition perfection voidable under strong-arm clause and as violation of stay; perfection did not relate back prepetition). Another example of general interest is perfection of a purchase money security interest. Under the Uniform Commercial Code, as enacted in most (if not all) states, a lender providing purchase money that perfects its purchase money security interest within the stated time after the debtor takes possession of the goods has a perfected security interest as of the date the security interest attached. UCC 9-301(2). Giving postpetition notice of this perfection (and filing the requisite Form UCC-1) will not violate the stay. **See** House Report, *supra* endnote 2, at 371.
104. Section 362(b)(12).
105. **See,** for example, *A. H. Robins Co.* v. *Piccinin,* 788 F.2d 994 (4th Cir.), *cert. denied,* 479 U.S. 876 (1986); *In re Johns-Manville Corp.,* 40 B.R. 219 (S.D.N.Y. 1984); *In re Johns-Manville Corp.,* 33 B.R. 254 (Bankr. S.D.N.Y. 1983).

106. See *id*.
107. See *Westinghouse Cred. Corp.* v. *Page (In re Page)*, 6 CBC2d 776 (D. D.C. 1982). But see *In re Twist Cap., Inc.*, 1 B.R. 284 (Bankr. M.D. Fl. 1979), in which the court stayed drawing under the letter of credit reasoning that the letter of credit was property of the estate. Subsequent cases have rejected the holding in *Twist Cap*. See, for example, *Kellogg* v. *Blue Quail Energy, Inc. (In re Compton Corp.)*, 831 F.2d 586 (5th Cir. 1987); *Zenith Laboratories, Inc.* v. *Security Pac. Nat'l Trust Co. (In re Zenith Laboratories, Inc.)*, 104 B.R. 667 (Bankr. N.J. 1989). Note, however, that an unsecured creditor who has been given a letter of credit in the applicable preference period may find that payments under the letter of credit are avoidable as preferences, at least to the extent that the debtor's reimbursement obligations to the letter of credit issuer became secured in the preference period. See *In re Compton Corp., supra*.
108. Section 362(c).
109. *Id.;* House Report, *supra* endnote 2, at 343.
110. Section 362(d).
111. For purposes of determining whether there is an equity cushion that provides the secured creditor with adequate protection, junior liens are disregarded. See, for example, *Pistole* v. *Mellor (In re Mellor)*, 734 F.2d 1396 (9th Cir. 1984); *In re Nashua Trust Co.*, 73 B.R. 423 (Bankr. D. N.J. 1987).
112. See, for example, *In re Southerton Corp.*, 46 B.R. 391 (M.D. Pa. 1982) (amount of equity cushion should be considered in context of rate at which interest accrues, among other things); *Hagendorfer* v. *Marlette*, 42 B.R. 17 (S.D. Ala. 1984) (9.3% equity cushion with respect to one of debtor's properties and 12.2% equity cushion with respect to another of debtor's properties found inadequate to provide adequate protection); *Federal Land Bank* v. *Carson (In re Carson)*, 34 B.R. 502 (D. Kan. 1983) (11% is sufficient equity cushion to provide adequate protection).
113. Senate Report, *supra* endnote 38, at 54. See *Prudential Ins. Co.* v. *Monnier Bros. (In re Monnier Bros.)*, 755 F.2d 1336 (8th Cir. 1985). It has already been observed that the methodology of valuing a secured claim is left to the discretion of the court. See section on The Secured Claim, *supra*. It is consistent with that discretion to give courts latitude to determine which value the secured creditor is entitled to have preserved.
114. Section 363(d)(2). To determine whether the debtor has equity in the collateral under Section 362(d)(2), courts have included junior liens. See, for example, *United Fin. Co.* v. *Cote (In re Cote)*, 27 B.R. 510 (Bankr. D. Or. 1983) (all liens deducted from value of property); *La*

Jolla Mortgage Fund v. *Rancho El Cajon Assoc.*, 18 B.R. 283 (Bankr. S.D. Cal. 1982) (same). But see *Central Florida Prod. Credit Ass'n.* v. *Spring Garden Foliage, Inc. (In re Spring Garden Foliage, Inc.)*, 15 B.R. 140 (Bankr. M.D. Fla. 1981) (junior liens are to be disregarded).
115. *United Sav. Ass'n* v. *Timbers of Inwood Forest Assoc., Ltd., supra* note 94 at 375-76 (emphasis in original). **See,** for example, *Grundy Nat'l Bank* v. *Tandem Mining Corp.*, 754 F.2d 1436 (4th Cir. 1985).
116. Section 362(e).
117. Section 362(f).
118. Bankruptcy Rule 4001(a)(3).
119. Section 362(g).
120. House Report, *supra* endnote 2, at 344.
121. *See D-1 Enterprises, Inc.* v. *Commercial State Bank*, 864 F.2d 36 (5th Cir. 1989). Counterclaims that go to the validity of the secured creditor's lien may more appropriately be part of a hearing on a motion seeking to lift the stay. **See** *Cheshire County Sav. Bank* v. *Pappas (In re Pappas)*, 55 B.R. 658 (Bankr. D. Mass. 1985).
122. Courts may also stay proceedings under their broad equitable powers. **Compare** *Explorer Drilling Co., Inc.* v. *Martin Exploration Co. (In re Martin Exploration Co.)*, 731 F.2d 1210 (5th Cir. 1984) (stay lifted automatically but court implicitly reinstated stay under Section 105 equitable powers) **with** *Grundy Nat'l Bank* v. *Looney*, 823 F.2d 788, 792-93 (4th Cir.), *cert. denied*, 484 U.S. 977 (1987) (equitable powers cannot revive terminated stay provisions unless court affirmatively determines stay is "necessary or appropriate"). However, courts will undoubtedly be less willing to circumvent Section 362 in light of the Supreme Court's ruling in *Timbers, supra* endnote 94.
123. Section 363(c)(1).
124. Section 363(b).
125. Section 102(a).
126. Section 363(f).
127. Section 363(c)(2).
128. Section 363(a); **see** subsection, Lien on the Property of the Debtor's Estate.
129. Section 363(c)(4).
130. Section 363(f)(3).
131. See, for example, *Richardson* v. *Pitt County (In re Stroud Wholesale, Inc.)*, 47 B.R. 999 (E.D.N.C. 1985); *The Mutual Life Ins. Co. of New York* v. *Red Oak Farms, Inc. (In re Red Oak Farms, Inc.)*, 36 B.R. 856 (Bankr. W.D. Mo. 1984).

132. **See,** for example, *In re Terrace Gardens Park Partnership,* 96 B.R. 707 (Bankr. W.D. Tex. 1989); *In re Beker Indus. Corp.,* 63 B.R. 474 (Bankr. S.D.N.Y. 1986); *Hatfield Homes, Inc. v. Pennview Sav. Assoc. (In re Hatfield Homes, Inc.),* 30 B.R. 353 (Bankr. E.D. Pa. 1983). It should be noted generally that there seems to be confusion in the case law about what protection Section 363(f) provides the secured creditors. The difference in opinion about whether the sale price must be greater than the debt secured by the liens or greater than the "value" of the liens is raised here and in the text accompanying this endnote. Consistent with this confusion, there seems also to be some question about whether the provision permitting a sale of collateral without a secured creditor's consent if the secured creditor could be compelled to accept a "money satisfaction" of its claim means "full" money satisfaction. **See,** for example, *In re Stroud Wholesale, Inc., supra* endnote 131. The editors of *Collier* suggest that, if the sale is out of the ordinary course of business, the sale proceeds must be sufficient to repay the debt secured by the property with some left over for the estate. **See** 2 *Collier on Bankruptcy* ¶ 363.07 at 363-32-32.1 (15th ed. 1990). Ultimately, the secured creditor may be forced to look to the adequate protection provision of Section 363(e) and its ability to bid on its debt under Section 363(k) for protection.
133. **See** *Citicorp Homeowners Serv., Inc. v. Elliot (In re Elliot),* 94 B.R. 343 (E.D. Pa. 1988); *Pelican Homestead & Sav. Ass'n v. Wooten (In re Gabel),* 61 B.R. 661 (Bankr. W.D. La. 1985).
134. Section 363(e).
135. **See** House Report, *supra,* endnote 2, at 345: "Most often, adequate protection in connection with a sale free and clear of other interests will be to have those interests attach to the proceeds of the sale." **See also** *Chase v. Bridges (In re Bridges),* 19 B.R. 847 (Bankr. D. Me. 1982); *Circus Time, Inc. v. Oxford Bank & Trust, U.S. (In re Circus Time, Inc.),* 5 B.R. 1 (Bankr. D. Me. 1979). Note that, if the secured creditor's security documents or as noted in endnote 28, *supra,* applicable state law, create a lien in proceeds, its lien in the sale proceeds of its collateral attach automatically, at which point it is entitled to adequate protection for its cash collateral. **See** Section 552(b); **see also** subsection, Lien on the Property of the Debtor's Estate, *supra.* Courts sometimes speak of the sale price as being the highest and best price and, therefore, that a lien in the proceeds is adequate protection. **See** *Seidle v. Modular Paving, Inc. (In re 18th Ave. Dev. Corp.),* 14 B.R. 862 (Bankr. S.D. Fla. 1981) (sale permitted); *In re Hatfield Homes, Inc., supra* endnote 132 (sale not per-

mitted). **See also** *In re Red Oak Farms, Inc., supra* endnote 131 (sale not permitted because price is not fair market value).
136. **See,** for example, *In re Karl A. Neise, Inc.,* 16 B.R. 602 (Bankr. S.D. Fla. 1981) (substitute lien in postpetition inventory and accounts receivable is adequate protection); *In re Serbus,* 48 B.R. 5 (Bankr. D. Minn. 1984) (granting replacement lien in new dairy cows purchased with cash collateral and paying over of proceeds from prior sale of cows, is adequate protection with respect to lien in livestock, but substitute lien in new crop of grain not yet grown for lien in cash collateral representing proceeds of old crop not adequate protection). But **see** *In re Red Oak Farms, Inc., supra* endnote 121 (substitution of cattle, cash, and leasehold interest with purchase option not adequate protection for interest on land being sold at less than full market value).
137. Section 363(k).
138. Section 364(d).
139. Section 1128(a).
140. Section 1126(f).
141. Section 1124.
142. Section 1124(l). **See** *In re Barrington Oaks Gen. Partnership,* 15 B.R. 952 (Bankr. D. Utah 1981) (finding that any alteration of rights constitutes impairment; the concept of impairment created by Section 1124 is not governed by a valuation standard). **See also** *In re Elijah,* 41 B.R. 348 (Bankr. W.D. Mo. 1984).
143. Section 1124(2). **See,** for example, *In re Entz-White Lumber & Supply, Inc.,* 850 F.2d 1338 (9th Cir. 1988) (plan may cure all defaults without impairing creditor's claim; such defaults include, but are not limited to, defaults resulting in acceleration); *In re Madison Hotel Associates,* 749 F.2d 410 (7th Cir. 1984) (Section 1124(2) permits the plan to reinstate the original maturity of a claim or interest as it existed before the default without impairing such claim or interest). **See also** *In re Blackwelder Furn. Co.,* 31 B.R. 878 (Bankr. W.D.N.C. 1983).
144. Section 1124(2) (A)-(D).
145. Section 1124(3).
146. See *In re Orlando Tennis World Dev. Co.,* 34 B.R. 558, 560 (Bankr. M.D. Fla. 1983).
147. See *In re Entz-White Lumber & Supply, Inc., supra* endnote 143; *In re Southeast Co.,* 868 F.2d 335 (9th Cir. 1989); *In re Arlington Village Partners, Ltd.,* 66 B.R. 308, 316 (Bankr. S.D. Ohio 1986).
148. *See In re Elijah, supra* endnote 142 at 351 (because a finding of nonimpairment means a creditor cannot vote on a plan, impairment

should be broadly construed); *In re Madison Hotel Associates, supra* endnote 143 at 418 (7th Cir. 1984) (Section 1124 defines impairment in the broadest possible terms and carves out three narrow exceptions).
149. See *In re Barrington Oaks Gen. Partnership, supra* endnote 142. **See also** *In re Jeppson,* 66 B.R. 269, 294 (Bankr. D. Utah 1986) (any change in legal, equitable, or contractual rights creates impairment). It is worth noting, however, that leaving a claim unimpaired by curing defaults in respect of that claim under the exception provided by Section 1124(2) does not impair a creditor's claim, even though it may entail altering a contractual acceleration clause. **See** *In re Taddeo,* 685 F.2d 24, 28-29 (2d Cir. 1982); *In re Entz-White Lumber and Supply, Inc., supra* endnote 143 at 1341; *In re Madison Hotel Associates, supra* endnote 143 at 420.
150. Section 1129(a)(7)(A)(i).
151. Section 1129(a)(7). Section 1129(a)(7) provides that the holder of an impaired claim or interest must either accept the plan or the plan must provide that it will receive or retain under on account of such claim or interest, property of a value, as of the effective date of the plan, that is not less than the amount that such holder would so receive or retain if the debtor were liquidated under Chapter 7 on such date.
152. Section 1126(g).
153. Section 1126(c).
154. Section 1126(d).
155. Section 1126(b) provides, in part, that a vote for acceptance or rejection will be counted only if the solicitation of acceptances and rejections has been either in compliance with applicable nonbankruptcy law (in the case of a plan proposed and votes obtained in respect of a so-called prepackaged Chapter 11 plan) or, in the absence of such law, in compliance with Section 1125(a). It is also worth noting that it is very important for creditors who oppose a plan to vote to reject that plan. Although it has been widely criticized as inaccurately construing Section 1126, one recent case has found that a creditor who fails to vote on a plan can have its inaction deemed to constitute an acceptance. See *In re Ruti-Sweetwater, Inc.,* 836 F.2d 1263 (10th Cir. 1988). It is also worth noting that, despite the absence of any language in the Code suggesting that inaction on behalf of a creditor may be construed to constitute an acceptance, in *In re Szostek,* 886 F.2d 1405, 1413 (3rd Cir. 1989) the Third Circuit found "[t]he general rule is that the acceptance of the plan by a secured creditor can be conferred by the absence of an objection." But **see** *In re Friese,* 103 B.R. 90, 92 (Bankr. S.D.N.Y. 1989) (disagreeing with *In re Ruti-*

Sweetwater, supra, and finding "where the class fails to vote, it should not be deemed to accept the plan" but the plan may nevertheless be subject to confirmation under the cramdown provisions); *In re M. Long Arabians,* 103 B.R. 211 (9th Cir. BAP 1989) (declining to follow *In re Ruti-Sweetwater, supra,* "to the extent it holds that a creditor is 'deemed' to have accepted the plan.").

156. Section 1122(a). Claims or interests placed within a class need not be homogeneous but merely substantially similar. **See** *In re Martin's Point Ltd. Part.,* 12 B.R. 721 (Bankr. N.D. Ga. 1981).
157. Section 1123(a)(4). **See,** generally, Riesenfeld, *Classification of Claims and Interests in Chapter 11 and 13 Cases,* 75 Cal. L. Rev. 391 (1987); Anderson, *Classification of Claims and Interests in Reorganization Cases under the New Bankruptcy Code,* 58 Am. Bankr. L.J. 99 (1984).
158. See *In re Gillette Assoc., Ltd.,* 101 B.R. 866, 878 (Bankr. N.D. Ohio 1989).
159. Section 101(4).
160. See House Report, *supra* endnote 2 at 413-18.
161. Section 101(15).
162. See, for example, *In re Sullivan,* 26 B.R. 677 (Bankr. W.D.N.Y. 1982).
163. See, for example, *In re Commercial Western Fin. Corp.,* 761 F.2d 1329, 1338 (9th Cir. 1985); *In re Sullivan, supra* endnote 162 at 678. **But see** *In re Palisades-on-the-Desplaines,* 89 F.2d 214 (7th Cir. 1937) (finding under the Act that claims against different property may be classified together if they are in the same location, were purchased at approximately the same location, were purchased at the same time, and therefore are worth approximately the same amount.
164. See *In re Holthoff,* 58 B.R. 216 (Bankr. E.D. Ark. 1985); *In re Martin's Point, Ltd. Part., supra* endnote 156 at 727.
165. See, for example, *Hanson v. First Nat'l Bank of South Dakota,* 828 F.2d 1310, 1313 (8th Cir. 1987); *In re Barash,* 658 B.R. 504 (7th Cir. 1981).
166. See, for example, *In re Northeast Dairy Coop. Fed'n, Inc.,* 73 B.R. 239 (Bankr. N.D.N.Y. 1987); *In re Atlanta West VI,* 91 B.R. 620 (Bankr. N.D. Ga. 1988); *In re Planes, Inc.,* 48 B.R. 698 (Bankr. N.D. Ga. 1985); *In re Rochem, Ltd.,* 58 B.R. 641 (Bankr. D. N.J. 1985). But **see** *Granada Wines, Inc. v. New England Teamsters & Trucking Indus. Pension Fund,* 748 F.2d 42, 46-47 (1st Cir. 1984), citing, *In re Los Angeles Land & Invs., Ltd.,* 282 F. Supp. 448, 453 (D. Haw. 1968), *aff'd,* 447 F.2d 1366 (9th Cir. 1971) (the general rule regarding classification is that all creditors of equal rank with claims

against the same property should be placed in the same class, and that separate classifications for unsecured creditors are only justified where the legal character of their claims is such to accord them a different status from other creditors).
167. See *In re U.S. Truck Co.*, 800 F.2d 581, 586 (6th Cir. 1986).
168. See *Hanson v. First Nat'l Bank of South Dakota, supra* endnote 165 at 1313.
169. See *In re Huckabee Auto Co.*, 33 B.R. 132, 141 (Bankr. M.D. Ga. 1981); *In re U.S. Truck Co., Inc., supra* endnote 167 at 586 (6th Cir. 1986) (finding that even though the evidence supported classifying a creditor separately from other creditors whose claims were of a similar legal nature and against the same property, the court stated that there "must be some limit on a debtor's power to classify creditors . . ."). **See also** *In re Jersey City Medical Center*, 817 F.2d 1055 (3d Cir. 1987) (agreeing with the "general view" permitting the grouping of similar claims in different classes while maintaining that the classification of claims or interests must be "reasonable").
170. Interpreting the classification procedure under the Bankruptcy Act, the court in *In re Le Blanc*, 622 F.2d 872, 879 n.9, *reh'g denied*, 627 F.2d 239 (5th Cir. 1980) found that, as a general matter, "classification in a plan should not do substantial violence to any claimant's interest. The plan should not arbitrarily classify or discriminate against creditors." **See also** *In re AG Consultants Grain Div., Inc.*, 77 B.R. 665 (Bankr. N.D. Ind. 1987).
171. See, for example, *In re Ward*, 89 B.R. 998 (Bankr. S.D. Fla. 1988); *In re 1000 Intern. Bldg. Assoc., Ltd.*, 81 B.R. 125 (Bankr. S.D. Fla. 1987); *In re S & W Enter.*, 37 B.R. 153 (Bankr. N.D. Ill. 1984).
172. Section 1129(a).
173. See, for example, *In re Valley Park Group, Inc.*, 96 B.R. 16, 21-22 (Bankr. N.D.N.Y. 1989); *In re Future Energy Corp., supra* endnote 84 at 481 (Bankr. S.D. Ohio 1988).
174. Section 1129(a)(8).
175. Section 1129(a)(7); **see,** generally, *In re Wilhelm*, 101 B.R. 120 (Bankr. W.D. Mo. 1989); *In re M.S.M. & Assoc., Inc.*, 104 B.R. 312 (Bankr. D. Haw. 1989).
176. See Fortgang & Mayer, *Valuation in Bankruptcy*, 32 U.C.L.A. L. Rev. 1061, 1063-66 (1985).
177. Section 1129(a)(8).
178. Section 1129(b)(1).
179. Section 1129(a)(10).

180. See Klee, *All You Ever Wanted to Know about Cram Down under the New Bankruptcy Code,* 53 Am. Bank. L.J. 133, 142 (1979).
181. **See,** for example, *In re Acequia, Inc.,* 787 F.2d 1352, 1364 (9th Cir. 1986); *In re Martin,* 66 B.R. 921, 929-30 (Bankr. D. Mont. 1986).
182. See *In re Wilhelm, supra* endnote 175 at 123 (Bankr. W.D. Mo. 1989). **See also** *In re Greystone III Joint Venture,* 102 B.R. 560, 571 (Bankr. W.D. Tex. 1989) (the requirement that a plan not "unfairly discriminate" with respect to a dissenting class parallels the requirement that all creditors within a given class must be treated the same; the phrase "unfairly discriminates" is a term of art, with a specialized meaning consistent with the operation of Section 1122(a)); *In re Dilts,* 100 B.R. 759 (Bankr. W.D. Pa. 1989) (in order not to discriminate unfairly, a plan must allocate value to each class in a manner consistent with the treatment afforded to other classes with similar legal claims against the debtor; a plan that purports to modify a first mortgage by reducing its interest rate and extending the term of repayment period, while junior mortgages on the same property remain unimpaired, discriminates unfairly in violation of Section 1129(b)(1)); *In re Aztec Co.,* 107 B.R. 585 (Bankr. M.D. Tenn. 1989) (the court preferred the broader meaning of unfair discrimination and held that, "to the extent the legislative history endorses a restricted application of the unfair discrimination standard in § 1129(b)(1), it is inconsistent with the unambiguous language of the statute . . ." *Id.* at 589; the court further held that not all discrimination is prohibited by § 1129(b)(1) but only "unfair" discrimination, and found Chapter 13 cases interpreting the fairness of discrimination among classes under § 1322(b)(1) of the Code, *supra* endnote 1, useful for guidelines and analysis of § 1129(b)(1); although the court allowed separate classification of the code-created deficiency claim to nonrecourse undersecured claim and other unsecured claims, it found that disparate treatment of the two types of classes would result in "unfair discrimination"); *In re Eisenbarth,* 77 B.R. 228 (Bankr. D. N.D. 1987) (plan that proposed to pay unsecured trade creditors in full, while paying unsecured institutional creditors only 10 percent of their claims, discriminated unfairly).
183. Section 1129(b)(2)(A)(i).
184. Section 1129(b)(2)(A)(ii).
185. Section 1129(b)(2)(A)(iii). It is worth noting that, with respect to a class of unsecured claims, the fair and equitable standard set forth in Section 1129(b)(2)(B) of the Code requires that (i) the plan provide that the holders of such claims receive or retain on account of such claims property of a value, as of the effective date of the plan, equal to

the allowed amount of such claims or (ii) no holder of an interest junior to the claims of such class may receive or retain under the plan any property on account of such junior claim or interest.
186. *In re Murel Holding Corp.*, 75 F.2d 941 (2d Cir. 1935).
187. 124 Cong. Rec. 32,406-07 (1978). It is worth pointing out that, even though the legislative history indicates that abandoning the collateral which secures a claim will generally be sufficient to satisfy the indubitable equivalent standard, the case law is not uniform on this point. **Compare** *In re Sandy Ridge Dev. Corp.*, 881 F.2d 1346, 1350 (5th Cir. 1989) (since the value of a secured claim is equal to the value of the collateral, and since "common sense tells us that property is the indubitable equivalent of itself," a plan that provides that a secured creditor will receive the collateral satisfies the "indubitable equivalent" requirement; the fact that property values are declining is irrelevant, since at any given moment in time the creditor's secured claim is equal to the value of the collateral; cases holding that transfer of property satisfies the "indubitable equivalent" standard only if property is the equivalent of cash are incorrect) **with** *In re B.W. Alpha, Inc.*, 100 B.R. 831 (N.D. Tex. 1988) (confirmation of a plan calling for secured creditor to take the collateral in satisfaction of its secured claim was denied, since the plan did not give the creditor the "indubitable equivalent" of cash payment, where evidence showed that the creditor would need some five years to realize the amount of the secured claim); *In re ThorneBrook Dev. Corp.*, 96 B.R. 350 (Bankr. N.D. Fla. 1989) (surrender of collateral to secured creditor in full satisfaction of claim is not the "indubitable equivalent" of the claim, notwithstanding that the collateral had stipulated value in excess of creditor's claim, where it would eliminate claims of creditor against guarantors and the creditor may never realize full satisfaction of its claim). It is also worth noting that, if the proponent of a plan uses abandonment to satisfy Section 1129(b) with respect to a class of recourse secured claims, the members of the class have a right to a determination of the value of their collateral pursuant to Section 506(a) as of the date of abandonment. The purpose of the valuation would be to determine the allowed amount of their unsecured claims. Prior to the abandonment, for purposes of classification of claims and to determine the unsecured portion of its claims, any party in interest may request the court to determine the value of the collateral and to allow the class to vote its deficiency claims as provisionally allowed. **See** Bankruptcy Rule 3012.
188. 124 Cong. Rec. H 11,103 (Sept. 28, 1978); S 17,420 (Oct. 6, 1978).
189. Cases considering the question of what constitutes the indubitable

equivalent of a secured creditor's claim include: *In re Sun Country Dev., Inc.*, 764 F.2d 406 (5th Cir. 1985) (distribution to secured creditor of 21 secured notes issued by debtor in exchange for release of creditor's first lien on 200 acres of property owned by debtor was indubitable equivalent); *In re Pikes Peak Water Co.*, 779 F.2d 1456 (10th Cir. 1985) (plan providing for oversecured creditor to retain its lien without receiving payments for three years, after which the mortgage would be paid in full or reinstated may constitute the indubitable equivalent); *In re Hoff*, 54 B.R. 746, 753 (Bankr. D. N.D. 1985) (replacement lien on after-acquired livestock and crops grown is not the "indubitable equivalent" of lien on livestock and crops presently existing, since just one crop failure would leave the secured creditor's interest unprotected); *In re Pine Lake Village Apt. Co.*, 21 B.R. 478 (Bankr. S.D. N.Y. 1982) (30-year self-liquidating note in the amount of secured claim is not the indubitable equivalent even when the interest rate is 15.75 percent a year, when the debtor's net income only barely covers the debt service payments); and *In re Planes, Inc., supra* endnote 166 (plan proposing to pay undersecured creditors from sales of its collateral as they occur did not provide present value of claim; therefore, plan could not be crammed down).

190. House Report, *supra* endnote 2 at 414.
191. See *In re Evans Prod. Co.*, 60 B.R. 863, 876 (S.D. Fla. 1986).
192. See, generally, Note, *The Proper Discount Rate under the Chapter 11 Cramdown Provision: Should Secured Creditors Retain Their State Law Entitlements?*, 72 Va. L. Rev. 1499 (1986).
193. See *In re Park Ave. Partners Ltd. Part.*, 95 B.R. 605, 613 (Bankr. E.D. Wis. 1988); *In re 360 Inns, Ltd.*, 76 B.R. 573, 585-94 (Bankr. N.D. Tex. 1987); *In re Camino Real Landscape Maint. Contractors, Inc.*, 818 F.2d 1503, 1505 (9th Cir. 1987); 5 *Collier on Bankruptcy*, ¶ 1129.03(4) (15th Ed. 1989).
194. See *In re 360 Inns, Ltd., supra* endnote 193 at 587-88 (finding a discount rate 2.5 percent above prime fair and equitable). **See also** *In re Park Ave. Partners Ltd. Part., supra* endnote 193 at 613 *citing* 5 *Collier on Bankruptcy* ¶ 1129.03[4][f][i] (15th ed. 1987); *In re Camino Real Landscape Maint. Contractors*, 818 F.2d 1503, 1505 (9th Cir. 1987) *citing* 5 *Collier on Bankruptcy* ¶ 1129.03 [4] [f] [i] at 1129-65 (15th Ed. 1987); *In re Southern States Motor Inns, Inc.*, 709 F.2d 647, 651 (11th Cir. 1983), *cert. denied*, 465 U.S. 1022 (1984), *citing* 5 *Collier on Bankruptcy* ¶ 1129.03 at 1129-65 (15th ed. 1982); *United States v. Neal Pharmacal Co.*, 789 F.2d 1283, 1285 1985 (8th Cir. 1986).

195. **See,** generally, 5 *Collier on Bankruptcy* § 1129.03(f)(ii) (15th Ed. 1989); **see also** *In re Fiberglass Indus., Inc., supra,* endnote 40, at 742 (Bankr. N.D.N.Y. 1987) (where plan calls for debtor to retain and continue using a secured party's collateral, a going-concern analysis is the proper approach to valuing that collateral).

196. See *Ahlers* v. *Norwest Bank of Washington (In re Ahlers),* 794 F.2d 388, 399 (8th Cir. 1986), *rev'd on other grounds,* 485 U.S. 197 (1988) ("For purposes of the reorganization plan, the value of collateral is to be determined at the time for confirmation of that plan."); *In re Mikkelsen Farms, Inc.,* 74 B.R. 280, 289 (Bankr. D. Or. 1987) ("A determination of the allowed amount of a secured claim for the purposes of applying the provisions of [Section] 1129(b)(2)(A)(i) . . . should be as of the effective date of the plan."). But **see** *In re Beard,* 108 B.R. 322 (Bankr. N.D. Ala. 1989) (proper date for determining allowed amount of secured claim is the date the debtor's Chapter 11 petition is filed).

197. Section 1111(b)(2).

198. Section 1111(b)(1)(A). The other situation in which the nonrecourse creditor's claim will not be recourse is when its collateral is to be sold in the Chapter 11 case or pursuant to the plan. For reasons discussed in the text, *infra,* the recourse creditor is also not permitted to make the election in that situation.

199. **See** 124 Cong. Rec. 32,406-07 (1978).

200. Section 1111(b)(1)(A).

201. Bankruptcy Rule 3014.

202. *Id.*

203. **See** *In re Keller,* 47 B.R. 725 (Bankr. N.D. Iowa 1985).

204. Section 1111(b)(1)(B).

CHAPTER 9

OTHER CONSIDERATIONS IN DEALING WITH A TROUBLED COMPANY

John F. Horstmann III, Esq.
S. Fain Hackney, Esq.
Duane, Morris & Heckscher

The primary focus of many chapters in this book is the federal bankruptcy code (11 U.S.C. Section 101 *et seq.*, the Bankruptcy Code). However, players in the troubled company arena should be aware of the many federal and state statutes that create a complex regulatory overlay to both out-of-court workouts and bankruptcies. Within the confines of this chapter, it is impossible to discuss every potential problem. A number of important considerations will not be addressed, such as the impact of the Financial Institutions Reform, Recovery and Enforcement Act of 1989 (FIRREA) on savings and loans; foreign laws and treaties regulating transactions in the international arena; and the certification and reimbursement regulations applicable to health care providers.

The issues covered in this chapter will be limited to the following subjects: (1) retiree benefit claims and pension liability, (2) federal and selected state environmental laws, and (3) the Federal Plant Closing Act.

AN OVERVIEW OF PENSION, EMPLOYEE, AND RETIREE BENEFITS CONSIDERATIONS IN THE CONTEXT OF TROUBLED COMPANIES

The Employee Retirement Income Security Act of 1974 (ERISA) was enacted for the purpose of protecting private pension plans and assuring workers that their private pension plans would be a source of retirement income. Before the enactment of ERISA, there were virtually no regulations to ensure that the benefits promised under the terms of defined benefit plans would be provided. As a result, employees were often deprived of their pension benefits upon plan termination. To protect defined benefit plans, ERISA mandates minimum funding requirements, regulates the investment of plan assets, and limits the access of employers to plan assets. In addition, the Pension Benefit Guaranty Corporation (PBGC) was established under ERISA to administer a plan termination insurance program and guarantee that workers receive certain benefits under defined benefit plans. As the result of the establishment of minimum funding standards and the creation of liability for failure to adhere to those standards, claims and potential claims under ERISA have become extremely important in corporate workouts and bankruptcy cases.

The obligation to make pension contributions is mandated by ERISA and the Internal Revenue Code (IRC). ERISA was amended by the Pension Protection Act of 1987 (PPA) to require employers to make quarterly estimated payments for plan years beginning after December 31, 1988. Failure to make plan payments in accordance with the provisions of ERISA and the IRC can have serious consequences. For example, failure to fulfill the minimum funding requirement results in the imposition of a "first tier" excise tax of 10 percent of the funding deficiency for single-employer plans or an excise tax of 5 percent of the funding deficiency for multiemployer plans. A multiemployer plan is one that is the subject of collective bargaining and to which more than one employer is required to contribute. Single-employer plans comprise all defined benefit plans that are not multiemployer plans, including plans to which more than one employer contributes so long as such plans are not created through collective bargaining.

A plan's funding deficiency, which forms the basis for the excise tax, is calculated by examining the current year's charges and credits to the funding standard account, including any funding deficiencies from prior years. Thus, for example, a funding deficiency in 1989 that remains unpaid at the end of 1990 will be subject to a 10 percent excise tax in 1989 and in 1990. A plan complies with the minimum funding requirement if, as of the end of a plan year, it does not have an accumulated funding deficiency in its funding standard account. A plan's funding standard account consists of a variety of complex credits and charges, and it must contain at the end of the plan year sufficient value to fund the pension plan.

An additional "second tier" excise tax of 100 percent of the accumulated funding deficiency is levied if an accumulated funding deficiency is not eliminated before the end of a "taxable period."[1] The taxable period ends on the earlier of the date the first tier tax is assessed or the date on which notice of the first tier tax is sent. Practically, this means that notices for first and second tier excise taxes are sent simultaneously. The second tier tax can be avoided if a contribution is made to the plan that eliminates the accumulated funding deficiency within 90 days after the second tier tax notice is mailed. The 90-day correction period can be extended if the employer files a petition in the tax court or files a bankruptcy petition. In addition, a lien is imposed on all assets of the employer and members of its "controlled group" for funding contributions in excess of $1 million that remain unpaid for 60 days or more.[2] The lien has the same status as a federal tax lien—that is, its priority is based on the date on which the lien is imposed.

ERISA provides that the employer and the members of its "controlled group" are jointly and severally liable for failure to make plan payments. The *controlled group* is defined as businesses under common ownership or control, regardless of corporate structure.[3] Treasury regulations define more precisely the members of the controlled group. The controlled group includes trades or businesses under 80 percent common ownership, affiliated service groups, and certain other related employers as defined in the Treasury regulations. An affiliated service group means a group consisting of an organization that primarily performs services ("service organization"), and one or more other organizations, which are either (1) shareholders of the service organization that regularly perform services for or with the service organization or (2) owned 10 percent or more by certain employees or officers of the service organization and perform services historically performed in such service field by employees.[4] An example of an affiliated service group would be a medical doctor and a corporation he or she established, of which he or she is more than a 10 percent owner, for the purpose of providing secretarial, nursing, and other services to this practice. For purposes of ERISA liability, the doctor's medical practice and the corporation he or she established would be members of the same controlled group.

There are instances in which employers experiencing substantial business hardship[5] may be granted a waiver by the IRS to permit the employer to pay current funding obligations over future years. In determining whether an employer under a single-employer pension plan is experiencing temporary substantial business hardship, the business condition of the employer and its controlled group will be considered. The business condition of the controlled group is not considered for a waiver request by a multiemployer pension plan. Prior to the enactment of the PPA, funding waivers were granted to certain troubled companies, like LTV Corporation, Chrysler Corporation, and International Harvester Company. The PPA limited to a certain extent the use of funding waivers, but they are still available. The grant of a waiver allows an employer to stretch the payment of required funding over a 5-year period, in the case of single-employer plans, and over a 15-year period for multiemployer plans. In addition, a funding waiver stays the imposition of the excise tax on accumulated funding deficiencies. The decision of whether to grant funding waivers is made by the Secretary of the Treasury.[6] However, the PBGC must be given notice of and an opportunity to comment on applications for waivers of funding deficiencies, with certain limited exceptions. Notice of the application for waiver of funding deficiencies must also be given to each participant, beneficiary, and organization representing employees covered by the plan.

If the employer defaults in its agreed upon payment schedule with the IRS or with any other condition of a funding waiver, the IRS may revoke the waiver. In addition, a significant benefit improvement will automatically revoke any prior waivers. The revocation of the waiver causes the unamortized balance of the waived funding deficiency to become a current obligation. In addition, revocation permits the IRS to assert that the excise tax liability can be calculated from the date required contributions would have been due in the absence of a waiver. This invariably results in the imposition of a 100 percent excise tax penalty.

Liability on Termination or Withdrawal from a Plan

Pension plans can be terminated in several different ways, some of which may result in the imposition of liability on the employer or the plan sponsor and the controlled group.

The first way in which pension plans can be terminated is the institution by the PBGC in federal district court of proceedings to terminate a single-employer plan. The PBGC is required to institute proceedings to terminate a single-employer plan if it determines that the plan does not have sufficient assets to pay benefits currently due.[7]

The PBGC has discretion to institute proceedings to terminate a plan if (1) the plan has not met the minimum funding standards, (2) the plan will not be able to pay benefits when due, (3) the PBGC's future loss will increase unreasonably if the plan is not terminated, and (4) a reportable event has occurred under ERISA § 4043(b)(7).

Second, a plan can be terminated by the employer itself. A single-employer plan can be terminated in two ways. First, it can be voluntarily terminated by the plan sponsor by having the plan administrator provide 60-day prior written notice to affected parties and filing a certification with the PBGC that the plan is sufficient to pay all benefit liabilities. This so-called standard termination procedure is not available if the plan is underfunded. Second, an employer that wants to terminate its pension plan can apply for a "distress termination." To qualify for a distress termination of a single-employer pension plan, the employer and its controlled group must (1) be a debtor in a liquidation case under the Bankruptcy Code or state law or be a debtor in a reorganization case under the Bankruptcy Code or state law in which the court approves plan termination on the basis that, if plan payments continue, the employer will be unable to reorganize, or (2) convince the PBGC that, unless the plan is terminated, the employer will be unable to continue to operate or that the pension payments are unreasonably burdensome as the result of a decline in the number of employees participating in all single-employer plans to which the employer contributes. In addition, to comply with the requirements for a distress termination, the plan administrator must provide written notice to all affected parties at least 60 days prior to termination.

Under the Multiemployer Pension Plan Amendments Act of 1980 (MEPPAA), liability is incurred when there is a complete or partial withdrawal from a multiemployer plan. A complete withdrawal occurs when an employer permanently ceases to have an obligation to contribute to the plan or permanently discontinues all covered operations under a plan. In general, a temporary cessation of the obligation to contribute or of covered operations will not result in a withdrawal.

Examples of complete withdrawals would be an employer's liquidation of its assets or selling of all of its covered operations to an unrelated third party, or the employees' membership in a union that decertifies, disclaims representation, or is replaced by a different union. A withdrawal does not occur if, for example, a parent corporation is no longer obligated to contribute to a plan to which the parent and its subsidiary jointly contribute, so long as the subsidiary continues to be obligated to contribute to that plan.[8] Similarly, a withdrawal does not occur if there are certain limited changes to the corporate structure, such as (1) transfer of covered operations to a subsidiary of the contributing employer, (2) incorporation of a sole proprietorship, (3) change of the ownership interests of a partnership, or (4) a change of identity, form, or place of organization, liquidation of a subsidiary into its parent or merger, consolidation, or division.

In certain instances, a decrease in an employer's obligation to contribute to a plan is substantial enough to trigger a partial withdrawal, even though a complete withdrawal has not occurred. A partial withdrawal can occur in two ways: (1) through a 70 percent contribution decline over a three-year testing period or (2) through a partial cessation of the employer's contribution obligation.

Upon termination of a single-employer plan, whether through a PBGC termination or distress termination, the employer and its controlled group are jointly and severally liable, on the termination date, to the PBGC for the total amount of unfunded pension liability, plus interest from the termination date. This liability gives rise to a lien on the assets of the employer and the controlled group, up to a maximum of 30 percent of the net worth of the employer and its controlled group.[9] This lien has the priority of a federal tax lien under IRC Section 6323. In addition, the employer is liable to the successor plan trustee (which might be the PBGC) for all delinquent contributions, including amounts that were subject to waivers and extensions.

In a multiemployer plan, the withdrawing employer is immediately liable for its allocable share of unfunded vested benefits.[10] There are at least four different methods for calculating an employer's allocable share, which will not be reviewed in detail here.[11] As in the case of single-employer plans, the withdrawing employer and all members of its controlled group are jointly and severally liable to the plan for the withdrawal liability.

Treatment of Retiree Benefit Claims in Bankruptcy

On June 16, 1988, Congress enacted the Retiree Benefits Bankruptcy Protection Act of 1988 (RBBPA) in response to the attempt by LTV Corporation to discontinue medical benefit payments to its approximately 75,000 retired employees and to treat those health and welfare benefit claims as prepetition unsecured claims in its bankruptcy case. RBBPA replaced temporary legislation that Congress had passed on November 3, 1986, requiring trustees and debtors-in-possession in Chapter 11 cases to maintain retiree medical benefits on existing levels until October 15, 1987. This stopgap legislation prevented LTV and other companies from terminating retiree medical benefits after filing for Chapter 11 bankruptcy protection.

The cornerstone of RBBPA is a new section of the Bankruptcy Code, Section 1114, which applies to all bankruptcy cases filed on or after June 16, 1988. All bankruptcy cases filed before that date remain subject to the stopgap legislation filed in response to the LTV case.[12] The retiree benefits that are covered by Section 1114 include "payments to any entity or person for the purpose of providing or reimbursing payments for retired employees . . . for medical, surgical, or hospital care benefits, or benefits in the event of sickness, accident, disability, or death under any plan, fund, or program. . . ." Section 1114 provides that retiree benefits cannot be modified and must be timely paid unless (1) the authorized representative of the retiree consents to the modification or (2) the bankruptcy court orders modification of the benefits pursuant to certain standards set forth in Section 1114.

The authorized representative with the authority to compromise the retiree's right to receive benefits is the retiree's labor union, or, if the retirees are nonunion, a committee of retirees appointed by the bankruptcy court. If the modification of retiree benefits is court ordered, the court must determine that (1) the employer has made a proposal to the authorized representative of the retirees; (2) the proposal is based on the most complete and reliable information available at the time the proposal is made; (3) the modifications proposed are necessary to permit the reorganization of the debtor and assures that all creditors, the employer, and all affected parties are treated fairly and equitably; (4) the employer has met and conferred with the authorized representative in good faith and attempted to reach mutually satisfactory modifications to the retiree benefits; and (5) the authorized representative has refused without good cause to accept the proposal. Even if the court determines that all of the steps listed above have occurred, it may not order a reduction in benefits to a level lower than that proposed by the trustee or debtor-in-possession. In addition, the authorized representative of the retirees is permitted under Section 1114 to petition the court for an increase in benefits at any time after an order modifying the benefits has been entered.

Treatment of Claims for Pension Benefits in Bankruptcy

As was discussed earlier about plan terminations outside of a bankruptcy case, an employer-debtor in a bankruptcy case can also apply for a "distress termination" and, if successful, cease making pension payments during the bankruptcy case. The PBGC may seek to restore the terminated plan to its prior status "as the result of such circumstances as the [PBGC] determines to be relevant."[14] The PBGC's authority to restore terminated plans has become an important issue in the context of "follow-on plans." For example, in the bankruptcy case of LTV Corporation, LTV sought to terminate its pension obligations by sending notice to the PBGC shortly after its bankruptcy filing, stating that it did not have the ability to fund its pension plans. The plans were ultimately terminated and LTV employees became eligible to receive guaranteed benefits from the PBGC. However, the union representing LTV's non-management employees commenced an adversary action in the bankruptcy case, alleging that LTV had breached its collective bargaining agreement, because the benefits provided by the PBGC were not as comprehensive as those that LTV was obligated to provide under the collective bargaining agreement.

The litigation with the union was settled pursuant to an agreement that provided the LTV employees would receive certain benefits in addition to those provided by the PBGC. The PBGC objected to this arrangement as a follow-on plan, which permitted LTV Corporation to provide additional benefits to its employees while the PBGC paid a substantial portion of the cost of the pension benefit package as a guarantor of the terminated plans. For this reason, the PBGC attempted to reinstate the terminated plans; but the bankruptcy court prevented it from doing so, ruling that the PBGC's decision to reinstate the terminated plans was arbitrary and capricious. The PBGC appealed the ruling by the bankruptcy court. On appeal, the United States Court of Appeals for the Second Circuit ruled further that follow-on plans are not impermissible and that "collective bargaining agreements can establish a contractual obligation to provide pension benefits, following termination of a plan, in excess of the amounts guaranteed by the PBGC."[15]

Priority of Claims

Retiree Claims
All retiree benefits incurred during a bankruptcy case before a plan is confirmed are entitled to administrative expense priority—that is, the retirees are entitled to payment in full before prepetition unsecured creditors are paid. If any retiree benefits are paid between the date on which the bankruptcy petition is filed and the date on which the plan is confirmed, those payments are not offset against other unpaid benefit claims arising either as the result of modification of the benefits or for future payments under the plan. The special treatment granted to retiree claims has been criticized, because it removes the economic incentive of the authorized representative to agree to modify benefit payments prior to plan confirmation unless

there is a risk of liquidation. In addition, it has also been argued that this treatment provides unsecured creditors with an incentive to seek the conversion of a reorganization case to a liquidation case before the company depletes its cash resources or the administrative expenses eliminate the prospect for a distribution to unsecured creditors.

Pension Claims

The PBGC has asserted in a number of bankruptcy cases that all pension liability that becomes due after a bankruptcy petition is filed is entitled to administrative expense priority. Bankruptcy courts have generally allowed administrative expense priority for funding obligations that become due postpetition so long as the actuarial calculations are adjusted to reflect actual labor rendered postpetition, rather than basing such calculations on prepetition service.[16] However, in the context of both multiemployer and single-employer plans, courts have consistently declined to allow the PBGC full administrative expense status for its claims arising from postpetition termination of a plan and the resulting payment of guaranteed benefits.[17] In denying administrative expense status, courts reason that, although the plan termination may occur postpetition, the claim is actually based on obligations of the debtor arising prior to the filing of the bankruptcy case.

AN OVERVIEW OF ENVIRONMENTAL CONSIDERATIONS IN THE CONTEXT OF TROUBLED COMPANIES

During the last decade, the impact of environmental statutes and regulations on troubled company situations has been dramatic. Secured lenders and purchasers of troubled businesses have become increasingly wary of unintentionally incurring liability for the often extraordinary cost of environmental cleanup of contaminated sites.

The principal federal statute involving hazardous waste cleanup is the Comprehensive Environmental Response, Compensation, and Liability Act of 1980 (CERCLA), more popularly known as the *Superfund statute*. CERCLA empowers the federal government to clean up hazardous waste sites. The Environmental

Protection Agency (EPA) has the primary responsibility for hazardous waste cleanup. Cleanup costs are financed either from the Hazardous Substance Response Trust Fund (the Superfund) or by "responsible parties."

If there has been a release or a threatened release of a hazardous substance, the EPA has several options. First, the EPA itself may clean up the hazardous waste site using Superfund monies. Second, by obtaining a court order or an administrative order, the EPA may require the responsible parties to stop the release or to clean up the hazardous waste under a plan approved by the EPA. Third, the EPA itself, or a state or political subdivision through an agreement with the EPA, may clean up the site and sue responsible parties for reimbursement.

To impose liability under CERCLA, three major factors must exist: (1) a "hazardous substance," a "contaminant," or a "pollutant" has been released or there is a threat of release; (2) the release or threatened release has caused or may cause harm to persons or the environment; and (3) the company or entity responsible for the release or threatened release is one of the categories of "responsible parties" liable for cleanup costs. Litigation under CERCLA usually centers on whether the third factor has been demonstrated.

Under CERCLA, there are four categories of "responsible parties" who can be liable for cleanup costs: (1) current owners or operators of a site where there is any hazardous substance; (2) past owners or operators of a site containing a hazardous substance who owned or operated that site during a period when there was a disposal of any hazardous substance; (3) persons who arranged for the treatment or disposal of any hazardous substance taken to that site (whether or not they intended the substance to be treated or disposed of at that site); and (4) persons who transported any hazardous substance for treatment or disposal at that site if they chose the site as the place of treatment or disposal. The issue of who can be considered an "owner or operator" of a hazardous waste facility is frequently litigated.

Liability of Shareholders, Officers, Directors, and Successor Entities

A corporation may be liable as the owner or operator of a hazardous waste site; but its officers, directors, and shareholders are not liable solely by virtue of their positions. An officer, director, or shareholder can become liable if he or she is directly involved in the acts giving rise to environmental liability. Examples of direct involvement would include direction of, approval of, or cooperation in the acts of releasing hazardous substances.

The United States Court of Appeals for the Second Circuit has imposed liability on a person who "approved of" the release of hazardous substances.[18] In that case, an individual established a corporation for the purpose of purchasing certain property for a condominium development. The purchaser was aware, at the time of the acquisition, that there were five storage tanks containing approximately 700,000 gallons of hazardous waste located in the center of the property. In addition, there were six smaller tanks containing hazardous waste located both below and above ground. Although the purchaser was aware of the existence of chemicals in the storage tanks, he did not participate in the generation or transportation of the hazardous waste.

The purchase agreement permitted the purchaser to cancel the agreement following the completion of an environmental study. The environmental study revealed that the cost of environmental cleanup would range from $650,000 to $1,000,000 before any condominiums could be built on the property. Nevertheless, after asking for a waiver of liability from, and being turned down by, the New York State Department of Environmental Conservation (DEC), the purchaser took title to the property while it continued to be operated as a hazardous waste storage facility. The operators of the hazardous waste storage facility remained on the property for approximately three months after the purchaser obtained title. During that three-month period, almost 90,000 gallons of additional hazardous chemicals were added to the storage tanks, and several leaking drums of chemicals were brought onto the site. The purchaser of the property finally evicted the tenants, but he took no further action on the site for five months. After five months, the purchaser asked the DEC to enter the site and attempt to mitigate the "life threatening crisis situation." After incurring cleanup costs, the DEC attempted to recover its costs from the purchaser.

The court imposed liability on the purchaser despite the fact that the purchaser had not caused the presence or the release of hazardous waste at the site. The court imposed liability because (1) the purchaser knew that hazardous waste had been dumped on the property and could readily have foreseen that hazardous waste would continue to be dumped after he took title to the property and (2) the purchaser did not take sufficient precautions to prevent further dumping of hazardous waste. The inaction of the purchaser, in his capacity as shareholder of the corporation that purchased the property, rendered him liable for cleanup costs.

On a similar theory, the vice president of a corporation who arranged for the transport and disposal of hazardous waste was held personally liable under CERCLA for cleanup costs.[19] Liability was assessed not based on a demonstration of negligence in carrying out his corporate functions but solely on the basis that the corporate officer participated in the disposal of hazardous waste. Thus, individuals who, in their capacity as officers, directors, or shareholders, have the opportunity to "participate" in release or disposal of hazardous waste should exercise a high degree of care to assure that all environmental requirements are met.

In addition to assessing liability against shareholders, officers, and directors, entities that become successors by purchase or merger can also be liable for cleanup costs under CERCLA. A successor entity may be held liable for the acts of the seller if (1) the purchaser buys all or substantially all of the assets of the seller and continues essentially the same business operations as the seller or (2) the sale is deemed to be a de facto merger. For example, a corporation that purchased the assets of a failing enterprise, which was being sued by the EPA for violations of the Federal Insecticide, Fungicide, and Rodenticide Act, was held liable for the fines assessed against the seller.[20] The purchase agreement provided for the sale of substantially all of the corporation's assets and the assumption of the corporation's trade liabilities. The agreement did not include the assumption of the corporation's liabilities to the EPA. Nevertheless, the United States Court of Appeals for the Ninth Circuit ruled that the EPA had authority to extend liability to the successor corporation to achieve the purposes of the statute. In its holding, the court noted that the president of the buyer corporation was the same person as the president of the selling corporation and the buyer corporation continued in the same line of business, namely the distribution of pesticides.

If management intends to acquire a company or substantially all of its assets and intends to continue its operation, management should conduct a detailed due diligence analysis for any actual or potential environmental liability that may attach to the buyer company.

Liability of Lenders

Lenders to companies that incur CERCLA liability can also be held liable for cleanup costs in certain factual situations. The definition of "owner or operator" under CERCLA expressly excludes "a person, who without participating in the management of a . . . facility, holds indicia of ownership primarily to protect his security interest in the . . . facility." Thus, a lender that merely holds a lien on assets containing hazardous waste is not liable for CERCLA cleanup costs. However, a lender can become liable through its actions.

For example, a court has held that a mortgagee/lender was not liable for CERCLA cleanup costs if, after the mortgagor/borrower defaulted on its obligations under the mortgage, the lender merely maintained close financial controls, visited the property regularly, prepared regular reports on operations, and participated in the identification and location of potential purchasers for the property.[21] However, the court also ruled that, once the mortgagee foreclosed on the mortgaged property and became the owner of the property, the mortgagee, as owner, was liable for cleanup costs. In addition, although the court did not find liability based on the lender's preforeclosure activities, the court noted that a lender could be held liable for its preforeclosure activities if it exercised control over the borrower.

The EPA has attempted to assert liability against a lender who arranged for equipment in which it had a security interest to be auctioned. The EPA has argued that the lender was responsible for $400,000 of cleanup costs because, in connection with the auction and removal of the equipment, drums containing hazardous materials were damaged and asbestos lining in pipes was knocked down and released in the facility.[22] The court determined that the lender was not a responsible party under CERCLA prior to the equipment auction, because the lender had not foreclosed on the facility. The court did not decide whether the lender was liable under CERCLA as an "owner or operator" of the facility by virtue of the damage to the storage drums and the release of asbestos in connection with the auction and removal of the equipment. Both the lender and the EPA have appealed the court's decision: the lender, on the grounds that a lender should not be liable for exercising its rights to sell its collateral, and the EPA, on the grounds that a lender can be liable as an "owner or operator" based on its actions.

The EPA has also attempted to recover its cleanup costs from the proceeds of a secured creditor's collateral.[23] The EPA has asserted its right to recovery on the grounds that (1) if the lender sought to sell the drums that were subject to the lender's security interest, the lender would have had an obligation under CERCLA to abate the hazard caused by its collateral, and (2) the EPA's actions benefited the lender. However, the court rejected the EPA's arguments on the grounds that the lender was not liable to abate the hazard caused by its collateral. The court reasoned that, since the lender was not an "owner or operator" under CERCLA, even if it had foreclosed on and sold its collateral, the lender would not have been liable for cleanup costs. Without evidence that the lender had participated in the management of the facility, the court was unwilling to assess liability simply based on a lender's exercise of its rights to its collateral.

Practice Points for Environmental Issues

Identification of Potential Environmental Liability
One of the most important ingredients in successfully avoiding unwanted environmental liability is obtaining adequate information. The extent of the information-gathering process will necessarily depend on the details of the transaction—for example, the cost, the nature of the business, the age of the business, and the nature of the seller. However, regardless of the details of the transaction, certain steps can be followed generally to minimize the risk of environmental liability.

If the transaction involves the acquisition of developed or undeveloped real estate or of an operating facility, an important initial step is the development of a site history. The most easily accessible source of information regarding a site is the people who are familiar with the site. Employees, neighbors, local environmental and health officials, and past and present on-site management can often be great sources of information regarding the history of the site and the purposes for which it has been used.

Based on interviews with these people and on an evaluation of any information that they supply, the next step is to develop a chronology of operation at the site, categorized by (1) location of operation, (2) flow of substances at each location, and (3) identification of any potential hazardous substance at each location. If the site has been used for the storing or disposal of any substances, one should identify each substance stored or disposed of and determine whether such substance is potentially hazardous. A *hazardous substance* under CERCLA is defined as any substance designated as hazardous or toxic under the Clean Air Act,[24] the Clean Water Act,[25] the Resource Conservation and Recovery Act of 1976,[26] the Toxic Substances Control Act,[27] or any substance designated from time to time by the EPA as posing a "present substantial danger to the public health or welfare or the environment."[28] A list of the substances considered to be hazardous by the EPA is published in volume 40 of the Code of Federal Regulations under the applicable sections and can also be obtained by writing to the EPA at the following address:

EPA
Freedom of Information Officer
A-101
401 M Street, S.W.
Washington, D.C. 20460

After identifying the potentially hazardous substances at the site, one should evaluate any aerial photographs or publicly available site surveys for underground tanks or pipes that could have generated hazardous substances.

After developing a site history from available data, a physical inspection of the site should be made by a person familiar with the physical manifestations of environmental problems. Both active and inactive areas of the site should be inspected. During the site inspection, all potential "discharge" locations should be identified, including underground storage tanks, underground piping, transfer or pumping stations for raw materials or other product, buried drums, and the like. Once these discharge locations are identified, the best method of inspecting each discharge location should be determined. In addition, all aboveground storage areas for hazardous substances should be visually inspected and identified. Examples of these are tanks, drums, pipes, and warehouses. Last, after identifying discharge locations and ground storage areas, a decision should be made about whether soil or groundwater testing is desirable or necessary.

A final area of review is public documents. The type of public documents that should be reviewed are reports to federal and state environmental agencies, such as monitoring reports, permit applications or renewals, CERCLA notifications, community complaints, and filings with the Securities and Exchange Commission. These documents are all public records and most can be obtained by filing a request for records with the EPA freedom of information officer at the address listed on page 317 or with the EPA regional office located in your area. The request should "reasonably describe" the records being sought. Under normal circumstances, the EPA will respond within 10 working days.

Internal reports can also be a useful source of information and should be carefully reviewed. Examples of these internal reports are health and safety audits, insurance claims, information requests from federal or state environmental agencies, permit compliance records, including work papers to prepare compliance reports, and any analyses of raw material inventories or the substances that are used to convert the raw materials into finished goods.

Cleanup

If, after conducting the analysis described above, the company determines that it, rather than the EPA or some other third party, should clean up and dispose of hazardous or potentially hazardous substances, that process should include the following procedures:

1. Identify and separate all hazardous substances into individual categories.
2. Separately package and label each hazardous substance.
3. If substances are not to be transported to permitted waste disposal facilities, determine whether the substances can be handled by high-temperature incineration or chemical treatment.

4. Take the substances that are to be transported to permitted landfills.
5. Obtain certificates of destruction for materials that are incinerated and certificates of disposal for those that are chemically neutralized, biologically treated, or landfilled.
6. Rinse all tanks and machinery from which hazardous substances have been removed and safely dispose of the runoff.

By following the steps given above, a company can reduce the risk that the cleanup process will create more environmental problems than were in existence prior to cleanup. If the company is unsure of how to proceed, local environmental officials or an environmental consultant should be consulted.

Selected State Statutes

In addition to the federal environmental statutes, such as CERCLA, a number of states have enacted their own environmental statutes. For example, New Jersey has enacted the New Jersey Environmental Cleanup Responsibility Act (ECRA), which is administered by the New Jersey Department of Environmental Protection (DEP).[29]

Certain provisions of ECRA are triggered by a closing, a termination, or a transfer of an "industrial establishment" engaged in operations involving hazardous substances. A *closing* or *termination* is defined under ECRA as the cessation of all operations that involve the generation, manufacture, refining, transportation, treatment, storage, handling, or disposal of hazardous substances and wastes, including any temporary cessation for a period of not less than two years. A *transfer* includes a change of ownership through statutory merger, sale of a controlling stock position, initiation of a bankruptcy proceeding, or transfer of title pursuant to foreclosure proceedings. Specifically excluded from ECRA are corporate reorganizations "not substantially affecting ownership of an industrial establishment."

For a property to be considered an "industrial establishment," it must have one of the Standard Industrial Classification (SIC) numbers identified in ECRA. The applicable ECRA SIC code numbers are 22–39 inclusive, 46–49 inclusive, and 51 or 76. These SIC codes include most manufacturing operations and companies engaged in operations involving hazardous substances and wastes, with certain limited exceptions, such as retail gasoline stations (SIC code 55) and automobile repair and body shops (SIC code 75). Certain classes of operations within the listed SIC codes are exempt from ECRA compliance requirements, such as the wholesale distribution of printing and writing paper, the wholesale distribution of farm product, and those companies involved in the transportation of freight and cargo. In addition, companies with ECRA SIC codes may petition the New Jersey DEP in writing for an exemption on the grounds that the industrial establishment does not pose a risk to public health and safety.

The definition of "hazardous substances" under ECRA includes the list of hazardous substances and toxic pollutants adopted by the EPA in the Clean Water Act and petroleum products and fuel oil storage facilities (excluding retail fuel oil sales facilities and gasoline stations).

Assuming that ECRA is applicable, certain notices must be provided to the DEP. The first notice submission required is a general information submission (GIS), which is due within five days of the public release of the decision to close or sell the industrial establishment. The GIS should include the identity of the company, its applicable SIC code, a description of the industrial establishment's historical operations, a list of federal and state permits, and a list of any enforcement actions against the establishment. The second notice that is required under ECRA is a site evaluation submission (SES), which must be filed within 45 days after the action triggering ECRA compliance. An SES is an environmental evaluation of the facility, which includes a site history since 1940, a list of all permits issued since 1940, a scaled map identifying the locations of hazardous waste, a detailed description of current operations, descriptions of the types and locations of hazardous waste storage facilities, an inventory of hazardous substances at the site, a detailed sampling plan (consisting of a description of geographic and hydrogeological characteristics of the site and an evaluation of environmental information), and a decontamination plan if the facility is to be closed.

If the GIS and SES submissions are complete to the satisfaction of the DEP, then within 45 days, the DEP either issues a negative declaration or requires the preparation and implementation of a cleanup plan. A negative declaration is a written statement by the DEP that there has been no discharge of hazardous waste at the site or that, if there has been, all hazardous waste has been cleaned up in accordance with DEP standards. A negative declaration is effective for a maximum of 60 days and less if the information submitted changes. To avoid having to ask the DEP more than once for a negative declaration, it is important that the timing of the request coincide with the proposed transfer or shutdown.

The penalties for noncompliance with ECRA can be severe. Failure to comply with ECRA is grounds for voiding any sale transaction and imposes strict liability on the owner, without regard to fault, for all cleanup costs. In addition, officers may be personally liable if they knowingly direct or authorize a violation of ECRA. Thus, if management is contemplating the shutdown of an industrial establishment in New Jersey or a bankruptcy filing that would involve industrial establishments in New Jersey, every effort should be made to comply with ECRA.

Like New Jersey, many other states, particularly those with a strong industrial base, have enacted their own environmental legislation. New York and California, for example, have both passed environmental legislation that requires those involved in the shutdown or transfer of certain types of businesses to take certain actions to ensure that environmental damage is abated.

AN OVERVIEW OF THE FEDERAL PLANT CLOSING ACT

On February 4, 1989, the Federal Plant Closing Act, officially known as the Worker Adjustment and Retraining Notification Act of 1988 (WARN), became effective. At the time of its enactment, President Ronald Reagan, who had vetoed the legislation, called WARN "a ticking time bomb in the back seat of any medium size or larger company."[30] Many special interest groups, such as the National Association of Manufacturers, lobbied strongly against WARN, because of the substantial costs of complying with the legislation. Opponents of the legislation argued that the additional costs imposed by WARN would contribute to the financial problems of troubled businesses and would cause employers in some industries to hire more part-time workers. Because WARN has been in effect for such a brief time, the legal and financial impact of the legislation has not been fully assessed, and it is difficult to demonstrate whether the long-term objectives have been accomplished.

In essence, WARN requires that employers who fall within its parameters must provide 60-day prior notice to employees, unions, state dislocated worker agencies, and local governments of a "plant closing" or "mass layoff."

To assist employers in interpreting WARN, the Department of Labor issued regulations concerning the implementation of many aspects of WARN (the DOL Rules).

The legislation and regulations provide that covered employers consist of all business enterprises employing 100 or more full-time employees, or which employ 100 or more part-time employees, who in the aggregate work at least 4,000 hours a week, exclusive of overtime hours. Nonprofit organizations are included in the definition of employer; but federal, state, and local public service companies are not. If an employer has temporarily laid off employees but those employees are expected to be recalled, the laid off employees are included in the counting of employees.

Triggering Events

Both a plant closing and a mass layoff trigger WARN. As defined in the legislation, a *plant closing* includes (1) the permanent or temporary[31] shutdown of a single site of employment or (2) a permanent or temporary shutdown of one or more facilities or operating units within a single site of employment, if the shutdown results in an employment loss of 50 or more full-time employees during any 30-day period.

A *mass layoff*[32] is defined as a reduction in the work force that results in an employment loss at any single site of at least 33 percent of all full-time employees, with a minimum number of 50 full-time employees. The 33 percent minimum requirement does not apply if 500 or more full-time employees will be affected by the layoff.

Notice Requirements

Notices under WARN must be given to the chief elected officer of the "affected employees" union, or, if the employees are not represented, to the individual "affected employee." The definition of affected employee is very broad, so employers may be required to give notice to some employees who might not ultimately be terminated. The DOL Rules provide generally that an *affected employee* is one who may reasonably be expected to suffer an employment loss as a result of a plant closing or mass layoff. Because it is often difficult for an employer to identify 60 days before an anticipated layoff those employees who are likely to lose their jobs, employers should be overinclusive in sending notices to affected employees.

There are certain exceptions to the notice requirements. For example, notice is not required if a temporary facility is closed, or if the layoffs are the result of the completion of a particular project and the employees were hired with the understanding that their employment was limited to the duration of the facility or project. Employers who hire employees at a temporary facility or on a project basis should enter into written employment contracts with such employees, which contain language making it clear that their employment is temporary.

Contents of the Notice

If an employer intends to notify employees of a plant closing or mass layoff, the notice must contain: (1) the name and address of the plant where the closing or mass layoff will or may occur; (2) the nature of the planned action, closing, or layoff; (3) the anticipated date of the first separation, first layoff or termination of employees, and the anticipated schedule for making subsequent layoffs or terminations; (4) the job titles of positions to be terminated and the names of the workers currently holding those jobs; (5) a statement about the applicable bumping rights, if any; and (6) the name, address, and telephone number of a company official to contact for additional information. The notice should also contain the name, address, and telephone number of federal, state, and local dislocated worker assistance agencies.

Implementation of WARN

Suppose management of a company believes that, within 60 days, a bankruptcy petition will be filed that will result in the reorganization of the company but that will also result in a mass layoff. Under the provisions of WARN, the company should give notice to its employees of the mass layoff. However, complying with WARN might jeopardize the likelihood of reorganizing the company. Under these circumstances, management should consider several options.

First, management should determine the economic impact of providing the WARN notice and should calculate the maximum monetary liability that would be incurred under WARN. Under WARN, courts cannot enjoin a plant closing or mass layoff, and, thus, the maximum exposure for failure to comply with WARN is readily ascertainable.

Second, either before or after sending the WARN notice, management may wish to negotiate incentive compensation arrangements with key employees. These arrangements should contain language whereby the employee expressly waives his or her rights to damages under WARN. There is nothing in WARN that prohibits a waiver of its provisions.

Third, management should consider having affected employees resign voluntarily by offering generous severance pay and early retirement packages. These two options may be less costly to the employer than providing the notice required by WARN.

Shortening of Notice Period

In addition, management should consider whether the circumstances of the layoff or shutdown allow the 60-day notice period to be shortened. There are three circumstances under which the 60-day notice requirements may be shortened.

First, under the so-called failing business exception, the WARN notice period may be shortened if an employer is actively seeking new capital or business that would enable the employer to avoid or postpone a planned shutdown or layoff, and the employer reasonably believes that "giving the notice required would have precluded the employer from obtaining the needed capital or business."[33] The DOL Rules provide that the employer "must have been seeking financing or refinancing through the arrangement of loans, the issuance of stocks, bonds, or other methods of internally generated financing; or the employer must have been seeking additional money, credit, or business through any commercially reasonable method." Employers intending to rely on this exception should keep careful and detailed records of their negotiations for new business or capital. The burden is on the employer to show that it falls within this exception. The DOL Rules have further limited this exception by stating that the resources of the entire company should be examined when applying the failing business exception. Therefore, it is not enough to demonstrate that one facility or operating unit was failing if capital was available from elsewhere in the company.

Second, 60 days' notice is not required "if the closing or mass layoff is caused by business circumstances that were not reasonably foreseeable as of the time that notice would have been required."[34]

Third, the notice period may be shortened if the plant closing or mass layoff is due to any form of natural disaster. With respect to all three exceptions, WARN provides that the employer must give as much notice as is practicable, along with a "brief statement of the basis for reducing the notification period."[35]

Penalties Under WARN

WARN provides that any employee who loses his or her job as the result of a plant closing or mass layoff and does not receive timely notice of the closing or layoff from the employer is entitled to collect from the employer back pay for each day of violation at the higher of the employee's average rate of pay during the last three years of his or her employment or the final rate of pay received by such employee. In addition, the employer is liable for any benefits to which the employee would have been entitled if the employee had retained his or her employment during the WARN notice period, including the cost of medical expenses actually incurred during the employment loss that would have been covered had the employment loss not occurred. An employer's liability is reduced by (1) any wages paid by the employer to the employee for the period of the violation, (2) any voluntary and unconditional payment by the employer to the employee, and (3) any payment by the employer to a third party on behalf of the employee for the period of the violation. For example, if an employee (1) earns $100 a day (assuming that such amount is higher than the average regular rate received by such employee during the last three years of his or her employment), (2) receives 30 days' notice of a plant closing and continues to be employed and receive wages during the 30 days prior to the plant closing, and (3) receives a $500 severance payment from the company to which he or she is not otherwise entitled, then such employee would be entitled to $2,500 in damages from the employer. The only further limitation on the amount an aggrieved employee can receive under WARN is that an employee can receive compensation for no more than one half of the days the employee was employed by the employer. For example, an employee who only has been employed for 70 days prior to a plant closing or mass layoff would be entitled to collect a maximum of 35 days' back pay.

Employers can be subject to a civil penalty of up to $500 a day for failure to notify the local governmental unit of a plant closing or mass layoff. This penalty can be avoided if the employer pays the damages due to terminated "affected employees" within three weeks of the shutdown or layoff. Punitive damages are not available under WARN.[36]

The filing of a bankruptcy case does not exempt the debtor-in-possession or trustee from complying with WARN. If the bankruptcy case is initiated for the sole purpose of liquidating all of the assets of the estate, certain comments to the DOL Rules indicate that the liquidating trustee may be exempt from complying with WARN.

State and Municipal Plant Closing Laws

A number of states and municipalities have adopted their own plant closing laws that are not preempted by WARN. Therefore, employers should be aware that, in addition to complying with the WARN notice requirements, they may also be required to comply with more stringent state and municipal notice requirements. As of April 1, 1990, a number of states have adopted their own plant closing laws, including Connecticut, Hawaii, Maine, Maryland, Massachusetts, Michigan, Tennessee, and Wisconsin.

CONCLUSION

The nonbankruptcy code issues involving troubled businesses and restructuring efforts are complex and the applicable statutes and regulations are intricate. In this chapter, we have given an overview of some of the pitfalls of which persons involved in turnarounds and workouts should be aware, but there are many others. The risks of inadvertent noncompliance with the applicable statutes and regulations can be serious and costly for the company and its managers. We recommend that persons responsible for the smooth operation of the restructuring effort consider the following:

1. Obtain complete and accurate data on existing and potential pension, environmental, and plant closing matters immediately.
2. If such data are incomplete or if current compliance in these areas is in doubt, then a management team member should be designated to make immediate compliance a top priority.
3. The management team member responsible for compliance should participate in decisions involving layoffs, plant closings, mergers, asset sales, and labor contract negotiations.
4. In considering the desirability of a workout versus a bankruptcy, determine the impact of pension, environmental, and WARN notice matters on the likelihood of a successful reorganization.

ENDNOTES

1. I.R.C. § 4971(b) (1988).
2. Employee Retirement Income Security Act, 29 U.S.C.A. § 1302(f) (West 1985 & Supp. 1989). The Employee Retirement Income Security Act, 29 U.S.C.A. §§ 1001-1461 (West 1985 & Supp. 1989), shall be cited hereafter as ERISA.
3. ERISA § 302(c)(11).
4. I.R.C. § 414(m)(2) (1988).
5. The factors to be considered in making a determination of substantial business hardship are set forth in ERISA § 303(b) and I.R.C. § 412(d) (2).
6. ERISA § 302(a).
7. ERISA § 4042(a).

8. PBGC Op. letters 81-41 (December 16, 1981) and 82-13 (April 12, 1982).
9. ERISA § 4068(a).
10. ERISA §§ 4201, 4211.
11. See ERISA §§ 4211(b), 4211(c)(2)-(5).
12. *In re Patrick Cudahy, Inc.*, 88 Bankr. 895 (Bankr. E.D. Wis. 1988) (stopgap legislation applied retroactively to case filed between lapse of legislation on October 15, 1987, and effective date of new law on June 16, 1988).
13. 11 U.S.C. § 1114(a) (1988).
14. ERISA § 4047.
15. *Pension Benefit Guaranty Corp. v. LTV Corp. (In re Chateaugay Corp.)*, 875 F.2d. 1008, 1017 (2nd Cir. 1989).
16. *Columbia Packing Company v. Pension Benefit Guaranty Corp. (In re Columbia Packing Company)*, 81 Bankr. 205 (D. Mass. 1988).
17. See *Trustees of Amalgamated Ins. Fund v. McFarlin's Inc.*, 789 F.2d 98 (2nd Cir. 1986); *Pension Benefit Guaranty Corp. v. LTV Corp. (In re Chateaugay Corp.)*, 87 Bankr. 779 (S.D.N.Y. 1988).
18. *New York v. Shore Realty Corp.*, 759 F.2d 1032 (2nd Cir. 1985).
19. See *United States v. Northeastern Pharmaceutical & Chem. Co.*, 810 F.2d 726 (8th Cir. 1986).
20. *Oner II, Inc. v. EPA*, 597 F.2d 184 (9th Cir. 1979).
21. *Guidice v. BFG Electroplating and Manufacturing Co.*, No. 86-2093, 1989 WL 197105 (W.D. Pa. Sept. 1, 1989).
22. *United States v. Fleet Factors Corp.*, 724 F.Supp. 955 (S.D. 1985).
23. *In re T.P. Long Chem., Inc.*, 45 Bankr. 278 (Bankr. N.D. Ohio 1985).
24. 42 U.S.C.A. § 7412 (West 1983 & Supp. 1989).
25. 33 U.S.C.A. §§ 1317(A), 1321(b) (2) (A) (West 1986 & Supp. 1989).
26. 42 U.S.C.A. § 6921 (West 1982 & Supp. 1989).
27. 15 U.S.C.A. § 2606 (West 1982 & Supp. 1989).
28. 42 U.S.C.A. § 9602(a) (West 1983 & Supp. 1989).
29. N.J. Stat. Ann § 13:1K-6 to 13:19-17 (West Supp. 1989).
30. *New York Times,* March 19, 1989, ¶ 3, at p. 1, col. 2.
31. The length of time for a "temporary" shutdown is not specified.
32. The definition of a mass layoff is set forth at 20 C.F.R. § 639.3 (1989).
33. 29 U.S.C.A. § 2102(b)(1) (West Supp. 1989).
34. 29 U.S.C.A. § 2102(b)(2)(A) (West Supp. 1989).
35. 29 U.S.C.A. § 2102(b)(3) (West Supp. 1989).
36. *Finnan v. L.F. Rothschild & Co.*, 726 F.2d 460 (S.D.N.Y. 1989).

CHAPTER 10

STABILIZING THE WORK FORCE; CONTROLLING THE INFORMATION FLOW

Michael S. Sitrick
Sitrick and Company, Inc.

THE NEED FOR EFFECTIVE COMMUNICATION IN CRISIS SITUATIONS

"Why would a company operating under Chapter 11 need public relations counsel?" you might ask. This is a logical question, since most people's perception of public relations is that the profession is promotionally oriented and most firms' areas of expertise are concentrated in that area.

Indeed, very few executives and even fewer public relations firms either understand or are experienced in the area of bankruptcy communications, as this area of the practice has come to be known. Many claim to have crisis communications expertise, but have limited hands-on experience; and often the experience they do have is sandwiched between promoting the biggest hot fudge sundae in the world and touting the latest new fall fashion. The fact is that, as a senior corporate executive, I had a difficult time finding a firm that I had confidence could provide support or counsel in major crises situations. Not that there weren't any. They were just few and far between.

The purpose of public relations in a Chapter 11 is to ensure that perceptions are the same as fact. Two of the most important tasks in a troubled company situation are stabilizing the work force and controlling the information flow.

Facts can be presented and reported in a variety of different ways. How an individual situation is presented can significantly influence the way it is reported. This isn't to say that you should stray from the facts or in any way mislead. However, there are a number of ways to look at and present each individual situation. Each fact should be examined and every angle explored.

It's very seldom a company that must seek the protection of the bankruptcy court finds itself suddenly in need of chapter protection. More often than not, weeks and months of red ink precede the filing and days, weeks, and months of bank and creditor negotiations.

Vendors begin requesting cash on delivery. Customers start questioning whether they can depend on you for that fall order. Employees put off buying a new house. Calls from the media begin, asking whether the company is considering filing bankruptcy.

Rumors begin growing in frequency and size faster than Jack's proverbial beanstalk. No matter how preposterous, they seem to be given credence by at least some of the company's constituencies.

Unfortunately, rumors of a company's demise, if left unattended, can help ensure that the prediction comes true. In a troubled company, and particularly in a Chapter 11 situation, it is not uncommon to find employees leaving in great numbers in the belief that liquidation and unemployment are imminent. People begin worrying about whether they will have a job, rather than about how to best do their job. Productivity, generally, is severely reduced; morale often sinks to an all-time low.

Most companies' reaction to a severely troubled situation is to keep their heads low . . . to minimize communications. "We really don't have anything we can tell people," is a common response. And so they say nothing.

But the grapevine doesn't remain silent. Rumors move from vendor to customer, from banker to investor; employees begin wondering how long they'll have a job. Soon the media begins smelling blood, and stories about your company's shaky condition begin appearing with increasing frequency.

At first, the stories only appear in a local trade publication; then a major market daily begins writing about you. The next thing you know stories of your troubles or your imminent demise begin appearing on the television news, in *Business Week,* and in *The Wall Street Journal.*

Customers begin canceling orders. Vendors take your cash, but don't ship you goods, instead applying the funds to monies previously owed.

Now the banks won't extend your terms for fear the additional funds will just be used to pay off trade debt. Before you know it, you have no choice but to file.

The lawyers head down to the court, file the papers, and issue a standard boilerplate release. That evening, local radio and television stations in each of your markets tell the world that your company has declared bankruptcy.

The next morning, half your stores don't open because your people don't understand what a Chapter 11 means. Your customers immediately begin making alternate arrangements for goods. Your business is paralyzed and in a state of panic.

Sound farfetched? It isn't. Just compare the day-after results of the Wickes Chapter 11 filing with that of Braniff and you can easily see the difference that good communications can make.

THE BRANIFF WAY VERSUS THE WICKES WAY

The day after Braniff filed, there was pandemonium. Employees didn't know if they should show up for work, so many didn't. Planes weren't flying. Reservations desks were not attended; phones weren't properly manned. It took days to get things back to normal, but they never really were the same.

At Wickes, which filed on a Saturday, all 3,200 retail outlets and 100 manufacturing locations were open that following Monday. All desks and phones in all offices and stores were manned. In a little over two and one-half years, the company emerged from Chapter 11 in what the bankruptcy judge called in open court "a miracle."

Coincidence? I think not. Throughout the reorganization process, communications was a top priority. The results speak for themselves.

At Wickes, the communications plan was designed to minimize the impact of the filing on the day-to-day operations of the business.

An explanation of what a "chapter" means and what it doesn't mean was given. Also, information was disseminated as to why the filing was necessary and what the company's various constituencies could expect.

The Friday night before the company filed, Wickes top managers were flown to the corporation's headquarters city for a meeting with the company's new chairman and chief executive officer. Information packets were handed to each attendee. The packet contained an agenda for the meeting; a list of whom each attendee was to call immediately after the meeting, along with that person's telephone number; a suggested script for that phone conversation; a suggested schedule for employee meetings, including where and when each meeting should be held; a copy of the news release to be issued the following morning; a memorandum from the chairman instructing that all media calls be referred to a central point; a copy of a letter from the chairman to each employee; a copy of the mailgram sent to each store and company location; a list of whom to call for answers to various questions and inquiries; and likely questions from employees, vendors, and customers, along with the appropriate answers.

Key members of management and bankruptcy counsel were on hand to answer questions. Immediately following the meeting, the managers were dispatched to their rooms to call their *top* people to let them know what was going on.

Midafternoon, mailgrams were sent to all Wickes locations. Included was an explanation of what was happening and why; the fact that filing Chapter 11 did not mean that they were going to lose their jobs; that it did not mean there was no chance for advancement. Employees were told what to do if a bank, for some reason, should refuse to cash their checks or should return their checks, and what to do if a vendor tried to reclaim goods.

Reporters were called Friday afternoon to determine where they would be over the weekend, in case they were needed. Media briefings were prepared, complete with likely questions and appropriate answers.

Saturday morning, after the documents were filed, releases were messengered to key publications and one-on-one interviews were scheduled with reporters.

Simultaneously, teams of corporate and division management were dispatched to the field, along with bankruptcy counsel, to repeat the Friday evening meetings first thing Monday at critical locations across the country.

At 6 A.M. Monday, two letters and a copy of the press release were on every employees' desk: one letter was from the chairman explaining what had happened and why, what the filing meant, and what it didn't mean; the other letter was from their local manager telling them at what time a meeting would be held to tell them, in person, what was contained in the chairman's letter and to answer any questions they might have.

By Tuesday morning, employee morale was at the highest point it had been in months. A new spirit was pumping through the company. A belief ran throughout the organization that it could win.

The monthly newsmagazine was replaced with a weekly newsletter, reporting both the good and the bad news. Employees began sporting buttons reading "This Team Wins."

Weekly letters were sent to vendors, advising them of the company's increasing cash position. Procedures were established to ensure that shareholder and bondholder calls were answered; and regular communiques, though austere, were sent to each holder of the company's securities.

News coverage shifted dramatically. From ailing, troubled, struggling Wickes, stories began reporting management's efforts to resuscitate the company, reduce expenses, increase its cash position, and repair its businesses. Vendors began shipping on credit. You could feel and see the tide begin to turn.

Clearly, there was more going on than just public relations to bring about these results. But keeping the company's publics informed, controlling the information flow, stemming the rumors, and keeping employees motivated were among the most critical elements of reorganization effort.

In the first several months, barely a day went by when the company didn't have to squelch the rumor of a lumber store closing in Monroe, Louisiana, or a furniture store going out of business in Chicago. Often, by the time the company would get wind of this rumor, the employee population of that store would be in absolute panic. More often than not, the rumor was false.

One of the ways that the communications group made sure that it was up to date on everything that was transpiring was to give reporters and store managers staff members' home phone numbers.

"I would rather be awakened in the middle of a night," I told a reporter one time, "and have a chance to correct a misperception, than to wake up in the morning only to find that an incorrect story had been printed, leaving us to try and undo the damage that had been done."

This resulted in a lot of calls at 5 A.M., being that Wickes was headquartered in California; but the company contained the problem and, ultimately, most reporters would call before they would write.

DEVELOPING A CRISIS COMMUNICATIONS PROGRAM

In fact, in almost every case in which I have been involved, management has been able to significantly aid the recovery process, to stem employee exodus, and to achieve requisite stability through the development of a crisis communications program to enhance the flow of information throughout the organization. While each situation is different and no two plans are alike, nearly all communications plans feature a series of timely actions and materials, which keep the employees and the rest of the corporation's publics informed and help increase management credibility.

We often recommend, for example, the following key actions:

1. *Create a crisis team to address communications issues.* In anticipation of the filing, assemble a task force of professionals to prepare a complete package of materials. Include letters to employees, answers to crucial employee questions, press releases, explanations of the Chapter 11 process and reorganization, and letters to customers, bankers, creditors, and vendors. The preparation and contents of this package are kept strictly confidential until the exact hour of disclosure.

2. *Make the lawyers part of the communications team.* This may sound strange, coming from a public relations professional, but a good bankruptcy lawyer can be one of the most valuable members of the public relations team. Beyond his or her contributions in the development and refinement of information, the bankruptcy attorney's insights into the politics and strategy of the case are critical to the development and implementation of a communications program. It is imperative that you not do anything which, while it may benefit the public relations effort, will hurt you in court or in the negotiations of your plan. The two objectives should not be mutually exclusive. Quite the contrary, an effective public relations effort should aid the company in both its plan negotiations and reorganization.

3. *Restrict who can speak to the media.* While this may appear to the uninformed as "muzzling," its primary purpose is to ensure accuracy and consistency in the dissemination of information. The last thing a company needs in a troubled situation, where rumors often outnumber products produced per hour, is for someone who is not fully informed on an issue to be quoted in the media on behalf of the company. Facts change rapidly in crisis environments. It is important that the person who is speaking on behalf of the company be the one who is the most likely to be consistently and accurately informed.

4. *Refer all media calls to a central point. Make sure that the person handling the calls is well informed about the company, its people, and its products.* This accomplishes several objectives: it ensures that media calls will be answered promptly and responsively; it will help to ensure that calls are being referred to and answered by the right people within the company; and it makes handling media calls someone's responsibility.

5. *Make sure there are procedures and provisions to handle shareholder, bondholder, vendor, customer, and all other pertinent calls.* During the first weeks of the Wickes Chapter 11, the communications department alone received more than 1,000 calls a week.

6. *Decide what you want the story to be.* This sounds routine, but it is very rarely done. Every time you issue a major press release, you should decide how you want the story to play. What is the message you want to transmit? What is the story you want to tell?

7. *Prepare for questions.* What are the likely questions that you will be asked by the media as a result of your announcement? Don't get caught unprepared. Write down both the likely questions and answers. Have them reviewed by other members of your management team and by your lawyers.

8. *Schedule management and employee meetings around the official court filing.* Just prior to announcement of the filing, crisis team members should summon senior officers and managers for a meeting to (1) explain what is going to happen and why and (2) hand out assignments. A special package of management materials should be assembled to provide a point-by-point discussion for meetings to be held with staffs and for actions that need to be taken in the first critical days of the Chapter 11 period. Emotional issues —how to deal with employee concerns—is a vital part of the presentation.

9. *Follow up every oral presentation with written materials.* To assure that the message is heard accurately, it is essential that key points made in live presentations be duplicated in written form. Distribute a letter to every employee, under the chief executive officer's signature, that reinforces the information employees receive from their managers.

10. *Maintain an open door policy/Increase senior management's visibility to employees.* Virtually every employee survey that has ever been taken indicates that employees want to maximize contact with senior officers. This fact is especially true during a crisis. It is imperative that employees feel that management is accessible. In the weeks following the Chapter 11 filing, senior executives must make it a point of being accessible to employees. Facilities should be visited with regularity, especially stores and other key locations, and letters must be regularly circulated to keep your people informed.

11. *Replace fear with information.* Even though employees will receive communications packages on the first day after the filing, it is important to recognize that most people will be able to absorb only a small amount of information. To reinforce the original messages and assuage fears of wholesale layoffs or major changes in operations, it is helpful to produce and distribute a newsletter or some other type of publication within the first two weeks after the filing occurs. In my experience, this companywide publication often becomes the vehicle by which every employee can obtain updates on the reorganization or can ask questions that will be answered in print.

12. *Disseminate both the good and the bad news.* If you are going to be effective, you must have credibility with your people. They must feel like part of the team. Disseminate the good and the bad news and provide explanations and rationales for both.

13. *Control the rumor mill.* In the absence of information, the rumor mill runs rampant. Keep speculation to a minimum by providing hot lines and feedback programs that allow employees to seek answers on an ongoing basis.

14. *Emphasize the positive aspects of continued employment without diminishing the severity of the situation.* In the midst of a crisis, there is a tendency to concentrate on the negatives and to forget the positives. Employees need to be reminded that their benefits continue, their work continues—that it is essentially "business as usual." In some situations, reorganization has actually improved the opportunities for advancement, not reduced them. Providing reassurance to employees about the positive aspects, while affirming the seriousness of the reorganization process, helps employees to achieve a balanced perspective.

15. *Strategize for continued motivation and maintenance of employee base.* If the above actions have been undertaken, stabilization and virtual "business as usual" can occur within a few months of filing Chapter 11. Once this critical phase has peaked, it is important to continue the momentum created by the urgency of the filing and to plan for new programs to build motivation and productivity. These programs may take many forms, from breakfast meetings with management and sales competitions to feedback and recognition programs.

16. *Provide a vehicle for employee suggestions.* Whether it's a suggestion box in the stores or an employee hotline at headquarters, provide some way for employees to share their ideas. Some of the most important ideas in business have come from the people in the field. They deal with the problems every day. Employees, more often than not, know the truth about what's going on and have a good perspective on what went wrong.

17. *Acknowledge the successes where and as they occur.* With the pressure of reorganization, it becomes all the more important that the hard work of employees be recognized throughout the organization. Employees should be kept informed of high sales, new contracts, and other signs of "recovery." Recognize exceptional performance with meaningful rewards.

18. *If at all possible, avoid holding press conferences. Instead, hold one-on-one interviews with key reporters, even by phone, if necessary. Designate spokesmen for secondary publications or reporters.* As a rule, reporters don't like press conferences. Those who do their homework don't like to share the results of their work.

Thus, they'll often call back with the really relevant questions after the fact. A bigger risk is that one reporter will ask a zinger or particularly tough or embarrassing questions . . . or you will make a statement you wish you hadn't and, instead of just appearing in one publication, it will appear in many.

19. *Consider a weekly cash statement for your vendors via a letter from your chief financial officer.* You might want to release it occasionally to the media.

People often ask what, in my view, is the most important element in turning around a business. It generally only takes me a second to answer. "It's the people," I tell them. Quoting my friend, turnaround expert Sandy Sigoloff, I say, "Building trust, obtaining commitment, and motivating people to have the will to win."

Public perception plays a very important part in the reorganization process. The way you handle your communications can make the difference between whether you win or you lose.

HOW TO HIRE PUBLIC RELATIONS COUNSEL

On July 25, 1988, while senior vice president of communications at Wickes, I wrote an article for a public relations trade newspaper, which it headlined, "The good, the bad and the ugly."

In this article, I wrote:

> Over the last few years, as head of communications for what was at one time the second largest company to successfully reorganize under Chapter 11, I have met with a number of senior level PR people, either to fill a senior level job at Wickes or to listen to an agency pitch. When asked how they would handle a specific project, the judgement exhibited by the vast majority of them gave me the shivers when I thought of them giving counsel to major corporate leaders.

Later in that article, I told what I look for in a PR professional:

> First and foremost I look for judgement. In this business, you can't take back mistakes. A misquote given to a newspaper—or worse, a wire service—is out there for the world to see.
>
> I look for people who have the sense to ask when they don't know, who aren't afraid to tell a reporter on deadline they will get back to

him, because they don't have the answer, who won't wing it under pressure. Most of all, who think before they speak about the different ways that a comment can be taken.

I look for integrity. All you have in this business is your reputation. My reputation and the reputation of my company is directly affected by the integrity of the people representing us.

The people I work with have to have news sense. They must understand what makes a good story. They must be able to sift through all the details and pull out the pearl. Similarly, they must be able to gauge, when questioned by a reporter, what he or she is looking for and even why.

They must also be able to write. Mine is a hands-on staff. All of us practice nearly every facet of our craft. While my job has expanded beyond PR, I still write news releases, place stories, handle media inquiries, and even—on occasion—stuff envelopes.

Finally, I look for people who like what they are doing. I have found that those who like what they do are almost always the best at what they do.

While I was not specifically talking about agency selection in this article, the same principles apply. The staff working on your account should exhibit all of those qualities. But in a Chapter 11 they must have more. Remember, early on in my article I said you can't take it back. The first few weeks of a Chapter 11 are clearly the most important in setting perceptions. While damage can be undone, it is somewhat difficult to do so.

Thus, the following questions should be asked when first considering an outside firm:

Should we hire an outside firm?

1. Do we have someone on staff who is experienced in Chapter 11 public relations and communications?
2. Do we have the public relations and communications expertise necessary to strategically develop the communications message?
3. If our staff is experienced in this area, do we have enough people to handle the initial workload requirements.

Questions to ask an outside firm

1. What other Chapter 11 situations have you been involved in?

2. Can you give us the name of two bankruptcy attorneys you have worked with in prior cases that we or our attorneys can call?

3. What type of actions do you generally take in a situation like the one we are in?

4. Who would be directly involved on a day-to-day basis with our management?
   a. in the beginning;
   b. once the case is underway.

5. Do you have any experience dealing with the financial media, the investment community, shareholders or bondholders?

6. Can we talk with the CEO or some other member of senior management with whom you have worked in a similar situation before?

7. Can you tell us a little bit about your firm?
   a. How long have you been in business?
   b. What other type of work do you do?

I ended my July 1988 article as follows: "The job sounds relatively easy and straightforward. That's part of the problem. PR is a profession that sounds like anyone can do it. A lot of people do, but not very many do it well."

Communications in a Chapter 11 is not something with which you can gamble. Choose your communications counsel as you would any other critical member of your professional team. Your company's survival could depend upon it.

CHAPTER 11

HOW TO TURN AROUND A CORPORATION PLAGUED WITH MASS TOXIC TORTS

J. Gregg Miller, Esq.
Francis J. Lawall, Esq.
Pepper, Hamilton & Scheetz

INTRODUCTION

Commencing in the early 1980s, an innovative approach to the use of bankruptcy law began to emerge for companies facing financial disaster resulting from mass toxic tort liabilities. In 1982, Johns-Manville Corporation, UNR Industries, Inc., and Amatex Corporation each filed Chapter 11 bankruptcy petitions as it became apparent that their products liability insurance coverage would not be sufficient to pay for all present and future tort claims. Each of these companies had been involved in the production of asbestos products, which resulted in thousands of products liability lawsuits being brought against them. In 1985, A. H. Robins Company filed a Chapter 11 petition as a result of its production of the Dalkon Shield. The alternative for each of these companies was the exposure of operating assets to execution by judgment creditors. Since that time, all of these former debtors have successfully emerged from Chapter 11 and, in the process, have implemented plans of reorganization that generate the greatest possible return to creditors while preserving the underlying business free of mass toxic tort liabilities.

In the past, many companies faced with overwhelming liabilities that were related to mass toxic tort have routinely liquidated. This result occurred in large part because the company was unable to effectively deal with all of the problems related to a particular defective product in a single forum. Often, these liabilities included not only claims presently pending against the company but also those claims certain to arise at a future date, which were nevertheless related to a product long ago discontinued by the bankrupt company. In circumstances such as this, particularly when the operating company remains fiscally healthy but for the toxic tort liabilities, innovative techniques for reorganization will most benefit the debtor and its creditors alike. This type of reorganization avoids the unnecessary and inefficient liquidation of a healthy company, the value of which to creditors is maximized as a going concern.

To reorganize, substantial advanced planning, experienced counsel, and a strong working knowledge of the issues and parties involved is necessary. The following is a highlight of the numerous challenges likely to be encountered while reorganizing a company faced with mass toxic tort liabilities and some proposed solutions to the problems that may arise.

PARTIES

Unlike most insolvency situations, a company facing substantial exposure from toxic tort liability will often have the ability to plan the bankruptcy filing well in advance of the event itself. An important element in the planning process is the creation of a multidisciplined team of professionals who are familiar with bankruptcy issues in addition to other areas of the law. On behalf of the debtor, the following professionals are likely to be necessary.

Bankruptcy Counsel

As in any bankruptcy case, counsel must be thoroughly familiar with Chapter 11. Bankruptcy counsel must also have a working knowledge of tax, trust, and related areas of the law that frequently arise in this type of reorganization.

Corporate Counsel

To assist the debtor with day-to-day advice concerning legal issues not related to the Chapter 11, the company may find it necessary to retain general counsel to handle routine legal issues and to assist bankruptcy counsel when a nonwaiveable conflict is encountered. Normally, the debtor's prebankruptcy general counsel is the appropriate person for this position. It is important that such counsel be thoroughly familiar with the mass toxic tort litigation and the parties involved.

Tax Counsel

In addition to normal tax issues that arise in a Chapter 11, the intricacies of I.R.C. Section 468B, as discussed later, render the use of qualified tax counsel essential during the course of the proceeding. Section 468B permits a mass toxic tort debtor to receive a current tax deduction for payments made pursuant to a plan into a qualified "settlement fund" or trust for tort claimants, regardless of the future time period it takes for the fund or trust to make payments to the underlying tort claimants.

Actuary

A key element in the reorganization will be a report and eventual testimony from an actuary concerning the present and future mass toxic tort liabilities that the debtor can anticipate. This evidence will often establish that the company's expected liabilities dwarf the value of its assets. This information will be essential to negotiations concerning the eventual dividend and distribution to the company's creditors, also in a possible cramdown, as discussed below.

Investment Banker

The investment banker will be necessary to conduct the going-concern and liquidation analyses of the company, which will be used by creditors to determine whether sufficient funding for a plan of reorganization has been offered. The investment banker should also prepare a business plan to establish the viability of the proposed plan of reorganization. The investment banker may also play a key role in obtaining the postconfirmation financing likely to be necessary as part of the reorganization.

Committees of Tort Claimants and Trade Claimants

Common to all Chapter 11 bankruptcy cases will be the unsecured creditors' committee and its counsel. The unsecured creditors' committee will normally consist of the company's seven largest unsecured creditors. Unique, however, will be a committee composed of the mass toxic tort claimants. Typically, as in asbestos-related cases, mass toxic tort claimants are represented by their litigation counsel in the bankruptcy case. It is not unusual for a single attorney to represent thousands of individual claimants.

Guardian or Legal Representative for Future, Unknown Tort Claimants

Also unique to this type of bankruptcy case will be the appointment of a guardian *ad litem* for future claimants. The guardian *ad litem* is responsible for negotiating a plan of reorganization on behalf of those persons who have not yet manifested a disease but nevertheless can ultimately anticipate a claim arising against the debtor's assets. For this reason, these persons are often referred to as *future claimants*.

Without the appointment of a guardian *ad litem,* a potential risk exists that the assets of the debtor will be exhausted long before future claimants are able to recover for their injuries. The guardian *ad litem* also serves an important role by satisfying constitutional due process concerns that arise as a result of the determination of the rights of unknown persons not otherwise represented in the bankruptcy. Because the guardian *ad litem* represents a class of persons whose status will remain undecided throughout the course of the case (see Future Claims, below), he or she is often in a good position to act as an intermediary among the debtor and the various creditor groups during negotiations involving the plan of reorganization.

PLANNING FOR BANKRUPTCY

Prior to bankruptcy, one of the most important tasks that the company must accomplish is the identification of the remaining available insurance coverage to satisfy the present and anticipated future claims. Part of the analysis should include a determination about what defenses or restrictions particular insurance companies may interpose in an effort to avoid payment. Often, an insurer may refuse payments under a particular policy provision, despite the company's belief that substantial coverage remains. The insurance policies should also be analyzed to determine whether they include a "duty to defend" the company in litigation. The obligation of the insurance company to pay all litigation costs over and above the policy limits represents a substantial asset of the estate.

An important player in determining the rate of exhaustion of available insurance coverage is litigation defense counsel. Litigation counsel should be able to provide insight into how long the remaining insurance coverage will be sufficient to satisfy existing liabilities.

It is important to note that the bankruptcy petition should, if possible, be filed well in advance of the exhaustion of remaining insurance coverage. The primary reason for doing so is that the remaining insurance coverage will be a primary asset in funding the trust, which will later be substituted as the vehicle for resolving the mass tort claims. Typically, after the bankruptcy petition has been filed, the debtor will seek to liquidate the remaining insurance policies together with a premium representing the value of the insurer's responsibility for defending the company in litigation. The insurer's incentive for "buying out" the insurance policy is to eliminate all further responsibility for the cost of defending or paying liability claims, or both, against the debtor. In conjunction with a buyout of the policy, the insurer will expect an injunction to be issued by the bankruptcy court prohibiting mass tort claimants from seeking payment from the insurer.

Insurers will typically resist liquidation of their policies after bankruptcy. One reason for this position is the beneficial effect of Section 362 of the Code, which stays all prebankruptcy litigation, including that related to the mass tort liabilities, thereby substantially eliminating the costs the insurer was otherwise paying under the policy. Therefore, because of the defenses that are likely to be interposed, the debtor should commence negotiations with its insurers immediately following the filing of the bankruptcy petition.

One of the obvious problems in filing a Chapter 11 is the negative effect it may have upon both short-term and long-term sales. As a result, the decision to file cannot be publicly discussed. Nevertheless, the company must try to avoid placing litigation counsel in a position where settlements with counsel for tort claimants have been substantially negotiated but not fully consummated prior to bankruptcy. A bankruptcy court is unlikely to allow a postpetition payment, even though all other aspects of the settlement were concluded prior to the bankruptcy filing. As a result of such unfunded settlements, substantial animosity is created with the plaintiff's counsel, which may spill over into the bankruptcy proceeding.

With proper advanced planning, the debtor will often have substantial time to prepare the operating company for bankruptcy. Prior to filing, the company should carry out all changes in the operation and management of the company that will result in increased efficiencies. Most changes, including necessary capital improvements, that are not in the ordinary course of business cannot be undertaken without bankruptcy court approval. The company should also attempt to conserve cash, where possible, during and after the bankruptcy filing. This is particularly important, because of the expensive nature of this type of reorganization. Due to the numerous professionals that are required, and the fact that the debtor will be responsible for paying the fees of its professionals, as well as those of the official committees, the overall cost of reorganization is likely to be substantial. It appears, however, that as more of these types of cases are completed the overall cost of reorganization will decline as a result of increased efficiency gained through experience.

FUTURE CLAIMS

One of the most difficult issues faced by a company in bankruptcy as a result of mass toxic tort liability involves future claims. Claimants falling into this category have been exposed to the product giving rise to the mass toxic tort liability, but they have not manifested a disease or injury prior to the filing of the bankruptcy petition. The controversy over the status of these persons as claimants under Section 101(4) of the Bankruptcy Code continues. If this class is deemed not to hold a claim as defined under Section 101(4), then the liability cannot be resolved or discharged until a future date. As a result, in a traditional bankruptcy case, such a future claimant could pursue the debtor even after the reorganization has been completed. The company attempting to reorganize, however, must be able to assure itself that, once the bankruptcy proceeding has been completed, it will no longer face liability as a result of its prior distribution of the defective product. Should the courts determine that all persons who have been exposed to the defective product hold claims under Section 101(4), regardless of whether an injury has presently manifested, then all of their claims could be treated in a manner consistent with most other bankruptcy cases. Unfortunately, no court has definitively addressed this issue under Section 1141 of the Code, which defines the scope of the discharge which a debtor obtains in Chapter 11. Therefore, the response to the future claims problem involves the issuance of an injunction pursuant to Section 105 of the Bankruptcy Code and a "channeling order," which requires that all liabilities resulting from the defective product, whether past, present, or future, be asserted against a fund or funds created to process, defend, and resolve those liabilities.

The consideration provided by the reorganized company for the injunction and the channeling order is the payment to creditors of the company's going-concern value, plus a share of the future earnings of the reorganized company. In addition, creditors may receive an equity position in the reorganized company or the existing management/shareholders may contribute additional capital to maintain their ownership position. As a result, the claimants' return is related directly to the future performance of the company. The reasoning behind this format is that the debtor is worth more to creditors as a continuing business, rather than through liquidation. By using the actuarial reports, in conjunction with the going-concern and liquidation valuations, it can be established that creditors will receive a greater return if the company is allowed to continue to operate. Since the company cannot operate if it faces the risk that the litigation will be ongoing after the bankruptcy proceeding has ended, the injunction must be issued. The injunction is deemed binding upon future claimants, because they are represented by the guardian *ad litem*. The future claimants have an additional incentive to support this type of reorganization, because the alternative is often a distribution on a first-come, first-served basis, which results in the premature exhaustion of the company's assets long before many of the claims have matured.

In the reorganizations of large publicly held companies, tort claimants have often sought and obtained an equity position in the reorganized company. In the smaller companies, however, which are often run by entrepreneurs, tort claimants have focused primarily upon an income participation in the reorganized entity payable to the trust fund. Because the smaller companies are usually owned and operated by the same group of people, an equity position by the fund is viewed as a disruptive influence that will directly impact upon the companies' future performance. Therefore, to accommodate the concerns of both the tort claimants as well as the existing management of the debtor, a minimum annual payment is given to the fund by the reorganized company, which can increase based upon future performance. This creates a win/win situation for both management and future claimants, each of whom retain an interest in seeing that the company thrives.

CLAIMS BAR DATE

In every Chapter 11 case, a final date for filing proofs of claim against the estate must be established. Unless a creditor's claim is listed within the debtor's schedules of assets and liabilities as not being contingent, unliquidated, or disputed, the creditor must file a proof of claim on or before the date established by the court or lose its right to recover from the debtor. In a bankruptcy case involving mass toxic torts, a claims bar date is also established for all creditors. However, the only effect that the failure to file a proof of claim will have upon personal injury claimants is the loss of the right to vote upon the plan. This is done largely because the status of future claimants under Section 101(4) of the Code has not been determined. Thus, rather than trying to distinguish between present and future claims, all personal injury claims are treated uniformly. Such tort-related claims nevertheless remain subject to applicable state and federal statutes of limitations as modified by the Bankruptcy Code. Future claimants are not permitted to vote on the plan.

By not eliminating a tort claimant's right to recover as a result of the failure to file a proof of claim, notice of the activities within the bankruptcy case can be given directly to the tort claimant's counsel and through publication. Often, bankruptcy counsel will not have the names or addresses of each individual claimant. It is under these circumstances that representation of numerous tort claimants by a single plaintiff's attorney can result in significant efficiencies to the estate.

In conjunction with the claims bar date program, debtor's counsel should determine the areas of distribution of the defective product to better identify all groups that should be put on notice of the bankruptcy and the claims bar date. Once the geographic areas are identified, publication notice of the claims bar date should be undertaken in those newspapers and periodicals most likely to reach that particular group of persons. Counsel should also identify all of the other manufacturers and codefendants normally involved in the mass toxic tort litigation.

THE PLAN OF REORGANIZATION

The plan of reorganization should be designed to free the reorganized company from all tort-related liabilities, thereby enhancing the profit participation payments to the trust. The operating business, therefore, must be protected by the injunction. Thus, the injunction is a condition precedent to, and an essential element of, the plan; without the injunction, not only the plan but the reorganized company's survival would be impossible.

Under the plan, the debtor normally assigns those indemnity and contribution claims that it had against other manufacturers and distributors of similar defective products to the trust. The plan, therefore, contemplates that the trust will press, in the name of the debtor, those tort-related claims that the company has already asserted against other parties and channel the proceeds from such claims to the trust fund. To the extent that outstanding claims continue to exist against the debtor's insurers, such claims are also assigned to the trust. Concurrently, the trust fund assumes all of the debtor's present and future tort-related liabilities and is directed to hold and administer the assets made available under the plan and to provide an alternative dispute resolution mechanism.

After confirmation, the reorganized company is required to cooperate with the efforts of the trust funds to collect such claims against third parties, by providing documents, records, and factual testimony where necessary. However, the trust is the sole party responsible for collecting the claims and paying the attendant costs and attorneys' fees.

To better address the tort-related claims, the plan should establish at least one class, distinct from other unsecured conditions, that consists of all tort-related claims, including any indemnity and contribution claims.

To preserve and maximize the assets of the debtor for distribution to claimants, punitive damages are disallowed in most cases under the plan. Payment of punitive damages would diminish the funds available for the compensation of tort claimants, present and future, and could seriously delay or perhaps prevent compensation of future tort claimants.

Apart from the tort claimants, general unsecured claimants, through their committee, must negotiate a settlement with the debtor. This aspect of the reorganization is consistent with all bankruptcy cases. A tension, however, does exist between the tort claimants and the general unsecured creditors about the status and priority of their respective claims. If all of the tort-related liabilities, both present and future, were treated as present "claims" under the Bankruptcy Code, then the combined total would likely exceed those claims held by the general unsecured creditors and, therefore, substantially dilute the potential return. As a result, on a strict liquidation basis, the tort claimants normally expect to receive the largest percentage of the debtor's assets. It should be kept in mind that the proceeds of the liquidated insurance policies are viewed by the tort claimants as belonging to them alone. In a liquidation, general unsecured creditors would have no entitlement to insurance proceeds. Nevertheless, in the course of negotiating a consensual plan of reorganization, the actual dividend paid to general unsecured creditors will often be the result of compromise among all of the parties and not necessarily based upon a strict pro rata distribution analysis.

Normally, a debtor will favor a consensual plan whenever possible. This is particularly true in this type of case, because of the importance of the injunction sought pursuant to Section 105 of the Code. The bankruptcy court will certainly be more amenable to issuing the injunction when it is supported by the groups that are most directly impacted. Future claimants will also benefit, in light of the profit participation that will bring additional assets to the estate; and general unsecured creditors benefit, because a negotiated settlement may result in a dividend exceeding that in a liquidation. Therefore, logic and self-interest suggest that a consensual plan is the appropriate result.

CONFIRMATION OF THE PLAN

To confirm the plan of reorganization, the bankruptcy court must independently determine that the plan is in the best interest of all classes of creditors and equity security holders impaired by the plan. The "best interest" test requires that the bankruptcy court find that the plan provides to each member of each impaired class of claims and interests a recovery having a value at least equal to the value of the distribution each such person would receive if the debtor was liquidated under Chapter 7 of the Code.

To calculate what members of each impaired class of unsecured creditors and equity security holders would receive if the debtor was liquidated, the bankruptcy court must first determine the aggregate dollar amount that would be generated from the debtor's assets if the Chapter 11 case was converted to a Chapter 7 case under the code and the assets were liquidated by a trustee in bankruptcy (the "liquidation value"). The liquidation value consists of the net proceeds from the disposition of the assets of the debtor supplemented by the cash held by the debtor and recoveries on actions against third parties. In a reorganization involving mass toxic torts, such claims may consist of contribution or indemnity claims, or both, against other manufacturers of similar products.

The liquidation value available to general creditors would be reduced by (*a*) the claims of secured creditors to the extent of the value of their collateral and (*b*) by the cost and expenses of the liquidation, as well as other administrative expenses of the debtor's estate. The debtor's costs of liquidation under Chapter 7 would include the compensation of a trustee, as well as counsel and other professionals retained by the trustee; disposition expenses; all unpaid expenses incurred by the debtor during the Chapter 11 reorganization proceeding (such as compensation for attorneys, financial advisers, and accountants) that are allowed in the Chapter 7 proceeding; litigation costs; and claims arising from the operation of the debtors during the pendency of the Chapter 11 reorganization and Chapter 7 liquidation proceedings. The liquidation itself would trigger certain priority claims, such as claims for severance pay, and would accelerate other priority payments, which would otherwise be payable in the ordinary course. These priority claims would be paid in full out of the liquidation proceeds before the balance would be available to pay general claims or to make any distribution of equity interests.

In liquidation, the distinctions between general unsecured creditors and tort claimants would likely be eliminated. In addition, a liquidation would likely generate a significant increase in general unsecured claims, such as contract rejection claims. Further, in liquidation, the value of the debtor's inventory and accounts receivable would drop substantially.

Once the percentage recoveries in liquidation of secured creditors, priority claimants, general creditors, and equity security holders are ascertained, the value of the distribution available out of the liquidation value is compared with the value of the property offered to each of the classes of claims and interests under the plan to determine if the plan is in the best interest of each creditor and equity security holder class. Typically, in the reorganization of a company facing mass toxic tort liabilities, where the operating assets of the company are otherwise financially sound, the going-concern value of the company will far exceed the liquidation value of the company. Therefore, reorganization will produce the greater return to creditors. As a result, a consensual plan of reorganization will often emerge, because each class of creditors tends to be in a better position as a result. For example, by consenting to a plan, general unsecured creditors and present tort claimants may avoid significant delays in payment caused by prolonged litigation involving the valuation of claims and the status of future tort liabilities in bankruptcy. Future tort claimants face the possibility that the debtor's assets will be exhausted before their claims mature. Classes of interest, such as equity security holders, would likely receive nothing in a liquidation.

As noted, future tort claimants do not vote on a plan in this type of reorganization, because their status as claimants under the Bankruptcy Code remains undecided. Nevertheless, their position as asserted by the guardian *ad litem* will carry substantial weight. In the event the guardian *ad litem* does not agree with the proposed distribution of assets in the plan, various litigation alternatives are available that will serve to delay the reorganization and greatly increase the overall costs, thus reducing the amount of assets available for distribution. Since the "clients" of the guardian *ad litem* consist solely of future claimants, it is the guardian *ad litem* who will be most interested in the future profit participation and, therefore, the prosperity of the reorganized company.

VOTING ON THE PLAN

At the time of voting on the plan, there will be thousands of present personal injury tort claimants and hundreds of property damage tort claimants who will have filed proofs of claim. Most of these claimants will assert, in their proofs of claim, liabilities in the amount of $1 million or more for each claim. It would unduly delay administration of the case to attempt to reduce each claim to a precise dollar value through the normal proof of claim objection process or by means of a jury trial of each personal injury claimant's cause of action. How then are each of these claims to be valued in dollar terms to weight them for voting purposes? The Bankruptcy Code provides that each class of claims must accept the plan by a vote of a majority in number and two thirds in dollar amount of all claims in each class. The compromise that has been reached in mass toxic tort Chapter 11 proceedings is to value the claims of personal injury claimants for voting purposes at $1 per claimant. With respect to property damage claims, the approach has been to give each claimant a vote of $1 multiplied by the number of properties alleged to have been damaged by the injurious material. For example, in asbestos cases, if the property damage claimant is the owner of several buildings, the claimant's dollar value will be calculated by multiplying the number of buildings alleged to have been damaged by $1 per building. In this manner, a plan of reorganization may be expeditiously approved without the precise liquidation of each and every personal injury and property damage claim.

CRAMDOWN

In the event some of the creditor groups do not consent, the debtor can still obtain a confirmed plan of reorganization. Under Section 1126(f) of the Bankruptcy Code, a claimant who is paid in full is deemed not to be "impaired" under a plan. Such a creditor is assumed to have accepted the plan of reorganization for purposes of voting. In a reorganization involving substantial present and future tort liabilities, however, it is not possible to provide for repayment to every creditor in full. As a result, certain impaired classes are likely to exist. If those impaired classes do not vote in favor of acceptance of the plan, the code contains provisions for confirmation of a plan, as long as at least one impaired class of claims has accepted it. These "cramdown" provisions are set forth in Section 1129(b) of the Bankruptcy Code.

A plan may be confirmed under the cramdown provisions if, in addition to satisfying the usual requirements of Section 1129 of the Code, it (1) "does not discriminate unfairly" and (2) "is fair and equitable, with respect to each class of claims or interests that is impaired under, and has not accepted, the plan." As used by the code, the phrases *discriminate unfairly* and *fair and equitable* have narrow and specific meanings unique to bankruptcy law.

The requirement that a plan not "discriminate unfairly" means that a dissenting class must be treated equally with other classes of equal rank. The plan will not discriminate unfairly with any class of claims or interests if no class is afforded a treatment that is disproportionate to the treatment afforded other classes of equal rank.

The fair and equitable standard, also known as the *absolute priority rule,* requires that a dissenting class receive full compensation for its allowed claims or interests before any junior class receives any distribution. In the event of a cramdown, the absolute priority rule will prohibit existing shareholders of the company from receiving any distribution or retaining their shares of stock unless the equity security holder gives up its prior interest and makes a substantial capital contribution that is both necessary and sufficient to make the plan a success. In addition, the dissenting class of impaired claims must receive an amount at least equal to that amount such claimant would otherwise have received if the debtor had been liquidated under Chapter 7 of the Bankruptcy Code. As a result of this provision, the amount of payment made by the debtor to fund the plan will normally be equal to the going-concern value of the company. The going-concern value must be higher than the liquidation value. Otherwise, logic dictates that the company should be liquidated to afford creditors the highest return. If less than going-concern value is paid, then remaining shareholders will receive a distribution equal to the remaining value of the company, contrary to the absolute priority rule. Initially, the purpose of obtaining the liquidation and going-concern values of the company is to support the proposition that the company is better off dead than alive to its creditors. The going-concern value will later serve as the basis for determining that the remaining shareholders do not receive a "windfall" as a result of their retention of an equity position in the company, despite the existence of impaired classes of creditors.

THE TRUST FUND

Following the successful reorganization of the debtor, the fund must be created in order to process, defend, and resolve the present and future tort claims arising from the debtor's prior manufacture and distribution of the defective product. The Johns-Manville, UNR, Amatex and Robins cases have each established trust funds for this purpose. The trust funds are established pursuant to state law with continued oversight by the bankruptcy court. The duties of the trust fund include processing and payment of claims, liquidation of assets assigned under the plan to the trusts, such as insurance and third-party claims, and the investment of liquidated assets.

One of the most difficult challenges with which the trust must deal is the efficient processing and payment of claims. The principal strategy that the trust must follow is a form of alternate dispute resolution that eliminates or greatly reduces the use of the court system. One of the factors that should facilitate this process is the representation of large numbers of claimants by a single attorney or firm. The use of computers also promises to expedite and economize the resolution of claims.

Various alternatives have been considered in order to avoid some of the problems that are unique to the trust fund format. These problems include the fiduciary obligations imposed upon trustees and the cost of liability insurance. One possible alternative to a trust fund is the creation of a nonprofit corporation or similar legal entity that does not utilize trustees. Many states have enacted immunity laws for directors of nonprofit corporations for liability arising out of ordinary negligence. It is unclear, however, whether these laws will insulate a director from unanticipated liability related to claims resolution and eliminate the need for insurance entirely. Until a solution to this problem is finally resolved, it is recommended that the plan of reorganization contain broad provisions that permit the bankruptcy court to exercise jurisdiction over the trust postconfirmation. By retaining jurisdiction, the trustees can seek court approval of most major decisions made in connection with the trust, thereby avoiding criticism at a later date. It is also recommended that the original agreement that creates the trust be drafted to provide the trustees with sufficient latitude to resolve issues as they are encountered. This will be important during the early stages of the trust, when most of the unique and difficult issues will be encountered.

I.R.C. SECTION 468B TAX ISSUES

In partial response to the Johns-Manville Chapter 11 and other mass toxic tort bankruptcies, Congress enacted § 468B as part of the Tax Reform Act of 1986. Typically, the trust funds that are created in a mass toxic tort bankruptcy are designed to qualify under I.R.C. § 468B. If they qualify, two of the consequences that result are: (*a*) the payments made by the debtor to the trust of its own funds (not the insurance proceeds) pursuant to the tax plan are tax deductible to the debtor in the year of each such payment, as opposed to the year in which payment is made to each underlying tort claimant;

(*b*) the trust is so treated as a separate entity from the reorganized company that earnings on the funds after receipt from the debtor are taxable to the trust and not to the reorganized company. The trust, if it qualifies under § 468B, is then taxable at a lower rate than the reorganized company under present law.

If the trust does not qualify under § 468B, it is deemed a "grantor trust" of the reorganized company, and two of the adverse consequences would be:

1. The reorganized company could not take a tax deduction in the year of each payment to the trust; rather, the deduction would be delayed until the year the funds were actually paid to the claimants by the trust.
2. Earnings on funds by the trust after receipt from the reorganized company would be taxed at the reorganized company's higher tax rate.

As a result of I.R.C. § 468B, the debtor is able to make increased contributions to the trust, which result in a greater return to individual creditors. The debtor gets an immediate tax deduction in the year of each contribution it makes to the trust, and, as a result, the debtor is able to shelter its income from taxation at an earlier date than it would otherwise obtain. This enhances the position of both the debtor and the creditors/trusts in the early years' postconfirmation of the plan.

Internal Revenue Code § 468B provides as follows:

§ 468B. Special Rules for Designated Settlement Funds

(*a*) In General. For purposes of § 461(h), economic performance shall be deemed to occur as qualified payments are made by the taxpayer to a designated settlement fund.
(*b*) Taxation of Designated Settlement Fund.
  (1) In General. There is imposed on the gross income of any designated settlement fund for any taxable year a tax at a rate equal to the maximum rate in effect for such taxable year under § 1(e).
  (2) Certain Expenses Allowed. For purposes of paragraph (1), gross income for any taxable year shall be reduced by the amount of any administrative costs (including state and local taxes) and certain other incidental expenses of the designated

settlement fund (including legal, accounting and actuarial expenses)—
- (A) which are incurred in connection with the operation of the fund, and
- (B) which would be deductible under this chapter for purposes of determining the taxable income of a corporation.

No other deductions shall be allowed to the fund.

(3) Transfers to the Fund. In the case of any qualified payment made to the fund—
- (A) the amount of such payment shall not be treated as income of the designated settlement fund,
- (B) the basis of the fund in any property which constitutes a qualified payment shall be equal to the fair market value of such property at the time of payment, and
- (C) the fund shall be treated as the owner of the property in the fund (and any earnings thereon).

(4) Tax in Lieu of Other Taxation. The tax imposed by paragraph (1) shall be in lieu of any other taxation under this subtitle of income from assets in the designated settlement fund.

(5) Coordination with Subtitle F. For purposes of subtitle F—
- (A) a designated settlement fund shall be treated as a corporation, and
- (B) any tax imposed by this subsection shall be treated as a tax imposed by section 11.

(c) Deductions Not Allowed for Transfer of Insurance Amounts. No deduction shall be allowable for any qualified payment by the taxpayer of any amounts received from the settlement of any insurance claim to the extent such amounts are excluded from the gross income of the taxpayer.

(d) Definitions. For purposes of this section—
(1) Qualified payment. The term "qualified payment" means any money or property which is transferred to any designated settlement fund pursuant to a court order, other than—
- (A) any amount which may be transferred from the fund to the taxpayer (or any related person), or
- (B) the transfer of any stock or indebtedness of the taxpayer (or any related person).

(2) Designated settlement fund. The term "designated settlement fund" means any fund—
- (A) which is established pursuant to a court order and which extinguishes completely the taxpayer's tort liability with respect to claims described in subparagraph (D),

(B) with respect to which no amounts may be transferred other than in the form of qualified payments,
(C) which is administered by persons a majority of whom are independent of the taxpayer,
(D) which is established for the principle purpose of resolving and satisfying present and future claims against the taxpayer (or any related person or formerly related person) arising out of personal injury, death, or property damage,
(E) under the terms of which the taxpayer (or any related person) may not hold any beneficial interest in the income or corpus of the fund, and
(F) with respect to which an election is made under this section by the taxpayer.

An election under this section shall be made at such time and in such manner as the Secretary shall by regulation prescribe. Such an election, once made, may be revoked only with the consent of the Secretary.

(3) Related person. The term "related person" means a person related to the taxpayer within the meaning of § 267(b).

(e) Nonapplicability of Section. This section shall not apply with respect to any liability of the taxpayer arising under any workers' compensation act or any contested liability of the taxpayer within the meaning of § 461(f).

(f) Other Funds. Except as provided in regulations, any payment in respect of a liability described in Subsection (d)(2)(D) (and not described in Subsection (e)) to a trust fund or escrow fund which is not a designated settlement fund shall not be treated as constituting economic performance.

(g) Clarification of Taxation of Certain Funds. Nothing in any provision of law shall be construed as providing that an escrow account, settlement fund, or similar fund is not subject to current income tax. The Secretary shall prescribe regulations providing for the taxation of any such account or fund whether as a grantor trust or otherwise.

At the time of publication of this book, the Internal Revenue Service had not adopted any regulations clarifying I.R.C. § 468B and the issues arising thereunder. One issue that arises under this section is the question whether future earnings of the reorganized debtor fall within the definition of "qualified payment." The definition of qualified payment excludes "the transfer of any stock or indebtedness of the taxpayer (or any related person)." Informal advice received from the Internal Revenue Service indicates that a court-ordered stream of payments from the future earnings of the reorganized debtor do constitute qualified payments and are not viewed as "stock or indebtedness" of the taxpayer. However, counsel for the Committee of Asbestos-Related Disease Claimants and counsel for the guardian for unknown future claimants, who will be the beneficiaries of the personal injury trust fund, may argue for the issuance by the reorganized debtor of one or more instruments evidencing the obligation of the reorganized debtor to make payments from its future earnings. Further, they may argue for collateralization of this obligation. It is possible that a tax problem might arise where the instrument, be it collateralized or uncollateralized, was transferred directly to the "designated settlement fund" or trust. Creative counsel for the Chapter 11 debtor may devise one or more methods of avoiding the tax problem, while satisfying the legitimate demands of the personal injury claimants. One such method may be the creation of an escrow to hold the instruments or collateral, or both, and that would be activated only in the event there was a default in the court-ordered stream of payments established pursuant to the plan.

Another issue arises out of the use of the term *designated settlement fund* in the singular, without any recognition that more than one fund may be required to account for the disparate interests of the personal injury claimants, on the one hand, and the property damage claimants, on the other hand. The personal injury claimants will undoubtedly want a separate settlement fund or trust fund to be established, separate and apart from any settlement fund or trust fund for the benefit of property damage claimants. Is the establishment of *two* funds a violation of I.R.C. § 468B? Informal indications from the Internal Revenue Service suggest that the establishment of two funds or trusts does not violate the provisions of I.R.C. § 468B.

What if one or both of the funds proves to be overfunded at the end of the time period when future tort claims, if any, cease to arise and are paid? I.R.C. § 468B(d)(2)(E) appears to clearly preclude any reversionary interest on the part of the reorganized debtor. However, there appears to be no preclusion of the possibility of the shifting of funds from one trust to another. Therefore, if the property damage fund proves to be overfunded, especially in view of the fact there is no such thing as a "future property damage claim," there would appear to be no prohibition in I.R.C. § 468B of a "spillover" provision from the property damage trust to the personal injury trust.

Finally, what is the tax effect on the debtor of the collection of substantial proceeds of products liability insurance policies by the debtor *during* the Chapter 11 proceedings? Assuming the debtor has substantial untapped balances remaining on its products liability policies on the Chapter 11 filing date, the debtor will want to collect those balances from the insurance carriers, plus a premium for any costs of defense saved by those carriers, as mentioned above. The total collection effort during the Chapter 11, but prior to finalization of a plan, will undoubtedly result in a fund of millions of dollars, which all parties will want to be held in escrow, perhaps by the clerk of the U.S. Bankruptcy Court, until the plan of reorganization is confirmed and the § 468B trusts actually spring into being. In the meantime, it would appear that the funds in the hands of the clerk of court would, at least arguably, be taxable to the debtor, whereas the debtor will never receive a direct benefit from those funds. This dilemma may be solved one of two ways. Either the settlement funds may be invested in tax-free instruments, or all the parties to the bankruptcy proceeding must agree that any taxes payable by the debtor on earnings of the insurance proceeds held in the settlement funds shall be payable by those funds before they are turned over to the § 468B trusts.

CONCLUSION

The reorganization of a company faced with mass toxic tort liability presents a unique challenge and opportunity for all of the parties involved. By filing the bankruptcy petition, much needed attention is focused upon the problems created by the litigation, which, in turn, forces those involved to explore viable solutions and alternatives. The ideas and suggestions set forth within this chapter are by no means the definitive answer to the problems encountered. Rather, they should serve as a springboard for further innovation, geared toward avoiding the needless and inefficient liquidation of viable businesses. The balance struck by this model, however, presents a promising step in the right direction. As demonstrated herein, through the injunction, the debtor is able to survive, and, in the process, enable claimants to realize a greater return by sharing in the reorganized company's future success.

CHAPTER 12

THE ROLE OF THE UNSECURED CREDITORS' COMMITTEE IN WORKOUTS AND REORGANIZATIONS

Joel B. Zweibel, Esq.
Adam C. Harris, Esq.
O'Melveny & Myers

Texaco. LTV. Eastern Air Lines. Manville Corporation. Federated and Allied Department Stores. Integrated Resources. Southmark. Lomas Financial Corp. Revco. During the past decade, these entities, as well as thousands of others, have found it necessary to seek the protections afforded by the reorganization provisions of the bankruptcy laws. They are also reflective of the size and nature of the entities that are now routinely becoming debtors under Chapter 11 of the Bankruptcy Code. These entities each have thousands of unsecured creditors—trade creditors, employees, lenders, debenture holders, ticket holders, retirees and pensioners, landlords, and so on—all of whom are directly impacted by a bankruptcy filing. Individually, these creditors, as a general rule, lack the resources necessary to effectively protect their interests during the course of a reorganization or a workout. It is this function that the unsecured creditors' committee is designed to perform for the benefit of all of the debtor's general unsecured creditors.

The unsecured creditors' committee is a group of creditors, appointed by the United States trustee (in a Chapter 11 reorganization) or selected by the unsecured creditor body (in a workout), bearing the responsibility to represent, as a fiduciary, the interests of all unsecured creditors. The burden undertaken by the creditors' committee is substantial and will require the committee to become deeply involved in virtually every aspect of the workout or Chapter 11 case, including, but not limited to, a thorough review of the debtor's financial affairs, a review of every substantial asset disposition and other out of the ordinary course transactions, and the negotiation of a restructuring plan or plan of reorganization that maximizes the recovery for unsecured creditors. Whether the context is an out-of-court restructuring, a prepackaged Chapter 11, or a traditional Chapter 11 case, the creditors' committee can play a pivotal role in determining the success or failure of the exercise. Its working relationship with the debtor, its determination of whether the debtor can be reorganized, and its ability to sway the vote of the unsecured creditor body generally can ultimately determine whether a restructuring plan or plan of reorganization will be achieved.

How one views the role of the creditors' committee may depend on the perspective from which the issue is approached. From the perspective of the debtor, the creditors' committee provides a vehicle through which the debtor can efficiently negotiate with its unsecured creditor body. Generally, however, a debtor prefers such a committee to be nonintrusive as far as the business operations are concerned. Conversely, to the unsecured creditors, the creditors' committee is their representative, with a fiduciary duty to all unsecured creditors, charged with the responsibility of protecting the interests of its constituents. And in performing this role, an effective creditors' committee will be a careful monitor of the debtor's operations. In either event, it is clear that the unsecured creditors' committee, acting on behalf of unsecured creditors generally, provides a mechanism for the debtor to negotiate with its creditor body, to avoid duplicative negotiations with individual creditors, and to move more quickly toward a consensual restructuring plan or plan of reorganization.

The purpose of this chapter is to provide debtors, potential acquirors, workout specialists, and others who may become involved in workouts or reorganizations with a comprehensive overview of the role of the unsecured creditors' committee. This discussion of who may serve on the creditors' committee, how it is formed, what its powers and duties are, what its expectations will be vis-à-vis the debtor, and other matters discussed more fully below should provide a sound understanding of the role, and importance, of the unsecured creditors' committee in workouts and reorganizations.

FORMATION OF THE UNSECURED CREDITORS' COMMITTEE

Statutory Unsecured Creditors' Committee in Chapter 11 Reorganizations

Under prior law, no provision existed mandating the formation of a committee to represent the debtor's unsecured creditors in a reorganization case. In enacting the Bankruptcy Code,[1] Congress provided, in Section 1102(a)(1), for the appointment in each Chapter 11 case of a creditors' committee to represent the interests of unsecured creditors. Pursuant to the statute:

> As soon a practicable after the order for relief under Chapter 11 of this title, the United States trustee shall appoint a committee of creditors holding unsecured claims and may appoint additional committees of creditors or of equity security holders as the United States trustee deems appropriate.[2]

On its face, the statute provides for the appointment of an unsecured creditors' committee in all Chapter 11 cases. However, it should be noted that in some smaller cases, no creditors' committee is ever appointed. The reasons for this are varied but often reflect the belief of both the creditors and the United States trustee that the substantial time, effort, and costs associated with the appointment and meaningful functioning of a creditors' committee is unwarranted in light of the small probability that the debtor will be reorganized.

While Section 1102(a)(1) "mandates" the appointment of an unsecured creditors' committee, Section 1102(b)(1) of the Bankruptcy Code purports to designate who should be appointed to that committee. Pursuant to Section 1102(b)(1), the unsecured creditors' committee:

> . . . shall ordinarily consist of the persons, willing to serve, that hold the seven largest claims against the debtor of the kinds represented on such committee, or of the members of a committee organized by creditors before the commencement of the case under this chapter, if such committee was fairly chosen and is representative of the different kinds of claims to be represented.[3]

While the statute suggests that the creditors' committee should be comprised of the persons, willing to serve, that hold the seven largest claims against the debtor, the legislative history of the statute indicates that this language is precatory;[4] thus, the creditors' committee may have a different composition so long as it is representative of the unsecured creditor body generally.

As a practical matter, whether or not the Bankruptcy Code requires it, the creditors' committee should be comprised of those persons who hold the largest unsecured claims against the debtor, and who thus have a substantial economic interest in negotiating a restructuring plan or plan of reorganization that maximizes the recovery for unsecured creditors generally. The rationale is that those persons who have the largest unsecured claims also have the most to lose and will, therefore, be effective representatives for all unsecured creditors (especially for those with lesser interests) in their efforts to negotiate acceptable recoveries with respect to their own claims. They will also generally be the creditors who can afford the time and expense of active membership on a committee.

Additionally, a creditors' committee comprised of the holders of the largest unsecured claims will generally command the respect of the unsecured creditor body as a whole and deference from the smaller unsecured creditors to the decisions made by the creditors' committee in negotiating a plan of reorganization. Conversely, large unsecured creditors, who may have leverage over the debtor not shared by smaller creditors, would not likely give deference to the results of negotiations conducted by a creditors' committee comprised of smaller claimants. In that case, the larger unsecured creditors might seek to negotiate treatment for their own claims. That result—separate negotiations by the debtor with the creditors' committee and then individually with the holders of substantial unsecured claims—is one of the problems that the mandatory appointment of a creditors' committee with a large claim holder composition was designed to avoid. An inappropriately comprised creditors' committee may thus defeat the purpose of appointing the committee in the first instance.

The Unsecured Creditors' Committee in the Out-of-Court Workout

In contrast to the statutory requirement mandating the appointment of a committee to represent the interests of unsecured creditors in a Chapter 11 case, the formation of a creditors' committee in the context of an out-of-court workout is generally left to the initiative of either the company or the larger unsecured creditors. Recently, the formation of unsecured creditors' committees in out-of-court workouts has become more prevalent, as debtors and creditors alike realize the benefits and efficiencies that can result.

As is the case with statutory committees under Chapter 11, the persons participating on the creditors' committee in a workout situation must be sufficiently representative of the unsecured creditors having the most substantial economic interests in the case. Therefore, the creditors' committee in a workout will also usually be comprised of those entities that hold the largest unsecured claims against the debtor. The rationale for this is the same as with the statutory committee appointed in a Chapter 11 case. If the creditors' committee chosen is representative of the largest unsecured creditors, the negotiations they conduct, which will determine the recovery to be received both on their own claims and those of all other general unsecured creditors, will also inure to the benefit of the less-substantial creditors. Further, other unsecured creditors will likely respect the judgment of the creditors' committee in negotiating the restructuring plan, and the debtor will not be forced to conduct separate negotiations with individual unsecured creditors.

Unsecured creditors' committees operating in the out-of-court workout context may encounter greater difficulties in attempting to protect the interests of the unsecured creditor body than their statutory counterparts under the Bankruptcy Code. As will be more fully discussed below, the Bankruptcy Code provides a statutory creditors' committee with powers not automatically possessed by a creditors' committee in an out-of-court workout situation. These powers include, but are not limited to, the right to retain counsel, accountants, and other financial advisors at the estate's expense, and the ability to investigate thoroughly the debtor's financial affairs. A creditors' committee in an out-of-court workout will not enjoy these privileges unless the debtor agrees to provide them. And while these arrangements are becoming more routine, the creditors' committee cannot be assured that the debtor will be agreeable.

Additionally, creditors' committees in out-of-court workouts will often encounter other difficulties that their statutory counterparts need not confront, such as communicating with the creditor body generally, and negotiating with the debtor regarding how to deal with creditors who are unwilling to accept the restructuring proposal. Unlike a Chapter 11 plan, whose acceptance and confirmation is governed by the requirements of Sections 1126 and 1129 of the Bankruptcy Code,[5] an out-of-court restructuring proposal can be held up by a single creditor that refuses to accept the proposal. In that case, the debtor and creditors' committee may need to formulate a method for obtaining such creditor's acceptance, possibly through reinstatement or payment of that creditor's debt, or taking the risk that the recalcitrant creditor will not ultimately upset the restructuring accepted by a substantial majority.

Finally, during the course of an out-of-court restructuring, the statute of limitations with respect to avoidance or other causes of action that might benefit the debtor (and ultimately the creditors) will continue to run. In the event a determination is made that an out-of-court restructuring is not feasible, the statute of limitations with respect to such actions may have expired, thereby impacting the potential recoveries for unsecured creditors. The same is not true in a Chapter 11 case. Under Bankruptcy Code Section 108(a), so long as the period within which to file the action has not expired prior to the filing date, the debtor may commence the action at any time up until the later of (1) the end of such period or (2) two years from the order of relief.[6] Therefore, a creditors' committee in an out-of-court restructuring must be alert to these potential problems so as to preserve the benefits of those actions for its constituents.

Continuation of Pre-Chapter 11 Creditors' Committee after Chapter 11 Filing

In those instances where the attempted out-of-court workout is not successful and a Chapter 11 case is commenced (voluntarily or involuntarily), questions arise about whether the creditors' committee formed during the attempted workout period can continue as the statutory committee. In this situation, depending on the amount of time spent attempting the restructuring, the existing creditors' committee may have (1) conducted a substantial amount of due diligence with respect to the debtor's business and operations, (2) obtained a working knowledge of the debtor's situation, and (3) undergone negotiations with the debtor toward a restructuring plan. It is also possible that the debtor and creditors' committee will have formed a working relationship. The formation of a wholly new creditors' committee after the Chapter 11 filing, in these instances, would be costly and inefficient. Therefore, to the extent possible, the creditors' committee formed prepetition should remain intact.

Bankruptcy Code Section 1102(b)(1) provides that a creditors' committee formed prior to the Chapter 11 case may continue postpetition if it was "fairly chosen and is representative of the different kinds of claims to represented."[7] Bankruptcy Rule 2007[8] provides certain guidelines that, if followed, will allow the court, upon application of a party in interest, to determine that the prepetition creditors' committee satisfies the requirements of Section 1102(b)(1). The guidelines set forth in Bankruptcy Rule 2007 require, among other things, that the committee must have been selected by a majority in number and amount of creditors (1) who hold allowed, undisputed, fixed, liquidated, unsecured claims, who do not have an interest materially adverse to the interests of creditors, and who are not insiders and (2) who were present or represented at a meeting, of which all unsecured creditors having claims over $1,000, or the 100 largest unsecured creditors, had at least five days' notice in writing.[9]

Where the selection of the prepetition creditors' committee

does not strictly comply with the Bankruptcy Rules, the United States trustee must determine whether the committee, as constituted, was "fairly chosen" and "representative of the different kinds of claims to be represented" by the committee.[10] Practically, in these instances, the United States trustee is likely to appoint to the statutory creditors' committee most, if not all, of those persons who served on the creditors' committee formed prior to the filing. The United States trustee's appointment should be influenced to a large extent by the benefits to be derived from continuing the relationship developed between the creditors' committee and the debtor prior to the filing and by the desire to minimize costs by eliminating the duplication of substantial efforts that may have already been made by the creditors' committee and its members prior to the commencement of the case. In determining the composition of the statutory committee, however, the United States trustee may add additional members to the prepetition committee, or otherwise change its composition, to ensure adequate representation of the various types of claims to be represented by the committee.

Despite the clear language of Section 1102(a)(1), which vests in the United States trustee the authority to appoint the members of the creditors' committee,[11] the court is often called upon to determine whether the committee is representative of the unsecured creditor body. Prior to the enactment of the Bankruptcy Judges, United States Trustees and Family Farmer Bankruptcy Act of 1986, Section 1102 contained a subsection (c), which provided that the court, on request of a party in interest, could change the membership and size of a creditors' committee if the membership was not representative of the different kinds of claims to be represented.[12] While Section 1102(c) has been repealed, bankruptcy courts continue to play a role in determining the composition of the creditors' committee, relying, in some instances, on their broad equitable powers under Section 105(a).[13] Further, bankruptcy courts retain the authority to review decisions made by the United States trustee with respect to the adequacy of representation, and may, upon request, direct the appointment of additional committees, or the reconstitution of existing committees, to assure adequate representation.[14]

Qualifications of Committee Members

Separate and apart from the issue of the committee's composition is the question of what qualifications a person must have to serve on the creditors' committee. In determining who may serve on the committee, the United States trustee must only establish that the entity to be appointed is a "creditor" holding a "claim" against the debtor that is unsecured. To more fully understand these qualifications, however, reference must be made to the definition of certain terms, such as *creditor, claim,* and *person,* as set forth in the Bankruptcy Code. For instance, the definition of "person" in Section 101(35) of the Bankruptcy Code excludes governmental units generally, but includes for purposes of Section 1102 governmental units which, *inter alia,* acquire an asset from a person as a receiver or liquidating agent of that person. Thus, for example, the Pension Benefit Guaranty Corporation, as a governmental unit, is not qualified to serve as a member of a creditors' committee because it is not a "person."[15] Conversely, the Federal Deposit Insurance Corporation, as receiver for the Federal Savings and Loan Insurance Corporation Resolution Trust Fund, which is also a governmental unit, is qualified because it acquired an asset from a person (i.e., the savings and loan institution) as a receiver or liquidating agent of that person.

A number of issues may arise regarding the propriety of appointing to the creditors' committee persons who are not only unsecured creditors of the debtor but also have collateral relationships with the debtor, or who have interests adverse to the debtor. Into these categories fall persons who, besides being unsecured creditors, are also (1) insiders,[16] (2) equity holders, (3) competitors,[17] (4) union members,[18] (5) parties holding disputed claims,[19] and (6) parties in litigation with the debtor. Instead of adopting a *per se* rule requiring exclusion, courts have adopted a case-by-case approach to determine whether a particular unsecured creditor with a collateral, and potentially adverse, relationship with the debtor may participate on an unsecured creditors' committee.[20] In at least one case, however, the appointment of such person to the creditors' committee was specifically conditioned upon that person's exclusion from any committee discussions relating to the creditor's collateral relationship with the debtor.[21] The debtor, thus, should be aware that the unsecured creditors' committee may have members holding interests adverse to the debtor.

The Eastern Air Lines creditors' committee is a good example of this problem. In Eastern, the United States trustee appointed to the creditors' committee a representative from each of Eastern's three unions—the Air Line Pilots Association, International (ALPA), Transport Workers Union–Local 553 (TWU), and the International Association of Machinists and Aerospace Workers (IAM)—on the grounds that each of these unions represented a constituency holding substantial claims against Eastern for, *inter alia,* wages, benefits, and pension plan contributions. The appointment of the unions to the unsecured creditors' committee was particularly unsettling for Eastern for a number of reasons. First, Eastern maintained that it was the strike by the IAM, and the subsequent sympathy strikes by ALPA and the TWU, that forced Eastern to file for reorganization. Additionally, Eastern's proposed business plan, which it was obligated to disclose to the creditors' committee, contemplated the hiring of individuals to replace all striking workers and indicated the progress Eastern was experiencing in obtaining those replacements. Finally, as will be discussed more fully below, the debtor in a Chapter 11 case is obligated to provide to the creditors' committee a substantial amount of information, often confidential or proprietary in nature. Eastern was particularly unsettled about the prospect of disclosing to the representatives of its three unions information of this type, which Eastern feared the unions would use to further their own interests. To partially alleviate this problem, Eastern requested, and the union representatives agreed, to absent themselves from those portions of the debtors' presentations to the creditors' committee that related to matters on which their interests were adverse.

An additional problem that has recently come to the fore is whether persons who purchased unsecured claims against the debtor at a substantial discount prior to the commencement of the Chapter 11 case may be appointed to the creditors' committee. There is no statutory prohibition against such appointment; nor is there any case law that would support the exclusion of such creditors. In fact, the language of the statute, as previously discussed, supports the conclusion that such persons are qualified to serve on a creditors' committee. The presence of such persons on the creditors' committee, however, obviously creates tensions. In distinction to the trade creditor, or to the debenture holder who purchased at or close to par, the claims purchaser has generally invested in the debtor at a much lower level of risk and is usually interested primarily in making a short-term return on the investment. To obtain this return, in many cases, the recovery for unsecured creditors need not approach 100 percent. Further, claims purchasers have no continuing business relationship with the debtor and, thus, have little interest in whether the debtor is reorganized or liquidated.

Finally, an issue that relates primarily, but not exclusively, to persons who buy and sell claims against the debtor, is whether a creditors' committee member may continue to buy and sell claims while serving on the committee. This issue is of particular importance to investment banking or brokerage houses that hold claims against a debtor, and whose brokers may wish to continue trading debentures and other securities of the debtor for their clients' accounts during the Chapter 11 case. Generally, committee members, as fiduciaries for all unsecured creditors, should not buy and sell claims against the debtor for their own account during the Chapter 11 case. In the case of an investment banking or brokerage house, to the extent the brokers do continue to trade in the debtor's debentures or securities for their client's accounts, the person who represents that entity on the committee should establish procedures to ensure that no information received in his or her capacity as a committee member is disseminated or available to those engaged in trading the debentures or securities.

POWERS AND DUTIES OF CREDITORS' COMMITTEES

Bankruptcy Code Section 1103[22] sets forth the powers and duties of a statutory creditors' committee appointed under Section 1102(a). The extent to which those powers are exercised, and the role that the creditors' committee may seek to play in any particular Chapter 11 case, will necessarily depend upon a number of factors, including the size of the case, the complexity of the debtor's financial affairs and, to a great extent, the cause for the debtor's financial difficulties. It will also depend on the activism of the chairman of the creditors' committee and its other members, as well as the committee's counsel and financial advisors. In almost every case, the debtor will feel that the creditors' committee's role is intrusive and is beyond the scope of what is necessary under the circumstances. However, the debtor must realize that the committee, acting as a fiduciary body for the benefit of all unsecured creditors, must carefully and diligently exercise its responsibilities as required by law. To that end, most creditors' committees will seek to delve deeply into the debtor's business and operations, as opposed to performing only a cursory review.

In the case of a debtor that is substantially insolvent, the creditors' committee's role will generally be much broader, focusing not only on recapitalization but also on the possible sale of underperforming or nonperforming assets and changes to the debtor's operations. The creditors' committee will certainly prepare a liquidation analysis to use as a benchmark for determining whether a reorganization or liquidation will provide a greater recovery for unsecured creditors, and it may seek to take an active role in pursuing fraudulent transfer and preference actions (which the debtor might not otherwise wish to pursue) as a means to enhance the recovery for unsecured creditors. Finally, in such cases, it is not uncommon for the creditors' committee to suggest changes in management.

Conversely, in the case of a debtor whose difficulties stem primarily from insufficient cash flow, the creditors' committee's role may be narrower, focusing on how to best recapitalize the debtor in order to achieve more realistic cash flow projections. This does not mean, however, that the creditors' committee will not undertake a substantial review of the debtor's business and operations. This analysis will still be required in order for the creditors' committee to determine the reorganization structure that provides the maximum return for unsecured creditors.

In almost all cases, the debtor will view the creditors' committee's requests for information, involvement, and constant review as a burden on its very existence. Nevertheless, the debtor must understand that the creditors' committee's actions are essential to the exercise of its fiduciary duty and the protection of the interests of unsecured creditors generally. Conceptually, the creditors' committee is a watchdog over the debtor's operations during the Chapter 11 case, and the debtor has little choice but to adapt to the situation.

The Creditors' Committee Is a Party in Interest

Pursuant to Bankruptcy Code Section 1109(b),

> A party in interest, including the debtor, the trustee, *a creditors' committee,* an equity security holders' committee, a creditor, an equity security holder, or any indenture trustee, may raise and may appear and be heard on any issue in a case under this chapter. [Emphasis added.][23]

As a party in interest, the creditors' committee, acting as a fiduciary for all unsecured creditors, can be expected to become involved in all significant aspects of the Chapter 11 case. Thus, the creditors' committee is likely to request the opportunity to undertake, in advance, a substantive review of all out of the ordinary course transactions proposed by the debtor, such as the sale, use, or lease of assets. In addition, the creditors' committee may become involved in litigations between the debtor and other parties in an effort to protect the interests of the creditors and the estate.

The Texaco Chapter 11 case presents a good example of a creditors' committee becoming actively involved to impact ongoing litigation between the debtor and a third party. Texaco's Chapter 11 filing was caused, in large part, by the approximately $10 billion state court judgment obtained by Pennzoil, based upon a claim that Texaco tortiously interfered with contractual relations between Pennzoil and Getty. Upon Texaco's filing for relief under Chapter 11 of the Bankruptcy Code, Pennzoil's claim became a prepetition general unsecured claim against the Texaco estate, which Pennzoil could not enforce because of the automatic stay.[24] While Texaco used the protection of the bankruptcy laws to hold Pennzoil at bay while it prosecuted appeals through the various state and federal courts, the creditors' committee engaged in direct discussions with Pennzoil in an attempt to reach a settlement. Ultimately, the creditors' committee's involvement forced Texaco to agree to a settlement with Pennzoil, thus bringing the Chapter 11 case to a more prompt conclusion.

Authority to Employ Attorneys, Accountants, and Other Professionals

Pursuant to Section 1103(a) a creditors' committee is authorized to employ, with the court's approval, one or more attorneys, accountants, or other agents to represent or perform services for the creditors' committee.[25] Depending on, among other things, the size and complexity of the case, the business in which the debtor is engaged, and the issues central to the reorganization, the creditors' committee may deem it necessary to employ one or more professionals who are specialists in the debtor's industry.

Generally, the creditors' committee will select one or more attorneys to represent the committee as a whole, while individual committee members may retain separate counsel. Employment of independent creditors' committee counsel will provide the creditors' committee with objective legal advice, which can then be used in the exercise of its fiduciary duty to all unsecured creditors. Further, the employment of separate creditors' committee counsel will avoid potential conflicts that might otherwise arise if one law firm represents both the creditors' committee and an individual committee member.

Representation of both an individual creditor and the creditors' committee is not, however, precluded *per se*. Pursuant to Bankruptcy Code Section 1103(b), an attorney

> . . . may not, while employed by [a] committee, represent any other entity having an adverse interest in connection with the case. Representation of one or more creditors of the same class as represented by the committee shall not per se constitute the representation of an adverse interest.[26]

Therefore, whether an attorney can represent both the creditors' committee and an individual creditor hinges on whether the interests of those two entities are adverse. The more common practice, however, is for the creditors' committee to retain separate independent counsel.

In most Chapter 11 cases, the creditors' committee will seek to employ an accounting firm with expertise in reorganization proceedings. Among other things, creditors' committees generally rely upon their accountants to review and report on all financial information prepared by the debtor or its accountants, including financial statements, cash flow projections, and statements of assets and liabilities. In addition, the creditors' committee may request its accountants to undertake a review of the debtor's business to determine what changes, if any, could be made to improve the debtor's operations and cash flow. Further, in many cases, the creditors' committee will utilize its accountants to target underperforming or nonperforming segments of the debtor's business with a view toward the sale or cessation of such operations. Finally, the creditors' committee will usually look to its accountants to (1) prepare a liquidation analysis, (2) review the debtor's books and records for potential voidable transactions and unenforceable claims, and (3) render such other assistance as may be necessary in connection with the prepetition accounts, conduct, property, liabilities, and financial condition of the debtor, including the operation and financing of its business and the desirability of its continuance.

In addition to counsel and accountants, creditors' committees in most large Chapter 11 cases will seek to retain investment bankers or other financial advisors, including those with special expertise in the debtor's industry. For example, in the Lomas Financial Chapter 11 case, the creditors' committee retained a special real estate advisor, as well as accountants and investment bankers. The creditors' committee will generally look to these professionals to (1) evaluate proposed sales of assets; (2) review the financial and economic reasonableness of the debtor's business plans, operating forecasts, and long-range projections; (3) evaluate, negotiate, and structure the terms and conditions of a plan of reorganization, with particular emphasis on the terms and value of any debt, equity, or equity-related securities proposed to be issued under such plan; and (4) advise the creditors' committee on the financial and economic interests of its constituency in relation to the interests of other parties in the Chapter 11 case. The creditors' committee's investment bankers may also be authorized, with the debtor's consent, to seek third-party purchasers for all or substantially all of the assets or stock of the debtor. This, however, is the exception rather than the rule, as these transactions are generally initiated by the debtor's investment bankers.

Unlike the situation in an out-of-court workout, where the issue of who pays the costs and expenses of the creditors' committee's professionals is the subject of negotiation, in a case under Chapter 11 the fees and expenses of the creditors' committee's professionals are paid by the estate. Pursuant to Bankruptcy Code Section 330(a), the court may award to any professional employed under Section 1103:

> (1) reasonable compensation for actual, necessary services rendered . . . based on the nature, the extent, and the value of such services, the time spent on such services, and the cost of comparable services other than in a case under this title; and
> (2) reimbursement for actual, necessary expenses.[27]

Pursuant to Section 331 of the Bankruptcy Code, the creditors' committee's professionals (as well as a trustee, an examiner, the debtor's attorney, or any professional employed under Sections 327 or 1103) may apply for payment of interim compensation not more than once every 120 days after the order for relief, or more often if the court permits.[28]

Recently, some courts have permitted the creditors' committee's professionals (as well as the professionals employed by the debtor and others), to receive payment of a percentage of their fees and expenses on a monthly basis upon the submission of reasonably detailed billing statements. Payments received on a monthly basis are, however, subject to the submission of interim applications seeking approval of compensation and reimbursement of expenses pursuant to Bankruptcy Code Section 331. Additionally, all payments are subject to the submission and approval of final fee applications. Orders authorizing monthly payments to the creditors' committee's professionals and others of a percentage of billable time plus all disbursements have been entered by the courts in such cases as Public Service Company of New Hampshire and Eastern Air Lines.

Consultation with the Debtor Concerning the Administration of the Case[29]

Much to the dismay of most debtors, the creditors' committee will likely request the debtor to provide to the committee's professionals, on a regular basis, substantial and detailed information regarding the debtor's business and operations. While the debtor may feel that these requests are overly broad and intrusive, the receipt of such information provides the creditors' committee with the understanding of the debtor's business necessary to properly carry out its fiduciary duty to all unsecured creditors. In many instances, the creditors' committee will request the debtor to make periodic presentations regarding its business and operations and may seek to have its professionals institute a monitoring procedure through which the creditors' committee can keep close watch on the debtor's operations.

Under the Bankruptcy Code, the debtor-in-possession—not the committee—is authorized to operate the debtor's business.[30] However, in many instances, particularly where the debtor is insolvent, the economic reality is that the true owners of the bankrupt entity are the creditors, not the prepetition common equity holders. Therefore, the creditors' committee has a substantial interest in monitoring and, if possible, improving the operation of the debtor's business. Accordingly, based upon the information provided by the debtor to the creditors' committee and its professionals, the creditors' committee will often make recommendations to the debtor's management concerning, among other things, potential asset sales and the desirability of ceasing some or all of the debtor's operations.

In this respect, the creditors' committee's role is to act as an advisor, providing management with the creditors' views about how the business may be improved and an acceptable plan achieved. In most cases, the debtor and creditors' committee will establish a mutually acceptable procedure whereby the creditors' committee obtains all the information it feels is necessary to perform its functions, and the debtor is not overly burdened by the creditors' committee's participation in the day-to-day operations of the business.

In futherance of this aspect of the creditors' committee's role in the Chapter 11 case, the debtor will generally prepare and present to the creditors' committee a detailed long-term business plan setting forth the debtor's anticipated future operations, cash flow, and net income. The preparation and presentation of a business plan (generally five years) is a precursor to the negotiation and filing of a plan of reorganization. Generally, the business plan will provide the creditor's committee with the debtor's evaluation of its assets and liabilities, as well as its operating plan and business projections, and furnishes the basis for negotiating the terms of securities to be issued under the plan. After the business plan is presented, the committee should direct its financial advisors to meet with the debtor to review the reasonableness of the assumptions underlying the business plan and the debtor's projections and to report their findings to the creditors' committee. Where the creditors' committee's financial advisors find that the debtor's business plan is likely to result in a viable reorganized entity, the committee and the debtor may then move forward to negotiation of a plan of reorganization predicated on that business plan. On the other hand, if the debtor's business plan is believed to be overly aggressive or not feasible, the creditors' committee may insist that the debtor make certain changes or seek to proceed with a liquidation.

Investigation of Financial Affairs

Bankruptcy Code Section 1103(c)(2) provides the creditors' committee with broad authority to

> investigate the acts, conduct, assets, liabilities, and financial condition of the debtor, the operation of the debtor's business and the desirability of the continuance of such business, and any other matters relevant to the case or to the formulation of a plan.[31]

This provision is the cornerstone of the creditors' committee's powers to compel the debtor to provide all information the creditor's committee reasonably deems relevant to its analysis of the debtor's business.

From the perspective of unsecured creditors generally, it is essential that the creditors' committee conduct a diligent inquiry into the financial affairs of the debtor and into the debtor's continued viability going forward. To effectively negotiate a plan of reorganization providing unsecured creditors with the maximum recovery possible, the committee must have so firm a grasp of the debtor's financial affairs that the value of the debtor can be determined and a plan of reorganization negotiated on that basis. Determining the value of the enterprise will ordinarily require the creditors' committee's professionals to meet with the debtor's financial personnel, so both parties can negotiate a plan of reorganization from a common information base and a business plan that the committee is satisfied with. This is the essence of the creditors' committee's role, and the result that the Bankruptcy Code seeks to achieve by providing the creditors' committee with the power to investigate the debtor's financial affairs.

In addition to providing the creditors' committee with a complete information base from which to negotiate a plan of reorganization, investigation into the debtor's financial affairs is also necessary to determine what assets, if any, should be sold, operations discontinued, or if the debtor should be liquidated or sold to a third party. Further, this investigation may reveal corporate mismanagement, conflicts of interest, or other matters that might lead the creditors' committee to seek the appointment of a trustee or examiner.

One problem that often arises in connection with the creditors' committee's investigation of the debtor's financial affairs is the debtor's unwillingness to provide the creditors' committee with proprietary or confidential information in the absence of reasonable assurances that the information will not be released publicly. This problem is exacerbated in the so-called high profile cases, where the release of proprietary or confidential information is more likely to have a direct impact on the debtor's business. Creditors' committees may take any number of steps to provide the debtor with the assurances it seeks. First, the bylaws adopted by the creditors' committee should ordinarily contain a provision, agreed to by all members, prohibiting the release of any proprietary or confidential information received from the debtor.[32] Second, although it is not technically necessary in view of the common bylaw provision, each member of the creditors' committee may be requested by the debtor to execute a confidentiality agreement. Finally, with respect to particularly sensitive information, the debtor may agree to provide the information only to the creditors' committee's professionals and not to the committee members generally. While this procedure obviously interferes with the creditors' committee's ability to investigate the debtor's financial affairs, and should thus be opposed by the committee, it is an option of last resort in instances where the debtor has otherwise refused to provide the information.

The debtor's concerns regarding the maintenance of confidentiality are often linked directly to who the members of the creditors' committee are. In those cases where certain members of the creditors' committee hold interests that are adverse to the estate (i.e., competitors, trade unions, parties in litigation with the debtor), maintaining confidentiality will likely be a bigger problem, requiring the use of the more extreme protective measures.

Negotiation of a Plan of Reorganization[33]

Clearly, the most important role of the creditors' committee is to negotiate with the debtor regarding the treatment to be provided to unsecured creditors pursuant to a plan of reorganization. In this regard, it is essential that the creditors' committee be perceived by the debtor as the legitimate representative of the significant economic interests in the Chapter 11 case. If it is not, the debtor will likely seek to negotiate directly with the holders of the most substantial unsecured claims that are not on the creditors' committee, thus defeating the purpose of having a creditors' committee to negotiate for the benefit of all unsecured creditors. Even where the creditors' committee is comprised of the holders of the most substantial unsecured claims, the debtor may nevertheless seek to negotiate directly and separately with individual committee members. Creditors' committees should, where possible, discourage this practice. Negotiations between the debtor and creditors' committee members with respect to their individual claims may result in the creation of factions within the committee. Except in the unique case, the creditors' committee should resist individual negotiations between committee members and the debtor, since this reduces the leverage that the committee has as a unified negotiating body, and defeats the purpose of having a creditors' committee to represent the interests of all unsecured creditors.

Maintaining the legitimacy of the creditors' committee is essential to the effective negotiation of a plan of reorganization. Furthermore, it is important because general unsecured creditors rely upon the creditors' committee to negotiate the most favorable plan possible. As a general rule, individual unsecured creditors have insufficient information regarding the debtor's business and operations to effectively negotiate the treatment of their claim under a plan of reorganization, thus leaving the debtor with a distinct advantage. Additionally, individual creditors, unless they are the holder of a substantial unsecured claim, lack the leverage necessary to compel the debtor to provide the information required to effectively negotiate for better treatment under a plan. Finally, the vast majority of unsecured creditors hold relatively small claims and, thus, are generally unwilling or unable to finance the costs associated with substantial negotiations over treatment under a plan.

The provisions of the Bankruptcy Code attempt to balance the players on what is frequently an uneven playing field. In contradistinction to the individual creditor, the Bankruptcy Code provides the creditors' committee with the resources it needs to effectively negotiate on behalf of all unsecured creditors. The Bankruptcy Code provides that the cost of counsel, accountants, and other professionals is to be paid for by the estate.[34] The Bankruptcy Code further provides the creditors' committee with the power to demand the production of all the information it deems necessary,[35] and the professionals to analyze it, so the committee may negotiate on a fully informed basis. Finally, the creditors' committee, acting as a fiduciary body for the benefit of all unsecured creditors, has substantial leverage in negotiations, especially where the debtor seeks to retain some or all of its prepetition equity interest. The committee also has substantial leverage based on its ability to recommend to its constituency whether to support or reject any plan proposed by the debtor. Thus, the provisions of the Bankruptcy Code attempt to place at the disposal of the creditors' committee everything it needs to protect the interests of all general unsecured creditors and to maximize their recovery through negotiation of a plan of reorganization, or otherwise.

As additional leverage in plan negotiations, and to truly level the playing field, creditors' committees have recently used the threat of seeking to terminate the debtor's exclusive period within which to file a plan. Pursuant to Bankruptcy Code Sections 1121(b) and (c), the debtor has an initial exclusive 120-day period within which to file a plan of reorganization and an additional 60-day period within which to solicit acceptances.[36] Generally, in most larger cases, the debtor will seek one or more extensions of exclusivity[37] to allow its business to stabilize and to give the debtor an opportunity to prepare a business plan, provide the creditors' committee with any information requested and the time to analyze it, and negotiate the terms of a plan reorganization. Exclusivity, however, is also a safe haven for the debtor that can be held over its creditors as a threat to substantially delay the payment of their claims unless the creditors accede to the debtor's position.

Where the creditors' committee has established a working relationship with the debtor, is receiving the information requested, and is engaged in plan negotiations with the debtor, the creditors' committee will generally support the debtor's requests for extensions of exclusivity. If, however, the debtor is intransigent or otherwise refuses to work with the committee, or is viewed by the creditors' committee as being unreasonable either in refusing to provide the information requested or in its stance in plan negotiations, the creditors' committee may oppose the debtor's request for an extension and seek to file its own plan.[38] The possibility of losing its exclusive right to file a plan, which is perceived by most debtors as a loss of control over the Chapter 11 case, will often force an otherwise intransigent debtor to the negotiating table.

This was the approach taken by the creditors' committee in the Texaco Chapter 11 case. There, the creditors' committee was engaged in substantial discussions with Pennzoil regarding the resolution of Pennzoil's claim. When Texaco moved to extend exclusivity, the creditors' committee responded by seeking the entry of an order modifying Texaco's exclusivity to permit the creditors' committee and the equity holders' committee (but not all parties in interest) to file a plan. The court nominally granted Texaco's request, but substantively made a major change by providing in the order that, if the official committees could reach an agreement with Pennzoil on a plan, the court would terminate exclusivity and permit the plan to be filed. It is generally recognized that this perceived loss of control forced Texaco to abandon its pure litigation approach to obtain United States Supreme Court review of Pennzoil's state court judgment and, instead, to negotiate a settlement with Pennzoil as the basis of a plan of reorganization that brought the Chapter 11 case to a prompt conclusion.

Similarly, in the Public Service Company of New Hampshire Chapter 11 case, the bankruptcy court terminated the debtor's exclusivity when it became apparent that the debtor and the State of New Hampshire were unable to resolve their differences, a resolution that the debtor asserted was a prerequisite to the filing of a plan. After exclusivity was terminated, a number of different parties seeking to acquire the debtor filed plans of reorganization. Each party attempted to win the creditors' committee's support of its plan by providing enhanced treatment for the unsecured creditors and other parties in the case. In essence, the plan of reorganization process became a bidding war, where each plan sponsor sought the support of the creditors' committee and other parties in interest. The result was a substantial enhancement to the recovery for unsecured creditors and other parties at the expense of the debtor.

Before beginning plan negotiations, there are a number of issues the creditors' committee must resolve internally, not the least of which is how the negotiations with the debtor will be conducted. Depending on the size of the creditors' committee, the committee may determine to elect a plan subcommittee, comprised of members representing the general types of claims that are the constituents of the committee (i.e., trade claims, lenders, debenture holders, and so on), to conduct (with the committee's professionals) the negotiations with the debtor. These negotiations will ordinarily be subject to periodic reporting to, and the ultimate approval of, the entire creditors' committee. Use of a plan subcommittee is generally viewed by the debtor and the committee as more efficient and, thus, more desirable.

Regardless of who actually conducts the negotiations for the creditors' committee, the committee, prior to commencing negotiations, must identify the issues it feels must be addressed in the plan and a negotiating strategy geared toward reaching the desired result. What the issues are will differ in each case. Those most common, however, are the amount and form of consideration to be received under the plan (i.e., cash, debt, or equity securities), provisions for the resolution and payment of disputed claims, the payment of postpetition interest where the debtor is solvent, reporting and financial covenants where debt securities are to be issued, a continuing committee postconfirmation, and the extent of the bankruptcy court's retained jurisdiction.

Appointment of a Trustee or Examiner

Pursuant to Bankruptcy Code Section 1103(c)(4), the creditors' committee may request the appointment of a trustee or examiner if the result of its investigation of the debtor's financial affairs, or other circumstances in the case, warrant such action.[39] The standards for the appointment of a Chapter 11 trustee are set forth in Bankruptcy Code Section 1104(a). Pursuant to that section, a trustee may be appointed

> (1) for cause, including fraud, dishonesty, incompetence, or gross mismanagement of the affairs of the debtor by current management, either before or after the commencement of the case, or similar cause, but not including the number of holders of securities of the debtor or the amount of assets or liabilities of the debtor; or
>
> (2) if such appointment is in the interests of creditors, any equity security holders, and other interests of the estate, without regard to the number of holders of securities of the debtor or the amount of assets or liabilities of the debtor.[40]

Appointment of a Chapter 11 trustee to operate the debtor's business results in the immediate displacement of current management and vests in the trustee the power to operate the debtor's business and manage its properties in the exercise of the trustee's reasonable business judgment.[41] Appointment of a trustee also terminates the debtor's exclusive right to file a plan of reorganization under Bankruptcy Code Section 1121.[42]

A request by the creditors' committee to appoint a trustee in a Chapter 11 case is a dramatic step that should not be taken lightly. Before filing such a motion, the creditors' committee must consider the potential ramifications of its actions, including the litigation that is likely to ensue in connection with obtaining the order appointing the trustee, and the effect that a change in management might have on the debtor's business and the potential recoveries for creditors. The creditors' committee must also consider the likelihood of success on the merits, and the impact the making of the motion will have on the creditors' committee's relationship with the debtor, and the committee's influence in the case generally, in the event it is denied.

As a general rule, bankruptcy courts are reluctant to appoint trustees in Chapter 11 cases for a number of reasons. First, the appointment of a trustee runs counter to the presumption in the Bankruptcy Code, and Sections 1107(a) and 1108 specifically,[43] that the debtor will continue to operate its business and manage its properties during the course of the case. Second, the appointment of a trustee, who will displace existing management, will often be viewed as a destabilizing event that might jeopardize the debtor's ability to reorganize.

Finally, courts are generally reluctant to appoint a trustee in a Chapter 11 case because of the adverse impact such appointment will have on the reorganization process itself. Appointment of a trustee can slow the progress of the case while the trustee and his professionals familiarize themselves with the debtor's business. Further, the application for such an appointment usually results in substantial litigation among the parties, which may both sidetrack the reorganization and have a destabilizing effect on the business.

As an alternative to the appointment of a trustee, the creditors' committee may seek the appointment of an examiner pursuant to Bankruptcy Code Section 1104(b). Unlike the appointment of a trustee, the appointment of an examiner is a much less dramatic step, which may have little, if any, effect on the business generally. Further, in contrast with the role of a Chapter 11 trustee—whose function is to operate the debtor's business in accordance with his or her reasonable business judgment—the examiner's involvement in the Chapter 11 case is specifically defined by the order authorizing his or her appointment. Thus, courts tend to look more favorably on motions for the appointment of an examiner, as evidenced by the number of recent cases in which examiners have been appointed, including Eastern, Public Service Company of New Hampshire, Southmark, and Revco. On the other hand, the appointment of an examiner may have a substantial impact where the mandate given the examiner by the court is broad, and, among other things, authorizes the examiner to take such steps as he or she may deem reasonable to facilitate a consensual plan.

The standards that must be met for the appointment of an examiner are set forth in Bankruptcy Code Section 1104(b). Pursuant to that section:

(b) If the court does not order the appointment of a trustee . . . on request of a party in interest . . . the court shall order the appointment of an examiner to conduct such an investigation of the debtor as is appropriate, including an investigation of any allegations of fraud, dishonesty, incompetence, misconduct, mismanagement, or irregularity in the management of the affairs of the debtor of or by current or former management of the debtor, if—

(1) such appointment is in the interests of creditors, any equity security holders, and other interests of the estate; or
(2) the debtor's fixed, liquidated, unsecured debts, other than debts for goods, services, or taxes, or owing to an insider, exceed $5,000,000.[44]

The motion seeking the appointment of an examiner should specify the nature and extent of the investigation that the moving party would like the examiner to conduct, and it will often cite specific examples of transactions that justify such investigation. The resulting court order appointing the examiner (assuming it is granted) should be narrow, limiting the scope of the examiner's investigation to the areas specified. On occasion, however, such as in the Eastern Air Lines case, courts have provided examiners with broad mandates, directing not only an investigation into specific areas but also granting carte blanche to the examiner to take such actions as he or she deems necessary to resolve all disputes between the parties and facilitate a consensual reorganization.

Unlike many of the other parties in interest in a Chapter 11 case, the creditors' committee may be uniquely situated to determine whether the appointment of a trustee or examiner is warranted. As discussed earlier, the creditors' committee may request, and is entitled to receive from the debtor, access to a significant amount of information regarding the debtor's business and operations. This will generally include a review of the debtor's books and records, as well as an analysis of any transactions between the debtor and its affiliates or insiders. The conclusions reached upon completion of these tasks will place the creditors' committee in a position to determine whether the appointment of a trustee or examiner is appropriate.

Creditors' committees may also use the threat of the appointment of a trustee or examiner as leverage in negotiations over a plan of reorganization. To the extent the creditors' committee makes good on its threat and files a motion for the appointment of a trustee or examiner, most courts, in the first instance, will opt for the less-drastic alternative of appointing an examiner to facilitate plan negotiations. It is worthwhile to note that the Bankruptcy Code does not specifically authorize the use of examiners for this purpose.[45] The lack of express statutory authority, however, has not stopped courts from authorizing examiners to become involved in plan negotiations as part of their mandate, as evidenced by the appointment of examiners for this purpose, among others, in UNR Industries and Eastern Air Lines.

In deciding whether to move for the appointment of a trustee or examiner, the creditors' committee must weigh the pros and cons associated with each. In connection with the appointment of a trustee, the creditor's committee must take into account the destabilizing effect that the appointment of a trustee might have, especially in high profile Chapter 11 cases. Additionally, the creditors' committee must consider the substantial litigation that will ensue in the event management is unwilling to consent to the creditors' committee's request. Further, the committee must consider the possible loss of influence in the case, as well as the substantial additional costs that could result. On the other hand, the creditors' committee may determine that the benefits associated with the appointment of a trustee far outweigh the potential adverse impact. These benefits might include enhanced public perception of the viability of the entity and the elimination of management, which may be incompetent, or which may have taken actions detrimental to the interests of creditors. It may also enhance the debtor's ability to reorganize by providing the suppliers, customers, and other parties who do business with the debtor with an increased level of confidence in the debtor's viability and the likelihood of its reorganization.

The appointment of an examiner, unlike a trustee, is in most instances less intrusive and, thus, presents the opportunity to obtain the benefits of an independent investigation without substantially impacting the debtor's business. However, the creditors' committee must evaluate, prior to moving for the appointment of an examiner, what impact that appointment might have on the creditors' committee's control over the issues that will be the subject of the examiner's investigation. Once appointed, the examiner's directive will be to investigate and report to the court on the specific matters identified. Fundamentally, once an examiner is appointed, the issues under investigation will no longer be within the substantial control of the creditors' committee. Thus, the creditors' committee may lose the leverage it might otherwise have to use these matters in plan negotiations. Additionally, the examiner's mandate may turn out to be much broader than the committee had initially anticipated, thus further diluting the creditors' committee's power and influence.

As a final matter in evaluating whether to proceed with a motion for the appointment of either a trustee or an examiner, the creditors' committee must take into consideration the fact that it may have little or no control over the selection of the person to be appointed. Further, any trustee or examiner appointed in a Chapter 11 case has a responsibility to all parties in interest and may not be beholden to any particular constituency, including the one who requested his or her appointment. This is an unquantifiable factor that must be considered by the creditors' committee in deciding whether to move for the appointment of a trustee or examiner.

Prosecution of Derivative Actions

In many Chapter 11 cases, the debtor will have potential causes of action against affiliates, its parent company or principals, or preference or fraudulent conveyance actions against third parties, which the debtor may be unwilling to prosecute. In each of these instances, prosecution of the cause of action could result in a substantial benefit to the estate and unsecured creditors. In the debtor's view, however, prosecution may be detrimental to ongoing business relationships or to relationships with its affiliate or principal. Where the debtor unjustifiably refuses to pursue these causes of action, the creditors' committee may need to take the initiative and seek court authorization to prosecute the actions derivatively, in the name of the debtor and for the benefit of the estate.

The ability of the creditor's committee to prosecute derivative actions on behalf of the estate has become increasingly important in light of the large number of leveraged buyouts that have resulted in Chapter 11 filings. In these instances, the unsecured creditors may seek to assert claims against the lending banks and other institutions—with whom the debtor may want to continue doing business—on the theory that the leveraged buyout constituted a fraudulent conveyance. That action, clearly, cannot be prosecuted by the debtor, which was itself a participant in the leveraged buyout and, thus, the creditors' committee may be the only party with standing to prosecute such action for the benefit of the estate.[46]

Case law in this area has provided a standard for determining those instances in which the creditors' committee should be authorized to prosecute a derivative action for the benefit of the estate. Thus, the creditors' committee may seek court authorization[47] to prosecute a derivative action where it can be shown that a colorable claim exists against a third party and that the debtor has unreasonably refused to bring the action.[48] Where this can be shown, the creditors' committee should be authorized by the court to initiate and prosecute the action, in the name of the debtor, for the benefit of the estate and its creditors.

As referred to earlier, the actions that the creditors' committee will generally seek to prosecute will often be against affiliates, insiders, lending institutions, and others with whom the debtor has had an ongoing business relationship. While the debtor, from a business perspective, may believe it reasonable to forego the cause of action in favor of continuing its business relationship, from a creditors' perspective, the increased recovery that might be received if the action is successfully prosecuted (or settled) might substantially outweigh the speculative benefits that the debtor expects to receive. Existing creditors, which may or may not continue to do business with the debtor, will probably not be convinced that speculative future benefits from an ongoing business relationship outweigh the benefits to be derived through prosecution of the action. This is especially true where the proposed recovery to creditors under a plan is substantially less than the face amount of their claims. Additionally, in many cases, the recovery of preferences or fraudulent conveyances may be an essential element to the recovery to be received by creditors pursuant to a plan of reorganization. Thus, it is the obligation of the creditors' committee to analyze potential claims and determine whether they should be brought.

THE CREDITORS' COMMITTEE AS ALLY OR ADVERSARY

Prior to the commencement of a Chapter 11 case, it cannot be determined with any reasonable degree of certainty whether the creditors' committee and the debtor will be allies or adversaries. Fundamentally, most creditors will favor a reorganization that will provide them with an ongoing business relationship. On the other hand, few creditors are willing to sacrifice the payment of a substantial portion of their claims simply to achieve a reorganization. Thus, within the creditor body (particularly between debenture holders and trade creditors) there is an inherent tension between recovery and reorganization. How the creditors' committee ultimately proceeds will depend on the circumstances of the case.

In almost every case, the creditors' committee, at least initially, will be supportive of the debtor's efforts to stabilize the business, to prepare a business plan, and to engage in negotiations regarding a plan of reorganization. To this end, the creditors' committee will generally work with the debtor for at least some time. However, the creditors' committee may, at some point, determine that the path being pursued by the debtor towards reorganization is not in the best interest of creditors or will result in a recovery for creditors that is substantially below what could be achieved through alternate paths, including sale of the entity or liquidation. Thus, the debtor and the creditors' committee may be allies or adversaries depending on the circumstances of the case.

In most cases, after substantial negotiations, the creditors' committee and the debtor will reach agreement on a consensual plan of reorganization. On the other hand, certain cases, including Texaco and Public Service Company of New Hampshire, provide examples of what can happen when the creditors' committee disagrees with the path that the debtor has chosen to pursue. In both of those cases, the creditors' committees decided to pursue a different course, or assist a third party (judgment creditor or acquiror), in an effort to obtain the maximum recovery for unsecured creditors. The Texaco Chapter 11 case, discussed earlier, is one significant example of the creditors' committee parting ways with the debtor and undertaking its own path toward reorganization. By initiating discussions directly with Pennzoil (which Texaco was unwilling to do) and causing the court to modify exclusivity, the creditors' committee forced Texaco into a settlement that brought the Chapter 11 case to a prompt conclusion, avoided the very substantial risk of an adverse result in the United States Supreme Court, and maximized the return for unsecured creditors. As a further example, in Public Service Company of New Hampshire, third-party acquirors approached the creditors' committee and other major parties in interest for their support in what ultimately turned into a bidding war for the company. At that point, the debtor's proposed plan of reorganization was pushed to the side as the potential acquirors jockeyed for the support of the creditors' committee. In these instances, the debtors lost the support of the creditors' committee and, thus, found themselves without control over the proceedings and being forced into positions they would not have been in had there been no creditor representative to force their hand.

CONCLUSION

The creditors' committee, as a fiduciary body representing all of the debtors unsecured creditors, was designed by Congress to provide an effective counterforce to the debtor during the course of a Chapter 11 reorganization. Congress vested the creditors' committee with substantial powers and duties in an effort to eliminate the debtor's leverage over its creditor body and to create a level playing field for the negotiation of a Chapter 11 plan of reorganization. While the debtor will no doubt view the creditors' committee as intruding on its province to manage its business, the debtor should realize that working with the creditors' committee, instead of fighting with it, will ordinarily result in a much more expeditious resolution of the Chapter 11 case. In sum, the creditors' committee's assignment in a Chapter 11 case is to act as a monitor over the actions of the debtor and to negotiate to protect the interests of all unsecured creditors through a plan of reorganization. The creditors' committee and debtor will often disagree on how to reach the ultimate goal of a successful reorganization and, thus, at times may be allies, and at other times adversaries. However, both parties will realize early on that working together and negotiating points of contention will increase the likelihood of a prompt and successful reorganization—for the benefit of all concerned.

ENDNOTES

1. The Bankruptcy Code was initially enacted as the Bankruptcy Reform Act of 1978 (Pub. L. No. 95-598). The Bankruptcy Reform Act of 1978 has since been amended by the Bankruptcy Amendments and Federal Judgeship Act of 1984 (Pub. L. No. 98-353) and the Bankruptcy Judges, United States Trustees and Family Farmer Bankruptcy Act of 1986 (Pub. L. No. 99-554). The Bankruptcy Reform Act of 1978, as amended, is more commonly referred to as the *Bankruptcy Code*. All statutory citations are to the provisions of the Bankruptcy Code currently in effect, unless otherwise specified.
2. 11 U.S.C. Section 1102(a)(1).
3. 11 U.S.C. Section 1102(b)(1).
4. The House Report states that:

    Subsection (b) [of Section 1102] contains precatory language directing the court to appoint the persons holding the seven largest claims against the debtor of the kinds represented on the creditors' committee. . . .

    H.R. Rep. No. 595, 95th Cong., 1st Sess. 401 (1977).
5. See 11 U.S.C. Sections 1126 and 1129.
6. 11 U.S.C. Section 108(a) states that:

    If applicable nonbankruptcy law, an order entered in a nonbankruptcy proceeding, or an agreement fixes a period within which the debtor may commence an action, and such period has not expired before the date of the filing of the petition, the trustee may commence such action only before the later of—
    (1) the end of such period, including any suspension of such period occurring on or after the commencement of the case, or;
    (2) two years after the order for relief.

7. 11 U.S.C. Section 1102(b)(1).
8. Bankruptcy Rule 2007 states, in relevant part, as follows:

    (a) Appointment. In a . . . chapter 11 reorganization case, on application of a party in interest and after notice as the court may direct, the court may appoint as the committee of unsecured creditors required by § 1102(a) of the Code, members of a committee selected before the commencement of the case in accordance with subdivision (b) of this rule.

(b) Selection of Members Committee. The court may find that a committee selected by unsecured creditors before the commencement of a . . . chapter 11 case satisfies the requirements of § 1102(b)(1) of the Code if:

(1) it was selected by a majority in number and amount of unsecured creditors who may vote under § 702(a) of the Code and were present in person or represented at a meeting of which all creditors having unsecured claims of over $1,000 or the 100 unsecured creditors having the largest claims had at least five days notice in writing, and of which meeting written minutes reporting the names of the creditors present or represented and voting and the amounts of their claims were kept and are available for inspection;

(2) all proxies voted at the meeting for the elected committee were solicited pursuant to Bankruptcy Rule 2006 and the lists and statements required by subdivision (e) thereof have been filed with the court; and

(3) the organization of the committee was in all other respects fair and proper.

9. *Id.*
10. See 11 U.S.C. Section 1102(b)(1).
11. See 11 U.S.C. Section 1102(a)(1).
12. Former section 1102(c) provided, in relevant part, that:

On request of a party in interest and after notice and a hearing, the court may change the membership or the size of a committee . . . if the membership of such committee is not representative of the different kinds of claims or interests to be represented.

13. See *In re First Republicbank Corp.,* 95 B.R. 58, 60-61 (Bankr. N.D. Texas 1988). Bankruptcy Code Section 105(a) provides, in relevant part, that:

The court may issue any order, process, or judgment that is necessary or appropriate to carry out the provisions of this title [11]. . . .

14. *In re Sharon Steel Corp.,* 100 B.R. 767, 776 (Bankr. W.D. Pa. 1989); *In re Texaco,* 79 B.R. 560, 566 (Bankr. S.D.N.Y. 1987); *In re Public Service Co. of New Hampshire,* 89 B.R. 1014, 1021, and n.9 (Bankr. D. N.H. 1988); *In re McLean Indus.,* 70 B.R. 852, 856-59 (Bankr. S.D.N.Y. 1987).

15. *In re Mansfield Tire & Rubber Co.*, 39 B.R. 974 (N.D. Ohio 1983).
16. **Compare** *In re Vermont Real Estate Invest. Trust*, 20 B.R. 33 (Bankr. D. Vt. 1982) (spouse of debtor's former president being sued by the debtor, with her husband, for mismanagement and fraud entitled to serve on creditors' committee where spouse was third-largest creditor) **with** *In re Daig Corp.*, 17 B.R. 41, 42 (Bankr. D. Minn. 1981) (holder of largest claim of any of the debtor's suppliers was denied the right to sit on creditors' committee where the creditor's chief operating officer was the father of the debtor's chairperson), and *In re Swolsky*, 55 B.R. 144, 145-46 (Bankr. N.D. Ohio 1985) (creditor, whose wife was Chapter 11 debtor's vice president, bookkeeper, and office manager, was denied membership on creditors' committee).
17. **Compare** *In re Plant Specialties, Inc.*, 59 B.R. 1 (Bankr. W.D. La. 1986) (competitor permitted to participate on creditors' committee) **with** *In re Wilson Foods Corp.*, 31 B.R. 272 (Bankr. W.D. Okla. 1983) (denying competitor's appointment to creditors' committee).
18. **Compare** *In re Altair Airlines, Inc.*, 727 F.2d 88 (3d Cir. 1984), *In re Northeast Dairy Cooperative Federation, Inc.*, 59 B.R. 531 (Bankr. N.D.N.Y. 1986), and *In re Enduro Stainless, Inc.*, 59 B.R. 603 (Bankr. N.D. Ohio 1986) (permitting unions to serve on statutory creditors' committee) **with** *In re Allied Delivery Systems Co.*, 52 B.R. 85 (Bankr. N.D. Ohio 1985) (denying union's request for appointment to creditors' committee).
19. *In re Grynberg*, 10 B.R. 256 (Bankr. D. Colo. 1981).
20. **See** cases cited in endnotes 16 through 19, *supra*.
21. **See** *In re Vermont Real Estate Invest. Trust*, 20 B.R. 33 (Bankr. D. Vt. 1982) (spouse of debtor's former president being sued by debtor, along with her husband, for fraud and mismanagement, entitled to serve on creditors' committee on condition that she be prohibited from participating in any discussions of the committee regarding the lawsuit).
22. 11 U.S.C. Section 1103.
23. 11 U.S.C. Section 1109(b).
24. **See,** generally, 11 U.S.C. Section 362(a).
25. 11 U.S.C. Section 1103(a).
26. 11 U.S.C. Section 1103(b).
27. 11 U.S.C. Section 330(a).
28. 11 U.S.C. Section 331 states that:

> A trustee, an examiner, a debtor's attorney, or any professional person employed under section 327 or 1103 of this title may apply to the court not more than once every 120 days after an order for relief in a case under this title, or more often if the court permits, for

compensation for services rendered before the date of such an application or reimbursement for expenses incurred before such date as provided under section 330 of this title. After notice and a hearing, the court may allow and disburse to such applicant such compensation or reimbursement.

29. See 11 U.S.C. Section 1103(c)(1).
30. See 11 U.S.C. Sections 1107(a) and 1108, which authorize a debtor to remain in possession of its assets and to continue operating its business and managing its properties during a Chapter 11 case.
31. See 11 U.S.C. Section 1103(c)(2).
32. In fact, the bylaw provision should cover not only information received from the debtor but also information and documents generated by the creditors' committee, its professionals and members, as well as the deliberations of the committee itself. The following is an example of a standard confidentiality provision:

> All (*a*) nonpublic information, documents, and matters of whatever nature and kind disclosed to the committee, (*b*) information or documents generated by the committee, or by the professionals employed by the committee, or by members of or counsel to the committee for the use of the committee, and (*c*) committee discussions and the minutes thereof are confidential and shall not be disclosed or revealed to third parties. Notwithstanding the above, a member may share any such information, documents, and matters with its attorneys and financial consultants, provided that any such information, documents, and matters shall be used only in connection with the conduct of committee business, and provided further that the person or entity receiving such disclosure agrees to be and is bound by these rules of confidentiality. To comply with their obligations as members, members who are from time to time contacted by constituent unsecured creditors or are otherwise obligated to report to such creditors may impart to such creditors public information supplied by the debtor or such other information as the chairman or the committee, on advice of counsel, may approve.

33. See 11 U.S.C. Section 1103(c)(3).
34. See 11 U.S.C. Sections 1103(a) and 330.
35. See 11 U.S.C. Section 1103(c)(2).
36. Bankruptcy Code Section 1121 provides, in relevant part, that:

> (a) The debtor may file a plan with a petition commencing a voluntary case, or at any time in a voluntary case or an involuntary case.

> (b) Except as otherwise provided in this section, only the debtor may file a plan until after 120 days after the date of the order for relief under this chapter.
>
> (c) Any party in interest, including the debtor, the trustee, a creditors' committee, an equity security holders' committee, a creditor, an equity security holder, or any indenture trustee, may file a plan if and only if—
>
> > (1) a trustee has been appointed under this chapter;
> >
> > (2) the debtor has not filed a plan before 120 days after the date of the order for relief under this chapter; or
> >
> > (3) the debtor has not filed a plan that has been accepted, before 180 days after the date of the order for relief under this chapter. . . .
>
> (d) on request of a party in interest made within the periods specified in subsections (b) and (c) of this section and after notice and a hearing, the court may for cause reduce or increase the 120-day period or 180-day period referred to in this section.

37. See 11 U.S.C. Section 1121(d).
38. See 11 U.S.C. Section 1121(c).
39. 11 U.S.C. Section 1103(c)(4).
40. 11 U.S.C. Section 1104(a).
41. See 11 U.S.C. Section 1108.
42. See 11 U.S.C. Section 1104(c)(1).
43. See endnote 30, *supra*.
44. 11 U.S.C. Section 1104(b).
45. See 11 U.S.C. Section 1104(b), which authorizes the appointment of an examiner to

    > . . . conduct such an investigation of the debtor as is appropriate, including an investigation of any allegations of fraud, dishonesty, incompetence, misconduct, mismanagement, or irregularity in the management of the affairs of the debtor of or by current or former management of the debtor. . . .

    Nothing in Section 1104(b) purports to authorize the appointment of an examiner for the purpose of facilitating plan negotiations.
46. *In re Ohio Corrugating Co.*, 70 B.R. 920 (Bankr. N.D. Ohio 1987).
47. The majority of courts have held that the creditors' committee must obtain court authorization before commencing the action. *In re Automated Business Systems, Inc.*, 642 F.2d 200 (6th Cir. 1981). **See also** 2A *Collier on Bankruptcy* § 47.03 at 1744.1 (14th ed. 1978); *Gochenour* v. *George and Frances Ball Foundation*, 35 F. Supp. 508 (D.C.

Ind. 1940), *aff'd,* 117 F.2d 259 (7th Cir.), *cert. denied,* 313 U.S. 566 (1941); *In re Toledo Equip. Co.,* 35 B.R. 315 (Bankr. N.D. Ohio 1983); *In re Evergreen Valley Resort, Inc.,* 27 B.R. 75 (Bankr. D. Me. 1983).

Some courts, however, have held that a creditors' committee has an implied right to commence such suits. See *In re Jones,* 37 B.R. 969 (Bankr. N.D. Tex. 1984); *In re Monsour Medical Center,* 5 B.R. 715 (Bankr. W.D. Pa. 1980).

48. *In re Xonics Photochemical, Inc.,* 841 F.2d 198 (7th Cir. 1988); *In re Automated Business Systems, Inc.,* 642 F.2d 200 (6th Cir. 1981); *In re Jones,* 37 B.R. 969 (Bankr. N.D. Tex. 1984).

CHAPTER 13

THE LAWYER'S ROLE IN REPRESENTING THE DISTRESSED COMPANY

Myron Trepper, Esq.
Willkie, Farr & Gallagher

The role that counsel to a financially troubled entity plays in a workout is better defined in terms of responsibility than role. Since most lawyers do not lack for ego, there is a tendency to define one's role in any engagement in such terms as *key, essential,* or *critical.* This may be a liability in a major workout where it is necessary to sublimate one's personality to a process, to guide rather than force, and to lead through calm analytical skills rather than by overaggressive, ego-gratifying displays of unnecessary advocacy.

Since no two lawyers will approach a case in precisely the same way, this chapter is intended to describe the responsibility and role of the debtor's lawyer from the perspective of one who has toiled in that vineyard for almost 20 years and who has had the opportunity to play a role in many major workouts and observe the process as managed by others as well as myself. As a preliminary matter I would suggest that, as with most complicated issues, there is no single "right way" to do things. Flexibility of thought and attitude are critical characteristics for one who would successfully represent a distressed enterprise in a crisis environment. There follow some suggestions for playing an effective and constructive role in a major turnaround situation.

UNDERSTAND THE BUSINESS

Most insolvency specialists have had no prior relationship with the client. If the company has previously been a client of the lawyer's firm, it is likely that the relationship has been established by other attorneys who have dealt with the client on other issues and under extremely different circumstances. If the company is not a firm client, then an entirely new relationship must develop, not only with management but with the company's regular counsel and other advisors. It is extremely important that the advisory relationship get off on the right foot. A formal judicial reorganization proceeding or an out-of-court workout is a lengthy, arduous, and often intense undertaking. Personal and professional antagonisms can only exacerbate an already difficult situation and should be avoided.

Make an effort to understand your client's business and its position in its industry. Assess as early as possible the gravity of the financial crisis that has caused your involvement. The prospects for the successful reorganization of a troubled company may be measured in many circumstances by the type of business involved. Some businesses can survive a restructuring with no substantial adverse effect on their ongoing operations, while with others even the intimation of financial difficulties portends disaster. While generalizations are always suspect, it appears that certain enterprises can better withstand the damage to a business that is inevitably entailed in a reorganization or restructuring.

Companies operating retail businesses that typically suffer the effects of a cyclical economy are able, generally (but not always, as is demonstrated by the recent demise of B. Altman & Company, Alcott & Andrews, Frost Brothers, and others), to work through the reorganization environment successfully. Since these businesses are consumer driven and, therefore, likely to maintain a revenue stream if adequate merchandise is on hand, the effects of a financial crisis can be more easily weathered while the process of restructuring the business is commenced. The recent publicity attendant to the mammoth Allied and Federated cases seems to confirm this prevailing attitude, although those businesses may be of such magnitude as to be sui generis for analytic purposes.

Likewise, manufacturing businesses that can continue to obtain raw material supplies and maintain output while restructuring can, in many instances, benefit from a debt moratorium environment, using the opportunity to terminate inefficient operations, reduce costs, and generally improve their competitive position.

At the other end of the spectrum are businesses whose foundations are constructed upon customer confidence and perceptions of economic strength and confidence, such as financial services businesses that solicit, hold, and invest the funds of others. Enterprises, such as these, are likely to be damaged most severely, and in most instances irreparably, by even the hint of financial difficulties. Since many of these businesses or their operating affiliates may be subject to regulatory control at the federal or state level, prospects for successfully reorganizing their capital and business structures are, in most instances, extremely bleak.

The experienced advisor will endeavor to quickly learn as much as possible about the nature of the client's business to provide competent counsel. It is critical that counsel bring an element of objectivity to the situation. Advocacy can and should come in due course, once an overall game plan is developed. Your client must understand what is possible. There is simply no room for an unreasonably optimistic outlook in the early days of a financial crisis. Clinical analysis must be undertaken and a realistic near- and long-term strategy must be established.

UNDERSTAND THE LEGAL ENTITY AND DEBT STRUCTURE

An attorney must not only understand the client's business but must also quickly gain an understanding of the client's legal entity and debt structure. In today's world of complex recapitalizations and highly leveraged transactions, an understanding of the corporate structure, the various debt obligations, and where they reside is critical to effectively advising the client. Recognizing the different legal rights of creditor groups, depending on the nature of their indebtedness and their obligor, is absolutely essential to developing a credible approach to restructuring.

If an entity has a traditional holding company/subsidiary structure and the indebtedness to be restructured affects the holding company only, the negotiating dynamic is significantly different than where subsidiaries have guaranteed or are jointly liable for the debts of their direct and indirect affiliated corporations.

If as in most instances some debt is secured, other rules of engagement are operative between the borrower and the secured creditors and among the secured and unsecured creditors and the company. The debtor's lawyer must quickly grasp the relative strengths and weaknesses of the client's position vis-a-vis creditors, secured and unsecured, and the strengths and weaknesses of the positions of various creditor groups in relation to other groups. It is extremely difficult to debate with and attempt to harmonize the views of creditors in a workout unless you have an in-depth understanding of their legal and practical positions. Therefore, the reorganization lawyer must be a relatively quick study.

Review the documents that are immediately available, ask questions, and listen carefully to the responses. Interview your client, assimilate as much as you can as quickly as possible, and try not to interrupt, which is difficult for most of us. In recounting the circumstances that have created the immediate financial crisis, your client will often ramble and reach further back in history than the situation warrants. Try to be patient, since history can be important. Guide the discussion, do not dominate it.

If as in most instances the reorganization lawyer is one of the last outside advisors to be brought in, try to utilize the learning curve of other outside advisors who may have been on the scene longer than you. Talk to the company's accountants, investment bankers, consultants, and any other advisory resource available. You will gain much from these discussions, since these advisors are likely to be more dispassionate and have better understood the situation than the client. They probably have had exposure to creditor representatives and are certainly likely to be more objective than the business people. They will also have formed preliminary views about the quality and depth of management, of which more will be said later.

DEVELOP AN UNDERSTANDING OF CASH AND FINANCING RESOURCES

Critical to your initial analysis is the identification of the company's sources of cash, whether internally generated or obtained from third-party financings. Without question, cash is the key component in any workout. No matter how inherently viable a business may be, I have never seen one that runs without cash. As a general rule, the party in control of the cash will have the greatest influence on the outcome of the workout.

It is important to grasp the financing resources and needs of the company. Since most businesses operate with the support of credit arrangements generally provided by banks or commercial finance companies, an initial inquiry should focus on the current status of the debtor's credit facilities. You should determine quickly whether credit lines are available to be drawn upon. If there are no existing defaults and there is a borrowing base, a quick decision should be made on whether to draw under existing facilities, even if the company has adequate cash to meet its current and near-term needs. Bear in mind that a downward spiral in operations probably has not reached its low point in the early stages of a workout, and, therefore, the company may well be within borrowing formulas established under existing loan agreements.

However, the rate of decline generally accelerates rapidly, and covenant defaults are often upon you more quickly than anticipated. In addition, the company probably has not yet made the financial statement adjustments that may be dictated by its fiscal crisis, and therefore, it will not be clear whether net worth maintenance and similar loan agreement tests have been breached. During this period, the company will have its last unobstructed opportunity to obtain cash under its existing facilities, and every effort should be made to draw on existing credit lines and build a war chest of cash with which to enter the negotiating arena. Rest assured that, if your client fails to obtain the cash available to it under existing facilities, the terms of lending under new facilities will be significantly less favorable.

Often, some of the more interesting negotiating dynamics occur early in a workout, when a financially distressed borrower that is not in default under existing credit lines seeks to obtain funds under its existing facilities. Lenders that have carefully monitored the deteriorating financial condition of their borrower may often take a hard-line position when a borrowing is requested. This may be your first major confrontation. If a borrower can obtain funds available to it, even if the funds are not immediately required for use in the business, it should in almost all instances press for the cash. Lenders must think long and hard about refusing to advance in the absence of a tangible default under a contractually committed facility, and you should take advantage of this circumstance before it disappears in a cloud of actual or technical defaults.

It may be almost too basic to note, but it is critical to assure that all of the company's cash is deposited in accounts maintained at institutions that are not creditors. Almost all lending and deposit agreements create a contractual right of offset for the institution. Under Section 553 of the Bankruptcy Code, this right to offset creates a secured claim, which would require a debtor-in-possession to provide adequate protection[1] to the lender to obtain a release of funds. It would be extraordinarily embarrassing for the reorganization specialist to leave his or her client vulnerable to offset when the opportunity to move funds to safer harbors is readily available.

INVOLVING THE CONSTITUENCIES

It is important to maintain a constructive dialogue with your client's institutional creditors. This effort should focus on making major creditors a part of the early workout process. A company's bank lenders, secured or unsecured, are the most likely sources of ongoing financing for the troubled enterprise. Many times, participating in newly constructed financing mechanisms enables existing lenders to improve their position in the workout. The most obvious improvement device is to convert unsecured debt to secured debt. Very often a lender group will provide badly needed interim financing only if its current unsecured position is fully secured by previously unpledged assets. Because of an emergent condition, a lender may be looked to for a relatively small credit line and, as part of the negotiations, will demand security for new advances and for its current position, which is likely to be much larger in dollars. This practice, which is often designed to provide a borrower with enough cash and credit lines to labor through a relatively short period, helps the lender immensely. It can improve its position and keep its borrower alive (albeit in extremis) until the opportunity to challenge its liens in a subsequent bankruptcy is better insulated.[2]

In advising your client, be sure you understand the strengths and weaknesses of the lender's position. If the lender is unsecured, bargain hard for a facility that will sustain your client for a reasonable period in an out-of-court environment before agreeing to pledge previously unencumbered assets. You won't have this opportunity again, since the pledge is not likely to be dissolved voluntarily.

If lenders are secured when you are first engaged, examine the lender's position carefully. Be sure that all liens are properly perfected. For example, if a part of the collateral is a pledge of an ownership interest in a subsidiary, has the lender actually taken physical possession of the stock certificates representing such ownership? Very often recently modified financings are done hurriedly, and sometimes the entire package is not put together before new money is advanced.

Check the timing and funds flow. Were the liens recently granted? Are the banks secured by guarantees from affiliates that may have received no economic benefit from the advances?[3] You won't have a lot to work with in your initial negotiations, and you need any advantage you can identify. The intensity of your advocacy must be related to reality. Simply threatening a precipitous bankruptcy filing will get you little benefit and may impair your ability to effectively negotiate a reasonably structured financing for the client. It will also in most instances cause your client, which is trying to avoid bankruptcy, some serious business problems and could affect your relationship with the lenders for the long term.

It is important to understand that, in negotiating a new facility, lenders obtain additional measures of control over your client. Once economic terms have been agreed upon, the lenders will begin the painful process of modifying existing covenants to tighten controls on the company and to add new covenants and events of default that are designed to reflect the current situation, all of which are designed to put the borrower in an extremely restricted business environment. In this type of negotiation, the experienced workout lawyer's advice is critical. It simply makes no sense to agree to lending terms and covenants that are unduly restrictive and harmful, if not fatal, to the restructuring effort. Signing up for a deal that you know will result in a default in a very short time is irresponsible, and counsel and other advisors should negotiate vigorously for reasonable terms. Unless compelling business reasons exist, you should not permit your client to agree to a recast financing that will cripple its ability to operate, no matter what oral assurances of future flexibility you hear from lenders and their counsel.

I have too often seen a desperate client accept a lender's assurance that the company can always come back later for covenant relief, only to find a chronic condition of amnesia prevailing when you return to the bargaining table. Also remember that people you deal with today may be transferred to different positions or leave the institution by the time you next confront the lender. It is hard to hold a new person to a predecessor's commitment.

An important consideration in this element of the process is to help your client in preparing its presentations to lenders to support financing. The projections, cash flows, and budgets your client provides will be the maximum it will receive and rarely will you obtain what you request. Leave reasonable negotiating room, no matter how difficult the environment and how immediate the need.

Use other creditor groups as your ally. If creditor groups have organized and are active, keep their attitudes and positions in mind. Bear in mind that lenders seeking to improve their position about the company are also improving their position against other creditors. When overreaching starts, you need to consider the position of others. You should not construct a deal that your client cannot explain, support, and defend to other creditor groups. If you've done your job responsibly, others may be unhappy; but, unless they are prepared to create a new facility and make funds available on more favorable terms they cannot criticize you and your client if the bargain reasonably reflects the situation.

ADVISING THE BOARD OF DIRECTORS

The board of directors of a troubled company finds itself in a unique and normally uncomfortable position dictated by many factors. Most directors, no matter how long their tenure with a company, do not and are not expected to have intimate familiarity with the day-to-day operations of the business. Therefore, a financial crisis is likely to be more a late-arriving surprise to the board than to management, and simply comprehending the magnitude and complexity of the situation and possible alternative solutions is a major undertaking.

A financial crisis takes a substantial toll on directors of a financially troubled company. It requires increased commitments of time and more intense analytical activity under tighter time constraints than directors are accustomed to accommodating. Further exacerbating the environment are concerns about requirements of public disclosure of significant events and possible personal exposure of the directors to shareholders and others.

It is most important to try to focus the board on the current situation and its solutions and the legal environment in which the board now is functioning. Since I am not an expert in the securities laws, I try to make sure that an experienced securities lawyer is part of the team so the board has continuing advice on the requirements of the securities laws and other corporate governance issues.

Encouraging a board not to dwell on history and diverting the directors attention away from irrelevant issues is often a major task. You must make the board understand the delicate balance it confronts. The directors certainly must have the enterprise, its employees, and the customers as a primary concern; but they must understand that, if the company is insolvent or is sliding inexorably towards insolvency, their primary perspective of representing shareholders exclusively must be altered. Directors must be counseled that they are beginning to undertake new obligations to creditors who, in an insolvency situation, are arguably becoming shareholders, albeit involuntarily.

Conceptually, it is often difficult to bring directors of a floundering enterprise to the realization that their fiduciary obligations are undergoing a significant metamorphosis. Most individuals who serve as directors have enjoyed considerable success in their careers and are likely to be persons of substantial financial means with major roles in other ventures. They are often unsuited to a role as a senior crew member on a ship that may be taking on water. It is essential that the reorganization lawyer communicate effectively and forcefully with the directors.

Since most directors of public companies perceive their primary obligation correctly to be that of the guardian of the interests of the company's shareholders, it often comes as a surprise to these individuals that courts have held that directors of an insolvent corporation owe a primary fiduciary duty to the corporation's creditors. Directors must understand that it may be that this shifting of duty occurs prior to actual insolvency, as the company's financial results and balance sheets erode on an accelerated basis.[4]

Given the new environment in which the board is operating, it is most important to impress upon the members what responsibilities the board has and the role it must play in the restructuring effort. You must counsel the board that the principles by which it has traditionally guided itself may not be operative. Courts that have held that the assets of an insolvent corporation are considered to be held in trust for the benefit of the entity's creditors have generally held that the directors, as trustees, must exercise such care and skill as a man of ordinary prudence would exercise in dealing with his own property.[5]

This standard of care is more stringent than the business judgment rule generally applicable to directors and, therefore, requires a greater circumspection by the board and a more intense and comprehensive analysis of problems and issues than many boards are accustomed to be undertaking. The crisis environment attendant to economic adversity always places greater demand on the time and efforts of the directors than their traditional roles previously dictated. Boards faced with these issues should seek the most sophisticated and experienced professional advisory services available.

As an advisor, you must appreciate that most often you are a new face with no corporate family history. The personal relationships between independent and management directors often have developed over many years and the environment can be emotional, superheated, and delicate. You must try to avoid the creation of a siege mentality. Try to clinically analyze the situation, not only from a legal rights point of view but from a strategic viewpoint. Give the board precise analyses of the current situation from the perspective of someone who has been there before. I have found that long complicated lectures assessing legal rights and analyzing case law is the fastest route to losing the attention of an already agitated group. Directors assume that you know what you're doing or you wouldn't have been hired. They need you to give them concise views of the alternatives available and to help them develop a strategy. You are not there to run a two-week seminar on fraudulent conveyances, use of cash collateral, and other esoterica. These issues can be discussed in a short-form analysis while you help the board help management to constructively approach the workout.

It is helpful for the board to understand the difference between the judicial and nonjudicial environment. Attempting an out-of-court restructuring is a difficult exercise, in general, and the board must understand the differences between the Chapter 11 and out-of-court alternatives. First, the board must appreciate that, unless a trustee is appointed under Chapter 11, which rarely occurs, the corporate governance of the enterprise is unaltered. It is surprising that many sophisticated businessmen believe that Chapter 11 means the automatic appointment of a trustee, which of course it does not.[6]

Try to explain to directors that continued service on the board after a Chapter 11 filing may be to their benefit. In the first instance, their business judgment on particular issues will be reviewed and challenged by creditor representatives appointed for that purpose, and, ultimately, be scrutinized by a bankruptcy court. Moreover those directors who continue to serve may be more likely to continue to be indemnified by the corporation pursuant to its bylaws.[7] The board must understand its obligations and responsibilities and must appreciate, as well, the problems that management is confronting on a daily basis.

COUNSELING MANAGEMENT

Senior management of a troubled company can be likened to advance platoons taking heavy artillery in an unfamiliar environment. First and foremost try to become a part of a team. Don't be overbearing and pedagogical. Take time to understand the problems and the people. If at all possible, sit quietly with management and try to make the managers understand what they are likely to encounter. Major workouts are long and often frustrating. Few complex financial problems can be resolved quickly and simply.

Make management understand that its traditional business relationships are changing. The banker the managers went to for loans has probably transferred the file to a workout group within the bank. The interests of the new person assigned to the credit are completely different, and the style and attitude of the workout specialist is likely to be diametrically opposite to the lending officer.

Condition management for the almost insatiable desire of creditors to receive current and understandable financial information about the company. It is important that management understand that creditors normally don't pay much attention to an enterprise that keeps its obligations current. When defaults occur, creditors usually have some catching up to do. Generally, the demands of creditors for information range from intolerable to totally unrealistic. The only demands more extreme than these are the time frames that run a spectrum from "today," "by the end of the week," to at most "within 10 days after the end of a month."

Counsel your client to accommodate these requests by inviting creditors and their advisors to meet with you and understand what can be produced and when. Use the creditors' advisors as your agents when you can. Make sure professionals, such as accounting firms, investment bankers, and other consultants, help you with creditors in this area. Ask them to help design formats for presentation of information that is acceptable to them and, therefore, should be acceptable to their clients. You will not find a perfect format or schedule; but you can be sure that exclusionary policies will be damaging to your client's efforts, while a process of inclusion will aid you immensely.

It is important to try to allocate responsibility among senior management and line employees. The requirements of a workout create demands upon a company that rarely can be satisfied by a management team that is operations oriented. I strongly recommend that management try to designate a reorganization team having little or no responsibility for day-to-day operation of the business and almost exclusive responsibility for dealing with the demands of creditors and their advisors. This group should be led by a level-headed senior financial officer who has experience dealing with financial institutions and complicated financial problems. The individual should understand the company, its capital structure, and the problems that caused the financial crisis. Beyond this senior manager, the rest of the team should come from inside the company, if possible. It is often enlightening to a senior management group to find that buried within multilayered overhead structures are extremely talented people who have previously been isolated in specialty areas or otherwise underutilized. These resources should be tapped and encouraged. If the staffing is inadequate, extra expense should be incurred by bringing people in from outside the company or by using the resources of advisors, such as accounting and consulting firms. You cannot fashion a restructuring proposal until everyone in the workout is working off the same page of underlying financial facts. The faster you get there, even if it means increased expense in the near term, the more successful the effort is likely to be.

If you can isolate a reorganization group, you must also understand the problems of operations. Reorganization lawyers need to be more proactive than traditional advisors. You're not there solely to tell your client whether a transaction or a strategy has legal flaws or risks. You have to challenge business decisions, question the strategies, and generally help guide the process. Major decisions, such as the sale of a significant business unit or asset, the alteration of a historical business focus, and similar issues, must be viewed in the context of the overall near, intermediate, and long-term perspective of the workout.

It is rare that a single decision in a large complicated restructuring can be identified as the cause of success or failure of the program. Each decision leads to the next and drives the process in a particular direction. Your client must understand that it must carefully and clinically analyze its business and assets to develop a strategic approach to the restructuring.

Management bred in an environment of ready access to the capital markets to fund long-term growth and interim working capital must be reoriented to the arduous environment of crisis management. The reorganization lawyer, together with other experienced advisors, must help develop a new attitude toward the business and the future. Realism in its starkest sense must often replace unrealistic views of the future. Present values tend to control over the long-term values. Tensions abound—and the lawyer is in the middle.

Possibly the most important decision management and the board must make in this regard is whether to pursue the out-of-court restructuring or to seek Chapter 11 protection. Your counsel here is absolutely critical.

IN OR OUT OF COURT

The strategic considerations of whether to seek a nonjudicial restructuring and recapitalization of a troubled enterprise, versus immediate commencement of reorganization proceedings under

Chapter 11 of the Bankruptcy Code, have become more difficult and challenging in recent years. The highly leveraged transactions that were prevalent in the 1980s have, in their concentration on new forms of debt, created a new emphasis on previously infrequently utilized mechanisms available under the securities laws, which may enable an enterprise to accomplish an expeditious restructuring without the increased burden and substantially greater costs of judicial reorganization. These transactions may be accomplished through the vehicle of exchange offers, pursuant to which private and publicly held debt and equity of an entity is exchanged for combinations of cash and of new and substantially different securities (usually more concentrated in the form of equity) in recapitalizations designed to enable the issuer to avoid bankruptcy proceedings and recast its balance sheet in a manner more consistent with its cash flows, debt capacity, and asset base.

The reorganization lawyer must understand the availability of these alternatives as an approach to a client's financial problems. Historically, insolvency specialists were inclined to pursue and recommend a Chapter 11 proceeding in almost all cases, other than those where there was a single creditor or a very small group of creditors with whom to negotiate, or where substantially all of the debt was secured by the assets of the debtor. In those relatively unusual and limited situations, it was generally prudent to pursue negotiations with small groups, since the Chapter 11 environment would not significantly change the negotiation dynamics or meaningfully alter the relative bargaining positions of the parties. Where, however, the reorganization lawyer encountered a complex debt and capital structure, with multiple creditor and equity classes to reorganize, each having independent claims against and interests in the enterprise and, in most situations, differing legal rights among themselves, the conventional wisdom was generally that a comprehensive restructuring could not be achieved without judicial intervention.

It is difficult to suggest that there has been a major structural change in today's environment, but it is certainly clear that there is a more conducive atmosphere for out-of-court solutions today, and it is most important for the lawyer retained to help a troubled company to carefully guide the client through the alternatives. There is no reason to recommend a precipitous leap into a Chapter 11 proceeding unless business circumstances or pending creditor actions offer no alternative. If your client's problems are identifiable and possibly curable by a debt readjustment that can be designed and implemented with dispatch, this alternative should be carefully explored and pursued. This is where experienced counsel can play a pivotal role.

There is a tendency on the part of management to be unwilling or unprepared to start a dialogue with the entity's major creditors. This is understandable, since management is accustomed to dealing with creditors in a totally different environment, where institutions and individuals were discussing details of new money facilities and trade credit terms, rather than dealing with obligations in actual or technical default. The lawyer and other outside advisors must take a great measure of control in this area. Key creditor groups should be identified. In the traditional structure, there will probably be a syndicate of banks holding senior claims often secured by some or all of the borrower's assets. Inquiry should be made about whether the client has had communication with these creditors, whether a group has been organized, whether advisors to the group have been engaged, and whether the institutional responsibility for the credit has been transferred from the originating lending officer or group to the lender's workout or equivalent department. This can be important information, since discussions with workout specialists representing financial institutions are markedly different than discussions with the parties originally responsible for making and monitoring the loan.

Counsel should begin a dialogue with lenders and their advisors as soon as possible. When representing a creditor, an interest holder, or a potential investor in a workout, I take great comfort in knowing that the debtor has engaged competent, experienced advisors who will bring a fresh and hopefully objective approach to the problem. Creditors and their legal and financial advisors are by the nature of the relationship in an adversarial position to you and your client. As in any potentially contentious environment, the reorganization lawyer has the opportunity to become part of the problem or part of the solution.

* Filing a Chapter 11 petition should in most instances be the last step taken after a careful inquiry is made about whether reorganization out of court is feasible and, if it is determined to be possible, after reasonable efforts to accomplish a nonjudicial restructuring

have been attempted. How much time and effort is expended on an out-of-court alternative varies from case to case, but some guiding principles are generally applicable.

As previously suggested, assess the nature of the business you are representing. If Chapter 11 is more likely to be destructive to the enterprise, efforts at an out-of-court solution should be aggressively pursued. Interrogate the client and consult with other advisors to the company on this issue. Almost every management considers Chapter 11 proceedings to be the end of the world and will argue endlessly that values in the business will deteriorate exponentially once the petition is filed. While this may be the case in a special circumstance, it is more likely that steps can be taken and strategies developed to significantly ameliorate the expected disastrous effects of a Chapter 11 proceeding. This is where the lawyer as psychologist takes over, since it is sometimes hard to define the point when an executive's business logic begins to be clouded by personal emotions.

It is often much easier to argue about why Chapter 11 will be a disaster than to plan for and analyze damage-control strategies in contemplation of a Chapter 11 proceeding. You are often dealing with fragile personal egos. Highly successful business people, who have previously enjoyed and basked in the limelight of success and the financial rewards that accompany it, are often unable or unwilling to deal with the public admission of business reversal that is a part of the workout process. Being overbearing and unnecessarily inflexible here won't help at all. Long hours of discussion and analysis are needed before the game plan is developed and the team is prepared to execute it.

As part of this process, you must assess whether your client's problems can be solved out of court. To do so, you again must know what needs to be done. Most troubled companies will have to reduce their size and scope to reorganize successfully. Generally, assets will have to be sold. You must analyze with your client the many issues attendant to asset dispositions and the prospect of selling major assets or business segments where the financial distress and the otherwise tenuous condition of the seller is publicly known.

It may be more appropriate to sell assets in a Chapter 11 proceeding than as part of a nonjudicial workout. Since the out-of-court environment is far more uncertain in result and duration, buyers of assets have the upper hand in most negotiations. Generally, the longer the process, the greater the deterioration in the business, and the more inclined the seller becomes to shed assets at prices that may be significantly less than their real value, especially if the cash is needed to finance operations and restructuring.

It may be far more difficult to sell assets in the out-of-court arena, because an insolvent or nearly insolvent seller may not be able to make the representations and warranties that are standard in an asset or stock sale transaction. Usually, counsel to a purchaser will be extremely concerned about risks to a buyer acquiring property from a financially troubled seller. These concerns are generally addressed by requests for opinions of seller's counsel regarding possible fradulent conveyance attacks and other related issues. These opinions, representations, and warranties are usually unavailable, or, if available, are couched in such equivocal terms that the buyer may perceive itself at significant risk and will either refuse to proceed or seek to reflect the increased risk in a severe price reduction.

Moreover, the sale of an asset or business segment may require formal consents or waivers from creditors holding security interests in the assets or having contractual covenants in agreements, indentures, or other instruments that prohibit sales or limit the ability to sell assets without prior approval. Negotiating these consents is usually very difficult and may result in creditors seeking to exact preferential treatment with respect to the proceeds of sale, thereby increasing tensions with other groups in the workout.

As a general legal matter, Chapter 11 solves this problem. Section 363 of the Bankruptcy Code provides for sales of assets out of the ordinary course of business after a full hearing in the bankruptcy court; and it further provides that, if a sale is approved, the assets may be conveyed free and clear of liens and encumbrances of any nature. Buyers are enamored of this section and procedure, since they obtain a judicial insurance policy. Creditors generally prefer the procedure, because the proceeds of sale are most often held subject to further proceedings in the Chapter 11 case, unless there is an undisputed secured claim to the proceeds, in which event the secured creditor is ecstatic, because it is likely to receive the proceeds.

Boards of directors and management can likewise take great comfort in this approach, since the court will generally not approve a sale until after an evidentiary hearing, which reviews the business judgment underlying the determination to sell. Therefore, in approving a sale, a court will be endorsing the business judgment of management and the board. Moreover, all bankruptcy courts, except in extreme emergencies, require (1) evidence that all reasonable efforts have been made to sell the asset and that the price being paid constitutes the best price and transaction available and (2) a hearing process that contemplates a full auction allowing a final opportunity for higher and better offers, even when presented with a fully negotiated transaction. For all these reasons, the bankruptcy court is no longer a forum for bottom-fishing bargain hunters but, rather, more a forum for maximizing asset value. If major asset sales are contemplated in a restructure, it is likely that Chapter 11 is the more viable solution.

Reducing the size of the business usually means more than simply adopting an asset divestiture program. If the economic analysis dictates a smaller, leaner core business around which to restructure, which in almost all situations is the operative case, then an overhead reduction program is also required. Reducing overhead in a troubled company is a cumbersome and painful exercise. Achieving massive expense reductions in a nonbankruptcy environment is often problematical. Working with the client and other advisors to help devise an overhead reduction program and forcing the implementation of the project is another responsibility that counsel must undertake.

Determinations of what is needed to reduce overhead will be a significant element in the decision about whether to pursue the out-of-court route. If cost cutting means reducing the number of employees by hundreds or even thousands, it is necessary to determine the cost of layoffs or terminations in terms of severance obligations and other costs. This is a painful process, since you are dealing with people, not buildings and equipment. Making judgments solely on the basis of dollar costs is impossible for management, since the business people have an emotional stake in their employee community and often have strong personal ties with individuals destined for termination. Here objectivity from outside advisors is especially important. If severance costs as part of an overhead reduction program are projected in the millions of dollars (remember—control the cash) a Chapter 11 filing must be considered. Employees terminated prior to a filing are creditors having only limited priority for payment of severance, bonuses, and other accurals.[8] Paying higher sums for severance may be the right emotional decision but the wrong business decision. The client needs help here.

Cost reduction often means eliminating premises and equipment held under long-term leases. Breaching these agreements can often create huge claims. These types of claims are more easily dealt with in Chapter 11 proceedings, where they are simply unsecured claims and, more significantly in the case of real property leases and employment contracts, subject to statutory damage limitations.[9]

For example, if a retail chain wants to reorganize by closing hundreds of unprofitable stores, realistic advice would require the lawyer to recommend a Chapter 11 filing, since negotiating with hundreds of lessors to settle their claims is simply not feasible. If, however, a business operates from three locations held under lease and projects future operations from only one, it may well be possible to settle with lessors on favorable terms by using the spectre of a Chapter 11 filing as a meaningful bargaining tool.

Perhaps the most important assessment to be made in determining the likelihood of success and desirability of nonjudicial approach versus bankruptcy proceedings lies in an understanding of the obligations you will be unable to affect out of court, and whether their continued existence will adversely affect the ability of the enterprise to operate after restructuring. It is difficult, if not impossible, to renegotiate obligations held by persons or entities that you cannot organize into a cohesive representative group. Claims against a company in pending litigation arising in the ordinary course of business fall into this category. Each litigation risk must be assessed on its own merits, rather than as part of a class of secured or unsecured debt. Contingent unliquidated claims in mass tort or environmental cases are not likely to be settled out of court and, as we have seen in cases such as Manville and A. H. Robins, may be reason enough to discard a nonjudicial alternative.

If a company has a large and diverse population of ordinary course trade creditors and cannot achieve a viable restructuring without a settlement of this debt, it is unlikely that an out-of-court proposal should be considered, unless creditors participating in the restructuring are prepared to accept less for their claims to enable these obligations to receive more favorable treatment. It is simply not possible to negotiate with hundreds of suppliers and service organizations in different businesses without a statutory procedure that classifies and adjusts claims. The reorganization lawyer must force this analysis and make strong and cogent arguments to move the analytical process in the appropriate direction.

If major contractual relationships, such as collective bargaining agreements, supply contracts, equipment leases, and consulting and employment agreements, cannot be terminated or significantly restructured out of court, the company must understand that Chapter 11 provides an ideal, if somewhat burdensome, environment for dealing with all of these issues with the aid of the court. In all of these discussions you must lead and recommend. Your efforts should provide the client with a full range of alternatives and a concise analysis of the positives and negatives relating to all issues.

You must in this process involve the major creditors and their representatives as well. Keeping these people posted on your progress is essential, since you must assume that they are doing their own benefit-versus-burden study, but with less current data and a more superficial understanding of the business. If creditors for borrowed money, such as banks and bondholders, perceive that you and your client are approaching the restructure in a responsible analytical way, they will be more likely to work with you and the company and maintain and recommend continuing standstill arrangements. Keep them out of the process and you will most assuredly encourage litigation and probably insolvency proceedings.

The foregoing discussion may leave you with the impression that few if any structures are conducive to out-of-court restructurings, and that your responsibility is to demonstrate that fact to the client. In fact, such is not the case. There are many situations where an exchange offer mechanism is the better and more suitable approach and should be pursued. Many of the well-publicized leveraged buyout transactions in recent years have left the major concentration of liabilities in a small number of holders. Usually, you find a substantial senior debt position held by banks and insurance companies and a large amount of publicly held debt securities issued in connection with recent financings. There are many modifications and subsets of this structure, including unpaid bridge loans made available by investment banks and different levels of seniority in public debt instruments. Often banks are secured, sometimes holding hard assets as collateral, but often having only pledges of the ownership interests of their borrower in subsidiaries and affiliates.

If the debt to be restructured is held primarily by institutions and public debt holders, and if adequate relief to make the business viable can be achieved by dealing only with those constituencies, you have a realistic opportunity for an out-of-court settlement. It is important that counsel recognize this quickly. You should not be intimidated by huge numbers on the debt side. In fact, the more debt there is the greater the incentive to focus on a prompt solution. The key to most of these transactions is identifying the intrinsic value on the asset side and working to educate your client, the major creditors, and any other key constituencies about the best method of conveying that value in a restructure, while maintaining a viable enterprise. This is a major undertaking. Competent reorganization counsel should lead here. You need to be present at all key meetings. You have to become a responsible missionary carrying a credible message, supporting your client's position, and goading and prodding both your client and the major creditor groups to achieve a reasonable and fair result.

If the company elects to pursue an exchange offer, you must have a reasonably in-depth understanding of what is possible under the securities laws. Such an analysis is beyond the scope of this discussion, but any lawyer who proposes to responsibly advise a troubled company should have a sufficient comprehension of the exchange offer provisions of the securities laws to effectively advise the client.[10] You should involve experienced securities lawyers in this process and employ the advice and counsel of investment bankers whose experience may well be invaluable. Again emphasize the team approach. Use all the resources available and, if necessary, go outside the existing advisory group for more help. You are in a crisis atmosphere, and the idea is to give the process the best possible chance of succeeding. Sparing extra expense at this time may deprive the company of its best opportunity to reorganize and may put your client in an unfavorable position in the future.

PREPACKAGED CHAPTER 11

This discussion would not be complete without a comment on the newest reorganization commodity, the "prepackaged Chapter 11." This terminology is generally used to describe a process pursuant to which approval of an exchange offer is solicited in a manner that permits the debtor to use the consents obtained as acceptances for a Chapter 11 plan having essentially the same terms as the exchange offer. This strategy, which is particularly directed at publicly held debt and equity, is designed to enable the debtor to obtain the necessary numerical and dollar majorities of voting creditors to satisfy the requirements of the Bankruptcy Code, although a higher consent percentage is expressed as a condition for the consummation of the exchange offer transaction.[11] There is an obvious *in terrorem* benefit to this strategy, since it would suggest that nonconsenting creditors will risk being bound by a Chapter 11 plan in any event. These prepackaged deals or so-called quickie Chapter 11 cases are proferred as unique and creative alternatives. In fact, the results appear mixed at best. I believe the concepts to be contradictory. It is almost impossible to prepackage these complicated deals, and Chapter 11 is never quick, especially in a complicated case. In advising the client on the wonders of prepackaged alternatives, conservatism should be your credo. It is always useful to develop a consensus whether in or out of court. The more supportive creditors are for an out-of-court plan, the more likely some form of that plan will be successful in court and the less likely that recalcitrants will be able to sabotage the ultimate result. However, it is professionally unwise to suggest that the Chapter 11 process, no matter how well staged, will be expeditious.

In today's economic world, where claims against reorganizing companies are traded in an active market by sophisticated investors, your constituency is often a moving target. Let your client know that successful prepackaged deals should be defined more in terms of extraordinary and even miraculous. Self-serving comments by debtors and their advisors that they have created a unique and unusual solution to the reorganization process should be viewed with extreme skepticism.

CHAPTER 11—THE END OR THE BEGINNING?

Having either discarded the out-of-court alternative after appropriate analysis or having elected to recommend Chapter 11 proceedings to the client for various reasons, counsel's role as advisor and advocate in the Chapter 11 case becomes more expansive and demanding. It is, in fact, in Chapter 11 proceedings that the lawyer's role becomes the most potent and where your client becomes most dependent upon you. This is clearly unfamiliar territory to the company and your advice, counsel, and day-to-day availability are most critical. Representing a major company in a reorganization proceeding can be among the most demanding, time-consuming, and pressure-intensive engagements a lawyer and his or her firm can undertake. The process of reorganization under Chapter 11 of the Bankruptcy Code has clearly become a sophisticated legal alternative and litigation strategy in recent years and has attracted and developed some of the most skilled and competent business lawyers and litigators practicing today.

Where Chapter 11 was previously viewed as the harbinger of liquidation, it is now generally perceived as a procedure for resuscitation and revitalization of a troubled and debt-burdened company, especially one with sound identifiable core operating businesses. The recent national publicity surrounding the Chapter 11 proceedings commenced by Allied Stores and Federated Department Stores constitutes a classic example of the increasing perception that Chapter 11 proceedings are a proper and appropriate statutory framework in which to effectuate the rehabilitation of a financially troubled enterprise. These cases follow other enormously successful mammoth reorganizations conducted in recent years and help to debunk the historical perception of Chapter 11 as a haven for corporate misfits with damaged and unappealing assets. Although the results of the Allied and Federated cases and many other pending reorganization cases are not yet fully known, it is abundantly clear that Chapter 11 proceedings are a most acceptable and indeed appropriate strategic business exercise.

No matter how acceptable and even desirable the process has become, few clients are prepared for the burdens it imposes upon the business, its management, and its counsel. As reorganization counsel, the lawyer and his or her firm generally become the focal point of activity. The debtor's attorneys must be prepared to assume substantial burdens on behalf of the client and undertake responsibility to the various creditor groups and, most significantly, the bankruptcy court.

One of the principal benefits of the structure of the Bankruptcy Code is that a reorganization case usually is supervised by a single judge throughout its administration. The fact that a single judicial officer oversees a proceeding from its inception is of great benefit to a debtor, since the court develops an intimate familiarity with the business and legal issues confronting the reorganization. Counsel to the debtor is in a critical position here. Bankruptcy courts have become accustomed to dealing with sophisticated debtor's counsel. Since it is the debtor that generally initiates most activity before the court, the debtor and its counsel set the tone and course of a proceeding. Retaining absolute credibility with the court is critical. Making applications for relief, which in your judgment have little or no prospect for success, but are nonetheless proffered because your client insists, will generally impair your client's credibility and cause the court to question your judgment. It is essential that the debtor and its management understand what is reasonably achievable and appreciate that a bankruptcy court must perform a massive judicial balancing act throughout a reorganization. The court must weigh the interests of all affected constituencies on all issues. Debtor's counsel should help the court in that effort by trying to bring a balanced perspective to all issues and to fit each particular issue into the larger framework of the reorganization. There is no better way to create overt hostility to your client in a reorganization case than being excessively confrontational on each and every issue, no matter its magnitude.

Chapter 11 has as its most essential purpose the rehabilitation of a financially distressed enterprise. Therefore, the courts are generally oriented toward affording a debtor a reasonable opportunity to reorganize. In the early stages of a reorganization case, most bankruptcy judges will lean heavily toward granting relief to the debtor on most issues where stabilization of the business is at stake. Experienced bankruptcy judges have come to understand the somewhat chaotic environment that often accompanies a filing and are generally prepared to deal with emergency applications for interim and final relief on issues critical to the continuity of the business.

The skilled practitioner should understand this generally prevailing attitude and be prepared to employ the judicial arena to the advantage of the client and, ultimately, the reorganization itself. Debtor's counsel should be prepared to deal with predictable issues immediately after a filing occurs. You should anticipate your client's needs for ongoing financing and have so arranged with current lenders or with a new financing source for all necessary working capital facilities that hearings to approve such financings can be scheduled within days of the actual filing date and, if necessary, so interim relief can be obtained on the date of filing.

You should make sure that all precautions are taken to assure that payroll and other employee-related expenses and standard benefits are covered, and that banks which process payroll and payroll related items are permitted to clear checks, even if they were issued prior to the filing date. Never let the employees suffer economically as an immediate result of a filing. They will ultimately be asked to expend extra effort in a crisis environment, and some of them may lose their jobs in the future as cost-cutting measures are effected. Their morale is likely to be low, and they will harbor great uncertainty about their future. You simply can't let their payroll checks bounce as well.

Be assured that courts understand these problems, and most judges will deal quickly and efficiently with sensible, reasonably considered, and properly presented requests even on very short notice. Judges and experienced practitioners understand that a complicated reorganization case will take a long time to conduct and conclude, and that a debtor must have reasonable leeway to get the program underway in the early months. Understanding these dynamics is critical, since a debtor and its counsel are the court's main focus. If you are constantly scrambling and have no clear focus and prepared strategy, the court will have a skeptical view of the acumen of management and the skill of counsel, thereby making your job even more difficult.

You must bear in mind that a reorganization is in essence a series of compromises. A skilled debtor's lawyer should try to find a reasonable middle ground on most issues, no matter your adversary. Bankruptcy courts generally will endeavor to find means for compromise on most issues that are not clear cut. Bankruptcy judges appreciate an intelligent approach to consensual resolution of issues so each and every controversy does not require lengthy hearings and time and expense to the estate, with concomitant burdens upon the court. This, of course, does not suggest that you must give more than is necessary to an unreasonable and intransigent adversary simply to achieve a consensual resolution of an issue. Bankruptcy judges are generally very attuned to issues, and they can perceive and deal with overaggressive lawyering as well as any jurists I have ever encountered. Use this knowhow to your advantage. Try to find a way to let the court know what efforts at compromise were made and where the discussions were terminated. Generally, being the proactive proponent of positions gives you the opportunity to get your client's proposal on the record early and to try to demonstrate the reasonableness of the debtor's exercise of business judgment on the issue at hand and the legal underpinnings supporting it. Where the issue warrants, try to let the court know that your client has been flexible, and that confrontation was not your goal at the outset, but has been dictated by the results of good-faith efforts to resolve issues before seeking the intervention of the court.

Expose management to the court process as early as possible. Let senior executives observe early hearings and develop a feel for the courtroom dynamics, the judge, and the lawyers representing other major constituencies in the case. This will generally help them to understand the somewhat cumbersome nature of the process and be more patient when things take longer than they should. Most bankruptcy judges will, in their ever-burdensome efforts to balance competing positions, allow each party in interest to make its own record on an issue before the court, in some cases no matter how relevant the comments are to the issue at hand. This lengthy process is often frustrating to clients who view it as a lawyer's visibility contest, with no resultant benefit to anyone but the speaker himself. Nonetheless it is an inherent part of the practice and must be dealt with.

Immediately after a filing, debtor's counsel should meet with a group of employees designated by management to explain what has occurred and what it means to them. I have had occasion to address many such groups, numbering as few as a dozen up to as many as 500, and have found that a short understandable explanation of Chapter 11 and its benefits and burdens is of great value. Allow employees to ask questions: communicate with them on a nonlegal basis, try to talk their language; and make them understand that their company is still there, that management is still in control, and that they have not been taken over by a group of lawyers and accountants, although those people will be more visible than in the past. Encourage management to have periodic update sessions with employees and to keep them apprised of significant events. Designate several senior management personnel—usually lawyers on an in-house legal staff, or treasurers and controllers—to whom questions relating to the Chapter 11 proceeding and its effect on the business are to be directed. These managers should then communicate with counsel. It is extremely inefficient and costly for multiple employees to have direct access to counsel, since such contacts will result in numerous different employees asking the same or similar questions, often of several different lawyers at your firm. Inevitably you will get mixed views, crossed signals, and unnecessary confusion. Setting up effective lines of communication and allocating responsibility for it, both at the client and at your firm, can enhance and accelerate the stabilization process. The early months of a case go by very quickly and once things settle down the business of reorganization can commence in earnest.

One of the most difficult attitudes to overcome in a debtor's reorganization case is the tendency on the part of management to become complacent and somewhat comfortable with the protective cocoon offered by the Bankruptcy Code and the court process. Once the company has stabilized its business, the counsel has developed a procedure for dealing with court hearings and submissions, and the client has become accustomed to the time delays inherent in obtaining judicial relief, it is important that counsel keep the process moving lest he or she and the client lose control.

Of paramount importance here are the so-called exclusivity provisions of Section 1121 of the Bankruptcy Code.[12] This section and the case law that has and continues to interpret it may be the most critical to your client's achievement of its reorganization goals. To maintain and extend the statutory exclusivity initially granted by law, you must demonstrate reasonable and good-faith progress towards business and debt restructuring. While extensions of the exclusivity period are generally routinely granted early in a case, it is far more difficult to obtain extensions after the first 12 months of a proceeding, unless most major constituencies consent.

Your client must understand that, while the statute is generally oriented toward the debtor and rehabilitation, it is by no means a one-way street. To maintain control and to keep creditors or others from proposing or sponsoring a reorganization plan, you must demonstrate progress in efforts to develop a credible business plan for the company and, from that base, to formulate alternative scenarios for a plan or plans of reorganization. Here again, continuing dialogue with creditors through committees appointed in the case is absolutely essential. Unlike the out-of-court environment, creditors have a place to voice their dismay if they are being delayed, deluded, or simply have had it with an incompetent or noncommunicative management. If you are doing your job, you should not have to defend your client from attacks of this nature.

While the lawyer's role is very important, guiding a client through a Chapter 11 proceeding should not be solely the lawyer's responsibility. Urge the company to assemble solid, experienced advisory groups, including lawyers, accountants, investment bankers, consultants, and others. Do your best to involve all the advisors in all general strategy sessions and in the approach to most of the key issues that arise. If a group was working together in an out-of-court effort, try to keep it together during the judicial proceeding. Elicit the views of other experienced professionals and try to harmonize them with yours and with those of other advisors. Constructive debate among advisors regarding the approach to and resolution of issues is useful and often very helpful to management, which must make the ultimate business judgment about the appropriate direction to take. Argumentative free-for-alls among professionals are counterproductive and often destructive to the process. Again, the team approach and a calm analytical dialogue is usually the best solution. You must be able to develop consensus, rather than foster contention. You will probably have many other transactions in your future and many other reorganizations in which to display your skills. This is your client's only reorganization, and often the future of a major business is hanging in the balance. The truly professional advisor will recognize this and approach his or her role accordingly.

CONCLUSION

I introduced this chapter by suggesting that *responsibility* was a more suitable term than *role* in describing the position of the company's counsel in a workout, and I truly believe it is an appropriate distinction.

In counseling a company in financial distress whether in the judicial or nonjudicial arena a lawyer must have a unique perspective. When you represent a single client in a typical transaction or litigation, your role is clear and unequivocal. You work for and on behalf of your client and focus all of your skills on your client's interests, leaving your counterpart on the other side to deal with his or her client's position.

In a workout, you assume more global responsibility. Your first and most critical obligation is to your client, but your client has many faces and incarnations for you to consider. There is the board, management, and perhaps thousands of employees, all of whose interests are implicated in the workout.

The reorganization specialist also must assume a responsibility to the shareholders and creditors of the company. They and their representatives expect counsel to bring a degree of objectivity to a crisis and to guide a troubled ship through heavy seas without precise navigational equipment. Your legal abilities are important; however, you must expect in a sophisticated workout that a large number of skilled lawyers will be involved on behalf of all constituencies, and you should assume that a relatively equal level of understanding of the law is present on all sides. Therefore, the real premium is on the ability to communicate, to moderate, to compromise when dictated, and to aggressively pursue adversarial positions when there is no reasonable alternative.

Reorganizations and restructurings are basically a process of definition and allocation. The effort is designed to define the enterprise that is your client and determine its real present value and potential future value and then to fairly and equitably allocate that value among creditors and equity holders. Few if any businesses are worth more in liquidation than in reorganization, and counsel to the company, therefore, has a significant leverage position to employ. You and your client are in control of the assets and, therefore, if you act responsibly (that word again) you can keep control of the process and significantly influence its ultimate outcome.

No matter how the redefinition and reallocation process turns out, counsel should be able to look back upon it as a well-managed and professionally handled engagement, which left everyone involved a bit dissatisfied with the outcome as it affects their individual interests. If everyone is to some degree unhappy, then the overall result was undoubtedly fair and was achieved responsibly.

ENDNOTES

1. Section 361 of the Bankruptcy Code (11 U.S.C. § 361) delineates several nonexclusive methods for providing adequate protection of an interest in property, including periodic cash payments and liens on otherwise unencumbered property (replacement liens) but does not permit the granting of an administrative expense claim as the sole method of providing adequate protection. All of such methods are cumbersome, take often critical time to put into place, and unduly advantage a previously unsecured creditor. Therefore, the need to keep cash in safe harbors is obvious.
2. Pursuant to Section 544 of the Bankruptcy Code (11 U.S.C. § 544) a trustee (including a debtor in possession under Chapter 11) succeeds to and is cloaked with the rights and powers of certain actual or hypothetical creditors.

    Section 544 provides:

    (a) The trustee shall have, as of the commencement of the case, and without regard to any knowledge of the trustee or of any creditor, the rights and powers of, or may avoid any transfer or property of the debtor or any obligation incurred by the debtor that is voidable by—

    (1) a creditor that extends credit to the debtor at the time of the commencement of the case, and that obtains, at such time and with respect to such credit, a judicial lien on all property on which a creditor on a simple contract could have obtained such a judicial lien, whether or not such a creditor exists;

    (2) a creditor that extends credit to the debtor at the time of the commencement of the case, and obtains, at such time and with respect to such credit, an execution against the debtor that is returned unsatisfied at such time, whether or not such a creditor exists; or

(3) a bona fide purchaser of real property, other than fixtures, from the debtor, against whom applicable law permits such transfer to be perfected, that obtains the status of a bona fide purchaser and has perfected such transfer at the time of the commencement of the case, whether or not such a purchaser exists.

(b) The trustee may avoid any transfer of an interest of the debtor in property or any obligation incurred by the debtor that is voidable under applicable law by a creditor holding an unsecured claim that is allowable under section 502 of this title or that is not allowable only under section 502(e) of this title.

These avoiding powers can be employed to recover preferences pursuant to Section 547 of the Bankruptcy Code and to set aside fraudulent transfers pursuant to Section 548 of the Bankruptcy Code. The trustee's avoiding powers are subject to certain limitations set forth in Section 546 of the Code and time periods provided for in Sections 547 and 548 thereof. Substantially all recast financings in a troubled credit are negotiated with these statutory provisions in the forefront of the process.

3. Developing case law in the area of fraudulent conveyances would seem to indicate that a guarantee by an otherwise healthy entity of obligations of a financially distressed parent company or other affiliate where the guarantor received no economic benefit from a restructured financing may be voidable as a fraudulent transfer. See *E. G. Rubin* v. *Manufacturers Hanover Trust Company*, 661 F.2d 979 (2d Cir. 1981).

4. Case law in this area is not uniform in its approach. See *Clarkson Co. Ltd.* v. *Shaheen*, 660 F.2d 506, 512 (2d Cir. 1981), *cert. denied*, 445 U.S. 990 (1982) (under New York law, insolvency is sufficient to invoke directors' duty to creditors, not the corporation's imminent or foreseeable liquidation); *Bovay* v. *H. M. Byllesby Co.*, 38 A.2d 808, 813 (Del. 1944) ("An insolvent coporation is civilly dead in the sense that its property may be administered in equity as a trust fund for the benefit of creditors. . . . The fact which creates the trust is insolvency, and when that fact is established, the trust arises and the legality of acts thereafter performed will be decided by very different principles than in the case of solvency.") (citations omitted). Generally, a corporation is considered insolvent if the present fair saleable value of its assets is less than the amount that would be required to pay its probable liability on its existing debts as they become absolute and matured, or if the sum of its debts (including contingent liabilities) is greater than the fair value of all its properties. See 11 U.S.C. Section

101(31); N.Y. Debtor and Creditor Law, § 271 (McKinney 1945); *In re Gott,* 3 B.R. 404, 408 (Bankr. N.D. Cal. 1980).

In contrast, other courts have held that directors of an insolvent corporation do not assume a fiduciary duty to creditors if the corporation remains a going concern and is not in the process of liquidation. **See,** for example, *In re Calton Crescent Inc.,* 80 F. Supp. 822, 824 (S.D.N.Y. 1948) (directors are not trustees for the creditors of an insolvent corporation if it is still a going concern) *aff'd,* 173 F.2d 944 (2d Cir.), *aff'd sub. nom., Manufacturers Hanover Co.* v. *Becker,* 388 U.S. 304, 311-12 (1949) ("even during insolvency corporate assets are not in any true and complete sense, trusts") (citation omitted).

5. **See,** generally, Cook and Schwartz, "At a Troubled Company, Officers and Directors Owe Creditors First," Nat'l L.J. (March 16, 1987) at 22. The so-called prudent man standard is more stringent than the ordinary "business judgement" rule. **See** *Bovay,* 38 A.2d at 813. Under the business judgment rule, management of a corporation is immunized from liability in a corporate transaction undertaken within the power of the corporation and the authority of management where there is a reasonable basis to indicate that the transaction was made in good faith. **See** *Black's Law Dictionary* (West, 5th ed., 1979) at 181. Therefore, a deteriorating financial environment puts more pressure on the discretion that must be exercised by directors.

6. Section 1104 of the Bankruptcy Code (11 U.S.C. § 1104) provides in pertinent part:

> (a) At any time after the commencement of the case but before confirmation of a plan, on request of a party in interest or the United States trustee, and after notice and a hearing, the court shall order the appointment of a trustee—
>
> (1) for cause, including fraud, dishonesty, incompetence, or gross mismanagement of the affairs of the debtor by current management, either before or after the commencement of the case, or similar cause, but not including the number of holders of securities of the debtor or the amount of assets or liabilities of the debtor; or
>
> (2) if such appointment is in the interest of creditors, any equity security holders, and other interests of the estate, without regard to the number of holders of securities of the debtor or the amount of assets or liabilities of the debtor.

In major reorganization cases it is uncommon to see the appointment of a trustee, because of the generally disruptive effect such an appointment has on the reorganization proceedings.

7. **See,** generally, Harris, "The Impact of Bankruptcy on Liability of Corporate Directors," 5 Bankr. Dev. J. 289, 295–96 (1987) (hereafter "Harris"). Evolving case law is not uniform in this area. Courts have recognized that to deny ongoing indemnification would discourage continued service, which, at some courts, have ignored the practical consequences in favor of a strict legal interpretation. **See** *In re Baldwin-United Corp.,* 43 B.R. at 461-62 (litigation expenses of current directors may be given first priority as administrative expenses where the continued service of the directors is crucial to the success of the reorganization—potential detriment to such directors in denying priority is not a factor for consideration). **See** *In re Amfesco Industries, Inc.,* 81 B.R. at 786 (bankruptcy principle of equality of distribution overrides chilling effect). **See,** also, *Christian Life Center Litigation Defense Committee* v. *Silva (In re Christian Life Center),* 821 F.2d 1370, 1374 (9th Cir. 1986) (postpetition legal fees of officers was a general unsecured claim, not an administrative expense claim or subordinated claim, because the claim for indemnity arose from prepetition acts of such officers).

    On a practical level, it is often possible to obtain approval for indemnification for continuing officers and directors with the support of major creditor groups, if the reorganization is being efficiently managed.

8. Bankruptcy Code Section 507(a)(3) (11 U.S.C. § 507) grants statutory priority to certain claim for wages, salaries, severance, and other forms of compensation, with a maximum entitlement of $2,000 per individual, if the compensation is applicable to a period which is not more than 90 days prior to a Chapter 11 filing.
9. **See** Bankruptcy Code Section 502(b) (11 U.S.C. § 502).
10. **See,** generally, Section 3(a)(9) of the Securities Act of 1933 and related provisions.
11. With respect to a class of claims, Section 1126 (c) of the Bankruptcy Code (11 U.S.C. § 1126) provides that: "A class of claims has accepted a plan if such plan has been accepted by creditors, other than any entity designated under subsection (e) of this section, that hold at least two thirds in amount and more than one half in number of the allowed claims of such class held by creditors, other than any entity designated under subsection (e) of this section, that have accepted or rejected such plan." **See,** also, Section 1125 (d), which provides, with respect to a class of equity interests, that "A class of interests has accepted a plan if such plan has been accepted by holders of such interests, other than any entity designated under subsection (e) of this section, that hold at least two thirds in amount of the allowed interests of such class

held by holders of such interests, other than any entity designated under subsection (e) of this section, that have accepted or rejected such plan."

Subsection (e) of Section 1126 provides for the disqualification of votes not cast in good faith.

12. Section 1121 of the Bankruptcy Code (11 U.S.C. § 1121) provides that—

(a) The debtor may file a plan with a petition commencing a voluntary case, or at any time in a voluntary case or an involuntary case.

(b) Except as otherwise provided in this section, only the debtor may file a plan under after 120 days after the date of the order for relief under this chapter.

(c) Any party in interest, including the debtor, the trustee, a creditors' committee, an equity security holders' committee, a creditor, an equity security holder, or any indenture trustee, may file a plan if and only if—

(1) a trustee has been appointed under this chapter;

(2) the debtor has not filed a plan before 120 days after the date of the order for relief under this chapter; or

(3) the debtor has not filed a plan that has been accepted, before 180 days after the date of the order for relief under this chapter, by each class of claims or interests that is impaired under the plan.

(d) On request of a party in interest made within the respective periods specified in subsections (b) and (c) of this section and after notice and a hearing, the court may for cause reduce or increase the 120-day period or the 180-day period referred to in this section.

CHAPTER 14

THE ACCOUNTANT'S ROLE IN THE WORKOUT ENVIRONMENT— REPRESENTING THE DEBTOR

Donald E. Thomas*
Price Waterhouse

THE 1990s—FUTURE OPPORTUNITIES FOR ACCOUNTANTS

The 1980s will be remembered by business historians as the decade of the leveraged buyout, or LBO. An LBO is a commercial transaction in which a relatively high level of debt is incurred to finance an acquisition with the acquired company's future cash flow or proceeds from conversion of assets, or both, dedicated to retire the acquisition debt. Typically, in an LBO, the acquired company's assets are pledged to secure all or a portion of the financing. In many large LBOs, shareholders of a publicly traded company receive a premium price for their shares and the company is taken private.

The statistics on LBOs during the past 10 years are impressive. According to a *Business Week* article (September 11, 1989) concerning LBOs, "Corporate America in this decade has retired $500

---

* I would like to personally thank my associates Neil Murdoch, Kelly Biar, and Carmen Eggleston for assisting me in reviewing various drafts of this chapter.

billion in equity while piling on almost $1 trillion in debt. Interest payments absorb 30 percent of cash flow, according to Merrill Lynch & Company, surpassing by several percentage points the records reached during the worst two postwar recessions." Some of the largest corporations in America were taken private in leveraged transactions to include such companies as Safeway Stores, Inc., RJR Nabisco, Inc., Revco D. S., Inc., and Beatrice Company.

In the 1960s, these leveraged acquisitions involved "bootstrap financings," where the majority of the purchase price was obtained from borrowed funds, either through financial institutions or sellers. The magnitude of leveraged purchase transactions exploded in the 80s and the rules of the acquisition game were rewritten. Many articles and speeches have been prepared to address the reasons why the LBO became so popular in that decade. Among many things, the decade will be remembered as one of the longest sustained periods of economic prosperity without a major recession. Existing tax laws, which allowed significant deductions for interest on borrowed funds and depreciation resulting from the write-up of assets to fair market value, produced a strong bias toward the utilization of debt financing as opposed to equity. A bullish stock market held out the prospect that a company could be taken private and then resold to the public several years later at a substantial profit. Also, during the later part of the decade, interest rates on a relative basis were less expensive than the cost of equity capital.

Loan portfolios in many commercial banks had soured, because of concentrations in such troubled industries as oil and gas, real estate, and commercial loans to less-developed countries. These commercial banks were eager to rebuild their portfolios with the high-margin secured loans that were commonly used in large LBOs. These bank loans often commanded significant up-front fees, as well as attractive spreads over the cost of funds, and were secured by virtually all of the assets of the acquired company. The savings and loan industry expanded rapidly in the 80s due to deregulation and the increase of individual federally insured deposit levels to $100,000. Brokered deposits were easily obtained through highly sophisticated national networks. Aggressive savings and loan institutions were able to achieve significant deposit growth by paying higher interest rates, which in turn forced them to take substantial risks in expanding their loan portfolios. These institutions loaded up on "junk bonds," which often provided the "mezzanine financing" (the financing layer between the secured debt and equity) in an LBO transaction.

Junk bonds were considered below investment-grade quality and often had interest rates of 300 to 600 basis points above the United States Treasury securities of comparable maturities. These junk bonds were used extensively to finance many of the large LBOs. Toward the end of the decade, the competition for large acquisitions that involved the use of junk bond financing became intense. Hostile takeovers became commonplace as companies were "put into play." Billions of dollars of "blind equity pools" were created for acquisition purposes, and investment bankers reaped enormous fees to suggest or force takeovers. There were simply more financing dollars available than large attractive deals, and bidding wars became commonplace.

Terms of various debt instruments used in a takeover became more and more complex to tailor the target company's future cash flows and asset sales to the cash interest payment and principal amortization schedules. It was not uncommon to find more exotic forms of debt securities, including such names as discount notes, convertible notes, "payment in kind" or "PIK" securities, general reset notes, junior and senior subordinated debentures, and zero-coupon debentures. These generally unsecured notes and debentures often provided the mezzanine financing layer that was necessary to meet the purchase price and fill the difference between the secured senior debt generally provided by commercial banks and the equity layer from blind investment pools. Because of higher acquisition prices and the need to sell off major businesses or assets to retire the significant acquisition financing, many of these debt securities were designed to have little or no cash interest paid or principal amortization in the initial years. Debt securities often deferred cash interest payments or allowed the debtor to pay the interest with similar securities in lieu of cash. Many of these specially structured debt securities became ticking time bombs waiting to explode in the 1990s, when the timing of asset sales and resulting prices fell short of expectations yet cash interest payments and amortization were still required. Although problems did occur in the mid-1980s with certain junk bond issues that were used to finance

LBOs, they were quietly refinanced or traded without capital market disruption. With the continued explosion of new deals and general euphoria, these problem junk bonds created little concern and were often not even noticed.

According to a *Wall Street Journal* article (October 20, 1987), "On October 19, 1987, the Dow Jones Industrial Average plummeted an astonishing 508 points, or 22.6 percent, to 1738.74. The drop far exceeded the 12.8 percent decline on the notorious day of October 28, 1929, which is generally considered the start of the Great Depression." Herein began the start of the sobering process necessary to cure the buyout intoxication that occurred in the 1980s. Quickly the market began to distinguish between high-quality and low-quality junk bonds, and trading became virtually nonexistent for the lower-quality bonds. Announcements of new hostile or friendly takeover deals declined dramatically, and commercial banks began to be very nervous about modifying terms on existing senior secured debt or participating in new deals. Portfolio managers of pension funds, insurance companies, mutual funds, and savings and loan institutions began in earnest to reduce their exposure in junk bonds. The 1987 Southland Corporation management-led buyout, which occurred shortly after the stock market crash, faced difficulty in being completed, and additional sweeteners in the form of higher yields had to be offered to get the deal closed. Even though the previously unquestioned "highly confident" letters were issued in the announced UAL Corporation management-led buyout in 1989, the transaction aborted, because the syndicated financing could not be completed. Compounding the junk bond market problems was the failure of many savings and loan institutions throughout the country. Many of these institutions had significant concentrations of junk bonds in their portfolios. Under currently proposed regulatory guidelines, savings and loan institutions would be required to reduce their junk bond portfolios over a five-year period.

Possibly the most significant impact on the junk bond market was the financial failure and subsequent bankruptcy filing of Drexel Burnham Lambert on February 13, 1990. Ironically, this investment banking firm, which had been a pioneer in developing the junk bond market to finance LBOs and in maintaining important trading liquidity for many outstanding junk bonds, was a victim of its own creation. Drexel failed because it was unable to roll over its short-term credit facilities due to, among other things, a large problem junk bond portfolio. To set the perspective for the 1990s, according to a *Time* magazine article (February 26, 1990), "The roughly $200 billion in junk bonds currently outstanding are held as follows: insurance companies 30 percent, mutual funds 30 percent, pension funds 15 percent, foreign investments 9 percent, savings and loan institutions 7 percent, individuals 5 percent, corporations 3 percent, and securities dealers 1 percent. It has been estimated that the future default rate for junk bonds will be 10 percent." Many have since suggested that the future default rate could be much higher.

In the early 1990s, many of the PIK securities, zero-coupon bonds, and other forms of debt securities will require cash interest payments and principal amortization but, with very tight cash flows and disappointing asset sales, many companies will be unable to roll over or refinance this debt. More defaults and bankruptcies are predicted. New legal interpretations concerning the status of a creditor accepting an exchange offer, if the debtor subsequently filed for bankruptcy protection, will further upset the junk bond market. There were several examples of spectacular LBO failures in the late 80s and early 90s, including Revco D. S., Inc., Campeau Corporation, Resorts International, Inc., Southmark Corporation, and Integrated Resources, Inc. All of these companies ultimately sought the protection of a Chapter 11 bankruptcy filing.

THE CHANGING ROLE OF THE ACCOUNTANT

Many people have used various names to describe a troubled debt restructuring, including *workout, corporate recapitalization,* or *financial restructuring*. The traditional role of the accountant representing a debtor in a workout environment could have been classified in three general areas: accounting services, tax services, and general business consulting. In the early 1980s, the accountant's involvement with a troubled debtor typically occurred when an audit client experienced financial difficulty and had to consider unaccustomed means to financially survive. The accountant was generally brought in to assist the client with the interpretation and application of certain accounting guidelines and tax regulations that would surface in a financial restructuring. Often an exchange offer (the process of exchanging new debt securities for old debt securities) was considered a viable approach to reduce the financial pressure of excessive debt and avoid bankruptcy. Financial projections, related assumptions, and other disclosure information for the public exchange offer had to be prepared by the debtor, reviewed by the accountant, and presented to the Securities and Exchange Commission for approval before submitting the offer to various creditors and stockholders.

In any major financial restructuring where debt is compromised or forgiven, or new equity is issued to existing creditors, the tax consequences are significant. The accountant was often engaged to analyze the tax consequences of a potential gain from cancellation of indebtedness and the effect on existing and future tax attributes that resulted from the compromising of debt and recapitalization. The accountant played a critical role in assisting management in the development of a tax-efficient recapitalization plan that minimized income recognition and maximized the value of future tax attributes. This challenge became even greater when, through the Tax Reform Act of 1986, some of the flexibility in the use of net operating loss carryforwards (NOLs) was reduced.

And finally, in the traditional role, the accountant found himself or herself suggesting approaches to a financially troubled client to improve operational efficiency and cash flow. This advice often included the review of systems, methods and policies in the areas of cash management, inventory planning and control, billing operations, including accounts receivable collection, disbursing activities, including accounts payable, and import/export operations.

In the late 80s, more comprehensive advice from the accountant was sought by the debtor who experienced financial difficulty, because of excessive financial leverage, including those debtors having undergone an LBO. The role of the accountant shifted from providing the necessary technical accounting and tax advice to more of a problem-solving advisory role. Many accountants had been forced into this new role by their clients suffering financial difficulties, while other more progressive accountants had started to recognize the need for this type of specialized advisory service and had aggressively marketed this service and their skills to both audit clients and nonclients.

THE NEW ROLE OF THE ACCOUNTANT

As the workout environment became more sophisticated and challenging, the services provided by various professionals, including accountants, investment bankers, management consultant groups, and lawyers, began to overlap. The traditional lines of demarcation disappeared. Professionals were viewed as problem solvers with various technical skills and working experiences. The accountant now has the opportunity to significantly expand his or her services from the traditional accounting, tax, and general consulting areas. The services that today's accountant can provide to a financially troubled debtor can generally be classified as those that are financial in nature and those that are operational in nature. This chapter concentrates more on the financial restructuring services. A general summary of select services that an accountant can provide to a debtor are:

Select Operational Restructuring Services

- Analyze the debtor's industry and recommend strategic changes that can improve operating performance.
- Analyze the debtor's major business segments and recommend divestitures of businesses that do not meet profit objectives.
- Recommend methods for improving internal accounting and management controls, management information systems, and organizational structure.
- Analyze overhead and other costs and recommend changes to conserve cash and improve cash flow.
- Analyze the financial impact of any existing or proposed joint venture arrangements, capital expenditure programs, or capital infusions.

Select Financial Restructuring Services

- Analyze and review the various credit relationships, including loan agreements, notes, debentures, mortgages, and other debt.
- Develop a microcomputer model to project financial performance and cash flows under various business assumptions and financial restructuring plans.

- Develop alternative financial restructuring plans and assist management in the selection of the most appropriate plan.
- Assist management in structuring the pricing, terms, and special conditions of any new debt or equity securities to be offered in an exchange offer.
- Prepare a written financial restructuring proposal to include industry analyses, recapitalization term sheet, pro forma balance sheet, financial projections and related assumptions, and valuation of any new debt and equity securities offered.
- Compare and contrast the proposed financial restructuring proposal to any creditor counterproposal or other plans that have been completed or are under negotiation in the marketplace.
- Prepare a detailed analysis of the tax consequences of the cancellation of debt, net operating loss carryforwards, and adjustments in other tax attributes resulting from the financial restructuring proposal.
- Conduct a cost/benefit analysis of the expected results of a bankruptcy filing.
- Perform various valuations that are required if a partial liquidation of the debtor or sale of business segments is selected.
- Assist in the proper application of accounting principles.

In providing services to the debtor, there are many cases when both the operational and financial problems are interrelated and must be addressed simultaneously. It should also be clearly noted that the accountant's role is to provide objective advice to the debtor. The debtor must take responsibility for the final business decisions. Several of these operational and financial services outlined above are discussed in greater detail.

Operational Restructuring Issues

A key issue in any workout is to identify immediate ways to improve cash flow by reducing or delaying cash expenditures and by increasing or accelerating cash receipts. The accountant can quite often draw on his or her firm's knowledge of certain key industries and, as a result, be able to suggest to a debtor various ways to improve profitability and resulting cash flows. For example, one fairly straightforward analysis would be to review overhead and determine where reductions are possible or preferable. Quite often the reduction of overhead is an emotional issue for the debtor, and an independent third-party review with resulting recommendations may be welcomed. The accountant can also independently evaluate operating management and make appropriate recommendations where personnel changes may improve operational efficiency and profitability. Many times, financial problems can result from basic operational problems. For example, a thorough analysis of costs, transfer pricing, or overhead allocations may demonstrate to management that certain subsidiaries, divisions, or product lines may not be as profitable as first believed. A recommendation to drop a product line, sell a division, or liquidate a subsidiary may, in itself or when combined with the renegotiation of credit lines, resolve the financial crisis. There may be further ways to assist the debtor in providing consulting advise on long-term strategic planning issues, such as the development of new business lines, suggesting niche markets, and establishing international operations to augment or replace declining domestic sales.

Financial Restructuring Issues

Many financial restructuring issues that a troubled debtor must consider have accounting, tax, and general business implications. The accountant who has experience in financial restructurings is in an excellent position to provide these needed specialized services to the debtor. In the simplest of terms, a financial restructuring is required when the debtor is unable or will become unable to meet future financial obligations, generally debt service requirements. The most common financial restructuring approach is to convert a portion of debt to equity and modify the remaining debt terms to include compromising the interest rate, scheduled amortization payments, and various loan covenants. There are, of course, many financial restructuring approaches that can be considered, often resulting in very complex plans.

Even though the financial restructuring or traditional workout is done outside of the bankruptcy environment, in most cases pending or threatened litigation exists. The pending or threatened litigation can be the threat of foreclosure on assets, enforcement of a lien or judgment, or the ability for the creditor to force the debtor into bankruptcy. In fact, in the simplest of terms, bankruptcy is no more than a financial restructuring conducted under the provision of the federal Bankruptcy Code and under the supervision of the federal bankruptcy court. The unique bankruptcy rules, regulations, and procedures are unknown or confusing to most debtors, and the process of bankruptcy can be lengthy. Further, there is the possibility that decisions on the fate of the debtor may shift to the creditors. This loss of control, expense of the proceedings, and potential damage to the "business franchise" are several of the major reasons why bankruptcy is often avoided and used only as a last resort.

Accounting Issues for Troubled Debt Restructurings

Certain specific accounting and disclosure issues exist in a troubled debt restructuring. One must first make a distinction between a "troubled debt restructuring" or simply a modification of the terms of a debt. Second, one must determine whether assets or an equity interest will be transferred by the debtor to the creditor in full or partial settlement of a debt. Each of these actions have important accounting implications.

For certain restructurings consummated after December 31, 1977, *Statement of Financial Accounting Standards No. 15* (*SFAS No. 15*), "Accounting by Debtors and Creditors for Troubled Debt Restructurings," may apply. Under *SFAS No. 15*, a restructuring of debt constitutes a "troubled debt restructuring," if the creditor for economic or legal reasons related to the debtor's financial difficulties grants a concession to the debtor that it would not otherwise consider. That concession either stems from an agreement between the creditor and the debtor or is imposed by law or a court. Many troubled debt restructurings involve modifying debt terms to reduce or defer cash payments required of the debtor to alleviate short-term cash problems and to improve the prospect that the debtor can eventually repay the creditor. Or the creditor may accept a transfer of assets or stock of the debtor, because the creditor believes that arrangement will maximize the recovery on the existing loan relative to other options. After emotions subside, it is axiomatic that a creditor will accept a financial restructure proposal that maximizes its future recovery. A debt restructuring is not necessarily a troubled debt restructuring, even if the debtor is experiencing some financial difficulty. In general, a debtor that can obtain funds from sources other than the existing creditor at market interest rates, at or near those for nontroubled debt, is not involved in a troubled debt restructuring.

A troubled debtor restructuring may include, but is not necessarily limited to, one or a combination of the following:

1. Transfer from the debtor to the creditor of certain assets including third-party receivables, real estate, or fixed assets to partially or fully satisfy a debt. This would include a transfer under a foreclosure or repossession proceedings.

2. Issuance or granting of an equity interest to the creditor to partially or fully satisfy a debt. This would not include equity created by the conversion of debt under the terms of the original indenture.

3. Modification of the terms of a debt, such as one or more of:
 a. Reduction (absolute or contingent) of the stated interest rate for the remaining original life of the debt.
 b. Extension of the maturity date or dates at a stated interest rate lower than the current market rate for new debt with similar risk.
 c. Reduction (absolute or contingent) of the face amount or maturity amount of the debt as stated in the instrument or other agreement.
 d. Reduction (absolute or contingent) of accrued interest.

SFAS No. 15 provides that a transfer of assets to a creditor to settle a debt can create an extraordinary gain called *gain on restructuring*. This gain would be calculated as the excess of the debt over the "fair value" of the assets transferred by the debtor. Fair value of assets is measured by their market value, if any active market exists. If no active market exists, then selling prices in a similar market may be helpful. Gains on restructuring are classified as an extraordinary item net of related taxes in the income statement. If the fair value of the asset transferred exceeded that asset's carrying value, then that difference is accounted for as a gain or loss on transfer of assets, not as a component of the gain on restructuring of a debt.

If an equity interest is transferred to a creditor to satisfy fully or partially a debt, then a gain on restructuring can occur and that gain would likewise be classified as an extraordinary item, net of related taxes, in the income statement. The gain is calculated as the excess of the debt over the fair value of the equity interest transferred. Various valuation techniques, including the income approach (discounted cash flow) and market approach that analyzes comparable companies in the same industry can be used to value the equity interest transferred to the creditor. The value of the transferred equity will be effected by, among other things, the percentage of outstanding stock transferred, whether or not any restrictions are placed on the sale of the stock, and the type of equity transferred that could be in the form of convertible debt or convertible preferred stock, common stock, or warrants. Accountants can play a role in valuing the assets or equity transferred to partially or fully satisfy a debt and also in determining and directing the proper application of the required accounting principles.

A debtor in a troubled debt restructuring involving only modification of terms of a debt and not involving a transfer of assets or an equity interest shall account for the effects of the restructuring prospectively from the time of the restructuring. The debtor does not change the carrying amount of the debt at the time of restructuring, unless the carrying amount exceeds the total future cash payments specified by the new terms. The total future cash payments include both principal and interest. The new effective interest rate shall be the discount rate that equates the present value of the future cash payments specified by the new terms with the carrying amount of the debt. If, however, the total future cash payments specified by the new terms of the debt (including both principal and interest) are less than the carrying amount of the debt, the debtor shall reduce the carrying amount to an amount equal to the total future cash payments specified by the terms and a gain on restructuring shall be recognized. Thereafter, all cash payments under the terms of the debt shall be accounted for as a reduction of the carrying amount of the debt, and no interest expense shall be recognized on the debt for any future period between the restructuring and the maturity dates.

For each period in which the financial statements are presented, a debtor shall disclose either in the body of the financial statements or in the accompanying footnotes the following information about a debt restructuring:

1. For each restructuring a description of the principle changes in terms or the major features of the settlement, or both.
2. Aggregate gain on restructuring of debt and the related income tax effect.
3. Aggregate net gain or loss on transfers of assets recognized during the period.
4. Per share amount of the aggregate gain on the restructuring of debt net of the related income tax effect.

Impairment of Asset Values

Often, a financially troubled debtor may have major assets that are no longer worth the current carrying amount on the balance sheet. These assets have suffered an impairment in value. This is particularly critical when a substantial amount of purchase goodwill may have been created in an LBO. Quite often, substantial goodwill is created in an acquisition, due to the fact that the purchase price paid exceeded the fair market value of the assets less liabilities. *Accounting Principles Board Opinion No. 16 (APB No. 16)*, "Business Combinations," deals with the accounting treatment of the two major types of business combinations: "purchase" and the "pooling of interests." The purchase method for a business combination is accounted for as the acquisition of one company by another. The difference between the cost of an acquired company and the sum of the fair values of tangible and identifiable assets less liabilities is recorded as goodwill. Goodwill represents, in a financial sense, the excess earnings ability of a company. When a debtor suffers financial difficulties, this future excess earnings ability may no longer exist, and consequently goodwill may be impaired.

Write-downs of operating assets including goodwill are required when there is a permanent impairment in value of that asset. The accountant can assist the financially troubled debtor by reviewing the impairment, if any, of productive assets that may have occurred. The Securities and Exchange Commission has taken the position that an asset write-down is currently required if it is probable that future cash flows will be less than the net book value of that asset. Cash flows can be calculated on either a gross or discounted basis. Aggregate future cash flows can include reasonable estimations of future revenue increases, cost reductions, and other factors that may effect the profitability of that asset over time. If the discounted approach is utilized, then an appropriate discount rate must be selected. Accountants must often review the calculations by management or third parties concerning the future cash flows from these potentially impaired assets. If there are significant writedowns, retained earnings would be immediately reduced, but future earnings should be higher, since future depreciation or amortization expenses will be less.

Quasi Reorganization

Another approach often considered by a financially troubled debtor outside of bankruptcy is a quasi reorganization. The general accounting guidelines for quasi reorganization are found in *Accounting Research Bulletins Chapter 7 (ARB Chapter 7)*, "Capital Accounts." A quasi reorganization occurs when a corporation in financial difficulty modifies its capital structure outside of a formal bankruptcy proceeding. Following a quasi reorganization, the debtor is considered, from an accounting standpoint, to have a "fresh start," and future net income and the reporting of dividends will be clearly delineated. Although the elimination of a retained earnings deficit in a quasi reorganization may perhaps obscure historically significant financial information, the accounting treatment is generally accepted, because assets are established at more realistic values.

A quasi reorganization typically involves the following steps:

1. Shareholder approval.
2. A valuation of each asset, and, if the current fair value of any asset exceeds the carrying amount, that asset is written down to fair value. Assets that are considered to have value greater than the carrying amount are generally not changed.
3. The deficit in retained earnings resulting from asset writedowns, and any accumulation of historical operating losses, is eliminated against the debtor's paid-in-capital account.
4. If the debtor's paid-in-capital account at the time of the quasi reorganization is insufficient to absorb the accumulated retained earnings deficit, then the par or stated value of the capital account stock is first reduced to establish a paid-

in-capital account, which can then be used to absorb the charge from eliminating the deficit in retained earnings.
5. The retained earnings following a quasi reorganization is dated for a period of 10 years.

The Securities and Exchange Commission's stated position on quasi reorganizations is:

1. Retained earnings must be completely eliminated.
2. Upon consummation of a quasi reorganization, no deficit can exist in any equity account.
3. The entire procedure must be known to all persons that are entitled to vote on such matters. In many cases this will require stockholders' approval, and the appropriate consents to the transaction must be obtained in advance in accordance with applicable corporate charter and bylaws.

In essence, the quasi reorganization accomplishes the restatement of assets in terms of present conditions and the resulting modification of the capital accounts with the prospect that a future reorganization will not be needed. A fresh financial start is achieved, since the debtor's assets have been reduced to more realistic values and the retained earnings account is initially established at zero. Clearly, there are many valuation issues that must be addressed, as well as the technical application of accounting principles in a quasi reorganization. The accountant can provide assistance in both the valuation and technical accounting areas.

General Tax Issues

The tax rules and regulations relative to a financial restructuring are most complex and are discussed in greater detail in Chapter 6 and in other technical literature. However, tax considerations are critical to any financial restructuring of a debtor and are discussed in the following general terms in this chapter.

Many financial reorganizations include issues that relate to forgiveness of debt or a conversion of debt to equity. The most valuable assets of a financially troubled debtor are often its tax attributes, including net operating losses (NOLs) and investment tax credit carryovers (ITCs). The future cash flows of a debtor will be directly impacted by the extent to which these tax attributes can be preserved. Under the existing tax laws, more favorable tax treatment is given to a debtor in bankruptcy than to a debtor reorganizing outside of bankruptcy. Unfortunately, the differences in tax treatment in certain cases will be the single most important reason for the debtor to file for bankruptcy protection. The two major sections of the Internal Revenue Code (I.R.C.) that most often affect tax attributes in a financial restructuring are Sections 108 and 382.

In general, a debtor taxpayer must include, in taxable income, income from debt forgiveness or conversion (cancellation of indebtedness income, or "COD income") unless specifically excluded. Section 108 provides that a debtor in bankruptcy may exclude all COD income from taxable income, and that an insolvent company may exclude COD income to the extent of its insolvency. In general, COD income is the excess of the face value of the debt over the fair value of the assets exchanged. Such assets may include cash, property, new debt, or equity securities. Insolvency is defined as the excess of liabilities over the fair value of the debtor's assets immediately prior to the discharge of indebtedness. There may be certain assets, such as goodwill, or other intangibles not recorded for financial reporting purposes that should be considered in valuing a debtor's assets. Thus, the accountant can assist the debtor in determining the extent to which the company may be insolvent for tax purposes. To the extent that COD income has been excluded from taxable income, tax attributes must generally be reduced whether the taxpayer is in or out of bankruptcy. Tax attributes (NOLs, ITCs, capital loss carryovers, basis reduction in depreciable property, and the like) must be reduced in the specific order outlined in the Internal Revenue Code.

One of the more significant exceptions to the recognition of COD income is referred to as the *stock for debt exception*. This exception applies to insolvent taxpayers (to the extent of insolvency) and to taxpayers in bankruptcy who issue their own stock in exchange for debt. In general, the exception essentially assumes that, in the calculation of COD income, the value of the stock exchanged is equal to the amount of debt discharged, rather than its fair value. Solvent taxpayers must use the fair market value of the stock issued in the calculation of COD income. The stock for debt exception does not apply where a de minimis amount of stock is issued or where the value of the stock issued to different unsecured creditors is disproportionate.

Section 382 limits the amount of tax attributes that can be used annually when there has been a change of control, which often is the case in debt restructuring. An ownership change occurs when the percentage of the stock of the loss corporation owned by one or more 5 percent shareholders has increased by more than 50 percentage points over the lowest percentage owned by such shareholder at any time during a three-year testing period. In general, the annual limitation under Section 382 is determined by multiplying the federal long-term tax exempt rate by the value of the company immediately prior to the restructuring. Certain debtors emerging from bankruptcy are permitted to use the value of the company immediately after the restructuring in determining its limitation. This limitation may effectively preclude the timely use of a debtor's tax attributes. A large NOL may be preserved, but the application of Section 382 may significantly limit the use of this NOL by fixing a low annual limitation. It should be noted that a Section 382 stock ownership change could be triggered by the issuance of warrants, certain types of convertible securities, the granting of a large net profits interest, or accelerating high interest debt. For tax purposes, the definition of equity is broadly interpreted and these types of securities or interests could represent disguised equity.

PRESENT VALUE/RECOVERY MATRIX OF RESTRUCTURING ALTERNATIVES

One of the most commonly asked questions, when a debtor clearly recognizes and accepts the fact that financial problems exist, is, What are the alternatives and which alternative should be pursued? Directors and officers must clearly evaluate various options and make a decision on the best alternative that maximizes shareholder values. Options are often varied and can range from sale of the entire company, sale or liquidation of various business segments, orderly liquidation of the entire company, the filing of a Chapter 11 bankruptcy, or reducing the outstanding debt burden through an exchange offer.

As an alternative to a bankruptcy filing, exchanges offers have been common in financially troubled LBOs. In an exchange offer, new securities are offered in exchange for old securities, which are typically in default or that will be in default through the passage of time. The financial projections, related assumptions, and narrative explanation of the exchange terms must be properly disclosed, and, if public securities are involved, filed with the SEC. To accept the exchange offer, existing creditors must believe that the fair market value of the newly offered securities will exceed the potential economic recovery of other alternatives, including bankruptcy. Generally, exchange offers are difficult to accomplish, because of the basic fact that a dissenting creditor cannot be forced to accept an exchange offer, as would be the case in bankruptcy. Under the federal Bankruptcy Code, a dissenting creditor may be forced to accept a formal plan or reorganization if his or her class of creditors vote in favor of the plan by two thirds in dollar amount and over 50 percent in number. There are also special "cramdown" provisions that can force a class that has voted against the plan to be governed by the plan of reorganization. However, the threat of bankruptcy can be the catalyst to get an exchange offer completed, due to the costs and time delays that are inherent in most bankruptcy proceedings.

Recently, Chief Judge B. R. Lifland of the United States Bankruptcy Court for the Southern District of New York rendered a decision in the LTV Corporation bankruptcy case that could dramatically affect the willingness of a existing bond creditor to except an exchange offer. According to Judge Lifland, a bond creditor that accepts an exchange offer may have compromised his or her legal claim if the debtor subsequently files for bankruptcy. For example, a $1,000 bond held by a creditor originally issued at $900 may only be worth $200 today, because of the debtor's existing financial problems. The creditor may accept, through an exchange offer, a new $1,000 bond, which is only worth $250, the $750 being classified as "original issue discount." In this example, if the debtor files bankruptcy immediately after the exchange offer, the decision rendered by Judge Lifland is that the creditor would have a claim of only $250 against the bankrupt estate. The $750 original issue discount would represent unmatured interest that would not accrue during the bankruptcy proceedings. This would be in contrast to the creditor's prior position of having a full legal claim of $900, if he or she had not accepted the exchange offer. If this decision stands, exchange offers will become even more difficult to accomplish.

A very useful tool that can be developed by an accountant in explaining various restructuring alternatives to a board of directors and management is a "Present Value/Recovery Matrix of Restructuring Alternatives." An example of a summarized matrix schedule is shown on the facing page. This summary matrix schedule displays the calculated present values and potential recoveries for the seven creditor and stockholder groups under four different restructuring alternatives. The restructuring alternatives include the sale of three divisions, orderly liquidation of the entire company, a Chapter 11 bankruptcy filing, and an exchange offer with a 80 percent and 90 percent acceptance. This matrix schedule was developed utilizing a discounted cash flow model that integrated the debtor's financial projections with various valuation calculations.

The type of creditor and stock group and their respective outstanding securities are stated in the various columns and include the face value, current market value, and the current market value to face value ratio for each of the securities. In the case of the revolving bank debt and bridge term bank debt, the market value is below the face value, due to the fact that the discount rate applied to the future projected principal and interest payments was higher than the interest rates charged by the banks. In this example, the discount rate selected represents the risk inherent in collecting the future interest and principal payments. The other debts, preferred stock, and common stock represent publicly traded securities with daily quoted prices. Due to the financial difficulty experienced by XYZ Company, the current trading values of these securities are significantly below the face amounts.

Under the four major alternatives, the projected present value of each restructuring alternative and the percentage recovery (present value divided by face value) has been calculated. The numerous present value calculations would be made in separate supporting schedules, and they would represent the present value of the package of cash, assets, securities, or equities that would be offered to each creditor and stockholder group. For example, the current subordinated discount debt group with a face amount of $400 million is projected to receive a present value of $185 million, representing a 46 percent recovery under an exchange offer if there

Present Value/Recovery Matrix of Restructuring Alternatives for XYZ Company ($ millions)

					Alternatives		Exchange Offer	
Type of Security	Face Value	Current Market Value	Current Market Value to Face Value	Sale of Three Divisions	Liquidation	Bankruptcy	(90% Acceptance)	(80% Acceptance)
Senior secured revolving bank debt	$750	$725	97%	$725/ 97%	$700/ 93%	$715/ 95	$730/ 97%	$730/ 97%
Senior secured bridge term bank debt	500	470	94	470/ 94	450/ 90	460/ 92	475/ 95	470/ 94
Senior subordinated debt	400	180	45	195/ 49	180/ 45	185/ 46	200/ 50	180/ 45
Subordinated discount debt	400	175	44	180/ 45	175/ 44	179/ 45	185/ 46	160/ 40
PIK subordinated debt	300	90	30	105/ 35	80/ 27	75/ 25	100/ 33	75/ 25
Preferred stock	275	50	18	60/ 22	45/ 16	45/ 16	65/ 23	40/ 15
Common stock	—	15	—	20/0	0/0	5/0	25/0	15/0

is a 90 percent acceptance. The $185 million would represent the present value of a package of new securities to include cash, assets, securities, and equity that would be exchanged for the existing subordinated discount debt.

If reasonable cash flow projections, discount rates, and assumptions are utilized in conjunction with the application of appropriate valuation techniques, this schedule can be a critical tool to a board of directors. If this financial model is properly integrated then, for example, a change in the gross profit margin of the debtor will automatically calculate the present values and recoveries of all creditor and stockholder groups under a proposed exchange offer. Also, if the package of securities is altered for any creditor or stockholder group, the effects to the other groups will be automatically calculated. This will allow the user of this matrix schedule to experiment with various security packages to be offered to each group and then analyze the resulting recovery percentages. The recovery percentages should track the legal priorities of each group, with the more senior creditor receiving a higher percentage recovery than a junior creditor.

Often, in a troubled debt restructuring, the existing creditors become the "economic shareholders" of the debtor, since the exercise of the creditors' legal claims against the debtor's assets will often leave little, if any, value to the existing common shareholders. Due to this fact, the board of directors' existing fiduciary duty to the current shareholders must now also be expanded to recognize these economic shareholders. This Present Value/Recovery Matrix of Restructuring Alternatives will assist the board of directors in reaching a decision about which restructuring alternative should be selected. The emotions of making certain decisions are removed, and the alternative selected should be the restructuring alternative that projects the highest present value recovery to the majority of the creditors and stockholder groups. In this example, the 90 percent exchange offer would represent the best restructuring alternative and should be selected.

CONCLUSION

The role of the accountant in assisting a financially troubled debtor will continue to expand in the 1990s. No longer is the accountant viewed only as a resource of technical advice for accounting, tax, and reporting matters. His or her expertise may also include valuations, assistance in the structuring of new securities to be exchanged for old securities, and advice on identifying and analyzing various financial restructuring alternatives. The accountant can also advise the debtor on operational issues to include better cash management practices, strategic direction, and overhead reduction. The independent accountant should be viewed as an objective problem solver. The lines of demarcation between accountants, investment bankers, management consultants, and lawyers are disappearing. In the future, the financially troubled debtor will engage the professional who can provide the variety of technical skills and experiences that must be brought to bear in a troubled debt restructuring.

CHAPTER 15

THE ACCOUNTANT'S ROLE IN THE WORKOUT ENVIRONMENT—REPRESENTING THE CREDITOR

Dominic DiNapoli
Partner
Price Waterhouse

INTRODUCTION

The role of the accountant in workouts and bankruptcies has changed significantly over the last several decades. In sickness and in health, companies rely on their independent accountants for expert auditing, technical accounting, and tax advice. These core professional services remain the cornerstone of the company-accountant relationship. However, the increasing complexity of business, finance, and corporate strategy has created the need for accountants to serve as business advisors, financial consultants, and corporate strategists. Nowhere is this trend more evident than in the workout environment in which the independent accountant's role has expanded to represent not only companies but their creditors, lenders, bondholders, equity security holders, or other parties in bankruptcy situations.

As the 1990s begin, businesses continue to be confronted with tighter cash flows and higher financial leverage due to the wave of leveraged buyouts in the 1980s. Combined with a sluggish economy, this environment portends a growing number of loan defaults, followed by workouts and bankruptcy filings. As a result, there will be an increasing need for accountants with the technical skills and business expertise necessary to guide management of troubled companies or their creditors through the perilous waters of restructuring, reorganizing, or liquidating. Accounting experts are needed to maximize the recovery on the parties' respective financial interests. The trained accountant must understand the myriad issues of financial conditions, operational inefficiencies, financial restructuring alternatives, and business strategies associated with workouts and bankruptcies.

This chapter will examine why the creditors of a troubled company, either individually or as a member of a creditors' committee, require their own accountant when a company attempts a turnaround/workout or files for protection under Chapter 11 of Title 11 of the United States Bankruptcy Code. The assistance and expertise required by the creditor in both instances will be examined in detail. In addition, the criteria to be considered in favoring either an informal, out-of-court restructuring or a bankruptcy filing will be reviewed.

CREDITORS NEED THEIR OWN ACCOUNTANTS

In almost all workout situations, the troubled company retains experts to provide it with accounting and consulting services. Too often, creditors fail to recognize the need for retaining their own professionals to act as independent advisors who provide the specialized consulting services that creditors require in a restructuring. Frequently, creditors are persuaded to use the existing sources of information provided by the company and its accountants. For a variety of reasons, this may not be the best alternative.

The Existing Accountants May Not Be Able to Provide an Objective Reassessment of the Situation

A company's financial difficulties are often the result of poor management or poor financial advice. In a workout situation, it may be necessary to reevaluate the competence of the current management. The existing accountants may be accustomed to the practices of the current management and therefore may be unable to assess the situation from an objective point of view.

The Debtor's Accountant May Not Be the Best Candidate to Conduct the Investigative Procedures

In some instances, irregularities may be the cause of the immediate problem. The debtor's accountant may be named as a defendant in lawsuits involving the troubled company because of alleged misconduct, negligence, or audit failures. Prior financial statements of the company, which were opined on by the debtor's accountants, may now be challenged. These types of circumstances often cloud the independence or objectivity of the debtor's accountant. In the early stages of a workout situation, it may not be possible for a creditor to determine if irregularities have taken place. For obvious reasons, it may not be in the company's or its accountant's best interests to report to the creditors any potential misconduct or irregularity that may have occurred during the accountant's tenure.

The Scope of Services to Be Performed May Be Restricted

Even in situations where the debtor's accountant is independent and competent to provide workout assistance, the scope of his or her services may be restricted or dictated by the debtor. The debtor's accountant may be requested by the debtor to present only information the debtor wants presented and to remain silent on other topics. For example, the debtor's accountant is under no obligation to disclose to the creditors any preferential transfers, as defined by 11 U.S.C. Section 547(b), that were made to officers, directors, or other insiders. In fact, it may be considered improper for the accountant to disclose such information without the consent of the debtor.

The Creditor's Accountant Works for the Creditor and Will Be More Responsive to the Creditor's Requests

In a workout or turnaround situation, the creditor's bane is a lack of timely, reliable, and accurate information. In order to properly evaluate alternative courses of action, creditors must have expert analyses to decipher complex data, and they must have access to the experience and unbiased judgment of trusted advisors. The priorities of the creditor's accountant are perfectly clear: inform, support, and advise the creditor in a timely, responsive, and professional manner.

Conflicts of interest, inherent restrictions in the scope of service, myopic views of past mistakes, and the age-old problem of serving two masters are just a few of the many reasons why the debtor's accountant should not be acceptable to the creditors. Not retaining separate accountants or "piggy-backing" accounting requirements with the debtor's accountant is, at best, imprudent and in the long run, cost ineffective. Clearly, creditors need their own accountants in workouts, turnarounds, and bankruptcy proceedings.

ACCOUNTANT'S ROLE—REPRESENTING THE CREDITOR IN AN OUT-OF-COURT WORKOUT

A company's financial crisis rarely occurs overnight, and the symptoms are often evident well before disaster strikes. Careful monitoring of a company's operating results, the results of its competitors and the industry in general, combined with frequent conversations with management regarding its current and future strategies, may reveal early warning signals of operating or financial problems. Management turnover, late filing of financial statements, declining market share, and failure to meet commitments and/or operating projections are indications that there may be just cause to question the stability of the company.

Once the creditor recognizes that an impending crisis may exist, professional assistance is required to evaluate the situation and determine an appropriate course of action. The accountant can function as the eyes and ears of the creditor by performing the hands-on analysis of the potential restructuring alternatives and, thereafter, by advising the creditor of his findings.

Upon the realization that a severe problem exists, the first step taken by the troubled company or its creditors is often to call a meeting of the creditors. At this meeting, the causes and potential solutions to the company's problems are discussed in order to explore the possibility of an out-of-court restructuring, which often requires a debt moratorium (a deferral of repayment) or other settlement of outstanding debts. At this meeting, professionals (accountants and lawyers) should be interviewed and retained.

Creditors require a full understanding of the financial condition of the company. There is a need for monitoring current operations, performing investigative accounting services, reviewing the company's plan to return to profitability, and assessing the viability of the enterprise.

To assist the creditor, the accountant must present a full picture of the troubled company—accurately determine the current financial status of the company, assess the commitment and competence of management, determine the causes of the financial difficulties, identify corrective actions that should be or are being considered, evaluate financial projections (cash flow and profit and loss), and regularly monitor company operations on behalf of the creditor.

The first tasks of the accountant engaged by the creditor in a workout/turnaround situation should be to identify and assess the measures taken by the debtor to immediately halt cash drains. The creditor's accountant must evaluate the efforts of the debtor to pinpoint the exact causes of the losses and to reduce overhead and discretionary spending. Early in the process, a determination must be made with respect to management's commitment and ability to execute a turnaround. There often are no easy answers and, therefore, it may be that new management must be retained to make the difficult personnel termination decisions and implement the required operational changes. Several options to be considered for a cash-generation or cash-conservation program in a crisis environment often include:

1. Sale of nonproductive assets.
2. Sale/leaseback of facilities.
3. Sale or cessation of noncore or unprofitable subsidiaries and lines of business.
4. Review of the accounts receivable policy in order to implement a program to accelerate collections.
5. Review of credit-granting policies and practices.

6. Review of the manufacturing process to determine if costs can be saved without affecting quality.
7. Reassessment of the marketing and advertising plans to determine if maximum benefits are being achieved for the spending levels.
8. Cessation of new hires.
9. Reduction of management's salaries.
10. Consolidation of job functions in order to eliminate excess staff.
11. Review of the effectiveness of the distribution and warehousing functions.

Following a review of a company's cash flow projections, the conclusion often reached is that the company needs additional financing. Sometimes the need is to bridge the time period required to execute an asset disposition or cost-cutting program. In many cases this immediate need also points out the longer term requirement for an infusion of new equity or long-term debt.

If financing is required, a careful analysis should be performed of the terms and conditions being considered in order to protect the creditors' interests. Lenders usually demand security and higher returns for loans to a company experiencing financial difficulty. Existing creditors often agree to extend new credit if they believe that the realization on the outstanding debt can be maximized and their position can be protected or enhanced by providing such credit.

After the cash losses are stopped, a determination must be made as to whether the company is viable and if a Chapter 11 bankruptcy filing may provide a more appropriate turnaround environment. In order to determine viability, an assessment must be made with respect to the company's long-term ability to generate funds to support its operations. Factors to consider include the industry in which the company operates and the company's competitiveness, management process, and ability to maintain an adequate capital base. In this process, the creditor must be satisfied with the accuracy and completeness of the financial information provided by the company. The books and records of the troubled company must be reviewed in order to assess the accuracy of the reported operating results of the company. The creditor's accountant should obtain an understanding of the accounting policies employed in areas that include the timing and method of recognizing revenue and expenses as well as the internal controls in place to safeguard assets.

Once the financial condition of the company has been assessed, other factors that may impact the viability of the entity must be addressed. An issue that must be addressed in every workout situation is whether management is adequate and/or competent. Signs of inadequate management include the following:

1. Insufficient management resources.
2. Management resistance to constructive change.
3. Ineffective organizational structure.
4. Poor communication and control.
5. Ineffective marketing/merchandising.
6. Inability to project/understand industry trends.
7. Lack of real sales growth.
8. Erosion of the customer base.

ACCOUNTANT'S ROLE—REPRESENTING THE CREDITOR IN A BANKRUPTCY PROCEEDING

The role of the accountant in a bankruptcy proceeding not only includes the activities in an out-of-court workout, but must be expanded to include also the activities, analyses, and creditor representation specific to the Chapter 11 bankruptcy proceeding. Relevant experience and a working knowledge of the provisions of the Bankruptcy Code are required for an accountant to protect a creditor's interest.

Section 1103 of the Bankruptcy Code (11 USC Section 1103), among other things, empowers a creditor's committee to conduct a broad investigation into the affairs of the debtor, its financial condition, and the prospects of its ability to continue as a going concern. In most instances, experienced professionals are retained to assist the committee in conducting these investigations.

Several of the more important issues in a bankruptcy proceeding that often require the services of an accountant are: determining the need for the use of cash collateral; review of financial schedules;

review of interim reports; analysis of preferences and fraudulent conveyances; and review of the business plan and plan of reorganization. Discussion of each of these issues follows.

Cash Collateral

One of the first motions filed by a debtor in a bankruptcy proceeding is a motion for the Use of Cash Collateral or Postpetition Financing. In order for a debtor to use the cash collateral of a secured lender (such as collections from accounts receivable), consent from the lender or an order from the court authorizing such use must be entered.

Financial Schedules

The Bankruptcy Code requires a debtor to timely file a schedule of assets and liabilities, a statement of financial affairs, and a list of executory contracts with the court. The schedules of assets and liabilities is a list of all assets of and claims against the debtor as of the petition date. This schedule is comprised of the following sections:

1. Schedule A-1—those creditors having priority claims such as wage claims up to $2,000 earned within 90 days of the petition date, certain contributions to employee benefit plans, deposits made by individuals up to $900, and certain outstanding taxes.
2. Schedule A-2—those creditors holding security interests in the assets of the debtor.
3. Schedule A-3—all other creditors having unsecured claims without priority.
4. Schedule B-1—all real property in which the debtor has an interest.
5. Schedule B-2—all personal property of the debtor.

Schedules A and B are significant documents because they contain the assets and liabilities in the order of priority that they must be dealt with in a plan of reorganization or liquidation. The accountant should review each schedule and compare the contents to the debtor's books and records to determine if they are accurate and complete.

The statement of financial affairs contains a series of 21 questions that must be answered by an officer of the debtor. The questions cover a broad range of financial and legal bases and should be reviewed by the accountant and counsel retained by the creditors.

The list of executory contracts contains all contracts to which the debtor is a party that have not yet been fully completed. These obligations, because of possible termination claims, must be carefully reviewed. In the case of onerous contracts, the debtor should attempt to renegotiate the terms or reject the contract. Favorable contracts should be assumed or assigned for value. In order to assume or assign, defaults must be cured and adequate assurance of future performance must be provided.

The creditors' accountant should independently assess the validity of any analyses used in support of rejection or assumption of an executory contract by the debtor because an assumption of a contract in the postpetition period may give rise to an administrative expense that is senior to general unsecured creditors.

Interim Reports

Each debtor-in-possession must file interim reports with the U.S. Trustee. In many cases, the debtor meets with the U.S. Trustee to discuss the reporting requirements and an agreement is reached on the content and frequency of the reports based on the debtor's ability to comply. The creditors' accountant should monitor such negotiations to ensure that the agreement reached will provide sufficient and timely information.

In Chapter 11 proceedings, the debtor usually files monthly operating results including actual balance sheets, actual monthly results of operations prepared on an accrual basis, and a schedule of receipts and disbursements. These monthly reports should be designed to enable interested parties to monitor the operating results of the debtor and to gain insights into whether the operations are deteriorating.

Although these reports are often helpful, creditors are best served if their professionals are working closely with the debtor to monitor the operating results on a more frequent basis. For this reason, the creation of a weekly "Flash Report" that provides timely, relevant financial and operating information should be considered. Significant operating variances should be investigated, disbursements should be reviewed for their appropriateness, and material changes in the balance sheet accounts should be analyzed by the creditors' accountant.

Another significant role of the creditors' accountant is to review past transactions of the debtor. The accountant must review the historical books and records for evidence of concealment of assets, insider transactions, and transactions executed for less than fair consideration.

Preferences and Fraudulent Conveyances

Preferences and fraudulent conveyances are two of the most powerful tools threatened and used in a Chapter 11 proceeding. The accountant can play an important role in defending or initiating an attack on creditors, insiders, lenders, shareholders, and others.

Preferences

Section 547 of the Bankruptcy Code (11 USC Section 547) contains the tests that must be satisfied in order to defend or recover on a preference. Briefly, the intention of this section is to protect all creditors from other creditors who may have been unfairly preferred with respect to payments on their debt within 90 days preceeding the filing of the Chapter 11 petition, and within one year if such creditor can be considered an "insider."

The highlights of the most significant provisions of Section 547 for the determination of a preferential transfer are:

1. On or within 90 days before the filing of the Chapter 11 petition (one year for an insider), a creditor received a transfer of an interest (cash, assets, guarantee, etc.) of the debtor in property.
2. The transfer was made for or on account of an antecedent debt, not in the ordinary course of business, and not in accordance with normal business terms.
3. The transfer was made while the debtor was insolvent—the fair value of its assets was less than its liabilities. (Off-

balance-sheet assets and liabilities should also be factored into the determination of solvency, i.e., contingent liabilities from lawsuits, potential lease liabilities, favorable leases, etc.).
4. The transfer enabled such creditor to realize more than he would have received in a Chapter 7 liquidation.

The accountant's role should include analyzing the debtor's books and records to identify transfers of assets and the preparation of a liquidation analysis to assist in quantifying and recovering preference payments.

Fraudulent Transfers
Section 548 of the Bankruptcy Code (11 USC Section 548) contains the tests that must be met to prove a fraudulent transfer. This section of the Code gained significant importance from the *U.S.* v. *Gleneagle Investment Co.* decision, 565 F. Supp. 556, where the judge ruled that under certain circumstances, a leveraged buyout could be considered a fraudulent conveyance.

Below is a summary of the significant provisions of Section 548 of the Bankruptcy Code:

1. Within one year before the Chapter 11 filing, a transfer of an interest was made or an obligation was incurred.
2. The transfer was made with the actual intent to defraud; or
3. The debtor received less than reasonably equivalent value for the transfer or incurrence of the obligation; and
   a. The debtor was insolvent or rendered insolvent by the transaction; or
   b. Was left with unreasonably small capital because of the transaction; or
   c. Intended or believed that the debts incurred were beyond the debtor's ability to service as they matured.

In most cases, a leveraged buyout involves the incurrence of a high level of debt secured by the assets of the company. The proceeds of the debt are raised by the acquirer of the company to purchase the stock from the existing shareholders. During the past five years, as many highly leveraged companies defaulted on their debt, creditors have successfully proved that the shareholders, not the company, received value for the debt incurred. The transactions, therefore, may be considered fraudulent conveyances because the debtor did not receive reasonably equivalent value and was rendered insolvent. There are numerous exceptions that must be considered prior to launching or defending a preferential transfer or fraudulent conveyance attack. The creditor's accountant plays a critical role in the analysis of these claims.

The Business Plan and Plan of Reorganization

After the debtor has had time to use the provisions of Chapter 11 to put its house in order, a business plan is prepared and provided to the creditors for their review. It is usually an operating plan which forms the basis for the plan of reorganization. The plan typically addresses the adjustments required to the debt and equity structure of the company in order for the company to emerge from bankruptcy.

The accountant, with the knowledge gained from investigations conducted and the monitoring role performed, should have a sufficient understanding of the debtor's business to provide an objective assessment of the assumptions underlying the operating plan. Significant disagreements over the company's projections are likely. The accountant can use his experience and understanding of the historical information developed from earlier analyses to assess whether available data either supports or disputes the assumptions employed in the plan. The assumptions and action plans must be reasonable in order for the debtor to achieve the projected results.

It is important to determine if the company's operational problems have been adequately addressed. This involves assessing the impact of the cost-cutting and revenue-enhancing measures undertaken by the company and evaluating what management realignments have taken or should take place. The workout accountant should consider adding professionals with specific industry expertise to his team in order to address industry related or specific technical issues such as industry trends, product design, the manufacturing process, and the numerous tax issues that often arise.

External factors affecting the company should also be assessed. An evaluation must be made with respect to the industry in which the company operates, including an assessment of its strategic position vis-à-vis that of its competition. Questions that must be answered include:

- What impact will internal changes have on the company's position in the marketplace?
- Is there now a weakness that competitors are (or will be) attempting to exploit?
- Is there adequate understanding of the behavioral patterns of its customers?
- Have the current and potential new markets and products been evaluated?

Based on the cash flow projected in the operating plan, a calculation of the level of debt that can be serviced is performed. In many reorganizations, creditors are given a combination of cash, notes, and equity securities. Section 507 of the Bankruptcy Code (11 USC Section 507) provides the order of priority of claims against which payments are to be made.

Negotiations of the terms and value of distributions to creditors and equity holders under a plan of reorganization are frequently topics of the most heated discussions between the parties in interest. However, the negative impact on operations caused by the uncertainty as to the debtor's viability due to the Chapter 11 proceeding, compounded by the litigation and other administrative costs of the proceeding, often motivates the parties to reach an expeditious compromise.

In most cases, a creditor should not agree to a plan of reorganization that would yield him less than what he would receive if the company were liquidated in a Chapter 7 proceeding. A creditor can object to confirmation of the plan (Section 1129 of the Bankruptcy Code (11 USC Section 1129) provides the requirements that must be met in order to confirm a plan), or if the debtor's exclusivity period for filing a plan has expired or has been terminated, the creditor may file his own plan of reorganization.

In some cases, creditors may not agree with the valuation analysis prepared by the debtor and used as the basis for formulating its plan of reorganization. In such cases, the creditor's accountant should assist the creditor in formulating an independent valuation analysis.

If the creditor elects to file a creditor's plan of reorganization, the accountant and other professionals employed by the creditor should assist the creditor in the preparation of a plan of reorganization and if needed, demonstrate that the plan meets the requirements for confirmation as listed in Section 1129 of the Bankruptcy Code.

DETERMINING IF A WORKOUT OR CHAPTER 11 IS THE PROPER COURSE OF ACTION

Determining whether a workout or Chapter 11 is the proper course of action is a complex decision. However, certain criteria can facilitate this determination.

Criteria Favoring a Workout over Bankruptcy

The Company Is Viable
The creditors have determined that the assets of the company, the competency of management, and the market/business plan indicate the possibility of a profitable future.

Management Is Honest and Competent
The creditors have assessed the leadership of the troubled firm by evaluating the answers to these questions:

- Are they making a concerted effort to isolate the company's problems and take steps to resolve them?
- What is the history of the company's leaders?
- Have they encountered prior difficulties and prevailed?
- Are they overwhelmed by the precarious condition of the company and anxious to disassociate from it?
- Despite possible restructuring within the firm, does management instill the confidence that key employees need to effect a turnaround?

Cash Is Available
Any workout considerations will be seriously jeopardized by an immediate cash crisis. The creditor must determine that sufficient

cash or financing is available to support the day-to-day activities of the troubled company and allow enough time for the turnaround to gain momentum.

Management Is Willing to Address the Problem and Work with the Creditors
Management is willing to confront the difficulties that have affected the troubled company. Management remains accessible and maintains communications with the creditor and his advisor.

Publicity, Expense, and Time Associated with a Chapter 11 Filing Would Impair the Company's Viability
While a Chapter 11 bankruptcy filing does provide protection for the troubled company, it may impair the speed with which the company might recover. Funds that ideally could be used for the company's turnaround would be directed in part to the bankruptcy administration costs in a Chapter 11 proceeding. In addition, the adverse effect of such publicity on the company's customers, suppliers, contractors, and so on, may be the impetus that could push an already troubled company into extinction.

Criteria Favoring a Bankruptcy over a Workout

Management Is Dishonest and/or Incompetent
Observations and investigations made by the creditor and his accountant reveal a lack of trust in the leadership of the troubled firm. Management has developed an ineffectual strategy for resolving the crisis and has, in effect, admitted defeat.

Management Is Not Willing to Address the Issues
Management is unwilling or unable to examine and subsequently attempt to resolve the issues that adversely affect the firm. The creditor and his advisor have no reassurance that management is willing to adopt any new course of action to alleviate the current crisis.

The Company's Viability Is Questionable
If a study by the firm's creditors and advisors reveals that the troubled company has deteriorated to such an extent (due to mismanagement, excessive debt, market failure, etc.) that a collapse is imminent, bankruptcy may be the only solution.

Required Financing Is Not Available
If a study by the company's creditors and advisors reveals that, outside of bankruptcy, there are no funds available to assist in turning around the troubled company, then a Chapter 11 proceeding may be the preferable alternative.

There Is a Need to Stay Certain Creditor Actions
If it becomes apparent to the creditor and the accountant that other essential creditors are refusing to conduct business with the troubled firm, are pursuing litigation or seeking to execute judgments against the firm, or are otherwise disrupting the normal course of business of the firm, it may be necessary to advise the company to seek shelter in bankruptcy.

There Is a Need to Reject Onerous Contracts
When onerous external or internal contracts severely limit the firm's ability to rectify the crisis through changing vendors, altering product lines, reorganizing personnel, and so forth, bankruptcy may be the only means available to allow the company to relieve itself from these immediate demands.

There Is a Need for Control of the Company
The recovery time of a troubled company is a very volatile period. At any time, the crisis may be exploited by any number of internal or external factors. The creditor should be alerted if the troubled company's assets are being threatened by other creditors, if key employees are considering resigning, or if investors are seeking to split up parts of the company. Filing for Chapter 11 will give the failing company adequate time to consider the options.

There Is a Risk of Lender Liability Claims
Once in a Chapter 11 proceeding, there is little risk of a lender liability suit for postpetition actions, because of the court's oversight of the process.

CONCLUSION

As we go further into the 1990s, workout situations may become more commonplace and the creditor's need for experienced and knowledgeable accountants will continue to increase.

This chapter has demonstrated the creditor's need for an accountant to act as its business advisor as the troubled company faces a workout situation or, ultimately, a bankruptcy proceeding. To ensure that a creditor's interests are adequately protected, it is essential that the accountant be engaged as early in the process as possible. While the debtor's accountant may seem a likely choice to provide required information and analysis, given the contentious atmosphere that often surrounds a firm's financial crisis, it is almost always advantageous to the creditor to retain his own independent accountant. This experienced business advisor can function as the "eyes and ears" of the creditor to review financial information, assess the debtor's management, study the industry (and the troubled company's position in that industry), and help the creditor determine the course of action most likely to protect his interests. The services of the accountant will permit the creditor to make an informed decision as to whether the troubled company can benefit from a workout or must be guided into bankruptcy. Regardless of the decision, by monitoring and evaluating the performance of the troubled company, the accountant can play a valuable role in the reorganization process.

CHAPTER 16

THE INVESTMENT BANKER'S ROLE IN THE WORKOUT PROCESS

Carter S. Evans
Senior Vice President
Shearson Lehman Brothers, Inc.

It's quite a pleasure to have the opportunity to write about the investment banker's role in the workout process, given the nature of the changing environment we find ourselves in today. As I write this, Drexel Burnham Lambert has just folded up its tent and gone from financial wizard to financial oblivion. The demise of the Drexel firm is symptomatic of the times. We can't say from a conservative point of view that we didn't see all of this coming, because several of us had predicted the demise of Drexel when the junk bond Ponzi scheme unwound. We also predicted the demise of the Southland deal before the deal had closed, and such things as Integrated Resources often intrigued us about why people would lend them money. I have been involved with Southmark, which is an advanced case of blue smoke and mirrors, where it would appear both the blue smoke and the mirrors were leased. It's interesting to see how these companies evolved to the point they did and managed to obtain the levels of debt financing that came to be. Quite frequently we hear that a company has figured out a way to get around all of the old rules of thumb and essentially defy gravity. Usually, that is the first sign of a prospective new client for the investment banker in restructuring.

In the sections that follow, I intend to try to lay out the general framework for how an investment banker goes about a successful restructuring. However, I must quickly point out at the same time this is based largely on my good luck to be one of a great number of members of those groups who successfully restructured over two dozen companies, including Chrysler, International Harvester, Manville, Kaiser Aluminum and Chemical, and Texaco, among others. It's important to know that it is only as a member of a large group that one does accomplish a successful restructuring plan, whether it's in court or out of court—and I would just say with emphasis, "Let's do it out of court." It's much cheaper, much easier, and it saves everyone involved a lot of money, in spite of what some people in the junk bond community appear to believe in the current environment. As a general comment, the only time a bankruptcy should truly be necessary is in cases, such as Manville and A. H. Robins, where the amount of the claims could not be determined, other than through judicial proceedings. The other type of situation in which a bankruptcy is the only practical alternative is in those cases where a total loss of confidence dictates a filing. Examples of this include the bankruptcies of such companies as American Continental (Lincoln Savings), Baldwin United, Drexel Burnham, Equity Funding, Federated/Allied, W. T. Grant, and Integrated Resources—again, to name but a few—where either the providers of financial accommodations lose confidence or trade vendors refuse to ship on credit, creating a loss of liquidity. The former is often associated with situations where fraud or other chicanery has occurred.

With any large group of people, organizing them and getting them to work effectively together is critical. By fostering communication among the parties, the investment bankers perform a vital function in the process. That brings me to one other point that should be made as a preface to this chapter, namely that not since 1975 have we had such a raft of new participants in the restructuring/workout/bankruptcy process. Incidentally, that's when I joined this business—quite by accident, I might note. In any event, it takes a number of years for the people involved to gain the experience required to be able to tell the difference between situations that belong in bankruptcy and those that don't belong in bankruptcy and should be "worked out" in an out-of-court mode. It would have been easy to put Chrysler into bankruptcy proceedings, for example, but I doubt it would have emerged as anything but a mere shadow of its former self, like White Motor or Allis-Chalmers later. Both of the latter two companies are examples of situations where management either refused or was unable to successfully come to grips with the problems at hand.

EVALUATING THE SITUATION AND GETTING MANAGEMENT TO COME TO GRIPS WITH THE PROBLEM AT HAND

While this is a fairly long heading for the first section of this chapter, it's an incredibly important one in the restructuring process. The first step in the restructuring process is obtaining a client. It is surprising to most people that the managements of troubled companies usually do not believe they are in trouble. Therefore, calling on potential clients can be a little delicate. For example, a new client recently retained us and held the strong belief that, with a quick fix of its bank agreements and an equity offering, there would be no problem. Less than three weeks later, the company has come to the conclusion that a bankruptcy filing is inevitable and is rushing to get prepared. I have yet to come in contact with a troubled company where the management didn't say one of the following things:

- "It's only a temporary blip."
- "There's no real operating problem."
- "There's not really an operating problem here, it's just because of all the junk debt that we have a financing problem." (This one has only developed recently.)

As I said above, I have yet to encounter a company that got into financial difficulties that didn't have an operating problem, although A. H. Robins and Manville come the closest. They may vary in severity, however, but they all come with operating problems and they normally come with a group of management that has no experience in insolvency or restructuring and often little experience in running the company that's in trouble. Everyone has heard stories about people making a killing in bankruptcy, or they've all read various things about bankruptcy and how it makes all your problems go away. It's somewhat similar to what the Spaniards thought they were looking for in their search for the fountain of youth in Florida centuries ago. As we all know, there was no fountain of youth and as we all should know, there is no company in financial extremis that merely needs a quick stop at the fountain of youth. One of the most difficult issues for the outside experts—investment bankers, accountants, lawyers, consultants—to get management to focus on is the importance of readdressing strategies, readdressing cost structures, and readdressing marketing efforts. We all face these things as very difficult issues to get management to deal with when we embark upon the restructuring process with a new client. In fact, that is the principal reason why so many successful restructurings and bankruptcy reorganizations have involved a change in management.

Until we have been able to identify the source of the company's problems, critical elements that must be dealt with at the start of any assignment are how to increase the company's cash flows and profitability and reduce its needs for working capital. Before any restructuring work can proceed, the company's cash flow and liquidity must be stabilized. This may involve DIP financing, selling a business, or various other options, but negative cash flows cannot be permitted if a company is to be restructured.

PREPARING THE BUSINESS PLAN

The first thing we do normally as investment bankers when assisting in the preparation of a business plan is to look at comparable companies—comparable in some ways, in that they are in the same basic industry, and noncomparable in others, in that they don't have problems—and try to determine what the profile should be of a successful company in whatever industry it may be, whether it's retailing like Revco, Federated, Circle K, or others, or entertainment or media like SCI Television, Ingersol Community Newspapers, or real estate, like General Development, L. J. Hooker (which combines real estate with retailing), and Radice, or the airlines (which, although some have come upon problems now, more will be in difficulty by the time this book is published). Knowing which industries are going to be getting into trouble, and when, is an important part of the investment banker's role.

The most successful approach in this process is to identify early on what the company's core business should be when it is restructured and to look at potential capitalization structures that go with it. In an iterative process, it is then necessary to see which businesses can be kept and which are clearly to be put on the exit list. In this way, the debt capacity can be determined and a plan can be prepared.

DETERMINING DEBT CAPACITY

A fundamental part in the process of developing your strategy for restructuring is to determine the amount of debt that the company can reasonably handle, and this must allow for either a static scenario or the possibility that the company will continue in a downtrend or, third, that the company will experience strong growth before requiring additional working capital to finance receivables, inventories, or whatever the case may be. Naturally, the company should strive to achieve a capitalization structure that provides adequate cushion and flexibility. In dealing with creditors, and particularly the secured creditors, it's been my experience that they do everything in their power to saddle the company with as much debt as possible. The ability to fight off attempts by creditors to preserve debt claims is the central issue in most workouts. One of the tendencies common among creditor groups is to try to force the company to sell assets quickly and at whatever prices necessary to pay out their particular layer of debt. For example, banks with secured loans are always interested in trying to see their collateral sold and debt reduced, even if the collateral has to be sold at prices that are disadvantageous to other creditors more junior to them or to the equity holders in the company's future. Naturally, the other problem created by overzealous lenders is that, by creating amortization schedules, they clearly signal to the world that asset sales will have to take place, which leaves the company in a weak position to negotiate any sales of assets that it may desire to undertake.

In this type of environment it's probably better to have provisions in the loan agreement or indentures, as the case may be, that provide debt service from operating cash flow only and require that additional mandatory prepayments come out of any asset sales.

Such a structure can only be achieved if there is adequate credibility developed by the management in its ability to manage the company in accordance with the business plan. The investment banker's role in this process involves analyzing other companies—primarily the principal competitors of the debtor—to determine what their capitalization structures are and, using that as a guide for the debtor's capitalization structure, to determine what will be required to enable the company to compete. One problem overleveraged companies always encounter is the competitors bandying about their name and their burdensome debt situation, saying, "You don't want to buy a truck or a house or what have you from XYZ Co. 'cause they're not going to be in business much longer with all the debt they have." Or developing suitable capitalizations for companies that are in the reorganization process. This can be greatly mitigated, and the effect on the company's business of an overburdensome debt structure can be greatly reduced. Suitable interest coverage ratios must also be a part of the consideration in determining the company's debt capacity.

In the later stages of the LBO craze that we have all witnessed, we often saw companies issuing debt to the degree that their operating cash flow could not even meet interest requirements, let alone amortization requirements. The bankruptcy law has a method of dealing with this, in that the plan must be feasible, which includes the company's ability to handle its obligations after it emerges from Chapter 11. I guess as a general rule of thumb you would hope that the company's plan would be able to show (in most cases) debt coverage in the neighborhood of one and a half times its annual interest charges. Generally, this is determined by looking at EBIT (earnings before interest and taxes) in determining the ratio of EBIT to interest. There also must be enough capacity to service principal amortization requirements under the company's debt instruments. In numerous cases, we've seen people, whether it's creditors or companies, using EBIT and adding back depreciation to determine debt service capacity of a company. Most troubled companies severely restrict or eliminate their capital expenditures to preserve liquidity in the deterioration phase. This is the corporate equivalent of burning your furniture to heat your house and inevitably leads to the obvious conclusion. In most cases, depreciation should actually be spent if the company is to grow and thrive. Therefore, it's impossible to include depreciation as a part of the company's cash flow and should be avoided, except in those exceptional cases where it can be demonstrated to be appropriate.

CREDIT AGREEMENTS

The chief thing to remember in negotiating and developing credit agreements with the company's lenders (and basically it should be remembered in conjunction with the entire plan) is to keep it simple. While we can all develop complex structures and some people think that shows a sign of their creativity, it is very rare indeed that a complex structure is required or beneficial from a practical business point of view. In fact, often complex structures require excess management time and attention to administer and involve extra reporting and extra overhead. In addition, investors and research analysts find complex structures too confusing and time consuming, which has the direct effect of diminishing the market capacity for the company's securities, thereby reducing the liquidity sought by the creditors in the first place. The fundamental form of creditor agreements generally follows along the following pattern.

Revolving Credit Agreement

The basic revolving credit agreement should be maintained in place to finance the working capital needs of the company over a three- to five-year time horizon. While it would be nice to have it be otherwise, the creditors will try to put a very tight limit on the amount of additional credit, if any, available.

The natural inclination of lenders is to see all of their loans repaid over the course of some "normal" time frame. (*Normal* seems to be adjusting to the environment, having meant three to five years in the early 1980s and lately five to seven years.) The essence of a revolving credit is to meet seasonal borrowing requirements. As a company's financial condition improves over time, the amount of the credit can decrease. However, it is most likely that some amount of working capital financing will be present in virtually any company. Based on a suitable and competitive capitalization structure, it is often appropriate to leave a revolving credit in place with a "bullet" maturity that will be refinanced. If the borrower is operating profitably and discharging its other obligations as they come due, there will be little problem in rolling over a revolver at maturity. It is far more likely that additional lenders will compete for the business, which enables the company to improve pricing.

Tranche Pricing

Another creative device in the tools available is tranche, or tiered, pricing. This can be employed in situations where the lenders agree that a certain amount of debt can be handled comfortably by the borrowers and should be priced accordingly. Additional debt or layers of debt make the lenders nervous and, therefore, should be priced at higher rates, giving the company a powerful incentive to pay down the more expensive tiers while compensating lenders for levels of risk with which they are uncomfortable. Normally, this will yield the borrower an overall blended cost that is less than would otherwise be the case and diminishes the need for renegotiating as the health of the company improves and the debt is reduced.

Chameleon Debt

One form of debt that has seldom been used was invented in the International Harvester situation, which I have chosen to call *chameleon debt*. This is a dynamic form of paper that relies on the underlying assumption that as a company's financial health and operating results improve, its access to the public markets will also improve, but the company cannot commit to a date when it will have access to the markets. At the same time, creditors are unwilling to leave it up to management about when the time is right to go to market. Therefore, a segment of the debt is carved out. To minimize uncertainty in the market, the amount qualified for chameleon debt should be specified and an upper limit on pricing should be set in advance, along with a minimum and maximum term to maturity. Indenture terms, including covenants, can be agreed upon and the indenture written in normal public indenture form. Prior to that time it is a portion of one of the company's loan agreements, complete with normal bank-type covenants.

When the creditors' investment banker is prepared to commit to underwrite the debt within those prescribed to parameters, the company prepares a registration statement and the paper is sold. Should market conditions never permit the sale, it continues to be serviced under the terms prescribed by the loan agreement. This provides, within predetermined ranges, the dynamic ability for the company to return to market when the time is right. Numerous variations and refinements also can be applied to such an instrument. For example, in the Harvester situation warrants were made available such that up to 20 percent of the value of the debt and warrant unit value could be in the warrant. This feature accomplished two purposes: it enabled the interest rate needed to sell the debt to be reduced while increasing the attractiveness of the security to the universe of potential buyers to include both fixed-income fund managers, who always secretly wanted to be equity managers and diversified fund managers. This security was a tremendous success and liquified $100 million of bank debt. It also had the effect of stretching the maturity on that segment of the debt well beyond anything the lenders would have been willing to consider.

EXCHANGE OFFERS

As a means of creating new equity and deleveraging a company, exchange offers have become one of the more popular vehicles. Whether this popularity will continue is highly questionable. For example, exchange offers successfully completed, while never having been high in number, have been dropping recently and in their purest form have virtually become extinct. In the wake of Judge Burton R. Lifland's recent controversial decision in the LTV case, the classic type of exchange offer may be impossible. First, though, a review of the types of exchange offers may be helpful.

Debt for Debt

By far the most successful type of offer in numbers, the debt for debt exchange typically has been employed where existing debt was trading at a substantial discount from face amount and the issuer was viewed as having adequate cash flow to service the debt. For example, if an issue of $100 million of debt with an original coupon of 12 percent was trading at 60 percent of face due to the issuer's problems in reported earnings, it might offer to exchange $75 million of new 18 percent bonds with the same maturity. This would offer the attraction to bondholders of generating $13.5 million in annual interest payments versus $12.0 million on the old issue, and it would have the added benefit of trading at a price much closer to par or at par, yielding a pickup in actual market value for the holders. From the issuer's standpoint, it would have the benefit of reducing outstanding debt by $25 million, the gain from which it would shelter from the losses that caused the original debt to trade at a discount.

One problem with this type of exchange offer (besides the obvious one of increased annual debt service) is that the requirements of *FASB Statement No. 15* provide that the issuer recognize the gain on early extinguishment of debt over the life of the new issue, if the total payments to be made on the new debt equal or exceed the payments required on the old debt. In the example above, this would occur if both issues had 16⅔ years to maturity ($1.5 million annual interest cost divided into $25.0 million principal reduction) or if the new issue had a maturity date more than 1.85 years longer than the old issue or any combination thereof. The $25 million principal reduction would be treated as a deferred credit on the balance sheet and would have the effect of being amortized as a reduction of interest expense over the remaining life. The accounting treatment required under *SFAS No. 15* has the effect of showing no reduction in total reported liabilities, while generating a taxable gain. While the debt for debt type of exchange offer had been the most popular variety, the effects of *SFAS No. 15* have all but eliminated its utility.

Equity for Debt

Given the increased levels of leverage on corporate balance sheets resulting from the takeover wave of the 1980s and the necessity to reduce the annual cash cost to the issuer, equity conversion offers have shown a great increase in popularity, and they would probably continue to do so were it not for the LTV decision, which is described later. The same concept employed in debt for debt exchange offers underlies the methodology in equity type offers (e.g., the total value offered to the debtholders in new securities must exceed the current market value of the old securities). While pure equity for debt exchange offers are rare, the methodology employed is worth explaining. Let's assume a company's bonds are trading at 20 percent of face amount or $200 per $1,000 bond. At the same time, however, due to turnaround speculation, the same company's common stock is selling for $1 per share. Therefore, an exchange offer would curtail offering in excess of 20 shares of stock for each bond before giving effect to the dilutive effect on the stock price.

Based on a recent deal, assume a company has $140 million of public debt trading at $20, giving a market capitalization of the debt of $28 million. Assume also that the company has 15 million shares of common stock outstanding, which are trading at $0.75 per share, giving the stock a capitalization of $11,250,000. As an incentive to the bondholders, the company is willing to offer a 25 percent premium to get them to exchange the debt for new equity, as follows:

Market capitalization of debt	28,000,000
Divided by common stock price	0.75
Shares to yield parity	37,333,333
Multiplied by premium	125
	46,666,667

For purposes of this example, assume also that a minimum acceptance rate of 90 percent was put on the offer. The dilution would be calculated as follows:

New shares offered	46,666,667
Acceptance rate	90
New shares issued	42,000,000
Shares previously issued	15,000,000
New shares outstanding pro forma	57,000,000

Assuming the offer is successful, the stub of old bonds outstanding would increase in price to something approaching par value within a relatively short time afterwards, particularly if market participants believe interest can be paid currently (a necessity, since no one would be willing to accept common stock if the debt were to be in default). For this purpose, let's assume the bonds trade at 80 percent of face amount and the common falls to $0.625, yielding a new market capitalization as follows:

Old stockholders' ownership (15/57)	26.32%
Bondholders' ownership (42/57)	73.68%
New market capitalization:	
14,000,000 bonds @ 80	$11,200,000
Common stock @ $0.625	35,625,000
Total capitalization pro forma	$46,825,000

This example implies that by completing a successful recapitalization, the market capitalization of the debt and equity increases from $39,250,000 to $46,825,000 or 19.3 percent, which in actuality would not be surprising, given the improved financial condition of the issuer.

The tax effect of the above exchange would be to generate cancellation of indebtedness income (Bankruptcy Code Section 108) of $126 million ($140 million less $14 million), which if done properly can be offset by the company's net operating loss carryforwards. However, given the restrictions under Code Section 382 on changes in ownership, the company's ability to use any remaining NOLs in the future would be greatly restricted, given the greater than 50 percent change in ownership.

The LTV Decision

In January of 1990, Bankruptcy Judge Burton R. Lifland in the Southern District of New York ruled that certain debenture holders of the LTV Corporation would not receive a claim in bankruptcy equal to the face amount of the debt they received in an exchange offer. Instead, holders would be entitled to a claim equal to the value of the debentures received in the exchange plus unpaid interest. The difference between face value and the value of the debentures at the exchange date is unmatured interest, which compounds to the maturity date. Thus, in bankruptcy, the holder's claim is the value on the exchange date plus unpaid cash interest plus the portion of the original issue discount attributable only to the period between the exchange date and the bankruptcy date.

Unless an exchange offer removes the bankruptcy risk of a company, holders will be reluctant to exchange. No one will exchange a potentially larger debt claim arising from the issuance of a security for the much smaller claim caused by the erosion in value of the debt and the subsequent exchange. This ruling will have the effect of changing the exchange offer market. Debtors and their advisors are precluded from patching up the situation through an exchange offer and postponing the inevitable major restructuring to a future date. It appears likely that this will increase the popularity of prepackaged exchange offers.

Prepackaged Bankruptcy

Pursuant to Section 1126(b) of the Bankruptcy Code, acceptance of a reorganization plan obtained prior to filing the petition can be used if the nonbankruptcy law disclosure requirements relating to the offer or the disclosure requirements contained in Section 1125(a) have been fulfilled. Often referred to as a *walk through* or a *quickie* bankruptcy, this section has not seen great use. The concept is that, by structuring an exchange offer in the form of two alternative deals—one deal if the requisite level of acceptances are obtained out of court and a less attractive deal if it needs to be done in court—a sufficient number of holders and bonds will approve (e.g., a majority in number and two thirds in amount) to confirm a reorganization plan. The idea is that, by filing a bankruptcy petition and the plan of reorganization simultaneously, a company theoretically can be back out of court and reorganized within three or four months. From a practical point of view, it still would very likely take six months or more to complete a reorganization plan. This is particularly the case in instances where there is pending litigation, outstanding disputes with the I.R.S., or other significant contingent claims, where the amount of the claims must be adjudicated through a lengthy litigation process.

On April 16, 1990, the Republic Healthcare reorganization plan was confirmed by the bankruptcy court only four months after filing a prepackaged plan in December. To my knowledge, this is the largest and quickest case yet to be confirmed on this basis. I would note the plan is still subject to appeal as of this date.

TERM LOAN AGREEMENTS

It is perfectly appropriate in restructuring to convert a portion of a borrower's loans to term financing. It can most often be done in asset rich/cash flow poor situations, but need not be restricted to these. For example, in numerous real estate-oriented restructurings, amortization has been tied to the orderly disposal of excess real estate. Often lenders will create amortization requirements that make it impossible for a company to service the debt without the sale of a division or subsidiary occurring. This often has the perverse result of leaving the borrower with less cash flow available to service the remainder of its debt, but it may be the only means of making significant debt reduction or of obtaining agreement with the creditors.

The determining factor that often is the difference between whether sales of assets or businesses are required, not surprisingly, is the lenders' confidence and familiarity with operating management. Getting the credit providers to spend the time to become familiar with the operations, while a burden on management, is highly recommended. If the lenders get to know the operating management and they get to see the new products being produced, some attachment and loyalty will likely develop. While care must be taken with regard to proprietary information regarding products on the drawing boards, understanding the logical direction in which the company is headed and seeing its hopes for the future give claim holders something they can latch onto and form a bond with the company. It is impossible to make a sweeping generalization here, however. Manufacturing operations are best suited to this type of field trip, in my experience, and care should be used in selecting the factory sites and personnel to be visited. Particularly old facilities are generally best avoided, as are visits during summer shutdown periods or to plants that have inventory stacked to the ceilings. No one wants to watch grass grow, so something exciting or demonstrating particular skill is best.

VALUATION OF THE BUSINESS

In analyzing a company's restructuring opportunities, a critical part of the investment banker's role is to develop a valuation of the enterprise and of its component parts. Often other professionals must play a role in this process, such as real estate appraisers. The importance of this effort cannot be emphasized enough. It provides the critical answer to the question, "How big is the pie?" Unfortunately, gaining agreement on this issue among the stake holders and their investment bankers is not usually a process free from controversy. Naturally, more junior classes of claimants attempt to show that the value of the business is very large, thereby leaving more for them, while senior claimants will attempt to show minimal values, thereby dictating that they should receive the vast majority of the value available. Normally, the truth is to be found somewhere in between. Numerous protracted battles have occurred over valuation, and it is important to remember your investment banker will be the one called upon to testify about valuation in any court proceeding.

An example of the importance of valuation can be found in the Evans Products (no relation) bankruptcy proceeding. The equity holders were offered 15 percent of the new common stock in the form of stock and warrants to be distributed in Grossman's. Victor Posner, the controlling shareholder through his control of Sharon Steel, argued for control of the common. When no agreement could be reached, the lending group threatened to give the equity holders nothing and ask the court to apply the absolute priority rule. With no agreement forthcoming, a valuation battle ensued in court. (Our firm represented the lenders, to give you a hint at the outcome.) The result was that the court found insufficient value to cover the claims of the creditors and, therefore, awarded them all of the equity and wiped out Sharon Steel's interest.

Different valuation techniques can be applied in the same situation and radically different outcomes achieved. One company we are representing has different groups arguing values of the enterprise from $20 million to $80 million, all using the same numbers. Set forth below are some of the standard accepted valuation techniques and some of the ways they get applied.

Multiples of Cash Flow

Invariably, different groups argue over what amount of cash flow is available. They then will each hire experts, who will produce comparable company data that may show varying ranges of multiples. Care must be taken to identify viable comparable companies. Also, a careful review of the debtors' operations and analysis of the comparable companies' reports must be performed to eliminate nonrecurring items. Then an analysis of trading ranges over cycles should be performed to determine high and low trading multiples.

Multiples of Book Value

Multiples of a company's historical tangible book value can often be used, along with cash flow multiples, to corroborate valuation. Care must be so exercised that assets acquired many years prior to the valuation are given an appropriate current value. Also, the book value of the comparable companies being used must be examined to determine whether they contain inflated or deflated asset values as well.

Liquidation Value

There are two primary uses for determining liquidation value in a restructuring or reorganization scenario. The first is simply informational to let the stockholders know, at the appropriate time, what that alternative holds in store for them. The second use is the requirement in the Bankruptcy Code (Section 1129) that an impaired class must receive as much as they would receive under a Chapter 7 liquidation for a plan to be confirmed. Liquidation analyses are often highly theoretical and contentious issues. If properly documented, they can provide powerful negotiating tools. Often the trickiest parts of a liquidation analysis are valuing real property and estimating the tax impact of a total liquidation.

Once all the parties in a reorganization have determined values, they have various tactics they use to influence the outcome of a valuation dispute. The most common tactic for someone who is trying to increase the value attributed to a company is to take some measure of "normalized" earnings several years in the future, applying a multiple to those earnings, and discounting the value back to the present time. This can have the double-barreled effect of applying a high multiple and low discount rate such that an overly inflated valuation results. At the other end of the spectrum would be someone who takes the prior year's earnings, which were adversely affected by the company's problems, and applying a low multiple to them, thereby yielding a low valuation.

Expert testimony provided by investment bankers on valuation has often proven critical in the outcome of reorganization proceedings. Convincing arguments by a credible witness frequently have a significant impact on the bankruptcy judge.

CONCLUSION

In this chapter I have set forth many of the functions commonly performed by investment banking firms. Certainly, it is by no means an exhaustive list. For example, I have only touched on the liquidity that can be provided by investment bankers in underwriting securities created in the restructuring process, thereby creating the liquidity that creditors so often demand. By having competent investment banking advice early in a restructuring, the types of securities to be issued and the capitalization structure to support them can be developed. The investment banking advice provided to the debtor and the creditors is of great benefit in assuring that all parties are made reasonably comfortable that the timing and marketing of the securities is known in advance.

This should give a broad background of the critical role investment bankers play in the restructuring and reorganization process and the types of services they normally perform.

CHAPTER 17

CONSIDERATIONS FOR INVESTING IN TROUBLED LEVERAGED BUYOUTS

Robert F. Cushman, Esq.
James D. Epstein, Esq.
Pepper, Hamilton & Scheetz

INTRODUCTION

The leveraged buyout (LBO) industry has its origins in the 1960s; however, it was not until the 1980s, with the introduction and acceptance of noninvestment grade corporate debt (commonly known as *high-yield* or *junk* bonds), that the marketplace experienced unprecedented growth in both the number and value of LBO transactions. With this new financing technique, corporations realized that overnight they could greatly expand their existing operations. Further contributing to this growth was the recognition by financial institutions that opportunities existed to earn substantial fees in connection with LBOs by providing advice on structure and by acting as brokers and finders. In addition, the reemergence of merchant banking institutions in the United States, which not only acted as brokers, finders, and advisors to buyers and sellers, but also participated in LBOs by sponsoring the transactions (in many cases in partnership with the target company's—the "LBO company"—management) and by providing capital to fund the purchase price, also fueled this growth in LBOs.

In the late 1980s, the country began to experience a rise in the number of LBOs that were experiencing financial trouble. Although relatively few major LBOs have failed to date, the bankruptcy of Revco D.S., Inc., less than two years after completion of the original LBO transaction is an example of what can happen.

The purpose of this chapter is to outline the issues relating to the restructuring of an LBO company that is experiencing financial problems. This article will discuss the capital structure of a typical LBO company and the reasons why an LBO company is particularly susceptible to financial difficulties, the identity and competing interests of the parties involved in an LBO restructuring, certain tax issues related to restructuring an LBO company, and the susceptibility of an LBO company to a fraudulent conveyance challenge with respect to the original transaction or the subsequent restructuring. This chapter does not discuss the bankruptcy implications of an LBO restructuring in detail, because bankruptcy in general is explored more fully in other chapters of this book and the information and the analysis contained therein is readily transferrable to the LBO context.

CAPITAL STRUCTURE—REASONS FOR FINANCIAL DIFFICULTIES

Capital Structure in General

The capital structure of an LBO company typically consists of common stock equity, mezzanine financing (which includes subordinated debt and may also include preferred stock), and senior debt. The capital structure of an LBO company is generally so formulated that the cash flow expected to be generated by the operations of the acquired business will be sufficient to service the debt incurred in the transaction (including acquisition debt and working capital). The percentage makeup of each capital component is dependent upon, among other things, the risk-taking nature of the acquiring company or the LBO sponsor and by its lenders, the creditworthiness of the LBO company, and the size of the overall transaction. The common stock equity component of the capital structure typically provides from 5 to 15 percent of the total capital; the senior debt component typically provides from 50 to 60 percent of the total capital; and the mezzanine component provides the difference.

The senior debt component of the capital structure is generally fully secured by the assets of the LBO company. Historically, funds for the senior debt component have been provided by banks, insurance companies, and pension funds. The amount of this debt is based upon the value of the assets in the LBO company at any given time; consequently, it will typically take the form of a term facility to be repaid at specified intervals, as well as a revolving credit facility based upon the fluctuating value of the LBO company's assets, such as receivables and inventory. Generally, the equity component of the capital structure is provided by the acquiring company or the LBO sponsor, by other venture capital investors, senior management of the LBO company, employee stock ownership plans, and, in certain instances, the former stockholders of the LBO company. In addition, it is typical for the providers of the mezzanine financing to receive an "equity kicker" in the form of common stock or warrants to purchase common stock. In addition to the equity kicker, the mezzanine financing, which is generally obtained from insurance companies, pension funds, and, in certain instances, the former stockholders of the LBO company, will take the form of preferred stock or unsecured subordinated high-yield junk bonds. This subordinated debt may take the form of a combination of fixed-term notes, redeemable-term notes, convertible-term notes, payment-in-kind notes, or zero-coupon bonds. Generally, the mezzanine financing has principal maturities, which correspond to the points in time when there is anticipated cash flow. The use of zero-coupon bonds, which do not pay interest during their term, provides a mechanism to not only postpone the payment of principal but also to postpone the payment of interest until maturity, thus enabling the available cash flow to be used to service the senior and other mezzanine financing.

Prior to the placement of some or all of the mezzanine financing, it is possible that one or more financial institutions, typically the investment banking firms, which are acting as the financial advisor to the acquiror, will provide interim "bridge" financing for the transaction. This debt is typically short term and is to be repaid from the proceeds of the sale of junk bonds, which is expected to occur shortly after the completion of the acquisition. This form of financing became increasingly more popular during the latter portion of the 1980s, when acquirors were under increasing pressures from sellers to complete the transactions very quickly.

Reasons for Financial Difficulties

Since the success of an LBO company is based upon an expectation of operating cash flow, the inability of the LBO company to generate sufficient cash flow will generally be the basis of its financial trouble and ultimate failure. This problem will generally result from one or more of the following sources: an original purchase price that was too high when compared against the future cash flow which is actually generated by the LBO company; a downturn in the LBO company's business; a downturn in the industry in which the LBO company operates; a downturn in the economy in general; and rising interest rates. The first reason for a failure, paying too high a price, can stem from any number of factors. For example, some LBO transactions are undertaken by existing companies in the hopes of taking advantage of operating synergies between its existing business and the business to be acquired. If these synergies are not properly analyzed, the acquiring company could agree to pay too high a price as a result of a false expectation. Further, in today's world of high technology, companies are bought and sold partly on the basis of their existing technology and their position with respect to the development of future technology within their industry. This is inherently a speculative analysis, and the failure to properly analyze the technology being purchased, as well as how it translates into sales and earnings, could result in a buyer overvaluing the technology being purchased and, thus, paying too high a price for the LBO company.

A downturn in the LBO company's business may result from any number of reasons. For example, LBO transactions often result in so disrupting the LBO company's employees that there are significant management changes, whereby talented managers leave the LBO company shortly after the LBO is completed. Unless replaced with equally talented executives, the LBO company's operations could suffer. More importantly, a business downturn that effects the demand for the LBO company's products or services could result from changes in customer tastes, or, as with any business regardless of its capital structure, the introduction by a competitor of additional competing products and services.

As the 1980s were generally a period of economic growth, most LBO transactions would not be expected to experience financial trouble as a result of a downturn in the industry in which the LBO company competes or a downturn in the economy in general. However, some industries, such as the steel industry, the retail consumer products industry, and the automotive industry, have experienced difficulties recently and LBO transactions relating to these fields may be at risk.

A downturn in the economy is generally accompanied by increased interest rates. Such a downturn usually translates into there being less potential purchasers of the LBO company's goods and services and, thus, weakening sales. Generally, LBO debt is so structured that a significant portion of the debt is subject to interest rate fluctuations. Although interest rates during the 1980s have been more predictable than during the 1970s, any increase in interest rates could have a negative impact upon an LBO company, especially if there is an extremely small amount of common stock equity supporting the transaction. For example, the use of short- and medium-term debt may require refinancing after a limited period. Further, the interest rates on revolving credit facilities for working capital are generally tied to some index (i.e., LIBOR or the lender's reference rate). Consequently, higher interest rates at the time when debt is anticipated to be refinanced, or increases in the index rates during the term of a fluctuating rate credit facility, would increase the LBO company's interest expenses—putting greater demands upon the LBO company's available cash flow at the same time when its cash flow is weakening as a result of slowing sales of its products and services.

Further, in many instances, it is contemplated by both the acquiror and its lenders that at least a portion of the assets of the LBO company must be sold to reduce the overall debt burden of the LBO company. In these circumstances, the parties to the transaction do not expect the cash flow that may reasonably be expected to be generated from all of the current operations will be sufficient to service the debt incurred as a result of the LBO transaction; however, a leaner company with a smaller debt burden is expected to be successful. Increases in prevailing interest rates after the completion of the LBO transaction could effect the ability of the LBO company to complete any such divestitures or spin-offs. It is likely that a buyer of the unwanted assets will also finance the purchase with debt. As interest rates rise, the costs associated with the purchase of the assets will increase, with the likely consequences to the LBO company seeking to dispose of the assets being reduced sale proceeds available to repay debt. In the worst case, the LBO company may be unable to locate a willing buyer, since the costs of financing to the buyer will be too great, thus leaving it with an unmanageable debt burden.

Further contributing to the financial health of a company that has undergone an LBO are the actions taken by management and the board of directors to alleviate the problems resulting from paying too high a price, a downturn in the business, the industry or the economy, or an increase in interest rates. For example, the first reaction may be to cut operating costs and, to some extent, fixed costs, if possible. A decision to reduce employees and inventory, for example, could result in a decrease in sales and revenues, since there are fewer products to sell and fewer people to produce replacement products. These reductions would naturally cause sales and cash flow to be reduced, and, if the LBO company's borrowing capacity is dependent upon the level of inventory, its available lines of credit would disappear. Further, reduced sales means a reduction in receivables, which could also translate into reduced borrowing capacity, since a typical working capital line of credits is based, in part, upon the level of an LBO company's receivables. All of this would have a spiral effect, which would likely mandate additional reductions in employees, which would perpetuate the circle until the LBO company has failed.

PARTICIPANTS IN AN LBO RESTRUCTURING

There are several different participants in the restructuring of a financially troubled LBO company. These participants generally fall into one of several categories: equity holders, including management; current lenders, including holders of senior debt and mezzanine financing; and new investors, including the providers of new equity capital. Naturally, the interests of these participants vary among the different categories, and, while the participants within each category generally have similar interests, their interests, too, will vary.

Equity Participants

If an LBO company is experiencing financial trouble, the investment of the equity holders is at substantial risk. To the extent management has invested in the transaction, the managers share a similar risk and have an interest that is aligned with the other equity holders. However, some LBO sponsors may have so structured the original LBO transaction that much of their original equity infusion has already been repaid to them in the form of closing or other advisory fees. Consequently, the actual amount of money that they have at risk has been substantially reduced. In fact, it can be argued that, in many instances, the only portion of their equity participation at risk is their profit potential. Conversely, the management stockholders may continue to have their entire original equity investment at risk, as well as their profit potential, and it is the management stockholders who are usually less able to afford the loss of their investment when compared to the other equity holders.

Moreover, it is likely that, to a large extent, the management stockholders consist of the executives who have historically operated the business. Under these circumstances, their economic interests also include preserving their current compensation, which is a large component of their overall economic stake in the LBO company. These executives, in contrast to the other equity participants, may also be motivated by other noneconomic factors, including corporate loyalty, the interests of their co-workers, their reputation as executives, and their standing in the community. Consequently, the management stockholders will be less willing than the other equity participants to close plants, reduce employment, or undertake any other action that could reduce the size of the LBO company, because these actions could affect their reputation and standing.

As a result of the different financial and other interests of the various equity participants, tensions may become apparent among them during the course of the restructuring negotiations. Management will seek to pursue long-term goals at the expense of a short-term solution designed to salvage the various equity positions of the equity participants. Management, for example, may propose a course of action that would improve operations in the long run but would result in the dilution of the present equity. One alternative would be to propose that a debt holder convert a portion of its loans to equity, which would dilute the present equity holders. In management's view, this may be all that is necessary to turn the LBO company around, and the managers would be willing to be diluted if it meant job security.

On the other hand, the nonmanagement equity participants may recommend a course of action that involves the sale of substantial assets or divisions of the LBO company. This could create a source of conflict, because it directly effects the direction that the LBO company will be taking as a result of the restructuring. Generally, management will look toward preserving the LBO company's plants, assets, and divisions, while the other equity participants will see these as a potential sources of cash that can be utilized to reduce existing debt. Similarly, management will be disinclined to reduce employment, capital expenditures, and research and development because these will again effect the long-term growth potential of the LBO company, whereas the other equity participants will also view these as potential areas in which operating costs can be reduced and the available cash can be shifted to be used for the repayment of the existing debt.

In sum, it can be expected that management would advocate a one-time recapitalization of the LBO company so it can complete the restructuring and return its attention to operating the business. On the other hand, the other equity participants can be expected to advocate a series of steps to be taken over time, which include deferrals and reductions of interest and principal payments on the existing debt, and which minimize the dilution of its equity position in the LBO company.

Lenders as Participants

The next group of participants involved in the restructuring of an LBO company is the existing lenders, including the senior lenders and the mezzanine lenders. Generally, both groups of lenders will prefer granting the LBO company only gradual interim relief, which results in a deferral or extension of required payments, rather than a reduction in the payments. The LBO company, on the other hand, will be seeking an immediate and permanent reduction of debt. Naturally, the senior lenders that hold the secured position can be expected to be the more intransigent of the two lender groups. The mezzanine lenders, which are generally unsecured and subordinated in right of payment to the senior lenders, as a result, have a weaker bargaining position. They can be expected to be slightly more accommodating—but only if the LBO company's assets are not expected to generate sufficient liquidation proceeds.

The strategy of the LBO company is to convince its lenders that bankruptcy is a real possibility, and that the company is prepared to take such a course of action if its lenders are not cooperative during the course of the restructuring. Because of their senior secured position, the senior lenders should be less concerned about a bankruptcy than the mezzanine lenders, which are generally unsecured. However, in practicality, the senior lenders will seek to avoid foreclosing upon the LBO company's assets not only because of the delays attendant in obtaining the appropriate relief but also because of the risk that the assets being foreclosed upon will diminish in value as a result of the foreclosure action. Furthermore, lenders encounter the practical considerations of lender liability in determining whether to foreclose upon (and take control of) some or all of an LBO company's assets.

Because of its complications and procedural requirements, the bankruptcy of an LBO company is likely to result in substantial fees and expenses that would otherwise not be incurred in an out-of-court restructuring. If the LBO company's creditors, especially the mezzanine lenders, can be convinced that they will receive less in a bankruptcy than if an out-of-court restructuring is completed by the parties, then they will be more willing to compromise and come to a settlement of their claims. Recently, many companies that have sought to restructure their debt with their existing creditors have met with intransigent creditors that were willing to risk a bankruptcy proceeding, rather than accept what they believed was less than what they were rightfully entitled to.

New Investors as Participants

The next group of participants in the restructuring of a financially troubled LBO company is the potential new investors. Often, an LBO company is unable to solve all of its financial problems by restructuring its current debt, by selling assets or divisions and using the sale proceeds to repay existing debt, by restructuring operations and cutting costs, whose savings are used to repay existing debt, or by a combination of the foregoing. Under these circumstances, a new infusion of equity capital is required.

These funds may come from the existing holders or from new investors. It may also be possible to convince some or all of the LBO company's existing creditors to convert some of their debt holdings into equity of the LBO company. In any event, under these circumstances, the existing equity participants are likely to see their equity holdings diluted if new equity is obtained, no matter what the source.

In connection with a new equity contribution to the LBO company, a new investor will generally have two important concerns. First, the new investor will seek to identify the LBO company's problems and determine whether a new influx of equity itself will solve the problems, what additional actions will need to be taken in connection with solving the LBO company's problems (this may include a management change), and whether the LBO company's problems are capable of being solved in a reasonable time. Second, in connection with its investment, the new investor will seek to obtain a position senior to all of the other equity participants. In fact, the new investor, to the extent possible, may demand a position that is senior to the position of the mezzanine lenders.

A new equity investor is unlikely to infuse new equity capital into an LBO company whose business operations are not sound, whose problems (other than capital structure) are insurmountable, or whose competitiveness in its industry has been diminished by its neglect of capital expenditures and research and development activities. The easiest situation in which to obtain a new equity investor is the case where the LBO company's problems were created by the payment of too high a purchase price. In that situation, the LBO company's business is likely to be sound, and it is likely to have strong earnings before interest and taxes (EBIT). Under those circumstances, the new investor need only negotiate the highest percentage of the LBO company for its new equity infusion. On the other hand, if the LBO company has been losing market share in a sound industry and business climate, and its EBIT has been on the decline, it will be difficult to convince a new investor to infuse new equity—no matter how much of the LBO company it is offered and no matter how senior its position may be.

In addition to negotiating for senior status relative to the other equity participants, and, to the extent possible, to the mezzanine lenders, the new investors will also seek to be indemnified by the other participants against claims relating to the operation of the LBO company prior to the time when they make their investment, as well as claims relating to fraudulent conveyance challenges that may result from the original LBO transaction. Generally, the new investors will look not only to the equity participants for this indemnity but also to the senior and mezzanine lenders. This may or may not be acceptable to the other participants in the restructuring. If bankruptcy or other litigation remains a real possibility even after the restructuring is completed, the other participants can be expected to resist providing this indemnity.

Many of the available sources of new equity are investors that are experienced in investing in "turnaround" situations. These investors will neither expect an immediate return on their investment nor immediate progress in solving the problems of the LBO company. Further, they can be expected to provide expertise to the LBO company in helping it solve its problems.

Other Participants

In addition to the participants described above, other participants in the restructuring of an LBO are worth mentioning. These include stockholders and creditors of the LBO company prior to the original LBO transaction, the attorneys, accountants, investment bankers, and other advisors and consultants who participated in the original LBO transaction and advised the LBO company and the other participants since the original LBO transaction, as well as the attorneys, accountants, investment bankers, and other advisors who can be expected to participate in the actual restructuring of the LBO company. For example, the former stockholders of the LBO company who were paid for their equity interest in the LBO company in connection with the original LBO transaction may find themselves the subject of litigation relating to fraudulent conveyance issues. Furthermore, the attorneys who provided the legal advice, as well as the accountants and investment bankers who provided financial advice in connection with the original LBO transaction, may also find themselves the subject of litigation in connection with their roles in the original LBO transaction. Finally, the LBO company can expect that the costs of the attorneys and advisors retained by all parties in connection with the restructuring will be borne by the LBO company.

FEDERAL TAX ISSUES IN A RESTRUCTURING OF AN LBO COMPANY

Since the restructuring of a troubled LBO company will involve to a large extent the restructuring of its capital structure, and, principally, the deferral or forgiveness of indebtedness, the following discussion of the tax considerations relating to the restructuring an LBO company focuses upon the federal income tax consequences resulting from the modification and discharge of existing indebtedness. In addition, a troubled LBO company may, in many cases, generate net operating losses (NOLs), which can be used to shelter future income from federal income taxes, notwithstanding the fact that, upon completion of the original LBO, interest and depreciation deductions generated as a result of the transaction may be sufficient in many cases to shelter all or a substantial portion of the LBO company's income from federal income taxes. Consequently, the following discussion also will discuss the considerations relating to the use and preservation of NOLs in the context of a restructuring of an LBO company.

The following discussion of the federal income tax consequences of restructuring a troubled LBO company is not intended to be an exhaustive discussion of all of the potential tax consequences. Additional provisions of the Internal Revenue Code of 1986, as amended (the I.R.C.), are implicated in any such transaction. For example, the Tax Reform Act of 1986 added a concept to the code of taxing a profitable company in the situation where its income for financial accounting purposes exceeds its income for federal income tax purposes. This addition to the concept of an alternative minimum tax provides for a 10 percent tax on the difference between such a company's "book" income and its "tax" income. It should be noted, however, that, as a result of the Technical and Miscellaneous Revenue Act of 1988, an insolvent corporation or a corporation otherwise in bankruptcy that completes a restructuring pursuant to which stock is issued to its creditors should not create an alternative minimum tax problem as a result of such an issuance of stock.

Finally, the following discussion relates only to the federal income tax consequences of the restructuring of an LBO company. The state and local tax consequences (which will vary from jurisdiction to jurisdiction) need to also be considered but are beyond the scope of this chapter.

Discharges of Indebtedness

Where there is a discharge of indebtedness, the general rule under I.R.C. Section 61(12) provides that the debtor has ordinary income in amount equal to the amount of indebtedness that is forgiven since the debtor has received an economic benefit from the discharge. Consequently, the threshold question to be addressed in the context of restructuring an LBO company is whether the existing indebtedness is actually debt or some other form of security. This inquiry becomes of critical importance, because the tax laws give paramount weight to the substance and not the form of an instrument, such that the label placed upon a particular security will not control its tax treatment if it possesses characteristics that are more commonly associated with another type of security.

In an LBO, many mezzanine instruments that are labeled as debt have substantial equity characteristics. For example, the security may be convertible into equity at some time, or the payment of the principal amount may only occur based upon compliance with certain financial (particularly cash flow) tests. Further, in a restructuring, holders of mezzanine instruments may demand "equity kickers" to defer receipt of principal or interest payments due thereunder. Consequently, each case must be considered in light of its particular facts and taking into consideration all of the legal and other features of the particular instrument being reviewed. The determining inquiry will be whether the instrument provides for a definite cash flow to be paid, regardless of the success of the entity, or whether it entities the holder to participate in the profit potential of the business.

If an instrument is determined to be indebtedness, such that the rule under Section 61(12) of the tax code would apply, it was generally thought that such an application to an insolvent or otherwise bankrupt company in the process of restructuring would impair the restructuring process by imposing a significant tax burden upon an LBO company that is otherwise unable to pay the tax. As a result of this perception, Congress enacted the Bankruptcy Tax Act of 1980, which provided new rules permitting insolvent companies to restructure their existing indebtedness without immediate adverse tax consequences. This law provides for exceptions to the rule resulting in taxable income to the extent of the debt forgiveness.

The first exception (Section 108(a)(1)(A) of the tax code) applies if the indebtedness is discharged in a proceeding under Chapter 11 of the Bankruptcy Code, and if the discharge is either granted by a court or as part of a court-approved plan. The second exception (I.R.C. Section 108(a)(1)(B)) applies where a debtor is insolvent but is not in bankruptcy. For these purposes, the term *insolvency* means the excess of the LBO company's liabilities over the fair market value of the LBO company's assets, in each case measured prior to the discharge of the indebtedness. Further, under the second exception, the exclusion from taxable income is limited to the amount by which the LBO company is determined to be insolvent. Prior to the enactment of the Tax Reform Act of 1986, a third exception was also provided in the case of the discharge of indebtedness by a solvent company. However, this provision has since been repealed with respect to discharges occurring after 1986, except that it remains available with respect to indebtedness discharged by a purchase money lender where there is a corresponding reduction in the purchase price paid by the LBO company.

It is important to note that these exceptions to the general rule do not result in an exclusion of the amount of the cancelled indebtedness from the taxable income of the LBO company. Instead, it results in a deferral of income taxes by permitting the LBO company to use its other available tax attributes (such as NOLs, carryovers of general business credits, and capital losses) to shelter the income that would otherwise be taxable. The code sets forth the specific order in which each of the available tax attributes of an LBO company are used, except that insolvent and otherwise bankrupt companies may make certain elections that enable it to reorder the categories. Such an election may provide an insolvent or otherwise bankrupt LBO company with the flexibility to retain NOLs and other carryovers for future use, instead of using them currently.

In the case of a solvent corporation that is undertaking a restructuring, since enactment of the Tax Reform Act of 1986, the exception for sheltering of income resulting from stock for debt exchanges is available to solvent corporations only if they are in bankruptcy and stock for debt exchanges outside of the bankruptcy context generally result in an immediate recognition of income, to the extent that the fair market value of the stock exceeds the principal amount of the indebtedness. Consequently, there is an incentive for solvent corporations planning such a restructuring to consider making a bankruptcy filing.

In sum, the code will enable an LBO company to defer, but not avoid, the payment of federal income taxes in connection with a discharge of indebtedness. NOLs and other carryovers will be used currently to shelter the income resulting from the discharge of indebtedness and, consequently, will not be available to shelter the future income.

Modifications of Indebtedness

Often, as noted above, the lenders to a troubled LBO company will not agree to forgive all or a portion of the existing indebtedness, but, instead, will provide interim relief by agreeing to so modify the terms of the existing indebtedness that the LBO company can have at least a short-term opportunity to turn itself around. This can be accomplished by, among other things, a modification of the interest rate, the extension of the maturity date for both principal and interest, the modification of the relative priority among the various debt instruments, as well as modification of the security position of the various debt instruments.

Generally, the tax treatment of a modification of indebtedness will turn upon whether there is an exchange of one instrument for another. The Treasury Regulations provide that a modification of the terms of existing indebtedness results in an exchange of property, if the holder of the existing indebtedness receives an instrument that is materially different from the existing indebtedness. Consequently, the Internal Revenue Service has taken the position that a change in both the maturity date and the interest rate results in such an exchange. However, the Internal Revenue Service has taken the position that a mere change in maturity date would not, in and of itself, result in an exchange. Further, no guidance is currently available to determine whether a mere change in the interest rate will be deemed to be an exchange. It should also be noted that, as a result of the substance-over-form doctrine, it is irrelevant to the question of whether there has been an exchange in the context of a modification of indebtedness that the form of the modification is accomplished through an amendment of the existing documentaton or a substitution of one instrument for another.

Generally, under I.R.C. Section 1001, an exchange of indebtedness will be a taxable transaction resulting in gain, to the extent of the difference between the fair market value of the new indebtedness and the basis in the old instrument in the hands of the holder. However, the transaction may be able to be characterized as a recapitalization under the code, entitling the holder to at least some tax-free treatment, such that the holder will not recognize gain or loss except to the extent it receives other property in connection with the exchange, including accrued but unpaid interest and the difference between the principal amounts of the securities subject to the exchange.

Net Operating Losses

As noted above, an LBO company with significant NOLs can use these to shelter future income. Generally, NOLs can be carried forward for 15 years. However, the Tax Reform Act of 1986 imposed stringent limitations on the use of NOLs under certain circumstances. These provisions limit the amount of income that may be sheltered for federal income tax purposes to a formula-based amount, the result of which is to extend over several years the use of an LBO company's NOLs.

These new restrictions come into play as a consequence of certain ownership changes, which may come about as a result of an LBO company restructuring. For example, stock sales, stock redemptions and recapitalizations, issuances of stock options, and other taxable and tax-free reorganizations may all result in a change in ownership. Generally, if an LBO company suffers a change in ownership of more than 50 percent of the value of its stock, then the new limitations imposed by the Tax Reform Act of 1986 will be applicable. Further, if the LBO company is not able to meet the "business continuity" requirements, its NOLs may not be used at all to shelter future income.

These new limitations on the use of NOLs do not apply to LBO companies that are reorganizing under the bankruptcy laws, if the LBO company's shareholders and creditors receive at least 50 percent of the equity value and the voting power upon emergence from bankruptcy. However, under that scenario, the LBO company's NOLs are reduced by 50 percent of the amount of income that would have otherwise resulted from a discharge of indebtedness pursuant to a stock for debt exchange with its creditors had the LBO company neither been insolvent nor in bankruptcy.

FRAUDULENT CONVEYANCE ISSUES

It is likely that, when an LBO company experiences financial difficulties, the LBO company, as well as all the participants in the original LBO transaction, will encounter legal challenges from the creditors of the LBO company or from a trustee appointed in a bankruptcy context. These challenges are likely to come from a bankruptcy trustee or from the LBO company's trade and other unsecured creditors, as well as from its secured creditors, and will include creditors that held obligations both before and after completion of the original LBO transaction. The most likely avenue to attack an LBO transaction (which is heightened in a bankruptcy context) is to argue that the original transaction violated the applicable fraudulent conveyance laws.

The concern of most lenders, in the context of providing financing for an LBO transaction, is that the former shareholders of the LBO company will receive payment for their stock prior to the existing creditors being paid in full. To complicate matters, as described above, most LBO transactions involve granting to these new lenders a security interest in the LBO company's assets. Consequently, these new lenders must be concerned that the LBO company, on a post-transaction basis, is capable of meeting its obligations, since if it is unable to do so, the LBO transaction may be susceptible to fraudulent conveyance challenges by the creditors that held obligations prior to the LBO transaction or by a bankruptcy trustee.

A successful fraudulent conveyance challenge can void not only the new lenders' rights arising out of the LBO transaction, such as the validity and priority of its security interest and its rights to enforce obligations on loans incurred by the LBO company, but also the rights of the selling stockholders of the LBO company to retain the proceeds received by them in the LBO transaction or to enforce their claims to receive any deferred portion of the purchase price. As a result, in the context of the restructuring of an LBO company, the bargaining power of the pre-transaction creditors of the LBO company prior to the LBO transaction vis-à-vis the selling shareholders and the new lenders to the LBO transaction may be amplified by a threat of a fraudulent conveyance challenge. Accordingly, the parties to any such restructuring need to carefully consider potential fraudulent conveyance challenges in the context of both the original LBO transaction and the contemplated restructuring.

Statutory Framework

Generally, there are three different statutory schemes pursuant to which a fraudulent conveyance argument can be made: (1) Section 548 of the federal Bankruptcy Code (FBC), (2) the Uniform Fraudulent Transfer Act (UFTA), and (3) the Uniform Fraudulent Conveyance Act (UFCA). The UFCA is applicable in approximately one half of the states, including New York and California. The UFTA has been adopted by approximately one third of the states, including California. Generally, each of these statutes will render a transaction voidable as a fraudulent conveyance where (1) the LBO transaction was accomplished with actual intent to hinder, delay, or defraud a present or future creditor; or (2) the debtor received less than reasonably equivalent value and the debtor was either (a) insolvent on the date of the LBO transaction, (b) became insolvent as a result of the LBO transaction, or (c) is reasonably expected to incur debts in the future that are beyond its ability to repay. The principal difference between these three statutory schemes relates to the time period in which a claim may be brought. Under the FBC, only transfers or obligations made or incurred within one year prior to a bankruptcy filing are reviewable, whereas the UFTA has a four-year statute of limitations. The UFCA incorporates each particular state's statute of limitations, which is typically longer than one year.

The ability to void a transfer or an obligation on the ground that the LBO transaction was accomplished with actual intent to hinder, delay, or defraud a present or future creditor has only been found to be available in situations where there is evidence of gross overreaching. Consequently, the remainder of this section will discuss the question of whether adequate consideration has been given in the LBO transaction and whether the LBO transaction has resulted in an LBO company that is insolvent or has unreasonably small capital, thus providing a basis for voiding an obligation as a fraudulent conveyance. The lack of adequate consideration, coupled with either insolvency or unreasonably small capital, is the primary basis for challenging an LBO transaction as a violation of the applicable fraudulent conveyance laws.

Adequate Consideration

The determination of whether adequate consideration has been received in an LBO transaction focuses upon the benefits received by the LBO company. Generally, however, it is the selling stockholders, not the LBO company, that derive a direct benefit from the LBO transaction. The transaction is merely a mechanism in which to cash-out the selling stockholders. The LBO company will not derive any direct benefit from any dividend distribution or other payment to the selling stockholders as a result of the transaction. Funds that may be received by an LBO company from lenders will be used to pay the purchase price to the selling stockholders. This is true whether the funds are delivered directly to the selling stockholders or to the LBO company, which, in turn, redeems the equity interests of the selling stockholders.

Accordingly, since the LBO company does not receive any direct benefit from the LBO transaction, it is necessary to argue that it has received an indirect benefit to show that it has received adequate consideration. Several arguments have been advanced to attempt to prove an element of indirect benefit to the LBO company. For example, in an LBO in which management participates in the equity, it has been argued that the LBO company benefits from a more committed management group as a result of the incentive they have to increase the value of their equity interest. In the context of an LBO of a former publicly held company, arguments have been advanced that the LBO company benefits from avoiding the expense of complying with the securities laws that are applicable only to publicly held corporations. Finally, where an existing company buys an LBO company to expand its business and take advantage of increased effectiveness and synergies, these economic arguments can also be made.

In any case, the question of whether adequate consideration has been received by the LBO company is a question of fact to be determined under existing circumstances. Certainly, the lack of success of the business on a post-transaction basis will be an important factor to be considered in determining whether adequate consideration has been received. Only in the circumstance where there is a preexisting business relationship between the buyer and the LBO company will there be any likelihood that an indirect benefit received by the LBO company will be sufficient to justify adequate consideration. Consequently, in most instances, since there is no direct benefit received by the LBO company, the creditors' or the trustee's first hurdle in making a fraudulent conveyance claim (i.e., showing inadequate consideration for the LBO transaction) will normally be met. This does not, however, in and of itself make the LBO transaction voidable. The claimant must also show that the LBO company was insolvent at the time, rendered insolvent as a result of the LBO transaction, or had unreasonably small capital.

Insolvency

Generally, there are two traditional insolvency concepts: bankruptcy and equity. In the bankruptcy context, insolvency means an excess of total debts over total assets. In the equity context, insolvency means an inability to pay debts as they mature in the ordinary course of business. Insolvency as used in the FBC, the UFTA, and the UFCA, with respect to fraudulent conveyance analysis, all measure asset values against total liabilities, and, consequently, all refer to insolvency in the bankruptcy context. The UFTA does, however, also use insolvency in the equity sense, with respect to fraudulent conveyance analysis by creating a presumption of insolvency as a result of a debtor's failure to pay its debts as they come due.

A complication in applying the bankruptcy insolvency concept to the fraudulent conveyance context occurs as a result of the availability of multiple valuation standards that may be used to determine whether an LBO company is solvent. Should the debtor's assets and liabilities be measured as based upon a forced or orderly liquidation method or on the basis of a going concern? It seems appropriate only to use a liquidation valuation method where the debtor's business is at the threshold of failure. Accordingly, since it is unlikely, absent fraud, that such an LBO transaction would be completed that the LBO Company is in danger of collapse immediately after the transaction, the issue of the LBO company's solvency should be viewed utilizing the going-concern valuation method.

It is arguable that the best evidence of going-concern value would be the price paid in the LBO transaction, as adjusted for transfers made and obligations incurred without adequate consideration. The buyer typically furnishes some portion of the price paid for the LBO company by an equity contribution, and it is this portion of the LBO purchase price that should not be affected by any of the foregoing downward adjustments in the purchase price. Accordingly, it is this portion of the LBO purchase price that provides a minimum going-concern value immediately after completion of the LBO transaction, thus rendering the LBO company solvent for fraudulent conveyance purposes. It is worth noting that other traditional going-concern valuation methods may also be employed in this analysis. These include utilizing a multiple of historical earnings method or a multiple of discounted projected future earnings.

Unreasonably Small Capital

For an LBO company to be deemed to have unreasonably small capital, it is not necessary to show that it is unable to pay debts as they mature (i.e., insolvent in the equitable sense). Instead, the concept of unreasonably small capital is intended to test whether a debtor is likely to become insolvent at some future time. Consequently, the question of whether an LBO company has unreasonably small capital is one determined by the particular facts and circumstances existing at the time of the LBO transaction. The threshold question is whether the LBO company will have sufficient cash flow to properly operate its business in the future in a competitive environment.

Projections about the future business operations and cash flow of the LBO company made in connection with the LBO transaction are helpful in this analysis. In determining whether an LBO company has unreasonably small capital, courts will generally seek to determine the reasonableness of these projections, which should naturally take into consideration, among other things, interest rate fluctuations and the difficulties that may result from a decline in industry or in general economic conditions. Further, such factors as the need to curtail expenditures for research and development or for capital improvements to plant and equipment are relevant inquiries in determining whether an LBO company has unreasonably small capital. Where curtailments in these areas result in an LBO Company becoming so uncompetitive that it is likely to be insolvent in the foreseeable future, an argument can be made that it had unreasonably small capital at the time of the original LBO transaction.

Practical Considerations in the Fraudulent Conveyance Analysis

Many courts have been reluctant to impose liability for fraudulent conveyance problems arising in the context of an LBO transaction based solely upon the above-described elements, unless there is also some element of knowledge or intent to defraud. Even in the landmark case of *United States* v. *Gleneagles Investment Co.,* 565 F. Supp. 556 (M.D. Pa. 1983), the court imposed liability for constructive fraud but also found that there was an element of intentional fraud existing under the facts and circumstances of the case. In affirming the United States district court's ruling, the Third Circuit Court of Appeals relied in large part on the facts and circumstances that indicated an actual intent to defraud. Accordingly, it appears that the general purpose of the fraudulent conveyance statutory scheme is to void transfers and obligations that both have the effect of injuring a party and were also intended as such. Although these principals of fraudulent conveyance are clearly intended by courts to apply to LBO transactions, an LBO participant can protect itself, to some extent, from potential fraudulent conveyance liability by conducting an extensive due diligence investigation of the LBO company, its present financial condition, business, operations, and prospects, and, as a result of such an investigation, the LBO participant reasonably concludes in good faith that the LBO company meets the foregoing financial tests.

Finally, it is worth noting that each of the statutory schemes for fraudulent conveyance contains a "savings clause" that is intended to protect initial transfers in good faith to the extent that the transferee give value to the LBO company. Further, subsequent transfers (including those in the context of a restructuring) are also subject to the protections of these savings clauses, if the subsequent transferee gives value to the LBO company in good faith without knowledge that the initial transfer was voidable. As discussed above, however, in the context of an LBO transaction, it is difficult to find that the LBO company has actually received value as a result of the LBO transaction. Instead, it is generally the selling stockholders that receive the proceeds of the transaction and, consequently, the value. Accordingly, since the savings clauses are predicated upon the LBO company receiving value in the context of the LBO transaction, these clauses may be of little help in fending off a fraudulent conveyance challenge. Typically, an LBO lender will have a better argument than a selling stockholder that it provided value to the LBO company, especially if its loans were made to the LBO company directly. However, even the LBO lender's argument of providing value may be dubious at best, since, as noted above, the monies provided by it to the LBO company are ultimately used to pay the selling stockholders for their interest in the LBO company. Many courts will rule to collapse the loan transaction into the distribution to the selling stockholders by utilizing a substance-over-form argument, which recognizes that the LBO lender is aware that the proceeds of its loans will be used to pay the selling stockholders and not to benefit the LBO company itself.

EPILOGUE

Restructuring a troubled LBO company involves the interworkings of several factors. The legal constraints that surface relate not only to the forward-looking business objectives of the various parties to the restructuring but as a result of potential fraudulent conveyance issues, must be viewed in light of the past transaction. Very often the mere threat of raising fraudulent conveyance issues can, in and of itself, serve to break a logjam that may have surfaced in the negotiation of the restructuring or may serve to provide one or more participants in the restructuring with a premium position in the restructured company. It may also have the effect of providing a seat at the negotiating table for a participant who may not otherwise have one, such as a subordinated creditor that is subject to a standstill provision. However, such an approach must be considered very carefully as it will, no doubt, be viewed by all of the participants as a drastic approach.

An understanding of the root of the problems being experienced by the LBO company is also essential to the restructuring. As discussed above, an LBO company will experience financial difficulties for many different reasons, each of which will undoubtedly require a different solution. For example, paying too high an original purchase price can be solved by one set of steps, whereas problems resulting from ineffective management will require a completely different solution.

Probably the most important factor, however, which should be kept in mind by the participants in the restructuring of an LBO company is the different interests and objectives of the various participants in the restructuring. As noted above, each of the participants in such a transaction has a different agenda and set of objectives. This is true with respect to those participants who stand in basically the same position (e.g., the equity players in the transaction, while holding the same piece of paper, all have different objectives and goals relating to completion of the restructuring). Necessarily, a successful restructuring, one involving the least amount of pain and expense, requires a recognition of the different interests among the various parties and the institution of creative ideas to meet those objectives. It is the professional who recognizes this fact that will be successful in reorganizing an otherwise troubled LBO company.

CHAPTER 18

OPPORTUNITIES FOR INVESTING IN TROUBLED COMPANIES

Barry S. Volpert*
Goldman, Sachs & Co.

INTRODUCTION

The dramatic increase in the number and size of leveraged buyouts in the second half of the 1980s will lead to a corresponding increase in workouts and restructurings in the early 1990s. The financial turmoil associated with this trend should create numerous opportunities for savvy and flexible investors to earn attractive returns from investments in troubled companies. To succeed, these sophisticated investors must be able to identify opportunities, analyze the assets and liabilities of target companies, structure their investments creatively, and assess various investment risks.

The increase in the number of leveraged transactions in the 1980s has been unprecedented. Whereas in 1981 there were 99 leveraged buyouts for an aggregate of $3.1 billion, by 1988 there were 318 leveraged buyouts for an aggregate of $42.9 billion. The

---

* The opinions and analysis included in this chapter are solely those of the author and do not represent either opinions of or representations by Goldman, Sachs & Co. All information included here is from public sources. The author wishes to thank his colleagues at Goldman, Sachs & Co. for their assistance in the preparation of this chapter.

growth of the LBO phenomenon arose from several factors, including the spectacular success of certain early transactions, comparatively low price/earnings ratios, abundant availability of bank financing as other profitable lending opportunities dried up, and the development and growth of the junk bond market. As early deals were sold at substantial profits, money flooded into the LBO business. Over $25 billion of equity capital was committed to over 166 leveraged buyout funds. With so much money chasing deals, prices increased accordingly. The ratio of aggregate consideration to cash flow in transactions financed with public junk bonds increased from 6 to 7 times in a typical transaction in 1985 to 8 to 12 times in many transactions in 1988.

As a result of the high prices paid in leveraged acquisitions in the past five years, we can expect to see an unprecedented increase in the number of financially troubled companies in the next few years. This trend has clearly started, as the recent bankruptcies of such major corporations as Eastern Air Lines, Federated Department Stores, Allied Stores, Southmark, Integrated Resources, L. J. Hooker, and others demonstrate, despite the fact that the U.S. economy has been quite resilient through the first quarter of 1990. An economic recession would quickly send numerous other highly leveraged companies into financial distress.

Sophisticated investors should find many opportunities to capitalize on this phenomenon. The trick will be to identify opportunities and determine appropriate investment strategies without incurring undue risk. Identifying troubled companies as potential investment opportunities should be the easiest part of the process. Many of the troubled companies of the 1990s will have public securities, either debt or equity, which will trade at levels indicating their financial distress. Others companies with only private debt and equity will be harder to find. Yet certain of the leading bank lenders to LBOs and LBO sponsors are sure to have numerous prospects in their portfolios.

Investors will have to choose among several alternative investment strategies, depending on their appetite for risk, return, liquidity, and uncertainty, and on their patience and pocketbook. Those looking for the least risky investments will focus on senior claims, including bank debt, senior secured notes, and trade claims, where liquidation value sets a satisfactory floor for recoveries. Those seeking liquidity will focus on publicly traded securities, such as junk bonds and common stock, although this liquidity may prove illusory if there are few buyers. Investors seeking a controlling or influential position will seek the fulcrum securities in a troubled company's capital structure (i.e., those securities for which asset values imply a partial recovery in liquidation). Those seeking the greatest risk/reward trade-off may focus on preferred stock and junior subordinated debt whose values may reflect nuisance value and potential litigation value but not asset value.

Investors will also choose between primary and secondary investments. Rather than purchasing existing claims at a discount, investors may contemplate financing a company-led restructuring in return for a new senior debt position and an equity upside. There will be substantial economies of scale in workout investments in these scenarios, because the influence of large creditors far outweighs that of groups of small creditors with equivalent aggregate claims.

In each case, properly analyzing the credit of the troubled company is the critical step. Investors must assess the value of troubled companies' assets. This requires an assessment of merger market values, public market values, debt capacity, and liquidation values. This credit analysis must then review the liabilities of a troubled company, with particular regard for the intercreditor relationships in a company's capitalization, viz convenants, subordination provisions, and the like.

Further, the investment risks must be appropriately weighed. These include operating, financial, and legal risks. Operating risks include the risk that a business could deteriorate from its current condition, due to either external factors, such as a recession or increased competition, or internal factors such as management distraction, due to the financial distress or cash constraints on the business leading to reduced inventory levels. Either situation could cause the asset values to deteriorate quickly in a distressed company. Financial risks include the risk a troubled company is permitted under its financial covenants to take steps that would impair the credit of particular securities (e.g., by borrowing additional senior debt to repurchase junior debt at a discount). Last, legal risks necessarily include the unpredictability of the bankruptcy process, the ability of a debtor or company to delay a restructuring, and the general bias of the Bankruptcy Code in favor of debtors and against creditors.

Exploiting the opportunities to invest in troubled companies will require patient searching to find attractive opportunities, careful analysis of credit quality and risk, and thorough reviews of alternative investment strategies. The difficulty and complexity of the task should discourage most investors, leaving attractive opportunities for those who persevere.

INCREASED INVESTMENT OPPORTUNITIES IN TROUBLED COMPANIES

Background: Historical "Vulture" Investing

"Vulture" investing historically has been a stepchild of risk arbitrage. Through the 1960s and 1970s, little capital was raised specifically for investments in turnarounds. A few large bankruptcies attracted attention from investors, most notably Penn Central, but for the most part investing in troubled companies was not a popular strategy. Wall Street arbitrageurs reviewed securities of bankrupt companies as a sidelight.

There were several reasons for this neglect. First, most bankruptcies arose from poor operations, rather than deliberate undercapitalization. Investors, therefore, had to bet on operational turnarounds or liquidation proceeds, rather than financial restructurings. Second, most bankruptcies involved smaller companies, where there were limited opportunities to invest significant amounts of capital. Third, corporations rarely financed with secured debt. As a result, bankruptcies frequently evolved into negotiations among various classes of creditors over subordination provisions, and claims were more difficult for independent investors to assess.

The Leveraged Buyout Phenomenon of the 1980s

The growth of leveraged transactions in the 1980s was spectacular. By any measure, the increase in the number, size, and scope of highly leveraged transaction was unprecedented.

As Table 1 demonstrates, the number and size of corporate

TABLE 1
Number and size of Mergers and Acquisitions and Portion that Were LBOs

	Total Mergers and Acquisitions		Leveraged Buyouts		
	Number	Dollar Value* (mil.)	Number	Percent of Total	Dollar Value* (mil.)	Percent of Total
1981	2,329	$ 70,064.4	99	4.3%	$ 3,093.1	4.4%
1982	2,298	60,697.8	164	7.1	3,451.8	5.7
1983	2,391	52,691.4	230	9.6	4,519.0	8.6
1984	3,164	126,073.7	253	8.0	18,631.4	14.8
1985	3,437	145,464.3	254	7.4	19,339.9	13.2
1986	4,381	204,894.6	335	7.6	40,910.5	20.0
1987	3,920	177,203.3	270	6.9	36,069.2	20.4
1988	3,487	226,642.6	318	9.1	42,914.0	19.0
1989	3,482	237,814.8	350	10.1	62,266.9	26.2

* Based on the subset of total transactions that report a dollar value.

Source: *Mergers & Acquisitions*.

acquisitions increased from 2,329 transactions, with an aggregate dollar volume of $70 billion in 1981, to 3,482 transactions, with an aggregate dollar volume of $237 billion in 1989. Of these transactions 99, or 4.3 percent, were leveraged buyouts or similar transactions in 1981, whereas 350, or 10.1 percent, were leveraged buyouts or similar transactions in 1989.

This growth in highly leveraged transactions was driven by the availability of financing including bank debt, subordinated high-yield debt, and equity.

Bank Debt
Banks were increasingly eager to lend to leveraged buyouts as this became one of the few remaining highly profitable areas for them to lend. Investment grade companies had abandoned commercial banks in favor of the commercial paper market or shelf-registered senior notes. The Third World lending boom had led to a debacle. The commercial real estate market was overbuilt and overlent. This

left leveraged buyouts as one of the few areas where banks could earn substantial fees, typically 1 to 2 percent of the amount advanced, and wide spreads, typically 300 basis points over their cost of funds. In 1989, it was estimated that 15 to 40 percent of the profits of the largest American banks were earned in loans to leveraged transactions (see Table 2).

Junk Bonds
The growth of the high-yield market, however, overshadowed the substantial increase in banks' LBO lending as the prime driver of the LBO phenomenon (see Table 3). The story is familiar: Michael Milken of Drexel Burnham Lambert pioneered the original issue noninvestment grade bond in the late 1970s after observing that yields on downgraded "fallen angel" or small company noninvestment grade bonds overcompensated investors for the incremental historical default rate. Drexel built this market from $30 billion in 1980 to $82 billion in 1985 by financing companies that were rated less than BBB by the rating agencies. The most dramatic growth of the junk bond market, however, began in 1986 with the use of junk bonds to finance mergers and acquisitions. New issues of junk bonds increased from $3 billion in 1982 to $9 billion in 1983, to $16 billion in 1984, and $20 billion in 1985. Then, in 1986, new issues jumped to $46 billion, and they remained near that level thereafter. The total of all outstanding junk bonds at the end of 1989 exceeded $200 billion, with all major bracket investment banking firms having underwritten substantial amounts of high-yield debt (see Table 4).

Equity
The amount of equity dedicated to leveraged buyouts grew just as the high-yield bond market grew. Whereas such firms as Kohlberg, Kravis, Roberts & Company and Forstmann, Little & Company had the market to themselves in the late 1970s, the enormous returns earned in some early deals attracted an enormous amount of new capital. Among the most successful early deals was William Simon's acquisition of Gibson Greeting Cards from RCA in 1982 for $80 million, of which only $1 million was equity, and later sale of the company in a public offering for $330 million, a staggering 25,000 percent return on equity. By 1988, LBO funds had over $25 billion of equity committed to search for deals, representing $250 billion of

TABLE 2
Estimated Earnings Contribution of Highly Leveraged Transaction (HLT) Loans for Selected Banks, 1989 (dollars in millions)

	Lending Revenues	Commitment Revenues	Up-Front Revenues	Resale Revenues	Total HLT Revenues	1989 Operating Earnings	HLT Revenue as a Percent of Operating Earnings
BankAmerica Corp.	$ 22.8	$ 3.4	$16.3	$ 7.7	$ 50.2	$1,103.0	4.6%
Bank of Boston	56.6	1.4	30.5	5.5	94.0	70.4	133.5
Bank of New York	88.1	6.0	54.3	3.8	152.2	440.7	34.5
Bankers Trust NY	73.6	4.3	42.3	14.5	134.7	620.1	21.7
Chase Manhattan	65.7	12.5	33.1	8.9	120.2	560.0	21.5
Chemical Banking	62.4	3.7	40.7	21.4	128.2	417.2	30.7
Citicorp	113.4	6.2	75.5	25.9	221.0	1,527.0	14.5
Continental Bank	45.2	4.5	28.8	6.8	85.3	286.0	29.8
First Bank System	17.2	0.6	9.2	1.7	28.7	2.4	1,195.8
First Chicago	24.7	5.5	22.0	6.7	58.9	451.1	13.1
Manufacturers Hanover	85.8	4.8	37.8	5.6	134.0	383.0	35.0
J. P. Morgan & Co.	16.3	1.4	12.3	7.7	37.7	725.0	5.2
NCNB Corp.	21.3	1.0	8.7	7.9	38.9	447.1	8.7
Security Pacific	60.6	5.4	38.6	8.8	113.4	740.6	15.3
Wells Fargo & Co.	77.1	3.5	36.5	5.8	122.9	601.1	20.4

Assumptions:
(1) Midyear 1989 outstandings and commitments approximate annual averages.
(2) Up-front revenues based on outstanding plus commitments.
(3) Resale volumes on annual basis are twice first-half estimates.

Source: Salomon Brothers, Inc., based on company financial reports and their estimates.

TABLE 3
Growth of High-Yield Bond Market

	New Issues
Year	High-Yield Bond Issues (billions)
1988	37.1
1987	35.8
1986	45.6
1985	19.8
1984	15.8
1983	8.5
1982	3.2
1981	1.7
1980	2.1
1979	1.7
1978	2.1
1977	1.1

Source: Drexel Burnham Lambert.

TABLE 4
Total Outstanding High-Yield Bonds

Year	Total Size of High-Yield Market (billions)
1989	205
1988	183
1987	159
1986	125
1985	82
1984	59
1983	43
1982	35
1981	32
1980	30
1979	28
1978	26
1977	24

Sources: Drexel Burnham Lambert; Goldman, Sachs & Co.

buying power at 9:1 leverage. In addition, virtually every major investment bank was pursuing LBOs as a principal for its own account (see Table 5).

Much of this money looking for a home found one: in the form of much higher prices paid to acquire companies in 1988 and 1989. Credit standards were stretched at each level. Banks lent against cash flow projections instead of assets. Junk bond investors required lower interest coverage. Deferred interest bonds, such as zero-coupon bonds and pay-in-kind debentures, were sold for cash or distributed to shareholders to finance acquisitions at prices higher than those that a target's cash flow could support in the first few years following an acquisition. The theory was that earnings would improve faster than interest accrued, so the company would grow into its debt load. Equity investors targeted lower returns, or

TABLE 5
The Top 20 LBO Funds Rated by Equity Capital in 1989

Rank	Firm	Fund Size ($ million)
1	Kohlberg, Kravis, Roberts & Co.	$5,600
2	Forstmann Little	2,500
3	Morgan Stanley	2,250
4	Merrill Lynch	1,900
5	Acadia Partners	1,600
6	Thomas H. Lee	1,600
7	Butler Capital	1,400
8	Shearson Lehman Hutton	1,300
9	Robinson-Humphrey	1,250
10	Wasserstein Perella	1,060
11	Clayton & Dubilier	1,000
12	Continental Equity	1,000
13	First Boston	1,000
14	Manufacturers Hanover	1,000
15	Welsh Carson Anderson & Stowe	910
16	Blackstone Capital Partners	850
17	Prudential-Bache Interfunding	800
18	Donaldson Lufkin & Jenrette	750
19	Charterhouse Group	612
20	First Chicago	600

ostensibly targeted the same returns of 35 to 40 percent they had previously promised their limited partners, but used more aggressive assumptions for earnings improvements and exit multiples to show that an investment met their parameters.

The resulting increase in merger prices was significant. Whereas the average acquisition price was 18.0× earnings in 1985, average earnings multiples increased to 22.2× in 1986, 23.3× in 1987, 21.6× in 1988, and 20.9× in 1989. Acquisition prices in leveraged buyouts increased even more dramatically. Whereas a typical leveraged buyout in 1985 might have been completed at a price of six times cash flow (or EBIT, earnings before interest and taxes), by 1989, LBOs were frequently done at 10 to 12 times EBIT (see Table 6).

As acquisition prices increased, credit standards deteriorated for high-yield bonds. Pro forma EBIT interest coverage for these bonds, for example, declined from an average of 2.07× in 1982, to 1.35× in 1985, and to 0.71× in 1988 (see Table 7).

The Music Stops

In the last half of 1989, a confluence of events occurred, which suggest that the LBO boom of the 1980s is over and will be succeeded by a workout boom in the early 1990s. These included an increase in bankruptcies, the inability of several visible transactions to obtain financing, new research indicating that junk bonds may not be as creditworthy as had been previously assumed, and, finally, the failure and liquidation of Drexel Burnham.

TABLE 6
Acquisition Prices as Multiples of Earnings

	1981	1982	1983	1984	1985	1986	1987	1988	1989
Average P/E paid	15.6	13.9	16.7	17.2	18.0	22.2	23.3	21.6	20.9
Median P/E paid	12.7	12.1	14.5	14.2	14.7	18.4	19.9	18.0	19.0

Source: Mergerstat Review.

TABLE 7
Pro Forma Credit Statistics for Junk Bond Issuers, 1980–1988, Weighted by Principal Amount

	EBIT Coverage of Interest	EBITD Coverage of Interest	Debt as a % of Net Tangible Assets	Cash Flow as a % of Debt	Common Equity as a % of Capitalization	Percent of Total Volume Related to M & A Activity
1980	1.99×	2.73×	60%	17%	39%	11%
1981	1.96	2.89	62	22	35	5
1982	2.07	3.00	65	18	35	13
1983	0.78	1.72	72	13	35	22
1984	1.14	1.69	175	7	21	45
1985	1.35	1.81	100	9	22	75
1986	0.77	1.38	123	5	16	75
1987	0.69	1.18	151	2	3	82
1988	0.71	1.23	202	3	4	93

Source: IDD Information Services, Inc.: microfiche prospectuses, 10Ks, and annual reports.

TABLE 8
List of 10 Largest Bankruptcies in 1989

Company	Assets ($ billions)
Lomas Financial Corp.	$6.7
Southmark Corp.	5.0
Eastern Air Lines	3.8
Hillsborough Holdings Corp.	3.5
L. F. Rothschild Holdings, Inc.	2.8
Continental Information Systems Corp.	1.9
Resorts International, Inc.	1.0
L. J. Hooker Corp.	0.9
Residential Resources Mortgage Investment Corp.	0.8
Maxicare Health Plans, Inc.	0.7

Source: Turnaround & Workouts.

Bankruptcies

The substantial number of large bankruptcies in 1989 and early 1990 included the failure of many of the most visible highly leveraged transactions of the 1980s (see Table 8). The most spectacular of these bankruptcies, by far, was the collapse of the Campeau empire, including such well-known and profitable department store chains as Bloomingdales, Rich's, and Burdines. Campeau was the product of two LBOs, of Allied Stores in 1986 and of Federated Department Stores in 1988, and had liabilities in excess of $7 billion. Other significant bankruptcies included Eastern Air Lines, L. J. Hooker, Southmark, Lomas Financial, and Integrated Resources.

Financing Failures

In addition to these bankruptcies, there were several well-publicized failures to finance acquisitions in 1989. The collapse of the UAL leveraged buyout in October 1989, which sent the stock falling from near the $300/share acquisition price to below $150/share overnight, was the bellwether event. The deal collapsed when the commercial bank syndicate for the deal disintegrated and could not be replaced. Also noteworthy were several outstanding bridge loans from investment banks that could not be refinanced in the high-yield market. The bank and high-yield bond markets simply

TABLE 9
List of Selected Outstanding Bridge Loans (dollars in millions)

Company	Lender	Amount
American Medical International	First Boston	$600
Del Monte	Merrill Lynch	500
Ohio Mattress	First Boston	500
Prime Computer	Shearson Lehman Hutton	500
Caldor	Donaldson, Lufkin & Jenrette	460
Federated Department Stores	First Boston	257
	Paine Webber	95
	Dillon Read	48
		400
Jerrico	First Boston	230
Popeye's–Church's Fried Chicken	Merrill Lynch	173
First Gibraltar Savings	Shearson Lehman Hutton	155
Vitro/Anchor Glass	Donaldson, Lufkin & Jenrette	155
American Marketing	Shearson Lehman Hutton	100
Grand Union	Saloman Brothers	80

closed following the UAL debacle. This left many investment banks stuck with their bridge loans to companies that were acquired at peak 1988 and early 1989 prices and that owned businesses that were surely worth less in the new environment (see Table 9).

New Junk Bond Research
New research on default rates compounded the turmoil in the junk bond market. For years the leading studies of high-yield default rates by Edward Altman of N.Y.U.[1] indicated annual default rates for junk bonds of between 1 percent and 2 percent, significantly less than the 3 to 5 percent interest rate spread over Treasury securities for such debt. A new Harvard study by Paul Asquith, David Mullins, and Eric Wolff[2] showed that, while only 1 to 2 percent of the total outstanding junk bonds defaulted each year, this statistic masked the fact that cumulative default rates for junk bonds are much higher. Indeed, by the end of 1988, 34 percent of all junk bonds issued in 1977 and 1978, and 19 to 26 percent of all junk bonds issued in 1979–83, had defaulted. This much higher default rate had been obscured by the dramatic growth in total outstanding high-yield bonds each year. Although the Harvard study and the N.Y.U. study used similar data and reached consistent results, the implica-

tions for junk bond investors appeared contradictory and reduced investor confidence.

Drexel's Collapse
Finally, in February 1990, Drexel Burnham Lambert filed for bankruptcy and began liquidation of its assets. Although Drexel had lost market share to other underwriters, it remained the dominant player in high-yield bonds for both new issues and secondary trading. Over the six months prior to Drexel's collapse, the firm had reportedly reduced its market-making activity. This contributed to a general drop in trading levels of junk bonds as investors recognized how illiquid the market really was.

The result of these factors is an unprecedented situation in which numerous companies with strong operating qualities—management, market position, cash flow, and so on—have been acquired for uneconomic prices. These companies have debt loads they will not be able to service without dramatic earnings improvements. Many, if not most, of these companies will not be able to generate those earnings improvements, particularly if there is an economic recession. Thus, we can expect to see a number of strong operating companies in financial distress. Those companies will present the best opportunities for investment in troubled companies.

IDENTIFYING OPPORTUNITIES

Troubled companies can be identified through several sources. Troubled companies with public securities can be identified most easily by reference to public trading levels. Private companies in financial distress are harder to locate, but they can frequently be found through lenders, investors, or the press.

The junk bond market provides the best source of information on troubled companies. Absent a complete liquidity crisis, bonds will not ordinarily trade at yields in excess of 1,000 basis points (10 percent) above the Treasury curve unless the market anticipates some sort of financial distress. As of March 1990, there were at least 49 companies with publicly traded junk bonds trading at yields above 20 percent. These companies are good targets for analysis (see Table 10).

TABLE 10
Selected Issues with Bonds Trading at Yields Greater than 20 Percent in March 1990

Issuer	Coupon	Maturity	Price*	Yield†
Adams Russell	0/16.50%	1997	$30.00	26.4%
Adelphia Communications	0/16.50	1999	55.00	21.3
Allied Stores	10.50	1992	34.00	83.4
Allied Stores	11.50	1997	7.00	163.7
Ampex Group	13.25	1999	23.00	58.8
Bond Brewing	12.63	2006	29.50	42.7
Burlington Holdings, Inc.	0/16.00	2003	39.50	20.8
Ceco Industries, Inc.	0/15.50	2000	50.00	22.7
Cencom Cable	0/15.00	2000	37.00	23.5
Coast Savings & Loan	16.00	1994	85.00	21.3
Coleco Industries	14.38	2002	19.25	73.9
Coleco Industries	11.13	2001	19.25	73.9
De Laurentis Entertainment	12.50	2001	9.00	133.0
Dr Pepper/Seven Up	0/15.50	1998	20.00	38.1
E-II Holdings	12.85	1997	61.00	24.9
E-II Holdings	13.05	1999	59.00	24.6
Federated Department Stores	9.375	1992	50.00	42.6
Federated Department Stores	7.88	1996	43.00	24.1
Federated Department Stores	16.00	2000	8.00	186.9
Federated Department Stores	0/17.75	2004	N.A.	N.A.
Gillett Holding	13.875	1999	14.00	98.4
Griffin Resorts	13.50	1995	42.00	40.1
Griffin Resorts	13.88	1998	42.00	36.4
Harcourt Brace Jovanovich	0/14.70	2002	24.50	31.0
Harcourt Brace Jovanovich	14.25	2004	46.00	31.4
Heritage Media Corp.	0/13.50	1997	65.00	21.7
ICH Corp.	11.25	1996	53.00	26.6
Interco, Inc.	13.75	2000	24.75	55.9
Interco, Inc. (PIK)	14.50	2003	4.00‡	69.2‡
Jim Walter Corp.	13.75	2003	13.00	103.9
Jones & Laughlin	9.75	1996	63.00	20.3
Las Colinas	12.50	1992	46.00	54.8
LTV Corp.	15.00	2000	19.00	78.4
LTV Corp.	14.00	2004	22.00	63.4
M Corp.	6.13	1997	22.00	37.8
M Corp. Financial	11.50	1992	54.00	41.4
M Corp. Financial	10.63	1993	54.00	36.3
M Corp. Financial	9.38	2001	54.00	19.6
Macy, R. H. & Co.	14.50	1998	76.00	20.5
Macy, R. H. & Co.	14.50	2001	64.50	23.5
Macy, R. H. & Co.	0/16.50	2006	28.00	26.3
Magma Copper	18.00	1998	87.00	21.3
Memorex Telex	13.25	1996	45.00	35.5

TABLE 10 *(concluded)*

Issuer	Coupon	Maturity	Price*	Yield†
Morse Shoe	20.24%	1998	$43.00	49.0%
National Gypsum	14.50	2001	61.00	25.0
National Gypsum	0/15.50	2004	37.50	29.5
National Gypsum	11.38	1997	60.00	23.1
Pay Less Cashways	14.50	2000	64.50	23.8
Pay N' Pack Stores	13.50	1998	71.00	21.0
PCPI Funding Corp.	15.50	1998	44.00	38.2
Ralph's Groceries	14.00	2000	72.00	20.6
Resorts International	11.38	2013	19.00	59.6
Resorts International	16.63	2004	20.00	82.9
Revco D. S., Inc.	13.13	1994	41.00	43.2
Revco D. S., Inc.	12.13	1995	70.00	21.6
Revco D. S., Inc.	13.30	1996	17.00	80.9
Revco D. S., Inc.	13.30	2001	7.00	176.9
RJR Holdings	0/15.00	2001	36.50	20.1
RJR Holdings (PIK)	14.70	2007	61.75	20.6
RJR Holdings (PIK)	15.00	2001	66.00	20.9
SCI Television	15.50	1995	80.00	21.8
SCI Television	16.50	1997	20.00	83.2
Sealed Power	14.50	1999	67.00	23.3
Seven Up Co.	12.13	1991	79.00	29.9
Southland Corp.	0/16.50	1997	30.00	44.5
Southland Corp.	15.75	1997	22.00	72.7
Southland Corp.	16.75	2002	13.75	117.7
Southmark Co.	11.88	1993	15.00	105.7
Southmark Co.	13.25	1994	15.00	108.7
Supermarket General Holdings	0/13.13	2003	33.00	23.8
Supermarket General Holdings	14.50	1997	77.00	20.7
TW Food Services	0/17.00	2001	35.00	20.6
USG Corp.	13.25	2000	58.00	24.6
USG Corp. (PIK)	16.00	2008	40.00	28.5
Western Union Co.	16.50	1992	37.00	71.4
Wickes Cos.	15.00	1995	55.00	34.1
Wickes Cos.	11.88	2001	47.00	27.1
York Holding Corp.	0/17.50	2004	36.00	22.4

N.A. means not available.
* Estimated bid price as of 3/2/90.
† Bid yield to worst.
‡ Based on 3/9/90 estimated bid price.

Source: Goldman, Sachs & Co.

The public equity market provides another source of information for identifying troubled companies. The common stock of companies that have been through a leveraged recapitalization is often highly volatile (e.g., FMC, Owens Corning Fiberglas, Harcourt Brace Jovanovich). When these types of companies experience problems their stock can drop precipitously, alerting investors to potential opportunities. These companies often receive great scrutiny in the press as well.

Private companies are also targets for potential investment. The best sources of information on troubled private companies may be the financial sources that helped create their problems, viz LBO sponsors, commercial bank LBO lending groups, or large mezzanine investors (insurance companies, mutual funds, and so on). However, these lenders and investors in LBOs will not ordinarily provide information about troubled companies in their portfolio unless they are seeking additional investors.

METHODS FOR INVESTING IN TROUBLED COMPANIES

There are several potential strategies for investing in troubled companies. Investors must decide where in the capital structure to place their bets (e.g., senior debt, mezzanine debt, or junior debt, or preferred or common equity). They must also decide whether to invest in existing securities in secondary market transactions or in new instruments through direct investments in the target company. The choice among these alternatives will depend upon the investor's tolerance for risk, return objectives, desire for control, size of preferred investment, patience, and other factors. (See Table 11.)

Priority in Bankruptcy

The risk and potential return of an investment each increase as one moves lower in the capital structure. Investments in senior secured debt typically offer the greatest protection and the least potential returns. Conversely, equity investments offer greater risk and greater potential returns. In between these poles, the risk/return trade-offs may vary substantially.

TABLE 11
Objectives for Investments in Various Classes of Debt

Priority in Bankruptcy	Objective
• Senior debt	Attractive return on investment.
	Downside protection through asset coverage.
	Receive cash or creditworthy debt in a restructuring.
• Mezzanine debt ("fulcrum security")	Obtain ownership and control of assets.
	Initiate or influence restructuring.
	Downside protection through discounted purchase price and partial asset coverage.
• Junior debt/preferred stock	Attractive return on investment.
	Use ability to delay restructuring to obtain nuisance premium above underlying asset value.
	Pursue litigation.
	Downside risk of low position in capital structure offset by deeply discounted purchase price.

The most interesting investment strategy, perhaps, is to pursue ownership and control of a troubled company through purchases of its "fulcrum security" (see Table 12). The theory is as follows. For a solvent company, legal equity and economic equity are identical. Both rest with the common stockholders. Legal equity is the power to control the business. Economic equity is the ownership of residual economic upside and downside risk. For troubled or insolvent companies, legal and economic equity are separated. Common stock remains the legal equity, and its holders remain in control of the business. But debt securities, usually subordinated debt trading at deep discounts, represent the economic equity insofar as these securities absorb the benefits and costs of swings in the company's performance.

A fulcrum security is the economic equity of a troubled company. It is the security for which the fair market value of the assets of a company exceeds the book value of the liabilities senior to it but does not cover the fulcrum security as well.

The fulcrum security holders should often be able to obtain ownership and control of the company's assets as legal and economic equity are again united in a restructuring. The restructuring

TABLE 12
Illustrative Fulcrum Security

ABC Company			
Assets		Liabilities	
Business with $100 million of earnings before interest and taxes per year and modest growth. Merger market value @ 7× EBIT = $700 million		Bank debt	$ 600
		Senior subordinated debt	200
		Junior subordinated debt	100
		Total debt	900
		Common stock	100
Total assets	$700	Total debt and equity	$1,000

Fulcrum security = Senior subordinated debt
Implied value @ $700 − 600 = $100 = 50% of par

could occur through an exchange offer, a Chapter 11 proceeding, or otherwise.

Investing either above or below the fulcrum security may also be attractive under certain circumstances. An investment in senior debt, either secured or unsecured, can generate attractive returns if there is adequate asset coverage. Senior secured debt has the advantage of receiving postpetition interest if it is fully collateralized, and yet it may still trade at substantial discounts. For example, following the bankruptcy filing of Federated Department Stores in January 1990, Federated 9⅝ percent senior secured bonds due 1992 were trading at approximately 50 percent of par, for a 42 percent yield, assuming there is adequate security, while Allied Stores secured paper due 1992 traded at 35 percent of par for an 84 percent yield. The difference between these issues? The Federated bonds were perceived to be fully collateralized, at least as to principal and might receive postpetition interest, while the Allied bonds were almost certainly underwater.

In contrast, an investment in preferred stock or other junior securities that are worthless in a liquidation presents another risk/reward trade-off. The bankruptcy process is time consuming and expensive. These costs are effectively borne by the fulcrum security holders. Holders of junior instruments have leverage to extract a premium from other creditors in excess of their liquidation value, because they can threaten to delay proceeds, litigate, oppose an exchange offer, or otherwise harm the more senior creditors unless they are paid off. Further, in certain circumstances, the junior bonds may present an interesting opportunity to bet on the outcome of potential litigation. For example, in Allied Stores, the 11.5 percent subordinated debentures due 1997 traded at 7.0 percent of par following the bankruptcy filing. Most credit analysts believe the value of the company's assets is less than its senior debt, leaving nothing for the subordinated debt holders. However, Allied was considering a variety of fraudulent conveyance and other claims against various parties to the Campeau situation. The 7 percent trading price may represent the market's assessment of the expected value of these lawsuits.

Secondary or Direct Investments

A critical decision for investors in troubled companies is whether to invest in existing securities in secondary market transactions or to invest directly in the company in a negotiated primary transaction. Secondary purchases will also tend to be riskier and more uncertain but will also have higher potential returns.

An investment in existing securities has several advantages. Generally, it can be made at lower cost. An investor can gradually accumulate bonds at a discount in the open market. He or she may be able to accumulate a significant position before word leaks of this investment. Once the investment has been made, an investor who sought ultimately to obtain control of the company would have a significant cost advantage over the potential purchasers, and an assured profit if he or she was topped. Moreover, an acquisition of one third of an issue gives an investor the ability to block a voluntary reorganization plan and, thus, substantial leverage in negotiating a restructuring. Furthermore, an investment in secondary transactions does not require the acquiescence of management, which could otherwise resist.

Investing quietly in secondary transactions has several disadvantages as well. The outcome of such an investment is highly uncertain. The biggest risk is that the underlying business will deteriorate while under existing management, before the investor has an ability to influence company decisions. In addition, the company can undermine the value of an investment through financial transactions, even if the business is unaffected (e.g., by borrowing additional senior debt and using the proceeds to redeem junior debt relative to an investment). If the company is not in default, the investor has no power to do anything, although he or she may ultimately earn a good return from interest and principal payments on the bonds. Moreover, even if the company does default, the pro-debtor orientation of the Bankruptcy Code gives the company tremendous ability to delay a reorganization, to the detriment of existing creditors. In short, an investment in existing securities in secondary transactions may appear adversarial to existing management, and an investor who has already put up her or his money may have less leverage than one who has not and is ready to offer new capital to the company.

Investing directly in troubled companies has a different set of pros and cons. The key advantage of a direct investment is that no money is invested until the success of a restructuring has been determined. Management generally must cooperate for this to occur, so an investor will have the benefit of company information in assessing the credit. Moreover, the investment will have a "friendly" character, with the investor appearing as a white knight. The paradigm for this type of investment would be for an investor to lend new senior unsecured debt to a company that uses the proceeds to tender at a discount for its outstanding junk bonds. This is likely to become a common occurrence in the next few years as banks refuse to advance additional funds to companies seeking to capitalize on the discounted prices at which their junk bonds trade. Alternatively, such direct investment may be proposed for companies already in Chapter 11 by potential acquirors as part of an overall restructuring. This was the approach taken by the Bass group in its unsuccessful attempt to acquire Revco in 1989, by financing a complete reorganization that would give the group control of the company. Specifically, a partnership of the Basses, Acadia Partners, American Express, the Equitable, and Shearson Lehman Hutton proposed purchasing substantially all the stock of Revco (with $1.5 billion of liabilities subject to bankruptcy proceedings), for $150 million. The proposal was subject to approval of a reorganization plan the group proposed, which would have reinstated approximately $515 million in senior obligations and raised an additional $260 million in new indebtedness. Under their plan, unsecured creditors would have received approximately $260 million in cash but no equity in the company going forward. In effect, if their proposal had been accepted, the Bass group would have accomplished a leveraged buyout of Revco at a substantially lower price than the original deal, with much of the required financing already in place. Direct investments will typically be structured as senior unsecured debt or as senior debt that refinances the bank debt, where the lender receives an equity kicker and, perhaps, even control, in return for advancing the loan.

The disadvantages of the direct approach are a high cost and a lower probability of success. The cost will be higher, because disclosure requirements will force a company to announce that it is repurchasing its bonds. This disclosure will drive the price up above where the bonds could have been purchased in market transactions. Moreover, a direct investment will normally have to be structured to appeal to management and existing shareholders, and buying their support will reduce the potential return further. Finally, a publicly announced reorganization will attract attention from other investors and may lead to competition. This increases the risk of failure and can further reduce the return on investment by driving up prices.

Economies of Scale

There are significant economies of scale for investments in troubled companies. These arise from both practical and legal sources. A result is that large investors should have significant advantages and unique opportunities to capitalize on the increase in troubled companies in the next few years.

Bankruptcies can be time consuming and complicated. A creditor must make a substantial commitment of time and effort to pursue maximum recovery. In many recent cases, the junk bondholders have small positions that have been written down to market prices. By reference to those written-down values, no holders believe they have a sufficient economic stake to justify the cost of serving on creditors' committees or otherwise pursuing maximum recoveries. As passive investors, they are vulnerable to inadequate representation by indenture trustees and to forceful representation by other classes of creditors with different interests.

Large bondholders, therefore, will have a significant ability to influence their recoveries. Their large stakes justify the commitment of time and effort to pursue maximum recovery. Since there may not be other large holders, an investor with a significant stake may find himself or herself in control of a creditors' committee or driving a restructuring through its own proposals.

In addition, the legal power of a one-third holder of an outstanding issue to block a reorganization plan and the practical ability of such a holder to block an exchange offer give large investors much greater leverage to influence restructurings and, thereby, maximize recoveries or obtain control. In particular, the ability of a large investor to develop alternative restructuring proposals to those proposed by the debtor will allow large investors to avoid being presented with a fait accompli. An investor with the capacity and willingness to place a higher value on the assets of a troubled company than the debtor, and thereby to offer greater recoveries to creditors of such companies, can take control of a restructuring.

INVESTMENT RISKS

At least three types of risks are to be assessed for any investment opportunity in a troubled company: operating risk, financial risk, and legal risk.

Operating Risk

Operating risks are both the most important and the hardest to evaluate. An investor in secondary market transactions generally has no control over the operations of the business and must anticipate a significant delay in obtaining any such control. During the interim, there is a risk that the business will deteriorate and that the investor will be powerless to implement any measures to improve performances. Operations could underperform, due to intrinsic or extrinsic factors. Intrinsic causes could include management distraction, poor operating decisions, trade creditors' or customers' fears, or other such problems. Extrinsic causes of operating problems include all of the normal operating risks of a business, all of which are exaggerated by financial troubles.

Financial Risk

Financial risks include the risk that a company takes affirmative steps that impair the credit of particular securities. Usually, this will involve adding debt that is senior to the particular security (e.g., borrowing more senior debt to finance repurchases of debt that is junior or to "leapfrog" exchange offers in which junior subordinated debt is exchanged for senior debt at a discount to face value or lower coupon, effectively jumping over any intermediate layers of subordinated debt). This occurred, for example, in December 1988 when Southland Corporation exchanged over 90 percent of its $400 million of 18 percent junior subordinated discount debentures for 13.5 to 14.5 percent senior resettable pay-in-kind notes leapfrogging above $1.1 billion in other subordinated debt in return for a 350–450 basis point interest rate reduction.

Legal Risk

Legal risk refers to the uncertainty of the bankruptcy process and the ability of debtors to delay a restructuring while managing a business poorly. Note the paradox facing a debtor with respect to business risks: If a troubled company takes operating risks and succeeds, the benefit accrues to the shareholders; yet, if the company fails, the costs are borne by the creditors. This asymmetrical incentive encourages debtors to delay restructuring and to operate the business in a risky manner, which may be inconsistent with creditors' interests. The legal risk of investing in the debt of troubled companies is that they often have the legal ability within the bankruptcy process to maintain control of the company for a long time.

ANALYZING OPPORTUNITIES: CASE STUDY OF INTERCO, INC.

The process of analyzing an investment opportunity in a troubled company is similar to the analysis of other investments. First, the business of the troubled company must be assessed with respect to merger market values, public market values, debt capacity, and liquidation values. Second, the liabilities of the company must be reviewed to identify the fulcrum security and the rights, claims, and vulnerabilities of each outstanding security. Third, the operating, financial, and legal risks must be considered. Then an investment strategy can be determined and implemented. This process can be illustrated with respect to a troubled company with bonds trading at distressed prices in March 1990, Interco, Inc.

Background

Interco owns four main businesses—Lane Furniture, Broyhill Furniture, Converse shoes, and Florsheim shoes. In 1988, Interco recapitalized to defeat a hostile takeover bid by the Rales brothers. After failing to achieve targeted divestiture proceeds, Interco ap-

Financial Information

Market Adjusted Capitalization (in millions)

	Book Value	Price[a]	Market Value	Yield
Senior debt				
Bank debt	$ 727	60%	$436	N.A.
Medium-term notes and other senior debt	218	60[c]	131	33%
Total senior debt[b]	$ 945	60%	$567	
Subordinated debt				
13.75% senior subordinated debentures due 00	$ 396	30%	$118	51%
14.0% subordinated discount debentures due 03	246	7%	17	79
14.5% PIK debentures due 03	216	5	11	69
Total subordinated debt	$ 858	17%	$146	
Total debt	$1,803	61%	$713	

[a] Based on 3/9/90 estimated market price.
[b] Based on price of medium term notes, which are pari passu and are publicly traded.
[c] Based on 5/15/90 estimated market price. Includes industrial revenue bonds and notes payable. Medium term notes yield 7.95–8.875% and mature in 1991–93.

Valuation Parameters

Shoe and Specialty Retail Companies

	Multiple of EBITD (LTM)	Multiple of EBIT (LTM)	Multiple of 1990E Net Income[a]
Comparable public companies			
Edison Brothers Stores	N/A	N/A	12.9
Stride Rite Corp.	7.8×	8.2×	12.2×
U.S. Shoe Corp.	6.8	10.8	14.6
Timberland Co.	11.3	15.2	12.2
Reebok International Ltd.	7.3	8.0	10.0
Nike Inc.	7.0	7.3	10.5
L.A. Gear Inc.	7.7	7.7	8.9

	Multiple of EBITD (LTM)	Multiple of EBIT (LTM)	Multiple of Net Income (LTM)
Comparable transactions			
Nike/Cole Haan (5/88)	13.7	15.7	36.2
McCown De Leeuw/Van Doren (2/88)	5.1	5.4	11.1
Reebok/Avia Group (4/87)	25.2	26.5	58.4

Furniture Stores

	Multiple of EBITD (LTM)	Multiple of EBIT (LTM)	Multiple of 1990E Net Income[a]
Comparable public companies			
Bassett Furniture Industries	8.4×	11.0×	15.3×
Flex Steel Industries	5.4	7.3	9.8
LADD Furniture Inc.	9.9	11.7	11.9
La-Z-Boy Chair Co.	6.8	8.7	12.8
Miller (Herman) Inc.	6.0	7.9	10.5
Pulaski Furniture Corp.	5.8	7.2	9.3

Valuation Parameters (*concluded*)

	Multiple of EBITD (LTM)	Multiple of EBIT (LTM)	Multiple of Net Income (LTM)
Comparable transactions			
Legend Capital/ Ethan Allen (6/89)	7.6×	9.2×	16.1×
Masco Corp./ Universal Furniture (5/89)	10.7	13.4	15.5
Maytag/Chicago Pacific (1/89)	5.9	7.1	11.7

[a] Multiple of median IBES estimate.

Summary Income Statement

	1988	1989	LTM (11/89)
Sales	$1,996	$2,012	$1,758
EBIT	228	171	130

pears overleveraged and unable to cover its cash interest expense with earnings. As a result, its bonds traded at between 3 percent and 29 percent of par.

Analysis and Conclusion

Valuing the businesses of Interco at 6–7 times estimated earnings before interest and taxes (EBIT) of $130 million for the latest 12 months implies an underlying business value of $780–910 million. Applying the value to the capital structure in order of priority, there is insufficient value to cover the senior debt. Thus the fulcrum security is the senior debt, and the liquidation value of the subordinated debt is zero. This suggests that the 13.75 percent senior subordinated debentures are substantially overvalued at 30 percent of par and would be a poor investment. The market price of discount debentures and PIK debentures, which trade at approximately 3–5 percent of par, may accurately reflect their nuisance value, but these securities are also not a bargain. However, the medium term notes (MTNs), which are pari passu with the bank debt, trade at approximately 60 percent of par for a 33 percent yield to maturity. Applying this value to all of the $945 million of senior debt yields an implied market value of $567 million, or 4.4 times EBIT. This is substantially less than the underlying business value. In a liquidation, the MTNs should be repaid in full even sooner than their 1991–93 maturities, resulting in a higher yield. At minimum, the underlying business value should protect an investor in the MTNs in a downside scenario, allowing the investor to recoup his investment. Ironically, the MTNs might have more influence (but less value) if they were subordinate to the bank debt and therefore were the sole fulcrum security rather than sharing this position with the banks.

CONCLUSION

The leveraged buyout boom of the 1980s should produce a workout boom in the 1990s. While many strong operating companies face financial distress due to overburdened capital structures, there should be opportunities for savvy investors to exploit market imperfections. These imperfections will arise, because the phenomenon of the bankrupt or insolvent strong company is relatively new, because few investors will know how to recognize these imperfections, and because size and stamina will convey significant advantages to certain investors.

The keys to investing successfully in troubled companies will be to distinguish attractive opportunities where underlying asset values are not accurately reflected in market prices, to assess operational, financial, and legal risks, and to select optimal investment strategies for these situations. Investors with the capacity to make large investments and to take substantial risks, with the flexibility to accept attractive returns through multiple potential outcomes, and with the patience to wait for economic reality to be reflected in legal organization and market prices will be most successful at earning attractive returns through investments in troubled companies.

ENDNOTES

1. Edward I. Altman and Scott A. Nammacher, "The Default Rate Experience on High Yield Corporate Debt," *Financial Analyst Journal,* July–August 1985, pp. 25–41.
2. Paul Asquith, David W. Mullins, Jr., and Eric D. Wolff, "Original Issue High Yield Bonds: Aging Analyses of Defaults, Exchanges and Calls," March 1989, unpublished manuscript.

CHAPTER 19

ANALYZING FINANCIAL STATEMENTS FILED WITH THE SEC

Michael O. Gagnon
Partner
Price Waterhouse

INTRODUCTION

Companies whose securities are registered with the Securities and Exchange Commission (SEC) are required to provide a wide range of information to the public. This information, which extends well beyond the annual audited financial statements, can be successfully utilized by knowledgeable investors and creditors to identify companies that are at greatest risk of suffering severe financial difficulty in the near future.

    The purpose of this chapter is to outline the sources of information, required to be provided by SEC registrants, which might be useful to provide indications about a company's future financial health, discussed below, and to outline some basic analytical techniques that an investor might use to assess the risk of a deterioration in a company's financial position, resulting in the bankruptcy of the company (see the section, Analysis of Reports Filed by SEC Registrants, below). The section, Examples of Distressed Companies, below, demonstrates these techniques using as examples three companies that have experienced severe financial difficulties. Two of these companies have sustained large losses over an extended period and have been forced to announce the possibility that they may be forced into bankruptcy, while the third has resolved its problems and is now very profitable.

REPORTING REQUIREMENTS OF SEC REGISTRANTS

The principal reports required to be filed by SEC registrants, in accordance with the provisions of the 1934 Securities Exchange Act, are as follows:

Report	Filing Date
Annual Report on Form 10-K	Within 90 days after the end of the registrant's fiscal year-end.
Quarterly Report on Form 10-Q	Within 45 days after the end of each of the registrant's first three fiscal quarters.
Current Report on Form 8-K	5–15 calendar days after the date of the event in respect of which the report is being filed.
Annual Report on Form 20-F (foreign registrants only)	Within 180 days after the end of the registrant's fiscal year-end.

There follows a summary of the information required to be provided in each of these reports.

Annual Report on Form 10-K

The 1934 act specifies the information to be provided in the form of 14 "Items." The information to be provided by each of these Items is prescribed either by SEC Regulation S-X or SEC Regulation S-K.

Regulation S-X prescribes the content and format of the audited financial statements required to be provided by Item 8, "Financial Statements and Supplementary Data." The information required to be provided in accordance with the other Items, and certain supplementary financial information required by Item 8, is contained in Regulation S-K, which prescribed the nonfinancial statement disclosures required by SEC registrants. The disclosures required by Regulation S-K are unaudited.

The following is a summary of Items that are likely to be of most use to an investor attempting to assess a company's financial health.

Item 1—Business	Information about the development of the registrant's business since the beginning of the fiscal year for which the report is filed.
Item 2—Properties	Information regarding the location and general character of the principal plants, mines, and other materially important physical properties of the registrant.
Item 3—Legal proceedings	Information regarding any material pending legal proceedings to which the registrant is a party.
Item 6—Selected financial data	Certain selected financial data for each of the last five fiscal years of the registrant and any additional fiscal years necessary to keep the information from being misleading. The data to be disclosed is as follows: • Net sales or operating revenues. • Income from continuing operations per common share. • Total assets. • Long-term obligations and redeemable preferred stock. • Cash dividends per common share. Registrants may include additional items that they believe would enhance an understanding of and would highlight other trends in their financial condition and results of operations.

Item 7—Management's discussion and analysis of financial condition and results of operations (MDA)	A discussion of the registrant's financial condition, changes in financial condition, and results of operations for its latest three fiscal years. The discussion should provide the following information: • Discussion of favorable or unfavorable trends in results of operations or financial condition. • Infrequent events or transactions. • Discussion of general economic and industry conditions where such general trends influence the registrant's performance. • Discussion of known prospective information. The SEC stressed the importance of this in an interpretive release on MDA issued in May 1989. Registrants must disclose trends, demands, commitments, events, and uncertainties when both known to management and reasonably likely to have a material effect on an enterprise's financial condition or results of operations. The SEC stressed the distinction between the required disclosure of such information and of optional forward-looking information requiring anticipation of a future trend or event or of the impact of a known trend, event, or uncertainty where such impact is not reasonably predictable.

	• An assessment of the ability of a registrant to generate adequate cash from operations or other sources to meet its needs.
Item 8—Financial statements and supplementary data	The registrant is required to file audited annual financial statements meeting the requirements of Regulation S-X. This regulation requires that the registrant file: • A balance sheet as of the two most recent fiscal years. • Consolidated statements of income, of cash flows, and of stockholders' equity for each of the three most recent fiscal years. Regulation S-X also specifies the form and content, including disclosures therein, of the financial statements to be filed.

Annual Report on Form 10-Q

The interim financial information in a Form 10-Q need not be audited or reviewed by independent accountants prior to filing; however, if a review is performed, the registrant may so indicate, in which case a report from the independent accountant must be filed commenting on the results of such review.

Form 10-Q consists of two parts.

Part 1—"Financial Information"
- Income statements for the most recent fiscal quarter, the corresponding fiscal quarter in the preceding year, and the year-to-date periods for both years.
- Statements of cash flows for the year-to-date periods of the current and prior years.
- Balance sheets as of the end of the most recent fiscal quarter and as of the end of the preceding fiscal year.

- Management's discussion and analysis (MDA) of material changes in liquidity, capital resources, and results of operations. The MDA in Form 10-Q is intended to enable the reader to assess material changes in financial condition from the end of the preceding fiscal year to the most recent balance sheet presented and to compare results of operations for the current quarter and year-to-date periods with the corresponding periods of the preceding fiscal year. In performing the MDA for inclusion in Form 10-Q, the company may presume that the reader has read, or has access to, the MDA included in the company's Form 10-K for the preceding fiscal year. Accordingly, a reader should read the MDA included in a Form 10-Q in conjunction with that included in the preceding year's Form 10-K.
- Events that occurred subsequent to the end of the most recent fiscal year should be disclosed in the footnotes to the financial statements included in the Form 10-Q. Footnote disclosure, which is substantially duplicative of that in the audited financial statements included in the company's Form 10-K for the preceding fiscal year, may be excluded, except that disclosure of material contingencies is required in Form 10-Q, even though a significant change since year-end may not have occurred.

Part 2—"Other Information"
The information to be provided in Part 2 is:
- Material developments in connection with legal procedures.
- Material modification of rights of registrant's securities.
- Defaults on senior securities.
- Submission of matters to a vote of security holders.
- Exhibits and Reports on Form 8-K.
- Any other information that the registrant deems of importance to its security holders.

Current Report on Form 8-K

SEC registrants are required to file a report on Form 8-K when any of the following specified events occurs:

1. A change in control of the registrant.
2. The acquisition or disposition by the registrant or any of its majority-owned subsidiaries of a significant amount of assets other than in the ordinary course of business. (Historical and pro forma financial statements may be required if the acquisition or disposition meet certain size tests.)
3. The appointment of a receiver, fiscal agent, or similar officer in a bankruptcy act (voluntary or involuntary) or similar state or federal proceeding, or issuance of an order confirming a plan of reorganization, arrangement, or liquidation that has been entered by a court or governmental authority.
4. Changes in the registrant's certifying accountant.
5. The registrant may also report at its option any other event that it deems of importance to its security holders.
6. Resignations of the registrant's directors since the date of the last annual meeting of shareholders because of a disagreement with the registrant, with a letter describing such disagreement and requesting that the matter be disclosed.
7. Registrant change in fiscal year.

Annual Report on Form 20-F

Form 20-F is used by non-Canadian foreign SEC registrants for filing annual reports in accordance with the requirements of the act. For the most part, Canadian SEC registrants file their annual reports on Form 10-K.

The information to be included in annual reports on Form 20-F is similar to that to be included in Form 10-K. The following is a summary of the principal differences:

- Although the registrant is required to file audited financial statements for the same periods as a registrant filing on Form 10-K, these statements are not required to comply with United States generally accepted accounting principles or with Regulation S-X. The audited financial statements must include, however, a quantified reconciliation of the differences between United States and local accounting principles and a discussion of the nature of such differences. The reconciliation typically takes the form of a reconciliation of net income and stockholders' equity.

- The MDA should, of necessity, focus on the primary financial statements, prepared in accordance with local accounting principles; however, the registrant must discuss those differences between local and United States accounting principles that it believes are necessary for a full understanding of the financial statements taken as a whole.
- The effects of governmental economic, fiscal, or monetary policies that have materially affected, or could materially affect, their operations or the investment in their securities by U.S. nationals are specifically required to be discussed in the MDA.
- As noted above, the filing date for annual reports on Form 20-F is 180 days after the end of the registrant's fiscal year-end, whereas that for annual reports on Form 10-K is 90 days.

ANALYSIS OF REPORTS FILED BY SEC REGISTRANTS

Obviously, a considerable amount of information is available to the investor who wishes to assess the risk that a company in which he or she has invested, or is considering investing, will experience severe financial difficulty, resulting in its bankruptcy. This section discusses some of the techniques that an investor may use to utilize such information to assess such risk. An investor can generally make reasonably good predictions of companies likely to experience such difficulties by concentrating on the following basic techniques:

- Analysis of the audited financial statements (balance sheets, income statements, and statements of cash flows) of the relevant companies.
- Careful reading of the footnotes to the audited financial statements.
- Careful reading of the nonfinancial statement information included in a registrant's Form 10-K or Form 10-Q or Form 20-F, in particular the discussion of the registrant's business, the information regarding material pending legal proceedings to which the registrant is a party, and the MDA of financial condition and results of operations.

There follows a discussion of how each of these techniques can be utilized as a predictor of a company likely to experience severe financial difficulty.

Analysis of Financial Statement Information

The obvious starting points in analyzing a company's balance sheet, income statement, and statement of cash flows are the company's net profit before and after taxation, the company's cash flows from operations, the company's working capital (current assets less current liabilities), and the company's net assets (stockholders' equity). Generally, a company that is profitable and has a strong balance sheet is unlikely to experience severe financial difficulty. In certain circumstances, however, the financial condition of even apparently healthy companies can deteriorate rapidly. It is, therefore, important that the investor utilize the same analytical techniques for such companies as for companies whose financial health is not as apparent.

The following discussion is of some commonly used ratios that can be applied to a company's balance sheet and income statement to gauge its financial stability.

Balance Sheet Ratios

Long-Term Debt to Equity Ratio. This ratio, which is calculated as the ratio of long-term debt to long-term debt plus stockholders' equity, measures the extent to which a company has been capitalized by debt (commonly referred to as *leverage*). Although a ratio of over 33⅓ percent has traditionally been seen as an indication of a relatively high risk level, ratios of in excess of 50 percent and up to 90 percent have been not uncommon in recent years. This ratio should be used in conjunction with such income statement ratios as interest coverage, since a company with a high degree of leverage may have the ability to comfortably cover its interest and other fixed charges, even in the event of a decline in its earnings. An investor should be particularly wary of companies whose leverage has increased significantly over time. In such circumstances, the investor should evaluate the reasons for the increase and assess whether the company's earnings and cash flows are sufficient to service the increased debt.

Ratio of Current Assets to Current Liabilities. A ratio of current assets to current liabilities of less than 1.0 may indicate that a company is experiencing difficulties in paying its current liabilities as they come due. Generally a ratio of at least 1.5 is desirable, although companies whose current assets consist primarily of cash and receivables that can be collected quickly can require a ratio of less than this. As with all balance sheet ratios, the investor should carefully scrutinize the trend of the ratio over a period. For example, a company that has had a ratio of 1.0 for several years, and is consistently profitable, may be healthier financially than a company with a ratio of 1.5 that has declined consistently from 2.5 with a corresponding decline in profits.

Income Statement Ratios

Ratio of Earnings to Interest Expense. This ratio, which is calculated as the ratio of earnings before deduction of interest expense to interest expense, measures the extent to which a company's earnings cover its interest charges. A ratio of less than 1.0 indicates that the company needs to increase its earnings to meet its interest payments. There is no strict rule of thumb about what constitutes a "safe" ratio; however, an investor should carefully examine the quality of a company's earnings where the ratio is less than 2.0, since a deterioration in the company's earnings might mean that the company will have difficulty meeting its interest payments. This ratio also assists an investor to evaluate the company's prospects of obtaining additional financing should it need to do so, since banks and other sources of finance are obviously more likely to lend to a company whose earnings are several times interest expense.

Operating Income to Sales. This ratio, which is calculated as the ratio of operating income to sales, enables the investor to evaluate the extent to which a company's earnings are exposed to decreases in sales prices or to increases in raw material prices or to other costs not matched by sales price increases.

Where a company has an operating margin of less than 5 percent, it generally has very little maneuverability to respond, other than in the short term, to decreases in demand for its basic products or services or to price competition from its competitors. An investor should carefully evaluate the reasons why a company's operating margins are low, particularly where they have been declining steadily over a period of years.

Analysis of Nonfinancial Statement Information. An analysis of a company's financial statements utilizing the ratios described above should enable an investor to develop a good picture of a company's financial position. To fully comprehend the company's finances and prospects, however, the investor should carefully read the company's nonfinancial statement information in conjunction with her or his reading of the financial statements and related footnotes. All of the information included in the report being analyzed (10-K, 10-Q, 8-K, or 20-F) should be read carefully; however, as noted above, the discussion of the registrant's business, the information regarding pending legal proceedings, and the MDA are likely to be of particular interest. The information relating to these matters contained in the registrant's 10-K, 10-Q, or 20-F can enable the investor to:

- Assess the quality of a company's earnings.
- Assess a company's future prospects.
- Assess the adequacy of a company's short-term and long-term liquidity and capital resources.

The company's MDA should be scrutinized particularly carefully by investors. As noted above, in May 1989 the SEC issued an interpretive release on MDA (FRR 36). In the conclusion to the release, the SEC noted that:

> In preparing MDA disclosure, registrants should be guided by the general purpose of the MDA requirements; to give investors an opportunity to look at the registrant through the eyes of management by providing a historical and prospective analysis of the registrant's financial condition and results of opreations, with particular empha-

sis on the registrant's prospects for the future. The MDA requirements are intentionally flexible and general. Because no two registrants are identical, good MDA disclosure for one registrant is not necessarily good MDA disclosure for another. The same is true for MDA disclosure of the same registrant in different years. The flexibility of MDA creates a framework for providing the marketplace with appropriate information concerning the registrant's financial condition, changes in financial condition, and results of operations.

Of particular concern to management should be the timely reporting of prospective information. The SEC staff has demonstrated that it will apply perfect 20/20 hindsight when a material change or event has occurred and was not disclosed by the registrant in a timely manner.

The SEC noted the disclosure of prospective information that involves material events and uncertainties known to management that would cause reported financial information not to be necessarily indicative of future operating results or of future financial condition was a key area of noncompliance in MDA included in past filings of registrants.

In light of the SEC comments contained in this release, it is likely the prospective information provided by registrants in future filings will be more comprehensive, enabling an investor to make a more informed determination of the registrant's prospects.

EXAMPLES OF DISTRESSED COMPANIES

This section analyzes the financial statements of two companies that have either filed for bankruptcy or whose current financial position is such that there is a significant risk they may be required to file for bankruptcy in the future, and of one company that incurred significant losses for a period of three years but has since generated profits. The section analyzes the balance sheet and income statement ratios of these companies for a period of years and outlines how these ratios may have been used by an investor to predict the companies' future financial difficulties. All dollar amounts are in millions.

Company A

	Year Ended December 31				
	1988	1987	1986	1985	1984
Net profit (loss)	$ (216)	$ (59)	$ 200	$ 212	$ 160
Interest expense	$ 561	$ 208	$ 57	$ 57	$ 103
Stockholders' equity	$ (388)	$ (150)	$1,667	$1,497	$1,196
Working capital	$ (536)	$ (196)	$ 46		$ 256
Long-term debt	$1,315	$4,605	$ 623	$ 564	$ 885
Long-term debt to equity ratio	110 %	104 %	37%	27%	43%
Interest coverage	0.61	0.72	4.50	4.70	2.67
Operating margin	2 %	0 %	2%	2%	2%

There was a significant change in Company A's financial position during 1987. This change resulted from a leveraged buyout (LBO) of the company in July 1987, as a result of which the company's long-term debt increased by $3,982 between December 31, 1986, and December 31, 1987. This resulted in an increase in interest expense of $151 in 1987 and a further $353 in 1988. Again, dollars are in millions.

An investor considering making an investment in Company A's securities following the LBO in 1987 would have been primarily concerned to evaluate the prospect that the company could make the interest and principal payments on the debt resulting from the LBO from operating cash flows and asset sales.

In the MDA included in its December 31, 1987, Form 10-K the company outlined its plans to reduce the debt arising as a result of the LBO. These plans included sales of 1,000 of approximately 8,000 retail stores operated by it and the sale of several business units. The net realizable value of the stores and business units was approximately $637. Following these sales the company's operations would primarily comprise retail sales through its remaining stores. The company also indicated that in future years cash flow from operations, which was $322 in 1987, would primarily be used to pay interest on debt and for debt retirement.

During 1988, as indicated by its reports on Form 10-Q for the first three fiscal quarters of 1988, Company A successfully completed the sales of the units described above. Cash flows from operations, excluding interest expense, increased from $322 in 1987 to $593 in 1988. This increase was not sufficient, however, to absorb the increase in interest expense of $504 in 1988.

At December 31, 1988, the company's current liabilities exceeded its current assets by $536, and it had unused credit facilities of $315, which were due to expire by December 31, 1992. The company did not indicate in its 10-K for the year ended December 31, 1988, how it intended to continue to make interest and principal payments on its debt if cash flows from operations did not improve, and it did not outline in detail its plans to improve such cash flows. However, the company did say in the MDA that it expected to incur net losses over the next several years due to its high level of interest expense.

In the first fiscal quarter of 1989, the company's loss before taxes and extraordinary items increased from $114 in the corresponding period in 1988 to $138. As explained in the MDA to its first quarter 10-Q, this was due in part to lower gross margins, reflecting higher costs, and in part to increased interest expense, reflecting higher interest rates. This trend was also apparent in the second and third fiscal quarters.

In its third quarter 10-Q the company stated, for the first time, that if earnings from operations did not improve it would need to implement various cost-saving measures to satisfy certain covenants contained in its credit agreements. It also stated that during 1991 its working capital requirements might exceed its cash on hand and available credit facilities.

At this stage, it was obvious the company was experiencing significant financial difficulties that could result in its bankruptcy. This was confirmed by the announcement in early 1990 that the company was attempting to restructure its debt and would be required to seek relief under the U.S. Bankruptcy Code if such restructuring was not achieved. In its December 31, 1989, 10-K the company explained, in the liquidity and capital resources section of the MDA, that its problems arose from competitive pressure in its industry and an erosion of demand for its core products, which resulted in slower than anticipated sales growth. The company admitted that in 1988 its operations had been considerably less profitable than anticipated. However, this had been viewed as temporary. In 1989, the company realized that this adverse trend was likely to continue, resulting in the inability of the company to make the interest and principal payments on its debt commencing in 1991.

Company A's difficulties are fairly typical of those experienced by many companies that have incurred large amounts of debt in recent years in connection with LBOs. The success of such ventures usually depends on the ability of the company to successfully sell assets to reduce its debt burden, to improve operating margins through cost reductions, and to utilize cash flows from operations to pay the interest on its debt instead of for capital outlays.

Company A attempted to reduce operating costs through cutbacks in advertising and, at the same time, reduce capital spending on its retail outlets. It did this, however, at a time when the economy was weakening and its competitors were aggressively attacking its market share.

This resulted in reduced margins for the company's products. If the company's interest burden had been less, it could have withstood these lower margins; however, it required improved margins and revenues to pay the interest on its debt. It could only increase its revenues and improve its margins, in the long term, by increasing capital spending and maintaining advertising expenditures. Since the company could not do this and continue to pay the interest on its debt, it was required to seek to restructure its debt in early 1990.

The lesson from this example is that where the success of an LBO is dependent on increased revenues or operating margins, or both, a potential investor needs to skeptically evaluate management's plans to achieve its goals. Where such plans appear to the investor to be overly optimistic, he or she would be wise to avoid investment in the company.

At the end of 1984, there were certain similarities in the financial position of Company B and Company C (see the tables on pages 558 and 559). Some of these similarities were as follows:

- Each was in a mature industry and needed to make significant capital expenditures to reduce costs or to adapt to industry trends (Company B provides telex services and Company C mines copper and produces copper products).
- Each had incurred losses recently, which, if not reversed in

Company B

Year Ended December 31

	1988	1987	1986	1985	1984	1983	1982
Net profit (loss)	$(1,082)	$ (64)	$(529)	$ (371)	$ (63)	$ (58)	$ (86)
Revenues	$ 876	$802	$ 889	$ 983	$1,134	$1,044	$1,025
Expenses (excluding restructuring charges, asset write-downs, and interest)	$ 832	$772	$ 908	$1,038	$1,124	$ 966	$ 882
Restructuring charges and write-downs	$1,018	—	$442	$ 265	—	—	—
Interest expense	$ 111	$ 86	$ 91	$ 78	$ 74	$ 59	$ 60
Stockholders' equity	$ (892)	$236	$(281)	$ 282	$ 648	$ 757	$ 856
Working capital	$ (18)	$ 35	$(889)	$(921)	$ (15)	$ (17)	$ 52
Long-term debt	$1,067	$771	$ 718	$ 838	$ 953	$ 818	$ 697
Long-term debt to equity ratio	609%	76%	164%	75%	59%	52%	45%
Operating margin	5%	4%	(2%)	(6%)	1%	7%	14%
Interest coverage	0.40	0.35	—	—	1.14	1.3	2.4

Company C

Year Ended December 31

	1988	1987	1986	1985	1984	1983	1982
Net profit (loss)	$ 420	$ 206	$ 61	$ 29.5	$(267.8)	$ (63.5)	$ (74.3)
Revenues	$2,320	$1,612	$846	$887	$ 910	$ 952	$ 923
Expenses (excluding restructuring charges, asset write-downs, and interest)	$1,717	$1,346	$782	$829	$ 1,009	$ 1,009	$ 1,011
Restructuring charges and write-downs	—	—	—	—	110	—	—
Interest expense	$ 44	$ 48	$ 36	$ 46	$ 52	$ 52	$ 60
Stockholders' equity	$1,676	$1,338	$934	$891	$ 828	$ 981	$ 977
Working capital	$ 431	$ 305	$205	$170	$ 112	$ 132	$ 162
Long-term debt	$ 450	$ 398	$610	$448	$ 591	$ 600	$ 667
Long-term debt to equity ratio	21%	23%	39%	33%	42%	38%	41%
Interest coverage	13.7	5.5	1.8	1.3	—	—	—
Operating margin	26%	17%	8%	6%	(11%)	(6%)	(9%)

future years, would ultimately result in the company's bankruptcy.
- Each had relatively high, but not unmanageable, leverage.
- Each had low margins, which needed to increase to fund interest payments, capital expenditures, and working capital requirements.

There were also, however, some significant differences between the financial position of each company, which indicated that Company C was much stronger financially than Company B. The most significant of these were as follows:

- Company C had adequate working capital at December 31, 1984, whereas Company B had negative working capital.
- Company C's long-term debt to equity ratio had remained relatively steady from 1982 to 1984, despite the losses incurred. As explained in the MDA section of the company's 1984 10-K, this was due to sales of assets in peripheral businesses, injection of additional equity financing, and reduction of working capital. In the same period, Company B's long-term debt to equity ratio had increased from 45 percent to 59 percent, despite a reduction in working capital of $67.
- Each company stated in the MDA to its 1984 10-Ks that existing levels of operating profits would not be sufficient to fund future capital expenditure, working capital, and debt retirement requirements. It was apparent, however, that Company C had much better prospects of increasing operating profits to the required levels.

In its 1984 10-K, Company C outlined in detail what it had done to reduce costs to a point where it could break even, or to make a small profit, at current copper prices. The company also had available lines of credit with its banks, which it could utilize to pay for capital expenditures until such time as copper prices improved. In the first quarter of 1985, Company C made a small profit after interest expense, although copper prices did not improve. This trend continued throughout 1985 and 1986. In both of these years, copper prices remained steady; however, the company demonstrated that it could survive a sustained period of relatively low prices until such time as prices improved. In 1987, the price of copper increased significantly and has remained high since, as a result of which the company has generated significant net profits and has recommenced payment of dividends.

In its 1984 10-K, Company B stated that it was likely that it would continue to incur operating losses for the immediate future. The company also admitted that it did not have sufficient credit to fund such losses, capital expenditures, and debt repayments, primarily because of the cancellation by a bank in November 1985 of a line of credit that had been arranged two months earlier. Because of these factors, the company stated, in the footnotes to its 1984 financial statements, that continuation of its operations was dependent upon obtaining additional funding.

By December 31, 1985, Company B's position had worsened and continued to do so in 1986 through 1989, to the point where, in its December 31, 1989, 10-K, the company stated that failure to restructure its debt or to raise funds through asset sales could force it to seek protection under the Bankruptcy Code.

An investor who studied the 10-Ks of Company B and Company C for 1984 and the quarterly 10-Q filings for 1985 and 1986 could have identified the above differences between the companies' financial positions and prospects. This may have persuaded the investor that the potential return from an investment in Company C justified the risks assumed, and that a similar investment in Company B was not justified.

CHAPTER 20

UTILIZING CASH FLOW STATEMENTS AS AN ANALYTICAL TOOL

Gregory E. Bardnell
David R. Williams
Price Waterhouse

INTRODUCTION

For years, investment bankers, lawyers, accountants, and financial consultants have been trying to unlock the secrets to turning around financially distressed and troubled companies. In most cases, these troubled companies have a common problem. They are in a negative cash flow position that can be attributed to an endless variety of reasons. From product dissatisfaction to increased labor and overhead costs, the resultant shortage of cash can cause a crisis within the company. The key to a successful turnaround is to effectively reverse this negative cash flow. It is well known that cash, or its lack, can destroy even the best-run companies if not properly managed and monitored. The means and ability for an enterprise to generate cash flow in its operations and from other sources has been and should be of interest to investors and others interested in an enterprise. Matters of interest would include whether cash is generated from operations, from the sale of assets, or from further leveraging of the enterprise. The means in which cash flows are generated are often as important as the magnitude of cash flows generated.

This chapter is devoted primarily to understanding the usefulness of effective cash flow reporting as an analytical tool by turnaround management or by others needing to understand the enterprise's cash flow. Without this understanding, it may be difficult, if not impossible, to effectively understand the inherent problems a troubled company is experiencing. For example, it may be imperative that a troubled company reduce overhead to reach a break-even point on operations. If overhead is controlled by both management and outside third-party creditors, then an understanding of the underlying historical and prospective cash requirements of these groups is required to assist in the development of a useful workout strategy that reduces or eliminates negative cash flow. For it is cash, the lifeline of all business ventures, that is probably the most misunderstood asset in corporate America today.

This chapter will also discuss important analytical aspects of the statement of cash flows and its ability to be used as a historical analytical tool, as well as a potential basis to provide prospective financial information. The statement of cash flows can usually bridge the gap between cash flow projections and historical financial statements and the effects they have on each other. Initially, a background to the purpose of the statement of cash flows and its current implementation is discussed. A general discussion regarding cash flow reporting in the bankruptcy environment will also be discussed.

CASH

Cash is defined by Webster as "ready money; money or its equivalent paid promptly after purchasing"; by children, as an assortment of coins and bills; by adults, as a paycheck or a trip to the automatic teller machine. Cash is not so easily defined in business as most of us know it. Without cash, business on this planet could not exist, at least not as a global marketplace. That is why cash, no matter the denomination, is so important to business and the enterprises of the world. You can promise a person water, and that person will become more thirsty as time passes. Limit it, and the person will become desperate and act irrationally. Eventually, with no water, he or she will die. This analogy gives meaning to the business term of *liquidity*. A business must always be cognizant of its cash demands and its cash sources, because the consequences of an unexpected cash shortfall can be significant. In addition, creditors of a corporation have various legal remedies, which are often used as leverage against companies experiencing cash problems. The most drastic, and perhaps becoming more widely accepted, is forcing the company into involuntary bankruptcy.

SOLVENCY

The inability to adequately service debt requirements as they become due has significant legal ramifications, also. Insolvency in the equity sense refers to a debtor's inability to meet or pay obligations when they become due. Under current bankruptcy law, a definition of insolvency is contained in Section 101(31) of the Bankruptcy Code:

> Insolvent means . . . financial condition such that the sum of . . . (the) entity's debts is greater than all of such entity's property, at a fair valuation; exclusive of (i) property transferred, concealed, or removed with intent to hinder delay, or defraud such entity's creditors and (ii) property that may be exempted from property of the estate under Section 522.

This definition is commonly referred to as the *balance sheet test,* and, as such, a corporation is considered legally insolvent if it falls within the definition. It is particularly important for a company to understand all cash obligations, since the law allows the creditors to force the debtor into bankruptcy court under the condition that the debtor is generally not paying its debts as they become due. Thus, a petition may be allowed, even though the debtor is not bankrupt in the equity sense, under conditions where the debtor has the current funds to pay its debts but is generally not paying them.

It is quite possible for an enterprise to be temporarily unable to meet its current obligations but also be legally solvent. A business with a temporary shortage of liquid assets may be at the mercy of its creditors, regardless of whether its total position shows an excess of assets over liabilities. On the other hand, a debtor may be insolvent in the bankruptcy sense, with liabilities greater than the fair value of its assets, but temporarily paying its currently maturing debts. In this situation creditors are normally unaware of the debtor's financial distress; but, even if they were, they would be unable to organize and initiate proceedings to protect their interests. (See Grant W. Neston, *Bankruptcy and Insolvency Accounting: Practice and Procedure,* 3rd ed.)

GENERALLY ACCEPTED ACCOUNTING PRINCIPLES (GAAP)

GAAP provides guidelines for the preparation of financial statements, because it provides standards for both accounting and reporting, among other things. Each component of the financial statements plays a role in stating an enterprise's financial condition. The balance sheet and income statement are the result of the enterprise's double-entry accounting system (i.e., all entries must have an equal debit and credit). These GAAP basis financial statements reflect the use of the accrual method of accounting, which basically assumes related revenues and expenses should be recorded in the same period to create an equitable matching of revenues and expenses. The general concept for the matching of revenues and expenses is that, for revenue to be recorded, all expenses related to generating this revenue should be recorded in the same period. The accounting profession refers to this concept as the *matching principle*. This concept also recognizes the need to record such contingencies as reserves for litigation, future warranty expense, allowances for returned sales and allowances, and for bad debts from unrecoverable receivables. These contingencies, or accruals, are management's best estimate of future detriments. These contingencies have a current impact on the net income, however, and have a future affect on cash flows. Therefore, the statement of cash flows will not necessarily record expenses with the related revenues in the same period. This is an important accounting concept to be aware of when reviewing the income statement and the statement of cash flows. To understand the statement of cash flows, a working knowledge of the balance sheet and income statement should exist for the time period in question. The statement of cash flows is prepared primarily on the activity recorded in the balance sheet and the income statement.

The balance sheet and income statement are prepared in accordance with GAAP and based upon the accrual method of accounting. This means revenues can be recorded without cash being collected initially. Accrual accounting generally requires the recognition of revenue at the date the goods were delivered, not when the cash was received. The statement of cash flows recognizes cash inflow when the cash is received. In effect, the statement of cash flows can be interpreted broadly as a cash basis income statement. Obviously, this is important to parties-of-interest, because cash is what pays obligations, not net income. Net income reported may be significantly different than an enterprise's cash flows from operations.

GAAP had required a statement of funds flow (statement of changes in financial position) for many years. This statement was superseded by the new statement of cash flows.

THE "OLD" STATEMENT OF CHANGES IN FINANCIAL POSITION

Prior to 1988, financial statements were not required to contain a statement reflecting cash flows. Instead, financial statements prepared in accordance with GAAP included a statement of financial position (balance sheet), a statement of operations (income statement), a statement of changes in financial position (statement of changes), and a statement of owners' equity. The statement of changes included certain elements of cash flow information but did not address certain other important elements of cash flow information. As such, the reader of such historical financial statements was limited to obtaining an understanding through either the statement of changes or footnote disclosure for information related to the cash flows of the enterprise. Even registration statements required by either the 1933 or 1934 Security and Exchange Commission (SEC) acts were not very useful in this environment.

The statement of changes was established by *Accounting Principles Board (APB) Opinion No. 19* in 1971. APB opinions were predecessors to Financial Accounting Standards Board (FASB) statements and remain authoritative unless amended. The lack of clear objectives for the statement of changes caused a large degree of uncertainty in how to apply it in practice. This problem, and the growing significance of information regarding an enterprise's cash flows, as opposed to working capital, created the need for a movement away from reporting working capital changes.

The statement of changes was initially used to illustrate changes in working capital in relation to changes in balance sheet items. In recent years, some enterprises have used the same methodology described in the standard but have adopted a cash definition of funds. The statement of changes in financial position that was prepared using a cash definition of funds was not much different than the statement of changes that was prepared using a working capital definition of funds, because the same elements or items were disclosed in a different manner. The new statement of cash flows is substantially different than its predecessor.

Working capital, or the term *funds,* was an integral part of the statement of changes. Such language was too vague to get an accurate indication about the true liquidity of an enterprise's working capital. Cash and cash equivalents are the focus of the statement of cash flows, which allows the reader to see actual cash flows and not flows of working capital or funds. Cash equivalents can be defined as highly liquid instruments, readily convertible to known amounts of cash, that have a short-term maturity and are risk adverse to changes in economic conditions. Although *SFAS No. 95* sets no standards for cash equivalents, guidelines are provided and require an enterprise to disclose what it defines as cash equivalents. Commonly, cash equivalents are short-term investments, with original maturities of three months or less. Some examples are Treasury bills, commercial paper, and money market funds. As such, changes in these balances would be considered as a change in cash in the statement of cash flows.

STATEMENT OF CASH FLOWS

As a result of continued pressure by the public sector, development of a statement to understand the cash flows of an enterprise began. After many years of debating about its purpose and structure, the accounting profession agreed to study the issue and consider implementing a new financial statement for cash flows. The formation of a statement of cash flows was based on the inability of financial statement readers to readily ascertain an enterprise's historical cash flow performance. With debt replacing equity as the primary financing tool in the 1980s, combined with a long period of high interest rates, cash flow information became more important. In late 1988, the Financial Accounting Standards Board, the accounting profession's governing body, implemented and issued *Statement of Financial Accounting Standards (SFAS) No. 95* entitled "Statement of Cash Flows." This standard effectively replaced the statement of changes in financial position with a statement of cash flows for GAAP presentation of financial statements.

Since enterprises are relying more heavily on debt to finance activities, as opposed to equity, cash payments have become increasingly more nondiscretionary. With off-balance-sheet financing, such as operating leases, becoming more common, the statement of cash flows illustrates these cash effects. This is a clear example of a benefit of the statement of cash flows to a third-party reader interested in a company's ability to service debt.

The increased cash flow information is designed to better inform shareholders, creditors, and investors about the overall financial condition of an enterprise. These parties-of-interest typically review the balance sheet for a summary of assets, liabilities, and equity at a point in time, and the income statement for results of operations during a stated time.

It is important to understand that the income statement is prepared in accordance with generally accepted accounting principles (GAAP), on an accrual basis, and does not reflect the actual effects of net cash flows. As a result, inflation and the increased use of deferred revenues and expenses can distort the meaningfulness of an enterprise's financial performance as reflected on the income statement. This situation is most evident in the real estate industry, whereby large developers can recognize millions in revenues on gains from sales but only receive a fraction of the cash upon closing the sale, the remainder being due in the future. Thus, cash inflows will not match the revenues from these types of sales. This can also be seen in the wholesale/distribution industry to a smaller degree. Inventory balances, accounts receivable, and trade payables can all be managed to affect cash balances and earnings.

However, during its infancy, the statement of cash flows was not widely accepted. The initial lack of wide acceptance was probably due primarily to the lack of comparability of the data with prior years, even though prior year financial data was restated. The new elements disclosed in the statement of cash flows were not fully understood. This change in the elements disclosed in the statement of cash flows caused a delay in the use of it as an analytical tool. The statement of cash flows was more exact in its guidelines, unlike the statement of changes in financial position, which had a wide diversity in how it was applied in practice. Eventually, readers became more familiar with the statement of cash flows, which significantly reduced interpretation issues, a main concern with the statement of changes in financial position.

The statement of cash flows is a primary financial statement and is required for each period for which an income statement is presented. For example, in an SEC filing where an income statement is presented covering a three-year period together with comparative stub periods, the statement of cash flows should also be presented for these periods.

The purpose of the statement of cash flows is stated in *SFAS No. 95* in paragraphs 4 and 5:

> The primary purpose of a statement of cash flows is to provide relevant information about the cash receipts and cash payments of an enterprise during a period.
>
> The information provided in a statement of cash flows, if used with related disclosures and information in the other financial statements, should help investors, creditors, and others to *(a)* assess the enterprise's ability to generate positive future net cash flows; *(b)* assess the enterprise's ability to meet its obligations, its ability to pay dividends, and its needs for external financing; *(c)* assess the reasons for differences between net income and associated cash receipts and payments; and *(d)* assess the effects on an enterprise's financial position of both its cash and noncash investing and financing transactions during the period.

In particular, the use of related disclosures and information in the other financial statements plays a significant role in interpreting an enterprise's statement of cash flows. It is important to realize the effectiveness of the statement of cash flows is diminished dramatically, as well as the other individual statements, if the financial statements are not reviewed as a whole. Similarly, to understand an enterprise, you must be knowledgeable of operations, financing, and marketing to truly understand the whole enterprise.

SFAS No. 95 defines cash inflows and outflows as coming from three sources: investing, financing, and operating. These three sources allow the reader to analyze the three major components of an enterprise's business. It is important to understand what components of the enterprise's activities are represented in each activity to better analyze what the statement of cash flows is representing. As previously mentioned, the transactions must involve cash or they are not included in the body of the statement of cash flows. In certain cases, they are separately disclosed as noncash transactions. Noncash transaction disclosures are important, because they could affect future cash flows. An example would be the purchase of equipment financed by the seller directly. Assuming no down payment, this is a noncash transaction, because no cash was exchanged for the purchase and will create future cash outflows as the obligation is paid.

Investing activities are classified as purchasing or selling of debt or equity securities, making and collecting on loans, and the acquisition and disposition of property, plant, and equipment and any other assets that are used in the production of goods or services by the enterprise. This does not include any other assets that are part of the enterprise's inventory or assets that are sold regularly as part of operations. However, judgment is required for classifying certain activities. For example, if a company purchases a piece of equipment for the ultimate purpose of leasing it to a customer, the cash outlay would be classified as an investing activity. However, if the ultimate use of the purchased equipment were to sell to the same customer, the cash outlay might be considered inventory and an operating cash outflow.

Other examples of investing cash flow activities include partial payment, down payments, and capitalized interest related to property, plant, and equipment. In addition, although proceeds from the sale of disposal of debt or equity securities of other entities are investing cash inflows, interest income of dividend income earned on those securities are operating cash inflows.

Financing activities are classified as obtaining equity investments from shareholders/owners and any subsequent return of investment (i.e., dividends), borrowing or repayments of cash, and any other payments, due for resources obtained from creditors on obligations. Incurring debt issue costs is considered an operating cash flow, not a financing cash flow. However, if a company issues debt at a discount, the net-of-discount borrowing will be reflected as a financing cash inflow, with the amortization of the discount being reflected as a noncash reconciling item between net income and net cash flows from operating activities.

Operating activities are classified as all cash transactions that are not specifically defined as investing or financing activities. Operating activities generally include the producing of goods and services and their subsequent sale. In broader terms, cash flows from operating activities are the cash effects of transactions that provide net income or loss. Interest and dividend revenues and interest expenses are classified as operating activities, because they affect net income. Interest has characteristics of being a financing or investing activity; however, the premise is that most recurring income statement items are classified as operating activities. Only the principal portion of payments or receipts are classified as investing and financing activities. This will allow the reconciliation of net income to net cash flows to be shown in operating activities. The effect is that the investing and financing sections generally exclude the effects of the income statement and reflect only the appropriate changes in the balance sheet. Certain cash transactions may have characteristics of more than one cash activity, such as a cash payment on an item that could be considered either inventory or a productive asset. In this case, the activity that is likely to be the predominant source of the ultimate cash flow for the item will be used to determine the classification (investing, financing, or operating) of the payment.

It is important to keep in mind that an understanding of the industry in which the enterprise operates is necessary to analyze its financial statements. Banks and other financial institutions are in the business of lending money; accordingly, they will have significant investing and financing activities and less-significant operating activities. However, the interest they earn or pay is still shown as an operating activity.

One portion of the statement of cash flows is the reconciliation of net income to net cash flows. Since an intent of the statement of cash flows is to show the relationship between net income and net cash flows, the noncash income statement items must be removed from the net income figure at the top of the statement of cash flows to determine cash flows. This is done by identifying noncash items, such as depreciation and amortization, provisions for losses, allowance for bad debts, and gains (losses) on sale of assets. The gain (loss) on sale of productive assets is removed, because the amount of cash received, which in part makes up the gain (loss), is included in investing activities. The net income figure, with noncash items removed, is then reconciled to the balance sheet items affected by operating activities, such as inventory, accounts receivable, accounts payable, and the like.

As with many accounting standards, *SFAS No. 95* allows for two methods to be used in the development of the statement of cash flows. These methods are referred to as the *direct method* and the *indirect method*. The direct method is a more comprehensive approach that details gross cash receipts and payments related to operating activities and also provides a reconciliation of net income to net cash flows from operating activities.

The advantage of the direct method is that it is more comprehensive and more clearly shows the amount of cash flows in their operating activities. The indirect method simply provides the reconciliation of net income to net cash flows. Although the direct method is recommended, not all enterprises have the ability in their current accounting system to prepare such a statement. As such, most enterprises use the indirect method. Although both methods are useful, one should recognize the differences, because it will effect an analysis of the statement of cash flows. The investing and financing sections are identical for both methods.

READING THE STATEMENT OF CASH FLOWS

No matter which method is utilized to prepare the statement of cash flows, cash flows can be affected through management of various assets and liabilities. The effect on the financial statements of managing certain assets and liabilities can be dramatic and is essential to an understanding of cash flows.

For example, a decrease in inventory balances between years

will create a positive effect on cash flow from operating activities. This decrease in inventory could result from one event or a combination of several events. Be careful when interpreting what the fluctuations in inventory balances represent. To illustrate, the decrease could mean that the company has tightened inventory controls, thus not requiring a large balance of inventory to be on hand at any one time. Conversely, the decrease in inventory could mean that cash flow was short, and the company was not able to purchase adequate inventory from suppliers. If inventory balances are decreasing and the related liabilities are increasing, then the suppliers of the inventory are not being paid on a current basis. Will the suppliers suspend shipments to the enterprise? Where is the cash going from the sales of this inventory? The statement of cash flows may assist in answering where the cash may have gone. Maybe the cash was not yet received from the customers (i.e., accounts are increasing), or maybe the funds were used to pay down debt or acquire equipment. These scenarios create different reasons why cash flows could have increased from operating activities. The reader should know this and understand that there can be positive and negative reasons for the increases or decreases in cash flows once you know the changes in account balances.

The practice of extending a customer's receivables is, in most industries, a norm and convenience. Fluctuations in the accounts receivable balances between years can be an early warning sign to future cash flow problems. If the balance increases, it could mean an increase in sales or a loosening of the credit policy, due to weak sales or attempts to sell slow-moving inventory. A decrease could mean a decrease in sales or an improvement in the collection period of receivables. In any industry, whether sales volume is high or low, receivables management is an important business tool. Extending credit to borderline customers can maximize sales, but it can affect cash flows if uncollectible accounts become too large. These receivables are future cash flows and any impediment to their collection, such as a recession, can cause cash flow problems. These practices are what make accrual accounting ineffective, unless reconciled to actual cash flows. However, accrual accounting is part of the financial statements and must be understood.

Cash used in investing activities, such as capital expenditures, can be viewed in two ways: (1) large expenditures for the repair of producing assets to allow the company to maintain its current production levels or (2) expenditures to increase capacity for new or current products. This latter reason for the capital expenditure will allow the company to expand overall sales and, potentially, the company may be able to recover this capital expenditure through increased future cash flows. Therefore, it is important to try to understand the nature of such expenditures, not just the magnitude.

In most cases, large capital expenditures are financed through some sort of borrowing. There are two common kinds of borrowing: (1) directly from the sellers themselves or (2) from a third party, such as a bank. The borrowings from a bank are shown on the statement of cash flows as cash provided in financing activities from bank borrowings. The purchase of assets will be shown as capital expenditure in investing activities. If the seller provides financing, only the down payment or monies paid shortly before or after the purchase will be considered to be part of the cash transaction that will reflect investing activities. The remainder will be considered to be a noncash activity. The obligation will be paid in future periods as part of the financing activities and will be shown as payments on obligations. This concept is important to understand, because these two scenarios of financing reflect the same detriment to the company for future payments; in most cases, however, the reflection on the statement of cash flows is different. This type of noncash transaction is disclosed within the body of financial statements in the notes to the financial statements, if significant.

The financing activities in the statement of cash flows are also important to understand for consideration of future operations. This is the area where an enterprise will obtain funds to provide for future growth or to help it obtain the cash to provide for investment in operations, which potentially will generate cash. The section of financing activities will generally be a good barometer about the financial condition of the company currently and in prior years. The financing section can provide insight about where the enterprise is heading in the future. An issuance of long-term debt might be used to acquire another company, to cover obligations currently coming due, or to finance current operations that are not generating cash flows. These three scenarios show growth, maintenance, and losses, respectively, with each showing a current direction of the enterprise.

As noted above, many questions regarding "why" should be answered in the notes to the financial statements. The notes should disclose what the terms are for the enterprise's borrowings, so the reader can understand what its effect will be on the current and future cash flows. As also noted earlier, interest expense and dividends payable, whether the case may be equity or debt, will be part of the operating activities in the future and will have an impact on operating cash flows. As the emphasis has switched from equity to debt in the United States, the understanding of this section and overall cash flows and the implications to an enterprise will become significant in the coming years. The financing activity section, in combination with the operating activity section, will provide the reader and potential creditors and investors with the first signals of an enterprise that does not generate enough operating cash flows to satisfy current liabilities or obligations.

The reader of the statement of cash flows should also be cognizant of the enterprise's industry, the current economic events that affect that industry, and its business cycles. This can be very helpful in understanding the enterprise's cash flows. Industries with cycles longer than one year, such as those involved in long-term construction or contracting, can indicate deceptive cash flow information if not properly interpreted. Although the statement of cash flows has not been in use for very long, it is difficult to determine common industry practices in presenting it. Trends in specific industries have begun and the reader should become aware of these trends.

The statement of cash flows can also be a very useful tool in determining what potential future cash flows will be in comparison to historical cash flows. However, when used in this context, the statement of cash flows should not be used in isolation from the other financial statements. The statement of cash flows will allow the reader to understand what cash activities have taken place in previous years for an understanding of the direction or trends of the future. The cash flows provided and used during the previous fiscal years can normally be used as a starting point for estimating future cash flows. If, for example, cash flows from operations on a historical basis are positive, then there is a good indication that the enterprise has the ability to maintain positive cash flows and to service debt in the future. This assumes no significant events will occur and that the current balance sheet and income statement are correctly interpreted. On this same point, since interest is included within the operating activities of the statement of cash flows, this can be useful in understanding whether an entity has negative or positive operating cash flows. If it has negative cash flows for its operating activities, then interest expense may be impeding or "masking" positive operating activity before interest payments. Interest expense is sometimes considered the most important cash outflow in corporate America. Debt-burdened corporations are continually trying to meet servicing requirements without affecting operations, a task that is becoming more and more difficult for many enterprises.

A common practice of leveraged buyouts (LBOs) was to sell subsidiaries, after the purchase of an enterprise, to service the high debt obligations. This was under the assumption that, in some enterprises, the sum of the value of individual subsidiaries is greater than the value of the entire consolidated group. LBOs are typically structured whereby future operating cash flows or sales of subsidiaries or divisions, or both, are required to cover these large debt obligations. Based on such a strong reliance on future cash flows and situations where the critical assumption range is narrow, the problems of servicing LBO debt can quickly become evident.

As the enterprise's need for cash increases, options for the generation of cash begin to decrease. Financing alternatives also become difficult, and the remaining option commonly is to sell off assets of value. This could assist the company in generating cash flows to cover current obligations; however, this could create a detriment, by reducing the ability to generate future cash flows. Another factor is whether these assets have a viable market value. Many times, even desirable assets have no market, or, more appropriately, cannot attract an acceptable offer. When assets become difficult to sell, and positive cash flow is necessary, a workout or reorganization of the enterprise is eminent. The quicker this is recognized, the better chance the enterprise has of surviving a workout or bankruptcy.

With this in mind, the reader of the statement of cash flows should be able to understand the ramifications of cash events that have taken place in prior years and be able to develop what could be a trend about the future direction of the company. If the company is showing a desperation for cash or is unable to meet current operating obligations, then other sources of cash need to be considered.

This kind of review should allow the reader to understand and make preliminary conclusions about the enterprise in question. However, to effectively use the statement of cash flows as a reorganization or bankruptcy tool, one must understand more about the detail and inner workings of the statement of cash flows.

RATIO ANALYSIS

At this time, the calculation of some common ratios might be of importance to obtaining a basic understanding of some of the problems that may not be explicitly explained from reviewing the financial statements themselves. Provided in Exhibit 1 are some traditional ratios prepared for a hypothetical XYZ Industries. These ratios are given for 1989 and 1988 to provide comparisons between years. In addition to these standard ratios, the statement of cash flows provides additional information that may be useful for ratio analysis, as summarized in Exhibit 2. All of these ratios were based upon the financial statement attached as Exhibits 3-A through 3-D. The ratios are: cash flows from operating activities divided by sales, cash flows from operating activities divided by total assets, and cash flows from operating activities divided by annual interest payments. This allows a determination of what actual cash flows have occurred per sales dollar, what cash flows have occurred per total assets employed, and, importantly, what cash flows are being realized as compared to annual interest payments due. This also reflects actual cash inflows as compared to the balance sheet and income statement which are based on the accrual method. Another useful ratio is: cash flows from operating activities divided by total debt, which will determine how many years of operating activities are required to service the current debt principal balance.

These commonly used ratios and the new cash flow ratios can derive different results and could shed some light on why an enterprise with healthy income and revenues is unable to meet current cash requirements. This should assist in identifying areas where potential problems may exist or where additional analysis is necessary. This can be especially useful in a matter involving an enterprise subject to possible bankruptcy and restructuring when cash

EXHIBIT 1

XYZ INDUSTRIES
Ratio Analysis
Balance Sheet Income Statement

		1989	1989	1988
Liquidity:				
Current ratio $= \dfrac{\text{Current assets}}{\text{Current liabilities}}$		$= \dfrac{13{,}590}{6{,}630} =$	2.05	1.83
Quick ratio $= \dfrac{\text{Current assets (Less inventory)}}{\text{Current liabilities}}$		$= \dfrac{9{,}390}{6{,}630} =$	1.42	1.19
Capital structure:				
Debt-to-equity $= \dfrac{\text{Debt}}{\text{Equity}}$		$= \dfrac{4{,}762}{10{,}748} =$	0.44	0.51
Debt service:				
Debt service coverage $= \dfrac{\text{Operating income}}{\text{Annual interest pmts.}}$		$= \dfrac{2{,}375}{140} =$	16.96	21.00
Profitability:				
$\dfrac{\text{Net income}}{\text{Operating revenues}}$		$= \dfrac{1{,}473}{17{,}500} =$	8.4%	12.8%
$\dfrac{\text{Net income}}{\text{Total assets (avg.)}}$		$= \dfrac{1{,}473}{21{,}765} =$	6.8%	N.A.
$\dfrac{\text{Net income}}{\text{Equity (avg.)}}$		$= \dfrac{1{,}473}{9{,}862} =$	14.9%	N.A.
Turnover:				
$\dfrac{\text{Operating revenues}}{\text{Total assets (avg.)}}$		$= \dfrac{17{,}500}{21{,}765} =$	0.80	N.A.
$\dfrac{\text{Operating revenues}}{\text{Accts. receivable (avg.)}}$		$= \dfrac{17{,}500}{3{,}000} =$	5.83	N.A.

N.A. means not able to calculate with information provided.

flow problems are not obvious from the income statement or balance sheet.

These ratios can be extremely important in a bankruptcy or restructuring environment, due to the inherent emphasis on cash

EXHIBIT 2

XYZ INDUSTRIES
Ratio Analysis
Statement of Cash Flows,
1989

$$\frac{\text{Cash flow from operating activities}}{\text{Operating revenues}} = \frac{1{,}903}{17{,}500} = 0.11$$

$$\frac{\text{Cash flow from operating activities}}{\text{Total assets}} = \frac{1{,}903}{21{,}765} = 0.09$$

$$\frac{\text{Cash flow from operating activities}}{\text{Annual interest payment}} = \frac{1{,}903}{140} = 13.59$$

$$\frac{\text{Cash flow from operating activities}}{\text{Debt payments}} = \frac{1{,}903}{1{,}133} = 1.68$$

$$\frac{\text{Cash flow from operating activities}}{\text{Total long-term debt (avg.)}} = \frac{1{,}903}{4{,}659} = 0.41$$

and the enterprise's ability to pay obligations on a timely basis. A good understanding of the debt and the terms of the debt are critical. The understanding of the terms to the enterprise's debt is very important, because this will be the cornerstone of a reorganization analysis. You must understand the timing and amounts of those obligations to be able to do a comparison to expected cash inflows. This comparison will show where the enterprise will have deficiencies or surpluses.

QUALITY OF CASH FLOWS

Another useful analysis is the understanding of whether the cash flows are being generated by operations or through other means. The quality of cash flows can be determined by examining from which of the three activities (investing, financing, or operating) cash is being generated and by understanding the nature of the cash flow. If cash flows from operating activities are aided by increases in

EXHIBIT 3–A

XYZ INDUSTRIES
Cross-Referenced Balance Sheet
at December 31

	1988	1989	Change	Cross-Reference
Assets:				
Cash and cash equivalents	1,600	3,100	1,500	D
Accounts receivable (net of allowance for losses of $350 and $600)	2,700	3,300	600	E
Notes receivable	1,000	800	(200)	F
Inventory	4,500	4,200	(300)	G
Prepaid expenses and other	3,100	2,190	(910)	H
Current assets	12,900	13,590	690	
Other assets:				
Investments	3,300	3,450	150	I
Property, plant, and equipment, at cost	7,000	8,000	1,000	J,K
Accumulated depreciation	(4,210)	(4,575)	(365)	A,J,L
Net property, plant, and equipment	2,790	3,425	635	
Other assets	680	815	135	M
Goodwill and intangible assets	1,320	1,260	(60)	L
Total assets	20,990	22,540	1,550	
Liabilities:				
Accounts payable and accrued expenses	3,800	4,200	400	N
Interest payable	50	120	70	O
Income taxes payable	300	450	150	P
Short-term debt	500	600	100	Q
Short-term lease obligations	0	40	40	R
Dividends payable	0	0	0	
Other current liabilities	2,400	1,220	(1,180)	S
Current liabilities	7,050	6,630	(420)	
Other liabilities:				
Long-term debt	4,015	4,262	247	K,T,U
Long-term lease obligations	540	500	(40)	R
Deferred taxes	0	0	0	
Other liabilities	410	400	(10)	V
Total liabilities	12,015	11,792	(223)	
Stockholders' equity:				
Capital stock	4,500	5,300	800	W
Retained earnings	4,475	5,448	973	
Total stockholders' equity	8,975	10,748	1,773	
Total liabilities and stockholders' equity	20,990	22,540	1,550	

EXHIBIT 3-B

XYZ INDUSTRIES
Cross-Referenced Income Statement
For the Year Ended December 31

	1988	1989	Cross-Reference
Net sales	15,000	17,500	
Interest and other income	200	290	
	15,200	17,790	
Costs and expenses:			
Cost of sales	9,450	12,250	
Depreciation and amortization	375	525	A
S.G. & A.	1,800	2,000	
Interest expense	150	210	
Other expense	225	350	
Total expense	12,000	15,335	
Income before taxes	3,200	2,455	
Provision for income taxes	1,280	982	
Net income	1,920	1,473	B
Beginning retained earnings	2,955	4,475	
Net income	1,920	1,473	
Dividends	(400)	(500)	C
Ending retained earnings	4,475	5,448	

payables and decreases in assets, the quality of the cash flows may be questionable. Is the enterprise not paying vendors to increase cash and cash flow? If the overall increase in cash is due to financing activities, this could be "masking" operating cash flow deficiencies.

As a company relies more on financing and investing activities for cash, the company may become more desperate for cash in the future, unless future operating activities will be able to support the increased financing and investing activities. Generally speaking, however, once a company enters into a reorganization or bankruptcy, cash will not be generated in future periods from financing activities. The remaining avenues will greatly be limited to operating and investing activities. To increase cash inflows from operating activities generally requires a combination of time to implement a plan and cash for capital investments to improve operations. The

EXHIBIT 3–C

XYZ INDUSTRIES
Cross-Referenced Statement of Cash Flows, Indirect Method

	1989	Cross-Reference
Cash flows from operating activities:		
Net income	1,473	B
Adjustments to reconcile net income to net cash provided by operating activities:		
Depreciation and amortization	525	A
Provision for losses on accounts receivable	250	E
Gain on sale of equipment	(200)	J
Increase in accounts receivable	(850)	E
Decrease in inventory	300	G
Decrease in notes receivable	200	F
Decrease in prepared expenses and other	910	H
Increase in accounts payable and accrued expenses	400	N
Increase in interest and tax payable	220	O,P
Decrease in other liabilities	(1,190)	S,V
Increase in other assets	(135)	M
Net cash provided by operating activities	1,903	
Cash flows from investing activities:		
Capital expenditures	(960)	K
Sale of equipment	600	J
Purchase goodwill	0	
Purchase investments	(150)	I
Net cash used in investing activities:	(510)	
Cash flows from financing activities:		
Principal payments on long-term debt	(993)	U
Proceeds from short-term borrowings	100	Q
Principal payments on capital leases	0	
Proceeds from issuance of long-term debt	700	T
Proceeds from issuance of common stock	800	W
Purchase of treasury stock	0	
Dividends paid	(500)	C
Net cash provided by financing activities	107	
Net increase in cash and cash equivalents	1,500	D
Cash and cash equivalents beginning of year	1,600	D
Cash and cash equivalents end of the year	3,100	D

EXHIBIT 3-D

XYZ INDUSTRIES
Notes on Company Transactions

During 1989, the company completed the following transactions:
Number   Cross-Reference

1.	J	Sold equipment that had a gross book value of $500 and accumulated depreciation of $100 for $600.
2.	K	Bought $1,500 of equipment, paying $960 in cash and issuing long-term debt of $540.
3.	T	Issued $700 of long-term debt for cash.
4.	U	Retired $993 of debt, paying cash.
5.	W	Issued and sold $800 of common stock.
6.	R	Reclassified $40 of long-term lease obligations to short-term obligations.
7.	E	Increased allowance for bad debt from $350 to $600.
8.	L	Amortized $60 of goodwill.
9.	I	Purchased $150 of equity in XYZ Courier Service.
10.	Q	Borrowed $100 of short-term debt.
11.	C	Paid $500 of dividends.

enterprise rarely has either resource available at this point. Investing activities can derive cash from sales of assets, such as subsidiaries, divisions, or securities. The sale of productive assets will also generate cash flows; however, this could worsen the situation in the long term, if operations rely on these assets and cash flows. Before investing activities are used as a source of cash flows, an analysis of the effect on future cash flows as compared to the current net sales proceeds should be performed. Selling off a subsidiary might provide cash currently, but it might hurt the operating cash flows in future periods. It should be noted that, the longer a company takes to recognize the fact it needs to go through some sort of reorganization, the fewer options it will have in the future.

A review of the statement of cash flows and other financial statements at an early date will assist in identifying potential cash flow problems on a timely basis. This early detection of problems within an enterprise may head off larger problems in the future. A clever and beneficial way for a consultant to generate new work and provide his or her clients an important service may be from an analytical review of an enterprise's financial statements to identify potential areas of cash flow problems.

NONOPERATING/NONRECURRING ITEMS

Another option that could satisfy cash shortages is the possibility of restructuring debt into equity. This will allow an enterprise to reduce its nondiscretionary payments of interest and principal during a given period. The downside to this is that the enterprise could lose some or all of its control over its operations. An equity holder is considered an owner, which implies a vote in how the enterprise is operated. This type of transaction will generally be disclosed in the notes to the financial statements and may be obvious from reviewing the balance sheet. This will have a dramatic effect, in some cases, on what cash is being used for in the future and whether it will be able to service its existing debt after such a transaction.

Nonoperating transactions include investing and financing activities. Nonrecurring activities may be, at times, operating in nature, and they are one-time events where cash inflows or outflows have been derived. These nonrecurring items can also be reflected as net income for extraordinary gains and other items. These can mitigate the actual events that would have taken place without these nonrecurring items. Nonrecurring items are excluded from the analysis of cash flows to get a better picture of the actual activities that would have taken place during that period.

SAMPLE REVIEW

Included in Exhibit 4–A is a sample statement of cash flows using the indirect method for three companies. Examine each of the three companies and try to analyze what the statements of cash flows represent about each enterprise and what preliminary conclusions can be drawn and what inquiries should be made.

From reviewing Company A, the most obvious problems are that operating activities used $2,719 of cash and that $6,040 of cash was used for all activities. Net income was $1,966 and can be

EXHIBIT 4-A

Sample Statement of Cash Flows
Indirect Method

	Company A	Company B	Company C
Cash flows from operating activities:			
Net income	$ 1,966	$ 1,352	$ (5,741)
Adjustments to reconcile net income to net cash provided by operating activities:			
Depreciation and amortization	1,796	1,823	1,779
(Gain) loss on disposal of equipment	(589)		
Provisions for losses on accounts receivable			
Increase (decrease) in deferred taxes	1,061	687	
(Increase) decrease in accounts receivable	(3,471)	(2,030)	(13)
(Increase) decrease in inventory	(3,990)	1,378	(805)
(Increase) decrease in notes receivable			
(Increase) decrease in prepaid expenses and other	(191)	(76)	(625)
Increase (decrease) in accounts payable and accrued expenses	274	(1,076)	1,184
Increase (decrease) in interest and taxes payable	123	1,432	542
Increase (decrease) in other liabilities	302	(228)	1,754
Net cash provided by operating activities	(2,719)	3,262	(1,925)
Cash flows from investing activities:			
Capital expenditures	(2,253)	(672)	(5,570)
Sale of equipment	851		3,167
Purchase investments			
Net cash used in investing activities	(1,402)	(672)	(2,403)

EXHIBIT 4–A (concluded)

Sample Statement of Cash Flows
Indirect Method

	Company A	Company B	Company C
Cash flows from financing activities:			
Principal payments on long-term debt	$(1,161)	$(18,509)	$(3,802)
Proceeds from short-term borrowings			
Principal payments on capital leases			
Proceeds from issuance of long-term debt		25,000	8,000
Proceeds from issuance of common stock			661
Repurchased treasury stock	(562)		
Dividends paid	(334)		
Proceeds from stock options exercised	138	79	
Net cash provided by financing activities	(1,919)	6,570	4,859
Net increase (decrease) in cash and cash equivalents	(6,040)	9,160	531
Cash and cash equivalents beginning of year	9,978	818	228
Cash and cash equivalents end of year	$ 3,938	$ 9,978	$ 759

reconciled to net cash flows by adding back depreciation amortization of $1,796 and reducing net income by $589 for a gain on disposal of equipment. This results in the net income reconciled to net cash flow of $3,173. The remainder of the changes in the operating activities are balance sheet changes that affect net income. These changes create fluctuations in cash balances as a result of these account balances. The largest users of operating activity cash are accounts receivable and inventory. If sales are growing, then this may not be a concern, because both items result in future cash flows. If sales are not growing, then increases may be the result of bloated inventories or uncollectible receivables, or both. As mentioned earlier, increases or decreases in account balances generally can have several meanings, and one should determine which is the most accurate. The increase in deferred taxes is a function of actual tax liabilities, which are due subsequent to the current year. The company expended funds for capital expenditures, retirement of debt, purchases of stock and dividends, and had cash inflows from the sale of equipment. Most significantly, no new borrowings were required to fund operating cash flows. After a quick analysis of Company A, it appears that earnings are of good quality, because net cash used by operating activities is a result of delayed cash receipts on receivables and increases in inventories to support increased revenues. Additionally, the company expended cash on investing and financing activities without selling debt or equity.

Reviewing Company B shows positive net income and an increase in receivables, which represents future cash flows, assuming sales are growing. Inventory is down, and, depending on sales, the company may not have enough money to purchase inventory or the company may have made improvements to inventory controls. The decrease in inventory could be a direct correlation to the decrease to the payables. There is nothing explicit to indicate problems in quality earnings from operating activities. Investing and financing activities show that money was spent on capital expenditures and retiring debt. The debt was retired either because it became due or it became advantageous to retire early. If it did retire debt early, any gain or loss is in net income. Losses should be added back to net income, and gains should be subtracted from net income to arrive at the proper reconciliation to net cash flows. The $25,000 raised from the issuance of long-term debt was probably used to make the principal payments on the long-term debt. This could be an indication that the company was required to issue long-term debt to satisfy obligations coming due. Even though cash flows increased $9,160 during the year, $6,570 came from financing activities. The $3,262 from operating activity is a mixed bag, and it should be reviewed more scrupulously to determine what the potential operating activity cash flows would be in the future.

In reviewing Company C, right away we see a large net loss; however, if the loss is due to significant noncash items, then there may not be a significant cash problem. However, in this case, there are no significant noncash items, other than depreciation and amortization, that would help reduce the net loss. The primary increase in cash flows is due to an increase in the payable balances. This is not a positive indication. While inventory did increase, it did not increase to the extent that payables did. A company may be stretching payables, due to lack of funds or ability to pay current obligations. The company spent $5,570 on capital expenditures and sold $3,167 of equipment. We do not know why the equipment was sold, although, given the state of operations, we have to question what assets were sold and why. We should look into why these assets were sold and purchased during the year. The components of the financing activities show a $3,802 principal payment on debt and principal debts funded by new debt and equity offerings. Was this a refinancing at a higher interest rate? If higher interest rates have been incurred, this potentially could cut future earnings and future cash flows. Overall, the quality of cash flows from operating activities is weak. The main source of cash flows is depreciation and increases in a payable balance.

Of the companies presented, Company C entered into bankruptcy proceedings one year later, Company B restructured operations, and Company A prospered.

A useful analysis of the statement of cash flows is to break it down into sources of cash inflows and outflows from the three activities, as detailed in Exhibit 4–B. This summary analysis quantifies the dollars and percentages of where cash is being provided and used.

As discussed above, Company A has obtained nearly all (84 percent) of its cash inflows from operations, while Companies B and C are at 21 percent and 31 percent, respectively. Cash outflows show a similar effect between the companies. This analysis helps support the analysis of the statement of cash flows.

This analysis can also be used for an enterprise on a historical basis to show trends in cash inflows and outflows. This will show future trends and will allow the comparison of prospective information for reasonableness reviews. There could be situations where a statement of cash flows is not provided as part of a package of financial statements. In that case, being provided an income statement and balance sheet should provide a basis for developing an approximate statement. A statement can be created by computing the changes in balance sheet line items from year to year. Review and highlight the income statement for net income, depreciation/amortization, gains or losses on asset dispositions, and other general information that may disclose noncash transactions. In cases where detailed information is not available, use net changes in account balances line items, which are generally classified as investing and financing activities, such as debt and property, plant, and equipment. This will show numbers net and inquiries can be made later about the details needed to show the numbers gross.

Exhibit 3–C contains a statement with cross-references made to the income statement (3–B) and balance sheet (3–A), so you can follow what line items are used in comparing the statement of cash flows. Also contained is a brief synopsis of some notes to the enterprise's financial statements (3–D). As you will notice, some critical information can come from notes to the financial statements, especially if more detail is required. Upon reviewing Exhibit 3–C, notice the significant accounts balance changes and how they affect the statement of cash flows. Cash increased $1,500, which reflects overall positive cash flows. Notice the $1,000 increase in property, plant, and equipment. This reconciles to Exhibit 3–D in numbers 1 and 2. The beginning balance was $7,000 and the company purchased $1,500 of equipment and sold $500 of equipment for a balance of $8,000. The company paid $960 for the equipment and received $600 for the sold equipment, as reflected in Exhibit 3–C in the investing activities. Notice the financing of $540 provided by the seller. The gain on the sale of the equipment of $200 is calculated by taking the sale price of $600 less the gross book value of $500, less accumulated depreciation of $100. the disclosures on Exhibit 3–D provide the majority of the detail for the investing and financing activities, and the balance sheet and income statement provide the majority of the detail for the operating activities. As a reminder, an increase in an asset *costs* cash and an increase in a liability *saves* cash.

In situations where detail is not accessible, broad assumptions can be made to at least derive an outline of what the statement of cash flows would look like. This will allow the development of questions that would be needed to ask management about cash flows during this last period. The balance sheet line items that generally make up investing activities are investments in subsidiar-

EXHIBIT 4–B

Sample Analysis of Statements of Cash Flows
Indirect Method

	Company A	%	Company B	%	Company C	%
Inflows:						
Operations:						
Net income and noncash items	$ 3,762	60%	$ 3,175	10%	$ 1,779	10%
Accounts receivable and inventory	0	0	1,378	4	0	0
Accounts payable and accruals	397	6	1,432	5	1,726	10
Other	1,172	19	687	2	1,754	10
Total—operations	5,331	85	6,672	21	5,259	30
Investing:						
Sale of assets	851	13	0	0	3,167	19
Financing:						
Issuance of debt	0	0	25,000	79	8,000	47
Issuance of stock	0	0	0	0	661	4
Other	138	2	79	0	0	0
Total—financing	138	2	25,079	79	8,661	51
Total Inflows	6,320	100%	31,751	100%	17,087	100%

Outflows:						
Operations:						
Net income and noncash items	589	5	0	0	5,741	34
Accounts receivable and inventory	7,461	60	2,030	9	818	5
Accounts payable and accruals	0	0	1,076	5	0	0
Other	0	0	304	1	625	4
Total—operations	8,050	65	3,410	15	7,184	43
Investing:						
Purchase of assets	2,253	18	672	3	5,570	34
Financing:						
Payments on debt	1,161	9	18,509	82	3,802	23
Repurchases of treasury stock	562	5	0	0	0	0
Dividends	334	3	0	0	0	0
Other	0	0	0	0	0	0
Total—financing	2,057	17	18,509	82	3,802	23
Total Outflows	12,360	100%	22,591	100%	16,556	100%
Net change in cash and cash equivalents	$ (6,040)		$ 9,160		$ 531	

ies and investments in securities and property, plant, and equipment. Financing activities include equity and any long-term debt or short-term obligations. The operating activities section includes all balance sheet account items not included within financing and investing activities.

PROSPECTIVE INFORMATION

A significant portion of work of the consultants and advisors in reorganization and bankruptcy is to help management or the enterprise's creditors to determine future cash flows. This can be done by developing a prospective statement of cash flows. This can be a very complex and involved process, where many assumptions, whether broad or narrow, need to be made. Varying assumptions can cause wide-ranging effects on potential cash flows. Such factors include current and future economic conditions, financial market conditions, industry, competition, product line, and future innovations. Within each factor, any number of potential variables can cause the assumptions and their results to vary greatly. As a general rule, projections over a short term are more accurate than projecting over a longer term.

The first step in developing a prospective statement is to provide a list of assumptions that affect the above-mentioned factors. These assumptions should be made in the following areas: revenue levels, expense levels, interest rates (potential cost of obtaining cash in the future), receivable collection periods, schedule of terms for creditor payments, tax rates, capital expenditures, and future production levels. The difficulty in determining these assumptions can fall into two factors: the enterprise's overall capacity and the outside market effects. These factors need to be taken into consideration when determining all of the above assumptions, because each one has an impact on the assumptions to be made. As an example, the company could develop a plan to increase production of a product as a response to demand or entering new market areas. This increased production should provide more revenue and cash flow, with operating costs increasing only marginally. However, changes in market conditions or demand for the product could affect whether that enterprise could actually attain this goal.

Generally, reasonable assumptions will fall within a range, with a certain assumption possibly being the most reasonable within that range. Flexibility should be maintained to allow for revisions to assumptions as warranted by the facts in the matter. It is always better to start out making broad general assumptions and then become more specific. If you get specific too early, you may narrow the whole approach on the prospective cash flows.

As assumptions are made, it is critical that these assumptions be documented. The documentation should include any calculations, conclusions, and basis for that assumption decision. Documentation is important so, as changes occur, they can be efficiently implemented into the projections. Documentation will allow you to revise assumptions when a change in the enterprise's variables occurs. The documentation will show your conclusions and whether it should be revised to take the changes into account. A useful tool for setting up a model is on a spreadsheet, which will allow you to insert various assumptions into the spreadsheet, so different scenarios can be run. This can give you an idea of the range in which you are working or whether your assumptions are reasonable. As different scenarios are run, the assumptions should begin to narrow and the projections will become more defined.

Once these assumptions have been incorporated into the prospective balance sheets and income statements, the statement of cash flows is ready to be prepared, based on the assumptions and the prospective balance sheet and income statement. After the statement of cash flows is prepared, review it for general reasonableness.

This will allow you to get a first run on whether your assumptions make sense given the balance sheet and income statement, as compared to a statement of cash flows. This should also expose the nonoperating events in previous years and the unusual items that probably will not reoccur. The focus of your review of your prospective statement should be to determine critical or sensitive areas from your assumptions and how these assumptions are affected by economic and financial changes.

The following examples are prepared to give a general understanding about which type of assumptions are commonly used in building projected financial statements:

- A 5 percent reduction in sales and cost of goods sold.
- No sale of equipment.
- Depreciation and amortization are fixed charges.
- A 4 percent increase in expenses due to inflation (including salaries and wages).
- Tax rate 40 percent.
- Variable interest rates will rise 2 percent.
- No investments will be purchased.
- No ability to issue long-term debt or equities securities.

Each assumption above should be documented and a conclusion written to justify the assumption and the variables used to derive the assumption.

AICPA GUIDELINES

The American Institute of Certified Public Accountants (AICPA) has current guidelines relating to prospective financial information. Basically, this standard provides guidance to the preparer of prospective financial information.

CASH MANAGEMENT ORDERS

Finally, it is important to consider other areas utilizing cash flow statements, both historical and prospective. In the event an enterprise is voluntarily or involuntarily forced into filing for protection from its creditors under the Bankruptcy Code, with respect to bankruptcy, cash reporting requirements are virtually undefined. Typically, the reporting and use of cash is determined by the lawyers of the debtors' or creditors' committees on a case-by-case basis. This is accomplished through what are commonly referred to as *cash management orders*.

Cash management orders define the guidelines for the use of and reporting for cash. The orders can become very complicated in nature when dealing with complex corporate structures. One such example can be found in the Southmark Corporation bankruptcy (Case #389-36324-SAF-11, Northern District of Texas, Dallas Division). Due to the complexity of the corporate structure resulting from hundreds of separate entities, this order incorporated detailed cash reporting requirements relating to asset purchases and sales, projections of cash positions, including sources and use of funds, and various guidelines relating to the monitoring of cash balances held at subsidiaries on a daily, weekly, and monthly basis.

In addition to guidelines established on a case-by-case basis, U.S. trustees have established rules relating to the safeguarding and reporting of cash within bankruptcy. The rules relating to cash reporting tend to vary significantly from each federal bankruptcy district; however, all districts require that a debtor close all bank accounts and reopen them as debtor-in-possession (DIP) accounts. U.S. trustee rules require that DIP accounts are backed by U.S. securities. This protects creditors for the debtor in case the financial institution fails. In addition, U.S. trustees usually establish a list of the institutions that a debtor may use. In a bankruptcy proceeding where a significant amount of cash is in question, typically the attorneys and other professionals will file a motion with the court to allow the debtor to increase their flexibility in the types of investments that can be in DIP accounts. Depending on the risk of the investment, this increased yield can be significant to the creditor's estate.

CONCLUSION

The statement of cash flows is a very useful tool and will provide a greater benefit as members of the financial community become more comfortable with its presentation and content. As useful as the statement of cash flows may be, it is only a part of the financial statements required by GAAP. Each statement or disclosure represents a particular emphasis and purpose. The income statement shows revenues and expenses for a period; the balance sheet shows assets, liabilities, and equity at a point in time; the statement of cash flows shows the inflows and outflows of cash during the income statement period; and the notes to the financial statements show the material disclosures that are not explicitly shown in the body of the financial statements. The statement of cash flows and the other financial statements and disclosures are interrelated and their usefulness and value diminishes dramatically if used individually.

As discussed, the statement of cash flows can provide many insights about an enterprise's historical operations and can be used as a basis to review expected future operations. The inflows and outflows of cash are clearly stated in the statement of cash flows and allow the reader to determine the quality of cash flows. Operating cash flow is normally the highest quality. Understanding the cash flows and their quality will assist the reader in making decisions about extending credit, investing, and acquisitions or disposal. These decisions can be made based on historical information and on the reader's estimate of prospective information. If used appropriately, a statement of cash flows can allow the reader to identify early warning signs relating to an enterprise's ability to generate quality and continuing cash flows. This statement can be a tremendous tool in providing workout and turnaround services.

CHAPTER 21

ANALYZING CHAPTER 11 FILINGS

Ronald G. Vollmar
Partner
Price Waterhouse

INTRODUCTION

Beginning with the filing of a bankruptcy petition, a debtor is required to prepare numerous reports for review by the court, creditors, and others. Many of them are designed to provide interested parties with financial information sufficient to evaluate the operations and financial position of the debtor and, thus, assist them in answering the critical question, "Can the company reorganize?" The nature, content, and timing of these reports are largely determined by the U.S. trustee and the court in accordance with local rules. The reports of primary interest to creditors and other parties-in-interest are:

- Schedule of 20 largest unsecured creditors.
- Operating reports.
- Employment of principals and professionals.
- Plan of reorganization.
- Disclosure statement.

SCHEDULE OF 20 LARGEST UNSECURED CREDITORS

This schedule is to be filed with the debtor's bankruptcy petition and lists, as the title indicates, the debtor's 20 largest unsecured creditors. This report is important in two respects: first, it provides large creditors with a basis for determining whether the debtor acknowledges their claims and, second, it is used by the U.S. trustee in selecting an unsecured creditors' committee.

Section 1102 of the Bankruptcy Code requires the U.S. trustee to appoint a committee of unsecured creditors consisting of the seven largest unsecured creditors willing to serve. This committee represents all unsecured creditors and acts to protect their interests during the bankruptcy. The activities of this committee will vary widely from case to case; however, the committee's duties frequently include an ongoing review of the debtor's operations and financial condition, analysis of the various transactions that the debtor wishes to enter into, review and negotiation of the debtor's plan of reorganization, and, in some instances, development of a plan of reorganization.

OPERATING REPORTS

Within two days of filing a Chapter 11 petition, the debtor must file a report, which includes the following information:

- Estimated costs of operations for the next 30 days.
- Estimated profit or loss for the next 30 days.
- Cash available for the operation.
- How the debtor intends to fund its operations during the next 30 days.

After the initial prospective operating statement, the debtor is required to file operating statements at least monthly. These operating statements must include: (1) a statement of income or loss, (2) a reconciliation of cash from the beginning to the end of the period, (3) an itemized listing of accrued but unpaid obligations of the debtor, (4) a discussion of any significant change in the status or amount of inventories, and (5) the amount, if any, of the debtor's prefiling assets that have been liquidated and the disposition of the cash received.

In reviewing the debtor's operating reports, the three most important areas of interest to most creditors or parties-in-interest relate to the debtor's profitability, its cash position, and asset sales. In essence, these three areas all relate to the amount of cash currently available and the ability to generate cash in the future through operations or liquidation of assets.

The filing of a Chapter 11 petition often has an immediate adverse affect upon the company's operations, due to uncertainties over the company's ability to continue in business. It may be necessary for the debtor to quickly seek out alternative sources of supply for materials used in its business, because trade creditors may be unwilling to continue previous relationships or be willing to continue them only on a COD basis. At the same time, the company's customers often are concerned about the debtor's ability to provide quality products on a timely basis and to support product warranties or guarantees, or both. Also, the company's employees often become concerned about the security of their positions and, accordingly, are less productive. Thus, the results of operations during the first several months of operation often can provide an indication about the extent of these concerns and how the debtor has dealt with those concerns. A strong cash position can go a long way to alleviating these concerns.

When reviewing the operating reports, it is important to remember that, during bankruptcy, debtors are not required to accrue interest on unsecured claims and are generally not required to pay any principal or interest on such claims. Accordingly, interest expense and debt payments are greatly reduced during bankruptcy, thus having a positive affect upon profits and the debtor's cash position. When analyzing profitability trends, it is often helpful to do so on a pre-tax, pre-interest basis to assure a proper comparison.

PLAN OF REORGANIZATION

The debtor has the exclusive right to propose a plan of reorganization during the first 120 days of the bankruptcy. This period is often referred to as the *exclusivity period*. The court may extend the exclusivity period or, in unusual circumstances, shorten this period.

While the plan of reorganization is often proposed by the debtor, as a practical matter it is generally the result of intense negotiations with creditors and other parties-in-interest. This plan will describe the various classes of claims against the bankruptcy estate, which claims will not be satisfied in full (i.e., "impaired"), and how each class of claims will be treated in the reorganization plan. To be approved (i.e., "confirmed"), the plan must receive the favorable vote of each class of impaired claims, and of at least two thirds of the amount and more than one half of the number of claims, compared to the total amount and number of claims voting. The court may confirm a plan even though it did not receive the requisite favorable vote, if it can be demonstrated that: (1) at least one impaired class accepted the plan and (2) each impaired class of claims received not less than they would have in a Chapter 7 liquidation and if no class junior to it receives anything. This scenario is often described as *cramdown*.

DISCLOSURE STATEMENT

To solicit acceptance of a plan of reorganization, Section 1125 of the Bankruptcy Code requires that a written disclosure statement must first be provided to holders of claims or interests. This disclosure statement must have been approved by the court, after notice and hearing, as containing "adequate information." Adequate information, as used in this section, means information of a kind, and in sufficient detail, as far as reasonably practicable in light of the nature and history of the debtor and the condition of the debtor's books and records, that would enable a hypothetical reasonable investor typical of holders of claims or interests of the relevant class to make an informed judgment about the plan.

What constitutes "adequate information" is left to the determination of the court. Financial reporting and audit standards developed for solvent and continuing businesses are not necessarily relevant, since the required disclosures are to take into consideration the history of the debtor, the condition of its accounting records, and the needs of the holders of claims or interests in the case. In general, a public company with many creditors and stockholders would be expected to provide more comprehensive disclosures than would a privately held business with few creditors.

Disclosure statements provided by larger public enterprises often include the following types of information:

1. Summary of the plan of reorganization.
2. A description of the debtor's business.
3. Projected financial information.
4. Valuation or liquidation analysis.

The summary of the plan of reorganization generally is used to provide a nonlegalistic description of the plan. It will explain the various classes of claims and interests, which classes will receive less than their approved claim amount (i.e., which classes will be impaired), and what each class will receive. To obtain a complete description of the plan, the summary will almost always refer readers to the full plan of reorganization, which is usually included as an exhibit to the disclosure statement.

Disclosure statements often devote considerable attention to describing each of the debtor's major business segments, the market in which each segment operates, and the business and financial risks associated with each. These disclosures often include the debtor's explanations of the conditions that caused the debtor's financial difficulties, what steps have been taken to counter or mitigate those conditions, and in which businesses the company plans to operate after the reorganization. This discussion is often crucial to a complete understanding of the plan, since it describes what caused the company's downfall, how it reacted to those causes, and what the reorganized company is expected to look like going forward. It is common for debtors to liquidate or deemphasize certain of its prior business segments and to focus on one or more "core" businesses around which the company believes it can reorganize. Accordingly, the reorganized entity may be much different than the company that operated prior to bankruptcy.

Of primary importance in evaluating the feasibility of the proposed plan of reorganization are the financial projections included in the disclosure statement. Almost all debtors seeking to reorganize will provide the court and its creditors with its forecast of the results of operations, cash flow, and financial position for a period of several years after the assumed consummation of the proposed plan. An integral part of these projections is the assumptions upon which they are based. While financial projections are not specifically required under the Bankruptcy Code, the absence of such disclosures should be regarded with a high degree of skepticism. This forecast should be carefully studied, since the plan is often a delicate (and often intensely negotiated) balance between two competing concepts: (1) providing the maximum possible return to prepetition creditors, stockholders, and other parties-in-interest; and (2) providing sufficient financial stability and flexibility for the debtor to continue as a viable business enterprise after reorganization. It should be clear that these needs can only be satisfied out of the same bankruptcy estate, and that the more of the debtor's assets used to satisfy prepetition creditors the fewer resources the debtor will have to achieve long-term financial stability and to provide flexibility for the continuing entity. The court cannot approve a plan that it determines does not provide the debtor with a reasonable chance to successfully reorganize, and, of course, the creditors and other holders of claims are unlikely to approve a plan under which they believe they do not receive an equitable portion of the bankruptcy estate.

Prior to proposing a plan of reorganization, the debtor usually will have gone through an agonizing process of preparing a business plan. In the course of preparing such a plan, the debtor will be required to make difficult decisions, such as:

- Which business segments it believes should continue to be operated and which should more appropriately be liquidated, sold, or spun off.
- How many and what types of employees will be needed.
- Which operations or functions can be consolidated to provide cost savings.
- How the company's products should be marketed and to whom.
- The level of inventories necessary to support the company's continuing businesses, and so on.

Such a business plan is absolutely necessary to evaluate two critical issues: (1) does the debtor have a potentially profitable core business around which it can reorganize, and, if so, (2) what cash flows are likely to be available and what portion of those cash flows should be utilized to satisfy claims of prepetition creditors and parties-in-interest.

The issue of whether the debtor has a core business or a franchise around which to reorganize is sometimes overlooked. To reorganize, the debtor must demonstrate that its business can be profitable and can provide a reasonable return on the investments made by creditors and equity holders. In certain circumstances, the best way for a debtor to maximize its return on investment may be to liquidate. For example, this condition may exist in a situation where the company is in a highly competitive service industry where its employees are its only substantial asset, where products that the debtor produces serve a declining market or are technologically or physically obsolete, or where the company may be in a capital intensive industry with no way or means to obtain the funds needed to compete.

Because of the debtor's frequent desire to continue substantially on an "as is" basis, and because of the competing needs of creditors and others, the components of the business plan are often challenged during the course of negotiations between the debtor and the creditors' committee. It should be recognized that the needs even among creditors and equity holders will vary substantially. Certain creditors will simply want to "get out of the credit" as soon as possible, therefore desiring to maximize their short-term recovery, while others will take a longer-term view and believe that their ultimate return will be maximized by accepting a larger (but longer term) payout or an equity position, or both, in the reorganized company.

The projected financial information discussed above is only as good as the assumptions upon which it is based. To make valid projections of the future, the preparer must make explicit assumptions regarding every facet of the company's business. For example, assumptions will have to be made on the following for each period within the forecast period:

- The products or services that the reorganized company will offer for sale.
- The volume of products or services that will be sold and the sales prices that can be obtained for them.

- The costs at which raw materials can be obtained.
- The number of employees that will be required to manage the reorganized company and to produce the goods and services to be offered for sale.
- The wages and salaries that employees will be paid.
- The locations at which the company will maintain operations.
- The rate at which customers will pay their bills.
- The rate at which the company's vendors will be paid.
- The level of inventories required to support the expected sales.
- Expenditures that will be required for research and development.
- Expenditures that will be required for the purchase of capital assets.
- The amount and timing of proceeds from assets sales or sales of discontinued operations.
- Alternative sources of financing and related costs.
- Minimum cash balances required.
- The taxes payable on any income earned.

These and other explicit assumptions must be made for each future period presented. Changes in the assumptions can dramatically affect the projected results and significantly alter each creditor's assessment of what the plan will provide to him or her. Accordingly, it is extremely important to pay close attention to the assumptions to assess the reasonableness of the resulting projections. The following paragraphs will offer suggestions to assist in the evaluation of such assumptions.

1. In general, assumptions used should be somewhat conservative (i.e., not optimistic). While projections usually assume certain trends (e.g., steadily improving sales) or steady relationships (e.g., customers will always pay their bills in 60 days), in the "real world" business is subject to ever-changing conditions and business cycles that are impossible to predict. To illustrate, sales of operations or assets may take longer to consummate, a major customer may file bankruptcy, new products may be delayed, workers may go on strike, and so forth. A conservative approach in developing assumptions can provide a "cushion" against unexpected problems.

2. Projected results should be compared to those actually achieved in the past. Where they differ significantly, an explanation should be sought from the discussion of the business included elsewhere in the disclosure statement, in the assumptions themselves, or directly from the debtor.

3. Rather than focusing upon absolute amounts, it is often useful to examine trends and relationships, such as percentage changes from year to year or ratios of one projected amount to another.

4. It is often helpful to compare the results projected to those achieved by other companies in the same or similar business. In using these comparisons, it is important to note that the company to which the projections relate is often in a substantially weaker position than are more established competitors. It would be reasonable to expect that projected results would be lower than those achieved by competitors, at least in the short run.

5. One assumption often overlooked is management. Who will run the company? Without effective management, even an enterprise with great potential may fail.

6. While all of the assumptions may be critical, those affecting sales are often the most important. Not only is sales the starting point for determining profitability, it indicates the debtor's strategy for the future. The assumptions or other disclosures, or both, should describe the markets in which the reorganized company will compete, the expected market share the company will achieve, the pricing policies that the company expects to implement, and the changes in those expectations over the forecast period. Market share and pricing factors are generally interrelated; the higher the price, the lower the market share. The assumptions made must be consistent with other aspects of the plan. Additionally, projections that assume large percentage sales increases in early years should be viewed with a high degree of skepticism.

7. Assumptions made for cost of sales are generally based upon a percentage relationship to sales. Changes in this relationship from that actually achieved in a prior period or from year to year should be viewed carefully. To achieve a lower percentage, it implicitly would be necessary to achieve one or more of the following: (1) raise sales prices obtained from customers, (2) obtain more favorable purchase prices from vendors, (3) reduce labor costs either by increasing productivity or lowering wages, or (4) reduce overhead costs.

While all are possibilities, (1) and (2) above are highly unlikely. It is, in fact, often necessary to offer customers lower prices to obtain any market share lost during the bankruptcy. Additionally, it is uncommon for the company's vendors to offer to sell goods to the company at lower prices than in the past, especially after incurring a loss from the company's bankruptcy. Reductions in labor costs may be achieved through negotiations with representatives of labor; however, such reductions are uncertain at best. Alternatively, labor costs can be reduced through investments in technology or equipment, each of which has a significant and immediate cost that a debtor coming out of bankruptcy can seldom afford.

Overhead is one factor that often can be reduced in the longer term through consolidation of operations, closure of inefficient facilities, and the like. However, such actions often carry immediate costs that offset any short-term gains.

In summary, while the relationship of cost of sales to sales can be improved in the longer term, it is more likely that in the short term this relationship will be adversely affected. Dramatic improvements are, typically, unlikely.

8. Selling, general, and administrative expenses are often projected to be lower in the future than in the past. Such reductions may be achievable through consolidating operations or by reducing the number of levels of management. Reductions are sometimes based upon reducing the salaries and benefits of remaining management; however, this is often counterproductive. When streamlining the company's management, it is more important than ever to retain the best managers. If their salaries are reduced below competitive levels, it is likely that they will leave, with only the less-efficient managers remaining.

Projections of reduced costs for outside services, such as consultants, accountants, lawyers, public relations, and others, are common. While such services often come under closer scrutiny when a company has financial difficulties, this may be when they are most needed. Additionally, such savings often can be achieved only by permanently increasing internal staffs.

Reductions in selling costs can be achieved by modifying historic marketing methods. However, such changes are difficult to implement over a short period. Arbitrary reductions in sales personnel can be counterproductive, since it is likely that a company coming out of bankruptcy will have to work harder to maintain its customer base—let alone improve upon it.

9. The final line item on most income statements is the provision for income taxes. Often it is taken for granted that a company just coming out of bankruptcy will have substantial operating loss carryforwards, which can be utilized to offset taxable income. However this may not be the case. Operating loss carryforwards existing prior to the bankruptcy filing may be reduced by taxable gains that arise from the forgiveness of debt typically contemplated in the plan of reorganization (Section 108). Additionally, Section 382 of the Internal Revenue Code may restrict the utilization of such losses when a "change in control" has occurred. Such a change is common when major creditors are given large equity positions in the company in return for the forgiveness of debt. Even when no regular tax payments are due prior to the utilization of NOLs, alternative tax payments may be required. Income tax rules in reorganizations are often complex, and they may be subject to interpretation. Creditors' committees should closely review the assumptions about income taxes and, if necessary, retain professionals specialized in this area.

10. Assumptions regarding working capital may significantly affect the debtor's cash position in the future and, therefore, are important to review closely. Working capital is the excess of current assets over current liabilities and, like any other asset, must be financed in some manner. Current assets commonly consist of such items as cash, accounts receivable, and inventories, while current liabilities generally include accounts payable, accrued liabilities, payrolls payable, and the like. These assets and liabilities, because of their nature, generally are converted into (current assets) cash or require (current liabilities) cash within one year.

While not directly affecting profits, the speed at which customers pay their bills impacts the amount of cash a debtor has available for other purposes. The reduction or increase in the days receivables outstanding is tantamount to a decrease or increase in debt, since, if customers pay their bills faster, the debtor can pay its debts faster. The converse also is true. It also should be noted that, even when there is no change in the speed at which customers pay their bills, a portion of any sales increase will result in an increase in accounts receivable, and, as such, will result in an increase in amounts necessary to finance working capital.

Changes in inventories affect working capital in the same way as accounts receivable. There is always a balance that must be maintained between having enough inventory on hand to support sales to customers and having too much inventory. The types of inventories to be maintained are also important.

Such items as accounts payable, accrued expenses, and accrued payroll affect working capital in the opposite way from accounts receivable or inventories. If the payment of such items can be delayed, this has the same effect as a reduction in debt.

Significant changes in projected working capital between future periods, or as compared to prior levels, should be closely reviewed.

11. Depending upon the debtor's business, significant expenditures may be required for capital equipment and research and development. Most businesses require some level of such expenditures, and the projected amounts should be realistic and consider the future needs of the business. Expenditures for capital equipment and research and development can be temporarily deferred but only at the risk of even higher costs in the future.

In evaluating the reasonableness of projections in these areas, one should compare the projected amounts to those actually incurred in the past. Significant differences should be explained.

UTILIZATION OF CASH FLOWS

Once the analysis of the above 11 assumptions has been completed, the evaluator should have a good idea of the level of cash flows that the debtor can be expected to generate from its business. The next step in the assessment of the projections included in the disclosure statement relates to the utilization of those cash flows. In other words, the debtor's obligations under the proposed plan of reorganization must now be overlayed on the financial projections.

From a creditor's perspective, cash generated can be used principally to service debt, pay dividends, expand the debtor's business either through entry into other product lines or the purchase of other businesses, or be retained in the business. There must be a balance among the uses of cash to meet the needs of all concerned.

While some creditors might argue that all of the cash generated by a reorganized debtor should go to the payment of debt, this view is frequently shortsighted. For example, in major reorganizations, creditors are frequently provided a substantial equity interest in the debtor—now they are owners as well as creditors. Such creditors normally take these equity positions with the hope that they can sell their interests within a several-year period through a public or secondary offering after the market value of the company's stock has increased. Because the market value of equity is related to the expectation of receiving cash dividends, the value of this equity interest is adversely affected by the "overhang" of large amounts of debt, which essentially utilizes all or most of the company's cash flow to service debt.

Prior to voting to accept or reject the plan of reorganization, each creditor and party-in-interest must determine the value of the consideration offered in the plan. This is often not an easy task, due to the variety of debt and equity interests typically offered to creditors and others in a plan of reorganization. For example, it is not uncommon for a class of creditors to be offered a package of cash, subordinated debt, common stock, and warrants.

One way to value a package, such as that described above, is by using a discounted present value approach. This method requires one to project the cash flows that will accrue from each type of interest offered and then apply an appropriate interest rate to that stream of cash flows. This can often be done based upon the projected financial information and plan of reorganization discussed above.

The easiest asset to be valued is cash to be paid at consummation date. This amount would not require discounting, unless consummation was not expected for some time.

In valuing a debt issue, one must understand the terms relating to the payment of principal and interest for that particular issue. To illustrate, under certain debt arrangements, interest may accrue but be payable only out of a specified percentage of cash flows, while principal payments are due beginning only after several years. Because the liquidity of a debtor coming out of bankruptcy is weak, it is often not realistic to offer creditors and others the promise of immediate or fixed payments. However, it is possible to use the financial projections included in the disclosure statement to calculate what cash flows would be received if the projections were correct.

The discount rate used in determining the present value of debt service payments should take into account the following:

- Time value of money.
- Credit risk (the risk that payments will not be received in the expected amount).
- Uncertainty over the timing of those cash flows (payments may be received in a different period than projected).
- The possibility that the projections will prove to be incorrect (a judgment factor).

In other words, the greater the uncertainty that the holder of such debt will receive the amounts indicated as scheduled, the higher the discount rate. For example, the discount rate applied to scheduled payments relating to senior debt would likely be lower than that used in discounting subordinated debt payable only from excess cash flows.

As noted above, the calculation of value must also consider the reasonableness of the projections. If, after completing a review of assumptions supporting the financial projections, it is determined that those projections are optimistic, it would be appropriate to increase the discount rate applied. Possibly a more precise way of taking this uncertainty into account would be to calculate the cash flows under assumptions considered to be more reasonable.

The valuation of equity securities is much more subjective than that of debt, because there are no scheduled payment terms. For this reason, an exit value is often estimated, based upon projected earnings, or cash flows may be used as a basis for determining present value. For example, if the market price of the common stock of companies in similar industries approximate between 7 and 10 times earnings, it may be appropriate to estimate the amount that could be received from the sale of the equity investment after several years by applying the lower end of this range to "stabilized" earnings projected to occur in the future and then discount this amount back to the present. Other measures that can be used are based upon cash flows (e.g., market prices of common stock are frequently analyzed by computing a multiple based upon that company's common stock price and its cash flow). Discount rates applicable to equity should normally be higher than those used in discounting debt, since the debt must be repaid for the equity to have value.

The discount rate applied by individual creditors or parties in interest may take into account personal tax rates and financial conditions.

CONCLUSION

In summary, the creditor or party-in-interest should review closely the filings made by the debtor during a Chapter 11 filing. This review will enable these parties to make an informed and reasonable decision relating to two critical questions:

- Does the debtor have a profitable core business that will provide a basis for the reorganization?
- Does the proposed plan of reorganization provide reasonable compensation to creditors and others?

CHAPTER 22

EVALUATING MANAGEMENT

William J. Nightingale
President
Nightingale & Associates, Inc.
Stephen J. Hopkins
Executive Vice President
Nightingale & Associates, Inc.

INTRODUCTION

A timely evaluation and assessment of the competence and capabilities of management in place to effect a turnaround is usually an essential and critical requirement for creditors, shareholders, potential investors, and other "outsiders" involved in some way with a troubled company. Such an assessment is necessary for outside constituencies to determine how much weight, if any, to give to management's strategies, actions, and pronouncements. In addition, outsiders must obviously tailor their own strategies and tactics for dealing with the troubled company, based on their assessment of the competency of management in place to deal with the problems and crisis at hand and to effect a turnaround.

The fact that a company is in a workout or turnaround mode is a strong indication of likely severe past management problems, which may or may not still persist. This is not to imply that management currently in place will be unable to deal with the crisis and successfully achieve a turnaround. However, a crisis situation is no place for initial "on the job training" in turnaround management or an excuse for a management development program to improve managerial skills. If management in place was a major contributor to the problem at hand, and lacks flexibility to dramatically adjust management styles and approaches, or lacks the personality traits and managerial skills needed to deal with a crisis situation, the probability of a successful turnaround under their management direction is low. Experience, aptitude, solid judgment, and self-confidence are among the traits required to orchestrate a turnaround, and, generally speaking, these attributes are not acquired overnight.

Management, as used in the context of this chapter, means the key decision-making authority in the company. Most often, this is the chief executive officer (CEO); but in some situations major responsibilities and authorities may be shared with another ranking officer (chairman of the board or president, depending on which is CEO) or even other executives encompassing an office of the president. Except in general terms, this chapter does not deal with evaluation of the capabilities of second level (vice presidential) or middle management assigned to specific functional responsibilities. Such evaluation is often difficult, if not impossible, without meaningful on-site contact and involvement with these managers. In addition, above-average strength, or serious weakness, at the second level of management is usually a reflection of the competence and effectiveness of the CEO.

Contrary to some opinion, the key to quickly evaluating a management's ability to successfully cope with a troubled company situation is to focus on the judgment, personality, management style, candor and openness (or lack of same), and communication skills of the CEO and other key officers. This is in contrast to a focus on their knowledge of the specific business, industry experience, or perceived level of intelligence.

Based on work with many troubled companies, we conclude that problem situations are best handled by a CEO who is a generalist with the self-confidence to act decisively, quickly react to change, and who has the judgment and experience to focus on fundamental problems and opportunities and to prioritize them correctly. Assistance in obtaining the background, facts, and analysis usually required in dealing with the specifics of a troubled company situation, including financial restructuring assistance, can always be obtained from outside professionals.

This chapter provides a framework within which the effectiveness and appropriateness of the management of a troubled company can be readily evaluated. This chapter is organized by subject matter as follows:

General functions of management.
Management requirements in a crisis situation.
Initial evaluation of management effectiveness.
In-depth evaluation of management competence.
Effective management and the use of outside consultants.
Conclusion.

GENERAL FUNCTIONS OF MANAGEMENT

Key responsibilities of an effective management might be summarized as follows:

- Planning.
- Organizing.
- Integrating/coordinating.
- Measuring/controlling.
- Leading/motivating.

Planning

Planning encompasses both creating a general strategy for the business and developing specific action plans and tactics related to implementing the strategy.

In reviewing troubled companies, there seems to be little correlation between the amount of planning detail and company success. Some of the factors that separate the successful from the troubled company are listed below:

- Realism of the business plan and financial projections.
- Disciplined tracking of performance.
- Nature of corrective actions taken when performance deviates from plan.
- Timeliness of corrective actions taken when performance deviates from plan.

In a troubled company, planning is necessarily more short-term oriented than in a successful company environment. In addition, more top management input and review is required, all within a much shorter time frame than is true in most other business situations. Planning must focus on the actions required to effect a major change in the course of events and the fastest way of implementing these changes.

It is the responsibility of top management to ensure there are adequate "validity checks" of plan details and to ensure that plans are carefully integrated and coordinated among the various functional departments within the company.

Management cannot achieve satisfactory performance if there is either an inability or reluctance to plan realistically or to be judged on performance. Without a realistic plan, management is only reacting to past or current events, rather than attempting to control the future.

Organizing

Organizing encompasses recruiting, employing, and deploying the human resources required to (1) properly operate all functional areas of the business and, in the case of a troubled company, rapidly effect major change; (2) secure and deploy fixed and intangible assets in a manner required to achieve business objectives; and (3) install and implement adequate review and control procedures.

Three essential prerequisites for an effective organization include:

1. Competent management and employees.
2. A realistic business strategy and plan.
3. Clearly defined responsibilities, authorities, and accountabilities.

An ineffective or inefficient company organization, either in terms of quality of personnel or clearly defined responsibility assignments, reflects unsatisfactory top management.

Integrating/Coordinating

Integration and coordination are required to ensure that the sum of the activities of a company's functional departments and operations are coordinated to achieve the objectives of the company as a whole. Troubled companies frequently suffer from inadequate coordination between functions and departments, with the result that the failure of one function or department to perform becomes not only a surprise but results in undue disruption throughout the organization.

Measuring/Controlling

It is difficult, if not impossible, to achieve a plan if measurements and controls are not in place to measure performance, identify deviations from plan, and provide the information necessary on which to base corrective actions.

Inherent in good measurement and control systems is an assumption that:

- An organization is in place that clearly defines responsibilities and accountabilities.
- A series of reporting procedures with appropriate measurements of results and performance are in use throughout the company.

An absence of effective management information and control systems is probably one of the most common shortcomings found in troubled companies. The operative word here is *effective*. Many companies have elaborate management information and control systems that prove to be essentially ineffective for a variety of reasons, including bad data input, missed data input, and absence of actionable variance reports and management summaries. In other cases, management information and control systems can be so complex, cumbersome, and unwieldy that required information is not received in an actionable form on a timely basis.

The absence of an effective management information and control system is a serious reflection upon the competency and capabilities of top management. It telegraphs a lack of understanding of the need and urgency for reliable and timely information necessary to manage and control the business and maximize cash flows and profitability.

Conversely, the presence of a truly effective management information and control system in a troubled company is a pretty good indicator that management currently in place may well be capable of achieving a turnaround.

Leading/Motivating

While all organizations require strong leadership to be fully successful, the need for strong decisive leadership is compelling in a troubled company situation. Leadership implies the ability to manage change, to initiate actions instead of reacting to external events, and to influence and control future results. In a troubled company situation this may require a total redirection of the mission and strategic direction of a company. It certainly requires establishing new and different sets of priorities for the immediate future than were in existence in the past.

When objectives and priorities have been established that provide proper direction for a company, the leadership challenge for management becomes one of instilling members of the organization with the desire and commitment necessary to achieve and, hopefully, exceed established objectives.

Good management leadership also requires achieving a good balance between delegation of responsibility and authority to subordinates, and an abdication of responsibility by excessive delegation.

In summary, the key top management responsibilities for planning, organizing, integrating, measuring and controlling, and leading that are required for managing any entity are even more critical in a troubled company where major changes in the course of events must be achieved very rapidly.

MANAGEMENT REQUIREMENTS IN A CRISIS SITUATION

Effective management of a troubled company requires all the usual organizational, administrative, and leadership skills normally associated with any well-managed company. However, because a crisis atmosphere often exists, and because the time frame within which dramatic results must be accomplished is typically greatly compressed, certain other management characteristics and skills are usually necessary. These include:

1. Recognition of, major focus on, and understanding of cash flow management.

    The bottom line when it comes to viability and survival is how to go about squeezing out the last dollar fast.
2. An ability to quickly identify and consider all logical options including those which have been viewed as "unthinkable" or "impossible" in the past.

    This requires creativity and intuition, necessarily bolstered by self-confidence, in turn tempered with risk analysis and assessment.
3. The instinctive ability to rapidly identify, focus on, and initiate corrective action in those key areas of the company that are impacting cash flow and operating profit the most.
4. A recognition of the need for continuous contingency planning.

    It must be assumed that "what can go wrong will go wrong."
5. The skill to communicate frequently and realistically to all constituencies.

Each of the above management characteristics are briefly discussed below.

Cash Flow Focus

Immediate and near-term cash flow improvement actions often fall into one of the following categories:

- Identifying, correcting, or eliminating negative cash flow product line or other business segments.
- Reducing operating expenses.
- Improving inventory and accounts receivable turnover.
- Restructuring/selling assets.

Many troubled companies, not surprisingly, have poor cash flow forecasting capabilities for periods beyond a few days. Accomplishing significantly improved cash flow from the types of actions indicated above requires:

- Effective leadership at the highest management levels to ensure that disciplined cash flow forecasting is undertaken.

- Analyzing and incorporating the effects of planned corrective cash flow actions on total business operating results and cash flow.
- An objective evaluation of alternative strategic and operational tradeoffs.

Management implementation of some or all of the cash flow improvement actions listed above normally yields more improved results in a reasonable time frame than the frequent management response of "across the board" operating expense reductions; the latter response can often have a negative impact on profitable growing segments of the company or are not deep enough to fundamentally improve the situation, or both.

Consider All Options

A surprising number of troubled company CEOs have tunnel vision and are wedded to traditional points of view. Effective management of a truly troubled company in crisis requires that traditional strategies, tactics, and modes of operation be reexamined from the ground up. There can be no sacred cows.

Some CEOs and senior managers thrive on change and on deriving creative solutions to old and new problems. Unfortunately, some cannot take off their blinders or throw out their preconceived notions. The approaches discussed later in the section on Internal Evaluation of Management and the section on In-Depth Evaluation of Management can usually separate the two.

Focus on Key Areas Impacting Cash Flow and Profitability

Even the best-managed companies have many opportunities for revenue, profit, and cash flow enhancement and, thus, have many areas for management to properly direct its attention. Unfortunately, this problem is generally compounded in the case of the troubled company, where problems, and sometimes opportunities, are almost too numerous to mention.

Accordingly, it is all too easy for management to attempt to direct its efforts on so many problems and in so many areas that the net result is a total diffusion of effort and a lack of timely and effectual accomplishment anywhere.

Nowhere more so than in a troubled company situation must management be able to rapidly identify and focus on those key areas of the business that have the most near-term impact on cash flow and operating profit, and, surprisingly, they are often few in number.

The effective troubled company management ensures that sufficient personnel and human resources are focused in these areas to effect maximum change in the least amount of time. Ineffective managements continue to thrash.

Continuous Contingency Planning

It seems almost axiomatic that problems beget problems. In effect, the traditional operating modes and ratios normally utilized and relied on by managements of a profitable company often inherently will not suffice in a troubled company environment.

As additional problems surface, they in turn impact other areas of the company, which create still more problems, and so on. This situation is compounded by the difficulty of reliable forecasting, because so many unforeseen events occur as a result of the destabilization and disruption inherent in troubled company situations.

Accordingly, an effective troubled company management will prepare and update contingency planning on essentially a continuous basis. Likely or potential new problems will be anticipated, and contingency plans will be prepared in advance to minimize their impact to the extent possible.

Frequent Effective Communication

If one management characteristic could be singled out above all others as a prerequisite for a troubled company it would probably be credible management communications. In a turbulent company environment, credible communication is essential to maintain a semblance of stability and direction both with internal management and employees and externally with all outside constituencies who can influence future events. While communication is essential for generating and maintaining management credibility, communication without substance will not suffice.

The effective management must constantly communicate its strategies, objectives, projects, and priorities throughout the company on a repetitive basis. Organizations, especially large ones, have a strong tendency not to react rapidly to change. Management and employees have widely varying abilities to grasp the concept of change and to recognize what this means for them personally in terms of deviation from past culture, mode of operations, and performance requirements. To effect rapid change and ensure implementation of change throughout the company, frequent repetitive communication of objectives, projects, and priorities is required.

A troubled situation also will typically require a much wider dissemination of operating results and other previously confidential information than would normally be the case, so management and employees can see firsthand the progress, or lack of it, being made and the impact of, or need for, corrective action.

Clear, concise, repetitive communication brings to the surface the discrepancies between what is being communicated and what is being heard, and it helps ensure a continuing commitment to company goals, rather than protection of functional and individual turf.

Effective communication with external constituencies is also essential, if their cooperation is to be achieved in addressing and solving the company's problems where they have a role to play. As with internal management and employees, outside constituencies must be made to understand and, hopefully, concur with the company's strategies, objectives, plans, and priorities.

Credible communication also requires management to tell it like it is; a lack of candor or overoptimistic projections will quickly be discerned by all concerned, and management will lose the cooperation and support of those constituencies it needs most if a turnaround is to be successfully implemented.

INITIAL EVALUATION OF MANAGEMENT EFFECTIVENESS

A prerequisite for outsiders when first encountering a highly troubled company or a workout situation is to make an initial rapid evaluation of company management. While one measure for evaluating management performance is a comparison with industry results and trends and other objective standards, such measurements in a problem situation will almost always result in unfavorable conclusions. The question then becomes whether management in place has the ability to correct past management mistakes and unfavorable performance. Therefore, a preliminary checklist for initially evaluating management capability is useful, and often necessary, for outsiders to determine their actions and strategy going forward.

This section sets forth a set of Characteristics of a Problem Management, followed by a description of Characteristics of a Promising Management. These characteristics or guidelines, if you will, are usually effective in quickly evaluating the capabilities of top management in place in troubled companies even given very limited exposure and contact with that management.

Characteristics of a Problem Management

- Focus on rationalization and justification of past events and unsatisfactory operating results, rather than on immediate and near-term problem solving and action.
- Lack of facts and understanding of where the business is making and losing cash flow and operating profit.
- Focus on the revenue line, rather than on operating profit and cash flow.
- Lack of specific plans, goals, and timetables for addressing and correcting negative cash flow segments of the business.
- Focus on manipulation of reported operating results, rather than improving cash flow.
- The "wishful thinking syndrome" of assuming and projecting favorable results, in spite of:
    Consistently missing previous forecasts.
    An absence of detailed plans, timetables, and checkpoints for implementing changes required to improve past unfavorable trends.
- Lack of an ability to seriously consider the possibility of downsizing the business.
- Failure to fulfill promises to sell off divisions, operating units, or product lines and to downsize the business.

- Focus on personal ego gratification, rather than on decisive business actions and results. Some tipoffs include:

    Excessive use of the word "I."

    Blaming the problem on everyone but himself or herself.

    Inability to listen.

    Countering or dismissing every questioning remark with an excuse.

    High turnover rate of senior and middle management employees.
- Inadequate management control and information systems.
- Absence of performance measurement benchmarks maintained and reviewed on a regular basis.
- A penny-pinching focus on operating expenses, rather than on the total operating results of the business.
- Excessive turnover of second level and middle management.

    The "poor performance" of terminated or resigned employees is often cited as the reason for the company's current problems.
- The CEO makes or must clear most decisions, many of which are not deserving of CEO attention.
- The CEO surrounds himself with second level and middle management "yes men."

    Subordinates rarely question or challenge the CEO.
- Poorly qualified second level management accompanied by a reluctance of the CEO to make changes thereto.
- A passive reaction to events, rather than proactive initiation of change.
- A "firefighting" corporate environment.

    A multitude of special projects and task forces in place, with constant interruptions of all concerned to deal with the crisis of the moment.

Generally speaking, observations relative to the above management characteristics can be made very quickly with only limited exposure to a company's chief executive and senior officers. An astute observer's initial conclusions relative to the above checklist factors will prove to be correct in a majority of cases, and these can be subsequently confirmed if circumstances provide the in-depth exposure and time necessary to quantify them without a doubt.

Characteristics of a Promising Management

Not surprisingly, many of the characteristics of a promising management represent the flip side of the coin of those identifying a problem management. Recognizing a risk of redundancy, a checklist is shown below for quickly obtaining a measure of comfort and confidence that management in place is competent to deal effectively with the trouble at hand.

- Strong focus and attention on cash flow and on real, not managed, operating profits.
    Possesses facts and knowledge relating to cash flow and operating profit by division, product line, plant, customer configuration, geography, and the like as appropriate to the particular company situation.
- An obvious candor and willingness to readily admit past mistakes.
- An openness to new, even radical, ideas and suggestions from both insiders and outsiders.
- A clearly defined action plan, with timetables and performance measurement points in place.
- Responsibilities and authorities are clearly defined; obvious delegation to subordinates where appropriate.
- Clear definition and communication of the major strengths, problems, and opportunities of the company, with primary management focus and attention on these areas.
- Subordinates are encouraged to ask questions, challenge decisions, and make differences of opinion known.
- Management information and control systems are designed to facilitate operational decisions and actions.
    Variances from plan and prior periods are highlighted and summarized.
- Timely and effective communication with all constituencies, including:
    Internal senior management, middle management, and employees.

Creditors, suppliers, customers, shareholders, and other outside constituencies.
- The ability to think creatively and "throw the book away."
  Highly troubled situations normally do not lend themselves to traditional or historical solutions. A CEO who can consider and evaluate radical or totally untried approaches exhibits the flexibility that is often required in troubled situations.
- A "can do" attitude.
  Projects the aura that "nothing is impossible."
- The ability to identify and consider all logical options, including "thinking small."
  Downsizing is often the key to survival for a troubled company.
- An understanding and reliance on risk analysis.
  The downside risk as well as the upside potential is considered and evaluated for all major decisions.
- A recognition that sometimes money must be spent to make money.
  Finding a way to free up and spend scarce cash when the opportunity exists to leverage such expenditures into increased cash flow or operating profits.

An astute observer can often reach conclusions about the effectiveness, or lack of effectiveness, of management in place in a troubled company after only several hours of freewheeling discussion with the CEO and, if possible, with other top company officers, based on the checklists discussed above.

IN-DEPTH EVALUATION OF MANAGEMENT COMPETENCE

If for any reason a quick evaluation of management effectiveness as discussed in the previous section, Initial Evaluation, is not possible or appropriate, another technique and procedure can be used to reach the necessary conclusions in a matter of a few days, although it requires the utilization of knowledgeable and experienced outside consultants who must have access to the CEO and senior management.

This approach consists of conducting in-depth one-on-one interviews with the CEO and selected senior level and middle level managers. Generally, each interview takes approximately two to four hours, but sometimes can be accomplished in as little as an hour and, on other occasions, may require five hours or more.

The consultant utilizes a structured questionnaire that has been prepared in advance and asks the same questions of each manager interviewed. The questions focus on the company's overall condition and situation and are not presented as, or primarily intended to be, an evaluation of management per se. The types of questions used by the consultant will vary, depending on the situation and circumstances, but a number of key questions are generic to almost any troubled company situation. This procedure is generally extremely effective in quickly identifying the major problems and opportunities facing a troubled company, prioritizing them, and enabling consultants working internally for the company or for outside constituencies to identify most, if not all, of the key issues that require action and further investigation and careful monitoring. Although management assessment is only one of the objectives of this procedure, the collective response to these interviews provides a great deal of insight into assessing the ability of current management to successfully work out a troubled situation. The questions are open-ended and presented in such a way that they encourage free flowing and candid responses.

Each interviewee is assured that all of his or her comments and responses will be treated confidentially, and that the consultant's findings and conclusions will be based on the sum of input and responses received from all members of management who are interviewed, not any single manager, which indeed they are.

Some of the key questions that are utilized in overview interviews, regardless of the nature of the business or the company's specific situation, include the following:

- What are the company's major strengths?
- What are the company's major problems?
- What are the company's major opportunities going forward?
- Are there any obvious cost savings or profit improvement opportunities that are not being aggressively pursued?

- Are there any obvious growth opportunities that are not being aggressively pursued?
- Are there any products, product lines, models, manufacturing facilities, and so forth that should be discontinued?
    Why?
- Does the company have a good handle on costs and margins?
    By product, model, and so on?
- Considering management and organization:
    Is responsibility, accountability, and authority clearly defined?
    Any fuzzy areas?
    Do decisions seem to be consistently delayed or avoided anywhere in the organization for any reason?
    Are there any particular functions, departments, or employees performing in an exceptional manner that are generally unrecognized throughout the organization?
    Are there any particular functions, departments, or employees underperforming to the extent that they are holding back the progress and profitability of the entire company?
    What changes in management or organization, if any, would you make if you owned the company?
- If you owned the company, what changes would you make or what would you do differently?
    Where would you focus immediately to improve cash flow and operating profit?
- Does the company have an effective and actionable management information and control system in place?
- The most important question of all: What question should I have asked, but didn't?

Other questions specifically tailored to the situation and problems at hand should be included. These can generally be quickly determined after a few hours of conversation with the company's CEO, CFO, or one or two other senior officers.

In companies with "promising management" in place, there generally will be a high degree of consistency in the responses to the overview interviews, indicating that strategies, plans, and goals are clearly defined, communicated, and understood by the management ranks. In addition, a relatively few number of items will be listed for certain questions, such as major problems, major strengths, and major opportunities, which indicates a recognition and focus by management on the key factors impacting the cash flow and profitability of the business.

Conversely, a wide divergence of opinion among the members of management interviewed, often accompanied by long laundry lists of problems, strengths, and opportunities, generally indicates a lack of focus and direction by the senior management of the troubled company.

In sum, the technique and procedure of overview interviews with selected management conducted by a qualified and perceptive outside consultant is a highly effective approach to evaluating the effectiveness of management in place and to identifying and prioritizing key issues for immediate further action or investigation. It also has the advantage that it can be undertaken and concluded within a matter of days, and rarely more than several weeks, even for very large corporations.

EFFECTIVE MANAGEMENT AND THE USE OF OUTSIDE CONSULTANTS

A company's board of directors presumably has the best basis for evaluating management and understanding the extent to which management in place has (*a*) originated or contributed to the problems the company has incurred or (*b*) conversely, has those characteristics necessary to effect a turnaround. Unfortunately, all too often boards do not carry out their responsibilities in this regard. Even if they do, it is often difficult for outside constituencies, such as creditors, customers, shareholders, potential investors, and others, to obtain the necessary level of comfort that management in place is indeed qualified to effect a turnaround.

In such situations, utilization of an independent outside consultant is an effective and common approach to providing both a company's board of directors and outside constituencies, as appropriate, with an objective evaluation of management's effectiveness and its plans and actions to deal with the problems.

A consultant experienced in working with troubled companies in crisis situations can not only provide the company with additional management expertise and objective advice but also act as the catalyst to quickly effect business change. In addition, the consultant's findings and recommendations inherently provide, either directly or indirectly, an evaluation of management in place.

In some cases, the consultant's role is properly limited to providing an independent evaluation of management's business and action plans and financial projections (i.e., providing an objective third-party "second opinion"). In this role, the consultant can also assist with the documentation and communication required to enhance management's credibility with outside constituencies that the turnaround plan is realistic and can be successfully implemented.

At the other extreme are situations where the consultant is requested to replace the current management team or to assume specific interim management responsibilities.

Typically, company managements resist retaining outside consultants when requested to do so by interested outside third parties, such as lenders or creditors. Many objections are used to justify this resistance, often the cost of the consultant, but the underlying reasons generally relate more to a blow to managerial ego, the loss of control represented by the need for outside assistance, or concern that the consultant is really an "informer" for the party requesting such action. Obtaining management acquiescence in retaining a consultant can generally be made to appear less threatening and objectionable if the party requesting the action focuses on a special short-term need, such an independent evaluation of management's business plan, an improvement in turnover of working capital assets, or other specific cash flow improvement projects. It can be pointed out to management that the consultant can provide added credibility with outside constituencies and should help promote a better understanding of the details that bridge the gap between forecasts of future operational improvements and past unsatisfactory results.

CONCLUSION

If management in place in a troubled company does not have the personality traits and managerial skills normally required to deal with a crisis situation, the probability of success of that management achieving a turnaround is low. An evaluation of management's ability to successfully achieve a turnaround should not focus on a specific business knowledge, industry experience, or level of intelligence, but rather on personality traits and management skills and styles.

There are methods through the use of outside consultants to quickly assess whether management in place in a troubled company appears to have the capabilities and skills necessary to effect the turnaround, or whether the chances of the managers doing so are low.

Effective management and turnaround of a troubled company requires a variety of management skills and traits. Foremost among them are (1) the ability to focus on those key factors having the greatest impact on cash flow and operating profits, (2) a sense of priorities, (3) creativity in seeking new solutions to old or new problems, (4) an ability to establish and achieve rational organizational balance, (5) communication skills that generate credibility, and (6) the intangible but necessary quality of leadership and style that motivates employees through all echelons of the organization to work harder and smarter than they ever thought possible.

CHAPTER 23

PURCHASING FINANCIALLY DISTRESSED COMPANIES BEFORE BANKRUPTCY— PITFALLS

Bernard Shapiro, Esq.
Gregory A. Bray, Esq.
Gendel, Raskoff, Shapiro & Quittner

INTRODUCTION

The purchase of a financially distressed company presents the opportunity to acquire a business for a discounted price. However, the acquisition of such a company poses many dangers to the purchaser. This chapter will discuss some of those dangers—focusing primarily on the nature and scope of liability of the purchaser for the seller's obligations, the effect of the fraudulent conveyance laws on the transaction, and the consequences to the purchaser of a subsequent bankruptcy by the seller.

GENERAL RULES OF SUCCESSOR LIABILITY IN STOCK TRANSACTIONS AND ASSET PURCHASES

The most common methods used to acquire a company are stock transactions and asset purchases. A critical distinction between these two methods is the nature and scope of liabilities assumed by the buyer. In a stock transaction, the purchasing company becomes liable for all of the debts and obligations of the seller, known or unknown.[1] On the other hand, an asset purchase offers the buyer the opportunity to limit its responsibility for the seller's liabilities. The general rule in the United States is that, where one company sells or otherwise transfers any of its assets to another company, the buyer is not liable for the debts and liabilities of the seller simply by virtue of its succession to the ownership of the assets.[2]

The fact that a seller is financially distressed clearly means that it is burdened by substantial liabilities, known and unknown, liquidated or contingent. To minimize exposure to such claims, buyers often choose to structure an acquisition as an asset purchase, rather than as a stock transaction.

Exceptions to General Rule of Nonliability of an Asset Purchaser

There are four traditional exceptions to the general rule of nonliability for the purchaser of assets: (1) where there is an express or implied agreement to assume such debt, (2) where the circumstances surrounding the transaction warrant a finding that there was a consolidation or merger of the two corporations, (3) where the purchasing corporation is a mere continuation of the seller corporation, or (4) where the transaction was fraudulent in fact.[3]

Expressed or Implied Assumption of Liabilities
It is clear that a buyer may expressly assume certain obligations of the seller. Often, a buyer will want to assume those obligations necessary for the uninterrupted conduct of business, such as real property leases or service agreements. If so, the language in the purchase agreement must be drafted very carefully. The contract should specifically list the liabilities that the buyer is assuming and explicitly exclude any liabilities not so listed. Attempting to list the liabilities that the buyer is not assuming may result in the buyer's liability for unwanted contractual and tort obligations not specifically excluded by the agreement and that may not even have been in existence at the time of the acquisition.[4] However, a contractual disclaimer of tort liability will not protect the buyer from liability

(most important, product liability) if the transaction falls within one of the other exceptions set forth herein.[5]

Moreover, even if the buyer does not expressly assume a debt, liability for that debt may be implied if the representations or conduct of the buyer indicate an intention to pay the debt.[6] For example, published statements by the buyer to the seller's creditors that go beyond mere announcement of the sale and suggest a merger of the companies, or that advise the seller's creditors that their accounts will be assumed or serviced by the purchaser, can be construed as an assumption of the seller's creditors' debts as a matter of law.[7] Similarly, statements to the seller's employees about future employment and wages should be carefully drafted to avoid a finding that the buyer has impliedly agreed to hire all of the seller's employees or to assume responsibility for unpaid wages and benefits.[8] However, the fact that the buyer voluntarily pays *certain* debts of the seller, in and of itself, is not grounds for concluding that the buyer has assumed *all* of the seller's debts.[9]

Another factor considered by the courts is the effect of the transfer on the creditors of the seller. When a sale is made for inadequate consideration and leaves the seller with no assets, so creditors have virtually no chance of being paid, courts have found that the buyer has impliedly assumed the seller's liabilities.[10] This is not a well-defined doctrine and the few cases that find grounds for implied assumption are fact-specific.

De Facto Merger Exception
The second exception to the traditional rule of nonliability is where the transaction amounts to a de facto merger of the seller and buyer. The characteristics of such a merger are:

- The enterprise of the seller corporation continues, resulting in a continuity of management, personnel, physical location, assets, and general business operations.
- A continuity of shareholders resulting from the purchasing corporation's payment of shares of its own stock for the acquired assets, the stock ultimately being held by the shareholders of the seller corporation who then become a constituent part of the purchasing corporation.

- The seller corporation ceases its ordinary business operations and liquidates and dissolves as soon as legally and practically possible.
- The purchasing corporation assumes those liabilities and obligations of the seller ordinarily necessary for the uninterrupted continuation of normal business operations of the seller corporation.[11]

The key element of a de facto merger is the continuation of the selling shareholders' ownership interest,[12] since corporate liability traditionally adheres not to the nature of the business enterprise but to the corporate entity itself.[13]

Continuation Exception

The continuation exception is similar to the de facto merger rule. The test is whether there is a continuation of the corporate entity of the seller—not whether the buyer is continuing to operate the seller's business.[14] A "continuation" exists when there is a common identity of officers, directors, and shareholders in the seller and buyer.[15] An additional factor sometimes considered by the courts is whether the purchaser retains key employees, including officers of the seller. However, such employment, by itself, has not been sufficient to invoke this exception.[16]

Fraudulent Transfer Exception

The final exception is a fraudulent transfer. The type of transfer contemplated is not necessarily one made with an actual intent by the seller to defraud its creditors.[17] Fraudulent transfers are more fully discussed in a later section, Attacking the Transaction for Inadequate Consideration.

Product Liability Claims

The general rule of nonliability of an asset purchaser was conceived to protect the buyer from the financial liabilities, generally contractual in nature, that plague a distressed company. This rule has also been extended to tort liability, with one exception—product liability claims. The potential for successor liability in product liability cases is significantly greater than in other areas. Such liability is generally based upon two theories: (1) the "continuation of enterprise" doctrine, which is an extension of the continuation exception described above, and (2) the "product line exception."

The "continuation of enterprise" theory ignores the traditional requirement of continuity of shareholder identity between the seller and buyer. A cash transfer can give rise to successor liability under the following circumstances: (1) retention of the same employees, (2) retention of the same supervisory personnel, (3) retention of the same production facilities and the same physical location, (4) production of the same product, (5) retention of the same name, (6) continuity of assets, (7) continuity of general business operations, and (8) the successor holding itself out as a continuation of the previous enterprise.[18]

The purchaser whose transaction falls within these criteria can be liable for all product liability claims arising out of the seller's conduct, both known and unknown, whether or not the purchasing entity existed at the time of the manufacture and use of the defective product. Moreover, the purchaser will probably be liable for such claims, notwithstanding language in the purchase and sale agreement expressly providing to the contrary.[19]

Another means of imposing successor liability for product liability claims is under the "product line exception." This theory is premised on the belief that a corporation that acquires a manufacturing business and continues the output of its line of products, thereby benefiting from the reputation and goodwill of the seller, ought to be liable for defects in units of the same product line previously manufactured and distributed by the seller. The justifications for imposing such liability on the buyer are that: (1) the buyer, like the seller, is in a position to assume the risk spreading role assigned to the manufacturer of a product by strict liability theory; and (2) the destruction of the plantiff's remedies against the original manufacturer due to the sale of its assets to the buyer.[20]

Thus, the product line exception should be applicable only when the buyer acquires all, or substantially all, of the seller's assets, thereby contributing to the destruction of the claimant's remedies against the seller/manufacturer. If the seller is still in existence and able to respond to a damages claim, no successor liability should be imposed.[21]

SUCCESSOR LIABILITY FOR FAILURE TO GIVE ADVANCE NOTICE OF THE TRANSACTION TO THE SELLER'S CREDITORS: THE BULK TRANSFER LAWS

The purchaser of assets also may become liable to the seller's creditors under the bulk transfer laws. The bulk transfer laws require the purchaser of a business to give notice of the sale to creditors of the seller who might be relying upon the seller's assets for payment of their debts before the transaction is completed. While simple in principle, compliance is often difficult.

The requirement of advance notice of the sale is a unique safeguard for creditors, because it gives them an opportunity to challenge the transfer before it occurs. Its central purpose is to deal with two forms of common commercial fraud: (1) the merchant, owing debts, sells out his stock in trade to a friend for less than it is worth, pays his creditors less than he owes them, and hopes to come back into the business through the back door some time in the future; and (2) the merchant, owing debts, sells out her stock in trade to anyone for any price, pockets the proceeds, and disappears leaving her creditors unpaid.[22]

There are severe consequences for the purchaser of assets who does not provide notice as required: The transfer is ineffective to the seller's creditors and they may levy upon the transferred assets to satisfy their claims against the seller. In certain cases, the purchaser can even be held personally liable for the value of the transferred assets.[23]

Bulk transfers are governed by Article 6 of the Uniform Commercial Code (the UCC), which has been adopted, with variations, in all states (plus the District of Columbia and the Virgin Islands) except for Louisiana.[24] It is important to note, however, that various states have differing versions of Article 6 and care should be exercised to comply with the law of the state where the property is located.

Definition of Bulk Transfer

For a sale to be a "bulk transfer," all of the following conditions must be met: (1) the seller's principal business must be the sale of merchandise from stock; (2) the transfer must involve a major part of the materials, supplies, merchandise, or inventory of the seller; and (3) the transfer must not be in the ordinary course of the seller's business.[25]

Types of Businesses Covered
Article 6 is directed at companies whose principal business is the sale of merchandise from stock.[26] The sale of equipment is not subject to Article 6 unless: (1) it is made in connection with a bulk transfer of inventory and (2) a substantial part of the seller's equipment is being sold.[27]

Types of businesses that are generally not covered by Article 6 include farming, contracting, professional services, cleaning shops, barber shops, pool halls, hotels, and similar companies whose principal business is the sale not of merchandise but of services. Put another way, excluded businesses are those in which unsecured credit is not commonly extended on the faith of a stock of merchandise.[28] The authorities are divided over whether the sale of a restaurant or a bar is included. Certain states have amended Article 6 to expressly include restaurants.[29]

Types of Property Covered
In addition to covering only certain types of businesses, the bulk transfer laws only apply to the transfers of certain types of property—materials, supplies, merchandise, and inventory of the seller.[30] In other words, it applies to "goods." Transfers of investment securities, money, accounts receivable, chattel paper, contract rights, negotiable instruments, and choses of action are not intended to be covered by Article 6.[31]

Types of Transactions Covered
Article 6 is commonly referred to as a *bulk sales statute*. In actuality, Article 6 covers *transfers*. This term is not defined in the UCC, but courts consider it to mean more than just "sales." For example, in *Danning* v. *Daylin*,[32] the court held that an exchange of assets between merchants was a transfer subject to Article 6 because "[t]he dangers of a bulk transfer—either fraud or mere inadequacy of consideration—can as easily occur with an exchange as with a cash sale."

Nonetheless, there are certain types of transfers that are expressly exempted from Article 6's coverage.[33] The applicability of these exemptions to prospective purchasers of assets is discussed in Avoiding the Bulk Transfer Laws, below.

Size of Transactions Covered

Even if the seller's business is of the type covered by the bulk transfer laws, the transfer must also constitute a "major" part of the seller's materials, supplies, and the like. It is generally agreed that *major* means more than 50 percent by value.[34] It is not clear whether this means 50 percent of the total value of inventory in a particular state or 50 percent of the total overall value of inventory of the transferor. The cases that have addressed this issue are in conflict.[35] Because of the magnitude of liability resulting from a failure to comply with the bulk sale requirements, the prudent purchaser will view each store as a separate enterprise and comply with the bulk transfer laws of the state where the assets are located.

A recent case has also held that, when the seller liquidates its inventory in stages, the value of inventory sold to a certain purchaser should be compared to the value of the inventory at the time of the particular sale and not to the value of the inventory at the time the seller began to dispose of its assets.[36] Thus, it is possible to have more than one bulk transfer during a liquidation, and, if so, the final purchaser should comply with Article 6 no matter how much inventory is involved.

Transfer Must Not Be Made in Ordinary Course of Business

Notwithstanding that the transfer constitutes a "major" part of the seller's inventory, it is not a bulk transfer if made in the ordinary course of business. Courts have not agreed on the meaning of the "ordinary course." Some look to the seller's past business practices as well as industry practices.[37] Others define transfers in the ordinary course as only day-to-day operations and not transfers of a significant portion of inventory even though the transfer is common.[38]

Transfer of Equipment

The transfer of a substantial part of equipment of a business is subject to Article 6 if made in connection with a bulk transfer of inventory.[39] The applicability of Article 6 to such transfers has been narrowly construed in favor of the buyer. Acquiring an option to purchase inventory in connection with the purchase of equipment will not transform the asset purchase into a bulk transfer.[40] For an equipment sale to be a bulk transfer, the buyer of the equipment must have known, or had reason to know, at the time negotiations were completed, that "[a] substantial part of the seller's inventory has been or will be sold in a reasonably contemporaneous transaction."[41] While this is of no consequence to a party who purchases both inventory and equipment, who will obviously have such knowledge, it might provide some protection to the buyer of equipment who later learns that the seller made a bulk transfer of its inventory to a third party at or about the time the equipment was sold.

Notice to Creditors

If the proposed transaction is a bulk transfer, notice of the transaction must be provided to the seller's creditors. "Creditors" is broadly defined to include nonconsensual creditors and holders of unliquidated claims as well as trade creditors.[42] The seller, at the buyer's request, is responsible for preparing a list of its creditors together with their addresses and amounts owed. The list must be signed and sworn to under oath by the seller.[43] The buyer and seller are both responsible for preparing a schedule of property being transferred.[44] The buyer is then obligated to allow the seller's creditors to inspect the creditor list and property schedule for up to six months after the transfer, or to file the list and schedule with the appropriate public office for viewing by the creditors.[45]

In addition, the buyer is required to give written "notice" of the transfer at least 10 days before he or she takes possession or pays for the goods, whichever occurs first.[46] The notice must be given to all creditors shown on the list provided by the seller *and* to all other persons *actually* known by the purchaser to have a claim against the seller.[47] A purchaser who in good faith relies on the seller's verified list does not have an obligation to inquire about the existence of creditors not listed by the seller. The "responsibility for the completeness and accuracy of the list of creditors rests on the transferor, and the transfer is not rendered ineffective by errors or omissions therein unless the transferee is shown to have knowledge."[48]

The amount of information required in this "notice" depends upon whether the debts of the seller are to be paid in full as they fall due. If so, the notice generally explains that (1) a bulk transfer is about to be made, (2) provides the name and address of the seller and buyer, (3) states that the seller's creditors' debts will be paid when due, and (4) provides the address where to send bills.[49] This is commonly known as the *short form of notice*. If the seller's creditors will not be paid when their debts are due, however, much more information about the transaction, a "long form" of notice, is required.[50] Because of the risks attendant to noncompliance with Article 6, prudence dictates that the buyer use the long form of notice, notwithstanding the seller's promise to pay its creditors.

Payment of Consideration to Seller's Creditors

Some states require that the buyer, in addition to providing the seller's creditors with notice, ensure that the consideration being paid to the seller is used to pay the seller's creditors.[51] If the consideration is not enough to pay all of the seller's creditors in full, the buyer is responsible for making a pro rata distribution to them.[52] The buyer can comply with these requirements by holding the consideration until the debts are ascertained and paid, by depositing the consideration in an account subject to withdrawal only by his or her countersignature, or by depositing it with an independent escrow agent. If the seller's business is too complicated to implement these procedures, the buyer should consider depositing the funds with the appropriate court and interpleading the seller's creditors.[53] It should be noted that the insertion of a provision in the purchase and sale agreement that the seller will pay its creditors with the proceeds of sale will not satisfy the buyer's obligations under this section.[54]

Consequences to Purchase of Noncompliance with Bulk Transfer Law

The bulk transfer laws are cumbersome, time-consuming, and by their very nature designed to attract the attention of what may be a suspicious and hostile body—the seller's unsecured creditors—to the transfer. Nonetheless, the consequences to the purchaser of a failure to observe the requirements of Article 6 could be enormous. Failure to comply with Article 6 renders the transfer "ineffective against any creditor of the transferor."[55] The seller's creditors may "disregard the transfer and levy on the goods as still belonging to the transferor."[56] Moreover, some courts have held the noncomplying purchaser personally liable for the value of the transferred assets.[57] Thus, the buyer could end up paying twice for the same assets.

However, the only creditors who have standing to attack the transfer are those with claims based on transactions occurring before the transfer who did not receive the required notice.[58] A creditor omitted from the seller's list whose existence was unknown to the buyer should not be able to attack the transfer.[59]

Compliance with Article 6 is even more critical if the seller is financially distressed. All transactions involving troubled businesses should be analyzed with the possibility of bankruptcy in mind. Section 544(b) of the Bankruptcy Code provides the bankruptcy trustee with the rights and powers of any unsecured creditor of the seller who could avoid a prebankruptcy transfer under applicable nonbankruptcy law.[60] Thus, if a creditor could attack a noncomplying bulk transfer under state law, the trustee inherits that power. However, the trustee can avoid the *entire* transaction if it will benefit the creditors of the seller—even if the noncompliance was only as to a single creditor; whereas in a nonbankruptcy setting, the creditor could only avoid the transfer to the extent necessary to satisfy its individual claim.[61] In the alternative, the bankruptcy trustee has the right to recover from the purchaser the value of the assets transferred.[62]

The seller's bankruptcy will also increase the time period in which the transaction can be avoided. Under Article 6, the statute of limitations for setting aside a noncomplying transfer is six months after the purchaser takes possession, or, if the transfer was concealed, six months after the discovery thereof.[63] If the seller commences a bankruptcy before this six-month period has expired, the bankruptcy trustee will have an additional two years from the date of the bankruptcy filing to bring an action against the purchaser.[64]

A bankruptcy case often cited to purchasers who are tempted to ignore Article 6 is *Verco Industries* v. *Spartan Plastics*.[65] In the *Verco* case, the purchaser did not comply with the bulk transfer laws when it purchased the seller's assets. The seller subsequently filed for relief under the Bankruptcy Code, and the noncomplying transaction was set aside and the assets ordered returned to the seller for the benefit of its creditors. The purchaser had financed part of the transaction by giving a promissory note to the seller. The court held that the purchaser would remain liable on the promissory note, notwithstanding that the assets had been returned to the seller. The court acknowledged that the purchaser would have a claim back against the seller for any losses it suffered when the transfer was set aside, but that a condition precedent to the assertion of the set off would be the return of the assets to the seller.[66]

Noncompliance resulted in more disastrous consequences to the purchaser in *Stolba* v. *Mastrandrea*,[67] where the bankruptcy court held that a sale violated the bulk transfer laws. Since the purchaser had resold the assets, he was held liable for their value, which was determined as of the date of sale by the seller/debtor. The court refused to give the purchaser credit for (1) the portion of the purchase price paid in cash to the seller, since none of this cash was ever shown to have gone to the seller's creditors; (2) payments made to creditors; or (3) payments made to improve the business after the sale was consummated.[68]

Avoiding the Bulk Transfer Laws

Certain types of transactions are not treated as bulk transfers even though they might literally fall within its purview.[69]

General assignments for the benefit of creditors are exempt.[70] Such assignments are governed by state law (either by statute or common law) and generally involve a voluntary transfer by the debtor of all or substantially all its property to an assignee, in trust, for liquidation and equitable distribution to creditors.[71] Thus, the purchaser should consider acquiring the seller's assets from the assignee, with the proceeds of sale being distributed to the seller's creditors.

Transfers in settlement of a lien or other security interest are also exempt.[72] This provides the purchaser with an opportunity to acquire the seller's encumbered assets from the lienholder, thereby avoiding the bulk transfer laws. However, for such a transfer to be exempt, there must be an actual default under the security agreement by the seller whereby the lienholder has a right to foreclose.[73] Courts are divided about whether the secured creditor must actually foreclose on the property itself or whether the seller can directly transfer the assets to a third party (such as a purchaser) with the proceeds being paid by the third party to the secured creditor.[74]

Sales or transfers made by executors, administrators, receivers, or bankruptcy trustees and sales made in the course of judicial or administrative proceedings are also exempt.[75] This exemption often prompts the seller, sometimes at the purchaser's request, to file for protection under the federal bankruptcy laws, which provide a method for the sale of all, or part of, the debtor's assets within a reasonably short time.[76]

Transfers to a buyer who maintains a known place of business in the state and "who becomes bound to pay the debts of the transferor in full, gives public notice of that fact, and who is solvent after the [transfer]" are also exempt.[77] In addition to avoiding the bulk transfer laws, there are other benefits to acquiring a business in this manner. The purchaser should be able to attract the goodwill of the seller's creditors and suppliers that may be necessary to the uninterrupted flow of business by assuming, and demonstrating the ability to pay, their debts. Moreover, the purchaser will not have to produce as much cash to purchase the company, since part of the consideration will be the assumption of the seller's unsecured debt.[78] The danger here is very great, however. Unknown or unanticipated debts could turn the transaction into a disaster for the buyer.

There are other exemptions, but they do not present any significant opportunities for a purchaser of assets to avoid the bulk transfer laws.[79]

ATTACKING THE TRANSACTION FOR INADEQUATE CONSIDERATION: THE FRAUDULENT CONVEYANCE LAWS

The purchase of stock or assets from a financially distressed company presents the opportunity to acquire a company for a bargain price. The fact that the seller is in a precarious financial condition, however, can lead to the acquisition being set aside as a fraudulent conveyance if the consideration bears no reasonable relationship to the value of the property acquired.

A sale that is found to be a fraudulent conveyance will be set aside and the assets returned for the benefit of the seller's creditors. In certain circumstances, the purchaser may be held personally liable for the value of the assets acquired.

Codification of Law of Fraudulent Conveyances

There are four sources of fraudulent conveyance law: the common law, the Uniform Fraudulent Conveyance Act (the UFCA), the Uniform Fraudulent Transfer Act (the UFTA), and the federal Bankruptcy Code. Twelve states have adopted and still retain the UFCA. Twenty-two states have adopted the UFTA as a replacement for the UFCA. Section 548 of the Bankruptcy Code establishes a federal law of fraudulent conveyances that is quite similar to the UFTA.[80] In addition, Section 544(b) of the Bankruptcy Code also arms a bankruptcy trustee with the rights and powers of the debtor's unsecured creditors under state law to attack fraudulent conveyances.[81]

Financial Condition of Seller

Like the bulk transfer laws, the fraudulent conveyance laws are designed to prevent undue prejudice to the seller's creditors when the business is sold. Thus, the seller's financial condition is of prime importance in determining if a sale is a fraudulent conveyance. Even where there is no actual intent to hinder, delay, or defraud creditors, any of the following conditions, coupled with an unreasonably low purchase price, can constitute a fraudulent conveyance: (1) insolvency of the seller either before or immediately after the transaction, (2) the seller being left with inadequate capital after the transaction to engage in its business, or (3) the seller being unable to pay its debts when due after the transaction.[82]

Insolvency generally means that the fair value of the seller's assets is less than the sum of the seller's debts.[83] However, even if the seller is not "insolvent" at the time of the transaction, the subsequent financial condition of the seller must be considered, particularly in an asset purchase where the buyer's assumption of only limited liabilities of the seller can leave the majority of the seller's creditors with no means of being paid from the remains of the seller's company.

To avoid fraudulent conveyance liability, the purchaser should attempt to gather financial information and documentation establishing: (1) the seller's solvency both before and after the transaction, (2) that the seller is adequately capitalized, and (3) that the seller will be able to pay its debts as they mature after the transaction. The purchaser should not simply rely upon representations or warranties by the seller of its financial condition. Such promises will provide little comfort to the purchaser whose acquisition is set aside as a fraudulent conveyance and whose sole remedy is an unsecured claim against a financially distressed company that may be either headed for, or in, bankruptcy. The conventional approach by purchasers (and sellers) is to employ an investment banker and request a "fairness opinion." This is not a guarantee against attack, but the opinion is a strong element in the defense if an attack is mounted.

The conservative purchaser of all, or substantially all, of a distressed company's assets will assume that the seller's financial condition comes within one of the conditions described above and will endeavor to structure a purchase price that will withstand hindsight scrutiny.

Adequacy of Consideration

The UFCA defines this issue differently than the UFTA and the Bankruptcy Code Section 548. The UFCA requires the purchaser to pay "fair consideration" for the property, while the UFTA and Bankruptcy Code Section 548 require the seller to receive "reasonably equivalent value" for the property being transferred.[84]

Fair Consideration
In a sales transaction, fair consideration has been paid when the seller has received the "fair equivalent of the property conveyed and the purchaser's tender of the consideration was in good faith."[85] What constitutes fair consideration is determined from the standpoint of the seller's creditors.[86] However, fair consideration does not mean exact equivalent value.[87] Instead of concentrating

solely on the relative value of the assets transferred, courts have considered all of the surrounding circumstances to determine whether the consideration is fair.[88] One important factor is the effort of the seller to market the assets and the availability, or unavailability, of other purchasers.[89]

Fair consideration also means that the purchaser must act in good faith. "Good faith" has received several definitions: (a) an honest belief in the propriety of the sale; (b) no intent to take unconscionable advantage of others; and (c) no intent to, or knowledge of, the fact that the sale will hinder, delay, or defraud the seller's creditors.[90] If any of these factors is absent, lack of good faith is established and the conveyance fails.[91]

Reasonably Equivalent Value

The UFTA and the Bankruptcy Code Section 548 have substituted the term *reasonably equivalent value* for "fair consideration." Under this definition, the purchaser's good faith is irrelevant to a determination of the adequacy of consideration.[92] Whether a sale was made for reasonably equivalent value also depends upon the facts and circumstances of each case.[93]

Consequences to Purchaser of Fraudulent Conveyance

A sale that is a fraudulent transfer may be avoided by the seller's creditors, or, if the seller is in bankruptcy, the trustee, and the property returned for the benefit of the seller's creditors.[94] Under the UFTA and the Bankruptcy Code, the purchaser may, in the alternative, be held liable for the value of the assets fraudulently transferred.[95] While the UFCA does not provide for a money judgment against the purchaser, courts construing the UFCA have held the purchaser personally liable for the value of the assets when they cannot be recovered, or have decreased in value since the transfer, on the basis of the purchaser's lack of good faith or knowledge of the fraud.[96]

However, certain purchasers are protected from the effects of a fraudulent transfer. Under the UFCA, the seller's creditors may not set aside (1) a sale to an initial purchaser for "fair consideration" who was not aware of the seller's intent to defraud its creditors or (2) a sale to a subsequent purchaser for "fair consideration" who did not have knowledge of any fraud at the time of the purchase.[97] Moreover, under the UFCA, even if there was less than "fair consideration," the purchaser may retain the property as security for the consideration that was paid as long as it did not have any intent to defraud the seller's creditors.[98]

Under the Bankruptcy Code and UFTA, the initial purchaser is granted a lien on the transferred assets to the extent of the value given—as long as the purchaser acted in "good faith."[99] No liability is imposed upon subsequent purchasers who take for value and in good faith.[100] Thus, while the purchaser's good faith is not relevant under these statutes to a determination of the adequacy of consideration paid, it is the most critical factor in determining if the purchaser will have any protection from the effects of the fraudulent conveyance.

The resolution of good faith depends upon the circumstances of each transaction (i.e., whether the "transaction carries the earmarks of an arm's-length bargain").[101] The factors used to decide the good faith element of the fair consideration requirement in the UFCA are just as applicable in judging the purchaser's good faith under the Bankruptcy Code.[102]

A finding of actual intent to defraud will necessarily preclude the possibility of a lien, "because good faith does not exist where there is actual intent to defraud."[103] However, the absence of fraudulent intent does not mean that the transaction was necessarily entered into in good faith. The lack of good faith imports a failure to deal honestly, fairly, and openly.[104] Thus, the purchaser's knowledge of the seller's unfavorable financial condition at the time of sale, or position as an insider with control over the seller's finances, also can establish a lack of good faith.[105]

Particular Transactions

Foreclosure Sales
The matter of determining how much a purchaser must pay for assets in comparison to their fair market value has been addressed primarily in the context of foreclosure sales. Some courts construing bankruptcy fraudulent conveyance law have held that the payment of less than 70 percent of the fair market value of property at a foreclosure sale is an inadequate price as a matter of law, and,

therefore, the sale is a fraudulent transfer.[106] This 70 percent test has been extended to real property leases, in which the rent due is less than 70 percent of the fair rental value of the property.[107] It has also been applied to the foreclosure of personal property, such as inventory and stock, which is normally governed by Article 9 of the UCC.[108]

The 70 percent rule has not been universally adopted. One court has flatly rejected it, concluding that the sale price at a regularly conducted noncollusive foreclosure should be conclusively presumed to be the reasonable equivalent value of the property.[109] Still other courts have rejected any bright line rule and, instead, concluded that what is reasonably equivalent value should depend on the facts and circumstances surrounding the foreclosure sale.[110]

What does this mean to the purchaser of a distressed company? First, because the seller is in a precarious financial condition and, therefore, a likely candidate for bankruptcy, the purchaser must be prepared to justify the fairness of the transaction to the bankruptcy court. Even though the 70 percent test has its genesis in prebankruptcy foreclosure sales, it provides a relatively safe benchmark for the purchaser of a company to follow, given that bankruptcy courts have consistently held that, to pay fair value for the assets of a company in bankruptcy, the purchase price must be at least 75 percent of the value of the assets, absent extenuating circumstances.[111] The purchaser should have appraisals or other evidence to establish the fair value of the assets as of the date they are sold, since this is the relevant date for determining the fairness of consideration.[112]

Assuming or Directly Paying Some of the Seller's Outstanding Debts

Often the purchaser will assume or even directly pay some or all of the seller's creditors as partial consideration for the sale. The satisfaction of antecedent debt can constitute fair consideration or reasonably equivalent value.[113] Accordingly, assumption of the seller's debt may be considered "reasonably equivalent value" as long as the purchaser becomes personally liable for the payment of such debt and actually pays the creditors' claims when due.[114]

However, the payment of selected unsecured creditors with a portion of the purchase price may be a fraudulent transfer. In *Dean*

v. *Davis*,[115] the United States Supreme Court held that the making of a secured loan to enable the borrower to prefer a certain creditor over others (to avoid a criminal prosecution) was fraudulent when the lender knew of the borrower's intent and the borrower was thereby rendered insolvent.

Problems also arise when the purchaser assumes or pays a debt that is not the direct obligation of the seller but, rather, is an obligation of the principal or affiliated entity of the seller, or when the purchaser pays a debt for which the seller and principal are jointly liable. Transfers solely for the benefit of a third party are not adequate consideration.[116] However, payments directly made to a third party that indirectly confer an economic benefit on the seller can constitute fair consideration, if the value of the benefit approximates the value of the seller's property transferred.[117]

Thus, the purchaser must know the principal and secondary obligors of the obligations being assumed or paid, and, where the seller is jointly liable with a third party for payment of the obligation, be sure that sufficient value is conferred upon the seller.

Leveraged Buyouts

The typical leveraged buyout (LBO) involves the purchaser's pledge of the seller's assets as collateral to finance the acquisition of the company, with the proceeds of the sale being paid to the seller's shareholders.

Such transactions often leave the company with an unreasonably high debt to equity ratio, leading to insolvency or undercapitalization. The seller does not receive fair consideration or reasonably equivalent value for the sale of its assets, because the consideration was paid to the seller's shareholders instead of being retained by the seller—thus violating the rule that the transfer solely for the benefit of a third party will not constitute adequate consideration. Moreover, the purchaser cannot be in good faith under the UFCA if it pays the shareholders knowing that the seller will be rendered insolvent or undercapitalized.[118]

The seller's unsecured creditors become particularly incensed about LBOs, because the company is left unable to pay its debts while the seller's shareholders, who are generally not entitled to be paid unless and until the unsecured creditor's claims have been satisfied in full, were paid with the sale proceeds.[119]

The full scope of the purchaser's liability in an LBO has not yet been explored. The principal defendants in an LBO action have been the selling shareholders who received the consideration and the lender that financed the sale and received a lien on the seller's assets. The obvious remedy against the purchaser is to have it return the assets it acquired. There is another possible remedy, however. As set forth above, under the Bankruptcy Code, the trustee can instead recover the value of the property transferred.[120] "Value" is generally determined at the time of the transfer, rather than at the time of the recovery.[121] Thus, the purchaser could be jointly or severally liable with the seller's shareholders and the lender for the full value of the company before the transaction closed, or, alternatively, be liable for any decrease in value of the company after the assets are returned to the seller. While there do not appear to be any reported cases in which this remedy was used against the purchaser in an LBO, it should not be ignored.

THE HOT GOODS RULE: THE SELLER'S VIOLATION OF FEDERAL LABOR LAWS CAN PRECLUDE THE PURCHASER FROM SELLING OR USING GOODS

The creditors of a financially distressed seller are not the only parties who go unpaid. Often, the seller's employees have been underpaid or unpaid for some time prior to the purchaser's acquisition of the company. If the seller's treatment of its employees violated the wage and hour requirements of the Federal Labor Standards Act, the purchaser of goods that were produced during the period when the violations occurred will be prohibited from in any way introducing these goods into interstate commerce.[122] This rule applies as well to a foreclosing secured creditor.[123] The purchaser is exempt from this rule only if it acquires the goods for value without notice of the violation and "in good faith in reliance on *written* assurance from the producer that the goods were produced in compliance with the requirements [of the Federal Labor Standards Act]."[124]

This exemption is narrowly construed. Its goal is not to exempt innocent parties but only to protect persons from unwittingly violating the act for which they would otherwise be liable.[125] Consequently, the purchaser must, at a minimum, obtain in writing from the seller appropriate representations and warranties regarding the seller's compliance with the Fair Labor Standards Act up through the closing date. Given that the purchaser must also be acting in good faith, consideration should be given to conducting further due diligence by reviewing, among other things, the seller's payroll records and perhaps even interviewing random employees.

REPRESENTATIONS AND WARRANTIES BY THE DISTRESSED SELLER: STRUCTURING THE TRANSACTION TO MAXIMIZE THE PURCHASER'S POTENTIAL RECOVERY SHOULD THEY BE BREACHED

The typical purchase and sale agreement will normally contain many representations and warranties by the seller to the purchaser. Indeed, certain representations, such as the seller's compliance with the Federal Labor Standards Act, are mandated by law. Assuming these representations and warranties survive the closing, the purchase agreement will then require the seller to indemnify the purchaser for any damages arising out of the breach of these covenants. However, prudence dictates against relying upon such promises when the seller is financially distressed. Such a seller is likely to promise the purchaser the world when, practically speaking, the likelihood that the purchaser will actually collect a money judgment for any breach is remote.

Moreover, the threat of a subsequent bankruptcy by the seller further decreases the value of such representations and warranties. Once the seller files for bankruptcy, the purchaser will be enjoined from suing the seller for a breach of any of these covenants that occurred prior to the bankruptcy and will be relegated to filing a claim against the seller in the bankruptcy court.[126] The purchaser will have only an unsecured claim against the seller for its damages and will, in all likelihood, be required to accept a pro rata distribution (if any) along with the seller's other unsecured creditors in full satisfaction of its claim.

There are several ways for the purchaser to minimize this problem. First, the purchaser could insist upon the personal guaranties of the seller's principals to indemnify the purchaser for breaches by the seller (assuming the principals are solvent).

Second, the purchaser could bargain for a lien on any remaining assets of the seller or the assets of its principals as security to indemnify the purchaser for any breach of the covenants in the purchase and sale agreement. In the event of a bankruptcy by the seller or guarantor, the purchaser will have a secured claim for its damages to the extent of the value of the purchaser's interest in the collateral.[127]

Third, the purchaser can so structure the transaction as an installment purchase that all or some portion of the purchase price is paid over time. If the seller breaches, the purchaser can offset its damages against the remaining amount of the purchase price due the seller.[128]

Fourth, the purchaser can hold a portion of the purchase price in an interest-bearing escrow account for a specified period. The funds in such an account can be used to indemnify the purchaser for any damages, costs, and expenses that were not allocated to the buyer in the purchase and sale agreement.

Of course, the purchaser can best protect itself by conducting thorough due diligence to minimize the danger in relying upon the seller's representations and warranties on any significant issues.

CONCLUSION

The foregoing illustrations of the problems arising when one deals with a financially distressed company are not exclusive. Doing business with an insolvent entails considerable risk. A transaction with a business that is clearly troubled should be approached with care, even where it appears that the seller might well be solvent. Solvency is often determined by hindsight, after all, or most of the seller's illusions have proved flawed. In these situations, where warranties might well be valueless, it is often safer to structure the transaction under the protection of the Bankruptcy Code.

ENDNOTES
1. *Krull* v. *Celotex Corp.*, 611 F. Supp. 146, 148 (N.D. Ill. 1985).
2. 15 W. Fletcher, *Fletcher Cyclopedia of the Law of Private Corporations*, § 7122 (Perm. ed. 1983), and cases cited in footnotes 1 and 2 therein.
3. *Crawford Harbor Assoc.* v. *Blake Construction Co.*, 661 F. Supp. 880, 883 (E.D. Va. 1987) (citing *People's Nat'l. Bank of Rocky Mount* v. *Morris,* 152 Va. 814, 819, 148 S.E. 828, 829 (1929), quoting *Luedecke* v. *Des Moines Cabinet Co.*, 140 Iowa 223, 118 N.W. 456 (1908)); accord W. Fletcher, *supra* § 7122.
4. See *Keller* v. *Clark Equipment Co.*, 715 F.2d 1280, 1289-90 (8th Cir. 1983); *Philadelphia Electric Co.* v. *Hercules, Inc.*, 762 F.2d 303, 309 (3d Cir. 1985).
5. *Goldstein* v. *Gardner,* 444 F. Supp. 581, 583 (N.D. Ill. 1978); *Menacho* v. *Adamson United Co.*, 420 F. Supp. 128, 133 (D.N.J. 1976).
6. *Ladjevardian* v. *Laidlaw-Coggeshall, Inc.*, 431 F. Supp. 834, 839 (S.D.N.Y. 1977).
7. *Id.* at 840; *Long* v. *Home Service of Puget Sound, Inc.*, 43 Wash. App. 729, 719 P.2d 176 (1986); *Hoche Productions, S. A.* v. *Jayark Films Corp.*, 256 F. Supp. 291 (1966); W. Fletcher at § 7124.
8. See *Long,* 43 Wash. App. at 733-35, 719 P.2d at 180-81.
9. *Id.* at 734, 719 P.2d at 181; W. Fletcher, *supra* § 7124 and cases cited in footnote 8 therein.
10. *Blackinton* v. *United States (In re Securities Mfg. Co.)*, 6 F.2d 147, 148 (8th Cir. 1925); *In re Alamac Operating Corp.*, 42 F.2d 120, 122 (2d Cir. 1930); *Ladjevardian,* 431 F. Supp. at 839.
11. *Keller,* 715 F.2d at 1291; *Shannon* v. *Samuel Langston Co.*, 379 F. Supp. 797, 801 (W.D. Mich. 1974).
12. *Good* v. *Lackawanna Leather Co.*, 96 N.J. Super. 439, 452, 233 A.2d 201 (1967); *Shannon,* 379 F. Supp. at 801-02; *Bud Antle, Inc.* v. *Eastern Foods, Inc.*, 758 F.2d 1451, 1457-58 (11th Cir. 1985).
13. *Bud Antle,* 758 F.2d at 1458; *Travis* v. *Harris Corp.*, 565 F.2d 443, 447 (7th Cir. 1977).
14. *Bud Antle,* 758 F.2d at 1458; *Travis,* 565 F.2d at 447.
15. *Bud Antle,* 758 F.2d at 1458-59; *Weaver* v. *Nash International, Inc.*, 730 F.2d 547, 548 (8th Cir. 1984); *Mozingo* v. *Correct Manufacturing Corp.*, 752 F.2d 168, 175 (5th Cir. 1985).
16. *Bud Antle,* 758 F.2d at 1459; *Travis,* 565 F.2d at 447.
17. *Keller,* 715 F.2d at 1292; *Bud Antle,* 758 F.2d at 1457; Annotation, *Similarity of Ownership or Control as Basis for Charging Corporation Acquiring Assets of Another with Liability for Former Owner's Debts,* 49 A.L.R.3d 881, 883-90 (1973).

18. *Mozingo,* 752 F.2d at 175; *Turner* v. *Bituminous Casualty Co.,* 397 Mich. 406, 424, 244 N.W.2d 873, 883 (1976); *Rivers* v. *Stihl, Inc.,* 434 So.2d 766, 771 (1983); **see also,** *Cyr* v. *B. Offen & Co.,* 501 F.2d 1145, 1153 (1st Cir. 1974).
19. *Cyr,* 501 F.2d at 1153; *Turner,* 244 N.W.2d at 877; *Andrews* v. *John E. Smith's Sons Co.,* 369 So.2d 781, 785-86 (1979).
20. *Ray* v. *Alad Corp.,* 19 Cal.3d 22, 560 P.2d 3, 136 Cal. Rptr. 574 (Cal. 1977); *Ramirez* v. *Amsted Indus., Inc.,* 86 N.J. 332, 358, 431 A.2d 811, 822 (1981).
21. *Kline* v. *Johns-Manville,* 745 F.2d 1217, 1219-20 (9th Cir. 1984); *Roy* v. *Bolens Corp.,* 629 F. Supp. 1070, 1073 (D. Mass. 1986). Some purchasers insist that a seller who is in financial difficulty file bankruptcy so the sale may be made under 11 U.S.C. Section 363 (free and clear). This method of avoiding liability on the part of the purchaser has met with some success. **See** *Volvo White Truck Corp.* v. *Chambersburg Beverage, Inc. (In re White Motor Credit Corp.),* 75 Bankr. 944, 949-50 (Bankr. N.D. Ohio 1987); however, in *Nelson* v. *Tiffany Industries, Inc.,* 778 F.2d 533, 538 (9th Cir. 1985) the court stated that, where there is a collusive agreement that the seller file bankruptcy to insulate a purchaser from product liability claims, the purchaser would suffer liability.
22. U.C.C. § 6-101 Official Comment 2 (1987).
23. See *infra* chapter subsection, Consequences to Purchase of Noncompliance with Bulk Transfer Law.
24. Unless otherwise indicated, all references in this chapter are to the 1987 official text of the UCC. It should be noted that the sponsors of the UCC have recommended that Article 6 be repealed by the states and have proposed that such transfers no longer be governed by the UCC. However, a revised Article 6 has been promulgated for those states that intend to continue to regulate such transfers. As of the date of this chapter, no state has repealed Article 6 or adopted the proposed revisions thereto. Consequently, this chapter will only discuss the requirements of Article 6 in its present form.
25. U.C.C. § 6-102 (1987).
26. U.C.C. § 6-102(3) and Official Comment 2 (1987); *Summer* v. *Janicare, Inc.,* 294 S.C. 483, 485, 366 S.E.2d 20, 21 (S.C. Ct. App. 1988); *Macke Co.* v. *Pizza of Gaithersburg, Inc.,* 259 Md. 479, 492, 270 A.2d 645, 652 (Md. 1970).
27. U.C.C. § 6-102(2) (1987).
28. U.C.C. § 6-102 Official Comment 2 (1987).
29. J. White & R. Summers, Uniform Commercial Code, § 20-2 n.17 and accompanying text (3d ed. Prac. ed., vol. 2, 1988).

30. See U.C.C. § 6-103 (1987).
31. U.C.C. § 6-102 Official Comment 3 (1987).
32. *Danning v. Daylin, Inc.*, 488 F.2d 185, 188 (9th Cir. 1973).
33. See U.C.C. § 6-103 (1987).
34. *Wilkelund Wholesale Co. v. Tile World Factory Tile Warehouse*, 57 Ill.App.3d 269, 271, 372 N.E.2d 1022, 1023 (Ill. App. Ct. 1978). **See also** J. White & R. Summers, Uniform Commercial Code, § 20-2 n.24 and accompanying text. California has substituted the word *substantial* in place of *major*, which has been held to refer to transfers of as little as 5 percent of the value of the inventory. **See** *Danning* v. *Daylin*, 488 F.2 at 189; *Reed* v. *Anglo Scandinavian Corp.*, 298 F. Supp. 310, 313 (E.D. Ca. 1969).
35. *Leach* v. *Burns Brick Co. (In re Albany Brick Co.)* 12 U.C.C. Rep. Serv. (Callaghan) 165, 166-67 (D. Ga. 1972) (50 percent of the total overall value of inventory of the transferor required); **see also,** *Froehle, Livingston & Roth* v. *Stan Smith Enterprises, Inc.*, 2 U.C.C. Rep. Serv. (Callaghan) 1045, 1047-48, Ohio Ct. App. 1986); *contra National Bank of Royal Oak* v. *Frydlewicz*, 67 Mich. App. 417, 422, 241 N.W.2d 471, 474 (1976).
36. *Nichols Motorcycle Supply, Inc.* v. *Regency Kawasaki, Inc.*, 295 S.C. 138, 141, 367 S.E.2d 438, 440 (S.C. Ct. App. 1988).
37. *Murdock* v. *Plymouth Enter., Inc. (In re Curtina Int'l., Inc.);* 34 U.C.C. Rep. Serv. (Callaghan) 1311, 1319 (Bankr. S.D.N.Y. 1982); *AAB* v. *Loehmann's, Inc.*, 8 Bankr. 777, 778 (Bankr. S.D.N.Y. 1981).
38. *Danning*, 488 F.2d at 189 (9th Cir. 1973).
39. U.C.C. § 6-102(2) (1987).
40. *Ouachita Electric Coop. Corp.* v. *Evans-St. Clair*, 12 Ark. App. 171, 177, 672 S.W.2d 660, 664 (Ark. Ct. App. 1984) ("The bulk sales act does not purport to regulate agreements for the sale of inventory as opposed to actual transfers of inventory because until the inventory is sold, title to it . . . remains in the seller . . . [and] is subject to being levied upon by the seller's creditors.").
41. *Republic Steel Corp.* v. *Canyon Culvert Co.*, 104 N.M. 396, 398, 722 P.2d 647, 650 (N.M. 1986).
42. U.C.C. § 6-109(1) and Official Comment 1 (1987); *Stone's Pharmacy, Inc.* v. *Pharmacy Accounting Management, Inc.*, 812 F.2d 1063, 1065 (8th Cir. 1987); **see** *Chemical Bank* v. *Society Brand Indus., Inc.*, 624 F. Supp. 979, 980-81 (S.D.N.Y. 1985); **see also** U.C.C. § 1-201(12) (1987) (defining "creditor").
43. U.C.C. § 6-104(2) (1987).
44. U.C.C. § 6-104(1)(b) (1987).

45. U.C.C. § 6-104(c)(1) (1987).
46. U.C.C. § 6-105 (1987).
47. U.C.C. § 6-107(3) (1987).
48. U.C.C. § 6-104(3) (1987); *Ross* v. *Rodolpho (In re Villa Roel, Inc.)*, 57 Bankr. 835, 838 (Bankr. D.C. 1985) ("case law and the statute itself establish that a transferee's good faith reliance upon a transferor's affidavit that he has no creditors may be sufficient to remove the transferor's obligation to send out notice of the transfer."); *Adrian Tabin Corp.* v. *Climax Boutique, Inc.*, 34 N.Y.2d 210, 213, 356 N.Y.S.2d 606, 608, 313 N.E.2d 66, 67 (1974).
49. U.C.C. § 6-107(1) (1987).
50. U.C.C. § 6-107(2) (1987) states:

If the debts of the transferor are not to be paid in full as they fall due or if the transferee is in doubt on that point, then the notice shall state further:
a. the location and general description of the property to be transferred and the estimated total of the transferor's debts;
b. the address where the schedule of property and list of creditors (Section 6-104) may be inspected;
c. whether the transfer is to pay existing debts and if so the amount of such debts and to whom owing:
d. whether the transfer is for new consideration and if so the amount of such consideration and the time and place of payment; [and]
e. if for new consideration the time and place where creditors of the transferor are to file their claims].

Note: The words in brackets are optional.

51. U.C.C. § 6-106 (1987). This requirement has been adopted by Alaska, Florida (with variations), Idaho, Kansas, Kentucky, Maryland (with variations), Minnesota (with variations), Mississippi, Montana, New Jersey, North Dakota, Oklahoma, Pennsylvania (with variations), South Dakota, Tennessee, Texas, Utah, Virgin Islands, Washington and West Virginia. California has rewritten Section 6-106.
52. U.C.C. § 6-106(3) (1987).
53. U.C.C. § 6-106(4) and Official Comment 3 thereto (1987).
54. *Atlas Merchandising Co.* v. *Johnny's California Market, Inc.*, 25 U.C.C. Rep. Serv. (Callaghan) 1427, 1428-29 (1977).
55. U.C.C. §§ 6-104(1) and 6-105 (1987).
56. U.C.C. § 6-104 and Official Comment 2 (1987).
57. *Sbar's, Inc.* v. *New Jersey Art & Craft Distributors, Inc.*, 42 U.C.C. Rep. Serv. (Callaghan) 535 (N.J. App. 1985) (bulk sale purchaser who failed to comply with provisions of Article 6 may be ordered to satisfy

the debt owed by the transferor to creditor only to the extent of the fair value of the goods transferred); *Murdock v. Plymouth Enterprises, Inc. (In re Curtina)*, 23 Bankr. 969, 979 (Bankr. S.D.N.Y. 1982) (a transfer in violation of the bulk sales law obligates the transferee to account to the transferor's creditors for the fair value of the merchandise transferred, valued on the date of the noncomplying transfer); **but see,** *New Haven Tobacco Co. v. O'Brien*, 32 U.C.C. Rep. Serv. (Callaghan) 523 (Conn. App. 1981) (creditor of bulk transferor cannot recover the debt from the transferee since he has no personal cause of action against the bulk transferee); *Bill Vorhees Co. v. R & S Camper Sales*, 605 F.2d 888, 891-92 (5th Cir. 1979) (no personal liability, but discusses different theories on which personal liability might be based).
58. U.C.C. § 6-109(1).
59. *Fico, Inc. v. Ghingher*, 411 A.2d 430, 435, 18 A.L.R.4th 1077, 1084, 28 U.C.C. Rep. Serv. (Callaghan) 498, 503 (Md. App. 1980).
60. 11 U.S.C. Section 544 (b) (West, 1989).
61. See 4 L. King, M. Cook, R. D'Agostino & K. Klee, *Collier on Bankruptcy*, § 544.03 (15th ed. 1989).
62. 11 U.S.C. Section 550(a) (West, 1989).
63. U.C.C. § 6-111.
64. 11 U.S.C. Section 108(a) (West, 1989).
65. *Verco Industries v. Spartan Plastics (In re Verco Industries)*, 704 F.2d 1134 (9th Cir. 1983).
66. *Id.* at 1137-40.
67. *Stolba v. Mastrandrea (In re Pritchard)*, 8 Bankr. 688 (Bankr. C.D. Cal. 1984).
68. *Stolba*, 8 Bankr. at 691-92. (This case dealt with a superseded version of the Bankruptcy Code. Under Section 550(d) of the present Bankruptcy Code, the seller would retain a lien on the assets to secure the value of any improvements made after the sale if he or she was in "good faith." However, it seems doubtful that a seller who intentionally disregards the bulk sale laws would ever be in good faith.)
69. See U.C.C. § 6-103.
70. U.C.C. § 6-103(2).
71. *In re A & B Liquidating, Inc.*, 18 Bankr. 922, 924 (Bankr. E.D. Va. 1982); *Freeman v. Marine Midland Bank*, 419 F. Supp. 440, 447 (E.D.N.Y. 1976).
72. U.C.C. § 6-103(3).
73. *Stone's Pharmacy v. Pharmacy Accounting Management*, 812 F.2d 1063, 1066 (8th Cir. 1987); *Starman v. John Wolfe, Inc.*, 490 S.W.2d 377, 382 (Mo. App. 1973). (To be exempt under § 6-103(3), there must be a default by the seller and the proceeds of the transfer must be used

to extinguish the debt); *Hixson* v. *Pride of Texas Distributing Co.*, 683 S.W.2d 173, 178 (Tex. Ct. App. 1985). (For a transaction to fall within the exception in § 6-103(3), there must be evidence of default, resulting in the secured creditor having a present right to foreclose.)
74. **Compare** *Techsonic Industries* v. *Barney's Bassin' Shop*, 621 S.W.2d 332, 334 (Mo. App. 1981) and *American Metal Finishers, Inc.* v. *Palleschi*, 55 A.D.2d 499, 501, 391 N.Y.S.2d 170, 172 (1977) (both ruling that § 6-103(3) applies when assets are transferred to a third party and the proceeds are paid to the secured creditor), **with** *Starman*, 490 S.W.2d 377 (holding that the transfer must be to the holder of the security interest and not to a third party for the benefit of the secured creditor), **and with** *Ouachita Elec. Coop. Corp.*, 672 S.W.2d at 663 limiting the rule of *Starman* to narrow facts (i.e., consideration paid for the transfer was used to pay in part other parties for the benefit of the transferor, resulting in a preference to some creditors).
75. U.C.C. § 6-103(4) and (5).
76. 11 U.S.C. Section 363(b) (West, 1989). The leading case on the sale of assets in bankruptcy is *Committee of Equity Security Holders* v. *Lionel Corp. (In re Lionel Corp.)*, 722 F.2d 1063 (2d Cir. 1983).
77. U.C.S. § 6-103(6).
78. J. White & R. Summers, Uniform Commercial Code, § 20-2, p. 104.
79. U.C.C. § 6-102(1): transfers made to give security for the performance of an obligation; U.C.C. § 6-103(7): transfers that reflect changes in the form of ownership without any initial changes in substance; and U.C.C. § 6-103(8): transfer of property that is exempt from execution.
80. 11 U.S.C. Section 548 (West, 1989).
81. 11 U.S.C. Section 544(b) (West, 1989).
82. Uniform Fraudulent Conveyance Act §§ 4, 5, & 6, 7A U.L.A. 474, 504, 507 (1980); Uniform Fraudulent Transfer Act §§ 4(a) & 5(a), 7A U.L.A. 652, 657 (1989); 11 U.S.C. Section 548(a) (West, 1989).
83. Uniform Fraudulent Conveyance Act § 2(1), 7A U.L.A. 442 (1980); Uniform Fraudulent Transfer Act § 2, 7A U.L.A. 648 (1989); 11 U.S.C. Section 101 (31) (West, 1989).
84. Uniform Fraudulent Conveyance Act §§ 3-6, 7A U.L.A. 448-507 (1980); Uniform Fraudulent Transfer Act §§ 4(a)(2) and 5(a), 7A U.L.A. 652, 657 (1989); 11 U.S.C. Section 548(a)(2)(A) (West, 1989).
85. *Cohen* v. *Sutherland*, 257, F.2d 737, 742 (2d Cir. 1958).
86. *United States* v. *Gleneagles Co., Inc.*, 565 F. Supp. 556, 574 (M.D. Pa. 1983), *aff'd sub. nom. United States* v. *Tabor Court Realty*

Court, 803 F.2d 1288, *cert. denied sub. nom. McClellan Realty Co.* v. *U.S.,* 483 U.S. 1005, 105 S.Ct. 3229 (1987); *Hansen* v. *Cramer,* 39 Cal. 2d 321, 324, 245 P.2d 1059 (1952).
87. *John Ownbey Co., Inc.* v. *C.I.R.,* 645 F.2d 540, 544 (6th Cir. 1981); *Neal* v. *Clark,* 251 P.2d 903, 906, 75 Ariz. 91, 94 (Ariz. 1952); *Utah Assets Corp.* v. *Dooley Brothers Assoc.,* 70 P.2d 738, 741, 92 Utah 577, 583 (1937).
88. *Ownbey,* 645 F.2d at 545; *DeAragon* v. *Chase Manhattan Bank,* 457 F.2d 263, 266 (1st Cir. 1972).
89. *Neal,* 251 P.2d at 906.
90. *Sparkman and McClean Co.* v. *Derber,* 4 Wash. App. 341, 481 P.2d 585 (1971); *United States* v. *Tabor Court Realty Corp.,* 803 F.2d 1288, 1296 (3d Cir. 1986).
91. *Tabor,* 803 F.2d at 1296, *citing, Sparkman,* 4 Wash. App. at 348, 481 P.2d at 591.
92. Uniform Fraudulent Transfer Act § 4 Comment 2, 7A U.L.A. 652 (1989); *Pereira* v. *Checkmate Communications Co. (In re Checkmate Stereo & Electronics Ltd.)* 9 Bankr. 585, 591 (Bankr. E.D.N.Y. 1981), *aff'd,* 21 Bankr. 402.
93. *Consove* v. *Cohen (In re Roco Corp.),* 701 F.2d 978, 981-82 (1st Cir. 1983).
94. Uniform Fraudulent Conveyance Act §§ 9 and 10, 7A U.L.A. 557, 630 (1980); Uniform Fraudulent Transfer Act § 7, 7A U.L.A. 660 (1989); 11 U.S.C. Section 548(a) (West, 1989).
95. 11 U.S.C. Section 550(a) (West, 1989); Uniform Fraudulent Transfer Act § 8(b), 7A U.L.A. 662 (1989).
96. *Pereira,* 9 Bankr. at 593; *Flowers & Sons Development Corp.* v. *Municipal Court,* 86 Cal.App.3d 818, 825, 150 Cal. Rptr. 555, 559 (1978); *Damazo* v. *Wahby,* 269 Md. 252, 257-58, 305 A.2d 138, 141 (1973); *State ex rel.* v. Nashville Trust Co., 28 Tenn. App. 388, 422, 190 S.W.2d 785, 798 (1945); *Joseph P. Manning Co.* v. *Shinopoulos,* 317 Mass. 97, 100, 56 N.E.2d 869, 871 (1944).
97. Uniform Fraudulent Conveyance Act § 9(1), 7A U.L.A. 577 (1980).
98. Uniform Fraudulent Conveyance Act § 9(2), 7A U.L.A. 578 (1980).
99. Uniform Fraudulent Transfer Act § 8(d), 7A U.L.A. 662 (1989); 11 U.S.C. Section 548(c) (West, 1989). Section 548(d) further provides the purchaser a lien to secure the lesser of:

> (A) the cost, to such transferee, of any improvement made after the transfer, less the amount of any profit realized by or accruing to such transferee from such property; and
>
> (B) any increase in the value of such property as a result of such improvement, of the property transferred.

100. Uniform Fraudulent Transfer Act § 8(b), 7A U.L.A. 662 (1989); 11 U.S.C. Section 550(b) (West, 1989).
101. *Bullard* v. *Aluminum Co. of America*, 468 F.2d, 11, 13 (7th Cir. 1972).
102. See *Tabor*, 803 F.2d at 1299; *Jones* v. *J.E.G. Enterprises, Inc. (In re Greenbrook Carpet Co., Inc.)*, 22 Bankr. 86, 91 (Bankr. N.D. Ga. 1982).
103. *Consove* v. *Cohen (In re Roco Corp.)*, 21 Bankr. 429, 436 (Bankr. 1st Cir. 1982), *aff'd*, 701 F.2d 978 (1st Cir. 1983).
104. *Jones*, 22 Bankr. at 91 quoting *Southern Industries, Inc.* v. *Jeremias*, 66 A.D.2d, 178, 183, 411 N.Y.S.2d 945, 949 (2d Dept. 1978).
105. *Tabor*, 803 F.2d at 1296; *Jones*, 22 Bankr. at 91.
106. The leading case is *Durrett* v. *Washington Nat. Ins. Co.*, 621 F.2d 201 (5th Cir. 1980). **See also,** *First Federal Sav. & Loan* v. *Standard Bldg. Assoc.*, 87 Bankr. 221 (N.D. Ga. 1988); *In re Gaines*, 82 Bankr. 105 (Bankr. W.D. Mo. 1988).
107. *Thrifty Dutchman, Inc.* v. *Florida Supermarkets, Inc. (In re Thrifty Dutchman, Inc.)*, 97 Bankr. 101, 108 (Bankr. S.D. Fla. 1988).
108. *Brown* v. *Borchers & Heimsoth Construction Company, Inc. (In re Apollo Hollow Metal and Hardware Co., Inc.)*, 71 Bankr. 179, 183 (Bankr. W.D. Mo. 1987); Koger & Acconcia, *The Hulm Decision: A Milestone for Creditors*, 91 Com. L.J. 301, 317-320 (1986). However, there are provisions in the UFTA that preclude the avoidance of such transfers that are done in compliance with Article 9 of the UCC. Uniform Fraudulent Transfer Act §§ 4(a)(2) and (5), 7A U.L.A. 652 (1989). Thus, if the sale is "commercially reasonable" under Article 9, and not done to intentionally defraud the seller's creditors, it cannot be avoided under the UFTA.
109. *Lawyers Title Insurance Corp.* v. *Madrid (In re Madrid)*, 21 Bankr. 424 (Bankr. 9th Cir. 1982), *aff'd* on other grounds, 725 F.2d 1197 (9th Cir. 1984).
110. *First Federal Savings & Loan Assoc. of Bismark, Inc.* v. *Hulm (In re Hulm)*, 738 F.2d 323, 327 (8th Cir. 1984); *Bundles* v. *Baker*, 856 F.2d 815, 824 (7th Cir. 1988).
111. *In re Abbotts Dairies of Pa., Inc.*, 788 F.2d 143, 149 (3d Cir. 1986); *Willemain* v. *Kivitz (In the Matter of Willemain)*, 764 F.2d 1019, 1023 (4th Cir. 1985); *Greylock Glen Corp.* v. *Community Savings Bank*, 656 F.2d 1, 4 (1st Cir. 1981); *In re Rock Indus. Mach. Corp.*, 572 F.2d 1195, 1197 (7th Cir. 1978); *In re Karpe*, 84 Bankr. 926, 933 (Bankr. M.D. Pa. 1988).
112. *Greene* v. *Newman (In re Newman)*, 15 Bankr. 658, 660 (S.D.N.Y. 1981); *Day* v. *Central Fidelity Bank, N.A. (In re Appomattox Agri. Serv., Inc.)*, 6 B.C.D. 1239, 1241 (Bankr. W.D. Va. 1980).

113. Uniform Fraudulent Conveyance Act § 3(a), 7A U.L.A. 474, 650 (1980); 11 U.S.C. Section 548(d)(2)(A); *Coors of N. Miss., Inc.* v. *Bk. of Longview (In re Coors of N. Miss., Inc.)*, 66 Bankr. 845, 861-62 (Bankr. N.D. Miss. 1986); *Beldock* v. *Faberge, Inc. (In re S&W Exporters, Inc.)*, 16 Bankr. 941, 945 (Bankr. S.D.N.Y. 1982).
114. *Sandoz* v. *Bennett (In re Emerald Oil Co.)*, 807 F.2d 1234, 1238 (5th Cir. 1987); *Sol-Tabb, Inc.* v. *Total Acquisition Corp. (In re Total Acquisition Corp.)*, 29 Bankr. 836, 840 (Bankr. S.D. Fla. 1983).
115. *Dean* v. *Davis*, 242 U.S. 438, 441, 37 S.Ct. 130, 131-32 (1917).
116. *Rubin* v. *Manufacturers Hanover Trust Co.*, 661 F.2d 979, 991-92 (2d Cir. 1981); *Klein* v. *Tabatchnick*, 610 F.2d 1043, 1047 (2d Cir. 1979); *McColley* v. *Rosenberg (In re Candor Diamond Corp.)*, 76 Bankr. 342, 351 (Bankr. S.D.N.Y. 1987); *Martin V. Phillips (In re Butcher)*, 58 Bankr. 128, 130 (Bankr. E.D. Tenn. 1986).
117. *Klein*, 610 F.2d at 1047.
118. *Gleneagles*, 565 F. Supp. at 574. The *Gleneagles* cases are: *United States* v. *Gleneagles Inv. Co.*, 565 F. Supp. 556 (M.D. Pa. 1983) (*Gleneagles I*); *United States* v. *Gleneagles Inv. Co.*, 571 F. Supp. 935 (M.D. Pa. 1983) (*Gleneagles II*); *United States* v. *Gleneagles Inv. Co.*, 584 F. Supp. 671 (M.D. Pa. 1984) (*Gleneagles III*); and *United States* v. *Tabor Court Realty Corp.*, 803 F.2d 1288 (3d Cir. 1986), *cert. denied sub nom. McClellan Realty Co.* v. *United States*, 107 S. Ct. 3229 (1987).
119. For a detailed analysis of leveraged buyouts and fraudulent conveyance law, **see** Murdoch, Sartin & Zadak, *Leveraged Buyouts and Fraudulent Transfers: Life After Gleneagles,* 43 Bus. Law J. No. 1 (Nov. 1987).
120. 11 U.S.C. Section 550(a) (West, 1989).
121. *Wood, III* v. *Davis (In re Southeast Comm. Media, Inc.)*, 27 Bankr. 834, 841 (Bankr. E.D. Tenn. 1983); *Chrystler* v. *Mersman Tables, Inc. (In re Furniture Den, Inc.)*, 12 Bankr. 522, 527 (Bankr. W.D. Mich. 1981).
122. 29 U.S.C. Section 206 (1978); 29 U.S.C. Section 207 (1985); 29 U.S.C. Section 215(a) (1978).
123. *Citicorp Indus. Credit Inc.* v. *Brock*, 483 U.S. 27, 39, 107 S.Ct. 2694, 2702 (1987).
124. 29 U.S.C. Section 215(a) (1978).
125. *Citicorp*, 107 S.Ct. at 2699, n. 7.
126. **See** 11 U.S.C. Sections 362, 501 (West, 1989).
127. **See** U.S.C. Section 506 (West, 1989). There are procedures in the Bankruptcy Code for the estimation of unliquidated claims that could limit the recovery of the purchaser against a bankruptcy debtor who

is the principal obligor on the underlying debt. **See** 11 U.S.C. Section 502(c) (West, 1989). Similarly, the Bankruptcy Code imposes limitations on the allowability of claims against guarantors of obligations of the debtor. **See** 11 U.S.C. Section 502(e) (West, 1989).

128. **See** 11 U.S.C. Section 553 (West, 1989).

CHAPTER 24

INVESTING IN DISTRESSED SECURITIES

Edward I. Altman, Ph.D.*
Max L. Heine, Professor of Finance
Stern School of Business
New York University

The market for distressed firms' debt and equity securities has captured the interest and the imagination of the investment community like never before. Fueled by a substantial increase in the supply and diversity of bankrupt and near-bankrupt companies and the perceived sizable upside potential of securities selling at deeply discounted prices, investors are increasingly considering this area as one of the growth opportunities of the 1990s. The purpose of this chapter is to document and analyze this unique asset class, both in terms of a descriptive anatomy of the market's major characteristics and participants as well as an analytical treatment of its pricing dynamics and performance attributes. While we refer to distressed securities as a *market* and an *asset class,* we are fully aware that these labels are premature, due to the field's nascent condition and the lack of much rigorous research to date. In actuality, it is a market of securities of problem firms, which afford opportunities if

---

* This is a revised version of the Altman/Foothill report, "Investing in Distressed Securities: The Anatomy of Defaulted Debt and Equities," April 1990, Los Angeles, Calif. A more comprehensive version can be found in E. Altman, *Distressed Securities: Analyzing and Evaluating Market Potential and Investment Risk* (Chicago: Probus, 1991).

the problems are addressed successfully and where the current prices may be overdiscounted for the perceived problems.

Distressed securities can be defined narrowly as only those publicly held debt and equity securities of firms that have defaulted on their debt obligations or have filed for protection under Chapter 11 of the Bankruptcy Code, or both. We estimate that the market value of these securities as of the start of 1990 was approximately $13 billion ($11.5 billion in debt), comprised of 178 different issuing firms.

A more comprehensive definition would also include those publicly held debt securities selling at sufficiently discounted prices to be yielding a minimum of 10 percent over comparable maturity U.S. Treasury bonds (about 18 percent at the beginning of 1990). Viewed by this more liberal definition, at least $75 billion in par value of distressed and defaulted securities are outstanding, comprising several hundred issuers and over 600 issues. The market value of these public defaulted and distressed securities is probably about $45 billion. If one would also add the private debt with public registration rights, the private bank debt, and the trade claims of defaulted and distressed companies, the relevant population for investor consideration increases substantially, perhaps by three to four times. Therefore, private defaulted claims add about another $75 billion, with an additional $175 billion in distressed debt bringing the total book value of defaulted and distressed securities and claims to about $300 billion. We estimate the market value of these securities and claims to be about $200 billion. A summary of these estimates is listed below.

Estimated Public and Private Debt Outstanding of Defaulted and Distressed Firms (as of January 31, 1990)

	Book Value ($ billions)	Market Value ($ millions)	Market/Book Ratio
Publicly traded:			
Defaulted debt	$ 26.0	$ 11.5	0.44
Distressed debt	50.0	33.0	0.66
Privately placed:			
Defaulted debt	75.0	45.0	0.60
Distressed debt	150.0	112.5	0.75
Total public and private	$301.0	$202.0	0.67

The total public and private debt in book value terms swelled to about $320 billion as of June 1990.

Following a descriptive and analytical treatment of investors and current developments, we will analyze the performance attributes of investing in distressed securities. While we include equities, our focus will be on the performance of debt securities. We will also utilize information derived from a survey sent out to about 80 known (or thought to be) investors in distressed securities. Our response rate was excellent, with 56 responses, giving us insights into the size and age of these entities, their investment focus, required and minimum rates of return criteria, and their outlook for opportunities in this area.

SUPPLY OF DISTRESSED SECURITIES

Over the last 20 years, the American bankrupt company profile has been transformed from the small undercapitalized distressed firm situation to a system that increasingly involves large and, in some cases, huge enterprises having complex asset and liability structures. In a sense, 1970 was a watershed year, with Penn Central, Dolly Madison, and a few other relatively large companies filing for bankruptcy protection. There have been about 100 enterprises with over $120 million in liabilities that have filed for bankruptcy in the last 20 years (see Exhibit 1). In the 1970s, we experienced increasing numbers of sizable business failures in retailing, REITs, and railroads. In the early 1980s, the severe inflationary recession caused a consistently increasing number of failures, including manufacturers, airlines, farmers, and service firms of all types, followed by the energy industry collapse. The business failure rate rose from a low of 24 per 10,000 firms followed by Dun & Bradstreet in 1978 to 110 per 10,000 firms (1.1 percent) in 1983 and reached a high of 120 in 1986 (Exhibits 2 and 3). One would have to go back to 1932 for a year when the failure rate exceeded 100 per 10,000. Clearly, the economy, while enjoying an unprecedented consecutive number of positive GNP growth years over the last eight years, has also seen an increasing vulnerability to distress of firms in all size categories. This is due to severe chronic problems in a number of industries, the oil industry collapse, increasing global competition, a record number of business startups, deregulation, and the leverage excesses

EXHIBIT 1
Largest U.S. Bankruptcies (as of February 1990)

Company	Liabilities ($ millions)	Bankruptcy Date	Company	Liabilities ($ millions)	Bankruptcy Date
TEXACO, INC. (incl. capital subs.)	$21,603	Apr–87	AMAREX	$348	Dec–82
CAMPEAU CORP. (ALLIED & FEDERATED)	9,947	Jan–90	FOOD FAIR CORP.	347	Oct–78
LOMAS FINANCIAL CORP.	6,127	Sep–89	BUTTES OIL & GAS	337	Nov–85
LTV CORP. (incl. LTV INT'L NV)	4,700	Jul–86	GREAT AMERICAN MORTGAGE & TRUST	326	Mar–77
PENN CENTRAL TRANSPORTATION CO.	3,300	Jun–70	MCLOUTH STEEL	323	Dec–81
EASTERN AIR LINES	3,196	Mar–89	WORLD OF WONDER	312	Dec–87
DREXEL BURNHAM LAMBERT	3,000	Feb–90	MGF OIL	304	Dec–84
WICKES	2,000	Apr–82	U.S. FINANCIAL SERVICES	300	Jul–73
GLOBAL MARINE, INC.	1,800	Jan–86	HUNT INTERNATIONAL	295	Apr–85
ITEL	1,700	Jan–81	RADICE	291	Feb–88
PUBLIC SERVICE, NEW HAMPSHIRE	1,700	Jan–88	CHASE MANHATTAN MORT. & REALTY TR.	290	Feb–79
BALDWIN-UNITED	1,600	Sep–83	DAYLIN, INC.	250	Feb–75
INTEGRATED RESOURCES	1,600	Feb–90	GUARDIAN MORTGAGE INVESTORS	247	Mar–78
REVCO CORP.	1,500	Jul–88	WATERMAN STEAMSHIP CORP.	242	Dec–83
PLACID OIL	1,488	Apr–85	REVERE COPPER & BRASS	237	Oct–92
McLEAN INDUSTRIES	1,270	Nov–86	AIR FLORIDA SYSTEM	221	Jul–84
HILLSBOROUGH HOLDINGS (JIM WALTER)	1,204	Dec–89	CHICAGO, ROCK ISLAND & PACIFIC	221	Mar–75
BELL NATIONAL	1,203	Aug–85	HELLENIC LINES, LTD.	216	Dec–83
GHR ENERGY CORP.	1,200	Jan–83	WILSON FOODS	213	Apr–83
L. J. HOOKER	1,200	Aug–89	LION CAPITAL GROUP	212	Apr–84
MANVILLE CORP.	1,116	Aug–82	KDT INDUSTRIES	203	Aug–82
BRANIFF AIRLINES (1)	1,100	May–82	EQUITY FUNDING CORP. OF AMERICA	200	Apr–73
CONTINENTAL AIRLINES	1,100	Sep–83	DE LAURENTIS ENTERTAINMENT	198	Aug–88

Company	Amount	Date	Company	Amount	Date
W. T. GRANT	1,000	Oct-75	TRIAD AMERICA CORPORATION	198	Jan-87
CHARTER CO.	976	Apr-85	INTERESTATE STORES, INC.	190	May-74
ALLEGHENY INTERNATIONAL	845	Feb-88	FIDELITY MORTGAGE INVESTORS	187	Jan-75
NORTH AMERICAN CAR CORP.	841	Dec-84	HRT INDUSTRIES	183	Nov-82
SEATRAIN LINES	785	Feb-81	TECHNICAL EQUITIES CORP.	180	Feb-85
A. H. ROBINS	775	Aug-85	BRANIFF AIRLINES (2)	178	Sep-89
PENROD DRILLING	764	Apr-85	TEREX CORP.	176	Mar-83
STORAGE TECHNOLOGIES	695	Oct-84	LIONEL CORP.	175	Feb-82
CORAL PETROLEUM	682	May-83	OMEGA, ALPHA CORP.	175	Sep-74
MUCORP ENERGY	615	Jul-82	MARION CORP.	175	Mar-83
CONTINENTAL MORTGAGE INVESTORS	607	Mar-76	MICHIGAN GENERAL	170	Apr-87
EVANS	600	Mar-85	DART DRUG STORES	169	Aug-89
ALLIS CHALMERS	570	Jun-87	U.N.R. INDUSTRIES	165	Jul-82
UNITED MERCHANTS & MANUFACTURING	552	Jul-77	THATCHER GLASS	165	Dec-84
COLECO CORP.	536	Jul-88	TOWNER PETROLEUM	163	Sep-84
MAXICARE HEALTH PLANS	535	Mar-89	OTASCO, INC.	163	Nov-88
AM INTERNATIONAL	510	Apr-82	DRECO ENERGY	161	Jun-82
OPM LEASING	505	Mar-81	READING RAILROAD	158	Nov-71
BEVILL BRESLER SCHULLMAN	498	Apr-85	ANGLO ENERGY	155	Nov-83
SMITH INTERNATIONAL, INC.	484	Mar-86	BOSTON & MAINE RAILROAD	148	Dec-75
SAXON INDUSTRIES	461	Apr-82	WESTGATE-CALIFORNIA	144	Feb-74
COMMONWEALTH OIL REFINING CO.	421	Mar-78	PIZZA TIME THEATRE	143	Mar-84
W. JUDD KASSUBA	420	Dec-73	COOK UNITED, INC.	143	Oct-84
ERIE LACKAWANNA RAILROAD	404	Jun-72	COLWELL MORTGAGE & TRUST	142	Feb-78
WHITE MOTOR CORP.	399	Sep-80	PHOENIX STEEL CORP.	137	Aug-83
SAMBO'S RESTAURANTS	370	Jun-81	PACIFIC FAR EAST LINES	132	Jan-78
INVESTORS FUNDING CORP.	370	Oct-74	ALLIED SUPERMARKETS	124	Jun-77
TODD SHIPYARDS	350	Aug-87	PENN-DIXIE INDUSTRIES	122	Apr-80

EXHIBIT 2
Failure Trends

Year	Number of Failures	Total Failure Liabilities	Failure Rate per 10,000 Listed Concerns	Average Liability per Failure	Year	Number of Failures	Total Failure Liabilities	Failure Rate per 10,000 Listed Concerns	Average Liability per Failure
1927	23,146	$520,105,000	106	$22,471	1958	14,964	$ 728,258,000	56	$ 48,667
1928	23,842	489,559,000	109	20,534	1959	14,053	692,808,000	52	49,300
1929	22,909	483,252,000	104	21,094	1960	15,445	938,630,000	57	60,772
1930	26,355	668,282,000	122	25,357	1961	17,075	1,090,123,000	64	63,843
1931	28,285	736,310,000	133	26,032	1962	15,782	1,213,601,000	61	76,898
1932	31,822	928,313,000	154	29,172	1963	14,374	1,352,593,000	56	94,100
1933	19,859	457,520,000	100	23,038	1964	13,501	1,329,223,000	53	98,454
1934	12,091	333,959,000	61	27,621	1965	13,514	1,321,666,000	53	97,800
1935	12,244	310,580,000	62	25,366	1966	13,061	1,385,659,000	52	106,091
1936	9,607	203,173,000	48	21,148	1967	12,364	1,265,227,000	49	102,332
1937	9,490	183,253,000	46	19,310	1968	9,636	940,996,000	39	97,654
1938	12,836	246,505,000	61	19,204	1969	9,154	1,142,113,000	37	124,767
1939	14,768	182,520,000	70	12,359	1970	10,748	1,887,754,000	44	175,638
1940	13,619	166,684,000	63	12,239	1971	10,326	1,916,929,000	42	185,641
1941	11,848	136,104,000	55	11,488	1972	9,566	2,000,244,000	38	209,099
1942	9,405	100,763,000	45	10,713	1973	9,345	2,298,606,000	36	245,972
1943	3,221	45,339,000	16	14,076	1974	9,915	3,053,137,000	38	307,931
1944	1,222	31,660,000	7	25,908	1975	11,432	4,380,170,000	43	383,150
1945	809	30,225,000	4	37,361	1976	9,628	3,011,271,000	35	312,762
1946	1,129	67,349,000	5	59,654	1977	7,919	3,095,317,000	28	390,872
1947	3,474	204,612,000	14	58,898	1978	6,619	2,656,006,000	24	401,270
1948	5,250	234,620,000	20	44,690	1979	7,564	2,667,362,000	28	352,639
1949	9,246	308,109,000	34	33,323	1980	11,742	4,635,080,000	42	394,744
1950	9,162	248,283,000	34	27,099	1981	16,794	6,955,180,000	61	414,147
1951	8,058	259,547,000	31	32,210	1982	24,908	15,610,792,000	88	626,738
1952	7,611	283,314,000	29	37,224	1983	31,334	16,072,860,000	110	512,953
1953	8,862	394,153,000	33	44,477	1984	52,078	29,268,646,871	107	562,016
1954	11,086	462,628,000	42	41,731	1985	57,253	36,937,369,478	115	645,160
1955	10,969	449,380,000	42	40,968	1986	61,616	44,723,991,601	120	725,850
1956	12,686	562,697,000	48	44,356	1987	61,111	34,723,831,429	102	568,209
1957	13,739	615,293,000	52	44,784	1988p	57,098	36,012,765,369	98	630,719

Due to statistical revision, data prior to 1984 are not directly comparable with the new series.
p = preliminary.

EXHIBIT 3
Number of Failures

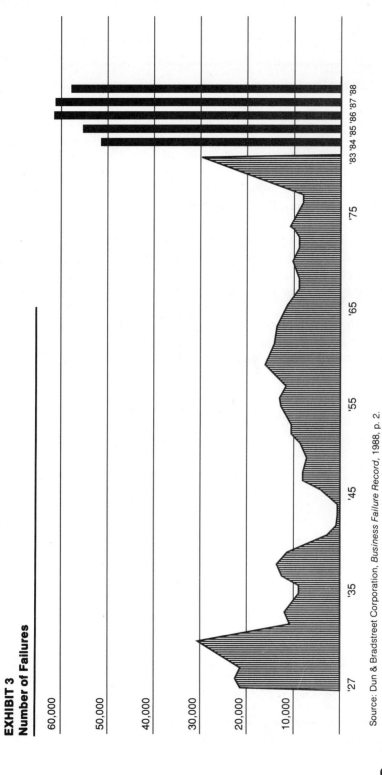

Source: Dun & Bradstreet Corporation, *Business Failure Record*, 1988, p. 2.

involving numerous corporate liability restructurings in the last few years.

The market for investing in distressed debt and equity securities has been growing dramatically, with an outstanding market value of defaulted securities of about $13 billion as of Februrary 1990 (Exhibit 4). The par value of the debt was about $26 billion. This compares with $4 billion in market value in 1984. The supply of defaulted debt has been swelled by over $35 billion par value of publicly traded straight debt in the last 5 years—$7.9 billion in 1989 alone and over $11.0 billion in the first 9 months of 1990. Several billion dollars of defaulted convertible debt and equities in the last few years add to the total.

And the near-term outlook bodes perhaps for even greater

EXHIBIT 4
Market Value of Securities Companies in Chapter 11 Reorganization and in Default* (as of January 31, 1990)

Exchanges	Value
AMEX:	
Bonds (19)†	$ 4,110,972,900
Convertible bonds (9)	356,894,550
Common stock (2)	33,634,500
Preferred stock (1)	678,100,875
Total (31)	5,179,602,825
NASDAQ:	
Bonds (101)	2,848,277,425
Convertible bonds (19)	85,177,200
Total (120)	2,933,454,625
NYSE:	
Bonds (36)	3,885,197,588
Convertible bonds (13)	162,507,350
Common stock (11)	389,390,406
Preferred stock (6)	279,115,688
Total (66)	4,716,211,032
Total all exchanges (217)	$12,829,268,482

* Includes coupon bonds trading flat.
† Number of companies is in parentheses.

Compilation: E. Altman and D. Chin, New York University, Stern School of Business.

"growth." While the par value of such issues has increased substantially, a noticeable reduction in recovery rates on the sale of debt just after default and the deteriorating prices on some issues has tempered the market value growth, especially among the senior subordinated and subordinated debt issues. We estimate that the average recovery rate on senior, senior subordinated, and subordinated public debt was 55 percent, 32 percent, and 32 percent, respectively, in the period 1985–89 but only about 23 percent for senior subordinated and subordinated debt in 1989 (Exhibit 5). The decline of recoveries on recent defaults of junior debt is probably due to the increased layers of debt and the general increase in the amount of indebtedness relative to asset values.

For several decades there has been curiosity and some interest for investors in bankrupt securities. Media stories of huge gains earned on bankrupt railroad and REIT securities and also on some equities (e.g., Toys-Я-Us) has fueled this attention. In addition to the interest of late caused by the sizeable increase in the breadth of this market, attention is being given by a relatively small number of professionals to deeply discounted but not defaulted debt issues and, even more intriguing, to the bank and trade debt claims of defaulted companies. Often, these issues have significant intrinsic value and potential profits.

To estimate the ratio of private to public debt, we examined the capital structures of 103 bankrupt firms. We found that this ratio was just under 4 to 1 for the entire sample and a bit over 3 to 1 for those firms (68) that had public debt outstanding. Among the large LBO defaults of late and for those expected to fail in the next few years, the ratio of bank debt to public debt is about 1.5 to 1.0, indicating that these defaults, caused mainly by leverage excesses, relied on public debt to a greater extent than did the more traditional business failure of the 1970s and of the early to mid-1980s. With several tranches of senior and subordinated debt, the recovery rates after default on the most junior issues have declined.

DISTRESSED SECURITY INVESTOR PROFILE

With the big increase in the supply of distressed securities and their likely continued growth, new investors and capital have been attracted. Our survey results indicate that at least $5 billion is under

EXHIBIT 5
Recovery Rates* on Defaulted Debt by Seniority (1985–1989)

Year	Secured		Senior		Senior Subordinated		Subordinated	
1989	$82.69	(9)†	$53.70	(16)	$21.53	(18)	$24.56	(29)
1988	67.96	(13)	41.59	(20)	29.33	(11)	36.42	(18)
1987	12.00	(1)	70.52‡	(29)	51.22	(9)	40.54	(7)
1986	48.32	(7)	40.84	(7)	31.53	(8)	30.95	(33)
1985	74.25	(2)	34.81	(2)	36.18	(7)	41.45	(13)
Arithmetic average	66.451	(32)	55.292‡	(74)	31.614	(53)	32.118	(100)

* Price per $100 of par value at end of default month.
† Number of issues is in parentheses.
‡ Without Texaco, 1987 recovery = $29.77.
  Arithmetic average senior recovery = $43.11.

Compilation: E. Altman and D. Chin, New York University, Stern School of Business.

active management by investment firms dedicated to the distressed securities field. Assorted other investors trade these securities, many times involuntarily. Of the responding companies that indicated their dollar commitment to distressed securities investing, the majority had between $20–$100 million under management. Many of these institutions are specialized groups of larger money management firms. While as many as 12 invested less than $20 million and 13 are investing $100–$300 million, just 2 with over $300 million are dedicated to this area. In 1990, two additional investment funds were capitalized at over $750 million each. A full list of investors will be available in the complete report on this market to be published in early 1991.

The investors represent numerous types of organizations, including private partnerships (the most common type), open-end mutual funds, closed-end funds, special groups within larger fund operations, broker-dealer pools of funds, departments of commercial and investment banks, arbitrageurs, and other firms looking to take over distressed companies at bargain prices. In addition, funds are always available from other investment vehicles that can be shifted to distressed securities purchases when opportunities present themselves. For instance, some LBO funds now seek other vehicles as the highly leveraged restructuring movement is reduced in scope and relegated to smaller, privately financed deals.

The overwhelming majority of these investors specialize in debt securities, with most investing between 85–100 percent of their assets in debt. In many cases, however, the initial debt purchase will evolve into an equity interest in a distressed exchange issue of bankruptcy reorganization. In addition, over 80 percent (46 of 56) of the respondents indicated that they analyze and either invest in or are considering investing in the private debt of distressed companies.

Most investors have become somewhat more active, as well as continuing to operate under the traditional passive investment strategy, indicating that they are more inclined now to seek either control of the restructuring process and even the company itself, as well as having an influence on the choice of management and setting the terms of the reorganization or the restructuring plan. This movement toward active, and even proactive, investing is one of the emerging trends in investments in general, and, in particular, in the distressed securities field. A prepackaged Chapter 11 (e.g., Resorts

International) is an example of this, as well as the creditor-motivated plan of Coleco Industries.

An increasing number of firms are relative newcomers to the field. Of 56 respondents, 8 were in business for less than one year and 19 for less than two years. A majority of portfolio managers of these new firms, however, had considerable experience in more established institutions before striking out with new institutions. While the number of new entities and inexperienced portfolio managers is troubling to certain established investors, experienced firms that have been in business for more than 5 years number an impressive 22, with 7 in business for over 20 years.

Just about anyone who has analyzed the distressed security market concludes this is not a market for amateurs and that, to attract new investment dollars, it is necessary to earn extraordinary returns. The risky nature of the business, the relatively poor liquidity of the issues, and the costly skills required lead to high minimum required rates of return as hurdle rates. We queried our distressed investors sample about their minimum and target rates of return. As expected, the target rates of return were, on average, higher than the minimum, although many respondents gave identical answers to both questions. The most common response was a target return of 30 percent and a minimum return of 20–25 percent. Indeed, 17 of 50 (about one third) respondents had a 30 percent target return, with the other two thirds split fairly evenly below and above 30 percent. About two thirds of the investors required a minimum rate of return of either 20 percent or 25 percent, with most of the remainder seeking higher returns.

RETURNS ON DISTRESSED SECURITIES INVESTMENT STRATEGIES

Along with the impressive increase in the market's size and diversity, perhaps the major interest in distressed public and private securities has developed from the reports of extremely attractive returns earned by a small number of astute investors. Despite the recent increase in new investors and capital, the formula for successful investing will continue to be a difficult set of fundamental valuation and technical legal/economic skills complemented by a patient and disciplined approach to asset management. These fundamentals are also important in the less-efficient private bank and trade debt markets, although negotiating skills will also be rewarded.

Our examination of past studies and new tests shows that extraordinary gains over relevant alternative investment opportunities can be earned with a disciplined and careful credit and asset valuation strategy, concentrating on firms where the probability of successful reorganization or restructuring is high.

Several studies on bankrupt equity securities have shown that returns from firms achieving a successful reorganization were exceptionally high, but that for the entire sample the overall return was about equal to relevant equity opportunity costs. Indeed, in many cases, the equity is essentially wiped out, with the old creditors becoming the new equity holders. The sample variability of these equity returns was extremely high.

Results from the few defaulted debt studies available show that excess returns (total returns adjusted for opportunity returns in other risky debt markets) start to be negative from about 18 months prior to default, become very steeply negative 5 months before, and tend to bottom out about 6 months after the default date. The excess returns then start to rise from month 6 to month 10, fall again from month 10 to 16, and then rise consistently to month 24 after default (see Exhibit 6). A strategy to buy just after default results in a positive excess return of about 7.5 percent over the two-year postdefault period, but the excess return was about 16 percent from month 6 to 24. Distressed exchange debt issues also show good recoveries but only after the 17th month after the exchange.

Our new tests concentrate on distressed, not defaulted, debt, whereby distressed is defined as a security with a current yield of 10 percent above comparable U.S. Treasury bonds. In all, 310 issues qualified over an 11-year sample period, 1978–89. Incredibly, over one half of these distressed securities eventually defaulted. The key to successful investing is either to avoid as many defaults as possible or to invest in those that do default but are successfully reorganized. Indeed, a "blind" naive strategy of investing in all distressed bonds yields very poor returns, but avoiding the minefields brings substantial rewards.

Exhibit 7 shows the results of some of our tests indicating

EXHIBIT 6
Cumulative Excess Returns on Defaults Only, 1977–1988

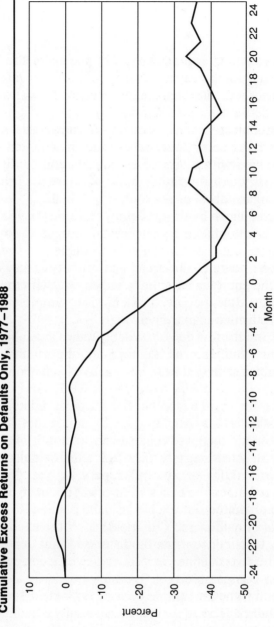

Source: G. Hradsky and R. Long, "High Yield Default Losses and the Return Performance of Bankrupt Debt," *Financial Analysts Journal*, July–August 1989, p. 46.

absolute and excess (residual) returns on the naive strategy (panel A). Panel B shows the exceptionally high returns possible (29.7 percent, 67.6 percent, and 90.3 percent for one, two, and three-year periods) if all defaults are avoided. Panels C and D show the returns when using an objective credit evaluation scoring system to eliminate the most risky securities. We use the Zeta® credit evaluation system. Note the impressive results, revealing very positive absolute returns but, due to the small sample size, not always statistically significant residual returns.

These tests show that a prudent, disciplined credit approach can be successfully utilized in the distressed security arena. Techniques like Zeta can be combined with other security selection approaches, including in-depth financial and legal analysis, to increase the relevant set of securities. Our tests do not, however, indicate returns after a reorganization takes place from a typical package of cash, debt, and new equity allocated to the old debt holder. Also, we utilize price debt reported by the rating services in their bond publications. Due to poor liquidity in many of these issues, actual prices may differ.

A DEFAULTED DEBT INDEX

We also constructed an index of defaulted debt securities on a market weighted (DDW) and an arithmetic unweighted (DDU) basis. My first attempt at this index (April 1990) comprised an initial sample of 23 defaulted debt issues in January 1986. Since the 1986 sample was so small, we have eliminated that year in our current compilation. Our index results cover the period January 1987 to July 1990. The two defaulted debt indexes plus return indexes on two other risky asset portfolios, the S&P 500 common stock index and the Merrill Lynch master composite high yield debt index, are shown in Exhibit 8. The annual returns as well as average number of securities in the index are shown in Exhibit 9. The number of issues in the index increased to 128 in July 1990.

The individual year returns in Exhibit 9 show two exceptional years (1987 and 1988) and one relatively poor year of performance (1989). Indeed, the annual rate of return on the market weighted index was as high as 37.9% in 1987 and 26.5% in 1988 and as low as

EXHIBIT 7
Performance Results for Various Strategies of Investing in Distressed Debt Securities (1978–1989)

A. Invest in All High-Yield Spread Issues

	Gross Return (%)/Months after Distress						Residual Return (%)/Months after Distress					
	6	12	18	24	30	36	6	12	18	24	30	36
Return	(7.2)	2.0	9.2	22.7	29.6	35.2	(14.1)	(15.2)	(16.4)	(9.7)	(12.5)	(18.1)
No. of issues	310	251	199	160	114	83	310	251	199	160	114	83
Significant (0.05)*							Yes	Yes	Yes	No	Yes	Yes

B. Invest in All Nondefaulting High-Yield Spread Issues

	Gross Return (%)/Months after Distress						Residual Return (%)/Months after Distress					
	6	12	18	24	30	36	6	12	18	24	30	36
Return	7.1	29.7	45.4	67.6	80.2	90.3	0.4	10.5	14.8	30.1	28.6	26.8
No. of issues	132	93	76	67	49	39	132	93	76	67	49	39
Significant (0.05)*							No	Yes	Yes	Yes	Yes	Yes

C. Invest in Positive Zeta Distressed High-Yield Issues

	Gross Return (%)/Months after Distress						Residual Return (%)/Months after Distress					
	6	12	18	24	30	36	6	12	18	24	30	36
Return	15.4	23.6	45.7	43.2	68.1	79.1	3.1	1.1	15.1	8.1	22.1	22.7
No. of issues	10	9	9	9	8	8	10	9	9	9	8	8
Significant (0.05)*							No	No	No	No	No	No

D. Invest in Zeta > −1 Distressed High-Yield Issues

	Gross Return (%)/Months after Distress						Residual Return (%)/Months after Distress					
	6	12	18	24	30	36	6	12	18	24	30	36
Return	17.6	24.2	37.3	44.9	68.4	72.9	5.4	1.0	7.9	9.8	20.7	23.8
No. of issues	31	29	26	24	17	16	31	29	26	24	17	16
Significant (0.05)*							No	No	No	No	Yes	No

* $t = \dfrac{\bar{X}}{\sigma/\sqrt{N}}$, at 0.05 level, approximately 2

Compilation: E. Altman and T. Ng, New York University, Stern School of Business.

EXHIBIT 8
Defaulted Debt Indexes* Performance versus High Yield[†] and S&P Stock Indexes (1987–1990)

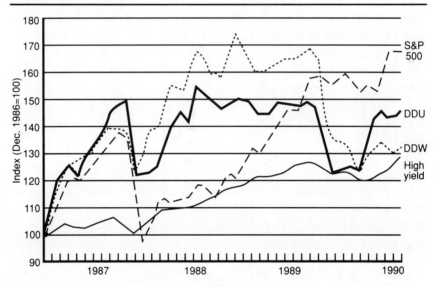

* Defaulted debt weighted index (DDW); Defaulted debt unweighted index (DDU)
† Merrill Lynch high yield composite index

EXHIBIT 9
Returns on Defaulted Debt Securities Indices (1987–1990)

Period	Average Number of Securities	Annual Return (market weighted average)	Annual Return (arithmetic unweighted average)	S&P 500 Stock Index	Merrill Lynch High Yield Index
1987	61	37.9%	24.0%	5.3%	4.7%
1988	89	26.5	20.7	16.6	13.5
1989	106	−23.0	−16.9	31.7	4.2
1990 (7 months)*	126	−1.3	19.1	3.4	4.3
1987–1990 Average (annual)					
Arithmetic	96	10.0%	12.0%	14.2%	6.7%

* Assumes 1990 total return is same as 7 month return.

Compilation by E. Altman and T. Genoyer, New York University.

−23.0% in 1989. The unweighted index returns were between +24.9% and −16.9%. The average annual return over the four-year period was 10.0% (weighted) and 12% (unweighted)—assuming 1990 returns so far are for the entire year. The defaulted debt indexes perform in a similar manner to the S&P 500 index with the latter recording a slightly higher average annual return of 14.2% for the four-year period. The high yield index had the lowest total return with an average annual return of 6.7%.

MARKET VALUE WEIGHTING AND RETURN BIAS

The market value indexes are based on the amount outstanding for each issue multiplied by its price at the start of each month. The index in my earlier report (April 1990) was calculated on weights based on prices at the end of the month. We have now determined that end-of-month weightings inflate the returns in each month. It is interesting how the statistical design of an index can have such a profound effect. For example, the previously reported annual rates of return for 1987 through 1989 were 53.0%, 44.5%, and 2.4%, respectively, versus those listed in Exhibit 9. Note that in every year the earlier reported returns are substantially higher. Clearly, the start-of-month weighting is the conventional methodology.

DIVERSIFICATION BENEFITS: CORRELATION WITH OTHER SECURITIES

One of the less obvious reasons for including distressed and defaulted debt issues in a larger portfolio of securities is the potential for adding a positive return asset class which also has relatively low correlations with other assets in the portfolio. The investor could then diversify across asset classes to reduce overall return variability.

An aspect of distressed security investing that has been relatively ignored is the relationship that it has within a larger portfolio of many different asset classes. If distressed security returns are relatively uncorrelated with other assets, investing in this area might very well afford attractive diversification attributes. And, we would expect that the firm unique risk of these securities is quite important in explaining their movement over time.

Our empirical results support the concept that somewhat attractive diversification benefits can accrue to the manager who invests in defaulted debt securities as well as other seemingly similar asset classes, such as equities and high yield bonds. Over the period 1987 to 1990, based on monthly total returns, the distressed security weighted average index displayed a moderate correlation with the S&P 500 equity index (correlation coefficient of 0.50 and an R^2 of 0.25), a somewhat higher correlation (0.59) with the Value Line equity index (which includes smaller stocks), and a lower than expected correlation (0.56) with the Merrill Lynch high yield debt index. While an R^2 of 0.25 is somewhat significant, the residual importance in explaining defaulted debt bond returns is quite large. The correlations are listed in Exhibit 10.

One example of how these benefits might work is for a pension fund portfolio manager to invest assets with different managers specializing in relatively safe investments like government bonds, as well as with more risky asset classes like equities, junk bonds, and defaulted debt indexes. While not a natural hedge, distressed securities do appear to have the potential to add a positive element to the overall risk/return tradeoff of a portfolio diversified across asset classes.

EXHIBIT 10
Correlation Matrix between Defaulted Debt Security Returns and Various Equity and High Yield Bond Returns

	Monthly Return Observations, 1987–1990			
	Defaulted Debt	S&P 500 Equity	Value Line Equity	Merrill Lynch High Yield
Defaulted debt	1.00	0.50	0.59	0.56
S&P 500 equity	0.50	1.00	0.87	0.56
Value line equity	0.59	0.87	1.00	0.69
Merrill Lynch (HY)	0.56	0.56	0.69	1.00

MARKET IMPORTANCE AND OUTLOOK

The bankruptcy-reorganization system in the United States is a unique process, affording rehabilitative opportunities to distressed, but not unproductive, entities. The market for distressed firm securities reflects this process and, in a sense, monitors the system's performance. By providing continuous feedback on the distressed company's progress, it actually helps facilitate the allocation of new capital to the most promising uses. Investors, operating in their own best interest, are unwittingly contributing to this process.

The outlook for the future is somewhat mixed in the short run, because the supply of new opportunities will likely exceed the amount of new capital allocated to distressed issues. This supply/demand situation has already contributed to some softening in prices in the last 14 months. In addition, several distressed investors have the impression that the relative number of promising new reorganizations is small, with too much money chasing these situations. While this phenomenon may exist in the near term, this observer and the vast majority of our respondents expressed enthusiasm and optimism about future profit potential, especially in the longer run. In addition, the market for private bank and trade debt claims promises to provide excellent prospects. The key, as always, is to be able to select the successful reorganizations and undervalued securities.

GLOSSARY OF TERMS

business failure rate The number of business failures in the economy per 10,000 firms listed by Dun & Bradstreet, New York City.

Chapter 11 The part of the Bankruptcy Code that specifies conditions and procedures for the reorganization of bankrupt companies.

defaulted securities Those securities of firms that have not met the prescribed interest/principal payments to debt holders. Includes all firms operating under Chapter 11, as well as others in default but not in bankruptcy.

distressed securities Those debt securities whose bonds are selling at a significant yield premium over risk-free securities (e.g., 10 percentage points above the government bond rate).

defaults: rates and losses The rate or proportion of debt that has defaulted. Losses consider the default rate adjusted for recoveries (see below) and one nonpaid debt coupon payment.

prepackaged Chapter 11 Where all debt and equity claimants agree to a bankruptcy reorganization plan prior to the actual bankruptcy filing.

private bank debt The debt of distressed and defaulted companies owed to commercial banks and other financial institutions.

private trade claims Other private debt primarily owed to suppliers of the distressed or defaulted company.

recovery rates The market value of defaulted debt just after default, adjusted for the fact that a coupon payment is also lost (i.e., the amount that would be received if the bonds were sold at the end of the default month minus one half of the annual coupon amount, all divided by the par value of the bonds).

reorganization The process by which a firm attempts to restructure its assets, liabilities, and equity capital to emerge from Chapter 11 as a going concern.

Zeta® scores Credit evaluation scores derived from a statistical model developed and distributed by Zeta Services, Inc., of Hoboken, New Jersey.

BIBLIOGRAPHY

Altman, E. I. "Financial Ratios, Discriminant Analysis and the Prediction of Corporate Bankruptcy." *Journal of Finance* 23 (September 1968), pp. 589–609.

———. "Bankrupt Firms' Equity Securities as an Investment Alternative." *Financial Analysts Journal* 25 (July–August 1969a), pp. 129–33.

———. *Corporate Bankruptcy in America*. Lexington, Mass.: Heath Lexington Books, 1971.

———. *Corporate Financial Distress: A Complete Guide to Predicting, Avoiding and Dealing with Bankruptcy*. New York: John Wiley & Sons, 1983.

———. "Investment Performance of Bankrupt Debt and Equity Securities: Preliminary Results." Presented at Max L. Heine Symposium on Investing in Bankrupt Securities, New York University, Stern School of Business, April 1989.

Altman, E. I.; R. Haldeman; and P. Narayanan. "Zeta Analysis, a New Model to Identify Bankruptcy Risk of Corporations." *Journal of Banking and Finance,* June 1977, pp. 29–54.

Altman, E. I., and S. A. Nammacher. "The Default Rate Experience on High Yield Corporate Debt." *Financial Analysts Journal*, July–August 1985, pp. 25–41.

———. *Investing in Junk Bonds*. New York: John Wiley & Sons, 1987.

Blume, M., and D. Keim. "Risk and Return Characteristics of Low Grade Bonds, 1977–1987." *Financial Analysts Journal*, July–August 1987, and updates. R. White Center working paper, 1989.

Business Failure Record. New York: Dun & Bradstreet Corp., 1988.

Casey, C.; V. E. McGee; and C. P. Stickney. "Discriminating between Reorganized and Liquidated Firms in Bankruptcy." *Accounting Review*, April 1986, pp. 249–62.

Clark, T. A., and M. Weinstein. "The Behavior of the Common Stock of Bankrupt Firms." *The Journal of Finance* 38, no. 2 (May 1983), pp. 489–504.

First Boston. "1990–1992: The Worst Case Scenario for Defaults." *High Yield Research*, November 27, 1989.

Hradsky, G., and R. Long. "High Yield Default Losses and the Return Performance of Bankrupt Debt." *Financial Analysts Journal*, July–August 1989, pp. 38–49.

Moeller, S. "Chapter 11 Filings: Good News for Investors." *AAII Journal*, April 1986, pp. 9–12.

Morse, D., and W. Shaw. "Investing in Bankrupt Firms." *The Journal of Finance* 43, no. 5 (December 1988), pp. 1193–1206.

Ramaswami, M., and S. Moeller. *Investing in Financially Distressed Firms: A Guide to Pre- and Post-Bankruptcy Opportunities*. New York: Quorum Books, 1990.

Shearson Lehman Hutton. "Bottom Fishers' Guide 4 to Distressed Corporate Bonds." January 10, 1990.

Standard & Poor's. Bond Guides, 1978–1989.

Vanderhoof, I.; F. Albert; A. Tenenbein; and R. Verni. "The Risk of Asset Defaults: The Report of the Committee on Valuation and Related Areas." *Society of Actuaries*, December 1989.

White, M. "Bankruptcy Costs and the New Bankruptcy Code." *The Journal of Finance* 38, no. 2 (May 1983), pp. 477–88.

CHAPTER 25

LEGAL CONSIDERATIONS OF PURCHASING SECURITIES

Jeffrey Sabin, Esq.
Mark A. Neporent, Esq.
Carol A. Weiner, Esq.
Schulte Roth & Zabel

INTRODUCTION

The onslaught of Chapter 11 bankruptcy filings by large publicly owned companies in the last decade, coupled with the apparent demise of leveraged buyouts, junk bonds, and corporate takeovers, has had a significant impact on investors that either hold securities of a debtor company or are interested in purchasing claims against or equity interests in a debtor company. The rights of these investors vis-à-vis the debtor and other creditors of the debtor are governed by the Bankruptcy Code and the Bankruptcy Rules, and, recently, a number of these statutory provisions have been the subject of judicial and congressional debate. This chapter addresses the legal issues that arise in connection with the rights of equity security holders under the Bankruptcy Code, the regulation of trading in claims against a Chapter 11 debtor, and the interplay of the Bankruptcy Code with the securities laws in connection with the distribution of equity securities pursuant to a plan of reorganization.

WHAT CONSTITUTES A SECURITY IN A BANKRUPTCY CASE

The definition of the term *security* under Section 101(43) of the Bankruptcy Code is open-ended and includes most forms of equity interests commonly considered to be securities, such as stocks, bonds, debentures, notes, certificates of deposits, and investment contracts that are required to be registered under the provisions of the Securities Exchange Act of 1934 (the '34 Act).[1] The interests of a limited partner in a limited partnership are also included in the definition. Congress did not intend the definition in Section 101(43) to be exclusive, and the courts have applied the characterization of the term to new kinds of documents and instruments on a flexible basis.[2]

The Bankruptcy Code, however, expressly excludes certain forms of interests from the scope of the definition of a "security." These interests include certain types of commercial paper (i.e., currency, drafts, bills of exchange, and letters of credit), commodity futures contracts and options related thereto, and evidences of indebtedness for goods sold or services rendered.[3] The exclusion of claims for goods sold and services rendered has been the focus of substantial debate as more and more investors seek to trade claims in bankruptcy free of the regulations imposed by the '34 Act. The thrust of the debate centers on whether the filing of a bankruptcy petition transforms claims against a debtor into speculative interests, which so resemble securities that the trading of such claims should be subject to regulations similar to those under the '34 Act.

The '34 Act does not expressly define the term *security* to include trade claims or other evidences of indebtedness for goods sold or services rendered, although, unlike the Bankruptcy Code, the '34 Act does not expressly exclude such forms of debt from its definition.[4] The phrase "evidence of indebtedness" is included in the definition of securities under the Securities Act of 1933 (the '33 Act) but was deleted from the definition under the '34 Act. The United States Supreme Court has addressed this definitional discrepancy and has held that various types of indebtedness, such as bank certificates of deposit and co-op shares, do not qualify as securities.[5]

The Supreme Court has recently determined that certain types of privately held demand notes qualify as securities under the '34 Act and, therefore, are subject to federal and state antifraud regulations.[6] In *Reves* v. *Ernst & Young*,[7] holders of certain uncollateralized demand notes issued by the Farmer's Cooperative of Arkansas and Oklahoma brought an action against Ernst & Young, the debtor's auditors, alleging that it had violated the antifraud provisions of the '34 Act by intentionally failing to follow generally accepted accounting principles that would have made the co-op's insolvency apparent to the note purchasers. Ernst & Young claimed that the notes were not securities under the '34 Act and, therefore, that the securities antifraud provisions of the '34 Act and state law did not apply. The Court found in favor of the note purchasers.

The Supreme Court explained in the *Reves* case that Congress's purpose in enacting the securities laws was to regulate investments in whatever form they are made. Because notes are used in both investment and noninvestment settings (i.e., commercial paper), the Court found that only notes used in the investment setting are securities under the '34 Act. To determine whether notes may be characterized as securities under the '34 Act, the Court relied on a modified version of the Second Circuit's "family resemblance" test.[8] Under that test, the Court begins with the presumption that every note is a security, but then applies the following four criteria to determine whether the note bears a "family resemblance" to one of a judicially crafted list of instruments that fall outside of the definition of a "security":[9] (1) the motivations that would prompt a reasonable seller and buyer to enter into the note transaction (i.e., the seller's purpose is to facilitate the purchase and sale of a minor asset or consumer good versus the raising of capital for general operational use; (2) the plan of distribution of the note (i.e., whether the note is offered to a limited number of investors or is subject to common trading for speculation or investment); (3) the reasonable expectations of the investing public (i.e., whether the public views the instrument as an investment device); and (4) whether the existence of another regulatory scheme significantly reduces the risk of the investment.[10] The Court held that the debtor's notes were securities, because the debtor sold the notes to raise working capital and the purchasers bought them to earn a profit in the form of interest, the notes had been so offered to a broad segment of the public that there was common trading, and the advertisements for the sale of the notes suggested that the public would perceive them as investment instruments (i.e., the notes were marketed as an "Investment Program"), and no risk-reducing factor or regulatory scheme that would make the application of the '34 Act unnecessary was evident.

The earlier reluctance of courts to broaden the definition of the term *security* to include commercial instruments of indebtedness in securities law litigation led at least one commentator to suggest that courts would be unlikely to reach a contrary conclusion in the bankruptcy arena.[11] The Supreme Court's decision in the *Reves* case, however, suggests that courts may be more determined to extend the scope of the '34 Act to trading practices not presently regulated by including within the scope of the term *security* various privately held evidences of indebtedness. Although the *Reves* decision does not directly impact on the purchase and sale of trade claims, it suggests that the trading of claims in bankruptcy may be susceptible to regulation under the securities laws. In the absence of specific congressional or judicial guidance on this matter, bankruptcy courts have begun to treat claims as securities in certain circumstances and are crafting their own claims trading regulations.[12]

RIGHTS OF EQUITY SECURITY HOLDERS UNDER THE BANKRUPTCY CODE

Overview

Holders of corporate shares or limited partnership interests are defined as *equity security holders* under the Bankruptcy Code, and their rights against the Chapter 11 debtor are referred to as *interests*.[13] All classes of interests are typically junior to all classes of claims (e.g., secured lender's claims, subordinated debt, and unsecured trade claims) in a bankruptcy case. The general principle contained in Section 1129(b)(2) of the Bankruptcy Code known as the *absolute priority rule*[14] requires that, unless otherwise agreed to by the holders of claims or interests in a particular class, classes of claims must be paid in full, in order of priority, before any class of interests may receive any distribution under a plan of reorganization.[15] Consequently, holders of interests may not receive any distribution under a plan of reorganization until all holders of claims have received the full amount of their allowed claims or have agreed to less favorable treatment.[16] As a practical matter, claim holders often consent to a reduced distribution under a plan of reorganization, allowing equity security holders to receive some type of distribution to avoid the cost and delay of cramdown litigation.[17]

Equity security holders whose interests are "impaired" under a plan of reorganization may vote to accept or reject the plan. The Bankruptcy Code generally provides that an interest is impaired under a plan of reorganization unless (1) the legal, equitable, or contractual rights incident thereto remains unaltered; (2) the maturity of the interest is reinstated, any and all defaults are cured, and the holder of the interest is compensated for damages sustained; or (3) the holder of the interest receives the greater of (*a*) the fixed liquidation preference of the interest and (*b*) the fixed redemption price of the interest.[18] A class of interests is deemed to have accepted a plan of reorganization if such plan has been accepted by holders of at least two thirds in amount of the allowed interests of such class.[19]

If a class of interests rejects a proposed plan of reorganization, the plan proponent, nevertheless, may impose or "cram down" the terms of the plan on the dissenting class of interests as long as the plan satisfies the requirements of Section 1129(b)(2)(C) of the Bankruptcy Code. To cram down on a class of interests, the proposed plan of reorganization must provide that each holder of an interest will either (1) be paid property of a value, as of the plan's effective date, equal to the greatest of the interest's (*a*) fixed liquidation preference, (*b*) fixed redemption price, and (*c*) value of such interest; or (2) receive at least the same value it would receive in Chapter 7 (liquidation), and that no junior interest shall receive any property under the plan or retain any interest in the reorganized debtor. Equity security holders are the easiest and most likely classes to be crammed down, because, typically, the liquidation value of a Chapter 11 debtor is less than the outstanding amount of its claims, so even under the standards of Section 1129(b)(2)(C) equity holders are not entitled to anything in exchange for their interests.

Shareholders' Meetings

Despite the equity holders' low position on the distribution ladder, equity security holders can have a significant role in the reorganization process. The management of a debtor-in-possession[20] continues to serve as a fiduciary for the equity holders, though it must also serve as a fiduciary for the creditors of the debtor's estate.[21] Accordingly, management of a debtor-in-possession, thus, is accountable to both creditors and interest holders.[22] This means that management is still governed to some degree by the corporate dictates of the debtor's shareholders. In this regard, courts generally permit shareholders to hold meetings and even initiate proxy fights during the pendency of a Chapter 11 reorganization case. For example, the courts have expressly held that shareholders of a Chapter 11 debtor may compel shareholders' meetings and oust current management, unless the shareholders' actions constitute a "clear abuse" of their rights.

In the *Johns-Manville* case,[23] the Second Circuit explained that "clear abuse" of shareholders' rights includes bargaining in bad faith and employing tactics that seriously jeopardize the debtor's rehabilitation. The court stated that the simple exercise of shareholders' rights to enhance their position in a reorganization case did not amount to clear abuse, and that such rights are not eliminated in a bankruptcy case.[24] The court did state, however, that where the debtor is insolvent and shareholders lack any equity in the corporation, "denial of the right to call a meeting would likely be proper, because the shareholders would no longer be real parties in interest."[25] The solvency of a debtor is often subject to extensive litigation.[26] Consequently, the practical significance of the Second Circuit's caveat must be determined on a case-by-case basis.

Equity security holders in a Chapter 11 case may seek to use their corporate governance rights in at least two ways. First, shareholders may seek to change management to enhance the possibility of creating a solvent and viable reorganized debtor and maximize the value of their equity interests. Second, shareholders may also seek to affect certain significant events during a bankruptcy case, such as the sale of an important asset, or to influence the proposed distributions under any plan of reorganization by compelling current management to more adequately provide for shareholders' interests or risk losing their positions. Given the fact that a Chapter

11 debtor has an exclusive period of no less than 120 days after the filing of a bankruptcy petition to propose a plan, the ability to control the proponents of such plan is significant.[27] As long as the shareholders' exercise of their powers does not jeopardize the debtor's reorganization, as prohibited by the rule enunciated in *Johns-Manville*, then shareholders may have a powerful weapon in controlling the terms and the fate of a debtor's plan of reorganization.

Under bankruptcy law, a director cannot be a member of an official creditors' or equity holders' committee, because the committees represent only one constituency and the director must represent all constituencies.[28] Consequently, if a director cannot be a member of an equity holders' committee, the equity committee should not be able to elect a director.[29] Despite this apparent anomaly, shareholders may, and indeed have, rearranged the management of a Chapter 11 debtor and thereby exerted control over the debtor and its ability to propose a particular plan of reorganization.[30]

Equity Security Holders' Committees

In addition to permitting continued corporate governance by shareholders on a limited basis, the Bankruptcy Code also provides that a court may appoint an official committee of equity security holders to represent the classes of interests.[31] Often, the equity holders' committee plays a significant role in developing a plan and in negotiating distributions on behalf of its constituents. The standard for appointing a separate official committee for equity holders is discretionary. The party requesting appointment must demonstrate that the typical creditors' committee (i.e., the committee of trade and other unsecured creditors) cannot adequately protect the equity holders' interests.

Once a committee is appointed by the United States trustee or the court, it will take part in the plan negotiation process. The equity committee may, for example, hire an investment banker or other professional to value the debtor and to negotiate the capital structure of the reorganized debtor to maximize the value of any new equity being issued under the plan. The equity holders' committee may also have a role in the valuation of the debtor's assets, which must be done at or prior to confirmation of a plan. The issue of valuation often dictates the allowed amount of claims (and, thus, the configuration of the classes that will vote on the plan) and the confirmability of the plan itself. Accordingly, the interests of equity security holders may be considered by the plan proponent and other parties-in-interest to avoid a fight on valuation or to enable the plan proponent to propose a consensual plan, rather than incur the expense and suffer the delay of seeking to confirm a plan under the cramdown provisions of the Bankruptcy Code. Where a debtor is insolvent, some courts have held that equity security holders lack standing as parties-in-interest to participate in certain aspects of the case, such as filing motions for disallowance of claims, avoidance of liens, and confirmation of reorganization plans, because, arguably, the equity security holders would have no pecuniary interest in the outcome of such matters.[32] No court has expressly held that the equity security holders of an insolvent debtor lack standing to demand and participate in a valuation hearing.

Shareholder Claims Based on Purchase/Sale of Stock

Section 510(b) of the Bankruptcy Code provides that an equity security holder cannot improve its position on the distribution ladder by asserting a cause of action against the debtor for rescission of, or damages arising from, the purchase or sale of the securities of the debtor or its affiliate, and that such claims are subordinated to the original claim or interest that was purchased or sold (except that a claim based on the purchase or sale of common stock has the same distribution priority as the common stock itself).[33] Thus, if an equity security holder files an action for damages arising out of the purchase of the debtor's preferred stock, then the resulting claim for damages will be subordinated to the claims of all other holders of preferred stock. The same cause of action based on the purchase of the debtor's common stock will result in a claim that is of equal priority as all other interests held by holders of the debtor's common stock.

TRADING OF CLAIMS IN BANKRUPTCY

In recent years, as more and more large corporate entities find themselves seeking the protection of the Bankruptcy Code, the market for the purchase and sale of bankruptcy claims has flourished. The reason is simple. Unlike the securities laws, the Bankruptcy Code permits the assignment of secured and unsecured claims by the holders of such claims to third parties, with few express restrictions and regulations. The potential benefit to an investor who trades in bankruptcy claims is the same as if he or she traded any other form of security: the investor will profit if the plan of reorganization provides the investor with a distribution (either in cash or securities, or both) of a value greater than the price at which he or she purchased the claim. In addition, some investors, who seek to take control of troubled companies, have used trading in claims as a means of acquiring all or substantially all of the newly issued stock of a reorganized debtor.

An investor who trades in this new market faces the risk that the Chapter 11 debtor will not reorganize but will be forced to convert to a Chapter 7 liquidation, in which case distributions tend to be smaller. Also, the reorganization may take so long that the investor's profit may be absorbed by his or her lost opportunity costs. The purchaser of a claim inherits all of the disabilities as well as the rights of the seller of such claim, and investors who purchase bankruptcy claims risk having such claims disallowed or reduced by the bankruptcy court for a variety of reasons, as discussed below. Finally, in view of the Supreme Court's recent decision in the *Reves* case, in the absence of congressional intervention, bankruptcy courts may be willing to impose restrictions on trading in certain types of claims similar to the restrictions on public securities in the '34 Act. The following is a discussion of the mechanics involved and the issues inherent in trading claims against a Chapter 11 debtor.

The Process

The process of purchasing bankruptcy claims begins with the negotiation and execution of an assignment agreement between the investor and the claim holder. Within a reasonable time after execution of the assignment agreement, notice of the transfer must be given to the bankruptcy court and the transfer must be approved pursuant to Bankruptcy Rule 3001(e) before the purchaser will be deemed substituted and recognized as the claim holder by the court. If the transfer is approved, the purchaser will succeed to all of the rights (i.e., the voting and distribution rights) of the original claim holder and will be subject to the same attacks on the transferred claim as would the original claim holder.

The Assignment Agreement

The assignment agreement can be fashioned to protect the claim purchaser from the various risks of the claim transfer, such as disapproval by the court of the transfer itself, disallowance or reduction of the transferred claim, or attack on the right of the purchaser to vote the claim due to insider trading or to other forms of bad faith conduct. As discussed later in the section on Bankruptcy Court Approval, courts have analogized trading in claims to trading in public securities. Consequently, some courts are becoming increasingly concerned with the potential "evils" of trading in claims and are no longer merely rubber-stamping their approval of claims transfers. Without court approval, an investor is prohibited from directly participating in the debtor's reorganization process or from receiving a distribution on the claim, because, despite the value of the assignment agreement, he or she is not deemed to be the record holder of the claim. Even if the transfer is approved under Bankruptcy Rule 3001(e), creditors objecting to the transfer may later attack it by contending that the purchaser's reason for or conduct in purchasing the claim amounted to bad faith and that the purchaser's vote on any plan should be disallowed pursuant to Section 1126(e) of the Bankruptcy Code,[34] or that the claims are subject to disallowance or reduction by attacks based on fraudulent transfers, preferential transfers, equitable subordination, or simple state law defenses to the indebtness evidenced by the claim.[35]

One way of protecting against the risks of disallowance or reduction of a purchased claim is to purchase only those claims in a bankruptcy case that have been allowed by the court. Of course, this limits the pool of claims from which to choose; but it also provides protection against the risk of having the claim subsequently reduced or disallowed.[36] Another means of protecting a purchase of a claim is for the investor to obtain a thorough set of representations and warranties in the assignment agreement, coupled with an indemnity from the seller covering any loss due to the reduction, disallowance, or subordination of the claim.

A more innovative mechanism for protecting the investor's interests is the use of a repurchase requirement or "put option." The put option was recently used in the purchase of a $75 million allowed unsecured claim in the *Wheeling-Pittsburgh Steel Corp.* bankruptcy case, where the claim was subject to a security interest held by the debtor and was conceivably subject to reduction by an offset if circumstances arose that enabled the debtor to foreclose on its security interest. The put option gave the claim purchaser the right to require the original claim holder/seller to repurchase any portion of the claim that was offset by the debtor. Of course, the selling creditor will typically seek to avoid including any representations or a put option in the transaction, but the triggering events and duration of such an option can be negotiated to protect the purchaser without unreasonably burdening the seller. These points are often the focus of intense and difficult negotiations between buyer and seller and are often resolved by adjustments in the discounted price of the claim.

A purchaser may also want to include an agency mechanism in the transaction to safeguard against two possible occurrences: (1) if a plan of reorganization is filed and voting is required prior to the bankruptcy court's entry of an order approving (or disapproving) the claim transfer and (2) if the bankruptcy court disapproves the claim transfer but the purchaser desires to be the beneficial holder of the claim. There is nothing in the Bankruptcy Code expressly prohibiting an agency relationship. The Bankruptcy Rules are silent about the effect of a bankruptcy court's denial of a motion to approve an assignment of a claim that is otherwise valid under state law. A bankruptcy court's refusal to approve a claim transfer under Bankruptcy Rule 3001(e) should not invalidate the assignment and render the agency relationship unenforceable. Such refusal should merely serve to maintain the ministerial status quo of the bankruptcy case. An assignment that is valid under state law, therefore, should be enforceable, despite a bankruptcy court's refusal to approve the claim transfer under Bankruptcy Rule 3001(e).[37] Accordingly, the assignment agreement should provide that, in either of the aforementioned events, the seller will act as the purchaser's agent, vote the claim only in accordance with the purchaser's instructions, and deliver to the purchaser any distributions made on such claim under any reorganization plan.

Bankruptcy Court Approval
The only Title 11-related provision that directly regulates claims transfers is Bankruptcy Rule 3001(e), which provides:

> (e) *Transferred Claim.*
> (1) *Unconditional Transfer before Proof Filed.* If a claim *other*

than one based on a bond or debenture has been unconditionally transferred before proof of the claim has been filed, the proof of claim may be filed only by the transferee. If the claim has been transferred after the filing of the petition, the proof of claim shall be supported by (A) a statement of the transferor acknowledging the transfer and stating the consideration therefor or (B) a statement of the transferee setting forth the consideration for the transfer and why the transferee is unable to obtain the statements from transferor.

(2) *Unconditional Transfer after Proof File.* If a claim other than one based on a bond or debenture has been unconditionally transferred after the proof of claim has been filed, evidence of the terms of the transfer shall be filed by the transferee. The clerk shall immediately notify the original claimant by mail of the filing of the evidence of transfer and that objection thereto, if any, must be filed with the clerk within 20 days of the mailing of the notice or within any additional time allowed by the court. If the court finds, after a hearing on notice, that the claim has been unconditionally transferred, it shall enter an order substituting the transferee for the original claimant, otherwise the court shall enter such order as may be appropriate.[38] [Emphasis added.]

The rule does not apply to bonds or debentures.

For claims that are transferred before a proof of claim is filed, all that is technically required is a statement of the transfer of the claim and disclosure of the consideration paid for it. Either the transferor or the transferee may file the proof of claim and the statement of transfer, and no court approval is required for the transaction.

Once a proof of claim has been filed, the transferee must file with the clerk of the court "evidence of the terms of the transfer." There are no guidelines in the Bankruptcy Rules about the disclosure required to satisfy the rule, but most courts require at least the identity of the assignor and assignee, the claim number, and the purchase price of the claim. The clerk must then notify the original claimant that objections to the transfer must be filed within 20 days. Technically, the rule provides that only the original claimant is entitled to receive notice and has the right to file an objection, presumably excluding third parties from objecting to the claim transfer. After 20 days, the court is technically required to approve the transfer if it finds, "after notice and a hearing," that the claim was "unconditionally transferred." The court need not hold a hearing unless a hearing is requested. Where the transferor waives his or her right to notice and a hearing in the assignment agreement, no other party may request a hearing. Courts have not always adhered to the technicality of this process, however, and third-party objections have been heard.[39]

Applying Bankruptcy Rule 3001(e) literally, the only issue to be decided by the court is whether the transfer was *unconditional*. If the court finds the claim was unconditionally transferred, then the court "*shall* enter an order substituting the transferee for the original claimant."[40] Again, there are no guidelines in the Bankruptcy Rules about what constitutes an unconditional transfer, and no courts have confronted the issue. Although not expressly set forth in Bankruptcy Rule 3001(e), it is probably an implied condition to approval that the claim transfer constitute a valid and binding assignment under applicable state law.[41]

There has been a recent trend by the bankruptcy courts, particularly in the Southern District of New York and the Western District of Pennsylvania, to regulate trading in claims by judicially expanding the regulations set forth in Bankruptcy Rule 3001(e). The first of these cases was *In re Revere Copper and Brass, Inc.*,[42] where Bankruptcy Judge Abram refused to approve claim purchases by Phoenix Capital Corporation, because of the huge discrepancy between the price Phoenix had paid for the claims and the distribution *The Wall Street Journal* estimated the debtor's proposed plan would provide to creditors. Phoenix had purchased numerous unsecured claims for approximately 20 cents on the dollar over a 30-day period prior to the date on which the debtor was purportedly going to file its plan. During that period, reports in the financial press suggested that unsecured creditors were to receive between 65 and 100 cents on the dollar under the debtor's plan. Judge Abram perceived that Phoenix, a sophisticated business entity, had taken advantage of less-sophisticated unsecured creditors who were unaware of the bankruptcy process and their rights in a Chapter 11 case and suggested that this violated the principle of adequate disclosure contained in Section 1125 of the Bankruptcy Code.[43]

Without citing any direct statutory or case authority, Judge Abram ordered Phoenix to give the assignor of each claim a 30-day option to rescind the assignment. It is noteworthy that Judge Abram did not find that Phoenix had traded on inside information. Apparently, the court was simply trying to create the proverbial level playing field for less-sophisticated trade creditors.

The *Revere* case decision was cited with approval in a recent opinion by Judge Cosetti in the *Allegheny International* case.[44] In the *Allegheny* case, the court refused to approve several claims transfers, because adequate information about the estimated value of the seller's claim was not disclosed. Judge Cosetti later rescinded his order and approved the claim transfers, but he ordered the *debtor* to inform future claims sellers of the estimated value of their claims prior to the entry of any order approving such claims transfers.[45]

Proposed Amendment to Bankruptcy Rule 3001(e)

The Committee on Rules of Practice and Procedure of the Judicial Conference of the United States recently approved certain amendments to Bankruptcy Rule 3001(e).[46] The following is a list of the significant changes to Bankruptcy Rule 3001(e) being proposed by the committee:

   a. Deletion of any reference in the rule requiring the *unconditional* transfer of a claim.
   b. Extension of the scope of the rule to claims based on bonds or debentures for transfers before a proof of claim has been filed.
   c. Deletion of the requirement that a statement of transfer be filed in connection with the assignment for transfers before a proof of claim has been filed.
   d. Exclusion from the scope of the rule only *publicly traded* bonds or debentures for transfers after a proof of claim has been filed.
   e. Limitation of the right to object to the transfer of claims to the transferor and requirement that the court substitute the transferee for the original claimant if the alleged transferor has not timely filed an objection, in each event for transfers after a proof of claim has been filed.
   f. Requirement that the court substitute the transferee for the original claimant as long as the court finds that the claim was transferred, other than for security, for a transfer after a proof of claim has been filed.

The amendments clarify a number of the elements of the rule that have been the subject of litigation, such as the standing of third parties to object to claims transfers and the discretion of the courts to deny approval based on other factors than whether the claim was transferred for security purposes. Indeed, the amendments suggest that the application of Bankruptcy Rule 3001(e) is, or at least should be, limited to the implementation of a ministerial function and is not intended to act as a substitute for securities law regulations. The amendments to Bankruptcy Rule 3001(e) must still be approved by the Supreme Court and the United States Congress.

Creeping Tender Offers

Claims transfers have also been disallowed on the grounds that wholesale purchases of claims are really disguised tender offers designed to enable the purchaser to take control of a debtor without the controls established by the securities laws. Section 14 of the '34 Act, commonly referred to as the *Williams Act,* contains provisions regulating tender offers.[47] The Williams Act requires, among other things, disclosure by the offeror and the target company of the tender offer and the offeror's intention to obtain control of the target company.[48]

An example of courts' concerns with creeping tender offers is found in Chief Bankruptcy Judge B. R. Lifland's order in the *LTV Energy Products* bankruptcy case.[49] In the *LTV Energy* case, an entity called Regal, Inc., formed a shell corporation for the purpose of making a broad-scale solicitation of the debtor's unsecured creditors, offering to purchase claims for 33 cents on the dollar. No disclosure was made of the acquiror's intentions in purchasing the claims. Over 400 creditors responded to the offer and, after consummation of the assignments, the acquiror/transferee filed with the court a notice of claims transfers under Bankruptcy Rule 3001(e). Judge Lifland refused to approve the transfers. It appears that the court's decision was based on two theories. First, a wholesale "tender offer" for claims filed against the debtor is actually a sub-rosa reorganization plan, in that creditors are solicited for, and agree to, cash in their claims at a discount. The tender offeror obtains acceptances of its "plan" without complying with the disclosure requirements contained in Section 1125 of the Bankruptcy Code.[50] Second, broad-scale claims transfers are, practically, a form of tender offer that ought to be regulated by the same type of disclosure requirements contained in the Williams Act.[51]

Insider Trading

Investors who are themselves insiders[53] or fiduciaries of the debtor may be prohibited from purchasing claims against the debtor, and any such transfers may be tainted as insider trading. Although the Bankruptcy Code does not expressly prohibit the debtor's fiduciaries from trading in the securities or claims of the debtor, the predecessor to the Bankruptcy Code contained specific prohibitions against such activity.[54]

Section 249 of the Bankruptcy Act limited the compensation of a fiduciary who traded in the debtor's claims or stock, and Section 212 of the Bankruptcy Act provided that a judge could limit the amount of any claim or stock acquired by a fiduciary of the debtor to the actual consideration paid therefor. Some courts have seen fit to employ their broad equitable powers to extend the prohibitions of insider trading contained in pre-code bankruptcy law to cases that arise under the Bankruptcy Code.[55] In today's judicial climate, it is unlikely that transfers by insiders of the debtor will be approved by the court.

The *Revere, Allegheny* and *LTV Energy* decisions, among others, are indicative of the bankruptcy courts' growing concern with the improprieties and inequities that may result from unsupervised and unregulated claims trading and with their willingness to judicially expand the requirements of Bankruptcy Rule 3001(e) as a means of regulating such activity. This is not to say that all claims transfers have been or will be subject to this type of judicial scrutiny. Indeed, a number of significant claims transfers were recently approved in the *Wheeling-Pittsburgh Steel* bankruptcy case without a specific requirement of the type of disclosure ordered in the decisions discussed above.[52] In addition, the Bankruptcy Court in the *Odd Lot Trading, Inc.* case recently approved 35 out of 36 claims purchases by AMROC Investments, L.P., finding that, under the express language of Bankruptcy Rule 3001(e), and in light of the proposed amendments thereto, the court is limited as to its inquiry into claims transfers.[53] The court in *Odd Lot* indicated that so long as the assignor/creditor is not mislead by the assignee's solicitation, the disclosure requirements of Section 1125 of the

Bankruptcy Code should not control approval of claims transfers.[54] Nevertheless, an investor should consider the following guidelines when seeking to purchase claims in bankruptcy:

1. Avoid mass solicitations of a debtor's creditors—solicitations should be limited in number and scope.
2. Avoid soliciting the debtor's insiders or fiduciaries (e.g., members of official committees), because these creditors are likely to be privy to inside information that might taint the transfer.
3. Include in the claim assignment agreement representations of the assignor that it is a sophisticated investor or business entity and that it is knowledgeable about the bankruptcy process and its rights as a creditor in a Chapter 11 case.

Claim Splitting

Section 1126(c) of the Bankruptcy Code provides that a class of claims is deemed to have accepted a plan of reorganization if it has been accepted by at least two thirds in amount and one half in number of the allowed claims held by creditors in such class who actually voted.[56] The requirement that a certain number of creditors accept a plan is a change from the requirements of the old Bankruptcy Act, and it may mean that an investor who purchases a controlling *amount* of claims may still not control the voting on a plan, because the investor is deemed to be a single claim holder for purposes of determining the *number* of acceptances or rejections.

An investor may not be able to "split up" his her conglomeration of claims to circumvent this voting rule. In a pre-code case, the court *In re Latham Lithographic*[57] refused to allow the partial assignment of a claim where the purpose of such "claim-splitting" was to increase the number of the creditors for voting on a liquidating trustee. The claim-splitting practice addressed in the *Latham* case has been cited by subsequent courts as an illustration of the evils that can result by trafficking in bankrupcy claims.[58] Thus, an investor may be restricted from purchasing or selling only a portion of a claim, or distributing her or his acquired claims to entities within its control, if the purpose of such actions is to multiply the number of creditors for voting purposes. Unfortunately, there is no case law under the Bankruptcy Code that clarifies whether a single investor who purchases multiple claims may be considered a separate claim holder for each claim in connection with tallying votes under Section 1126(c).[59]

Limiting the Amount of a Transferred Claim

A recent decision by Chief Bankruptcy Judge Lifland in the Southern District of New York may impact on a transferee's right to assert the full amount of the purchased claim against the debtor. In the *In re Chateaugay* case,[60] the court held that creditors who received notes at an original issue discount pursuant to a prebankruptcy exchange offer are allowed a claim in bankruptcy in an amount equal *only* to the fair market value of the debentures given up in the exchange, rather than the face value of the notes received. The court stated that any excess of the face value of the new original issue discount notes over the market value of the exchanged debentures represents unmatured interest, a claim for which is disallowed under Section 502(b)(2) of the Bankruptcy Code. The court noted that "the essential factor guiding this Court in making its determination of allowability is the underlying economic substance of the transaction."[61] The practical effect of this decision may be focused on the recipients of notes or securities in prebankruptcy exchange offers, whose allowed claims in a subsequent bankruptcy may be subject to reduction by original issue discount.

Voting the Transferred Claim

Section 1126 of the Bankruptcy Code governs the voting by a claim holder for the acceptance or rejection of a plan of reorganization. Section 1126(e) provides that a vote may be designated as a bad faith vote and may be disqualified for purposes of determining whether a plan has been accepted or rejected. Thus, even if a claims transfer is approved pursuant to Bankruptcy Rule 3001(e), a third party may later raise the issue of the transferee's bad faith under Section 1126(e) with respect to the voting of the claim and thereby limit the transferee's right to participate in the debtor's reorganization.

The Bankruptcy Code does not expressly define "bad faith" for purposes of disqualifying a vote, but several courts have considered the issue. In the *Featherworks* case,[62] a major creditor of the debtor held both a secured claim against the debtor and an unsecured claim for breach of warranty against the debtor and its affiliates. The debtor's affiliates settled the unsecured claim by paying the creditor $25,000 in cash, and the creditor simultaneously changed his previously cast rejection of the debtor's plan to a vote for acceptance of the plan. The court found that the payment by the debtor's affiliates was made to entice the creditor to change its vote, the creditor's vote was solicited in bad faith and the court refused to recognize the change of the vote. In essence, the debtor had paid "greenmail" to the creditor. Although the court recognized that good faith and self-dealing are not mutually exclusive, the court pointed out that "vote trafficking" and self-dealing *after the votes have been cast* are not permitted by the Bankruptcy Code.[63] Other courts have applied this standard of bad faith voting to cases where a creditor purchases claims to advance some "ulterior" motive, such as the destruction of a competing enterprise, blackmail, or pure malice.[64]

Each of the courts that have considered this issue, however, have been careful to point out that purchasing a claim to secure the approval or rejection of a plan of reorganization does not amount to bad faith and should not cause the disqualification of the claim holder's vote. The legislative history of the Bankruptcy Code seems to indicate that, where a creditor seeks undue advantage for itself only, disqualification of a vote is warranted.[65] On the other hand, where a creditor's actions will benefit its class or the estate as a whole, courts seem to be unwilling to disqualify the creditor's vote. Accordingly, even where an investor purchases claims against a Chapter 11 debtor with an eye toward taking control of the debtor, as long as the creditor's conduct during reorganization is geared toward supporting, rather than hindering, the reorganization effort, the disqualification sanction contained in Section 1126(e) of the Bankruptcy Code should not be imposed upon such creditor.

SECTION 1145 OF THE BANKRUPTCY CODE

Often, a plan of reorganization provides for the distribution to creditors and interest holders of securities, or cash and securities, of the reorganized debtor in exchange for their claims or interests in the Chapter 11 debtor. The Bankruptcy Code provides that a debtor may issue securities under a plan of reorganization without filing the registration statement required by Section 5 of the '33 Act, as long as the securities are being exchanged for a claim or interest in the debtor.[66] The Bankruptcy Code also provides a limited exemption for a creditor or interest holder acquiring such securities to resell them without complying with the registration requirements of the '33 Act.[67]

The following is a discussion of the registration provisions contained in the '33 Act and the criteria under which the issuance and sale of securities in bankruptcy and subsequent to confirmation of a plan of reorganization are exempt from such registration.

Overview of the '33 Act

Corporations or other issuers that offer and sell securities to the public must register such securities under the '33 Act[68] unless there is an available exemption. The primary purpose of this provision is to require full disclosure of all material information about securities offered to the public. Section 5 of the '33 Act prohibits any offer or sale of securities, including any public statements regarding such securities, until a registration statement is filed with the SEC and is declared effective.[69] If an issuer does not comply with the provisions contained in this section, such issuer may incur civil liability.

Sections 3 and 4 of the '33 Act provide for certain exemptions from the registration requirements contained in Section 5. The following is a list of transactions that are exempt from registration under the '33 Act:

1. Transactions by any other person than an issuer, underwriter, or dealer.[70]
2. Many dealer transactions that involve the trading of already outstanding securities.[71]
3. Transactions involving issuers that do not constitute public offerings.[72]
4. Transactions that constitute "intrastate offerings," which are sales of securities to persons who reside in a single state where the issuer is incorporated and doing substantial business.[73]
5. Transactions that constitute "small offerings" and do not exceed $500,000 in amount.[74]

The effect of these exemptions is that the only entities that must register under Section 5 of the '33 Act are issuers and underwriters.

Section 2(4) of the '33 Act defines an *issuer* as anyone who issues any type of security.[75] The definition of the term *issuer* is supplemented by Section 2(11) of the '33 Act, which adds that any entity that directly or indirectly controls or is controlled by an issuer is itself an issuer.[76]

Generally, an issuer does not issue its securities directly to the public but uses an intermediary, such as an underwriter. An underwriter is defined under Section 2(11) of the '33 Act as a person who has purchased securities from an issuer with a view to redistribution.[77] An underwriter either purchases the securities from the issuer and resells them to a dealer[78] for resale to the public or agrees to sell the securities on behalf of the issuer for a commission.

Section 1145 of the Bankruptcy Code

In addition to the exemptions contained in the '33 Act discussed above, Section 1145 of the Bankruptcy Code provides a limited exemption from certain of the '33 Act's registration and licensing requirements and from the registration requirements of any other state or local law.

Issuance of Securities under a Plan
Section 1145(a) of the Bankruptcy Code[79] exempts from registration the offer or sale of any security of a debtor, a successor to a debtor, or an affiliate of a debtor in a joint plan of reorganization, which securities are distributed under a plan of reorganization[80] and exchanged, in principal part, for securities of the debtor or for allowed claims or administrative expenses in the debtor's estate.[81] The rationale underlying the 1145(a) exemption is that a Chapter 11 debtor is required to provide both the court and its creditors and equity security holders with adequate disclosure in connection with its reorganization plan pursuant to Section 1125 of the Bankruptcy Code,[82] so compliance with the registration and disclosure requirements of the '33 Act, which are usually costly and burdensome, would be unnecessarily duplicative.

Section 1145(a) of the Bankruptcy Code refers to a debtor's "successor" or to an "affiliate participating in a joint plan" with the debtor. The Bankruptcy Code contains no guidelines on what constitutes a successor for the specific purposes of these sections, and there is only limited case law on the issue. The prevailing view is that a *successor* to the debtor is an entity that assumes the good will, property rights, and major assets of the debtor and will also undertake the debtor's liabilities and obligations pursuant to a plan of reorganization.[83]

An "affiliate participating in a joint plan" has also not been defined in the Bankruptcy Code. An *affiliate* is defined in Section 101(2) of the Bankruptcy Code to include an entity that directly or indirectly owns, controls, or holds, with power to vote, 20 percent or more of the outstanding voting securities of the debtor.[84] In the leading case on this issue, *Frontier Airlines, Inc.*, the bankruptcy court held that New York Air was an affiliate of the debtor, because it was a wholly owned subsidiary of the debtors.[85] The *Frontier Airlines* court also found New York Air to be an "affiliate participating in a joint plan" by virtue of the fact that New York Air was a proponent of the debtors' plan and its notes were being issued under a plan of reorganization in partial satisfaction of the unsecured claims of the creditors of the debtor's estates.[86] In reaching its conclusion, the court cited the *Amarex, Inc.*, case,[87] where the bankruptcy court explained that a broad application of Section 1145(a) is "in keeping with Congress' intent that reorganization be facilitated without the registration requirements of the '33 Act where adequate information is provided through the reorganization disclosure process."[88]

Although Section 1145(a) of the Bankruptcy Code provides that certain issuances are exempt from registration under Section 5 of the '33 Act, it does not apply to all issuances of securities by a debtor. The Section 1145(a) exemption is not available for an issuance of securities wholly in exchange for cash, property, or some other form of consideration, other than a claim (including an administrative expense claim) against or an interest in the debtor or an affiliate participating in a joint plan with the debtor.[89] The purpose of this requirement is to exempt from registration only the issuance and distribution of securities to claim holders or equity security holders of the debtor or its estate. This provision is not intended to exempt distributions by an issuer to the general public. The rationale is that only claim holders and equity security holders of the debtor receive a disclosure statement with respect to the issuance of the securities under a plan of reorganization; the general public has no access to information regarding the debtor or the issuer.[90]

Section 1145(a)(2) of the Bankruptcy Code exempts from registration the "offer or sale of any security that arises from the exercise of a subscription right or from the right of a conversion privilege when such subscription right or conversion privilege was issued under a plan."[91] This exemption is designed to facilitate the issuance of convertible securities, options, rights, or warrants pursuant to Chapter 11 reorganization plans. If, for example, a debtor's plan provides for the issuance of convertible preferred stock immediately convertible at the option of the holder into the debtor's common stock, in exchange for the cancellation of all unsecured indebtedness, the preferred stock issuance is exempt. Consequently, Section 1145(a)(2) allows the continuing offer of the underlying security and the sale that occurs upon conversion without registration under the '33 Act.[92]

Section 1145(a)(3) of the Bankruptcy Code provides a limited exemption for the sale of portfolio securities owned by the debtor, or its affiliate, on the date of the filing of the bankruptcy petition and sold pursuant to a plan of reorganization.[93] This exemption allows the debtor or trustee to sell or distribute its securities as long as the securities are of a company that is required to file reports under Section 13 or Section 15(d) of the '34 Act and that is in compliance with all requirements for continuance of trading those securities. Section 1145(a)(3) limits the amount of restricted securities that may be distributed to 4 percent of each class of restricted securities at any time during the first two years immediately following the date of the filing of the bankruptcy petition and to 1 percent during any 180-day period thereafter.[94] Section 1145(a)(4) exempts transactions by a stockbroker occurring within 40 days after the offer of securities pursuant to a plan of reorganization.[95] To qualify for this exemption, a stockbroker must provide the purchaser with a disclosure statement that is approved under Section 1125 of the Bankruptcy Code.[96] Finally, the Securities and Exchange Commission has concluded that the granting of beneficial interests in a liquidating trust to holders of claims against a debtor pursuant to a Chapter 13 plan is exempt from registration requirements where the sole purpose of the trust is to effect the orderly disposition and liquidation of the debtor's estate.[97]

Resale of Securities
One of the most important provisions in Section 1145 of the Bankruptcy Code is subsection (b), which provides the criteria under

which a creditor or equity security holder or other entity acquiring securities under a plan may resell them without complying with the registration requirements of the '33 Act.[98] This subsection is important, because the willingness of a creditor or interest holder to accept new securities under a plan of reorganization in exchange for debt or existing securities depends in part upon the liquidity of such new securities and the ability to utilize the public market. It is intuitive that the value creditors and interest holders may place upon newly issued securities under a plan decreases as regulatory restrictions on resale increase.

Section 1145(b) does not exempt the resale of such securities by an underwriter. Section 1145(b)(1)(A) defines *underwriter* to be a person who purchases a claim (including an administrative expense claim) against or an interest in the debtor with a view to distributing any security received or to be received in exchange therefor.[99] A person is also an underwriter for purposes of this section if he or she offers to sell securities offered or sold under the plan for the holders of such securities, or offers to buy securities offered or sold under the plan from the holders of such securities if the offer to buy is with a view to redistribution.[100] Courts generally have defined *distribution* as the process by which securities are transferred from the issuer into the hands of the general investing public.[101] Finally, a person is deemed to be an underwriter if he or she is an issuer, as that term is defined in Section 2(11) of the '33 Act.[102]

The limited resale exemption afforded by Section 1145(b) of the Bankruptcy Code only concerns creditors or interest holders with less than 10 percent of a class of the debtor's securities, because any creditor or interest holder who holds more than that amount is deemed a controlling person; under the '33 Act, a controlling person constitutes an issuer for purposes of the offer and sale of securities. Creditors acquiring in excess of 10 percent of a class of securities of the reorganized debtor under a plan of reorganization, therefore, will be subject to normal '33 Act registration requirements upon resale of the securities.

Finally, although Section 1145 of the Bankruptcy Code provides an exemption from the registration requirements of Section 5 of the '33 Act, it does not provide immunity from liability under the antifraud provisions contained in the '33 Act.[103] Section 1125(e) of the Bankruptcy Code provides a "safe harbor" for those who, in good faith, participate in the offer or sale, under a plan of reorganization, of securities of a debtor, an affiliate participating in a joint plan with the debtor, or securities of a newly organized successor to the debtor.[104] It should be noted that the Securities and Exchange Commission has issued a no-action letter stating that the safe harbor provisions of Section 1125(e) apply even if the successor is not "newly organized."[105]

The Role of the Securities and Exchange Commission

The Bankruptcy Code provides a more limited role for the Securities and Exchange Commission in Chapter 11 cases than did its statutory predecessor. Under the old bankruptcy act, the SEC played an active part in a debtor's reorganization process. For example, the court was required to submit reorganization plans to the SEC for examination, and the SEC provided the court with an advisory report on the fairness and feasibility of the plan.[106] Under the Bankruptcy Code, the SEC plays more of an amicus-type role. The SEC may (1) raise and be heard on any issue in a case,[107] (2) comment on the adequacy of the information contained in the disclosure statement,[108] and (3) object to confirmation of a reorganization plan if the principal purpose of the plan is to avoid the registration requirements of the '33 Act.[109] These provisions, coupled with current SEC policy, have resulted in a decrease in the SEC's participation in reorganization cases.[110]

On June 8, 1989, however, the SEC voted to review its role under Section 1109(a) of the Bankruptcy Code in reorganization cases involving publicly held debtor corporations, and the SEC has sought public comment on the issue.[111] The three areas in which the SEC is seeking public input in reassessing its role are as follows:

1. The extent to which more active SEC participation would contribute to a fair, efficient, and effective resolution of a Chapter 11 case and the extent such participation would impede the resolution of cases.
2. The extent to which SEC should play a more active role, under Section 1109(a), on behalf of investors in reorganization cases, rather than limiting its involvement to its present amicus-type role.
3. The desireability of the SEC proposing legislative changes concerning either its Section 1109(a) role in reorganization cases or in the statutory protections for public investors.[112]

Presumably, this reassessment has been prompted by the increased number of bankruptcy filings by publicly held corporations, as well as the effect on the securities market of such bankruptcy-related activities as trading in claims against a debtor. When this chapter was written, the SEC had not announced the results of its review and no legislation had been proposed that would modify the SEC's role in reorganization cases.

ENDNOTES

1. 11 U.S.C. Section 101(43)(A).
2. H.R. No. 95-595, 95th Cong., 1st Sess. 311-14 (1977); S.R. No. 95-989, 95th Cong., 2d Sess. 24-26 (1978).
3. 11 U.S.C. Section 101(43)(B).
4. 15 U.S.C. Section 78c(a)(10).
5. **See,** for example, *Marine Bank* v. *Weaver,* 455 U.S. 551 (1982) (bank certificate of deposit does not constitute a security); *United Housing Foundation, Inc.* v. *Forman,* 421 U.S. 837 (1975) (shares in a housing cooperative do not constitute a security).
6. *Reves* v. *Ernst & Young,* No. 88-1480 (U.S. Feb. 21, 1990) (LEXIS Genfed library, courts file).
7. *Id.*
8. **See,** for example, *Chemical Bank* v. *Arthur Anderson & Co.,* 726 F.2d 930, 939 (2d Cir. 1984). The Supreme Court rejected the Eighth and District of Columbia Circuits' use of the alternative test (referred to as the *Howey test*) to determine whether notes are securities, because it found that the Howey test addressed investment contracts, rather than notes.
9. Types of notes that have been deemed not to be "securities" include mortgage notes, short-term collateralized notes, notes evidencing loans by commercial banks for current operations, and notes delivered in consumer financing or as a means of formalizing an open-account debt.
10. *Reves.*
11. Fortgang and Mayer, *Trading Claims and Taking Control of Corporations in Chapter 11,* at 69 (1988).
12. **See,** later in this chapter, the section Trading of Claims in Bankruptcy.
13. 11 U.S.C. Section 101(15).
14. 11 U.S.C. Section 1129(b)(2).
15. One exception to the absolute priority rule may exist where an equity security holder makes a "substantial contribution" of new capital

into the debtor in exchange for which he or she retains an interest in the reorganized debtor of a value equivalent to the value of the new monetary investment. The infusion-of-new-capital exception is not a statutory exception and, while some courts recognize the exception, other courts have held that this judicially created exception violates the express provisions of the Bankruptcy Code. **See** *In re 222 Liberty Associates,* 108 B.R. 971 (Bankr. E.D.Pa. 1990) (recognizing the validity of the new value exception); *cf. In re Winters,* 99 B.R. 658 (Bankr. W.D.Pa. 1989) (declining to recognize the "infusion of new capital" exception to the absolute priority rule); **see** also *Norwest Bank Worthington* v. *Ahlers,* 485 U.S. 197 (1988) (declining to decide whether an exception to the absolute priority rule exists, but finding that the promise of future services does not constitute an infusion of new capital).
16. 11 U.S.C. Section 1129(b).
17. The term *cramdown* refers to the confirmation of a reorganization plan, notwithstanding the failure of one or more classes of claims or interests to accept the plan. It requires that the plan meet certain standards of fairness to the dissenting creditors for which the burden of proof rests with the plan proponent.
18. 11 U.S.C. Section 1124.
19. 11 U.S.C. Section 1126(d).
20. The term *debtor-in-possession* refers to a debtor (or a trustee) that remains in possession of the estate's property and is authorized to continue operating its business after the commencement of its bankruptcy case. **See** 11 U.S.C. Sections 1101(1), 1107, and 1108.
21. *In re V. Savino Oil & Heating Co.,* 99 B.R. 518 (Bankr. E.D.N.Y. 1989) (debtor-in-possession holds its powers in trust for benefit of creditors and shareholders); *In re Consolidated Rock Products Co.,* 36 F. Supp. 912 (S.D. Cal. 1941) (where debtor has been allowed to remain in possession of its properties and to operate its business, it has been a trustee for all interested parties including its creditors and its shareholders).
22. *In re Consolidated Rock Products Co.,* 36 F. Supp. 912 (debtor-in-possession deemed trustee for creditors and shareholders); *H. H. Sacks, Inc.* v. *Atherton,* 108 F.2d 173 (1st Cir. 1939) (creditors have right to require debtor-in-possession to exercise its powers for their benefit).
23. See *In re Johns-Manville Corp.,* 801 F.2d 60, 69 (2d Cir. 1986).
24. *Id.* at 64.
25. *Id.* at 65, n.6. **But see** *Saxon Industries Inc.* v. *NKFW Partners,* 39 B.R. 49 (Bankr. S.D.N.Y. 1984) (insolvency of debtor does not disenfranchise shareholders).

26. Generally, debtor is insolvent under the Bankruptcy Code if the sum of its debts is greater than all of its property at a fair valuation. **See** 11 U.S.C. Section 101(31).
27. A debtor-in-possession has the exclusive right to file a reorganization plan for 120 days after the date of the commencement of its Chapter 11 bankruptcy case, which period may be extended or reduced by the court for cause shown. If the debtor-in-possession files a plan within the exclusivity period, then the exclusive right continues to allow solicitation of acceptances of the plan until the 180th day after the petition date. During these exclusive periods, no other party may file or solicit acceptances of a competing plan. **See** 11 U.S.C. Section 1121.
28. **See** *In re Realty Associates Securities Corp.*, 56 F. Supp. 1008, 1009 (E.D.N.Y. 1944) (directors may not serve on bondholders' committee); *In re Penn-Dixie Industries, Inc.*, 9 B.R. 941, 944 (Bankr. S.D.N.Y. 1981) (equity holders' committee must be free from the influence of management).
29. Fortgang & Mayer, *Trading Claims and Taking Control of Corporations in Chapter 11*, at 98 (1988).
30. Most recently, in the *Allegheny International, Inc.*, bankruptcy case, shareholders succeeded in compelling a meeting, and, after initiating a proxy fight, elected 5 out of 11 directors.
31. 11 U.S.C. Section 1102(a)(2).
32. **See,** for example, *Willemain* v. *Kivitz,* 764 F.2d 1019 (4th Cir. 1985) (no standing for Chapter 7 debtor to challenge asset sale, because successful challenge would not render debtor solvent); *In re Evans Products Co.,* 65 B.R. 870 (Bankr. S.D.Fla. 1986) (equity class lacked standing to object to treatment of claims under Chapter 11 plan, because equity's recovery from the estate would remain the same no matter what the outcome). **But see** *In re TM Carlton House Partners, Ltd.,* No. 88-10774S (Bankr. E.D. Pa. Feb. 7, 1990) (LEXIS, Bkrtcy library, cases file) (court expressed reluctance to prohibit a party from avidly expressing a legal position based on lack of standing).
33. 11 U.S.C. Section 510(b).
34. The court may, upon the request of a party-in-interest, designate any entity or class whose acceptance or rejection of a reorganization plan was made or solicited in bad faith, and thereby disallow the vote when determining whether the plan has been accepted or rejected. **See** 11 U.S.C. Section 1126(e).
35. **See** 11 U.S.C. Sections 510(c), 547, 548, and 550.
36. The court has the power to reconsider allowance of a claim, but such action by the court is rare. **See** 11 U.S.C. Section 502(j).

37. See *In re Robert T. Noel Coal, Inc.*, 82 B.R. 778 (Bankr. W.D. Pa. 1988) (state law determines validity of postpetition assignment); *In re Oxford Royal Mushroom Products, Inc.*, 93 B.R. 390 (Bankr. E.D. Pa. 1988) (where court had not yet approved claim transfer but trustee received notice of transfer, the trustee was obligated to make distributions to assignee). **But,** *cf. In re Heritage Village Church & Missionary Fellowship, Inc.*, 87 B.R. 17 (Bankr. D.S.C. 1988) (bankruptcy court has authority to disapprove of valid state law assignment).
38. Bankruptcy Rule 3001(e).
39. For instance, in the *Wheeling-Pittsburgh Steel* bankruptcy case, Judge Bentz considered the objections of some of the debtor's secured creditors in making his determination of whether to approve the transfer of unsecured claims.
40. Bankruptcy Rule 3001(e)(2).
41. See *In re Oxford Royal Mushroom, supra* at endnote 37.
42. *In re Revere Copper and Brass, Inc.*, 58 B.R. 1 (Bankr. S.D.N.Y. 1985).
43. Section 1125(b) of the Bankruptcy Code prohibits solicitation of acceptances or rejections of a filed plan unless the solicitation is accompanied or preceded by a disclosure statement that contains adequate information for a typical investor to make an informed judgment about the plan.
44. *In re Allegheny International, Inc.*, No. 88-448, Memorandum Opinion and Order (Bankr. W.D.Pa. Oct. 13, 1988).
45. *In re Allegheny International, Inc.*, 100 B.R. 241 (Bankr. W.D. Pa. 1988).
46. See *Proposed Amendments to the Bankruptcy Rules,* Bankr. L. Rep. (CCH) No. 265, at 76 (Oct. 12, 1989).
47. 15 U.S.C. Sections 78m(d)-(e), 78n(d)-(f).
48. 15 U.S.C. Sections 78n(d)(1), 78n(d)(4).
49. *In re Chateaugay (In re LTV Energy Products)*, 86 B 227342-405 Slip op. (Bankr. S.D.N.Y. March 11, 1988).
50. 11 U.S.C. Section 1125(a).
51. In addition, the court found that Regal intended to propose a plan of reorganization that would pay other creditors in the same class as the transferors 100 cents on the dollar once Regal gained control of the debtor.

    Judge Lifland has since published his own chambers rules for the filing of notices under Bankruptcy Rule 3001(e), which require (1) disclosure of the consideration paid for the claim and (2) a statement by the assignee that it did not solicit the assignor via the use of misinformation.

52. *In re Wheeling-Pittsburgh Steel Corp., et al.*, No. 85-793 PGH, Order (Bankr. W.D.Pa. Oct. 5, 1989).
53. *In re Odd Lot Trading, Inc.*, 115 B.R. 97, 98 (Bankr. N.D. Ohio 1990).
54. *Id.* at 98.
55. Under the Bankruptcy Code, the term *insider* includes any director, officer, control person, general partner, or affiliate of the debtor. **See** 11 U.S.C.A. § 101(30) (West supp., 1989). An "affiliate" is defined as (1) an entity that directly or indirectly owns or controls 20 percent of the outstanding voting securities of the debtor; (2) a corporation 20 percent of whose outstanding voting securities are owned or controlled by the debtor or by an entity described in subsection (1) above; (3) a person whose business is operated under a lease or operating agreement by a debtor; or (4) an entity that operates the business of the debtor under a lease or operating agreement. 11 U.S.C. Section 101(2) (West, 1979, & supp., 1989).
56. See 11 U.S.C. Sections 612 and 649 (1976), repealed effective October 1, 1979.
57. **See,** for example, *In re Executive Office Centers, Inc.*, 96 B.R. 642 (Bankr. E.D. La. 1988)(an assignee's right to recover the full value of an assigned instrument may be limited where the assignment involved a breach of fiduciary duty and enabled the assignee to acquire the claim for inadequate consideration).
58. 11 U.S.C. Section 1126(c).
59. *In re Latham Lithographic Corp.*, 107 F.2d 749 (2d Cir. 1939).
60. **See,** for example, *In re U.S. Truck Company, Inc.*, 42 B.R. 787 (Bankr. E.D.Mich. 1984) (citing the facts in *Latham* as an example of the evils of trafficking in claims by insiders).
61. Under the Bankruptcy Act of 1898, at least one court held that an assignee of multiple claims can only be counted as a single creditor for voting on a composition. **See** *In re Messengill*, 113 F. 366 (E.D.N.C. 1902).
62. *In re Chateaugay*, No. 86B11270 *et al.* (Bankr. S.D.N.Y. Jan. 10, 1990) (LEXIS, Bkrtcy library, cases file).
63. *Id.*
64. *In re Featherworks*, 36 B.R. 460 (E.D.N.Y. 1984).
65. *Id.* at 463.
66. **See,** for example, *Young* v. *Higbee Co.*, 324 U.S. 204 (1945) (stockholders who selfishly rejected plan in exchange for consideration for themselves violated Bankruptcy Code); *In re P-R Holding Corporation*, 147 F.2d 895 (2d Cir. 1945) (when a purchase of a claim is made in aid of an interest, other than an interest as a creditor, such purchases may result in votes cast in bad faith).

67. The legislative history of the predecessor to Section 1126(c) of the Bankruptcy Code provides that the purpose of the good faith requirement is to prevent creditors from participating in voting on a plan who "by use of obstructive tactics and hold-up techniques exact for themselves undue advantages. . . ." **See** Hearings on Revision of the Bankruptcy Act before the Committee on the Judiciary of the House of Representatives, H.R. No. 6439, 75th Cong., 1st Sess., pp. 180–182 (1937).

68. 11 U.S.C. Section 1145(a).
69. 11 U.S.C. Section 1145(b).
70. 15 U.S.C. Section 77a *et seq.*
71. 15 U.S.C. Section 77e.
72. 15 U.S.C. Section 77d(1).
73. 15 U.S.C. Section 77d(3).
74. An example of a nonpublic offering is a "private placement" of securities with a large institutional investor. This exemption is available because, in a typical private placement, the persons receiving the securities have access to the kind of information that registration would disclose. **See** 15 U.S.C.A. § 77d(2) (West, 1981). **See also** *SEC v. Ralston Purina Co.*, 346 U.S. 119 (1953) (whether § 4(2) applies depends upon whether the person to whom the securities are being offered has access to the kind of information that registration would disclose).
75. 15 U.S.C. Section 77(c)(11).
76. 15 U.S.C. Section 77(b).
77. 15 U.S.C. Section 77b(4).
78. 15 U.S.C. Section 77(b)(11).
79. A question arises about whether a person is an underwriter, if such person buys securities from an issuer in a private transaction and then wishes to resell them. The SEC adopted SA Rule 144, which states that, for a person to *not* be deemed an underwriter, any sale by such person made during a six-month period may not exceed the lesser of 1 percent of the total number of units of the security outstanding, and, if the security is listed on the exchange, the average weekly trading volume for the preceding four weeks. Also, if such person bought the securities in a nonpublic transaction, he or she must have held the securities for at least two years before reselling them. **See** 17 C.F.R. § 230.144.
80. A *dealer* is defined as a person who acts as agent or principal to offer, buy, or sell or otherwise trade in securities issued by another. 15 U.S.C. Section 77b(12).
81. 11 U.S.C. Section 1145(a).

82. Section 1145(a) does not exempt from registration securities issued prior to filing of a plan of reorganization. See *In re The Diet Institute, Inc.*, SEC No-Action Letter, dated May 31, 1985.
83. Section 1145 "is available even if some cash or property is received for the security, so long as the security is exchanged principally for a claim against, or interest in, the debtor." See 5 *Collier on Bankruptcy,* ¶1145.01(e) at p. 1145-15 (15th ed. 1989).
84. Section 1125 of the Bankruptcy Code requires that all creditors and stockholders whose rights are to be affected by a plan of reorganization receive "adequate disclosure." *Adequate disclosure* is defined as: "information of a kind, and in sufficient detail, as far as is reasonably practicable in light of the nature and history of the debtor and the condition of the debtor's books and records, that would enable a hypothetical reasonable investor typical of holders of claims or interests of the relevant class to make an informed judgment about the plan." 11 U.S.C. Section 1125(a)(1).
85. See *In re Amarex, Inc.*, 53 B.R. 12 (Bankr. W.D.Okla 1985) (the "successor" language of U.S.C. Section 1145(a)(1) should be read broadly in view of the adequate information requirement in the disclosure process so as to encourage reorganization and relieve the debtor from strict compliance with securities laws); *In re Stanley Hotel, Inc.*, 5 C.B.C.2d 64 (Bankr. D.Colo. 1981) (an investment group acquiring the debtor's assets was deemed a successor and entitled to the Section 1145 exemption, because the group would "step into the boots" of the debtor by assuming *both* its assets and its liabilities).
86. 11 U.S.C. Section 101(2).
87. See *In re Frontier Airlines, Inc.*, 93 B.R. 1014, 1021 (Bankr. D. Colo. 1988).
88. *Id.* at 1022.
89. *In re Amarex, Inc.*, 53 B.R. 12 (Bankr. W.D. Okla. 1985).
90. *Id.* at 1021.
91. 11 U.S.C. Section 1145(a)(1).
92. 5 *Collier on Bankruptcy,* ¶1145.01[1] at p. 1145-4 (15th ed. 1989).
93. 11 U.S.C. Section 1145(a)(2).
94. *Id.* See also Phelan, Cheatham, *Issuing Securities under the New Bankruptcy Code; More Magic for the Cryptic Kingdom,* 11 St. Mary's L.J. 393, 428 (1979).
95. 11 U.S.C. Section 1145(a)(3); SA Rule 144 and SEC Rule 148 also provide an exemption from registration for portfolio securities of a debtor.
96. 11 U.S.C. Section 1145(a)(3)(C).

97. 11 U.S.C. Section 1145(a)(4).
98. *Id.* **See** also endnote 82 *supra.*
99. **See** *Nelson Bunker Hunt and Caroline Lewis Hunt,* SEC No-Action Letter, dated November 17, 1989.
100. 11 U.S.C. Section 1145(b).
101. 11 U.S.C. Section 1145(b)(1)(A).
102. 11 U.S.C. Sections 1145(b)(1)(B), (C).
103. The general public consists of those unsophisticated persons lacking in wealth that need the protections afforded by the registration and prospectus delivery requirements of the Securities Act. **See** *SEC* v. *Ralston Purina Co.,* 346 U.S. 119, 125 (1953).
104. See endnote 76 *supra.*
105. Section 17 of the '33 Act contains an antifraud provision that makes it unlawful to engage in fraudulent or deceitful practices in connection with the offer or sale of securities. 15 U.S.C. Section 77q.
106. Section 1125(e) provides:

 > A person that . . . participates, in good faith . . . in the offer, issuance, sale, or purchase of a security, offered or sold under a plan, of the debtor, of an affiliate participating in a joint plan with the debtor, or of a newly organized successor to the debtor, . . . is not liable, on account of such . . . participation, for violation of any applicable law, rule, or regulation governing . . . the offer, issuance, sale, or purchase of securities.

107. **See** *Computer Input Services, Inc.,* SEC No-Action Letter, March 16, 1984 (SEC stated that a newly formed successor to the debtor may distribute, without Section 5 registration or liability under Section 17 of the '33 Act, if in compliance with Section 1125(e) of the Bankruptcy Code, securities of a successor's parent corporation pursuant to a plan of reorganization).
108. 11 U.S.C. Sections 172 and 173 (1976), repealed effective October 1, 1979.
109. 11 U.S.C. Section 1109(a).
110. 11 U.S.C. Section 1125(d).
111. 11 U.S.C. Section 1129(d).
112. **See** Securities and Exchange Commission Annual Reports 1980–1983 at 3-4 (1983).
113. Notice, 54 Fed. Reg. 40760 (1989).
114. *Id.* at 40763.

CHAPTER 26

INTERNATIONAL WORKOUTS AND BANKRUPTCIES: ADDITIONAL CONSIDERATIONS

Donald R. Joseph, Esq.[*]
Partner
Baker & McKenzie

INTRODUCTION

"Global economic interdependence" is a phrase formerly heard only at economic summit conferences and at seminars for the corporate elite. The macroeconomics of foreign markets, flow of capital, currency fluctuations, and exploitation of raw materials have long been the source of scholarly research and debate. For all but the largest American businesses, however, and their lenders and advisors, the mysteries of doing business outside the United States have until recently remained just that.

Today, that luxury is no longer available. Even the smallest companies are being advised to "go international." Strategic business planning now includes some consideration of the advantages

---

[*] The author would like to acknowledge with appreciation the contributions of his Baker & McKenzie colleagues: Wallace R. Baker, Paris; Harold Margles, Toronto; James O'Donovan, Melbourne; and Alvaro Espinos, Barcclona.

and disadvantages of sourcing products or component parts from suppliers outside the United States; of introducing products or services for consumption in a non-U.S. marketplace; and of strategic alliances, such as a joint venture, equity, or debt relationship, with an overseas investor or industry participant. Virtually every aspect of business being conducted in the United States can now involve some foreign participation.

For example, it is not at all unusual to find a medium or even small United States corporation engaged in a joint venture or licensing arrangement with a Japanese investor, conducting *maquiladora* manufacturing operations in Mexico, selling into Europe, or otherwise entering into cross-border transactions. The increase of foreign capital into the United States by acquisitions of real estate or other property or businesses further binds the economies of the world's nations in a very basic way.

Add to this the monumental political and economic changes taking place globally. The massive shifts toward free economies in Eastern Europe and the Soviet Union, the reunification of Germany, and the effect in 1992 of the substantial breakdown of barriers within the European Community are some of the most dramatic examples. The end result is an acceleration of the already rapid pace of international commerce. This means opportunities for profit for American businesses and, therefore, incentive to pursue them. With such opportunities, however, come the attendant risks. And with those risks, particularly in light of the uncharted waters that await, come inevitable insolvencies or business failures. It is no great prediction to say that the international issues and problems of insolvency presented by the conduct of trade or business will proliferate in the years to come at an unprecedented rate.

Yet, unlike many other areas of international concern, ranging from customs and tariffs to national and regional defense to exploitation of natural resources, relationships among countries in matters of business insolvency have so far not produced a great deal of international cooperation. Scores of thorny legal issues are presented when a United States debtor, for example, files for Chapter 11 protection and seeks to protect the assets of its manufacturing division in Singapore; or, conversely, the representative of an Australian entity, pursuing insolvency relief in that jurisdiction, seeks to protect and distribute its assets located in the United States toward the end of a distribution in accordance with Australian laws and priorities.

These issues are the subject of the brief consideration given below. Unless and until the current draft Model International Insolvency Cooperation Act or some similar legislation based on the principle of universality is adopted by most of the world's primary mercantile nations, however, transnational insolvencies will remain for the most part an effort to harmonize and reconcile the often divergent laws and competing policies of insolvency in the affected jurisdictions. It should be apparent that any potential insolvency situation will require an examination, at a minimum, of the applicable insolvency and related laws of the jurisdiction(s) in which the debtor and its primary assets are located.

No attempt will be made here to address the specifics of any particular nation's insolvency laws,[1] particularly those of the United States discussed elsewhere in this book. Instead, the aim of this brief chapter is simply (1) to point out the lack of any unified and comprehensive body of law applicable to insolvencies having international aspects, (2) to consider the extraterritorial effect of U.S. bankruptcy law, and (3) to examine the methods by which a foreign insolvency representative may invoke the protections and jurisdiction of United States bankruptcy laws. Finally, a short comment on the draft Model International Insolvency Cooperation Act will consider the prospects for international insolvencies in the future.

THE U.S. DEBTOR HAVING ASSETS ABROAD

One of the fundamental protections provided to a debtor under the United States Bankruptcy Code is the *automatic stay*.[2] Immediately upon entry of an order for relief, the automatic stay generally prohibits creditors and any other parties from proceeding to recover on prepetition claims against a debtor seeking relief under the U.S. bankruptcy law. In broad terms, the automatic stay prohibits any act to commence or continue litigation based on prepetition claims; to obtain possession of or control over property of the debtor's estate (which carries an extremely broad definition);[3] to create, perfect, or enforce any lien against property of the estate; to enforce a judgment or perfect or enforce a lien; or to set off debts owing to the debtor against any claims against the debtor. Although certain exceptions apply, the immediate, mandatory, and comprehensive provisions of the automatic stay are intended to provide the debtor an opportunity to reorganize or liquidate in an orderly fashion, without a race by creditors to recover assets or to pursue litigation across the United States.

The underlying premise of the automatic stay, of course, is that such a liquidation or reorganization of a debtor in a United States bankruptcy proceeding will take place in accordance with the priorities and protections of the Bankruptcy Code. If the debtor entity and all of its assets are located in the United States, no international conflict of law or policy is likely to be presented by the implementation of the automatic stay. But what of the U.S. debtor having substantial assets in foreign jurisdictions? Are the same policies applicable? Will the effect of the automatic stay be recognized in those other jurisdictions? Will the U.S. debtor be able to protect and recover its assets for administration in the U.S. bankruptcy case? To what extent will the insolvency (or other) laws of the jurisdiction in which the assets are located by considered? In the event of conflicting laws or policies, which jurisdiction will control? These issues cannot be answered uniformly, but they will require a careful case-by-case analysis. It is possible, however, to address a key threshold issue: the applicability of the automatic stay in court-supervised insolvencies in foreign jurisdictions.

In a United States bankruptcy, the debtor's estate is defined to include all property of the debtor "wherever located." The broad language of Bankruptcy Code Section 541(a) can be read to mean that even assets of the debtor that are located outside the United States should be included in "property of the estate" and, thus, should be administered by the bankruptcy court. This interpretation finds support in similar language in the bankruptcy jurisdictional statute, which grants the district court in which a bankruptcy case is commenced "exclusive jurisdiction of all property, wherever located, of the debtor. . . ."[4] At least one commentator has expressed the opinion that these statutory provisions are intended to grant to the U.S. bankruptcy courts jurisdiction over assets located abroad.[5] Moreover, the predecessor of 28 U.S.C. Section 1334(d), Bankruptcy Act Section 11(a)(1), explicitly limited the bankruptcy courts' jurisdiction to their respective territorial limits. The omission of the prior narrower language from 28 U.S.C. Section 1334(d), in favor of the broader "wherever located" language, would seem to indicate a deliberate intent to invest the bankruptcy courts with worldwide jurisdiction.

Despite what appears to be the United States claim of worldwide jurisdiction, at least over a U.S. debtor's foreign assets, a U.S. bankruptcy proceeding has no force of its own outside the United States. It is clear that the bankruptcy court does not enjoy personal jurisdiction over a foreign creditor unless such creditor has certain minimum contacts with the United States.[6]

Without personal jurisdiction over the foreign creditor, the United States has no power to enforce the automatic stay with respect to foreign actions or creditors. This distinction is critical. If a creditor is subject to personal jurisdiction in the United States, the foreign creditor will also be subject to the automatic stay and its enforcement. Enforcement abroad nevertheless remains difficult, particularly where the local laws of the jurisdiction in which the U.S. debtor's assets are located allow the continued ability by a creditor to attach or otherwise realize upon assets of an insolvent entity. In that regard, even such apparently simple matters as service of legal documents becomes much more difficult. Note the impact of the Convention of the Service Abroad of Judicial and Extrajudicial Documents in Civil or Commerical Matters (commonly referred to as the *Hague Convention*), which provides that any document served abroad can be required to be translated into the official language of the country in which the document is served.[7] Depending on the translation issues presented and the scope of documents to be served, this preliminary step can itself become quite time consuming and expensive.

Even more difficult, and potentially disastrous for the U.S. debtor, is the situation in which its assets are being held, controlled, or affected in a foreign jurisdiction by a creditor that is not subject to personal jurisdiction in the United States. For example, one reported case, *Fotochrome, Inc., v. Copal Company, Ltd.*,[8] concerns a U.S. debtor that had filed for relief under Chapter 11 of the Bankruptcy Act, predecessor to the Bankruptcy Code. A restraining order was issued by the bankruptcy court comparable in effect to the provisions of the automatic stay under the Bankruptcy Code.

At the time of the restraining order, the debtor was subject to and was participating in a commercial arbitration proceeding in Japan. After its bankruptcy filing, the debtor refrained from continuing to act in the arbitration, which nevertheless proceeded forward. Subsequent to the issuance of the restraining order, a substantial award ultimately was rendered in favor of the creditor in the Japanese arbitration.

The United States Court of Appeals for the Second Circuit affirmed the lower court's ruling that, without "minimum contacts," no personal jurisdiction existed over the foreign creditor (until the creditor filed its own proof of claim in the United States bankruptcy proceeding based upon the arbitration award); and, therefore, the stay was ineffective. In this case, the foreign creditor filed a proof of claim in the U.S. bankruptcy case because the debtor had no assets located in Japan. While the debtor was unable to relitigate the arbitrated issues, it did at least maintain control of the administration of its assets, all of which were located in the United States, pursuant to the Bankruptcy Act. If the debtor had had assets located in Japan, it is safe to say that the Japanese creditor could have proceeded to enforce its award by applicable Japanese law, and such assets would have been lost to creditors participating in the U.S. bankruptcy.

Without personal jurisdiction over the creditor in the United States, then, the effectiveness of the automatic stay will be dependent upon the cooperation of foreign jurisdictions. International recognition of a country's laws and legal proceedings traditionally is accomplished by way of treaty. However, very few international bankruptcy treaties have been ratified to date. Two rare examples of such treaties are the Scandinavian Convention,[9] ratified by Denmark, Finland, Iceland, Norway, and Sweden, and the Bustamente Code of Private International Law,[10] ratified by 15 Latin American countries. In certain instances, other international agreements may have some application, such as the Hague Convention and the United Nations Convention on the Recognition and Enforcement of Foreign Arbitral Awards,[11] which was at issue in the *Fotochrome* case. Any consideration of an international insolvency, therefore, must include a search for applicable treaties and conventions.

In the absence of treaties or other specific bilateral or multilateral agreements, the law of the country in which the debtor's assets are located will determine whether the automatic stay will be recognized and enforced abroad. The extent to which the automatic stay will be recognized is as varied as the countries where debtor assets are located. Although "no country automatically gives full extraterritorial effect to a foreign insolvency law and to an adjudication pursuant thereto . . . no country seems totally to disregard the effects of foreign insolvencies."[12] Summarized below are a few examples of the diverse approaches taken by other countries to recognize foreign bankruptcy proceedings.

One of the most severe nonrecognition provisions is found in the Argentinian Insolvency Act. The act provides that

> insolvency proceedings abroad cannot be invoked against creditors whose claims are payable in the Republic, in order to contest the rights which they claim in respect to assets located in the territory, nor to avoid transactions which have been negotiated with the insolvent.[13]

Foreign creditors with claims in Argentina, then, are left solely to Argentinian internal law for their remedies. In such countries, creditors should give careful consideration before appearing locally to pursue those rights, if personal jurisdiction over the creditor does not yet exist.

A more moderate position regarding recognition is taken by England. Many English decisions have allowed United States trustees to collect assets of the estate located in England, provided such collection does not conflict with principles of local law.[14]

France, on the other hand, has given extensive effect to foreign adjudication of bankruptcies and has accorded extensive powers to foreign bankruptcy representatives. Formal recognition and enforcement of a non-French proceeding is achieved through a procedure known as *exequatur*. Through exequatur, a foreign representative is granted broad powers to collect assets in France. In this way, "the 'exequatur' extends the effect of a foreign bankruptcy proceeding to French assets, but only to the extent there has been no intervening adjudication or transaction in France."[15]

In Canada, there are no direct legislative provisions under Canadian bankruptcy law for the recognition or enforcement of foreign bankruptcy orders or judgments of foreign courts. Pursuit of assets located in Canada, therefore, depends upon the separate procedural and substantive laws of each of its provinces. In those provinces applying the common law, generally the United States bankruptcy trustee may administer property of the U.S. debtor located in Canada if there are no pending Canadian bankruptcy proceedings; if the debtor is, in the view of that court, subject to the jurisdiction of the United States bankruptcy court; and if the U.S. bankruptcy applies to property of the debtor, wherever located.[16] In addition, the reach of the U.S. bankruptcy representative in Canada may depend in a given province upon the character of the property itself (i.e., real or personal).

It is impossible, therefore, to summarize or predict the extent to which the automatic stay will apply to foreign creditors—or to assets of a U.S. debtor that are located in a foreign jurisdiction. Careful analysis must be made of the character of the asset; the nature of the creditor's claim; the basic "recognition" laws of the foreign jurisdiction (and, potentially, any applicable political subdivisions) with respect to foreign insolvency proceedings and representatives thereof; and, perhaps, even a comparison of the basic policies of the competing jurisdiction's insolvency laws. Under certain circumstances, as mentioned with regard to Canada, the U.S. debtor's representative may even find that a foreign court is construing the jurisdiction of the U.S. court to administer the assets of the U.S. debtor!

Although by no means all of these issues would be necessarily solved or eliminated, the availability in the foreign jurisdiction of a proceeding analogous to that under Bankruptcy Code Section 304 may at least provide the U.S. bankruptcy trustee or debtor-in-possession with a procedural avenue for advancing its claims. Consideration should now be given to that method by which foreign insolvency representatives may pursue claims against assets or debtors located in the United States.

THE FOREIGN DEBTOR HAVING ASSETS IN THE UNITED STATES

The Bankruptcy Code provides two methods for dealing with the increasingly common situation in which a foreign debtor within the jurisdiction of a foreign court has an interest in property located in the United States. The foreign debtor or its representative almost certainly will desire the assistance of the United States to protect its assets located in the United States from creditors racing to protect their own interests through attachment or appropriation of the debtor's U.S. assets, thus potentially upsetting the scheme of the foreign bankruptcy administration and distribution. Even the term *bankruptcy* itself, or any related concept, can vary in meaning from country to country. This discussion will use the word *bankruptcy* to mean the operative concept to invoke insolvency protection or administration in the jurisdiction where the debtor is primarily located. Often that protection will entail the appointment of a trustee, liquidator, or other representative. The U.S. concept of a debtor-in-possession is unusual. Provided the foreign representative meets certain requirements discussed below, the foreign representative may enlist the aid of the bankruptcy court either by commencing an ancillary proceeding pursuant to Bankruptcy Code Section 304 or by commencing a full bankruptcy case, voluntary or involuntary pursuant to Bankruptcy Code Sections 301 or 303.

U.S. Cases Ancillary to Foreign Proceedings

Since 1978, a qualifying foreign representative has had the option of petitioning the bankruptcy court for assistance in protecting its assets located in the United States from creditors pursuant to Bankruptcy Code Section 304. The bankruptcy court is granted broad authority to order any appropriate relief to a foreign representative.[17]

Filing a petition pursuant to Bankruptcy Code Section 304 does not commence a "full" bankruptcy case—that is, a case filed pursuant to Bankruptcy Code Section 301 (voluntary filing) or 303 (involuntary filing). Thus, for example, a foreign representative petitioning for an ancillary proceeding is not entitled per se to the protection of the automatic stay under Bankruptcy Code Section 362, nor is a foreign debtor entitled to a discharge of its debts upon completion of the Bankruptcy Code Section 304 case.[18]

The Confusion Prior to the Enactment of Section 304
Prior to 1978, U.S. bankruptcy law contained no provisions for the administration of a foreign debtor's assets located in the United

States, other than commencing a full bankruptcy case. Three key events stirred the United States Congress into enacting specific provisions that address the situation in which a foreign debtor owns assets in the United States: (*a*) the Herstatt matter, (*b*) the *Israel-British Bank* v. *Federal Deposit Insurance Corporation* case (the IBB case)[19] and (*c*) the *Banque de Financement* v. *First National Bank of Boston* case (the *Finabank* case).[20] These three events are discussed briefly below.

The Herstatt Matter. The problems inherent in a transnational bankruptcy became dramatically apparent in 1974 when Bankhaus I.D. Herstatt Kommanditgesellschaft auf Aktein (Herstatt), a major West German commercial bank, became insolvent. Chase Manhattan Bank held over $150 million in funds belonging to Herstatt at the time of its insolvency. The race among Herstatt's German liquidator and its creditors to gain control over the $150 million held by the United States bank has been described as "a transatlantic judicial calamity."[21] A group of Herstatt's creditors filed an involuntary bankruptcy petition in the United States, which ultimately was dismissed. Because of the novelty of the problems attendant to a transnational bankruptcy, and the lack of legislative provisions for the administration of the assets, the parties in interest eventually opted for an out-of-court settlement regarding the disposition of the funds held by Chase Manhattan Bank.

The IBB Case. The legal void regarding transnational bankruptcies still had not been filled by 1976 when the British banking corporation, Israel-British Bank (IBB), filed a voluntary bankruptcy petition in New York. The IBB case underscored the confusion that ensues when the bankruptcy court is required to apply U.S. bankruptcy law to foreign debtors.

IBB was engaged in the banking business in London. It did no banking business in the United States, nor was it licensed in any state of the United States to do such business. IBB did borrow Eurodollars and United States dollars from U.S. banks. It also maintained deposits in U.S. banks. Following IBB's financial troubles, IBB's creditors quickly commenced actions in the United States to recover amounts owed them by IBB. Two of IBB's creditors attached IBB's bank accounts in the United States and moved to dismiss IBB's voluntary bankruptcy petition on the grounds that IBB was not eligible to file such a voluntary petition.

The U.S. district court was confronted with the issue of whether IBB was a "banking corporation" and, therefore, excluded from filing a voluntary bankruptcy petition pursuant to former Bankruptcy Act Section 22(a) (now Bankruptcy Code Section 109). Because IBB was a banking corporation, albeit organized under the laws of England, a literal reading of Bankruptcy Code Section 22(a) might exclude IBB from filing. Taking this literal view, the district court dismissed IBB's petition.

The United States Court of Appeals for the Second Circuit recognized the need to look beyond the literal language of Bankruptcy Act Section 22(a) in light of the novel fact situation before it. The court of appeals reasoned that U.S. banking corporations are excluded from filing a bankruptcy petition because the liquidation or rehabilitation of U.S. banking corporations is under the regulation of federal or state governmental agencies. The liquidation or reorganization of foreign banking corporations, however, is not regulated by U.S. governmental agencies. Therefore, the court of appeals found the policy reasons for excluding U.S. banking corporations from being able to seek bankruptcy protection to be inapplicable to a foreign banking corporation. Consequently, the court of appeals held that IBB was entitled to file a voluntary petition and, "in so doing, [avoided] an inequitable result to [IBB's] creditors, including [those creditors] who have lost the race of diligence."[22]

The Finabank Case. One year after the Court of Appeals for the Second Circuit decided the IBB case, it was confronted with the *Finabank* case, another case involving transnational insolvency issues. Finabank, a Swiss bank, became insolvent in 1974. Finabank neither did business nor maintained any office in the United States. At the time, Finabank had approximately $12.5 million on deposit at a U.S. bank, prompting U.S. creditors to commence attachment proceedings against Finabank's assets located in the United States. An insolvency proceeding was commenced in Switzerland early in 1975. To protect its U.S. assets, Finabank filed a petition for arrangement in the United States under former Chapter XI of the Bankruptcy Act. Finabank's U.S. creditors brought a motion to dismiss the bankruptcy proceeding. The U.S. district court granted the motion to dismiss, because of Finabank's inability to comply with Bankruptcy Act requirements concerning the filing of a plan of arrangement and a complete list of creditors.

Finabank's inability to comply with the requirements of the former Bankruptcy Act was a direct result of the transnational aspects of its operations and subsequent bankruptcy. Thanks to the decision in the IBB case, there was no question of Finabank's ability to file the case. But Finabank could not file a plan of arrangement with the bankruptcy court until its plan of rehabilitation had been approved by the Swiss court in which the principal proceeding was taking place. In addition, Finabank was expressly prohibited by Swiss banking secrecy laws from divulging the identities of its individual depositors (and, as such, creditors in the U.S. case).

The court of appeals recognized that transnational bankruptcies present unique problems that the former Bankruptcy Act was not designed to address. To further the policy underlying the Bankruptcy Act (i.e., to promote the equal distribution of assets among all creditors similarly situated), the court of appeals reversed the district court's dismissal of the voluntary petition.[23] The Finabank decision, while representing a more enlightened and progressive response in a transnational insolvency case than most previous decisions, underscored all the more the need for a specific law to address, accommodate, and harmonize the administration of a foreign debtor's assets located in the United States with the principal bankruptcy case pending in the debtor's home jurisdiction. Indeed, the Finabank decision foreshadowed the enactment of Bankruptcy Code Section 304.

The Enactment of Bankruptcy Code Section 304

In 1978, Congress responded. The enactment of Bankruptcy Code Section 304 marked a significant change by the United States in its recognition of foreign proceedings. Prior to the enactment of Bankruptcy Code Section 304, the United States had displayed little interest in cooperation with foreign tribunals. In fact, one court has noted that, historically, the bankruptcy laws of the United States concerning foreign bankruptcy tribunals have been "hostile."[24]

The intent of Bankruptcy Code Section 304 clearly is to promote creditor equality in transnational bankruptcies,[25] and "to deal with the complex and increasingly important problems involving the legal effect the United States courts will give . . . foreign bankruptcy proceedings."[26] That section, while not providing total certainty of result, establishes a procedure for the administration of a foreign debtor's assets located in the United States and provides flexible guidelines to assist the court in fashioning appropriate relief.

The Operation of Bankruptcy Code Section 304 and Related Issues

Bankruptcy Code Section 304(a) allows the foreign bankruptcy representative to commence a case ancillary to a foreign proceeding by filing a petition with the bankruptcy court. Bankruptcy Code Section 101(21) defines a *foreign representative* as the "duly selected trustee, administrator or other representative of an estate in a foreign proceeding."

In a case commenced pursuant to Bankruptcy Code Section 304, the bankruptcy court is authorized to order a broad range of relief. Specifically, the bankruptcy court may enjoin the commencement or continuation of any action, or the enforcement of any judgment, against a debtor with respect to property involved in the foreign proceeding. The court may also order the turnover of property of the estate to the foreign representative. The bankruptcy court further is empowered to order "other appropriate relief."[27]

This broad grant of authority was used by one U.S. bankruptcy court to appoint a cotrustee in a case in which the foreign representative was tainted by a conflict of interest but could not be removed from the case. The court granted the cotrustee authority to evaluate the debtor's position and represent it to parties in interest.[28] In another case, a U.S. district court held that Bankruptcy Code Section 304 was broad enough to allow for an ancillary case to be filed for the purpose of discovery because "[a]llowing discovery will best assure an economical and expeditious administration of [the] estate."[29] The flexibility needed to confront problems associated with transnational insolvencies has created a climate in which the bankruptcy court "is free to broadly mold appropriate relief in near blank check fashion. . . ."[30]

Must the Foreign Debtor Qualify as a "Debtor" for United States Bankruptcy Purposes in Order to File an Ancillary Proceeding? At least two courts faced with the issue have concluded that the foreign debtor at issue need not fit within the definition of "debtors" eligible under Bankruptcy Code Section 109 to commence a full bankruptcy case. Because the focus of Bankruptcy Code Section 304 is on making U.S. bankruptcy courts available in aid of foreign proceedings, rather than requiring an actual U.S. bankruptcy administration, "it would make little sense to require that the subject of the foreign proceeding qualify as a 'debtor' under United States bankruptcy law."[31] One court reasoned that, because a foreign debtor is not per se granted the benefit of the automatic stay or a discharge (as is a qualifying debtor in a full bankruptcy proceeding), "Congress did not intend that 'debtor' eligibility under the Code be a prerequisite to Section 304 ancillary assistance."[32] The same court further found that a foreign debtor need only be subject, under applicable foreign law, to a proceeding commenced for the purpose of liquidating an estate, adjusting debts by composition, extension or discharge, or effecting reorganization.

Must the Foreign Debtor Have Assets in the United States? Must the foreign debtor actually own property in the United States to be eligible for ancillary assistance? Bankruptcy Code Section 304 does not explicitly address the issue. However, the question has subsequently arisen in at least four cases. Three courts decided that the foreign debtor must have assets in the United States to be entitled to relief,[33] while one court took the opposing view, finding it unnecessary for the foreign debtor to have assets in the United States to invoke Section 304.[34]

The distinguishing factor in these four cases appears to be the nature of the ancillary relief sought. The cases in which the presence of assets in the United States was required for the bankruptcy court to grant relief involved the turnover of assets and injunctions protecting property. The one case in which presence of assets in the United States was not required involved a Section 304 petition filed solely for the purposes of discovery. In that case, even though there were no assets in the United States, there was nevertheless a strong connection, because the foreign debtor had its management, legal counsel, and accountants and some records in the United States. These cases indicate the willingness of the U.S. courts to extend even the broad requirements of Section 304 to fashion orders for what the U.S. court believes to be appropriate relief.

What Venue Applies to Cases Ancillary to Foreign Proceedings? The proper venue for an ancillary proceeding under Section 304 depends in part upon the relief sought. A case brought to enjoin the commencement or continuation of an action or the enforcement of a judgment may be commenced only in the district court for the district where the action is pending against which the injunction is sought. If the objective of the foreign representative is to enjoin the enforcement of a lien against property or to require the turnover of property of the estate, the foreign representative must commence the case in the district court for the district where such property is found. Finally, in a case other than those specifically provided for above, a Bankruptcy Code Section 304 case may be commenced in the district court for the district where the debtor has its principal place of business or the district court for the district in which the debtor's principal assets are located.[35]

The Fundamental Principles Applied in Determining Appropriate Relief under Section 304. Once the Section 304 petition is filed, the court is directed to determine (upon the expiration of time to contest the petition or, if timely contested, trial of the matter[36]) whether to grant relief under Bankruptcy Code Section 304(b) by deciding "what will best assure an economical and expeditious administration of such estate"[37] consistent with six enumerated factors:

1. Just treatment of all holders of claims against, or interests in, such estate.
2. Protection of claim holders in the United States against prejudice and inconvenience in the processing of claims in such foreign proceeding.
3. Prevention of preferential or fraudulent dispositions of property of such estate.
4. Distribution of proceeds of such estate substantially in accordance with the order prescribed by [the Bankruptcy Code].

5. Comity.
6. If appropriate, the provision of an opportunity for a fresh start for the individual that such foreign proceeding concerns.[38]

The legislative history of Bankruptcy Code Section 304 articulates the flexibility available to a court in applying these factors to the specific circumstances in each case in order to arrive at a fair result. It describes the Section 304(c) factors as:

> [G]uidelines . . . designed to give the court maximum flexibility in handling ancillary cases. Principles of international comity and respect for the judgments and laws of other nations suggest that the court be permitted to make the appropriate orders under all of the circumstances of each case, rather than being provided with inflexible rules.[39]

Although these principles appear innocuous and noncontroversial, each in fact is capable of raising significant questions and, to some extent, may even be contradictory.

Just treatment. Any relief granted must be consistent with just treatment of all holders of claims against or interests in the foreign debtor's estate. Bankruptcy Code Section 304(c)(1) expresses the general requirement that all creditors be treated alike, notwithstanding their origin.[40] Determining "just treatment" is not so simple when, as can easily occur, the goals or creditor priorities of the foreign proceeding differ from those under U.S. bankruptcy law. "Just treatment" is not specifically aligned with the treatment afforded by the foreign jurisdiction, thereby introducing discretion in the U.S. bankruptcy judge.

Protection against prejudice and inconvenience. Bankruptcy Code Section 304(c)(2) directs the court to fashion relief consistent with the protection of claim holders in the United States against prejudice and inconvenience in the processing of claims in foreign proceedings. What constitutes prejudice or inconvenience? Courts interpreting *prejudice* have defined the term differently. The *Finabank* court understood prejudice to exist only if the main proceeding treated claims of U.S. creditors "in some manner inimical to this country's policy of equality."[41] Taken at face value, however, a decision based on "inconvenience" or "prejudice" would seem to be at odds with the principle of creditor equality contained in the "just treatment" test expressed above.

In noting this ambiguity and potential contradiction in construing "prejudice," one commentator has opined:

> Prejudice must be found in the rules governing the main proceeding, not in a shift of position caused by an act of a United States court in an ancillary proceeding. Furthermore, to turn section 304(c)(2) into an instrument preventing the turnover of attached assets goes beyond the scope of protection; it may prefer United States creditors over foreign claim holders, a concept completely irreconcilable with the ideas underlying section 304.[42]

Similarly, the vague concept of "inconvenience" has been the subject of some debate. The better reasoned interpretation of inconvenience should envision something more than the situation where a U.S. claim holder is required to pursue its rights abroad, because, in most Section 304 cases, the foreign debtor will have U.S. creditors who will have to pursue their claims abroad. Apparently adopting this viewpoint, at least two courts have stated that "inconvenience" must be more than just the necessity of filing a claim abroad.[43]

Prevention of preferential or fraudulent dispositions of property. This factor is a reference to, and perhaps an incorporation of, the causes of action created by Bankruptcy Code Sections 547 (voidable preferences) and 548 (fraudulent conveyances). One case analyzing Bankruptcy Code Section 304(c)(3) held that a foreign representative may assert only those avoiding powers vested in him by the law applicable to the foreign estate.[44] The court reasoned that, if Congress desired to vest a foreign representative with the avoiding powers of Bankruptcy Code Sections 547 and 548, it would have said so directly. The application of this factor, therefore, remains uncertain.

Distributions in accordance with Bankruptcy Code. Bankruptcy Code Section 304(c)(4) requires that the foreign proceeding distribute proceeds of the estate substantially in accordance with the order prescribed by the Bankruptcy Code. It is apparent, then, that the concept of "just treatment" becomes more and more closely tied to results that would occur under the U.S. bankruptcy scheme. At least one court, perhaps with tongue in cheek, has taken the broader view that the laws of the situs of the foreign proceeding need not be identical to the Bankruptcy Code if "there is nothing inherently vicious, wicked, immoral or shocking to the prevailing

American moral sense . . . [and the foreign laws] are not repugnant to our ideas of justice."[45] It would be nonsensical to conclude that Congress intended the bankruptcy court to require as a prerequisite for relief under Section 304 that the laws of the foreign jurisdictions substantially mirror U.S. bankruptcy law. Such a requirement would almost certainly make Bankruptcy Code Section 304 inapplicable in the vast majority of cases, since the likelihood of another country having substantially the same bankruptcy laws as the United States is slim at best.

Comity. Under the general principles of comity, as well as the specific provisions of the Bankruptcy Code, it has been said that the bankruptcy court should recognize a foreign bankruptcy proceeding, provided that the foreign law comports with due process and fairly treats claims of local creditors.[46] However, one court has emphasized that, in determining the appropriate relief in a proceeding ancillary to a foreign bankruptcy, the comity factor should not become the focal point, with the other statutory factors becoming subordinate or eliminated. Rather, all factors should be considered equally.[47]

Opportunity for a fresh start for a foreign debtor. Because the issue of what constitutes a "fresh start" generally applies only to individuals, it has not been common in cases of international bankruptcies. However, those concerned with international insolvencies under Section 304 should be aware of this additional factor and its ambiguities (what exactly is a fresh start, and how does it pertain to the often dissimilar laws of foreign jurisdictions?).

Related Bankruptcy Provisions. A full consideration of the desirability and effect of filing or responding to a Section 304 petition requires analysis of other related Bankruptcy Code provisions, briefly noted here.

Bankruptcy Code Section 305 provides that a foreign representative may request the dismissal or suspension of the ancillary case or full bankruptcy case if there is no pending foreign proceeding and if the factors specified in Section 304(c) warrant a dismissal or suspension. Pursuant to Section 305, one bankruptcy court suspended a Section 304 case in favor of a foreign proceeding under principles of comity, because the foreign jurisdiction's bankruptcy laws were inherently fair and not repugnant to U.S. bankruptcy concepts of distribution and liquidation.[48]

It can often be the case that a foreign representative will forego the option of filing a Section 304 petition if to do so would subject the foreign representative or its estate to personal jurisdiction in the United States generally. Such jurisdiction might allow U.S. creditors not only to circumvent the foreign proceeding but conceivably preempt (or at least compete with) the entire foreign administration. Therefore, Bankruptcy Code Section 306 provides that a foreign representative appearing in connection with a Section 304 case does not submit to jurisdiction of any court in the United States for any other purpose. However, the bankruptcy court may condition any order granting relief under Bankruptcy Code Sections 303 (the filing of an involuntary petition), 304, and 305 on compliance with orders of the bankruptcy court. The legislative intent behind Bankruptcy Code Section 306 was that the foreign representative should not be required to waive the ordinary jurisdictional rules of its home country, thus encouraging the foreign representative to take advantage of Bankruptcy Code Section 304.[49] However, the condition in Section 306 that relief requested by the foreign representative under Sections 303–305 may be conditioned on compliance with other orders of the bankruptcy court,

> is not carte blanche to the bankruptcy court to require the foreign representative to submit to jurisdiction in other courts contrary to the general policy of the [applicable] section. It is designed to enable the bankruptcy court to enforce its own orders that are necessary to the appropriate relief granted under section 303, 304, or 305.[50]

Should creditors who go to the time, effort, and expense of pursuing their claims in the foreign proceeding and receive a distribution be rewarded by receiving distributions in a United States ancillary proceeding without reduction based upon their receipt of foreign distributions? Congress decided no, in Section 508(a). If a creditor receives a distribution in a foreign proceeding, that creditor may not receive further distributions under a Section 304 case until other creditors of the same priority have received equal consideration. This provision is designed to prevent disproportionate recovery by a creditor who participates directly in the foreign bankruptcy proceeding. Oddly enough, this provision would seem to discourage to some extent the participation in the home jurisdiction's proceedings, at least when a Section 304 case is filed, although it is consistent with the universality principle of equal treatment of like creditors.

In addition to the broad discretion granted in the specific section discussed above, Bankruptcy Code Section 105 generally grants to the bankruptcy court the authority to issue any order, process, or judgment that is necessary or appropriate to carry out the provisions of the Bankruptcy Code. This broad grant of equitable powers allows the court, *sua sponte,* to take any action necessary to enforce court orders and prevent abuse of process.

Finally, parties interested in this area should keep in mind that Bankruptcy Code Section 304 was not intended to be the exclusive avenue of relief for a foreign debtor or its representative.[51] A foreign representative, instead, may commence an involuntary bankruptcy case by filing a petition in the United States under Bankruptcy Code Section 303(b)(4). In some situations, commencing a full bankruptcy case might not be an attractive alternative to the foreign creditor. Such a proceeding would be duplicative and costly if a foreign proceeding already is pending in another jurisdiction. The foreign debtor may itself also commence a full bankruptcy case by filing a voluntary petition under Bankruptcy Code Section 301, if it qualifies as a debtor under Section 109.

Shortcomings of the Ancillary Proceeding. The enactment of Bankruptcy Code Section 304 and the other provisions summarized above undoubtedly reversed the United States position of indifference to foreign bankruptcy proceedings and provided a recognizable method for foreign representatives to be heard. Even so, the impossibility of reconciling in advance the disparate bankruptcy laws of the world's nations and their application in today's increasingly complex transactional climate has inherently limited the ability of the United States to provide uniformity of result. Creation of flexible guidelines and reliance upon procedural due process and the wisdom of the bankruptcy bench therefore provides, it is hoped, resolutions that achieve fairness on a case-by-case basis. Yet the guidelines expressed in Section 304 are ambiguous and, at some level, contradictory. Because no one factor is to take precedence, a balancing test introduces additional uncertainty.

Furthermore, certain of the Section 304 factors have been criticized as being unduly favorable toward U.S. creditors and the application of U.S. bankruptcy principles even if contrary to those of the home jurisdiction. Although comity and just treatment have their place on the list, each of the other principles is directly or indirectly weighted in favor of the application of U.S. bankruptcy principles.

These criticisms have been a part of the debate surrounding the draft Model International Insolvency Cooperation Act (MIICA or the Model Act). Although not yet adopted in any jurisdiction as of this writing, MIICA continues the evolution of a more cooperative, efficient, and responsive method of addressing international insolvency issues.

THE MODEL INTERNATIONAL INSOLVENCY COOPERATION ACT

The Model Act, the current draft of which is dated November 1, 1988, is the product of efforts of a committee of the International Bar Association and was approved by that body in June 1989. In essence, the strategy of the committee is to press, by the efforts of its individual members, for adoption of the Model Act in as many jurisdictions as possible. This goal represents a formidable task, to say the least. Reports from committee members, with respect to their individual jurisdictions, reveal the complexities and variety of local reactions to MIICA, as well as the political labyrinth present in each of these countries, that must be negotiated prior to adoption. Even though MIICA itself does not create substantive rules of law for administration of insolvencies in the sense of establishing, for example, priorities for distribution or requirements for proposal and adoption of a plan of reorganization or rehabilitation, the Model Act generates controversy for reasons that vary from country to country. Add to that the fact that international private bankruptcy reform itself is likely not the highest legislative priority in any country, and the result is an uncertain future for MIICA.

A complete copy of the current draft of MIICA, with its official comments, is attached as an appendix. In essence, the structure of MIICA (which, as will be seen upon examination, is extremely brief) is to provide in each adopting jurisdiction a vehicle much like the ancillary proceeding provided by Bankruptcy Code Section 304, with some notable differences. The general concept underlying MIICA is to allow for a single administration of insolvency, based on the principle of universality in treatment of creditors' rights. Protection of the estate from dismemberment and equitable administration and distribution of assets are its precepts.

The Model Act differs from an ancillary proceeding under Section 304 in several notable respects: it specifically requires the local court to act in aid of and be auxiliary to the foreign proceedings,[52] in all countries that either (*a*) provide substantially similar treatment under the Model Act or (*b*) in which the local forum is proper and convenient, and the "home jurisdiction" will administer the assets consistent with the overall interests of creditors. (For the purposes of this discussion, *home jurisdiction* refers to the jurisdiction in which the full insolvency proceeding for the debtor was initially brought.) Notable by their absence are the additional factors identified in Bankruptcy Code Section 304(b), which would provide greater discretion to the local court in determining whether to act in a manner consistent with the foreign proceeding.[53] Nevertheless, it is intended that MIICA would leave substantial flexibility in foreign representatives to seek, and in the court to grant, appropriate relief. The Model Act is not intended to provide discretion to favor local creditors.

The Model Act also would take a more affirmative approach in its choice of applicable substantive law. Section 4 would require that, in an ancillary case commenced under MIICA, the court shall apply the substantive insolvency law of the home jurisdiction, "unless after giving due consideration to principles of private international law and conflict of laws, the Court determines that it must apply the substantive insolvency law of [its own] jurisdiction."[54] In this way, a court is impelled to apply the foreign law, except under limited circumstances based solely upon consideration of private international law and conflict of laws. No such restriction exists in the current version of Bankruptcy Code Section 304.

The Model Act would adopt the effect of Bankruptcy Code Section 306 and its limitation upon personal jurisdiction over the foreign representative commencing an ancillary proceeding,[55] and it would also allow the foreign representative to commence a full insolvency proceeding under local law if the ancillary proceeding is unavailable or is denied.[56] In such a full insolvency case, the substantive law of the local jurisdiction will apply.[57]

Finally, in recognition of the possibility of refinements in individual relationships among nations, MIICA Section 7 recognizes that treaties or conventions concerning matters of insolvency cooperation that have been ratified by the home jurisdiction and the jurisdiction in which the ancillary proceeding is sought, shall override the Act, unless otherwise provided in the applicable treaty.[58] Furthermore, although not specifically expressed in the text of the Model Act itself, the drafters of MIICA intend that the principle contained in Bankruptcy Code Section 508(a) be so adopted and applied that creditors who receive distributions in another jurisdiction do not receive additional distributions until creditors of equal priority receive equal payments.[59]

The Model Act represents a reasoned, thoughtful effort toward international cooperation in the administration of insolvencies. Based upon the principle of universality, it seeks the application of the law of the jurisdiction in which the original proceeding was commenced, except under limited circumstances. Yet, although its fundamental principles are inarguable and its procedural mechanisms are not intricate, MIICA faces major hurdles in its adoption. Even in the United States, where much of the structure of MIICA is familiar through the existing vehicle of Bankruptcy Code Sections 304, 306, and other provisions, the omission of the Section 304(b) factors is likely to be the source of much discussion. In addition, the tortuous process of proposal and adoption of legislation through Congress on any topic is, of course, completely unpredictable. The process becomes that much more difficult in countries having no current provisions analogous to Bankruptcy Code Section 304, or even to the Bankruptcy Code and in countries where skepticism of the United States structure already exists, and where much more fundamental political obstacles are presented (e.g., the recent changes in government in Japan and Mexico).[60] Additional problems are presented in countries having adopted internal legislation of their own which may overlap or compete with the effect of MIICA, such as Switzerland.[61]

CONCLUSION

The need for greater consistency in the disposition of international insolvency matters is undisputed. Currently, the debtor, creditor, or bankruptcy representative faced with an international insolvency must, in addition to dealing with the many business issues and legal complexities under domestic law, grapple with the added overlay of unfamiliar and often inconsistent laws and policies in another jurisdiction. Reconciliation and enforcement add further uncertainties, as well as further time and expense. Reported decisions in these areas that would assist interpretation and application are still relatively rare, even in such litigation-oriented societies as the United States.

Bankruptcy Code Section 304 does afford a foreign bankruptcy representative a vehicle for seeking relief appropriate to the particular issue, insofar as assets located in the United States are concerned. Although the principles of application of Section 304 are necessarily broad and, it can be argued, somewhat slanted toward protection of U.S. interests, the ancillary proceeding nevertheless provides a mechanism that is supported by judicial discretion and jurisdiction for enforcement in the United States. Given the impossibility of adoption of any uniform body of substantive insolvency law on a worldwide basis, one can only hope that, through the vehicle of the Model International Insolvency Cooperation Act or some similar legislation, the world community can agree upon at least this type of procedural structure. Such a structure would greatly assist in facilitating the resolution of the unique and pressing requirements of international bankruptcy administration for the benefit of all concerned. In the midst of these uncertainties, one fact can be counted on: the number, extent, and effect of international insolvencies will increase dramatically in the future.

ENDNOTES

1. For a brief digest of certain nations' laws pertaining to creditors' rights, **see** 1 *International Loan Workouts and Bankruptcies,* 111-364 (R. Gitlin & R. Mears ed. 1989).
2. 11 U.S.C. Section 362. Title 11 U.S.C. Sections 101 *et seq.,* will be referred to herein as the Bankruptcy Code.
3. Bankruptcy Code Section 541.
4. 28 U.S.C. Section 1334(d).
5. **See** Huber, *Creditor Equality in Transactional Bankruptcies: The United States Position,* 19 Vand. J. Transnat'l. L. 741, 772 & nn. 208-13 (1986).

6. See *International Shoe Co.* v. *Wash.*, 326 U.S. 310, 316, 66 S. Ct. 154, 158, 90 L. Ed. 95 (1945) (to subject a party to *in personam* jurisdiction, the party must "have certain minimum contacts with [the forum] such that the maintenance of the suit does not offend 'traditional notions of fair play and substantial justice.' ") (Citations omitted.)
7. Convention of the Service Abroad of Judicial and Extrajudicial Documents in Civil or Commercial Matters, November 15, 1965, art. 5, 20 U.S.T. 361, T.I.A.S. No. 6638.
8. 517 F.2d 512 (2d Cir. 1975).
9. November 7, 1933, 155 L.N.T.S. 136.
10. February 20, 1928, 86 L.N.T.S. 362.
11. 1970, 21 U.S.T. 2517, T.I.A.S. No. 6997.
12. Jaffe, *Chapter 11 Stategies and Techniques—Creditors Committees, Effective Use of Plan Provisions, Objections to Confirmation, Financing a Chapter 11 Case, "Cramdown" and How It Works*, 59 Tul. L. Rev. 1298, 1313 (1985) (citing Riesenfeld, *The Status of Foreign Administration of Insolvent Estates: A Comparative Study*, 24 Am. J. Comp. L. 288, 290 (1976)).
13. Jaffe, *supra* endnote 12, at 1313 (citing Argentinian Insolvency Act of April 4, 1972 (Law 19551), Article 4, XXXXIIV, A.D.L.A. (1972)).
14. See Jaffe, *supra* endnote 12, at 1314.
15. *Id.*
16. See *supra*, text accompanying endnote 5.
17. H.R. Rep. No. 595, 95th Cong., 1st Sess. 324-25 (1977);   S. Rep. No. 989, 95th Cong., 2d Sess. 35 (1978).
18. See *In re Georg*, 844 F.2d 1562, 1568 (11th Cir. 1988), *cert. denied sub nom. Parungao* v. *Georg,*—U.S.—109 S. Ct. 850, 102 L. Ed. 981 (1989).
19. 536 F.2d 509 (2d Cir.), *cert. denied sub nom. Bank of Commonwealth* v. *Israel-British Bank (London), Ltd.*, 429 U.S. 978, 97 S. Ct. 486, 50 L. Ed. 2d 585 (1976).
20. 568 F.2d 911 (2d Cir. 1977).
21. 1 *International Loan Workouts and Bankruptcies* 14 (R. Gitlin & R. Mears ed. 1989) (citing Morales & Deutsch, *Bankruptcy Code Section 304 and U.S. Recognition of Foreign Bankruptcies*, 39 Bus. L. 1573, 1574 (1984)).
22. 536 F.2d at 515.
23. 568 F.2d at 920.
24. *In re Toga Mfg., Ltd.*, 28 Bankr. 165, 167 (Bankr. E.D. Mich. 1983).
25. Report on the Commission on Bankruptcy Laws of the United States, H.R. Doc. No. 137, 93rd Cong., 1st Sess. 71 (1973).
26. *Cunard Steamship Co., Ltd.* v. *Salen Reefer Serv.*, 773 F.2d 452, 454 (2d Cir. 1985).

27. Bankruptcy Code Section 304(b).
28. *In re Lineas Aereas de Nicaragua,* 13 Bankr. 779, 780 (Bankr. S.D. Fla. 1981).
29. *Angulo* v. *Kedzep, Ltd.,* 29 Bankr. 417, 419 (S.D. Tex. 1983).
30. *In re Culmer,* 25 Bankr. 621, 624 (Bankr. S.D.N.Y. 1982).
31. See *supra* endnote 18; see also *In re Gee,* 53 Bankr. 891 (Bankr. S.D.N.Y. 1985).
32. *In re Georg,* 844 F.2d at 1568.
33. *In re Trakman,* 33 Bankr. 780, 783 (Bankr. S.D.N.Y. 1983); *In re Toga Mfg., Ltd.,* 28 Bankr. 165, 167 (Bankr. E.D. Mich. 1983); *In re Stuppel,* 17 Bankr. 413, 415 (Bankr. S.D. Fla. 1980).
34. *In re Gee,* 53 Bankr. at 898.
35. 28 U.S.C. Section 1410.
36. Bankruptcy Code Section 304(b).
37. *Id.* Section 304(c).
38. *Id.*
39. See *supra* endnote 17.
40. Huber, *supra* endnote 5, at 749.
41. 568 F.2d 911, 921 (2d Cir. 1977).
42. Huber, *supra* endnote 5, at 751.
43. *In re Gee,* 53 Bankr. 891, 903 (Bankr. S.D.N.Y. 1985); *In re Culmer,* 25 Bankr. 621, 630 (Bankr. S.D.N.Y. 1982).
44. *In re Metzeler,* 78 Bankr. 674, 677 (Bankr. S.D.N.Y. 1987).
45. *In re Culmer,* 25 Bankr. at 631.
46. *Victrix S.S. Co., S.A.* v. *Salen Dry Cargo,* 825 F.2d 709, 714 (2d Cir. 1987).
47. *Matter of Papeleras Reunidas, S.A.,* 92 Bankr. 584 (Bankr. E.D.N.Y. 1988).
48. *In re Axona Int'l. Credit & Commerce,* 88 Bankr. 597 (Bankr. S.D.N.Y. 1988).
49. H.R. Rep. No. 595, 95th Cong., 1st Sess. 325-26 (1977).
50. *Id.*
51. See *supra* endnote 26.
52. MIICA, § 1(b)-(c).
53. MIICA, § 5.
54. MIICA, § 3.
55. MIICA, § 4(b).
56. MIICA, § 7.
57. See MIICA, § 2, which while otherwise substantially identical in form to U.S.C. Section 304, omits the additional factors discussed above, thereby limiting the discretion available to the foreign court.
58. MIICA, § 4(a).

59. See Official Comment to Model International Insolvency Cooperation Act (Miscellaneous Comment § 3), in appendix hereof.
60. See Country Committee Reports of Committee J, International Bar Association, October 4, 1989.
61. *Id.*

APPENDIX

MODEL INTERNATIONAL INSOLVENCY COOPERATION ACT

Section 1
In all matters of insolvency, including bankruptcy, liquidation, composition, reorganization or comparable matters, a Court, in accordance with the provisions of this Act,

(a) shall recognize a foreign representative of the debtor or estate, provided that such foreign representative complies with the orders of such Court;
(b) shall act in aid of and be auxiliary to foreign proceedings pending in the courts of all countries that provide substantially similar treatment for foreign insolvencies as that provided by this Act; and
(c) shall act in aid of and be auxiliary to foreign proceedings pending in the courts of all other countries, if the Court is satisfied that:
  (i) the court or administrative agency having jurisdiction over the foreign representative is a proper and convenient forum to supervise administration of the property of the debtor; and
  (ii) the administration of the property of the debtor in the pertinent jurisdiction by the foreign representative is in the overall interests of the creditors of the debtor.

Section 2
(a) A foreign representative may commence a case ancillary to a foreign proceeding by filing a petition under this Act for purposes of:
  (i) obtaining an order to turn over to the foreign representative any property of the debtor or the estate in this jurisdiction;
  (ii) staying or dismissing any action or proceeding concerning the debtor or estate in this jurisdiction;

(iii) obtaining testimony or production of books, records or other documents relating to an insolvency;
(iv) obtaining recognition and enforcement of a foreign judgment or court order; or
(v) obtaining any other appropriate relief.

The Court may exercise such additional powers with respect to the matter as it could exercise if the matter had arisen within its own jurisdiction.

(b) Upon the commencement of an ancillary case, any currently pending related insolvency proceeding in this jurisdiction shall be consolidated with such ancillary case.

Section 3

In the event that ancillary proceedings pursuant to Section 2 are unavailable or denied, a foreign representative of the estate in a foreign proceeding concerning a person, may commence an insolvency proceeding against such person in this jurisdiction in accordance with the provisions of the applicable laws of this jurisdiction.

Section 4

(a) In any case commenced ancillary to a foreign proceeding as provided in Section 2, a Court shall apply the substantive insolvency law of the foreign court having jurisdiction over the foreign proceeding, unless after giving due consideration to principles of private international law and conflict of laws, the Court determines that it must apply the substantive insolvency law of this jurisdiction.

(b) A Court shall apply the substantive insolvency law of this jurisdiction in any insolvency proceeding brought by a foreign representative as provided in Section 3.

Section 5

An appearance in a Court by a foreign representative in connection with a petition or request under this Act does not submit such foreign representative to the jurisdiction of any Court in this jurisdiction for any other purpose.

Section 6

(a) "Foreign representative" means a person who, irrespective of designation, is assigned under the laws of a country outside of this jurisdiction to perform functions in connection with a foreign proceeding that

are equivalent to those performed by a trustee, liquidator, administrator, sequestrator, receiver, receiver-manager or other representative of a debtor or an estate of a debtor in this jurisdiction.
(b) "Foreign proceeding" means an insolvency proceeding, whether judicial or administrative, in a foreign country, provided that the foreign court or administrative agency conducting the proceeding has proper jurisdiction over the debtor and its estate.

Section 7
Any treaty or convention governing matters of insolvency cooperation, which has been ratified by this country and the country in which a foreign proceeding is pending, shall override this Act with regard to such matters between such countries, unless the treaty or convention shall otherwise provide.

OFFICIAL COMMENT TO MODEL INTERNATIONAL INSOLVENCY COOPERATION ACT

Statement of General Principles

The ultimate goal of model legislation for international insolvency cooperation is universality which envisions a single administration providing protection of the insolvent debtor's estate from dismemberment, and an equitable distribution of assets among both domestic and foreign creditors in liquidation, or the equitable administration of the estate in a reorganization, composition or rehabilitation proceeding. Insofar as possible, such universality should be the guiding principle of all efforts toward international insolvency cooperation, for it alone is truly compatible with the realization of equal treatment of all creditors, debtors, assets and liabilities, and the swift and effective administration of the estate. Within the parameters of this overarching principle, mechanisms must be provided for the recognition of foreign representatives, the stay of local proceedings, the production of documents and testimony, the integration of asset distribution and other forms of ancillary relief. In a world of increasing global integration and growth of true multinational business entities, these principles are the indispensable elements in attaining equity and fairness in international insolvency proceedings.

Statutory Comments

Section 1

Purposes. The purposes of Section 1 are to provide assurance and predictability that the foreign representative will be recognized by the Court; to require the foreign representative to comply with orders of the Court; to ensure that the Court will aid foreign proceedings in countries where a form of the model act (or similar legislation) has been adopted; and to encourage the Court to aid foreign proceedings in other countries, where the model act has not been adopted, provided that only two limited and very basic qualifications are satisfied.

Sources. Subsection 1(a) is derived from principles found in provisions of the laws of England (case law) and the United States Bankruptcy Code §304(a) and §306. Subsections 1(b) and (c) are similar in form to §29(2)(a) and (b) of the Australian Bankruptcy Act. The specific qualifications enumerated in Subsections 1(c)(i) and (ii) are similar to those in §316(5)(a) and (b) of the provisions on international insolvencies included in two recent bankruptcy bills introduced, but not adopted, in Canada (the "Canadian Bill"). The omission of a third qualification in the Canadian Bill was based upon comments in Report of the Canadian Committee - Special Project on International Cooperation in Bankruptcy Proceedings, IBA Committee J, 1987 (the "Canadian Report") at pp. 46–47.

Explanation. Section 1 supplies a foundation for the entire model act and its principle of universality by providing for recognition of foreign representatives, and by providing that the Court shall act in aid of and be auxiliary to foreign proceedings in all matters of insolvency. The scope of matters is sufficiently broad to include debtor rehabilitation as well as liquidation. The terms "in aid of" and "auxiliary to" clearly set forth the ideal role of the Court in relation to foreign proceedings, and the recognition of the foreign representative establishes the point of entry into the Court for that foreign proceeding and its representative. Subsection 1(a) requires the Court to recognize foreign representatives so that, even though the Court may have discretion in responding to the requests of the foreign representative, that representative is assured of recognition in order to place the request before the Court. The sole qualification to such recognition is that the foreign representative must comply with any Court orders; the Court could withdraw recognition if the foreign representative did not so comply.

Subsection 1(b) requires the Court to act in aid of and be auxiliary to courts in countries which have adopted the model act. This reciprocity provision will provide an incentive for countries to adopt the model act, or substantially similar treatment, so that its representatives will have a basis for depending upon the receipt of aid in those jurisdictions which have likewise adopted the model act.

Subsection 1(c) provides that the Court shall provide aid to courts of countries which have not adopted the model act, but which satisfy two fundamental qualifications: that the foreign proceeding is a proper and convenient forum and that administration in that proceeding is in the overall interests of the general body of creditors of the debtor. Such qualifications in no way provide special consideration for local parties, but rather establish a basic threshold of fairness and equity which is central to the concept of international insolvency cooperation. Certain additional factors which would arguably provide the Court with greater discretion to deny aid to the foreign proceeding, such as those found in United States Bankruptcy Code §304 and Canadian Bill §316(5), have not been included in the model act. Such omission is in response to commentaries received from a number of jurisdictions which criticize the United States provisions for giving too much discretion to the Court by enumerating multiple factors which the Court may consider, and thus allowing many alternatives for determining to deny aid to foreign proceedings.

Section 1 generally raises the issue of whether a Court would act in aid of and be auxiliary to foreign proceedings with regard to recognition and enforcement of foreign revenue (tax) or penal claims that are not currently recognized or enforced in many jurisdictions. The resolution of the issue must be left to the individual jurisdictions adapting the model act for adoption.

Section 2

Purposes. The purposes of Section 2 are to provide the framework for aid to a foreign proceeding by establishing the mechanism of a case ancillary to a foreign proceeding, in which the foreign representative may seek several types of relief; to set forth four of the most commonly sought types of assistance which foreign representatives may request; to ensure flexibility by allowing the foreign representative in an ancillary case to obtain any other appropriate relief in addition to the four enumerated types of aid; and to provide that any separate related proceedings pending in the jurisdiction shall be consolidated with the ancillary case.

Sources. Section 2 is similar conceptually and in form to §304 of the United States Bankruptcy Code, which similarly provides for cases ancillary to foreign proceedings without the commencement of separate bankruptcy proceedings. The model act deviates significantly from §304, however, by omitting the six factors to be considered by the Courts in determining whether to grant ancillary judicial assistance. No such factors are set forth in Section 2 of the model act. Such omission responds to the criticism of some bankruptcy practitioners that §304, as currently enacted, provides too much discretion to the Court by setting forth such criteria. Instead, the model act enumerates the types of aid which the foreign representative may seek in the ancillary case, once the Court has determined to act in aid of the foreign proceeding in accordance with limited guidelines set out in Section 1. The specific types of relief listed are derived from the comments of bankruptcy practitioners in response to the Special Project on International Cooperation and Bankruptcy Proceedings, IBA Committee J, 1987, and from certain statutory and other sources. Subsection 2(a) provides similar types of relief to those enumerated in the Canadian Bill at §316(3). Subsection 2(b) is derived from the Federal Statute on Private International Law Tenth Chapter; Bankruptcy and Composition Law of Switzerland, Articles 159 ff., and was stressed, along with Subsection 2(a) by the Switzerland Commentary on the Special Project on International Cooperation and Bankruptcy Proceedings, IBA Committee J, 1987.

Explanation. Whereas some statutes provide that foreign representatives may "seek orders," others provide that foreign representatives may "obtain recognition of foreign decrees," or may "seek necessary relief." Such provisions do not provide a flexible framework within which foreign representatives may obtain aid of many types and in many different forms, depending upon the needs which are generated by the foreign proceeding. The United States model of the "case ancillary to a foreign proceeding," provides just such a flexible mechanism within which the foreign representative may then take any number of actions and seek any number of different types of relief depending upon the particular needs of the estate. In addition, the concept of an "ancillary case" reemphasizes the universality principle by distinguishing this special type of case allowed for the particular purposes of aiding and being auxiliary to the foreign proceeding which remains the dominant and central administration for the debtor's estate. The enumeration of types of relief to be sought provides a starting point, based largely upon comments of bankruptcy practitioners with regard to the goals which foreign representatives are likely to bring to the ancillary case. The four enumerated types of relief will cover a very significant portion of the actions sought in ancillary cases, but Subsection 2(a)(v) provides the additional flexibility to foreign representatives to seek any other kind of appropriate relief. The last sentence of Subsection 2(a) provides the Court with full powers to provide relief and act in aid of the foreign representative and the foreign proceeding; however, this provision is not intended to provide the Court with discretion to favor local creditors or other local parties in interest. Subsection 2(b) is based upon the recognition that creditors or other parties in interest may commence either involuntary insolvency proceedings or related judicial or administrative proceedings in the recognizing jurisdiction, prior to the commencement of a case ancillary to a foreign proceeding. A foreign representative has the discretion to either allow such action to proceed, or to commence a case ancillary to the foreign proceeding, in which case, under the terms of Subsection 2(b), the separate proceeding brought by the creditor or other party in interest shall be consolidated with the ancillary case. Upon such consolidation with the ancillary case, the separate proceeding will be fully integrated into a single administration of the estate, and will be governed by the provisions of the model act. It is the intent of this provision to allow consolidation of any future actions similarly brought, following commencement of the ancillary case.

Section 3

Purposes. The purposes of Section 3 are to provide a further means for foreign representatives to enter the Court and seek relief, if the ancillary case is unavailable or is denied by the Court; and to ensure the broadest possible access of the foreign representative to the Court by allowing a full proceeding to be commenced in accordance with the laws of the Court's jurisdiction in the event that such proceeding is deemed necessary.

Sources. The United States Bankruptcy Code §303(b)(4) similarly allows a foreign representative to commence full proceedings in the United States. The Canadian Report at p. 46 strongly recommends such a provision and commends the United States Bankruptcy Code for so providing.

Explanation. The primary thrust of the model act is toward a central administration of the estate in one jurisdiction with ancillary cases in other jurisdictions as necessary. However, in the event that the Court declines to act in aid of a foreign proceeding and refuses to allow an ancillary case (under the provisions of Section 1(c)), this Section provides the foreign representative with an alternative course in which a full proceeding may be commenced against the debtor in accordance with the domestic provisions of the applicable statute of the jurisdiction. Section 3 has been drafted to clearly indicate the necessity of the foreign representative first considering and seeking to obtain ancillary relief under Section 2, and only in the event that it is unavailable, proceeding to initiate a full proceeding under Section 3. This construction further buttresses the universality principle and the emphasis which the model act places upon a central administration.

Section 4

Purposes. The purposes of Section 4 are to provide guidance to the Court with regard to the applicable substantive insolvency law for proceedings under the model act; to distinguish between the ancillary case and the full proceeding, by providing that the substantive insolvency law of either the foreign or local jurisdiction may be applied in an ancillary case whereas the substantive insolvency law of the local jurisdiction is applicable to the full proceeding; to encourage recognition of the law of the foreign jurisdiction insofar as possible in ancillary cases, but to provide for the possibility that such law may be improper in the local jurisdiction and thus not subject to being utilized; and to further confirm that a full proceeding initiated by the foreign representative is subject to the substantive insolvency law of the local jurisdiction and that such law will be the applicable law for the full proceeding.

Sources. Subsection 4(a) reflects a principle noted in the English Commentary to the Special Project on International Cooperation and Bankruptcy Proceedings, IBA Committee J, 1987 regarding Section 426 of the Insolvency Act 1986 of England. Subsection 4(b) sets forth the generally accepted principle of utilizing local substantive law when the benefits of a full local proceeding are sought by the person initiating the proceeding.

Explanation. It is clear that if a foreign representative has been denied the assistance of the Court in initiating an ancillary case, and has initiated a full bankruptcy proceeding under the laws of the local jurisdiction, then the applicable substantive law should be that of the local jurisdiction. In an ancillary case, the issue of applicable substantive law is more complex. Ideally, following the principle of universality in its purest form, the substantive law of the foreign court would govern the entire proceedings, including ancillary cases, whereas procedural matters would presumably be governed in the ancillary cases by the procedural law of the recognizing jurisdiction. However, the constraints of public policy or strongly supported local bankruptcy principles in the Court's own jurisdiction, may require that this basic principle be modified and, in some instances, that local substantive law be applied. The intention of the model act is that the Court should, whenever possible in ancillary cases, apply the substantive insolvency law of the jurisdiction of the foreign proceeding, and that the application of local substantive insolvency law should only occur in isolated and infrequent instances when the application of the substantive insolvency law of the foreign proceeding would violate public policy.

Section 5

Purposes. The purpose of Section 5 is to allow the foreign representative to appear in the Court for the limited purposes of obtaining ancillary relief, without the fear of being subject to the jurisdiction of the Court for other purposes.

Sources. Section 5 is patterned closely after United States Bankruptcy Code §306.

Explanation. In order to encourage foreign representatives to seek relief by initiating cases ancillary to the foreign proceeding, or, if necessary, to initiate a full proceeding, this section provides protection of foreign representatives from the Court assuming jurisdiction for other purposes. Such protection is limited to actions of the foreign representative prior to the commencement of the ancillary proceeding, and is not intended to prevent subjecting the foreign representative to claims or counterclaims validly raised after commencement of the ancillary proceeding. The intention of the model act is not only to provide access to the Court for the foreign representative, but to provide an efficient, equitable and safe mechanism for the foreign representative to use, in order to encourage a central administration of the estate and to foster the principle of universality. The protections which this section affords the foreign representative are important aspects of this effort.

Section 6

Purposes. The purposes of Section 6 are to define "foreign representative" and "foreign proceeding" clearly; to frame such definitions with sufficient flexibility to cover the various types of proceedings and the various roles which administrators may play under the laws of a variety of jurisdictions; and to allocate to the Court responsibility for determining that there is proper jurisdiction in the foreign proceeding.

Sources. The definition set forth in Section 6(a) is closely patterned after §316(1) of the Canadian Bill. The definition set forth in Section 6(b) is derived in part from United States Bankruptcy Code §101(22).

Explanation. It is the intention of the model act to include within the term "foreign representative" at Subsection 6(a) all of those persons who perform substantially equivalent functions in a foreign insolvency. Note, for instance, that the breadth of this definition allows it to include such unique concepts as the "debtor-in-possession" under the provisions of the United States Bankruptcy Code.

Subsection 6(b) defines "foreign proceeding" with sufficient breadth to include all types of judicial and administrative proceedings that exist in jurisdictions throughout the world. "Foreign proceeding" does not include private non-judicial receiverships or similiar actions that are not under the control of a judicial or administrative body. To meet the definition of "foreign proceeding" under the model act, the foreign court or agency conducting the proceeding must have proper jurisdiction. Determination that proper jurisdiction exists, and therefore that the proceeding is a "foreign proceeding" under the terms of the model act must be made by the Court. An underlying assumption of the model act is that the Court, guided by a forum non-conveniens approach, would concede jurisdiction to the foreign court or administrative agency in a jurisdiction having greater contacts with the debtor and its estate. In making its jurisdictional determination, the Court should be accorded maximal flexibility so that, for instance, it may consider whether improper forum selection or "shopping" has occurred in the choice of forum made by the debtor.

Section 7

Purposes. The purposes of Section 7 are to recognize that treaties or conventions may be adopted and ratified to govern the subject matter of the model act, and to provide that in such instance, the treaty or convention shall override the model act with regard to international insolvency matters between the ratifying countries.

Sources. Section 7 was drafted in response to comments of bankruptcy practitioners, some of whom advocate the adoption and ratification of treaties or conventions to effect international insolvency cooperation, and some of whom simply seek to clarify the relation of such treaty and the model act in those instances in which a treaty or convention is ratified following the enactment of the model act.

Explanation. Section 7 provides that if a treaty or convention is effected with regard to international insolvency cooperation, it will override the model act with regard to such matters between the ratifying countries. This new provision explicitly recognizes that bilateral or multilateral treaties or conventions may be effected as alternative means for establishing arrangements concerning international insolvency cooperation between countries. Enactment of the model act is not to be construed as prohibiting or deterring the adoption and ratification of such treaties or conventions; on the contrary, Section 7 explicitly addresses the issues of how to reconcile the later ratification of such a treaty by a country which has previously adopted the model act.

Miscellaneous Comments

1. Meaning of "Insolvency." The term "insolvency" has been used in the title of the model act, and throughout its text and official comment, to mean all of those various proceedings under all types of law and in various jurisdictions worldwide, applicable to actions regarding financial failure generally, including insolvency, bankruptcy, reorganization, composition, rehabilitation and any other such proceeding by whatever name.

2. Venue. A provision governing venue with respect to cases commenced ancillary to a foreign proceeding has not been included in the model act. It is presumed that venue will be determined by the Court in accordance with the applicable laws of the Court's jurisdiction.

3. Effects of Multijurisdiction Distribution. Although no marshalling provision has been included in the model act, the principles of universality and single insolvency administration dictate an equitable worldwide distribution. Thus, if a creditor receives payment or other satisfaction of a claim in a foreign proceeding, such creditor should not receive any payment in the Court's jurisdiction until other holders of claims who are entitled to share equally with such creditor, have received payment equal in value to the consideration already received by the creditor in the foreign proceeding. This comment is derived substantially from United States Bankruptcy Code §508(a).

INDEX

A

A. H. Robins Company, 341, 355, 418, 474
A. H. Robins/Dalkon shield litigation, 6, 341
Absolute priority rule, 689
Acadia Partners, 534
Accidents, and company financial health, 32
Accountant's creditor representation
　accountant's role in bankruptcy proceeding, 462–69
　accountant's role in out-of-court workout, 459–62
　creditors' need for own accountants, 457–59
　workout or Chapter 11 choice determination, 469–72
Accountant's debtor representation
　accountant's changing role in, 438–39
　accountant's new role, 440–50
　asset values impairment, 446–47
　and financial restructuring issues, 442–43
　future opportunities for, 434–38
　general tax issues, 448–50
　and operational restructuring issues, 441–42
　present value/recovery matrix, restructuring alternatives, 450–54

Accountant's debtor representation—*Cont.*
　quasi-reorganization, 443–48
　troubled debt restructuring issues, 443–46
Accounting issues, troubled debt restructuring, 443–46
Accounting Principles Board *Opinions No. 16* and *19,* 446, 566
Accounting Research Bulletins Chapter 7, 447
Accounts payable, and turnaround, 57–58
Accounts receivable
　and troubled company financing, 105–7
　and turnaround, 55
　valuation of, 216–17
Actuary, and toxic liability, 343
Additional working capital, troubled company, 107–8
Adequate consideration
　bulk transfer laws, 645–46
　fraudulent conveyances, 508–9
Adequate protection, secured creditor, 259–67
Affiliate defined, 706–7
Airline industry, analysis of and asset dispositions, 232–37
Air Line Pilots Association, 372
Alcott & Andrews, 401
Allied Stores, 363, 401, 474, 515, 525
Allis-Chalmers, 475

757

Allowed claim, secured creditor, 246–49
Ally or adversary, unsecured creditors' committee, 392–93
Alternative minimum tax and ACE adjustment, 189–90
Altman, Edward I., 27, 526, 663
Amarex, Inc. case, 707
Amatex Corporation, 341, 355
American Continental, 474
American Express, 534
American Institute of Certified Public Accountants (AICPA), guidelines to financial information, 594
Analytical framework summary, liquidation, 227–28
Ancillary proceeding shortcomings, 738–39
Applicable venue, foreign debtor with assets in United States, 733
Argentinian Insolvency Act, 725
Asquith, Paul, 526
Asset liquidations market data, 228–37
Asset sales, troubled company, 99–103
Assets taxonomy, liquidation, 202–6
Assets transfer, reorganization, 153–56
Assets values impairment, 446–47
Asset write-down, SEC, 446
Assignment agreement, trading claims, 695–96
Automatic stay
 and Bankruptcy Code, 721–24
 lifting of, 262–64
 and reorganization, 79–80
 and secured creditor, 261–65
Avoidance, bulk transfer laws, 642–43
Avoiding powers, and secured creditor, 251–59
Avoiding powers, reorganization, 83–85
Azzara, Gregory A., 244

B

B. Altman & Company, 401
Bad debt deduction timing, 194–96
Baker, Wallace R., 719
Balance sheet ratios, 551–52
Balance sheet strategies, and turnaround, 55–58
Balance sheet test, 564
Baldwin United, 474
Bank debt, and LBOs, 518–19
Bank financing, troubled company, 106
Bankhaus I.D. Herstatt Kommanditgesellschaft auf Aktein involency, 728
Bankruptcies, and LBOs, 525
Bankruptcy Act, 1980, 168, 723, 724, 729
 adequate disclosure, 700
 claims transfers, 695
 insider trading, 701–2
Bankruptcy and Insolvency Accounting Practice and Procedure (Neston), 566
Bankruptcy Code
 absolute priority rule, 689
 adequate disclosure, 698
 adequate protection, 81
 affiliate defined, 706–7
 after-acquired property clauses, 105
 ancillary proceedings, 727, 733, 738–39
 automatic stay, 721–24
 avoiding powers, 83, 251
 bad faith vote of reorganization plan acceptance, 703, 704
 and cash collateral, 81–82, 107
 Chapter 11 plan acceptance, 368
 comity, 736
 committee of equity shareholders, 692
 committee powers, 78
 conflict of interests, 91
 cramdown, 690, 693

Index   759

Bankruptcy Code—*Cont.*
creditor seeking undue advantage, 704
debtor and prepetition claims, 85
debtor and reorganization plan filing, 383–84, 386
debtor assets outside United States, 722, 726–27
debtor business operation, 379
debtor credit permitted, 82
debtor estate location, 722–23
debtor property seizure prohibited, 82
debtor rights and privileges, 100
disclosure statement, holders of claims or interests, 600
distribution, 735–36
equitable subordination, 84–85
equity security holder rights, 689–93
equity security holders' position improvement, 693
equity security holders' rights against debtor, 689
equity security interests committee, 692
ESOPs, 111
exclusivity provisions, 426–27
exemptions from Securities Act, 1933, 706–10
expense responsibility, 87–88
and foreign debtor with assets in United States, 726–28, 730–39
foreign representative definition, 731
fraudulent conveyance and transfer, 84, 101–5, 507, 644, 646
and fresh-start opportunity, 736
impairment of interests, 690
interests excluded, 687
involuntary filing, 727
just treatment, 734
legal considerations, securities purchases, 704–10
packaged reorganizations, 120–21

Bankruptcy Code—*Cont.*
party in interest, 374–75
preference provisions, 83–84, 105
prevention of preferential or fraudulent disposal of property, 735
proposed amendment to, 699–700
protection against prejudice or inconvenience, 734–35
and reasonably equivalent value, 645–46
registration exemption, debtor's securities, 706–7, 708
registration requirements, Securities Act, 1933, 704
reorganization, 120–21, 129
reorganization plan, 85–87
reorganization plan acceptance, 702
retiree pension claims, 308–9
rights and powers, bankruptcy trustee, 641, 644
rights of equity security holders, 686–87, 689–93
on sales of assets, 410
and SEC, 710
secured creditor election, 276–80
secured creditors, 276–80
and Securities Act, 1933, 704–5
securities purchases, 704–10
seller and reasonable equivalent value, 645, 646
"strong-arm" provision, 251–52
trustee appointment, 387
unmatured interest, 703
unsecured creditors' committee, 365–67, 370, 373, 376, 380, 598
unsecured creditors' committee professionals, 378
unsecured taxes with priority, 182
voluntary filing, 727, 729
Bankruptcy counsel, and toxic liability, 342
Bankruptcy Court approval, trading claims, 696–99
Bankruptcy defined, 727

Bankruptcy filing, 180–86
Bankruptcy Judges, United States Trustees, and Family Farmer Bankruptcy Act, 1986, 370
Bankruptcy over workout criteria, 470–72
Bankruptcy planning, and toxic liability, 345–46
Bankruptcy proceeding, creditor accountants representation in, 462–69
Bankruptcy Reform Act, 1978, 245
Bankruptcy Rules
  investors' and other creditors' rights, 686
  notice of securities transfers, 694–701, 703
  notice on automatic stay, 264
  prepetition creditors' committee, 369
Bankruptcy Tax Act, 1980, 503
Banks and other financial institutions, and turnaround, 63–66
Banque de Financement v. *First National Bank of Boston,* 728, 729–30, 734
Batch processing, 107
Beatrice Foods, 435
Benefits and risks, out-of-court workout, 75–77, 75–77
Biar, Kelly, 434
Bloomingdales, 525
Board of directors advising, lawyer's role, 407–10
Book value multiples, 488
Braniff, 331–34
Bray, Gregory A., 631
Bridge financing, 492
Bridge loans, 526
Bulk transfer laws
  avoidance of, 642–43
  bulk transfer defined, 636–39
  businesses covered by, 637
  noncompliance, consequences to purchase of distressed company, 640–42

Bulk transfer laws—*Cont.*
  notice to creditors, 639–40
  payment of consideration to seller's creditors, 640
Businesses covered, bulk transfer laws, 637
Business failure rate, 683
Business plan, accountant role in, 467–69
Business plan, turnaround, 61–62
Business plan preparation, investment banker, 476–77
Business valuation, investment banker, 487–89
Business Week, 230

C

Campeau Corporation, 438, 525
Canada, and foreign bankruptcy recognition, 725–26
Canadian SEC, required reports, 549
Cancellation of indebtedness (COD) income, 449
Capital structure, financial difficulties and, 491–95
Cases ancillary to foreign proceedings and enactment of Bankruptcy Code Section, 304, 730–39
  Finabank, 729–30
  Herstatt, 728
  IBB, 728–29
Cash
  availability of, 469–70
  as collateral, 265–66, 463
  control of, and turnaround and troubled company, 39–41, 53–54
  and financing resources understanding, and lawyer's role, 403–5
  importance of to business, 563–64
  as performance measurement, liquidation, 201–2
  and turnaround, 55

Cash flow
  focus on, management, 618–19
  multiples of, 488
  and profitability, management and, 619–20
Cash flow statements
  AICPA guidelines, 594
  cash, 563–64
  cash management orders, 594–95
  generally accepted accounting principles, 565–66, 568
  nonoperating/nonrecurring items, 584
  prospective information, 592–94
  quality of cash flows, 579–84
  ratio analysis, 577–79
  sample review, 584–92
  solvency, 564–65
  statement of cash flows, 567–77
  statement of changes of financial position, 566–67
Cash flow utilization, Chapter 11 filings analysis, 608–11
Cash management orders, 594–95
CEO, and crisis management team, 48–49
Chameleon debt, 480–81
Change of ownership, reorganization, 172–77
Changing role, accountant, 438–39
Chapter 11 as end or beginning, 422–27
Chapter 11 filings analysis
  cash flows utilizations, 608–11
  disclosure statement, 600–608
  operating reports, 598–99
  reorganization plan, 599–600
  schedule, 20 largest unsecured creditors, 598
Chapter 11 reorganization
  benefits of, 79–87
  compared with Chapter 7 liquidation, 77–79
  out-of-court workout as alternative, 74–77
  risks of, 87–90

Chapter 11 reorganization—*Cont.*
  warning signs and first steps toward, 73–74
  workout/bankruptcy decision, 92
  from workout mode to, 91–92
Chapter 11 reorganization, tax considerations
  alternative minimum tax and ACE adjustment, 189–90
  assets transfers, 153–56
  bad debt deduction, timing of, 195–96
  bankruptcy filing, 180–86
  creditor tax consequences, 190–96
  debt conversion to equity, 168–69
  debt forgiveness, consolidated groups, 177–80
  debt forgiveness income, 156–62
  debt modification, 190–94
  debtor tax consequences, 153–86
  debt restructure or modification, 162–68
  ownership change, 172–77
  partnership considerations, 186–88
  profitable company acquisition, 190
  property for debt exchange, 194–95
  purchase money debt reduction, 170
  related party debt acquisition, 170–71
  S corporation considerations, 188–89
  shareholder debt acquisition, 172
  stock for debt exchange, 195
Chase Manhattan Bank, 729
Chrysler Corporation, 305, 474
Circle K, 476
City Capital Associates, 229
Claims bar date, and toxic liability, 348–49
Claim splitting, claims trading, 702
Claims priority, retiree and pension benefits, 310–11
Classification, and secured creditor, 271–73
Clean Air Act, 317
Cleanup, hazardous wastes, 318–19

Clean Water Act, 317
Coleco Industries, 673
Collateral, value of, 250–51
Collateral pledged, troubled company, 105
Comity, 736
Commercial paper, 567
Committees of tort and trade claimants, and toxic liability, 344
Company control, need for, 471
Company viability, 469, 470, 471
Competent professionals engagement, troubled company, 41–42
Comprehensive Environmental Response, Compensation, and Liability Act (CERCLA), 1980, 311–12, 314–16
Confirmation, bankruptcy plan, 273–76
Consensual confirmation, bankruptcy plan, 273–74
Consolidated groups debt forgiveness, 177–80
Constituencies involvement, and lawyer's role, 405–7, 415–17
Consultants, and effective management's use of, 628–29
Consumer spending slowdown, 3–4
Continuation exception, nonliability, buyer of distressed company, 634
Continuous contingency planning, management and, 620
Controlled group, ERISA, 304–5
Control loss, and reorganization, 88–89
Conventional accounts receivable financing, troubled company, 106
Convention of the Service Abroad of Judicial and Extrajudicial Documents in Civil or Commercial Matters, 723
Converse, 229
Convertible-term notes, 492
Cook United, 6
Cooper Companies, assets liquidation, 230–31

Cooper Technicon, 231
Corporate counsel, and toxic liability, 343
Corporate recapitalization, 438
Corporate renewal, 5
Cost approach, asset valuation, 208
Cramdown, 600, 690
 and bankruptcy plan, 274–76, 354–55
Credit, and adequate protection, 267
Credit agreements, 479–81
Creditor actions, need to stay, 471
Creditor relations, and turnaround, 62–70
Creditors' C.O.D.s, and company financial health, 36
Creditors' need for own accountants, 457–59
Creditor tax consequences, reorganization, 190–96
Creeping tender offers, claims trading, 700–701
Crisis communications program, 334–38
Crisis management, 45–50
Crisis situation, management requirements in, 617–21
Cronin, Denis F., 244
Current assets to current liabilities ratios, 552
Cushman, Robert F., 490
Customer concentration, troubled company, 16
Customer dissatisfaction, and company financial health, 30

D

Dalkon Shield, 6, 341
Debt capacity determination, investment banker, 477–79
Debt-for-debt exchange, 481–82
Debt forgiveness income, reorganization, 156–62
 and bankruptcy filing, 180–81

Debt modification, and reorganization, 190–94
Debtor consultation, unsecured creditors' committee, 378–80
Debtor-in-possession (DIP) financing, 267
Debtor-in-possession operation, reorganization, 80–82, 379
Debt payment problems, and company financial health, 35–36
Debt restructuring or modification, 162–68
Debt-to-equity conversion, debt forgiveness income, 168–70
Debt to worth, and company financial health, 23
Declining margins, and company financial health, 25–26
Declining profits, sales, and per-unit sales values, and company financial health, 26–27
Decreasing market for goods or services, and troubled market, 22–23
De facto merger exception, nonliability, buyer of distressed company, 633–34
Defaulted debt index, 677–80
Defaulted securities, 683
Deferral of gain, sale to ESOP, 114–15
Deferred interest bonds, 522
Deferred maintenance, and company financial health, 30–31
Department of Labor, 322
Derivative actions prosecution, unsecured creditors' committee, 390–91
DiNapoli, Dominic, 456
Direct method, development of statement of cash flows, 572
Discharge of indebtedness, and LBO restructuring, 502
Disclosure statement, Chapter 11 filing analysis, 600–608

Dishonest or incompetent management, 470
Distressed companies, examples of, 554–61
Distressed securities investment
defaulted debt index, 677, 681
distressed securities defined, 664, 683
glossary of terms, 683
investor profile, 671–74
market importance and outlook, 683
returns on, 674–77
supply of securities, 665–71
Distribution
in accordance with Bankruptcy Code, 735–36
defined, 709
ESOP requirements, 112–13
Dividend deduction, and ESOPs, 115
Dolly Madison, 665
Dorsch, Jay A., 97
Drexel Burnham Lambert, 2, 5, 437–38, 473, 474, 519, 523, 527
Due process clause, Fifth Amendment, 259

E

Early stages, troubled company, 8–9
Early warning signals, troubled company, 7–8
Earnings before interest and taxes (EBIT), 478
Earnings-to-interest-expense ratio, 552
Eastern Air Lines, 363, 371–72, 378, 387–89, 515, 525
Economic growth rate, 4
Economies of scale, and troubled companies investment, 535–36
Effective communication, and management, 620–21
Eggleston, Carmen R., 152, 434
Elective bankruptcy rule, ownership change, 176–77

Employee benefits restructuring, ESOPs, 117
Employee retention, poorly planned incentives for in troubled company, 17
Employee Retirement Income Security Act (ERISA), 1974, 303–7
Employee stock ownership plans (ESOP)
  defined, 109
  distribution requirements, 112–13
  exception, ownership change, 117
  fiduciary considerations, 116–17
  leveraged, 110–15
  net operating loss, 115–16
  and ownership change, 177
Employee turnover rate, and company financial health, 31–32
England, recognition of foreign bankruptcies, 725
English Statute of Elizabeth cases, 102
Environmental Protection Agency (EPA), 311–12, 314–16
Epstein, James D., 490
Equipment transfer, and bulk transfer laws, 638–39
Equitable Life, 534
Equitable subordination, reorganization, 84–85
Equity, and LBOs, 519, 522–23
Equity-for-debt exchange, 482–84
Equity Funding, 474
Equity infusion, financing alternative, 125–27
Equity kicker, 492
Equity participants, LBO restructuring, 495–96
Equity shareholders' committees, 692–93
"E" reorganization, and bankruptcy filing, 184–85
ESOP exception, ownership change, 177
Espinos, Albaro, 719

Ethan Allen, 229
Evans, Carter S., 473
Evans Products, 487
Excessive leverage, troubled company, 14–15
Excess machinery and equipment, valuation of, 217
Exchange offers, 481–86
  junk bonds and, 123–24
  nature of, 118
  prepackaged Chapter 11 reorganizations, 120–21
  securities laws' concerns, 121–22
  tax considerations and, 124–25
  Trust Indenture Act, 1939, 118–20
Exclusivity period, 599–600
Exequator, foreign bankruptcy recognition proceedings, France, 725
Existing encumbrances treatment, troubled company, 100–101
Expenses elimination, and turnaround, 58–59
Expressed or implied liabilities assumption, buyer of distressed company, 632–33
External causes, troubled company, 19–23
External reporting indicators, company financial health, 38–39

F

Failure to penetrate key markets, troubled company, 15
Fair and equitable, bankruptcy plan, 274–75
Fair consideration, and bulk transfer laws, 645–46
Fair market value in use, liquidation, 207
Federal Fair Labor Standards Act, 650–51
Federal plant closing legislation, 321–26

Federated/Allied Stores, 4–5
Federated Department Stores, 363, 401, 474, 476, 515, 525, 532
Fiduciary considerations
 ESOPs, 116–17
 troubled company, 102–3
Finance, and crisis management team, 49
Financial affairs investigation, unsecured creditors' committee, 380–82
Financial documents, need for, 463–64
Financial Institutions Reform, Recovery and Enforcement Act, 1989, 302
Financial restructuring, 438
Financial restructuring issues, accountants, and 442–43
Financial restructuring services, accountant's, 441–42
Financial risk, troubled companies investment, 537
Financial statement information analysis, 551–54
Financing failures, and LBOs, 525–26
Fixed-term notes, 492
Florsheim, 229
Forced liquidation, 207
Foreclosure sales, and fraudulent conveyance, 647–48
Foreign competition, and troubled company, 21
Foreign debtor with assets in United States
 applicable venue, 733
 Bankruptcy Code and, 726–28, 730–39
 cases ancillary to foreign proceedings, 727–39
 Finabank case, 729–30
 Herstatt matter, 728
 IBB case, 728–29, 730
 qualification as debtor, 732
 shortcomings, ancillary proceeding, 738–39

Form 8-K, SEC, 548–49
Form 10-K, SEC, 544–47
Form 10Q, SEC, 547–48
Form 20-F, SEC, 549–50
Form UCC-1, and secured creditor, 251–52
Forstmann, Little & Company, 519
Fotochrome v. *Copal Company, Ltd.,* 723–24
Fraudulent transfers and conveyances, troubled company, 101–2
France, and foreign bankruptcy recognition, 725
Fraudulent conveyance, consequences to buyer, 646–47
Fraudulent conveyance issues
 adequate consideration, 508–9
 insolvency, 509–10
 practical considerations regarding, 511–12
 statutory framework regarding, 507–8
 unreasonably small capital, 510–12
Fraudulent conveyance laws
 adequacy of consideration, 645–46
 codification, 644
 particular transactions cited, 647–50
 purchaser protection under, 646–47
 seller's financial condition, 644–45
Fraudulent conveyances, and avoiding powers, 255–58
Fraudulent conveyance statutes, reorganization, 84
Fraudulent transfer exception, nonliability, buyer of distressed company, 634
Fraudulent transfers, 466–47
Fresh start opportunity, bankruptcy as, 736
Frontier Airlines case, 707
Frost Brothers, 401
Funds, 567
Future claims, and toxic liability, 346–48

G

Gagnon, Michael, 543
General Development, 476
General economic conditions, and troubled company, 20
General expense reduction, financing alternative, 127-29
General functions, management, 614-17
Generally accepted accounting principles (GAAP), 565-66, 568
Getty Oil, 375
Giacco, Richard J., 138
Gibbons, Peter J., 152
Gibson Greeting Cards, 519
Global economic independence, 719-20
Going-concern value, liquidation, 206, 219-27
Grapevine, and troubled company, 329-30
Great Depression, 437
"G" reorganization provisions, and bankruptcy filing, 183-85
Guardian *ad litem,* and toxic liability, 344, 353
Guidelines to financial information, AICPA, 594

H

Hackney, S. Fain, 302
Hague Convention, 723, 724
Hall-Mark Electronics, 231
Harris, Adam C., 363
Hazardous substance defined, 317
Hazardous wastes, troubled companies and
  cleanup, 318-19
  and Comprehensive Environmental Response, Compensation, and Liability Act, 1980, 311-12, 314-18
  leaders' liability, 315-16
  New Jersey action on, 319-21

Hazardous wastes—*Cont.*
  potential liability identification, 316-18
  shareholder and corporation liability, 313-15
Hertz, 232
High financing costs, and company financial health, 25
High-yield bonds, 490, 492
High-yield discount obligations, debt modification, 166-68, 193-94
Hilton International, 232
Honest and competent management, 469
Hopkins, Stephen J., 612
Horstmann, John F., III, 302
Hot goods rule, and financially distressed companies purchase, 650-51
Human relations, and crisis management team, 49-51

I

Identifying opportunities in troubled companies investment, 527, 530
Immediate steps, troubled company, 39-42
Impaired claim, and secured creditor, 270
In- and out-of-court activities, lawyer's role, 413-30
Income approach
  asset valuation, 207
  going-concern valuation, 224-26
Income statement
  ratios, 552-54
  strategies, and turnaround, 58
Incorrect shipments, and company financial health, 28
Indebtedness modification, LBO restructuring, 504-5
In-depth early evaluation, management, 625-28

Indirect method, development of statement of cash flows, 572
Industry conditions, and troubled company, 20
Ineffective management, troubled company, 11–13
Information flow control
 Braniff and Wickes experience with, 331–34
 crisis communications program, 334–38
 grapevine and troubled company, 329–30
Ingersol Community Newpapers, 476
Initial quick evaluation, management, 621–25
Innovative technology and obsolescence, and troubled company, 21–22
In re Chateaugay Corp., 123
In re Coastal Petrolem Corporation, 64
In re Latham Lithographic, 702
In re Revere Cooper and Brass, Inc., 698–99
In re V.N. Deprizio, 64
Insider trading, claims trading, 701–2
Insolvency, 157–58
 defined, 503
 and fraudulent conveyances, 509–10
Installment loan delinquencies, 4
Institutional Investor Study, SEC, 223
Intangible assets
 defined, 205–6
 personal property, and troubled company, 105
 valuation, 208–16
Integrated Resources, 363, 438, 474, 515, 525
Integrating/coordinating, management and, 615–16
Interco, Inc., 229–30, 538–41
Interest as equity security, 272
Interim financing, 492
Intermediate stages, troubled company, 9

Intermediate steps, troubled company, 42–43
Internal causes, troubled company, 11–19
Internal reporting, troubled company lack of timely, 18–19
Internal Revenue Code
 Section 61(12), debtor's ordinary income, 502–3
 Section 108, indebtedness and insolvency, 503
 Section 486B, toxic liability, 356–61
 Section 1001, exchange of indebtedness, 505
International Air Line Pilots Association, 372
International Association of Machinists and Aerospace Workers, 372
International Harvester Corporation, 305, 474, 480
International workouts and bankruptcies
 cases ancillary to foreign proceedings, 727–39
 foreign debtor with assets in United States, 726–39
 model international insolvency cooperation act, 721, 739–41, 745–55
 U.S. debtor with assets abroad, 721–26
Interstate Department Stores, 90
Inventory, and turnaround, 56
Inventory turnover slowdown, and company financial health, 25
Investing methods, troubled companies, 530–36
Investment banker, and toxic liability, 343–44
Investment banker and workout process
 business plan preparation, 476–77
 credit agreements, 479–81
 debt capacity determination, 477–79
 exchange offers, 481–86

Investment banker and workout
  process—*Cont.*
  situation evaluation, 475–76
  term loan agreements, 486
  valuation of business, 487–89
Investment opportunities, troubled
  companies
  analysis of, 537–41
  end of LBO boom, 523, 525–27
  growth of, 515–16
  historical vulture investing, 517
  indentification of, 527, 530
  and LBOs of 1980s, 517–23
  methods for, 530–36
  risks in, 516–17, 536–37
Investment risks, troubled companies, 536–37
Investment value, liquidation, 207
Investor profile, distressed securities, 671–74
Israel-British Bank v. *Federal Deposit Insurance Corporation*, 728–29

J

Johns-Manville case, 691–92
Johns-Manville Corporation, 341, 355, 363, 418, 474
Jones, Bob, 200
Junior debt, 531
Junk bond Ponzi scheme, 473
Junk bond research, 526–27
Junk bonds, 1, 2, 123–24, 490, 492, 519, 522, 527
Just treatment, Bankruptcy Code on, 734

K

Kaiser Aluminum and Chemical, 474
Kaiser Steel, 6
Kaufman, Henry, 2
King, Francis J., 200
Kohnbert, Kravis, Roberts & Company, 519
Kraftson, Raymond H., 138

L

L.J. Hooker, 476, 515, 525
Labor problems, and troubled company, 20–21
Labrum, Steve, 200
Late shipments, and company financial health, 28
Late stages, troubled company, 9–11
Lawall, Francis J., 341
Lawyer's role
  activity in and out of court, 413–20
  advising board of directors, 407–10
  Chapter 11 as beginning or end, 422–27
  constituencies involvement, 405–7, 415–17
  legal entity and debt structure, understanding of, 402–3
  management counseling, 10–12
  need to understand business, 401–2
  prepackaged Chapter, 11, 421
  understanding cash and financial resources, 403–5
Leading/motivating, management and, 617
Legal considerations, securities purchase
  equity security holders' rights, Bankruptcy Code, 689–93
  Section 1145, Bankruptcy Code, 704–10
  security defined, 687–89
  trading of claims in bankruptcy, 693–704
Legal entity and debt structure understanding, and lawyer's role, 402–3
Legal risk, troubled companies investment, 537
Legislation or politics, and troubled company, 19–20
Lender fatigue, 65
Lender liability risk 472
Lenders, as participants in LBO restructuring, 497–98

Lenders' liability, hazardous wastes, 315–16
Lerner, Stephen D., 97
Leveraged buyouts (LBO), 5–6, 434–36, 517–23; *see also* Troubled leveraged buyouts, investing in
  end of boom, 523, 525–27
  and fraudulent conveyance, 649–50
Leveraged ESOPs, 110–15
Liability
  hazardous wastes, 313–16, 345–48
  pension plan termination or withdrawal, 306–8
  successor, 631–35
Lifland, Burton R., 451, 481, 484
Lifting automatic stay, 262–64
Limitations, ESOPs, 111–12
Limited sources, supply of strategic materials, and troubled company, 22
Lincoln Savings, 474
Liquidation analysis, troubled company, 42
Liquidation options
  analytical framework summary, 227–28
  assets taxonomy, 202–6
  cash flow as performance measurement, 201–2
  going-concern valuation, 206, 219–27
  intangible assets defined, 205–6
  intangible assets evaluation, 208–16
  market data, asset liquidatins, 228–37
  risk factor, 200–201
  tangible assets defined, 205
  tangible assets evaluation, 216–19
  valuation fundamentals, 206–8
Liquidation value, 488–89
Lomas Financial Corporation, 8, 363, 377, 525
London Fog, 229
Long-term assets, short-term money, and company financial health, 24–25

Long-term debt-to-equity ratio, 551
Low morale, and company financial health, 31
LTV Corporation, 305, 308, 309, 310, 363
LTV decision, 481, 485–86

M

MacCrate, Jim, 200
Management counseling, lawyer's role, 410–12
Management defined, 613
Management evaluation
  crisis situation requirements, 617–21
  in-depth early evaluation, 625–28
  initial quick evaluation, 621–25
  key functions, management, 614–17
  management defined, 613
  outside consultants, effective management and, 628–29
Management inability to control events, and company financial health, 33
Management information systems, troubled company lack of, 18
Manville/asbestos resolutions, 6
Margles, Harold, 719
Market comparison approach, asset valuation, 207–8
Market data, asset liquidations, 228–37
Market importance and outlook, distressed securities, 680–82
Market value approach, going-concern valuation, 220–24
Mass layoff defined, 322
Matching principle, 565
Measuring/controlling, management and, 616–17
Medium term notes (MTN), 541
Merqerstat Review, 223
Merrill Lynch & Company, 435
Mezzanine debt, 531

Mezzanine financing, 436, 492, 497, 502
Milken, Michael, 519
Miller, Harvey R., 97
Miller, J. Gregg, 341
Miscellaneous assets, and turnaround, 56–57
Miscellaneous unsecured creditors, turnaround and, 69–70
Model International Involvency Cooperation Act, 739–41, 745–55
Money market funds, 567
Mullins, David, 526
Murdoch, Neil, 434

N

Named fiduciary, 116
National Association of Manufacturers, 321
Natural disaster, and troubled company, 22
Negative impact, troubled company asset sales, 123
Neporent, Mark A., 686
Neston, Grant W., 565
Net operating losses (NOLs)
  carryforwards, 439
  and ESOPs, 115–15
  and LBO restructuring, 501, 505–6
  as tax attributes, 448, 450
  and Tax Reform Act, 1986, 505
New investors, as participants in LBO restructuring, 399–500
New Jersey Department of Environmental Protection (DEP), 319–21
New Jersey Environmental Cleanup Responsibility Act (ECRA), 319–21
New role, accountant, 440–50
New value, 253
New York State Department of Environmental Conservation (DEC), 313

Ng, Johnson C., 97
Nightingale, William J., 612
No deemed exchange, debt modification, 166
Noncompliance, bulk transfer laws, 640–42
Nonfinancial statement information analysis, 553–54
Nonliablity, asset purchaser, exceptions to general rule, 632–34
Nonoperating/nonrecurring items, statement of cash flows, 584
Nonrecourse debt, reorganization, 153–55
Notice requirements, plant closing or layoffs, 323–25
Notice to creditors, and bulk transfer laws, 639–40

O

O'Donovan, James, 719
Off balance sheet financing, troubled company, 107
Omnibus Budget Reconciliation Act, 1989, 115–16
Onerous contract rejection, need for, 471
Operating income-to-sales ratio, 552–53
Operating reports, 598–99
Operating risk, troubled companies investment, 536
Operational analysis, and turnaround, 61
Operational restructuring issues, accountants and, 441–42
Operational restructuring services, accountant's, 440
Operations, and crisis management team, 49
Opportunities analysis, 537–41
Options considerations, management and, 619
Orderly liquidation, 207

Organizing, management and, 615
Original issue discount (OID), 123–24
 and debt modification, 191–93
 and existing debt, 163–66
Out-of-court workout
 accountant's role in, 459–62
 benefits and risks of, 75–77
 choice of or bankruptcy, 92
 and creditor accounts'
  representation in, 459–62
 moving to bankruptcy filing, 91–92
 and unsecured creditors'
  committee, 367–68
Overdue mortgage loans, 4
Ownership change, 172–77

P

Pan American, 233, 234–35
Participants, LBO restructuring
 equity, 495–96
 lenders as, 497–98
 new investors as, 499–500
 others, 500–501
Parties in planning for bankruptcy,
 and toxic liability, 342–44
Partnership tax considerations,
 reorganization, 186–88
Party in interest, unsecured creditors'
 committee as, 374–76
Payment-in-kind (PIK) securities, 123,
 436, 492
Payment of consideration to seller's
 creditors, and bulk transfer laws,
 640
Payroll taxes payment problems, and
 company financial health, 36
Penn Central, 665
Pennzoil, 375, 384
Pension benefits in bankruptcy,
 309–10
Pension Protection Act, 1987, 303, 305
Periodic reports, need for, 464–65
Personal property, and troubled
 company, 105

Phelps, Theodore G., 7
Phoenix Capital Corporation, 698
Plan development and
 implementation, turnaround,
 59–60
Planning, and management, 614–15
Planning by budgeting, troubled
 company lack of, 17
Planning problems, and company
 financial health, 35
Plant closing defined, 322
Posner, Victor, 487
Postpossession credit, reorganization,
 82–83
Potential environmental liability
 identification, 316–18
Powers and duties, unsecured
 creditors' committees, 373–91
Practical considerations, fraudulent
 conveyance analysis, 511–12
Preferences, 465–66
 defined, 64
 provisions for, reorganization,
 83–84
Preferential transfers, and avoiding
 powers, 252–54
Preferred stock, 531
Prepackaged bankruptcy, 485–86, 673,
 683
 Chapter 11, 11, 120–21, 421
Prepaid expenses, and turnaround,
 56
Prepetition claims and interest
 accrual, reorganization, 85
Present value/recovery matrix,
 restructuring alternatives, 450–54
Prevention of preferential or
 fraudulent disposition of
 property, and Bankruptcy Code
 Section 304, 735
Priority in bankruptcy, and troubled
 companies investment, 530–33
Private bank debt, 684
Private trade claims, 684
Problem identification, turnaround
 and, 51–53

Problem management, characteristics of, 622–24
Proceeds and after-acquired property, troubled company, 105
Product innovation, troubled company lack of, 16
Production problems, and company financial health, 28
Product liability claims, and buyer of distressed company, 634–35
Professional employees, unsecured creditors' committee, 376–78
Profitability measures, and company financial health, 25–27
Profitable company acquisition, and reorganization, 190
Promising management, characteristics of, 624–25
Property, plant, and equipment, and turnaround, 56
Property covered, bulk transfer laws, 637
Property-for-debt exchange, 194–95
Property lien, and secured creditor, 249
Property use, sale, or lease, and secured creditor, 265–67
Proposed amendment, Bankruptcy Rule 3001(e), 699–700
Prospective information, cash flows, 592–94
Prospects assessment, turnaround, 60–61
Protection against prejudice and inconvenience, 734–35
Publicity, expense, and time with Chapter 11, 470
Public Service Company of New Hampshire, 378, 384–85, 392
Purchase money debt reductions, debt forgiveness income, 170
Purchasing financially distressed companies
 bulk transfer laws, 636–43
 fraudulent conveyance laws, 643–50
 general rules of successor liability, 631–35

Purchasing financially distressed companies—*Cont.*
 hot goods rule, 650–51
 representations, warranties, distressed seller, 651–52
Pushing liabilities down, and turnaround, 57–58

Q

Qualified farm indebtedness, reorganization, 157
Qualitative indicators, company financial health, 27–32
Quality of cash flows, 579–84
Quantitative indicators, company financial health, 23–27
Quasi-reorganization, 443–46
Questionable company viability, 471

R

Radice, 476
Ratio analysis, 577–79
RCA, 519
Reactive management, and company financial health, 33
Reading statement of cash flows, 572–77
Reagan, Ronald, 321
Real estate, valuation of, 217–19
Real property, fixtures, and improvements, troubled company, 105
Reasonably equivalent value, and bulk transfer laws, 646
Receivables, and turnaround, 55
Receivables and payables aging, and company financial health, 24
Recognition timing, debt forgiveness income, 159
Recourse debt, reorganization, 155–56
Recovery rates, defaulted debt, 684
Redeemable-term notes, 492
Regulatory issues, and troubled company, 21

Reiss, M. Freddie, 7
REIT securities, 671
Related party debt acquisition, 170–71
Relationships with lenders,
    deterioration of, and company
    financial health, 37–38
Reliance Universal, 231
Reorganization, 683
  goal of fostering, 245–46
Reorganization plan, 85–87, 599–600
  and exchange offers, 120–21
  and negotiation, unsecured
    creditors' committee, 382–85
  preference provisions, 83–84
  shareholders' meeting, 692–93
  toxic liability, 349–54
Representations and warranties,
    distressed seller, 651–52
Republic Healthcare, 485–86
Resale of securities, 708–10
Resorts International, Inc., 438, 673
Resource Conservation and Recovery
    Act, 1976, 317
Restructuring defined, 5
Restructuring or modification, existing
    debt, 162–68
Retiree benefit claims in bankruptcy,
    308–9
Retiree Benefits Bankruptcy
    Protection Act, 1988, 308
Retiree benefits claims and pension
    liability
  claims priority, 311–12
  legislation concerning, 303–6
  liability on termination or
    withdrawal, 306–8
  pension benefits in bankruptcy,
    309–10
  retiree benefit claims in bankruptcy,
    308–9
Returns
  and company financial health, 28–29
  on distressed securities, 674–77
Revco, 363, 435, 438, 476, 534
Revenue Reconciliation Act, 1989,
    166, 189–90
Reves v. *Ernst & Young,* 688–89, 694

Revolving credit agreements, 479–80
Rework, and company financial
    health, 29
Rights of equity security holders
    under Bankruptcy Code, 686–87,
    689–93
Risk
  and benefits, out-of-court workout,
    75–77
  in Chapter 11 bankruptcy, 81–90
  as factor in liquidation, 200–201
  in troubled company investment,
    516–17, 536–37
RJR Nabisco, 435
Roaring Twenties, 1

S

Sabin, Jeffrey, 686
Safeguard Scientific turnaround
  background to, 138–40
  decision on, 140–44
  execution of, 144–51
Sales and marketing, and crisis
    management team, 49
Sample review, statement of cash
    flows, 584–92
Sands, David A., 44
Scandinavian Convention, 724
Schedule, 20 largest unsecured
    creditors, 598
SCI Television, 476
S corporation tax considerations,
    reorganization, 188–89
Scrap factors increase, and company
    financial health, 29–30
Secondary or direct investments,
    troubled companies, 533–35
SEC-required financial statements
  examples, distressed companies,
    554–61
  financial statement information
    analysis, 551–54
  Form 8-K, 548–49
  Form 10-K, 544–47
  Form 10-Q, 547–48

SEC-required financial
  statements—*Cont.*
  Form 20-F, 549–50
Secretary of commerce, 262
Section 1111(b) election, secured
  creditor, 276–80
Secured creditors
  adequate protection, 259–67
  allowed claim, 246–49
  automatic stay, 261–65
  avoiding powers, 251–59
  claims treatment, secured creditor's
    response, 268–70
  confirmation, bankruptcy plan,
    273–77
  fraudulent conveyances, 255–58
  and goal of fostering reorganization,
    245–46
  obtaining credit, 267
  preferential transfers, 252–54
  property lien, 249
  property use, sale, or lease, 265–67
  Section 1111(b) election, 276–80
  "strong-arm" provision,
    Bankruptcy Code, 151–52
  subordination, 258–59
  value of collateral, 250–51
  voting and classification, 270–73
Secured financing, troubled company,
  104–9
Securities Act, 1933, 121–23,
  704–11
Securities and Exchange Commission
  (SEC), 318
  analysis of information reported to,
    551–54
  on asset write-downs, 446
  exemption from registration
    requirements, 708
  Form 8-K, 548–49
  Form-10-K, 544–47
  Form 10-Q, 547–48
  Form 20-F, 549–50
  on quasi reorganization, 448
  registration statements, 566
  role in Chapter 11 cases, 710–11
  and statement of cash flows, 569

Securities Exchange Act, 1934, 122,
  687–89, 708
Securities laws' concerns, exchange
  offers, 121–22
Security defined, 687–89
Security Pacific Corporation,
  229
Seidemann, Robert S., 44
Seller's financial condition
  and bulk transfer laws, 644–45
  and fraudulent conveyance laws,
    644–45
Seller's outstanding debts paid, and
  fraudulent conveyance, 648–49
Senior debt, 531
Shapiro, Bernard, 631
Shareholder and corporate liability,
  hazardous wastes, 313–16
Shareholder claims based on
  purchase/sale of stock, 693
Shareholder debt acquisition, 172
Shareholders' meetings, and
  reorganization, 692–93
Sharon Steel, 487
Shearson Lehman Hutton, 534
Shifting consumer preferences, and
  troubled company, 22
Short form of notice, and bulk
  transfer laws, 640
Short-term business plan, troubled
  company, 42
Sigoloff, Sanford C., 1
Simon, William, 519
Sitrick, Michael S., 329
Situation evaluation, investment
  banker, 475–76
Slaughter, William A., 72
Solvency, 564–65
Southmark, 363, 438, 473, 515, 525,
  594–95
Southwest Airlines, 233, 236
Stages, troubled company, 8–11
State and municipal plant closing
  laws, 326
Statement of cash flows, 567–77
Statement of changes in financial
  position, 566–67

Statement of Financial Accounting Standards, No., 15 and, *95*, 443–44, 482, 567–72
Statutory framework, fraudulent conveyance, 507–8
Statutory provision, unsecured creditors' committee, 365–67
Stigma of bankruptcy, 90
Stock for debt exception, 449
Stolba v. *Mastrandrea*, 642
Storage Technology, 90
Strategic or scarce materials sources, troubled company, 16–17
"Strong-arm" provision, Bankruptcy Code, 151–52
Subordinated debt, 492
Subordination, and avoiding powers, 258–59
Successor liability, distressed company purchase, 631–35
Supply, distressed securities, 665–71
Supreme Court, on privately held demand notes as securities, 687–89

T

Tangible assets
  defined, 205
  personal property, 105
  valuation, 216–19
Tartakovsky, Yuli, 200
Tax attributes reduction, debt forgiveness income, 159–62
Tax benefit rule, debt forgiveness income, 158–59
Tax claims, and bankruptcy filing, 181–83
Tax consequences, creditor, reorganization, 190–96
Tax considerations
  income from debt cancellation, 124–25
  out-of-court or Chapter 11 reorganization, 152–95

Tax counsel, and toxic liability, 343
Tax incentives, leveraged ESOPs, 113–15
Tax issues
  accountants and, 448–50
  and LBO restructuring, 501–6
  and toxic liability, 356–61
Tax Reform Act, 1986, 172, 184, 501–2, 503, 504, 505
Technical Advice Memorandum 8837001, IRS, 168–69
Technical and Miscellaneous Revenue Act, 1988, 157, 502
Technical defaults, 37
Term loan agreements, 486
Texaco, 363, 375, 384, 392, 474
Texaco/Pennzoil litigation, 6, 375, 384
Texas Air Corporation, 233, 235–36
Thomas, Donald E., 434
Time and expense, and reorganization, 87–90
Time and money creation, and turnaround, 54–58
Timely and accurate information, lack of, and company financial health, 34
Toxic liability and turnaround
  bankruptcy planning, 345–46
  claims bar date, 348–49
  companies affected, 341–42
  cramdown, 354–55
  future claims concerning liability, 346–48
  parties involved in bankruptcy planning, 342–44
  reorganization plan, 349–51
  reorganization plan confirmation, 351–53
  tax issues, 356–61
  trust fund, 355–56
  voting, reorganization plan, 353–54
Toxic Substances Control Act, 317
Toys 'R' Us, 90, 671
Trade accounts payable, turnaround and, 66–69
Trading of claims in bankruptcy
  assignment agreement, 695–96

776 Index

Trading of claims in
bankruptcy—*Cont.*
  bankruptcy court approval, 696–99
  claim splitting, 702
  creeping tender offers, 700–701
  flourishing of sale and purchase of
    bankruptcy claims, 693–94
  insider trading, 701–2
  proposed amendment, Bankruptcy
    Rule 3001(e), 699–700
  transferred claim amount limitation,
    703
  transferred claim voting, 703–4
Tranche pricing, 480
Transactions covered, bulk transfer
  laws, 637–38
Transferred claims amounts limited,
  702–3
Transferred claims voting, 703–4
Tranfers in ordinary course of
  business, and bulk transfer laws,
  636
Transport Workers Union, 372
Trans World Airlines, 233, 235
Transworld Corporation, 232
Treasury bills, 567
Treatment of claims, secured creditor,
  268–70
Trepper, Myron, 400
Triggering events, plant closing or
  layoffs, 322
Troubled company
  actions concerning, 39–43
  early warning signals of, 7–8
  external causes of, 19–23
  financial health indicators
    qualitative, 27–39
    quantitative, 23–27
  internal causes of, 11–19
  stages of, 8–11
Troubled company, financing
  alternatives
  asset sales, 99–103
  employee stock ownership plans,
    109–17
  equity infusion, 125–27

Troubled company, financing
  alternatives—*Cont.*
  exchange offers, 118–25
  general expense reduction, 127–29
  secured financing, 104–9
Troubled debt restructuring,
  accounting issues regarding,
  443–46
Troubled leveraged buyouts,
  investing in
  capital structure, and financial
    difficulties, 491–95
  equity participants, 495–96
  fraudulent conveyance issues,
    507–12
  increase in LBOs, 491
  indebtedness discharges, 502–4
  junk bonds, 490
  lenders as participants, 497–98
  modifications of indebtedness,
    504–5
  net operating losses, 505–6
  new investors as participants,
    499–500
  participants, LBO restructuring,
    495–501
  tax issues, and restructuring, 501–6
  various participants, 500–501
Trust fund, and toxic liability, 355–56
Trust Indenture Act, 1939, 118–20
Trust liquidation, and bankruptcy
  filing, 185–86
Turnaround process; *see also* Toxic
  liability and turnaround
  accounts payable and receivable,
    55, 57–58
  and balance-sheet strategies, 55–58
  and banks and other financial
    institutions, 63–66
  business plan, 61–62
  cash control, 53–54
  creditor relations, 62–70
  crisis management, 45–46
  crisis management team, 46–50
  expenses elimination, 58–59
  miscellaneous assets, 56–57

Index **777**

Turnaround process—*Cont.*
  operational analysis, 61
  plan development and implementation, 59–60
  problem identification, 51–53
  prospects assessment, 60–61
  pushing liabilities down, 57–58
  Smith Scientific as example, 138–51
  time and money creation, 54–58
  turnaround defined, 5
Tyler Corporation, assets liquidation, 231

U

U.S. debtor with assets abroad, 721–26
Unavailability, required financing, 471
Undercapitalization, troubled company, 13–14
Understanding business, lawyer's role and, 401–2
Underwriter defined, 709
Unfair discrimination, and bankruptcy plan, 274
Uniform Commercial Code, 636, 637, 648
Uniform Fraudulent Conveyance Act (UFCA), 255–57, 507–8, 644–45, 646, 647
Uniform Fraudulent Transfer Act (UFTA), 507, 644–45, 646, 647
Unimpaired claim, and secured creditor, 268–70
United Airlines, 232, 234, 236
United Nations Convention on the Enforcement of Foreign Arbitral Awards, 724
United States v. *Gleneagles Investment Company*, 511
UNR Corporation, 341
Unreasonably small capital, and fraudulent conveyances, 510–11
UNR Industries, 389

Unsecured creditors' committee
  as ally or adversary, 392–93
  authority to employ professionals, 376–78
  and consultation with debtor, 378–80
  continuation of after filing, 369–70
  defined, 363–64
  derivative actions persecution, 390–91
  and financial affairs investigation, 380–82
  members' qualifications, 371–73
  in out-of-court workout, 367–68
  as party in interest, 375
  powers and duties of, 373–91
  reorganization plan negotiation, 382–85
  statutory provision for, 365–67
  trustee or examiner appointment, 386–90
Unusual allowances, and company financial health, 29
Unwillingness to address problems, management, 470
US Air, 233, 236
USG Corporation, assets liquidation, 230

V

Valuation, cramdown provisions, 275–76
Valuation fundamentals, liquidation, 206–8
Value Line, 229
Value of collateral, 250–51
Venue, foreign debtor with assets in United States, 733
Verco Industries v. *Spartan Plastics*, 641–42
Voidable preferences and lender liability considerations, troubled company, 108–9
Vollmar, Ronald G., 597

Volpert, Barry S., 514
Voting, bankruptcy plan, 270–71
Vris, Jane Lee, 244
Vulture investing, 517

W

W.T. Grant, 474
W.T. Grimm and Company, 223
Weiner, Carol A., 686
Westin Hotels, 232
Wheeling-Pittsburgh Steel case, 695–96
White Motor, 475
Wickes Furniture, 331–34
Williams Act, 700
Willingness to address problems, management, 470
Wolff, Eric, 526
Wong, Alana M., 719
Worker Adjustment and Retraining Notification Act (WARN), 1988, 321–26
Working capital, 567
  and company financial health, 24
  troubled company and additional, 107–8
Workout, 438
  defined, 5
  or Chapter 11 choice, accountants and, 469–72
  out-of-court, 75–77, 91–92, 367–68, 459–62
  workout/bankruptcy decision criteria, 469–70
Worton, Linda G., 72

Z

Zero-based budget, 59
Zero-coupon bonds, 123, 492, 522
Zeta scores, 677, 684
Z score, and company financial health, 27
Zweibel, Joel B., 363